THE ROUTLEDGE HANDBOOK
OF MATERIAL RELIGION

The Routledge Handbook of Material Religion places objects and bodies at the center of scholarly studies of religious life and practice.

Propelling forward the study of material religion, the *Handbook* first reveals the deep philosophical roots of its key categories and then advances new critical analytics, such as queer materialities, inescapable material entanglements, and hyperobjects that explode the small-scale personal view on religions.

The *Handbook* comprises thirty chapters, written by an international team of contributors who offer a global perspective of religious pasts and presents, divided into four thematic parts:

- Genealogies of Material Religion
- Materializing the Terms of the Study of Religion
- Entanglements, Entrapment, Escaping
- Hyperobjects, or How Ginormous Things Affect Religions

In these four parts, the study of material religion is redirected towards systematic, critical interrogations of the imbrication of religious structures of power with racial, economic, political, and gendered forms of domination.

From Spinoza's political theology to African philosophies of *ubuntu*; from the queer materialities of Mesoamerican religion to the Satanic Temple of the United States; from Islamic love and sacrifice in human-animal entanglements to Shia militants' attachment to weaponry; from epidemic cataclysm in Latin America to vast infrastructures and the gathering of millions in India's Kumbh Mela, the study of material religion proves to be the study par excellence of the human condition.

The *Handbook* is essential reading for students and researchers in religious studies, anthropology, history, and media studies, and will also be of interest to those in related fields such as archeology, sociology, and philosophy.

Pooyan Tamimi Arab is Assistant Professor of Religious Studies at Utrecht University.

Jennifer Scheper Hughes is Professor in the Department of History at the University of California, Riverside.

S. Brent Rodríguez-Plate is Professor, by special appointment, at Hamilton College, NY.

ROUTLEDGE HANDBOOKS IN RELIGION

**THE ROUTLEDGE HANDBOOK OF RESEARCH METHODS IN THE
STUDY OF RELIGION, SECOND EDITION**
Edited by Steven Engler and Michael Stausberg

**THE ROUTLEDGE HANDBOOK OF RELIGION,
GENDER AND SOCIETY**
Edited by Caroline Starkey and Emma Tomalin

THE ROUTLEDGE HANDBOOK OF RELIGION AND SECRECY
Edited by Hugh B. Urban and Paul Christopher Johnson

THE ROUTLEDGE HANDBOOK OF BUDDHIST-CHRISTIAN STUDIES
Edited by Carol Anderson and Thomas Cattoi

**THE ROUTLEDGE HANDBOOK OF EVOLUTIONARY
APPROACHES TO RELIGION**
Edited by Yair Lior and Justin Lane

THE ROUTLEDGE HANDBOOK OF RELIGION AND THE BODY
Edited by Yudit Kornberg Greenberg and George Pati

THE ROUTLEDGE HANDBOOK OF JUDAISM IN THE 21ST CENTURY
Edited by Keren Eva Fraiman and Dean Phillip Bell

THE ROUTLEDGE HANDBOOK OF MATERIAL RELIGION
Edited by Pooyan Tamimi Arab, Jennifer Scheper Hughes and S. Brent Rodríguez-Plate

For more information about this series, please visit: https://www.routledge.com/Routledge-Handbooks-in-Religion/book-series/RHR

THE ROUTLEDGE
HANDBOOK OF
MATERIAL RELIGION

Edited by
Pooyan Tamimi Arab, Jennifer Scheper Hughes and
S. Brent Rodríguez-Plate

Routledge
Taylor & Francis Group

LONDON AND NEW YORK

Designed cover image: Ana Teresa Fernández. 2011. *Borrando la Frontera (Erasing the Border).* Courtesy of the artist and Catharine Clark Gallery, San Francisco.

First published 2024
by Routledge
4 Park Square, Milton Park, Abingdon, Oxon OX14 4RN

and by Routledge
605 Third Avenue, New York, NY 10158

Routledge is an imprint of the Taylor & Francis Group, an informa business

British Library Cataloguing-in-Publication Data
A catalogue record for this book is available from the British Library

Library of Congress Cataloging-in-Publication Data
A catalog record has been requested for this book
Names: Tamimi Arab, Pooyan, editor. | Scheper Hughes, Jennifer, editor. | Plate, S. Brent, 1966 – editor.
Title: The Routledge handbook of material religion / edited by Pooyan Tamimi Arab, Jennifer Scheper Hughes, S. Brent Rodríguez-Plate.
Description: Abingdon, Oxon; New York, NY: Routledge, 2023. | Series: Routledge handbooks in religion; vol. 18 | Includes bibliographical references and index.
Identifiers: LCCN 2022060874 | ISBN 9780815385998 (hbk) | ISBN 9781032502441 (pbk) | ISBN 9781351176231 (ebk)
Subjects: LCSH: Material culture—Religious aspects. | Religion and culture.
Classification: LCC BL65.C8 R655 2023 |
DDC 200—dc23/eng20230512
LC record available at https://lccn.loc.gov/2022060874

ISBN: 978-0-8153-8599-8 (hbk)
ISBN: 978-1-032-50244-1 (pbk)
ISBN: 978-1-351-17623-1 (ebk)

DOI: 10.4324/9781351176231

Typeset in Bembo
by codeMantra

CONTENTS

Contents

Contents

NOTES ON CONTRIBUTORS

Ni Wayan Pasek Ariati is Director of The School for International Training (SIT), Indonesia. Trained as a scholar of religion, she is the author of *The Journey of the Goddess Durga: India, Java & Bali* (International Academy of Indian Culture and Aditya Prakashan, 2016) as well as many articles on religion and gender.

Ulrike Brunotte is Associate Professor at Maastricht University and adjunct Professor at Humboldt-University Berlin. Her research focuses on orientalism, gender and postcolonial studies, aesthetics of religion, and ritual theory and performativity. She is co-editor of *Orientalism, Gender, and the Jews. Literary and Artistic Transformations of European National Discourses* (de Gruyter, 2015) and author of *Das Wissen der Dämonen. Gender, Performativität und materielle Kultur im Werk Jane E. Harrisons* (Ergon, 2013).

Xiomara Verenice Cervantes-Gómez is Assistant Professor of Spanish and Portuguese and affiliated faculty in Women's and Gender Studies, Latina/Latino Studies, Religion, the Center for Latin American and Caribbean Studies, and the Unit for Criticism and Interpretive Theory. As a transdisciplinary scholar, she researches and writes in the interstices between Latin American and U.S. Latinx cultural studies, continental philosophy, performance studies, queer theory, and contemporary literature. Cervantes-Gómez currently serves on the editorial board of *Women & Language* and is co-chair of the Latin American Studies Association (LASA) Sexualities Section. She is completing her first monograph entitled, *Pasivo: Risks of Exposure in Bottom Mexicanness Performance*.

Patrick Eisenlohr is Professor of Anthropology, Chair of Society and Culture in Modern India at the University of Göttingen. He received a PhD in Anthropology from the University of Chicago and previously held positions at Utrecht University, Washington University in St. Louis, and New York University.

Tom Froese is Assistant Professor at the Okinawa Institute of Science and Technology Graduate University (OIST), where he heads the Embodied Cognitive Science Unit. He serves as Editor-in-Chief of the journal *Adaptive Behavior*. Froese has a Master of Engineering in Cybernetics and Computer Science, and a Doctor of Philosophy in Cognitive Science.

Emiliano Gallaga Murrieta is Professor of Archaeology and Anthropology at the Universidad Autónoma de Chiapas, Mexico. He previously served as a federal delegate at the INAH Chiapas Center (2006–2013) and as director and professor of the EAHNM, Chihuahua (2014–2019).

Ian Hodder was trained at the Institute of Archaeology, University College London and at Cambridge University where he obtained his PhD in 1975. After a brief period teaching at Leeds, he returned to Cambridge where he taught until 1999. In 1999 he moved to teach at Stanford University as Dunlevie Family Professor in the Department of Anthropology and Director of the Stanford Archaeology Center. In 2021, he moved to teach at Koc University.

Jennifer Scheper Hughes (editor) is Professor in the Department of History at the University of California, Riverside. She is a historian of religion focusing on Latin American and Latinx religions with special consideration for the spiritual lives of Mexican and Mexican-American Catholics. Her book, *The Church of the Dead: The Epidemic of 1576 and the Birth of Christianity in the Americas* (NYU 2021), was named one of the top five books on religion for 2021 (Publishers Weekly). Professor Hughes' first book, *Biography of a Mexican Crucifix: Lived Religion and Local Faith from the Conquest to the Present* (OUP 2010), explores the affective bonds that join devotional communities to vital and agentic objects of material religion. Her research has been supported by grants and fellowships, including the Radcliffe Institute for Advanced Study at Harvard University, UCHRI, and the Luce Foundation. With colleagues from UCSD, UCSC, and UCLA, Hughes received a $1million grant to support collaboration with California Indian tribal nations and communities in retelling the story of the California missions.

Duane Jethro is a Post-doctoral Researcher in the research project "Making Differences: Transforming Museums and Heritage in the 21st Century", at the Centre for Anthropological Research on Museums and Heritage, CARMAH, at the Humboldt University Berlin. He has published in *Material Religion*, the *International Journal of Heritage Studies* and *Tourist Studies*. Jethro is the author of *Heritage Formation and the Senses in Post-Apartheid South Africa: Aesthetics of Power* (Bloomsbury, 2020).

Kapya J. Kaoma (ThD, Boston University) is a Zambian Anglican Priest, Interdisciplinary Scholar, Visiting Researcher at Boston University Center for Global Christianity and Mission in Boston, USA, and Distinguished Visiting Professor at St. John's University College in Zambia. In addition to publishing academic articles and chapters on the integration of African traditional philosophy in ecological ethics and politics, he has authored and edited a number of books, including *Christianity, Globalization, and Protective Homophobia, The Creator's Symphony, God's Family, God's Earth: Christian Ecological Ethics of Ubuntu*, and *Raised Hopes, Shattered Dreams*. He has also written and spoken extensively about subjects in Mission history, the Anglican communion, gender and African culture, human rights and intercontinental LGBTQI+ politics.

Laurel Kendall is Chair of the Division of Anthropology at the American Museum of Natural History and Curator of Asian Ethnographic Collections at AMNH. Best known for her work on Korean shamans, Kendall is the author of many books and articles on popular religion, including, most recently, *Mediums and Magical Things: Statues, Paintings, and Masks in Asian Places* (University of California Press, 2021).

Laura Arnold Leibman is Professor of English and Humanities at Reed College and the author of *The Art of the Jewish Family: A History of Women in Early New York in Five Objects* (Bard Graduate Center, 2020), which won three National Jewish Book Awards. She held visiting positions at Bard Graduate Center, Oxford University, Utrecht University, and the University of Panama. Her latest book *Once We Were Slaves* (Oxford UP, 2021) is about an early multiracial Jewish family who began their lives enslaved in the Caribbean and became some of the wealthiest Jews in New York.

Amanda Lucia is Professor of Religious Studies at the University of California-Riverside. She is author of *White Utopias: The Religious Exoticism of Transformational Festivals* (2020), *Reflections of Amma: Devotees in a Global Embrace* (2014), and numerous articles.

Sharday C. Mosurinjohn is Assistant Professor in the School of Religion at Queen's University, Kingston, Ontario. She is a philosopher of religion with a focus on the phenomenology and ontology of new media as well as esoteric aesthetics. She has published several articles on New Religious Movements, contemporary spirituality, and so-called "cults." Mosurinjohn is the author of *The Spiritual Crisis of Overload Boredom* (McGill-Queen's University Press, 2022).

S. Romi Mukherjee is Professor in the Gallatin School of Individualized Study and Media, Culture, and Communications at New York University in Paris. He is also Visiting Lecturer in the Political Humanities at *L'Institut d'études politiques de Paris*.

Evander Price is a postdoctoral fellow at the Center for Religion and the Human at Indiana University, Bloomington. He received his doctorate in American Studies from Harvard University. His research focuses on apocalypse, monumentality, Anthropocene art, and environmental humanities. Currently, he is working on a book on the subject of Anthropocene monumentality.

Inken Prohl has been Professor of Religious Studies at Heidelberg University since 2006. She has been conducting fieldwork in Japan and Germany for several years. Her research interests focus on modern transformations of Buddhism, theories of "Material Religion," and artificial intelligence.

Katja Rakow is Associate Professor of Religious Studies at Utrecht University. Her research focuses on megachurches in the US and Singapore with a special interest in material religion, technology, and the use of texts in religious practices.

Allen F. Roberts is Emeritus Distinguished Professor of World Arts and Cultures at the University of California Los Angeles. Trained as a socio-cultural anthropologist, he specializes in sub-Saharan arts and humanities. Recent work includes *A Dance of Assassins: Performing Early Colonial Hegemony in the Congo* (Indiana University Press, 2013) and his edited volume to which he also contributed essays, *Striking Iron: The Art of African Blacksmiths* (Fowler Museum at UCLA, 2019).

Mary "Polly" Nooter Roberts (d. 2018) was an Africanist Art Historian, Professor of World Arts and Cultures at UCLA, and Consulting Curator of African Arts at the Los Angeles County Museum of Art. The Robertses conducted research together, co-authored scholarly treatises, co-curated museum exhibitions, and co-taught university courses. Their significant projects include *Memory: Luba Art and the Making of History* (Museum for African Art, New York, 1996), and *A Saint in the City: Sufi Arts of Urban Senegal* (UCLA Fowler Museum of Cultural History, 2003), while *Devotional Spaces of a Global Saint: Shirdi Sai Baba's Presence* (Routledge, 2022), to which the Robertses contributed essays, is dedicated to Polly's memory.

S. Brent Rodríguez-Plate (editor) is a Writer, Speaker, Editor, and Part-time College Professor whose books include *Blasphemy: Art that Offends* (Black Dog, 2006), *A History of Religion in 5½ Objects* (Beacon, 2014), and *Religion and Film: Cinema and the Re-Creation of the World* (Columbia University Press, 2017). His essays have been published in *Newsweek, Slate, The Los Angeles Review of Books, The Christian Century, The Islamic Monthly, The Huffington Post,* and elsewhere. He is a Board Member of the Interfaith Coalition of Greater Utica, NY; Executive Director of the Association for Religion and Intellectual Life; and Editor of the journal *CrossCurrents*. He is professor, by special appointment, at Hamilton College, NY.

Olaya Sanfuentes is Professor at Pontificia Universidad Católica de Chile where she works on Latin American material and visual culture and media. She is the author of *Develando el Nuevo Mundo Imágenes de un proceso* (Ediciones UC, Santiago, 2009). Her recent book chapters and articles include "The Vocabulary of Tenderness: Maternal Feelings towards the Christ Child among Spanish American Nuns", in *Emotion, Art and Christianity in the Transatlantic World, 1450–1800* (Brill, 2021); and "Otherness Underfoot, Enemies of Occidental Christian Culture Defeated by the Apostle St James", in *Ikon* (2022). She has also written narratives for museums and history books for children.

Roger Sansi is Professor of Anthropology at Universitat de Barcelona. He has worked on contemporary art and the concept of the fetish. Sansi is the author of *Fetishes and Monuments* (Berghahn, 2007), co-editor of *Sorcery in the Black Atlantic* (The University of Chicago Press, 2011), and author of *Art, Anthropology and the Gift* (Routledge, 2015).

Younes Saramifar is Assistant Professor of Inhumanities at Vrije Universiteit Amsterdam. He holds a doctorate in sociology and another in cultural anthropology. He is hitchhiking between acts of killing, violence, nonstate combatants and activists, and material expressions of everyday life. He crafts interdisciplinary approaches and finds himself perplexed by the weird and lesser explored corners of existence.

Vineeta Sinha is Professor and Head of Department at the Department of Sociology, at the National University of Singapore. Her research interests include Hindu religiosity in the diaspora, intersections of religion, commodification and consumption processes, the interface of religion and materiality, and religion-state encounters in colonial and post-colonial moments. Her publications include the following books: *A New God in the Diaspora? Muneeswaran Worship in Contemporary Singapore* (National University of Singapore Press, 2007), *Religion and Commodification: Merchandising Diasporic Hinduism* (Routledge, 2011), and *Religion-State Encounters in Hindu Domains: From the Straits Settlements to Singapore* (Springer, 2011).

Barbara Sostaita is the granddaughter of Pilar Villegas and Clementina Cesar. She comes from a lineage of women whose touch maintained the home and nurtured life. She received her PhD from The University of North Carolina at Chapel Hill and is an Assistant Professor in Latin American and Latino Studies at The University of Illinois at Chicago. She is completing a manuscript titled *Sanctuary Everywhere: Fugitive Care on the Migrant Trail.*

Tulasi Srinivas is Professor of Anthropology, Religion and Transnational Studies at The Marlboro Institute of Interdisciplinary Studies at Emerson College. She is author/editor of the award-winning books *Winged Faith: Rethinking Religious Pluralism and Globalization* (Columbia University Press, 2010), *Curried Cultures: Globalization, Food and South Asia* (University of California Press, 2012) and *The Cow in the Elevator: An Anthropology of Wonder* (Duke University Press, 2018). Srinivas serves on the boards of The American Academy of Religion, the American Anthropological Association, and The World Economic Forum, Davos.

Emiko Stock is a Visual and Historical Anthropologist at The American University in Cairo. Working with Chams (Cambodian Muslims) and Sayyids (descendants of the Prophet Muhammad), she traces passages between Sunnism and Shi'ism and Cambodia and Iran as a practice of history refracted in still and moving images.

Johan Strijdom is Professor of Religious Studies at the University of South Africa and editor of the *Journal for the Study of Religion*. His research focuses on critical terms and theories in the comparative study of religions, with particular attention to case studies from southern Africa.

Pooyan Tamimi Arab (editor) is Assistant Professor of Religious Studies at Utrecht University. He is the author of *Amplifying Islam in the European Soundscape* (Bloomsbury, 2017) and *Why Do Religious Forms Matter?* (Palgrave, 2022). Tamimi Arab is a board member of the Amsterdam Spinoza Circle and a member of the Young Academy of the Royal Netherlands Academy of Arts and Sciences.

Shaheed Tayob is Lecturer in the Department of Sociology and Social Anthropology at Stellenbosch University, South Africa. His research in the Anthropology of Islam focuses on the materiality of food practices and human-animal relations as a lens through which to understand the complex entanglements of ethics, religion, politics, and economy in India and South Africa. His recent journal articles and book chapters include work on the neoliberal transformation of halal in South Africa and a consideration of the ethics and politics of slaughter, order, and infrastructural neglect in Mumbai, India.

Pamela D. Winfield is Professor of Buddhist Studies at Elon University in North Carolina. She is the author of the award-winning monograph *Icons and Iconoclasm in Japanese Buddhism: Kūkai and Dōgen on the Art of Enlightenment* (Oxford University Press, 2013) and co-editor of *Zen and Material Culture* (Oxford University Press, 2017).

Yohan Yoo is Professor and Chair of the Department of Religious Studies in the College of Humanities at Seoul National University, South Korea. His research takes a comparative perspective on broad religious issues, ranging from purity and pollution, iconic and performative aspects of sacred books, and general theory and method in the study of religion, to myth and contemporary literature. He recently co-authored with James W. Watts a book titled *Cosmologies of Pure Realms and The Rhetoric of Pollution* (Routledge, 2021).

ACKNOWLEDGMENTS

We are grateful to Utrecht University for institutional support for this project. The editors and several of the authors came together at Utrecht in the summer of 2018 to explore what a new handbook of material religion might look like. At Utrecht, we thank Birgit Meyer especially, for supporting our vision for the project from the start, and then reading and thinking along with us. Hamilton College and the University of California, Riverside also provided funds in support of this publication.

It was no small feat to bring a labor like this to completion during the Coronavirus pandemic. We extend our gratitude to the contributing authors, for their diligence and patience. Their essays, complex and provocative, have helped us think better and more deeply. They offer readers nothing less than continents of meaning.

A tremendous debit is owed to the masterful Kirsten Janene-Nelson, for taking on the Herculean task of copyediting this handbook and doing so with both care and creativity.

Pooyan Tamimi Arab, Jennifer Scheper Hughes, and S. Brent Rodríguez-Plate

EDITORS' INTRODUCTION

The Pasts, Presents, and Futures of the Study of Material Religion

*Pooyan Tamimi Arab, Jennifer Scheper Hughes,
and S. Brent Rodríguez-Plate*

The phrase "material religion" is redundant. Religion is always already material.

Religion does not simply manifest in physical forms. Nor does religion operate from a theo-logic or anthropo-logic in which rational thought patterns and texts establish first-order constructions while material entities remain second-order, symbolic representations. "Religion" does not refer to content, and "material" does not refer to some container into which content is poured. Instead, religion is material through and through.

So, why preserve the descriptor "material" to modify "religion"? The study of material religion as such stands as a corrective to an interpretive approach to religion that has historically operated out of what amounts to a Platonist worldview, positing an abstract, immaterial realm in which true religion is found, usually discovered by reading texts. Traditionally, scholars of religion have contemplated manifold and abundant ritual engagements with the material world as all-too-human attempts to create a channel back to the invisible beyond, where material forms are mere shadows that only "matter" in so far as they refer to the deeper reality they refract and reflect.

In contrast and counterbalance, material religion as a theory and method works to upset this historical, hierarchical order by placing objects, things, and other manifest corporalities at the center of scholarly studies of religious life and practice. Indeed, studies in material religion often work from the premise that, in fact, materiality is primary while beliefs, ideas, and theologies are secondary. Granted, thoughts can shape materials, but it is the body (biological and otherwise) that first gives rise to thought.

As an interdisciplinary thematic sub-field, the study of material religion has coalesced since the end of the twentieth century. With this volume, we approach a field that has now come of age. In so doing, we build on—without attempting to supersede—previous collective efforts to codify and organize the field. David Morgan's edited collection *Religion and Material Culture* (Routledge 2010) may have been the first in this regard, with essays thematically categorized under "performance," "things," and "spaces." A few years later, Dick Houtman and Birgit Meyer's *Things: Religion and the Question of Materiality* (Fordham 2012) nuanced and expanded some of the categories by schematizing essays around "anxieties about things," "public space," "bodily fluids," and "digital technologies." Most recently, Vasudha Narayanan's edited *Wiley Blackwell Companion to Religion and Materiality* (2020) structured the study of material religion into broad topics such as "bodies," "performances," "spatiality,"

DOI: 10.4324/9781351176231-1

"mobility," "media," "food," and more. Together these works have identified and defined the key categories and analytics that have made the field of material religion accessible to and usable for a broad range of scholars.

Given the defining groundwork achieved in these prior collective volumes, we have sought to leverage the opportunities of the handbook genre toward other ends. From the beginning of this project, we have been self-conscious about the place of this "handbook"—both in relation to these other works and in relation to the current prevalence, even overabundance, of the handbook genre on the publication landscape. We refuse many, if not all, of the implications of the "handbook" genre. Instead, we work to subvert it. Our purpose is not to represent, consolidate, summarize, or frame or fix the boundaries of our field. Our volume does not serve as some sort of academic field guide: readers will find no maps or markers, no taxonomies. As editors, we are neither guardians of, nor evangelists for, the field of material studies of religion. Even as we wonder about the excess of handbooks on the publishing landscape, we wield the "handbook" genre and leverage its opportunities—breadth, inclusion, and dissemination—for other purposes. At the same time, we believe that the essays in our volume can collectively serve as an exploratory source for those who are new to the topic.

With this handbook, we retain an awareness of the constructions and categorizations of what we call material religion even as we urge the field in new directions. The essays and chapters within do not solidify the boundaries of material religion; in fact, some trouble them. We wonder about the limits of the field and seek to transgress them. We ask: What counts as material? Who gets to decide? How might those boundaries be expanded and redrawn? And even, what is religion? Perhaps most saliently, we shaped this volume to offer a critical interrogation of structures of power (racial, economic, political, gendered), as of the legacies of imperial and colonial domination. We perceive that the Protestant-normative ethos of Western studies of religion has as one of its inclinations a "de-politicizing" character inherited from its imbrication with capitalism. Our (re)turn to the material contradicts and contests this tendency. We hold that we can introduce normative evaluations while maintaining the study of material religion as a scientific endeavor.

Our *Routledge Handbook of Material Religion* traces some of its intellectual origins to a meeting at Utrecht University in the summer of 2018. At that seminar, a dozen scholars from around the world, including ourselves, discussed the "past and future" of material religion. From those conversations, we knew we wanted to highlight the many historical sources of this type of study, but what came out was a keen interest in pushing toward new directions for the future. S. Brent Rodríguez-Plate is the founding editor of the flagship journal in the field, *Material Religion: The Journal of Objects, Art, and Belief.* Pooyan Tamimi Arab is an anthropologist and philosopher who researches political ideals such as religious tolerance and the separation of church and state from a material religion perspective. Jennifer Scheper Hughes is a historian of religion in Latin America who writes within the mode of lived religion on the affective ties between devotees and images. When we extended invitations to others to contribute to our volume, we wanted to represent something of the global purview of scholars in the field.

We have shaped our conversation around four categories, clustering our thirty chapters loosely within four suggestive thematics. We start with a kind of "history" (Part 1, Genealogies), then work through some of the "terms" (Part 2, Materializing Terms), and end with two key areas that encompass some of the emerging work in the field (Parts 3 and 4, Entanglements and Hyperobjects). Within each category our authors explore and probe the given thematic from different perspectives, and each category includes a diverse set of critical interrogations. Within these, readers will encounter essays on both the material conditions and "conditionedness" of human existence—as well as the material consequences of embodied religious belief and practice: from the materiality of *ubuntu*, an African philosophy of humanity, to rifles as potent symbols of Shia communities devoted to the Islamic Republic of Iran; from environmental annihilation to queer materialities of Aztec religion; from the destruction of images and the impossibility of incarnation to the hypermateriality of the world's largest religious festival, India's Kumbh Mela. As many of the chapters in this handbook exemplify, there are a great plethora of ways to construct material religion as a field of study, and a variety of genealogies reveal its multiple historical trajectories.

This handbook is thus Janus-faced, gazing on the past and future with equal optical force and delivered here in the present. The contributions make an account of what has happened in this field and how it has been defined up to this point, including its genealogies and modes of classification. It also turns toward the state of the field with a focus on what is to come, pushing for new definitions, new approaches, new ways of generating smart, sophisticated scholarship—new ways of showing that, indeed, the term "material religion" is redundant. Grounded in the evidence of specific case studies, each chapter provides broad theoretical insights that are applicable to multiple situations.

Part I: Genealogies of Material Religion

For Part I, we asked contributors to reflect on the intellectual lines of descent that shape and define material religion as an academic approach, as well as to focus on unacknowledged genealogies. As a field of specific inquiry, the study of material religion began to develop in the 1990s, leading to the founding in 2005 of the dedicated scholarly journal *Material Religion*. Contributors to the field drew from earlier modes of reasoning as they materialized the academic study of religion. From twentieth-century thought, Mauss, Merleau-Ponty, and Bourdieu come to mind: on the body, perceptions, emotions, practices, and politics. Scholars of material religion may even refer back to Aristotle's conception of the human sensorium (e.g., Verrips 2008, 2010; Lambek 2013). Other founding influences came from the fields of anthropology, archaeology, art history, and cultural studies. Writing the genealogies of the study of material religion, we argue, contributes to the larger project of researching the genealogies of religion (e.g., Asad 1993; Masuzawa 2005; Chidester 2014).

Previous studies of material religion have not typically offered genealogies of the field, with few exceptions. Birgit Meyer and David Chidester, whose thinking is decisively informed by the imperial outreach of "the West," divide the field of material religion in relation to two fundamental trajectories: (1) a methodological recognition of performativity and the so-called affective turn, which goes against the now thoroughly interrogated "Protestant bias" in studies of religious sensibilities and sensations; and (2) an emphasis on the world-changing power of colonization (see, e.g., Meyer 2012 and Chidester 2018). The result is a critical analysis of religious phenomena, focusing especially on the relations of people whose lives are marked by encounters with religious pluriformity in colonial frontier zones. Toward this end, Chidester and Meyer identify early analysis of material religion in canonical thinkers and scientists such as Feuerbach and Durkheim, and thus contribute to our awareness of our field's long genealogy. They also develop the approach further: by showing how asymmetrical transnational interactions shaped what we think religions are (see Chidester's *Empire of Religion* 2014), and by exploring how the study of material religious forms contributes to understanding inclusion and exclusion in contemporary pluralist settings (in projects such as Meyer's *Religious Matters in an Entangled World*, which started in 2016 at Utrecht University and is ongoing; see: www.religiousmatters.nl).

The material religion approach did not gain influence in a political vacuum, nor did the theories on which it still relies. In making transparent some of the diverse genealogies of the field, we hope to reveal and interrogate some of its more problematic normative judgments, including those that may be hidden or embedded within its very concepts of critique and interpretation. Most material religion scholars have not made explicit nor unpacked the normative assumptions that orient their scholarship, preferring to use the concept of "critique" as a container for various political judgments. Casting the material perspective as a "new turn" further serves to obscure the methodological and normative judgments built into the approach. Genealogies, in the senses of Nietzsche and Foucault, do more than describe these contemporary perspectives' lineage of descent: they respond to contextual questions about identity, interests, and power. Who argued in such and such manner? What social relation brought them to think in this way? What did they stand to gain or lose? And what became of those affected by this or that style of reasoning? We thus point to analyses that exclude or marginalize the religious experience and purposes of historically dominated groups, such as women, Indigenous, Queer, and Black people, as well as of those who have been rendered invisible on the horizons of Western thought.

Pooyan Tamimi Arab's chapter on Benedictus de Spinoza (1632–1677) opens our authors' reflections in this part, proposing an interpretive model in which material religion becomes an analytical lens through which to critically re-engage founding works of traditional philosophy. Rather than thinking with philosophy, or contrasting philosophy to studies of material religion (e.g., Miller 2005: 14; Chidester 2018: 53), attending to genealogies allows us to turn the gaze back on to philosophers themselves to interrogate the role of material religion in the intricacies of their writings. Despite their profound influence on thinking of the religious as material, philosophies have rarely been researched by scholars of material religion. (An exception to the rule is Chidester's early work on philosophy, theology, and the senses; see Strijdom 2018 for an overview.) Nor have many philosophers written for the journal *Material Religion*. But what if the existing material religion approach is applied to critically re-evaluate its ancestors? What do Spinoza and other philosophers write about religious rituals, body techniques, and architecture styles, or about sacred books, spiritual dreams, and symbols? What do their philosophies reveal about the intellectual history of thinking about concepts such as immanence, mediation, and materiality? And, what do we learn from studying material religion in philosophical texts about the approach's normative inclinations vis-à-vis religious pluriformity?

The authors of this part of the handbook "re-member" philosophies and less widely recognized ways of thinking (cf. Meyer 2016). Some predate contemporary studies in material religion; others originate in non-Western contexts. By learning about potential blind spots, we aim to deepen and diversify the core conceptualization of the material approach to religion. Ulrike Brunotte's chapter introduces the performance and aesthetic-oriented studies of classicist Jane Harrison (1850–1928). In drawing attention to the work of this currently underestimated woman scholar, Brunotte renews the canon known to most material religion scholars. Pamela Winfield's chapter illustrates the capacity of the material religion approach to engage academic and religious traditions beyond a Western-centric timeline. Researching the history of Japanese Buddhist philosophy or the material culture of Zen, and rooted in Indian and Chinese theories of material culture such as art and architecture, Winfield presents an alternative history of philosophizing enlightenment in the material realm. Buddhist masters such as Kūkai (774–835) and Dōgen (1200–1253) are therefore not only relevant for specialists of Japanese history, but can also become points of reference for scholars working on material religion, thus providing a sense of the historical depth of the approach. Kapya

Kaoma's chapter similarly presents material religion as inherent in the African philosophical concept *ubuntu* by engaging with the work of the nineteenth-century Church of England missionary Henry Rowley (d. 1884). Kaoma argues that Rowley's openness to African cosmologies, appreciating the role of materiality therein, led to his work being sidelined by Africanists.

The possibilities for writing genealogies of material religion seem endless, so which should be written about? Our authors' choices appear to derive from desires to relieve us of ignorance and to criticize past and present prejudices. The impetus to criticize injustice is not a feature of all research in material religion studies—and it does not have to be—but political concerns are central to its theorization. This can be observed in the chapter by Xiomara Verenice Cervantes-Gómez, which calls attention to "promiscuous" genealogies that are excluded by conservative, clinically demarcated (versus transgressive) understandings of religion and the body. Cervantes-Gómez describes queer materialities of religion through the example of Aztec "anal theologies," reflecting on the contemporary reverberation of sex captured in the hieroglyphics of past sexual experiences.

It is beyond the capacity of one volume to retrieve all such previously neglected genealogies. Here we provide some examples of what could and should be included—not just so the mainstream genealogies of the transdisciplinary thematic field that is material religion can be made more critical and inclusive, but also to open up the possibility of seeing more than what single perspectives can offer. In *On the Genealogies of Morals*, Nietzsche himself reconciled his philosophy's relativism with the quest for objectivity:

> There is only a perspective seeing, only a perspective "knowing"; and the more affects we allow to speak about one thing, the more eyes, different eyes; we can use to observe one thing, the more complete will our "concept" of this thing, our "objectivity," be.
>
> (Nietzsche [1967] 1989: 119)

In a similar spirit, Johan Strijdom's analytical chapter clarifies the role that comparisons can play in defining the concept of material religion. Comparing is not an end in itself, argues Strijdom. It can become a critical act by making explicit the normative, essentialist, and in some cases oppressive judgments attached to the things humans consider sacred. Strijdom illustrates this with a discussion of the ways two South African monuments have been understood: the nationalist Voortrekker Monument and the post-apartheid-designed Freedom Park. When informed by genealogies and comparisons, taking a critical perspective is a way of seeing with many different eyes in striving to understand the contested dynamics of material religion—hopefully so that we scholars are prevented from making errors of judgment.

Part II: Materializing the Terms of the Study of Religion

Words and their meanings are unstable, changing over time. New technologies, social movements, and scholarly writing *about* words alter their definitions and usages for current environments. The second part of this handbook of material religion attends to the ways the terms used in the academic study of religious life and practice have evolved over time. Material religion theories and methods have caused scholars to rethink some of the ways traditionally significant terms in religious studies have shifted.

Just how much the meaning of terms shifts is well illustrated by a description of "material religion" in *The Eclectic Magazine of Foreign Literature, Science, and Art*, a nineteenth-century periodical based in New York. Edited by a series of Protestant ministers, the publication included an 1865 article on the "Battle of Lepanto" by Professor Eugène Rousseeuw Saint-Hilaire, Chair of Ancient History at the Sorbonne. Fought in 1571, the Battle of Lepanto pitted the "Holy League" (several European Catholic states united under Pope Pius V) against the (Muslim) Ottoman Empire. Saint-Hilaire suggests: "Material religion and spiritual religion met for the first time in decisive conflict, and spirit triumphed over matter, as Christianity triumphed over the Old World in a battle lasting not for one day but for three centuries" (Saint-Hilaire: 366). In this binary account, "material religion" is part of the Old World, connected to Islam—while Christianity is "spiritual," part of the emerging New World.

Rousseeuw Saint-Hilaire's use of the term "material religion" was not unusual for his time. Throughout English publications in the nineteenth century, the term appears consistently in the pejorative, used in essays to denigrate religious others, such as Muslims and Mormons, as well as other traditions, such as African traditions that were placed within an evolution of religion and connected with "primitive" practices.

At the start of the twentieth-first century, the term itself has evolved and is now used with increasing frequency in academic fields including anthropology, art history, history, sociology, and religious studies. In a key text on the topic, Matthew Engelke states that "all religion is material religion" (Engelke 2011: 209). There is a certain logic to this statement, but, as just noted, the meaning behind the terminology has not always been considered in the same way.

Terminology changes. Academia is notorious for producing more and more neologisms as ways of explaining novel events, behaviors, people, and things. There is a benefit to these new terms, since they stand as signs marking a state-of-the-art approach, pointing out a break with what comes before. The word "term" itself comes from the Latin and denotes an "end" or "limit" (as in, *terminus*). Terms have limits, and sometimes a limit has been reached and it is time for something new.

One of the ways material religion has impacted religious studies more broadly is by redefining many of the terms used in the field (see Plate 2015). While not comprehensive, the chapters in the second part of this handbook offer case studies to allow a rethinking of the terms that define and describe religious life and practice. The idea is that a redefining of these terms can help reanimate the older approaches. Together with the first part on genealogies, this part looks to the past in order to offer renewed takes on future studies.

As with the rehabilitating of the term "material religion," this part provides a reconsideration of a number of key terms that are often used by scholars while examining religious dimensions of life. Many terms that were developed as negative monikers have been rethought through a particularly material lens. Terms like "fetish," as the chapter by Roger Sansi demonstrates, were at one point solely pejorative descriptors—but in recent years have been rethought and put to use again as positive ways to rethink the complexity of religious life and practice. Relatedly, Laurel Kendall and Ni Wayan Pasek Ariati, in their chapter re-situate "animism" via Balinese masks, turning to the related action verbs "ensoulment" and "animation" to indicate more precisely the power of the activities undertaken. In such instances the re-materializing of terms shows that what were once words used to instantiate difference (i.e., "'Those' people use *fetish* objects, 'we' do not"), are turned around to demonstrate how all religious traditions are constituted in part by these once-pejorative terms.

Likewise, major terms that have been at the bedrock of religious studies (and theology) are rephrased to show what they look like when approached from a material studies perspective. In her contribution, Katja Rakow takes on an interrelated family of terms—centered around "book" and "scripture"—that also enfolds "words" and "text" into its orbit; materializing these terms entails shifting them from their semantic (and immaterial) understanding to the embodied practices of reading, holding, and sensing books-as-objects in multi-mediated ways. Emiko Stock's chapter on Cambodian Cham "texts" demonstrates that the idea of a "manuscript" shifts as we look at the fullness of lived, bodily religious life, one that resists the colonizing impulses of equating manuscripts with verbal language that must be read and interpreted by "literate" experts. Yohan Yoo thinks with and through the ever-prominent term "symbol" via indigenous Korean shamanistic practices, indicating that, while studies of religion have often suggested how symbolic structures retain a split between sign and signifier, in shamanistic *gut* rituals there is no split—the material and the divine are united. And Tulasi Srinivas takes on "ritual," finding its emergence across everyday life in Bangalore through the practice of eating *prasadam*, an idea and practice that has mythological roots but that takes on a variety of concatenations in real-life existence, since food itself transforms human bodies in observably physical ways.

Part II also reimagines some relatively new terms in the study of material religion. This includes "queer materialities," as highlighted in Sharday Mosurinjohn's chapter on The Satanic Temple. Mosurinjohn argues that the tactics of the Temple group activate a form of social resistance through decidedly material religion work, operating through non-binary spaces. Duane Jethro initiates a strong take on the term "heritage," which has been well-used in material religion studies but has not been as widespread in general scholarly approaches to the understanding of religious life and practice; "heritage" may, on Jethro's account, be an analogous term to the term "religion" itself.

Perhaps all this rematerializing of terms is what Allen and Polly Roberts proffer in their chapter as "brainsmithing," an ingenious neologism created by the African American artist Lonnie Holley when referring to transformational, postcolonial sculpture. Nonetheless, as Kendall and Ariati note, such terms, especially when given by outsiders, "must be deployed with caution lest they elide the sometimes messy and variable processes they are intended to define." Verbal language too is deeply material, not only in its mediatized forms but also in its impact on the religious worlds that use, and that are used by, the terms.

Part III: Entanglements, Entrapment, Escaping

The third part of this handbook is inspired by the work of archaeologist Ian Hodder in which he theorizes the human condition with the concept of "entanglement." The archaeological record shows, he argues, that from the time of human prehistory—much earlier than the advent of modern capitalism—relations of material dependency increased exponentially, leading to "entrapment." Echoing Horkheimer and Adorno's *Dialectic of Enlightenment*, Hodder's account of the human trajectory—from the first cave paintings to spiritual experiences in twenty-first-century museums—entails? instrumental reason's spinning out of control. This part kicks off with Hodder's chapter about archaeological research of human-thing dependency at a 9,000-year-old site in central Turkey, explaining why religious worldviews arise from fundamental material conditions. In response to phenomena beyond human control, and with which we may be so entangled that there is no escape—the wild, death, the future—religious practices help humans cope with uncertainty by manipulating the forces that make up their worldview.

Such material entanglements are a permanent characteristic of religions. Froese and Gallaga's chapter illustrates this in measuring entanglements in prehistoric Mexico, showing that religious practices were determined by the environment: material features set in motion self-reinforcing social processes of religious aesthetic formations. The relation between the material and the socially influenced human imagination is, from the Hodderian perspective, likely to be asymmetrical. The concept of entanglements, in other words, has the virtue of scrutinizing all too positive interpretations of the material religion nexus by focusing on the asymmetries of thing-human relations that make up inescapable networks.

No wonder, then, that scholars of material religion focus on mediation, arguing that for a religious phenomenon to be experienced as such, the material nature of mediation must fade into the background so as to make space for an experience of immediacy (Eisenlohr 2009, 2012). The religious can only then conjure a direct experience of the metaphysical forces or beings: the transcendent, gods, spirits, or ancestors. Such experiences of immediacy in many contexts go together with religious practitioners' awareness of fabrication processes. Anthropologist Vineeta Sinha's contribution illustrates a similar process. She describes how people make ritual objects work in modern India: by socially and mentally disentangling them from commercialization and commodification processes. Sinha argues that, in everyday Hindu religiosity in a fast-paced capitalist world, people need to unscramble the objects from their place in the chains of production and consumption to be able to have the attitudes that orient them toward Hindu religiosity.

To change our dependency on material things and to break free, argues Hodder in Nietzschean fashion, would require nothing less than to cross the bridge, to become something that goes beyond what it means to be human (Hodder 2012: 221). While we in material religion studies may point to the inescapable relations with matter, in many religious traditions the relation to the material is ambivalent at best, hostile at worst. Approaching Buddhism philosophically, Romi Mukherjee describes attempts to overcome entanglements and the rapaciousness of the entangled human ego by cultivating a positive relation toward immateriality in practices such as Tibetan monks wiping away mandalas after weeks of careful creation—itself an act of manipulating matter. Inken Prohl's chapter approaches the topic from what appears to be a diametrically opposed perspective. She scoffs at dematerializations based on preoccupations with supposedly deep philosophical works. These obviously do not reflect religiosity in everyday entangling with popular culture. They reflect, she writes, "the priorities of men's worlds." In *de facto* entangled religion and popular culture, differences between Siddhartha Buddha and Justin Bieber fall away. Historical research into such low cultural or mundane products as Christmas gift cards, in Olaya Sanfuentes's chapter on commodification and religion in nineteenth- and twentieth-century Chile, results in a similar theoretical outlook as Prohl's. Readers will have to decide whether they are convinced by Mukherjee to not posit the essentiality of the material—to make space for silence, void, and zero, against the human condition of entanglement; or whether they prefer Prohl's almost blasphemous mixing of religion and popular culture, which argues from a gender-critical perspective against their dichotomization. Some readers may be convinced by both.

Entanglements and entrapment are conditions often sought to escape because of their intrinsic violence. Articles published in the journal *Material Religion*, however, betray a tendency to focus more on tolerance than intolerance, to humanity rather than "inhumanity," and to steer away from the things of religious socialization in violence. Younes Saramifar's chapter on the "jewels of men"—from swords and bows to the AK47—describes masculinity and the materiality of weaponry in Muslim societies. Saramifar describes, for instance, how the Supreme Leader of the Islamic Republic of Iran, Ayatollah Khamenei, chooses to hold a Dragunov sniper rifle during Friday sermons to give tribute to marksmen deployed to fight ISIS (the Islamic State of Iraq and Syria). We hope that scholars of material religion will follow suit and produce more historical and ethnographic accounts of the roles weapons play in religious traditions in different times and places.

Another form of religious socialization in violence is animal sacrifice. Though religious studies is opening up to interdisciplinary approaches to animals (e.g., Schaefer 2015), much work is still to be done in this area. Anthropologist Shaheed Tayob gives a moving account of his Indian Muslim interlocutor's long care for his goat before having it slaughtered on the occasion of the feast of sacrifice that commemorates Prophet Abraham's submission to the will of God. Tayob's account does not reduce sacrifice to violence. Instead, he unsettles the reader by presenting an ethnographic description of a religious tradition that entangles violence and intimacy. Such accounts make us wonder, in good anthropological fashion: What can we learn from life's messiness, of people actually living with, caring for, and slaughtering animals?

Entanglements connect and, in the process, delineate possibilities of inclusion and exclusion. Part III closes with a chapter by anthropologist and Latin American studies scholar Barbara Sostaita. She presents *Borrando La Frontera*, a queer touch and transborder communion performance in which artist Ana Teresa Fernández used powder blue paint to "erase" the US-Mexico border wall. Sostaita describes the performance art alongside a weekly border Eucharist, described by the minister as an occasion in which people touch each other's fingertips on the other side of the wall as they pray together. The minister explains: "We then invite them to raise their hands and look at the sky as a reminder that God's grace is greater than the structures humans create for ourselves." Religious performances, Sostaita shows, do not only assist in coping with or escaping entanglements; they also serve an important public role by touching the heart and imagining another world.

Part IV: Hyperobjects, or, How Ginormous Things Affect Religions

The final set of essays recasts what we mean by "object" into a larger network—to interpret and extrapolate the object in a massive, excessive manner. What of those "things" that are so large in scale as to be spatially and temporally "ungraspable" by human perception (Morton 2013: 2)? Such "hyperobjects" are akin to Marcel Mauss's concept of total social facts, shaping human life and natural surroundings in a huge way, and being entangled with all major dimensions of societies such as the economy, ecology, politics, law, medicine, and religiosity. We write this introduction even as our planet confronts the hyperobject of the global COVID pandemic and its not-yet-legible future impacts.

From its origin, religious studies focused attention on sacred texts, doctrines, beliefs, and the realm of the interior. In distinction, the more recent approach of material religion seeks to turn religion inside out, to explore the ways religious people engage with objects, the things of the world that anchor devotional and ritual practice. In their focus on the object, scholars have been explicit in their critique of the Protestant normative impulse, which has historically either neglected, criticized, or misread the significance of religious objects for diverse communities. As the balance has shifted toward centering objects and materiality even more so than belief, at least one aspect of Protestant bias has been reified: the emphasis on personal devotion cast within a culturally particular, individualized—even atomized—frame. The objects of material religion that have preoccupied scholars are typically small, human-scale things. Eminently available for personal use, these objects sometimes pertain first and foremost to the intimate and interior worlds of devotees (Hughes 2020). Icons, stones, fetishes, portraits, prayer beads, household shrines, museum displays, tombs, magazines, clothing, statues, crucifixes, paintings, books, headscarves, relics, foods, cards, human bodies, and human bodily fluids: these are characterized by their accessibility and immediacy, all designed, enacted, and used primarily in individual or highly localized settings. Even media-oriented analyses are often relegated to user-experience studies, while new emphases on affect theory and cognitive studies in religion and ritual have continued to isolate individual responses to the material world. The particular emphasis on the personal, the interior, and the small-scale among US and Western European scholars may be a Protestant inclination, often deeply imbricated with the spirit of capitalism. Indeed, contemporary devotional cultures are often inflected by consumer capitalist culture, which weaves the spell of individual choice over vast and diverse global populations.

At the same time, there is an urgency to confront a particular set of unwieldy "objects" of extraordinary dimension and magnitude: environmental catastrophe, pandemic illness, the fracturing and fractal impact of vast-scale infrastructure projects like a 2,000-mile border wall. We invoke the term "hyperobjects," elaborated by philosopher and ecologist Timothy Morton, to consider the religious significance of those things that are "massively distributed in time and space relative to humans" (2013: 1). Morton's examples include global warming (because there is "no rational solution" to it; 2013: 135), all the Styrofoam on Earth (not just because of its ubiquity, but because of its longevity), and pollution (in its simultaneous diffusion and "sticky" adhesion). In its totality, the hyperobject is incomprehensible and even imperceptible to individual human beings. It is non-local by definition because its immediately perceived and specifically experienced impacts are only a very partial iteration of the object itself. Yet, its materiality is of enormous consequence and includes the threat of human, even biological, extinction. Even if hyperobjects are never fully perceptible, we are all nevertheless entangled within them: as Morton explains, hyperobjects are "viscous . . . they stick to the beings that are involved with them" (2013: 1).

Of what relevance, then, are "hyperobjects" to the study of religion, and to the study of material religion specifically? What can religious studies bring to bear in human grappling with immanent but not fully perceptible threats to existence? In our application, the scale of the hyperobject denies and refuses availability and access to the religious subject, yet it still has religious relevance. The lens of hyperobjects allows our field to confront a range of objects of massive scale and, in particular, to grapple with the scope of environmental devastation and the threat of human extinction. These are placed in relation to religious beliefs, practices, and experiences, bringing to bear the primary interpretive analytics of religious studies: ritual, performance, identity and belonging, illness and health, the unfathomable, and even death itself.

Through this part we retain the term "object" to reiterate its material nature and attribute ongoing salience to the ways that human bodies engage with these objects. But by "hyper" we mean to explode the personal view, to put these objects in connection with and contrast to social, economic, environmental, political, and/or cultural histories—even as they point beyond their abilities to be grasped in any clear way. The religious is never isolatable from these other forces—but neither are these organizing forces isolatable from their material structures, at both the infra- and super-structural levels. In this way, the theme of hyperobjects overlaps with our lens of "entanglements," revealing the accretions of power that occur when massive formations and assemblies congeal. Our language of entanglements points toward the intersections and interstices. The vocabulary of hyperobjects allows us to approach and contemplate the mass itself, even as we accept its ultimate incomprehensibility and inaccessibility.

The chapters in this part offer several ways to think about hyperobjects in relation to religious contexts and religious phenomena. Together these essays consider the irreducible mass of large-scale infrastructure projects, a canal and a temporary, ephemeral sacred city; the senses as hyperobject, the irreducible incomprehensibility of disease and global pandemics; demographic cataclysm, and the void of human extinction.

S. Brent Rodríguez-Plate explores infrastructure as hyperobject through the immense impact of the Erie Canal on religious life in the United States. For Rodríguez-Plate, the canal is a geological, geographical, artistic, technological, and religious hyperobject. Without it, deeply engrained beliefs about free will, sex, science, manifest destiny, equal rights, the environment, the afterlife, and the imminent end of the world would not retain such a hold on the US imagination.

Amanda Lucia considers as hyperobject the Kumbh Mela, the Hindu mega ritual at the confluence of the Ganga, Yamuna, and (mythological) Saraswati rivers in northern India. During the days of the Kumbh Mela an order of magnitude of 100 million devotees participate. For Lucia, as hyperobject the Kumbh Mela defies the boundary of the senses, extends to the horizon, and negates its own existence (in the construction and dismantling of the temporary sacred city). In a different tack, Patrick Eisenlohr directs his attention to sound as an "eventful, energetic force." Considering sonic performance especially in an urban context, Eisenlohr argues that sonic atmospheres, much as affects, "seize upon . . . envelope, and intermingle with felt-bodies." He interprets sonic performances as eventful materiality, materially sensed and socially linked, and as "half-things" that share with hyperobjects the quality of unsteadiness in time and place. In them, causality and effect collapse into "one immediate causality."

Jennifer Scheper Hughes's chapter considers the Mexican *"mortandad"*—the demographic catastrophe of the sixteenth-century—the result and consequence of European invasion. Hughes reveals the extent to which epidemics, as hyperobjects, are perceptible or absent in the historical record. Laura Arnold Leibman considers the virus as hyperobject, the "stickiness" of a global pandemic that entangled local Jewish communities in New York in 1822. Leibman applies the concept of hyperobject to reveal how a Yellow Fever outbreak threatened providential views of the universe and motivated a more urgent form of Jewish mysticism that imbued rituals with a corresponding hyperpower.

Our handbook closes with Evander Price's chapter on a hyperobject of immense absence: the void caused by extinction events. Price places into a shared interpretive frame sixty-five million years of seashell extinction, the emergence of Young Earth theories of evolution, and scientific efforts toward the resurrection of extinct species. For Price, the concept of extinction has resulted in theological movement toward reconciliation with the "abyss of time and death." Living as we do in the sixth great extinction event, an apocalypse during which the planet's human population goes over the threshold of ten billion before 2100, scholars of religion may indeed, like Price, serve as witnesses to our struggles and follies.

References

Asad, Talal. 1993. *Genealogies of Religion: Discipline and Reasons of Power in Christianity and Islam.* Baltimore, MD: Johns Hopkins University Press.

Chidester, David. 2014. *Empire of Religion: Imperialism and Comparative Religion.* Chicago, IL: University of Chicago Press.

Chidester, David. 2018. *Religion: Material Dynamics.* Oakland, CA: University of California Press.

Eisenlohr, Patrick. 2009. "Technologies of the Spirit: Devotional Islam, Sound Reproduction and the Dialectics of Mediation and Immediacy in Mauritius." *Anthropological Theory* 9 (3) (September): 273–296.

Eisenlohr, Patrick. 2012. "Media and Religious Diversity." *Annual Review of Anthropology* 41: 37–55.

Engelke, Matthew. 2011. "Material Religion." In *The Cambridge Companion to Religious Studies*, edited by Robert Orsi, 209–229. Cambridge: Cambridge University Press.

Hodder, Ian. 2012. *Entangled: An Archaeology of the Relationships Between Humans and Things.* Chichester: Wiley Blackwell.

Houtman, Dick, and Birgit Meyer, eds. 2012. *Things: Religion and the Question of Materiality.* New York: Fordham University Press.

Hughes, Jennifer Scheper. 2020. "Objects of Devotion: Intimacy and Material Relations in Mexican Catholicism." In *Religious Intimacies: Intersubjectivity in the Modern Christian West,* edited by Mary Dunn and Brenna Moore, 131–145. Bloomington, IN: Indiana University Press.

Lambek, Michael. 2013. "The Value of (Performative) Acts." *HAU: Journal of Ethnographic Theory* 3 (2): 141–160.

Masuzawa, Tomoko. 2005. *The Invention of World Religions: Or How European Universalism Was Preserved in the Language of Pluralism.* Chicago, IL: University of Chicago Press.

Meyer, Birgit. 2012. *Mediation and the Genesis of Presence: Towards a Material Approach to Religion.* Inaugural Lecture, Utrecht University, Utrecht, Netherlands, October 19.

Meyer, Birgit. 2016. "How to Capture the 'wow': R.R. Marett's Notion of Awe and the Study of Religion." *Journal of the Royal Anthropological Institute* 22 (1): 7–26.

Miller, Daniel, ed. 2005. *Materiality.* Durham, NC: Duke University Press.

Morgan, David. 2010. *Religion and Material Culture: The Matter of Belief.* London: Routledge.

Morton, Timothy. 2013. *Hyperobjects: Philosophy and Ecology after the End of the World.* Minneapolis, MN: University of Minnesota Press.

Narayanan, Vasudha. 2020. *The Wiley Blackwell Companion to Religion and Materiality.* Hoboken, NJ: Wiley Blackwell.

Nietzsche, Friedrich. [1967] 1989. *On the Genealogy of Morals: Ecce Homo.* Translated by W. Kaufmann and R. J. Hollingdale, edited with commentary by W. Kaufmann. New York: Vintage Books.

Plate, S. Brent, ed. 2015. *Key Terms in Material Religion.* London: Bloomsbury.

Rousseeuw Saint-Hilaire, Eugène. 1865. "The Battle of Lepanto." *Eclectic Magazine of Foreign Literature, Science, and Art,* 357–367.

Schaefer, Donovan O. 2015. *Religious Affects: Animality Evolution and Power.* Durham, NC: Duke University Press.

Strijdom, Johan. 2018. "'Senses': Assessing a Key Term in David Chidester's Analysis of Religion." *Journal for the Study of Religion* 31 (2): 161–179.

Verrips, Jojada. 2008. "Offending Art and the Sense of Touch." *Material Religion* 4 (2): 204–225.

Verrips, Jojada. 2010. "Body and Mind: Material for a Never-Ending Intellectual Odyssey." In *Religion and Material Culture: The Matter of Belief,* edited by David Morgan, 21–40. London: Routledge.

PART I

Genealogies of Material Religion

1.1

SPINOZA

Arch-Father of the Material-Religion Approach

Pooyan Tamimi Arab

I took great pains not to laugh at human actions, or mourn them, or curse them, but only to understand them.

(Benedictus de Spinoza (1677, Political Treatise, Chapter 1, §4)

The theories that inform the material-religion approach are derived from older scientific endeavors to study religion as a human, historical, or even natural phenomenon. They echo the Enlightenment and nineteenth-century materialist, historicist, and political critiques of religion, all of which led to a perspective that methodologically excludes the idea of transcendence. Simultaneously, colonial empires facilitated the anthropological examination of diverse peoples' beliefs, rituals, and experiences of something that they may call God, spirits, the sacred, or the transcendent. Given the historical backdrop to the recent material turn in the study of religion, what we are engaged in is, in fact, a process of constant reinterpretation of past materialisms in conversation with new standpoints and empirical studies. This was already clearly the case in theory-driven works by David Chidester (1992, 2018) and also in reflections by Birgit Meyer (2016) on the material-religion approach's resonance with scholars whom we should "re-member" through critical reevaluation—such as Feuerbach, Durkheim, Marett, and Cassirer. A genealogical reconstruction of the material-religion approach, in turn, leads to rereading these thinkers through a material lens. Looking closer, it appears that our ancestors wrote a good deal about material religion: about sacred buildings, magical strategies, and the body techniques of various traditions. And material religion almost always played a role in thinking about power and justice; it was never theorized in a political vacuum. A key figure in this regard is the Early Modern philosopher Benedictus de Spinoza (1632–1677), born of Portuguese Jewish descent in the relatively free and pluralistic Amsterdam of the seventeenth century. Spinoza is rarely cited by scholars who study material religion, but they do build on the so-called affective turn in the humanities and the social sciences, which safeguarded the theoretical significance of the sensing body against a too-reductive focus on texts and beliefs alone and allowed a critical stance toward the notorious "Protestant bias" in studies of religion. Affect theory's indebtedness to Spinoza is acknowledged, often indirectly, in references to Gilles Deleuze ([1968] 1992, [1970] 1988), Brian Massumi (2002), and Antonio Damasio (2003) in works by anthropologists, religious studies scholars, art historians, and political theorists. It is somewhat surprising, then, that Spinoza is

DOI: 10.4324/9781351176231-3

named only twice in the first fifteen volumes of the journal *Material Religion*, once by Stewart Guthrie (2007), who places the Early Modern philosopher in a lineage extending to Feuerbach and Freud, and once by Diana Espírito Santo (2019) via Deleuze.[1] I agree with Sally Promey, who, in her edited volume *Sensational Religion: Sensory Cultures in Material Practice*, suggests without elaborating that the intricacies of philosophers such as Spinoza should not be forgotten by those adopting a material-religion approach. Indeed, leaving out thinkers like Spinoza can lead to an oversimplified history of the senses and their relation to religious traditions in modernity (2014: 13). How so? In this chapter, I explain this point by drawing the general contours of Spinoza's theorization of what we presently call material religion.

A genealogical approach differs, however, from a historical and descriptive account of Spinoza's ideas and influence on later thinkers. A genealogy, in the sense developed by Nietzsche in *On the Genealogy of Morals* ([1887] 1996) and furthered by Foucault ([1971] 1978), always asks what a certain moral knowledge was produced for, by whom, with what interests and power relation to others, and, importantly, what governance outcomes were facilitated by a knowledge shift. Spinoza's analysis of religious phenomena was likewise not a purely objective endeavor, but was entangled with a normative aspiration to criticize religious excesses that turn violent, destabilize society, and limit citizens' freedom of thought. Thus, Spinoza's way of understanding material religion is at the outset embroiled in a political project of Enlightenment criticism, leading him to propose a purified Christian faith as the *religio patriae* of his ideal state. As heirs to Spinoza's philosophy, we too face the question of the extent to which the material-religion approach should or should not be deployed to criticize religious beliefs and practices.

I begin by highlighting Spinoza's views—which scholars working on material religion will find surprisingly recognizable: first, the equality of mind and body and the power of affects, as developed in the *Ethics*; and second, the fundamental role of human imagination in socially constructing religious meanings, as described in the *Theological-Political Treatise*. A focus on Spinoza's philosophy can thus better ground the material-religion approach. This includes Spinoza's views that scholars today may find problematic. The sharp distinction between internal and external religiosity comes to mind, with far-reaching political consequences in relation to religious minorities' right to public expressions. These are potentially positive on the one hand, because of the famed celebration of religious toleration as it existed in the Dutch Republic, but they are negative on the other, because Spinoza envisions the state as an unquestionable arbiter in religious matters—in other words, cultivating, managing, and imposing debatable limits on public religiosity. Despite the reservations we may feel today about using concepts such as "superstition" to describe undesirable beliefs and practices—since these conceptualizations have been exploited in unjust ways—I nonetheless believe Spinoza's critique of religion cannot be disavowed by scholars using the material-religion approach.

Mind–Body Equality

Promey referred to the *Ethics* because Spinoza's analysis of cognition disrupts all-too-facile outlines of Western philosophy as being overly dualistic—celebrating the mind, thought, and the inner experience of faith at the expense of the body and the senses. Such an interpretation of Spinoza makes sense, but it leaves out the complications of the philosopher's sharper theological criticism of rituals or ceremonies; a closer look reveals that theological concerns were embroiled in his thinking about cognition itself. The primary reason for Spinoza's non-dualism and non-denigration of the body could be described as the concept of mind–body equality, which was famously but misleadingly coined by Leibniz as the "parallelism" between the two (Yakira 2014: 59–71). Leibniz's metaphor of parallel suggests two separate entities that exist alongside each other, rather than a deep entanglement of the two. Spinoza, however, describes an identity relation in the famous proposition in Part 2 of the *Ethics*, proposition 7, a fundamental sameness that I understand as an equation rather than a parallel: "The order and connection of ideas is the same as the order and connection of things" (Spinoza, in Curley's translation, 1985: 451; all quotations hereafter refer solely to Curley's translations unless otherwise stated). From the discussion of God as Nature in Part I of the *Ethics* to that of the mind in Part II, in Part III Spinoza describes the human emotions as the center around which his project revolves, as well as—in Parts IV and V—their relation to the (im)possibility of becoming free through enlightenment. In contrast to religiously inspired resentment of the body—for example, the ascetic, in Nietzsche's thought—Spinoza praises the role of aesthetic stimulation in a wise person's life. In a beautiful passage worth quoting at length, he vividly describes this "plan of living" as follows:

> Nothing forbids our pleasure except a savage and sad superstition. For why is it more proper to relieve our hunger and thirst than to rid ourselves of melancholy?
>
> My account of the matter, the view I have arrived at, is this: no deity, nor anyone else, unless he is envious, takes pleasure in my lack of power and my misfortune; nor does he ascribe to virtue our tears, sighs, fear, and other things of that kind, which are signs of a weak mind. On the contrary, the greater the Joy with which we are affected, the greater the perfection to which we pass, i.e., the more we must participate in the divine nature. To use things, therefore, and take pleasure in them as far as possible—not, of course, to the point where we are disgusted with them, for there is no pleasure in that—this is the part of a wise man.
>
> It is the part of a wise man, I say, to refresh and restore himself in moderation with pleasant food and drink, with scents, with the beauty of green plants, with decoration, music, sports, the theater, and other things of this kind, which anyone can use without injury to another. For the human Body is composed of a great many parts of different natures, which constantly require new and varied nourishment, so that the whole Body may be equally capable of all the things which can follow from its nature, and hence, so that the Mind also may be equally capable of understanding many things.
>
> This plan of living, then, agrees best both with our principles and with common practice.
>
> (*Ethics IV*, P45, Scholium, Spinoza 1985: 572)

The ideal life described in the *Ethics* is disconnected from the gloomy and false beliefs promulgated by theologians' superstitious machinations; it is nourished instead by sensory pleasures that "every man may make use of without injury to his neighbor." The affects, in this vision, are essential precisely because they fundamentally impact both body and mind—the latter reaching a greater understanding through joyful aesthetic experience.

The material-religion approach reflects Spinoza's view of mind–body equality, and employs affect theory for its conception of the subject. This reliance on Spinoza is particularly salient in the related field called New Materialisms. Books such as *Vibrant Matter* (Bennett 2010), *The Posthuman* (Braidotti 2013), and *Pantheologies: Gods, Worlds, Monsters* (Rubenstein 2018) pay special attention to the subject as the resultant of ever-changing natural forces whose "human actions and appetites" can be studied—in Spinoza's famous opening words to the third part of the *Ethics*—"as if it were a Question of lines, planes, and bodies" (Spinoza

1985: 492). The subject is made by many contingent forces—or perhaps an "assemblage" of humans and things, as New Materialists sometimes put it. Such works understand affects in an anti-essentialist manner as being always in flux. Disassembling well-trodden boundaries between subject and object, and culture and nature, I understand this affective turn toward a complex (entangled) subject as an animalization of the human being (Schaefer 2015: 27). We only need to recall Deleuze's fascination with Spinoza and Bergson's philosophy of life— the latter having been developed in response to the Darwinian revolution (cf. Grosz 2007). The interest in animalization connects with Deleuze's meditations on Bacon's animated humans—religious creatures composed of meat and bones—in *The Logic of Sensation*: "What Bacon's painting constitutes is a *zone of indiscernibility or undecidability between man and animal*. Man becomes animal, but not without the animal becoming spirit at the same time, the spirit of man, the physical spirit of man" ([1981] 2003: 21; Figure 1.1.1). Consequently, criticizing anthropocentric understandings of nature and our place in it does not yield a loss of interest in studying art or religion, and should not be misidentified as a self-defeating endeavor for scholars interested in the humanities, which by definition focus on human perspectives (cf. Hazard 2013). Spinoza and later naturalists' critique of anthropocentrism matters because it changes the ways we see human perspectives and phenomena such as religious affects in the first place.

The New Materialists' spiritual (and in my opinion sometimes unconvincing) ideas of pantheism and panpsychism—that all physical objects have a "mind"—also revolve around conflicting interpretations of Spinoza. Jane Bennett, for example, understands Spinoza's concept of power or *conatus*—that each thing strives to persevere in its being—as deeming that all "bodies," which is to say all things in the universe, possess vitality (2010: 2). But such an anthropomorphization contradicts the critique of anthropocentrism and goes against the heart of what Spinoza is arguing for in the specific context of the seventeenth century. Spinoza's controversial point is, namely, not that matter is vibrant but, as Deleuze puts it, that the vibrant human spirit is physical—in other words, that the human mind is not superior to the body and thus cannot be disentangled from it. The suggested equality of mind and body acquires force, especially, because it disrupted and still disrupts thinking traditions that deem the former superior to the latter (cf. Bräunlein 2016). Spinoza goes even further, casting doubt on the extent to which the mind is able to overcome the body's compulsions, but this too questions the theologically posited superiority of the mind over the body, and ultimately questions the soul's power over a material realm (cf. *Ethics* III, proposition 2, scholium).

Moreover, if we turn to the broader field of affect theory—to which scholars of the material-religion approach and New Materialists relate—we can note that popular anti-essentialist readings of Spinoza's subject in late twentieth-century France and Italy are continuously debated. For example, Donovan Schaefer, taking up New Materialists as theoretical interlocutors, comments that "affect in this [Spinozist] sense images bodies as sandcastles, granulated conglomerates that are susceptible to radical reformation by the action of multidirectional waves washing over them" (2015: 41). Schaefer thinks, then, that radical readers of Spinoza who are critical of biological determinism make the mistake of arriving at and exaggerating its complete opposite—not unlike the behaviorists of the 1950s—going from determinism to a "hyperplasticity" in which it seems that in nature anything is possible (2015: 41, 97). Such a vision aligns with Rosi Braidotti's ideal of "post-human" and planetary ethics (2013), which to be effective require massive, unlikely transformations in human behavior. I see a cleavage between New Materialists' appraisal of Spinoza and his ethics and politics, which do not go so far and revolve around the free human, the *Homo Liber,* who is not an endlessly becoming *Liber* (Schneider 2019). For Spinoza, the human being cannot easily transcend itself, if at all.

Figure 1.1.1 Francis Bacon. 1965. *From Muybridge "The Human Figure in Motion: Woman Emptying a Bowl of Water/Paralytic Child Walking on All Fours."* Oil on canvas. Stedelijk Museum Amsterdam.

So, while Spinoza is known for criticizing anthropocentric epistemologies, the significance of the concept of the human in his philosophy should not be underestimated. The human, for Spinoza, entails a subject who is by default delimited rather than liberated by religious affects. This is most evident in Spinoza's pessimistic concept of the "multitude"—the superstitious majority who do not live under the guidance of reason, and whom he thought of as a lasting philosophical problem (Yovel 1989: 128–153). In a revealing letter dated 1674, four years after the publication of the *Theological-Political Treatise*, Spinoza explains where his account of sovereignty over the people differs from Hobbes's *Leviathan*:

> As far as Politics is concerned, the difference you ask about, between Hobbes and me, is this: I always preserve natural Right unimpaired, and I maintain that in each State the Supreme Magistrate has no more right over its subjects than it has greater power over them. This is always the case in the state of Nature.
>
> *(Letter 50, Spinoza 2016: 406)*

Going further than Hobbes's state of nature, which served more as a thought experiment than as an actual account of human history, Spinoza's state of Nature is tied to an uncompromising view of humans' place in the natural world, which they can never escape. Even in a so-called commonwealth—or, greater still, in a civilization—humans remain a perpetual threat to one another. Given these dark thoughts and the equality of mind and body, which is another way of placing the human mind within Nature, the kind of religious affects people experience can make the difference between peace and persecution, between joyous life and wretched existence.

Imagined Sacrality/Imagined Communities

To Promey's suggestion that the material-religion approach echoes Spinoza's mind–body equality, we can add that not only the *Ethics* but especially the *Theological-Political Treatise* matters to a genealogy of thinking about material religion. While affect theory is popular among humanities scholars broadly understood, Spinoza's theoretization of material religion is less known and commented on; perhaps because it was part of his "theological-politics," which in the seventeenth century referred to searching for political arguments in Scripture (Verbeek 2016: 8, cited in Krop 2021: 6). This is, in part, due to philosophers' interests themselves. A glance at the *Oxford Handbook of Spinoza* (Della Rocca 2017) shows no entries on material culture or the politics of physical religious manifestations. We may be tempted, in response, to separate the sciences that study material religion and aesthetic regimes of in- and exclusion from philosophy, the discipline that is often thought to put ideas above forms, essences above appearances, and the universal above the particular.[2] Yet, the stereotypical image of the philosopher who rejects the treacherous senses is incorrect, certainly in the case of Spinoza and other Early Modern thinkers who worried about what it would practically take to achieve religious peace.[3] That is why the first half of the *Theological-Political Treatise* is devoted to discussing the power of the human imagination (*imaginatio*) to create forms of prophecy, worship, and miracles. In doing so, Spinoza sharply contrasts a truly universal religion from the superstition (*superstitio*)[4] of the masses and the confused beliefs of people in the fictions they themselves designed (*humana figmenta*, Spinoza 1999: 66). In this scheme, the knowledge of the prophets is derived from "revealed" words (*verba*), signs (*hieroglyphica*), pictures (*figurae*), and visions (*imagines*) (Spinoza 1999: 82, 90). These forms are necessary elements of historical religions, argues Spinoza, because experiences of the divine can be authorized and experienced as real only when materiality and physicality impact the religious imagination. As art historians know, even the most imaginative painters relied entirely on reconfiguring sensuous material already encountered in the natural world. For example, consider Breughel the Elder's *The Fall of the Rebel Angels*, in which he depicts the Archangel Michael as a winged knight fending off the rebel angels—who are disfigured

Figure 1.1.2   Pieter Brueghel the Elder. 1562. *The Fall of the Rebel Angels*. Oil on panel. Royal Museum of Fine Arts, Brussels.

into fish- and frog-like creatures, with clam shell and butterfly wings and with plant body parts—as they fall from a heaven drawn as a sun-like sphere (Figure 1.1.2).

Thinking of texts more than paintings, Spinoza writes, "The Prophets perceived and taught almost everything in metaphors and enigmatic sayings, and *expressed all spiritual things corporeally*" (*omnia spiritualia corporaliter expresserint*, emphasis added), adding that the latter "agree more with the nature of the imagination" (*natura imaginationis*, Spinoza 1999: 110, 2016: 92). Put differently, prophets must adapt their revealed form of expression to the faculties of understanding of those people they wish to bring within their religion's fold. In contrast to Spinoza's concept of God as immanent and eternal Nature, to be understandable to the multitude these revelations must be anthropomorphic—such as can be found in the (improper) attribution to God of human properties like mind, heart, and body, or imagining God as a just king seated on a heavenly throne. For Spinoza, everyday religion is a historical, human, and imagined phenomenon. Therefore, when a Muslim believes in the authority of the *Hadith*, thinking that angels "really" enter and depart from mosques, this can be recognized from an etic perspective "as if" and "for them." Angels are, ultimately, figments of the mind, and in Spinoza's philosophy, this holds true for the concept of transcendence itself.

Spinoza clarifies his etic perspective in a fascinating passage wherein he explains what he means by the "sacred"—which is not only fabricated by human imagination but is also dependent on collective practice in order to remain meaningful:

> *Words have a definite meaning only from their use* [*Verba ex solo usu certam habent significationem*, emphasis added]. If they should be so organized that, according to their usage, they move the people reading them to devotion, then those words will be sacred. So will a

book written with the words organized that way. But if, afterward, the usage should be lost, so that the words have no meaning, or if the book should be completely neglected, whether from malice or because men no longer need it, then neither the words nor the book will be of any use. They will lose their holiness. . .

> *From this it follows that nothing is sacred or profane or impure in itself, outside the mind, but only in relation to the mind* [*Ex quo sequitur, nihil extra mentem absolute, sed tantum respective ad ipsam sacrum aut profanum aut impurum esse*, emphasis added].
>
> *(Spinoza 1999: 432, 434, 2016: 250)*

Spinoza, in short, applies his general analysis of the human mind–body and the affects to the religious imaginations and the social level of collective religious experience and meaning. His relativizing understanding of the sacred is reminiscent of both Durkheim and the later work of Wittgenstein, who wrote about the social construction of the sacred—that in principle anything can be made sacred[5]—and about social practices' role in making linguistic utterances meaningful (which Spinoza does not equate with truth). When Moses broke the first tablets, he merely broke the stones. Something that had been sacred was no longer, because the people's eyes had turned toward the Golden Calf:

> [W]hat he angrily hurled from his hands and broke was not the word of God—who could even think this of Moses and of the word of God?—but only stones. Though previously these stones were sacred, because the covenant was inscribed on them—that covenant by which the Jews had bound themselves to obey God—after they had made that covenant null and void by worshipping the calf, the stones no longer had any holiness.
>
> *(Spinoza 2016: 251)*

I am not concerned here with the adequacy of this interpretation of religious objects' power—wherein the power attributed to a calf dissipates the power of the tablets.[6] These thoughts, which derived from Spinoza's analytical gaze, shocked his contemporaries because the very idea of sacrality as attributed power is interpreted without any reference to transcendence. More than two centuries later, Durkheim in his positivist study of Australian totemism would similarly see sacred phenomena as being the results of *sui generis* social processes. Spinoza's work can thus be seen as a precursor to an anthropology of religion, especially given that he was aware of diverse ritual practices that tied with the sacred, such as dream interpretations, hearing divine voices, and sacrificial offerings. Like Durkheim, who never visited Australia, Spinoza learned about many of these practices through texts. For example, the vivid words of Virgil (Gale 2000: 105) describe the ancient practice of a seer or *haruspex* seeking meaning in reading the "steaming entrails" of a sacrificed animal. In the preface of the *Theological-Political Treatise*, Spinoza calls this practice a remarkable form of "superstition"—to think that God's decisions are written in animal intestines (*pecudum fibris inscripsisse,* Spinoza 1999: 58).[7] Moreover, even books and texts can be a form of material religion: that believers worship mere ink and paper makes those texts "sacred" in the social sense of the word—which he sharply distinguishes from the enlightened knowledge of philosophers.

These ideas revolve around the combined power of the imagination and rituals or "ceremonies" (*caeremoniae*, Spinoza 1999: 208); they also resonate with both Anderson's idea of "imagined communities" and, more recently, Meyer's "aesthetic formations" (2009), the latter of which imagine and give aesthetic shape to community identities. Spinoza argues that there exist as many practices as there are communities, which invent "countless things" that "interpret nature in amazing ways," through "ceremony and pomp" (*vanam cultu*), "external ceremony" (*externum cultum*) (Spinoza 1999: 60, 2016: 66, 68), and "representations" (*repraesentationes*) (Spinoza 1999: 124, 2016: 99). These ceremonies cannot exist in private precisely because their purpose is to establish and preserve the group. Their efficacy relies on certain methods (*methodo*) "to increase wonder at things, and consequently to impress devotion in the hearts of common people" (Spinoza 2016: 162). When style (*stylo*), devotion (*devotio*), and imagination (*imaginatio*) are brought together (Spinoza 1999: 260), they produce powerful beliefs in miracles, which become part of repeatable religious practices that maintain a stable sense of community identity. But these conventions, as Spinoza sees it, do not necessarily grant access to true, Enlightened religion, which consists of nothing more than charity and justice. Of course, Spinoza's perspective is influenced by a semiotic ideology that runs through Christian history, distinguishing the *adiaphora* or non-essential forms from what truly matters in religion (cf. Keane 2018). Spinoza derived the Enlightened distinction between internal and external faith, to which I turn next, from Protestant debates about Church and State.

Internal Faith/External Ritual

Dutch theologians of the seventeenth century had diverse interpretations of the relation between internal and external faith. This dichotomy contributed to developing a distinctly Protestant style, which was known to be rather austere. An extreme depiction of Protestant sobriety can be seen in the idealized church interiors by the painter Saenredam. In his *Interior of the Sint-Odulphuskerk in Assendelft* (Figure 1.1.3), the geometric order is contrasted only by the amorphic water stains on the white walls and the tiny burghers dressed in sober, fashionable black. The light, which fills up the entire space and was meant for reading God's

Figure 1.1.3 Pieter Jansz. Saenredam. 1649. *Church Interior of the Sint-Odulphuskerk in Assendelft*. Oil on panel. Rijksmuseum, Amsterdam.

Word, marks a subtle transition from the dark, medieval Catholic churches that spotlighted the altar. Spinoza's contemporary, the poet and scientist Christiaan Huyghens, once wrote about these paintings that it is "like looking at a portrait of God himself."[8] The church interior's representation of the divine as a greater, eternal space, in which transitory living beings dwell, is indeed hardly anthropocentric. Superseding Catholic superstitions, the church is stripped down to an essential task of housing a religious service and holding the dead (the tombstone of the painter's father can be seen in the foreground).

Spinoza suggested an even more radical version of the separation between interior faith and external worship, one that allowed him to disentangle religious rituals from the universal ethics that should form the core of the idea of religion as a concept not limited to historical Christianity. In the *Theological-Political Treatise*, he writes:

> As for the Christian ceremonies, viz., Baptism, the lord's Supper, the festivals, public statements, and whatever others there may be which are and always have been common to all Christianity, if Christ or the Apostles ever instituted these (which so far I do not find to be sufficiently established), they were instituted only as external signs of the universal Church, not as things which contribute to blessedness or have any holiness in them.
>
> *(Spinoza 2016: 146–147)*

Moreover, going against the Protestant ideology of *Sola Fide, Sola Gratia*—of salvation by faith and grace alone—Spinoza maintains that a truly good life is determined by good works above all, defending the centrality of the Epistle of James against orthodox contemporaries. Hence, neither particularistic doctrines nor rituals truly contribute to living a good life; and, even worse, in the age of religious wars and intolerance, men everywhere fought over various superstitions and externalities and forgot what truly mattered: love for one's neighbor. This moral idea lies at the heart of Spinoza's project.

To demonstrate the separation of internal from external worship, Spinoza refers first to religious others who live in solitude yet can live a good life without ceremonies and without being energized by the dominant group's rituals. From this thought about the religious other as an individual, which reminds us of Spinoza's own life, he steps to the level of a group that forms a religious minority, the Dutch who lived in Japan:

> We have an example of this in Japan, where the Christian religion is forbidden, and the Dutch who live there are bound by a command of the East India Company to abstain from all external worship.
>
> *(Spinoza 2016: 147)*

Spinoza argues that the Dutch can live good lives despite their solitude in Japan and despite their external worship being forbidden, not by the United East India Company (*Vereenigde Oostindische Compagnie*), but in fact by the Tokugawa regime's Sakoku Edicts. Around the time that Spinoza was born, the Japanese Shogunate forced the English, Spanish, and Portuguese to leave. Only the Dutch received permission to trade with Japan on the small island of Deshima, close to Nagasaki. The shogun allowed the Japanese to interact with foreigners only after all foreign rituals—"all external worship" (*omnis externus cultus*, Spinoza 1999: 226)—were subjected to strict rules and regulations. Public and visible Christian rituals were banned to protect the Tokugawa regime's cohesion and authority against Christian, especially Catholic, influences. Even private worship, such as praying before and after a meal, was forbidden; indeed, signs on the Dutch ships' masts warned passengers against bringing Bibles into Japan. The United East India Company advised its members to endure and serve God in one's "sacred and inner thoughts" (*ondertusschen betrachte een ijder met heijlige innerlijcke gedachten sijnen Godt te dienen*, Van Troostenburg de Bruijn 1884: 579–580). In an additional example, the Dutch were forced to demolish a building in Deshima because the entrance was decorated with the suspect inscription "anno domini 1640" (Mochizuki 2008: 319; see also Mochizuki 2009: 63–94).

In contrast to his contemporary Protestant authorities and Catholic critics,[9] Spinoza is remarkably silent about Japanese religious intolerance—which is intriguing given that he described Muslims as being authoritarian.[10] Nor does Spinoza comment on the United East India Company forbidding Muslims to publicly practice their religion, punishable by death, in South Africa, where they had been brought from the Molucca Islands to protect the Dutch colony in the Cape against the indigenous KhoiSan (Moosa 1995: 131).[11] That is because Spinoza's interest in the Japanese situations (and others) was to defend a point at home, a point about an ethical argument that appealed to an elite, mostly Protestant audience. The separation of internal and external worship, then, was carefully crafted to reassure the politicians, merchants, and religious authorities that the very work in which they might read these words—specifically its ideal of the freedom of inquiry, or *libertas philosophandi*—not only posed no threat to the state, it also did not oppose business overseas. The *Theological-Political Treatise* was, then, a pamphlet, a work of circumstance, as much as it was a philosophical masterpiece.

Governing Religious Pluralities

Though Spinoza sought to formulate a true, universal religion, scholars of material religion today do not. That does not make the approach politically neutral, however, since its critique of the so-called Protestant bias and of the Enlightenment advocacy of disenchantment is also a response to certain forms of epistemic domination that denigrate ecstatic—for example, noisy—religion (Schmidt 2000; Tamimi Arab 2017; Weiner 2014). The underlying normative ideal of the material-religion approach is to value not only the diversity of opinions and doctrines but also the diversity of religious forms themselves. All religious forms matter, whether forms of discourse or styles of architecture, dress, and cuisine. The material-religion approach's motto is that there are, in principle, no adiaphorous or indifferent religious forms; consequently, scholars using this approach show restraint in describing forms as being secondary, less meaningful, or deceitful. Such a recognition of pluriformity appears at first sight to be in harmony with Spinoza's praise of the free atmosphere of his city of birth in the closing chapter of the *Theological-Political Treatise*:

> Consider the city of Amsterdam, which, from its great growth and the admiration of all nations, knows by experience the fruits of this liberty. In this most flourishing Republic, this most outstanding city, all men, no matter what their nation or sect, live in the greatest harmony. When they entrust their goods to someone, the only thing they care to know is whether the person is rich or poor, and whether he usually acts in good faith or not. They don't care at all what his Religion or sect is, for that would do nothing to justify or discredit their case before a judge. Provided they harm no one, give each person his due, and live honestly, there is absolutely no sect so hated that its followers are not protected by the public authority of the magistrates and their forces.
>
> *(Spinoza 2016: 352)*

Amsterdam's ethnic and religious diversity meant that the Dutch Republic was by no means a homogenous Calvinist nation (Spaans 2021). The coexistence of Jews, Armenian and Greek Orthodox, Catholics, Lutherans, Quakers, and others was a fact of pluralism. Yet, Spinoza's ideal—to not care too much about religious difference—was a minimal one. A closer look at Spinoza's theoretization of material religion shows that he cherished such indifference or neutrality toward religious pluriformity more than he provided a positive evaluation of diverse public religious forms. The distinction between internal and external worship allowed him to understand the latter as primarily fulfilling a social function: to provide an aesthetics that forms a unique and coherent, whole society (*integra societas*, Spinoza 1999: 224). But that also made it possible to problematize religious minorities' material expression and practices as a threat to the ideal of a single nation within one sovereign territory.

About the Jews—who notoriously excommunicated and cursed him—Spinoza writes that "They separated themselves so from all the nations that they have drawn the hatred of all men against themselves, not only by having external customs contrary to the customs of the other nations, but also by the sign of circumcision, which they maintain most scrupulously" (Spinoza 2016: 124). Although Spinoza experienced bizarre events such as the postmortem circumcision of his grandfather (Kaplan 2016), he was not concerned about the violation of the body, as can be found in disputes about religion and children in Europe today. Spinoza worried that particularistic rituals and body techniques created identities that refused to be assimilated into a different majority. These can be so influential that they preserve an identity, in this case a Jewish one, when all else seems lost. He writes in the *Theological-Political Treatise*: "I think the sign of circumcision is also so important in this matter that I am persuaded that this one thing will preserve this Nation to eternity. . . . I would absolutely believe that some day, given the opportunity, they would set up their state again, and God would choose them anew" (Spinoza 2016: 124; Rosenthal 2016). Another example Spinoza gives is that a unique Chinese hairstyle preserved Chinese identity for "many thousands of years" (Spinoza 2016: 124).[12]

To manage and harness the social power of the religious imagination, Spinoza turns to the state in the hopes of creating a tolerant society by moderately taming diversity—which he saw as a natural, human phenomenon. For Spinoza, specific identities could pose a threat to the peace and order of the state, which should regulate the emotions of the people by instilling in them fear of punishment, hope of reward, and love of country. This view is not unlike the Japanese Shogunate theological politics mentioned earlier—the banning of public Christian rituals so as to preserve the regime's cohesion and, thus, authority. The nineteenth chapter of the *Theological-Political Treatise* makes clear "That the right concerning sacred matters [*jus circa sacra*] belongs completely to the supreme powers [*penes summas potestates omnino esse*], and that the external practice of Religion must be accommodated to the peace of the Republic, if we want to obey God Rightly" (Spinoza 2016: 332; Spinoza 1999: 604; Fukuoka 2018: 152–181). The state must actively regulate religious affairs, allowing diverse religious manifestations but also demonstrating its dominance in this regard by promoting certain national festivals and material forms at the expense of others. Spinoza not only holds that rituals harnessing the power of the imagination sustain identities, but also that they thus sustain the normative order of the state. In a remarkable passage, looking forward to Durkheim's concept of "collective effervescence" (Durkheim [1912] 1995: 218–220, 228, 424), Spinoza captures the sensation of religious nationalism: "Nothing wins hearts more than the joy which arises from devotion, i.e., from love and wonder together" (Spinoza 2016: 316).

Spinoza's adversaries are the orthodox theologians who sought to dominate state and society. To resist them, he did not argue for a separation of Church and State, but rather for granting the political authorities power over the definition, interpretation, and practice of religion (cf. Balibar 1998: 30; Nadler 2011: 74). To protect both freedom of thought and a relative freedom or neutrality of religion, he also pleaded for a state-organized religion of the people—which, as with historical religions, would effect a semi-rational civilizing of people into citizens united in an imagined social order under God's law (Yovel 1989: 129–131). This majority should be formed by specific feasts and a national aesthetic. It is important to note here that Spinoza's recommendation of *pietas* for the fatherland (Spinoza 1999: 614) is not only an inward sense of community and justice, but can also connote outward devotion and therefore material religion, as in the ancient Roman world from which he derives the term (Wagenvoort 1980: 1–20).[13] The practical consequences are spelled out in Spinoza's unfinished *Political Treatise*, in which he reasons that the religion of the state can coexist with others, but must clearly demonstrate its material superiority:

> In the Theological-Political Treatise we showed fully enough what we think about Religion. But at that time we did omit some things which that wasn't the place to discuss: namely, that all the Patricians ought to be of the same Religion, a very simple and most Universal Religion, such as we described in that Treatise. For it's very necessary to make sure that the Patricians aren't divided into sects, some favoring one group, others favoring others, and that they don't, in the grip of superstition, try to take away from their subjects the freedom to say what they think. Next, though everyone must be granted the freedom to say what he thinks, nevertheless large assemblies ought to be prohibited. Thus those who are attached to another religion must certainly be allowed to build as many houses of worship as they wish, but these should be small, of some definite size, and at some distance from one another. But it's very important that the temples dedicated to the national Religion be large and magnificent, and that only Patricians or Senators be permitted to officiate in their chief rituals. So only Patricians should be permitted to baptize, to consecrate a marriage, lay on hands, and unconditionally be recognized as Priests, and as defenders and interpreters of the national Religion. On the other hand, for preaching and administering the financial affairs of the church, and its daily business, the Senate should select some of the plebeians, who will be, as it were, the Senate's representatives; for that reason they'll be bound to render to the Senate an account of everything they do.
>
> *(Spinoza 2016: 587)*[14]

Concluding Remarks: Why Materialist Critique Still Matters

I have made the case that Spinoza is an arch-father of the material-religion approach. Spinoza's mind–body equality, his theory of affects, and his idea of the power of religious aesthetics to form communities and mediate access to an imagined divine are in basic accordance with contemporary studies. Spinoza did not denigrate the body or religious forms in an unreflective way, and he well understood their power. On the other hand, Spinoza may be a father with whom we feel compelled to argue, since his philosophy sometimes speaks from a distinctly earlier time—such as when he writes that "women do not, by nature, have a right equal to men's" (Spinoza 2016: 603). Similarly, distinctions between internal and external worship and true religion and superstition, combined with the Early Modern power of the state over public religiosity and the advocacy of a majoritarian national religion, go against the postcolonial scholarship that recognizes how such Enlightenment perspectives could justify the oppression of religious others categorized on a hierarchical scale of "world religions," where the perception of being "more material" lowered a tradition's status (Meyer 2012).

Moreover, in the past twenty years, Dutch intellectuals have increasingly invoked the name of Spinoza to secure a greater space for the rights of individuals and minorities within minorities, who yearn to liberate themselves from the suffocating grip of family, class, or ethno-religious community. In the understandable haste to secure a space for freethinkers and vulnerable sub-groups, especially women and sexual minorities, they sometimes hope to push religion, especially Islam, out of public life (Tamimi Arab 2017: 14; Van den Hemel 2020), which is both impossible and undesirable in a liberal-democratic constitutional state. Rather than celebrating this great philosopher's works uncritically, we would do them more justice by taking the time to grasp the arguments' justifications and to understand the historical situation in which they were made. A focus on material religion is, I hope to have shown, a good entry to the questions Spinoza addresses regarding the human being, religion, and politics—but that focus also makes us reflect on the theoretical basis and genealogy of materialist approaches in the study of religions.

A genealogical understanding, however, cannot lead to a simple abandonment of Spinoza's and other Enlightenment philosophers' critiques of religion; nor is materialist critique a thing of the past, either because its dark side has been acknowledged or because it is viewed as a boring fait accompli. This will always depend on context. Spinoza's time was one of religious wars and persecution, one in which political theology could both unify citizens of diverse persuasions and justify democratic government that stripped religious authorities of material power, church goods (*kerkelijke goederen*), and excessive political influence. It is no wonder that this perspective is today popular in other contexts too, outside the safety of the Netherlands, which is one of the richest countries in the world. In Brazil, for instance, where in the twentieth century the Catholic Church exerted political influence in destructive as well as liberating ways, the philosopher Marilena Chaui (b. 1941) produced Portuguese scholarship in defense of Spinoza's critique of superstition and religious authorities (Ribeiro 2021). In the Islamic Republic of Iran, established in 1979, translators of philosophical texts have been imprisoned, tortured, and murdered—a theocratic oppression that has made Spinoza increasingly popular. The American-Iranian historian and political scientist Ali Ferdowsi (b. 1950), translator of the *Theological-Political Treatise* into Persian (published in Tehran in 2017), produced it in the hope that the work would be read in Shia seminaries—not as a simple blueprint from the Dutch seventeenth century for a Middle Eastern country today, but to open up the mind to critical thinking (Mirzaei 2021). If the material-religion approach seeks to indeed de-center Europe, as is so often suggested, these thinkers' valuation of the European Spinoza becomes part of our story. For Spinoza's criticism of superstition as "delusions of the imagination" (*imaginationis deliria*, Spinoza 1999: 58, 2016: 66) was never written to target a vulnerable religious minority or to establish superiority over it, but to end the theological persecution of dissenters as God's enemies by God's self-appointed representatives on earth. The latter's negative desires and emotions—ambition, rage, vengeance, and hatred—can lead to a society's destruction. Spinoza's analysis, then, remains with us as a political critique of theologically motivated violence that exists to this day.

Acknowledgments

I am indebted to this volume's coeditors S. Brent Rodríguez-Plate and Jennifer Scheper Hughes; language editors Mitch Cohen and Kirsten Janene-Nelson; Birgit Meyer and our colleagues at Utrecht University; Henri Krop and many other Spinozists, and to the city of Amsterdam where I first encountered the philosopher at the multicultural Spinoza Lyceum High School.

Notes

1 Volume 15, issue 5, of *Material Religion* contains a short "In Conversation" piece I wrote to suggest Spinoza's relevance for both the material-religion approach and the body of literature called New Materialisms. This chapter is an expansion of that argument, based on both a lecture given for Spinoza Day in Amsterdam Paradiso (November 2018) and a presentation at the conference "Spinoza and Identity" in Rijnsburg (June 2019), where the philosopher once lived.

2 David Chidester, for instance, suggests in *Religion: Material Dynamics* that religion is "more like cooking than philosophizing," the former being a sensory practice vital to the "lower" passions that philosophers and theologians often criticize or ignore to the detriment of their analysis (2018: 53).

3 A historical-philosophical analysis of the importance of the senses and rituals is provided by Rainer Forst (2013), who, in his overview of different conceptions of tolerance, explains how in the Early Modern period, "indifferent matters" or *adiaphora* were denigrated and defended in treatises on tolerance.

4 Despite his critical attitude toward "superstition" and "ceremonies" versus true "religion," Spinoza also uses the word "religion" when he describes rituals. Henri Krop notes about this matter, "[I]n the *Tractatus* the adverbial form of 'religion'—*religiose* or even *religiosissime*—is frequently used to denote the way that different kinds of persons complied with a specific ritual, law, or ceremony, for example circumcision" (2019: 39).

5 "Sacred things are not simply those personal beings that are called gods or spirits. A rock, a tree, a spring, a pebble, a piece of wood, a house, in a word anything, can be sacred" (Durkheim [1912] 1995: 34–35).

6 For an analysis that unpacks the biblical story of the Golden Calf and the attribution of power to objects, see Sherwood 2019.

7 Piet Steenbakkers locates the expression *pecudum fibrae* in the ancient poetry of Ovid and Virgil, whereas Spinoza's criticism of superstition was inspired by Lucretius (private correspondence). The reading of a sacrificed animal's liver is also named, for example, in Ezechiel 21: 21.

8 Pieter van Os. "Expositie Pieter Saenredam: Portretten van God." *De Groene Amsterdammer*, 18 November 2000. I am indebted to Ben Visser's visual analysis (via private correspondence).

9 Jan A. B. Jongeneel observes that "[D]uring 1653–60, the Utrecht Provincial Synod vehemently opposed the edict of the Japanese authorities which forbade Dutch citizens during their stay at Deshima to worship and pray publicly, to observe the Sunday, to evangelize, and/or to hand out Christian literature. The VOC decided to live by this 'horrible decree,' and consequently to abstain from religious and missionary activities in the Japanese territory… After complaints of Voetius about the VOC strategy, the annual Utrecht Provincial Synod meetings viewed the price of hiding the Christian faith in 'pagan' Japan as too high. But from 1660 onwards, they seem to have stopped debating this issue" (2012: 21).See also Acta classis Utrecht 9–10 August 1653, Utrechts Archief, T 24-1, inv. nr. 3, 312–314.

10 In the preface to the *Theological-Political Treatise*, Spinoza writes that the "Turks," i.e., Ottomans but also Muslims in general, do not make sufficient space for philosophical argument or even for the possibility to doubt. Muslims appear several times in Spinoza's writings, often in negative terms. But though the philosopher saw the prophet Muhammad as a deceiver, he considered Muslims as equals in humanity. In Letter 43, written in February 1671, Spinoza suggests that what matters is that Muslims honor God by striving for justice and love of one's neighbor—disregarding their beliefs about Islam. Combining this with his criticism of the then existing Christianity as a mad religion (Letter 73), it becomes clear that what matters to Spinoza are love of one's neighbor and ethical action—which is in line with his praise for the Epistle of James.

11 It is unclear whether Spinoza knew about the religious prohibitions in South Africa. The only time he writes about a Black person, for instance, is in a letter in which he describes dreaming of a "black, scabby Brazilian" (Goetschel 2016). Because of his family's business, Spinoza was acquainted with Dutch presence across the world. Jonathan Israel explains that "Spinoza's father, Michael d'Espinoza, a substantial merchant in Amsterdam, had traded, using Dutch ships, with Morocco as well as Portugal, the Canaries and Brazil, while a cousin, Jacob d'Espinoza, spent many years in the Middle East" (Spinoza 2007: 5, n. 4). While various thinkers associated with Spinozism came to argue for a universal equality of human beings, including Spinoza's teacher Franciscus van den Enden, the latter suggested that this equality held "with the possible exception of the Hottentots at the Cape of Good Hope—if it were true they reportedly resemble an

unintelligent herd of cattle more than humans" (cited in Vink 2007: 36–37). For an account of the Dutch geographic imagination as an early form of cultural anthropology in Spinoza's time, see Van Bunge 2019.

12 Spinoza's biographer, Steven Nadler, writes that the stereotypical account of Chinese hairstyles is unfortunate and that such examples should perhaps not be taken seriously. From the perspective of the material–religion approach, these examples are part of Spinoza's attribution of power to the imagination and aesthetic formations; they also make Spinoza's politics understandable (Nadler 2011: 166–168).

13 On the Greek and Roman inspirations for Spinoza's materialism, see Vardoulakis 2020.

14 For an analysis of religion and the civil state in the *Political Treatise*, see Garber 2018. For a (too) charitable interpretation of Spinoza's national religion, see Lærke 2018: "The state administration of sacred matters thus turns into a delicate balancing act between both promoting and curbing religious diversity within the state, drawing the benefits from it while avoiding its inherent dangers. My argument in this chapter has been that the conception of a national religion in TP, Ch, 8, sect. 46, is Spinoza's practical guide to how to perform this balancing act" (p. 127).

References

Balibar, Etienne. (1985) 1998. *Spinoza and Politics*. Translated by Peter Snowdon. New York and London: Verso.

Bennett, Jane. 2010. *Vibrant Matter: A Political Ecology of Things*. Durham, NC: Duke University Press.

Braidotti, Rosi. 2013. *The Posthuman*. Cambridge, MA: Polity Press.

Bräunlein, Peter J. 2016. "Thinking Religion through Things: Reflections on the Material Turn in the Scientific Study of Religion\s." *Method & Theory in the Study of Religion* 28 (4–5): 365–399.

Chidester, David. 1992. *Word and Light: Seeing, Hearing, and Religious Discourse*. Urbana, IL: University of Illinois Press.

Chidester, David. 2018. *Religion: Material Dynamics*. Oakland, CA: University of California Press.

Damasio, Antonio R. 2003. *Looking for Spinoza: Joy, Sorrow, and the Feeling Brain*. Orlando, FL: Harcourt.

Deleuze, Gilles. (1968) 1992. *Expressionism in Philosophy: Spinoza*. Translated by Martin Joughin. New York: Zone Books.

Deleuze, Gilles. (1970) 1988. *Spinoza: Practical Philosophy*. Translated by Robert Hurley. San Francisco, CA: City Lights Books.

Deleuze, Gilles. (1981) 2003. *Francis Bacon: The Logic of Sensation*. Translated by Daniel W. Smith. London: Continuum.

Della Rocca, Michael, ed. 2017. *The Oxford Handbook of Spinoza*. New York: Oxford University Press.

Durkheim, Émile. (1912) 1995. *The Elementary Forms of Religious Life*. Translated by Karen E. Fields. New York: Free Press.

Espírito Santo, Diana. 2019. "The Ontogeny of Dolls: Materiality, Affect, and Self in Afro-Cuban Espiritismo." *Material Religion* 15 (3): 269–292.

Forst, Rainer. 2013. *Toleration in Conflict: Past and Present*. Translated by Ciaran Croni. Cambridge: Cambridge University Press.

Foucault, Michel. (1971) 1978. "Nietzsche, Genealogy, History." In *Nietzsche*, edited by John Richardson and Brian Leiter, 139–164. Oxford: Oxford University Press.

Fukuoka, Atsuko. 2018. *The Sovereign and the Prophets: Spinoza on Grotian and Hobbesian Biblical Argumentation*. Leiden: Brill.

Gale, Monica R. 2000. *Virgil on the Nature of Things: The Georgics, Lucretius and the Didactic Tradition*. Cambridge: Cambridge University Press.

Garber, Daniel. 2018. "Religion and the Civil State in the Tractatus Politicus." In *Spinoza's Political Treatise: A Critical Guide*, edited by Yitzhak Y. Melamed and Hasana Sharp, 128–144. Cambridge: Cambridge University Press.

Goetschel, Willi. 2016. "Spinoza's Dream." *The Cambridge Journal of Postcolonial Literary Inquiry* 3 (1): 39–54.

Grosz, Elizabeth. 2007. "Deleuze, Bergson and the Concept of Life." *Revue Internationale de Philosophie* 3 (241): 287–300.

Guthrie, Stewart. 2007. "Bottles Are Men, Glasses Are Women: Religion, Gender, and Secular Objects." *Material Religion* 7 (1): 14–33.

Hazard, Sonia. 2013. "The Material Turn in the Study of Religion." *Religion and Society* 4 (1): 58–78.

Jongeneel, Jan A. B. 2012. *Utrecht University. 375 Years Mission Studies, Mission Activities, and Overseas Ministries*. Studies in the Intercultural History of Christianity 154. Frankfurt: Peter Lang.

Kaplan, Yosef. 2016. "On the Burial of Spinoza's Grandfather and Grandmother." *Zutot* 13: 26–39.

Keane, Webb. 2018. "On Semiotic Ideology." *Signs and Society* 6 (1): 64–87.

Krop, Henri. 2019. "From Religion in the Singular to Religions in the Plural: 1700, a Faultline in the Conceptual History of Religion." In *Enlightened Religion: From Confessional Churches to Polite Piety in the Dutch Republic*, edited by Joke Spaans and Jetze Touber, 21–59. Leiden: Brill.

Krop, Henri. 2021. "The Tractatus Theologico-Politicus and the Dutch: Spinoza's Intervention in the Political-Religious Controversies of the Dutch Republic." *Philosophies* 6 (1), 23: 1–15.

Lærke, Mogens. 2018. "Spinoza on National Religion." In *Spinoza's Political Treatise: A Critical Guide*, edited by Yitzhak Y. Melamed and Hasana Sharp, 111–127. Cambridge: Cambridge University Press.

Massumi, Brian. 2002. *Parables for the Virtual: Movement, Affect, Sensation*. Durham, NC: Duke University Press.

Meyer, Birgit, ed. 2009. *Aesthetic Formations: Media, Religion, and the Senses*. New York: Palgrave.

Meyer, Birgit. 2012. "Mediation and the Genesis of Presence: Towards a Material Approach to Religion." *Inaugural Lecture*. Utrecht University, Utrecht, Netherlands, October 19.

Meyer, Birgit. 2016. "How To Capture the 'Wow': R. R. Marett's Notion of Awe and the Study of Religion." *Journal of the Royal Anthropological Institute* 22 (1): 7–26.

Mirzaei, Sina. 2021. "The Reception of Spinoza's Theological-Political Treatise in the Islamic Republic of Iran." *Philosophies* 6 (2), 42: 1–18.

Mochizuki, Mia M. 2008. *The Netherlandish Image after Iconoclasm, 1566–1672: Material Religion in the Dutch Golden Age*. New York: Ashgate.

Mochizuki, Mia M. 2009. "Deciphering the Dutch in Deshima." In *Boundaries and their Meanings in the History of the Netherlands*, edited by Benjamin Kaplan, Marybeth Carlson and Laura Cruz, 63–94. Leiden: Brill.

Moosa, Ebrahim. 1995. "Islam in South Africa." In *Living Faiths in South Africa*, edited by Martin Prozesky and John de Gruchy, 129–154. New York: St. Martin's Press.

Nadler, Steven. 2011. *A Book Forged in Hell: Spinoza's Scandalous Treatise and the Birth of the Secular Age*. Princeton, NJ: Princeton University Press.

Nietzsche, Friedrich. (1887) 1996. *On the Genealogy of Morals*. Translated by Douglas Smith. Oxford and New York: Oxford University Press.

Promey, Sally, ed. 2014. *Sensational Religion: Sensory Cultures in Material Practice*. New Haven, CT: Yale University Press.

Ribeiro, Viviane Magno. 2021. "From the Reality without Mysteries to the Mystery of the World: Marilena Chaui's Reading of Spinoza's Tractatus Theologico-Politicus." *Philosophies* 6 (2), 45: 1–20.

Rosenthal, Michael A. 2016. "Spinoza on Circumcision and Ceremonies." *Modern Judaism* 36 (1): 42–66.

Rubenstein, Mary-Jane. 2018. *Pantheologies: Gods, Worlds, Monsters*. New York: Columbia University Press.

Schaefer, Donovan. 2015. *Religious Affects: Evolution, Animality, and Power*. Durham, NC: Duke University Press.

Schmidt, Leigh Eric. 2000. *Hearing Things: Religion, Illusion, and the American Enlightenment*. Cambridge, MA: Harvard University Press.

Schneider, Daniel. 2019. "Spinoza on the Conditions of the Human Condition. The Significance of the Concept 'Homo' in Spinoza's Conception of 'Homo Liber.'" Paper presented at Spinoza and Identity, the second Netherlanders and Israelis Spinoza Seminar, at Erasmus University, Rotterdam, Netherlands, June 30.

Sherwood, Yvonne. 2019. "The Hypericon of the Golden Calf." In *Figurations and Sensations of the Unseen in Judaism, Christianity and Islam: Contested Desires*, edited by Birgit Meyer and Terje Stordalen, 57–76. London: Bloomsbury.

Spaans, Joke. 2021. "Spinoza in his Time: The 17th Century Religious Context." *Philosophies* 6 (2), 27: 1–12.

Spinoza, Benedictus de. 1985. *The Collected Works of Spinoza Vol. 1*. Translated by Edwin Curley. Princeton, NJ: Princeton University Press.

Spinoza, Benedictus de. 1999. *Oeuvres III. Tractatus Theologico-Politicus/Traité Théologique-Politique.* Text prepared by Fokke Akkerman, translated by Jacqueline Lagrée and Pierre-François Moreau. Paris: Presses Universitaires de France.

Spinoza, Benedictus de. 2007. *Theological-Political Treatise.* Translated and edited by Michael Silverthorne and Jonathan Israel. Cambridge: Cambridge University Press.

Spinoza, Benedictus de. 2016. *The Collected Works of Spinoza.* Vol. 2. Translated by Edwin Curley. Princeton, NJ: Princeton University Press.

Tamimi Arab, Pooyan. 2017. *Amplifying Islam in the European Soundscape: Religious Pluralism and Secularism in The Netherlands.* London: Bloomsbury.

Van Bunge, Wiep. 2019. "Geografie en filosofie: Olfert Dapper (1636–1689) en de Kring van Spinoza." In *Spinoza en Zijn Kring: Een Balans van Veertig Jaar Onderzoek,* edited by Henri Krop, 75–96. Rijnsburg: Uitgeverij Spinozahuis.

Van den Hemel, Ernst. 2020. "Iedereen een Eigen Spinoza? Over de Hedendaagse Populariteit van Spinoza en Ander Erfgoed." Amsterdamse Spinozakring. Accessed February 2021. Available at https://youtu.be/YFmoLqYxusk.

Van Troostenburg de Bruijn, Caspar Adams Laurens. 1884. *De Hervormde Kerk in Nederlandsch Oost-Indië Onder de Oost-Indische Compagnie (1602–1795).* Arnhem, Netherlands: Tjeenk Willink.

Vardoulakis, Dimitris. 2020. *Spinoza, the Epicurean: Authority and Utility in Materialism.* Edinburgh: Edinburgh University Press.

Verbeek, Theo. 2016. *Spinoza's Theologico-Political Treatise: Exploring "The Will of God."* Abingdon: Routledge.

Vink, Markus P. M. 2007. "Freedom and Slavery: The Dutch Republic, the VOC World, and the Debate over the 'World's Oldest Trade.'" *South African Historical Journal,* 59 (1): 19–46.

Wagenvoort, Hendrik. 1980. *Pietas: Selected Studies in Roman Religion.* Leiden: Brill.

Weiner, Isaac. 2014. *Religion Out Loud: Religious Sound, Public Space, and American Pluralism.* New York and London: New York University Press.

Yakira, Elhanan. 2014. *Spinoza and the Case for Philosophy.* Cambridge: Cambridge University Press.

Yovel, Yirmiyahu. 1989. *Spinoza and Other Heretics: The Marrano of Reason.* Princeton, NJ: Princeton University Press.

1.2

MATERIAL THEORIES IN JAPANESE BUDDHISM

What Kūkai and Dōgen Thought about Things

Pamela D. Winfield

Dualistic cosmologies clearly distinguish between physics and metaphysics—in other words, that which is above or beyond the physical realm. This vision presupposes a vertically oriented bifurcated cosmology and soteriological system that privileges the supposedly higher, immaterial spheres over and against the lower and lesser material dimension. Buddhist cosmology, by contrast, collapses this vertical bifurcation and locates realization squarely in and as the material world.

This chapter introduces two kinds of material theories and soteriological claims in Japanese Buddhism. It first discusses the material theory that the esoteric Buddhist master Kūkai (774–835) first introduced to Japan in the ninth century. It was premised on India's five elements (earth, water, fire, air, and space), with the sixth element of consciousness running through all five. Kūkai claimed that these six elements constitute the world-body of Buddhahood that preaches the dharma by its very nature (J. *hosshin seppō*). In contrast to Kūkai's esoteric system, this chapter also discusses the material theory that Zen Buddhist master Dōgen (1200–1253) later promulgated in Japan in the thirteenth century. It was premised on China's five phases (earth, water, fire, wood, and metal). Dōgen claimed that the generative and destructive interactions of these five phases also preach the dharma in and as insentient forms (J. *mujō seppō*). By tracing the genealogical influence of Indian and Chinese material theories on Japanese Buddhist texts, art, and architecture, this chapter offers two alternative, non-dualistic systems of thought that envision enlightenment here and now in the material realm. In order to contextualize the thought and practice of these two eminent Japanese masters, however, a fairly substantial introduction to Buddhist cosmology and soteriology is warranted.

Matter and Mind in Mahāyāna Buddhism

Anyone who has read Plato through Descartes can discern the fundamentally bifurcated cosmology of the European philosophical tradition. Many thinkers in this canon dualistically distinguish between matter and mind, real and ideal, physics and metaphysics, visible objects in space versus invisible thoughts in time. This dualistic substance ontology, in which matter and mind are considered to be two distinct ontological substances, is similar to other fundamentally dualistic cosmologies and soteriological systems. The Hindu philosophy of

DOI: 10.4324/9781351176231-4

Samkhya Yoga, for example, strictly distinguishes between pure spiritual principle (Skt. *puruṣa*) and impure material principle (Skt. *prakṛti*), and seeks spiritual liberation from the messiness of material embodiment. In addition, the relative dualism of Chinese cosmology bifurcates Heaven (C. *tien* 天) and Earth (C. *tu* or *di* 地) with the emperor's mandate of heaven mediating between the two, while also positing a dynamic, complementary interaction between the gendered binaries of *yin* and *yang*.

By contrast, later Mahāyāna Buddhist cosmology, which developed around the turn of the millennium in India, collapses the vertically oriented metaphysical divide into a singular horizontal plane. It completely rejects any substance ontology that reifies tangible matter versus intangible mind, as if they were somehow two unrelated ontological entities occupying either extreme of the heavenly ladder—to borrow John of Climacus's (579–649 CE) soteriological imagery. Its mutual integration of matter with mind and mind with matter automatically deflates the inherent value system that prioritizes the one over the other, and has significant implications for thinking about material religion.

Instead of a dualistic structure of Being, Mahāyāna Buddhism proposes a non-dualistic matrix of becoming. It asserts that visible matter and invisible mind are non-dual and interdependent agents in a dynamic and ever-unfolding process in which all things and events (Skt. *dharmas*) are free to karmically connect and influence one another ad infinitum. This cosmological vision is not static or fixed, but rather constantly swirling like a galaxy, or like an atom, or like the dharma wheel which comes to symbolize Buddhism.

Impermanence and Interdependence

Basic Buddhist doctrine teaches the fundamental principle that all things are impermanent and interrelated. All things and events naturally arise, abide, and pass away, and each of these transient forms depends upon everything else in the universe for its very temporary existence. As a result, the world is seen as a constantly recycling, ever-shifting, interdependent, co-conditioning latticework of life. In Buddhist parlance, this is called the "dependent-arising" of forms (Skt. *pratītya-samutpāda*). This is similar to Heraclitus's observation that one never steps into the same river twice, but it is more than a simple expression of impermanence. It is a profound recognition that it is important to be present and attentive to "being in the now," and to appreciate the fortunate confluence of influences that have coalesced to create the necessary causes and conditions that provide one's daily food and lodging and other basic necessities of life.

Because all things lack any permanent, fixed essence in this matrix of becoming, new forms are free to recombine and continually arise as unique amalgamations of karmically conditioned and conditioning factors. This includes the provisional notion of the self. In Buddhism, there is no substance ontology involved. The "self" is considered to be just an expedient label or convenient collective singular for all the aggregated elements of the body, mind, perceptions, sensations, and karmic imprints. These five aggregates (Skt. *skandhas*) that karmically clump up to constitute the provisional "self," however, are fundamentally impermanent and ever-changing, and thus are subject to loss and suffering. This is why Buddhism characterizes the three marks of existence as impermanence (Skt. *anitya*), suffering (Skt. *dukkha*), and lack of fixed selfhood (Skt. *an-ātman*).

According to Buddhism, like the Internet, the five aggregates and all other forms ultimately karmically link up with everything else within six degrees of separation or less. Like the image of Indra's Net in the *Flower Garland Sūtra* (Skt. *Avataṃsaka Sūtra*), every *dharma* is connected by a vast interlaced netscape of being. At every node there is a jewel, and every facet of every jewel reflects every other facet of every other jewel in the entire cosmic space-time continuum. This holographic and holochronic infinite regress of interpenetrating forms enfolds and unfolds universes within universes, times within times. Like a grand hall of mirrors, like a never-ending Russian doll, or like quantum super-string theory, these forms continually arise, abide, and pass away as self-renewing, ever-recycling threads in the interconnected web of becoming.

This recombinant system does not allow for any permanently abiding self or eternal soul. Buddhism offers a simple, fundamental insight: if constructs such as the "self" or the "soul" (Skt. *ātman*) are said to somehow possess a permanent, unchanging nature, then they would not ever change and they should be able to exist forever, independent from all other things in the universe. Since it is evident, however, that all things do change (including the five aggregates) and since they are obviously dependent upon other things (such as food, parents, and the sun) for their very existence, they must lack this presupposed but falsely attributed sense of permanent selfhood (Skt. *an-ātman*). This lack of fixed essence is what the Buddhists call "emptiness" (Skt. *śunyatā*), which actually allows things to interact, change, and become just what they are, such as they are at that moment (Skt. *tathatā*).

Emptiness and Suchness

In order to understand Buddhist material theories fully, one must first grasp the important anti-ontology of emptiness. Historically, this philosophy of emptiness (Skt. *śunyatā*) developed in reaction to early classical Indian schools of Buddhism. In particular, the Theravada "Tradition of the Elders," which was one of eighteen early schools of Buddhism and the only one to survive to the present day, set up a false dichotomy between the realm of phenomena (Skt. *saṃsāra*) and the realm of enlightenment (Skt. *nirvāṇa*). Samsara was cast as a vicious cycle of suffering through incalculable aeons of karmically compelled rebirths. Nirvana, by contrast, was the blissful release from this cycle. It was like extinguishing the flames of desire—including bodily desire—that fuel the actions (Skt. *karmas*) that determine one's future rebirths. Nirvana extinguishes the ego that feeds the action-reaction cycle that continually and exhaustingly propels one around the eternal wheel of transmigration ad infinitum.

Specifically, Buddhaghosa's fifth-century-BCE "Path of Purification" called *The Visudimagga* distinguishes between samsara's realm of form (Skt. *rūpadhatu*) and the realm of formlessness (Skt. *arūpadhatu*), and prioritizes the higher formless meditations (Skt. *dhyana;* Pali *jhāna*) that lead to the perfect state of nirvana. Awareness of the body drops off in the four higher meditative states in the realm of formlessness, where one sequentially perceives infinite space, infinite consciousness, infinite nothingness, and then neither perception nor non-perception (Harvey 2012: 331).

Then, according to early scholastic commentaries known as the *Abhidharma*, nirvana is attained when this fourth and final formless stage is transcended through insight, and one arrives at the absolute cessation of perception, sensation, and consciousness itself (Pali *nirodha samāpatti*). Extinguishing the desires and delusions of body, mind, sensation, and perception also liberates one's "mental formations" or karma. This is the last of the so-called five aggregates (Skt. *skandhas*) that temporarily clump together to make up one's provisional sense of self. Ironically, the overly psychologized mindfulness movement that is so popular in America today is heir to this early classical Theravada tradition of *vipassanā*-insight meditation, but paradoxically focuses only on the lower meditations with body in the realm of form (Wilson 2014: 152–156).

Around the turn of the millennium BCE/CE, however, later Mahāyāna Buddhists saw the soteriological setup of nirvana versus samsara as but another simplistic, reified good-versus-evil type of extreme dualism. In order to overcome this soteriological goal that contradicted Buddha's teachings about the Middle Path of moderation, balance, non-extremism, and non-duality, Mahāyāna Buddhists adopted a revolutionary philosophy predicated on a scientific innovation. They took up the ancient mathematical principle of "zero" (Skt. *śunya*) and philosophized it into "zero-ness" (Skt. *śunya-tā*) or "emptiness."

Before the Mesopotamian concept of zero was introduced to India via the Greeks in the late fourth century BCE (Kaplan 1999), the number line was envisioned as an infinite asymptote of increasingly minute fractions.[1]

... 1/4 1/3 1/2 1 2 3 4 ...

The neutral placeholder zero, however, completely revolutionized the number line.

... –4 –3 –2 –1 0 1 2 3 4 ...

Zero holds no inherent value in and of itself, but, by virtue of it, zero gives relative value to everything else around it. In addition, zero provides space for the recognition of negative integers, and thus the inverse of positive phenomena. Buddhist philosophers then applied this principle and concluded that *all* dualities—all positive and negative phenomena: samsara and nirvana, self and other, body and mind, hope and fear, generation and extinction—were actually connected and relativized to one another by virtue of this principle of zero or emptiness.

In addition to the common interconnections and radical relativity of all *dharmas*, the Buddhists applied another mathematical principle to one's false sense of permanent selfhood. Because multiplying by -1 yields its opposite, such that negating a negative yields a positive and vice versa, self-negation and self-deconstruction became the Buddhist's main *modus operandi* for realizing the ultimate relativity and non-duality of all things, including one's purported sense of self.

Early Mahāyāna Buddhist philosophers such as the semi-legendary Nagārjuna (first-through third-century CE) also went a step further and applied another mathematical principle to all phenomena to determine the ultimate emptiness of the self and all *dharmas*. It is well known that if one multiplies any integer by zero, all things are reduced to zero. "Zero-ing out" the selfhood of things and neutralizing the all-consuming importance of a falsely predicated permanent self, therefore, meant that all things could be affirmed as interconnected and actually empty of fixed essence. Conventionally speaking, all integers naturally assume their positions along the number line—but, ultimately speaking, they can all be reduced to the ground zero of emptiness.

As a result, by becoming a little less self-ish and a little more self-less, and by taking oneself out of the equation, *all* things became integral to the vast calculus of life. As a result of this cutting-edge Buddhist philosophical application of a scientific, mathematical innovation, the metaphysical divide between nirvana and samsara collapsed. If one could successfully and viscerally experience *śunyatā*, and see the zero-ness or emptiness of oneself and the world, then one would obtain enlightenment and perceive the forms of samsara as perfect, such as they were, at that very moment. With this transformed vision, one could discern that such ethereal notions as nirvana, enlightenment, or immaterial Buddha-nature cannot exist anywhere but in and as the *things* of the world themselves—people included. When correctly perceived, samsara *was* nirvana and nirvana *was* samsara. As the *Heart Sūtra* claims, "Form is emptiness, emptiness is form. Form is nothing other than emptiness; emptiness is nothing other than form." This fundamentally revalorized the world of material phenomena as non-dual with the world of enlightenment.

This comes close to the Eurocentric Christian idea of "heaven on earth" or Jesus's claim that "the Kingdom of God is within," but it does not presuppose a transcendent God who has simply been relocated or somehow immanentized on a lower plane. It is also distinct from the notion of avatars (like Krishna as the incarnation of Vishnu; or Jesus as the embodiment of God the Father). Nor does it have any of the overt political valences of ontocratic theology, in which the divine and material worlds are one and the same, insofar as the head of state (the Pharaoh, the Sun King of eighteenth-century France, or the Japanese emperor during World War II) rules as an embodied deity on earth. According to Buddhist doctrine, there technically is no deity to be embodied; such mental constructions as divinity are mere mental fabrications that cause as much suffering as they do solace.

This Mahāyāna Buddhist principle of emptiness has profound implications for material theory. Because everything is empty of fixed essence on the ultimate level, everything is mutually implicated in the whole karmically connected, co-conditioning matrix of flux and change. At the same time, however, on the conventional level, it also means that every single *dharma* is a wholly unique combination of factors as long as it lasts in its present form. This temporary uniqueness is what characterizes and distinguishes individual *dharmas* from one another on the conventional level. It is what gives them their so-called suchness or thusness (Skt. *tathatā*). This sentiment inverts the discourse of emptiness, which sounds a bit negative, to a more positively inflected discourse of suchness, which carries with it an appreciation for the uniquely compounded causes and conditions of each passing moment. According to this assertion, *dharmas* temporarily abide *such as they are,* as a once-in-a-lifetime collective singular that we can conveniently label and affix through language and abstract conceptual categories—but which is in fact never to be repeated in quite the same way.

Recognizing and celebrating the unique suchness of each individual form, including the distinctiveness of every fortunate human rebirth, means realizing that both self and world always and already are perfect such as they are. They always already embody Buddha-nature, and we always already are Buddhas. We just have to wake up to that fact through dharma practice.

This epistemological soteriology is based on waking up to that which is already there but which is obscured by delusion and ignorance. In this scheme, there is no question of a transcendent deity or even any sense of immanence, for that would presuppose a divine substance that has somehow gotten relocated or encased in coarse form down on the physical plane. Rather, in the Buddhist scheme, everyone always already possesses the potential to "become a Buddha in this very body" (J. *sokushin jōbutsu* 即身成仏). Furthermore, because all of nature already is the world-body of Buddhahood (Skt. *dharmakāya*; J. *hosshin* 法身), which preaches the suchness or thusness of things by its very nature for its own enjoyment (J. *hosshin seppō* 法身説法), even insentient matter such as "grasses and trees can become Buddhas" (J. *sōmoku jōbutsu* 草木成仏). This locates enlightenment squarely in and as the material realm.

With this clear Mahāyāna worldview in mind, the sections that follow will examine two main strains of Mahāyāna Buddhism, namely esoteric (or tantric) Buddhism and Zen Buddhism.

Esoteric Buddhist Material Theory

Esoteric Buddhism is a tantric form of Mahāyāna Buddhism that is known as the diamond or lightning "quick path" to awakening (Vajrayāna). It is a self-styled "secret teaching" (J. *mikkyō* 密教) that requires initiation. It originated in the eastern coastal region of India near Odisha (Orissa) and traveled via overland and maritime Silk Road trade routes into China by the early eighth century CE. It was then transmitted to Japan by the patriarch Kūkai (784–835), who studied in China from 804 to 806 CE and returned home to Japan with a treasure trove of esoteric sutras, ritual implements, relics, iconographic guides, and ritual manuals. The elaborate and highly symbolic ritual arts of esoteric Buddhism are designed to condense the Buddha's universal body, speech, and mind into the practitioner's microcosmic hand mudras, chanted mantras, and envisioned mandalas. This secret mikkyō tradition explicitly recognizes the non-duality of body and mind, and ritually deploys the breath (usually in the form of chanted mantras) to unify both.

When Kūkai returned to Japan after two years on the continent, he systematized the esoteric teachings and clearly articulated Indian Buddhist material theory in texts such as *Becoming a Buddha in This Very Body* (J. *Sokushin jōbutsugi* 即身成仏義), which he wrote in 817 at the age of forty-one. In this treatise, Kūkai describes the world-body of Buddhahood in terms of the Six Great Elements (earth, water, fire, air, space, and consciousness), that is, "all solids, liquids, gasses, heat, space, and the awareness to perceive them" (Winfield 2019: 246; *Kōbō Daishi Kūkai zenshū* 2: 246–247). This system was the most advanced physics of its day, as it explained the basic building blocks of all perceptible phenomena in the world.

The Six Great Elements of Indian esoteric Buddhism ultimately derived from Hellenistic models. The conquests of Alexander the Great introduced Greek material theories into the subcontinent in the fourth century BCE, which originally only posited four basic elements of earth, water, fire, and air—to which Aristotle (384–322 BCE) added a fifth quintessential element of ether. This material model became the basis of ayurvedic medicine in India, but, beginning in the late seventh century CE (Davidson 2002: 117–118), Indian esoteric Buddhism took these five elements of earth, water, fire, air, and space and recognized a sixth immaterial element of mind or consciousness, which ran through them all.

Architectures of Enlightenment

The genealogical legacy of this abstract Indian system of elements can be found in the symbolic architectures and visual arts of esoteric Buddhism in Japan. For example, the distinctive five-wheel tower (J. *gorintō* 五輪塔) in Japan is fashioned with five geometric shapes symbolizing the five elements (Figure 1.2.1). The square base represents the earth, the circle represents water, the triangle represents fire, the crescent shape represents air, and the so-called wish-fulfilling jewel shape (Skt. *cintamani*) represents space. It is understood that the sixth immaterial and invisible element of mind runs through all five building blocks of existence. This was explicitly diagrammed in Kakuban's (1095–1144) *Commentary on the Five Elements and Nine Syllables* (J. *Gorin kuji myō himitsu shaku* 五輪九字明秘密義釈), which indicates five Sanskrit seed syllables (Skt. *bija*) inscribed on the front of the stacked tower. The sixth Sanskrit *bija* for "mind" runs down the length of the five-element tower in the back.

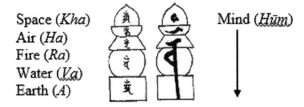

Space (*Kha*)
Air (*Ha*)
Fire (*Ra*)
Water (*Va*)
Earth (*A*)

Mind (*Hūm*)

Figure 1.2.1   Kakuban, twelfth century. *Gorintō* five-element stupa, with mind running through all five material elements. FRONT: *Bija* seed syllables for earth (*a*), water (*va*), fire (*ra*), air (*ha*), and space (*kha*) inscribed on the front. BACK: *Bija* seed syllable for the sixth immaterial element of mind (*hūm*) written on the back of the stupa, running through all matter.

In actual practice, the five-element *gorintō* tower has been used as a reliquary stupa or grave marker in Japan from at least the Heian period onward (794–1192) (Glassman 2018). Its mortuary usage aptly indicates the concept of "ashes to ashes, dust to dust," as all six elements disaggregate upon the physical death of the body, later to be karmically reconstituted in Buddhism's infinitely recycling system of ever-changing, causally conditioned, empty yet unique forms.[2]

Kūkai explains the origins of these *bijas* in his ninth-century treatise:

> As to the first line [of the *Mahāvairocana Sūtra*], "The Six Great Elements are interfused and are in a state of eternal harmony," the Six Great Elements are earth, water, fire, wind, space, and consciousness. The seed (*bija*) mantras for these words are: *A, Va, Ra, Ha, Kha, Hūṃ*. *A* stands for "that which is unborn (*anutpāda*)" which is the earth element; *Va*, for "that which language (*vāc*) cannot communicate" which is the water element; *Ra*, for "free from all defilements," which is the fire element (*rajas*); *Ha*, for "transcends causality" (*hetva*), which is the wind element; *Kha* for "void like space (*kha*)" which is the space element; and *Hūṃ*, for "I have realized," which represents the consciousness element.
>
> *(Hakeda 1972: 228)*[3]

That is, according to Kūkai, mind and matter interpenetrate one another, and each element also correlates with a sacred syllable, which contains the root or seed of a doctrinal truth (for example, the letter *A* for the idea of *A-nutpāda*, and so on). This correlation of elements with sounds and thoughts underscores the so-called Three Secrets of body, speech, and mind in esoteric Buddhism.

This material-mental theory also literally shaped the architectural contours of the five-story many-jeweled pagoda (J. *tahōtō* 多宝塔) of esoteric Buddhism in Japan. The prototypical sanctuary at Kōyasan monastery is a case in point (Figure 1.2.2). Established in 819 by Kūkai, Kōyasan is the headquarters of the esoteric Shingon Buddhist sect in Wakayama prefecture

Figure 1.2.2 The "Fundamental Great Pagoda" (J. *konpondaitō*) at Kōyasan, Wakayama Prefecture. Established by Kūkai in 819. Photo was taken in 2009 and made available by Wikimedia Commons.

to the southeast of Osaka. Its square earth base, circle water dome, triangle fire roof, and nine consecutive air rings lead up to the *cintamani* finial, an almond-shaped wish-fulfilling jewel representing space. Inside the pagoda, five resident buddhas arranged according to the cardinal directions collectively symbolize the sixth immaterial element of mind as they personify five distinct enlightened wisdoms. In the center, the cosmic "Great Sun" Dainichi Buddha 大日如来 (Skt. Mahāvairocana) symbolizes the all-encompassing enlightened and enlightening total wisdom. To the north, Fukūjōju (Skt. Amoghasiddhi) embodies mirror wisdom, to the west Muryōju (Skt. Amitābha) embodies equality wisdom, to the south Hōshō (Skt. Ratnasambhava) embodies observation wisdom, and to the east Ashuku (Skt. Akṣobhya) embodies action wisdom.

Images of Awakening

These symbolisms are also mapped out visually in Shingon's two distinctive Diamond and Womb World mandalas. Broadly speaking, this pair of elaborate paintings symbolize mind and matter and bring them together as "two that are not two" (J. *ni fu ni* 二不二). Specifically, the Diamond World mandala symbolizes the enlightened wisdom of the "Mind Only" or Yogacara school of Mahāyāna Buddhism. It illustrates perfect realization that has been acquired in the perfectly enlightened noumenal realm (Skt. *dharmadhatu*). In a complementary way, the Womb World mandala symbolizes the "Buddha-Womb" (Skt. Tathāgatagarbha) strain of Mahāyāna Buddhism. It proposes that the phenomenal world is empty of substance and therefore pregnant with potential. It is fertile ground for gestating our latent, embryonic mind of enlightenment (Skt. *bodhicitta*) through dharma practice. This mandala therefore illustrates the Buddha's compassionate, enlightening methods for birthing potential Buddhahood in and as the phenomenal realm. Taken together—as they are always displayed as a pair in Japan—these two mandala images symbolize the ends and means of realization, and bring together two main strains of pre-existing thought and practice within Mahāyāna Buddhism. As I have argued elsewhere:

> Both mandalas picture an ontology wherein mind and matter are inextricably linked. Within the Diamond World's central hall, four figures personifying the elements [of earth, water, fire, and air] outstretch their arms at each diagonal corner to embrace the fifth and sixth elements of space and consciousness, personified as Dainichi [the Great Sun Buddha] and his wisdom buddhas, respectively. The Womb World's central Lotus Court, likewise, illustrates the five elements as a band of rainbow colored light within which the sixth element of consciousness is represented by the wisdom buddhas.
>
> *(Winfield 2019: 247)*

Other iconographic clues also indicate the interpenetration of mind and matter in the twin yet non-dual mandalas. The deities in the Diamond World mandala sit in fully illuminated moon disks supported by lotus thrones, which have risen up through the muck of materiality to blossom into the full light of enlightenment. The figures in the Womb World mandala, inversely, sit on lotus thrones supported by moon disks, and the mandala's central red lotus flower features vajra spikes (symbolizing wisdom) jutting out in between each petal (symbolizing mikkyō's compassionate "quick path" methods for realizing Buddhahood in this very body). In addition, "[t]he namesakes of the Womb World Buddhas in particular evoke the qualities of the five elements in their poetic monikers. For example, Dainichi the "Great Sun" identifies with the element of space, "Flower-Opening King" identifies with water,

Table 1.2.1 The Five Elements of Esoteric Buddhism and their Associated Wisdom Buddhas in the Diamond and Womb World Mandalas

Dir.	Diamond Names	Wisdom	Elements		Womb Names
C.	Dainichi (Mahāvairocana)	total	(jewel shape)	Space	Dainichi (Great sun)
N.	Fukūjōju (Amoghasiddhi)	mirror	(half-moon)	Air	Tenkuraion (Heaven-Drum-Thunder-Sound)
W.	Muryōju (Amitābha)	equality	(triangle)	Fire	Muryōju/Amida (Immeasurable light/life)
S.	Hōshō (Ratnasambhava)	observation	(circle)	Water	Kaifukeō (Opening flower king)
E.	Ashuku (Akṣobhya)	action	(square)	Earth	Hōdō (Jewel pennant)

"Heaven-Thunder-Drum Sound" identifies with air, and so on," as outlined in Table 1.2.1) (Winfield 2019: 248).

It is for the above reasons that Kūkai concludes in his *Sokushin jōbutsugi* treatise:

> These Six Great Elements create all the Buddhas, all sentient beings, and the material worlds, that is, the Dharmakaya [world-body of Buddhahood] in Four Forms [of body, speech, mind, and all actions] and the threefold world [of enlightened beings, sentient beings, and insentient beings]. The Six Great Elements are the creating; and the Dharmakaya in Four Forms and the threefold world are the created. . . . Although there are differences such as coarse or subtle, large or small among the created, they are not external to the Six Great Elements. . . . Differences exist between matter and mind, but in their essential nature they remain the same. Matter is no other than mind; mind, no other than matter. Without any obstruction, they are interrelated. The subject is the object; the object, the subject. The seeing is the seen, and the seen is the seeing. Nothing differentiates them. Although we speak of the creating and the created, there is in reality neither the creating nor the created. What kind of intellectual determinations can be made of the eternal Order that is naturally so (*hōni no dōri*)?
>
> *(Hakeda 1972: 229–230)*

Zen Material Theory

Four centuries after Kūkai established mikkyō in Japan, Zen master Dōgen (1200–1253) imported Sōtō Zen Buddhism into Japan after studying in China from 1223 to 1227. Zen is a form of Mahāyāna Buddhism that emphasizes meditation. When the first Indian patriarch Bodhidharma introduced this practice to China in the sixth century CE, the Sanskrit term for meditation or "*dhyana*" was phonetically transliterated into Chinese as "*chan*" 禅. The Japanese pronunciation of this borrowed Chinese character 禅 is "*zen.*" When Dōgen brought the Sōtō (Ch. Caodong 曹洞) Zen lineage into Japan in 1227, he brought with him the then current Chinese system of material physics known as the "five phases" (Ch. *wu xing*; J. *gogyō* 五行).

In contrast to Kūkai's mikkyō and the previously discussed Indian system of earth, water, fire, and air, Dōgen's Zen is associated with Chinese material theory, which is premised on earth, water, fire, wood, and metal. Furthermore, instead of five stacked and static building blocks of existence as in India, Chinese material theory is premised on the dynamically unfolding and constantly changing Way of Nature (Ch. *dao*; J. *dō* 道), which is formally and institutionally known as Daoism in China. The Daoist emphasis on the flowing course of nature dovetailed nicely with Buddhist teachings on impermanence and the non-dualism of generation-extinction, and Daoist material theory greatly influenced Chinese Chan Buddhism during the Tang (618–907 CE) and Song (960–1279 CE) dynasties. This synergy demonstrates the sinification of classical Indian Buddhism.

The so-called "five phases" of the Chinese system constantly interact to generate and extinguish life in the self-renewing cycle of existence. It is neither good nor bad—it is simply the way vital energies ebb and flow in their natural rhythms. Historically speaking, this Chinese material theory influenced everything from *fengshui* geomancy to traditional Chinese medicine (TCM). Theoretically speaking, the five phases interact by either generating or overcoming one another, as diagrammed in Figure 1.2.3.

According to this diagram, the peripheral set of arrows indicates the generating flow of life, and the interior set of arrows indicates the degenerating process of decay. In terms of generating activity, wood gives rise to fire (in the sense that wood is fuel for the fire). Then, fire gives rise to earth (ash), earth gives rise to metal (such as mining ore), metal gives rise to water (condensation), water gives rise to wood (as water nourishes a tree), and the process continues ad infinitum. Conversely, in terms of life's inevitable and necessary process of death and decay, the interior set of arrows indicates that wood consumes earth (in the sense that trees consume nutrients and minerals from the earth). Then, earth consumes water (as in absorption or dams), water consumes fire (water extinguishes flames), fire consumes metal (melting), metal consumes wood (as in an axe chopping a tree), and so on ad infinitum.

It is important to remember, however, that in this Chinese system, these five material categories and interactive patterns of nature are highly generalized theoretical constructs. They do not only refer to literal woods, flames, grounds, minerals, and waters, but rather correlate with everything in the universe—from internal organs to the outer planets, from the cardinal directions (and center) to the five seasons (including the fifth added season of midsummer). Moreover, because these five phases outline the functional dynamics of natural processes, everything impacts everything else. A deficiency or an excess of *yin* or *yang* in any one of these five phases, for example, will trigger ripple effects throughout the entire organic system.

The legacy of the five phase system in Japan can be clearly seen in Zen master Dōgen's writings. How did Dōgen invoke and manipulate Chinese material theory as he set out to

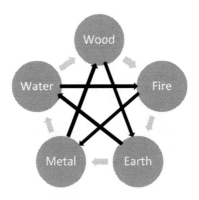

Figure 1.2.3 Peripheral arrows: Generating activity; Interior arrows: controlling/overcoming activity.

establish a new form of Zen monasticism in Japan? How did he see the non-duality of matter and enlightened mind in and as the monastic compound?

Dōgen first subtly invokes the five phases in his earliest fascicle *A Talk on Pursuing the Way* (J. *Bendōwa* 辨道話), which he wrote in 1231 at the age of thirty-one. He writes it just as he is about to embark on building his first monastery, Kōshōji, outside of Kyoto in 1233. He is eager to explain his newly imported form of Chinese Buddhism to his Japanese audience, and he seeks to obtain new donors and patrons who can help him "establish the bodhi-mind" in Japan. He also very clearly enumerates the material and human resources he needs to build a new monastery or *dōjō* (J. 道場)—that is, literally a place (J. *jō* 場) for pursuing the Way (J. *dō* 道). Even in this first fascicle, one can discern Dōgen's reliance on Chinese material theory to structure his thoughts about enlightenment. He writes that when a realized master (such as himself) brings the Buddhist teaching to a new place and constructs a new monastery:

> At this time, everything in the ten directions—the *soil and the earth, the grasses and trees, fences and walls, tiles and stones*—all perform the Buddha's work. Those who benefit from the *wind and water* produced by them are mystically assisted by the Buddha's subtle and inconceivable influence, and they immediately awaken to themselves. All beings who benefit from this *water and fire* spread the influence of the Buddha's original enlightenment, so that those living and talking with them are mutually endowed with the limitless Buddha-virtue.
>
> *(adapted from Dōgen, translated by Nishijima-Cross 1994: 1: 5–6)*

For his first monastic project at Kōshōji in 1233, Dōgen itemizes a series of two-character compounds that roughly match up with the five phases of Chinese material theory. Specifically, "*soil and earth*" (J. *dochi* 土地) corresponds to the earth phase. "*Grasses and trees*" (J. *sōmoku* 草木) is code speak for the wood phase. The next two compounds, "*fences and walls*" (J. *shōheki* 牆壁) and "*tiles and stones*" (J. *guwaryaku* 瓦礫), reference a famous phrase uttered by a late eighth-century Chinese Zen patriarch Nanyō Etchū 南陽慧忠 (d. 775), who stated, "Fences, walls, tiles, and pebbles are the mind of eternal buddhas" (Dōgen, trans. Nishijima-Cross 1994: 3: 254).[4] However, in the context of enumerating the basic materials needed to establish a new monastery in Japan, Dōgen's citation of Nanyō adds his own five-phase twist to this ancient famous phrase. In this new context, "*fences and walls*" that are built with axes, hammers, mallets, or other tools could well indicate the metal phase, and the monastery's "*tiles and stones*" may represent the phase of fire, since clay tiles are kiln-fired, and since they are held in place along the flammable roof eaves by stones. Finally, the whole monastic compound—and everyone's flaming desires within it—can be extinguished by "*wind and water*" (J. *fūsui* 風水) or the water phase, which is also a clear reference to the pseudo-environmental science of *fengshui* (Ch. 風水). Dōgen's additional mention of "*water and fire*" (J. *suika* 水火) is a stock reference to *yin* and *yang* that completes the standard Chinese cosmological scheme.

Most importantly, Dōgen states that these five phases "all perform the Buddha's work" and mystically benefit any sentient being living nearby. This seems to indicate that Dōgen believes that a kind of dynamic, enlightened energy automatically radiates out from the very material buildings and living buddhas of the Zen Buddhist monastery. According to Dōgen, this material energy assists and benefits all through the Buddha's "subtle and inconceivable influence" (J. *myōshi* alt. pron. *myōka* 冥資).

In this way, Dōgen puts his own Zen spin on Kūkai's old esoteric doctrine. Kūkai's ninth-century esoteric Buddhist doctrine of *hosshin seppō* (J. 法身説法) states that the world-body of Buddhahood (J. *hosshin* 法身) preaches the dharma in and as nature—which, as stated previously, was broken down into the five Indian elements of earth, water, fire, air, and space. However, in the thirteenth century, Dōgen riffs on this idea and instead advances a revised doctrine of *mujō seppō* (J. 無常説法), or the insentient preaching of the dharma. This Zen doctrine explicitly specifies that it is the insentient (J. *mujō* 無常) forms of nature that can teach the truth of emptiness and suchness to those with eyes to see it. Given the contemporary thirteenth-century Zen context, these insentient forms were defined in terms of the five Chinese phases of earth, water, fire, wood, and metal. For Dōgen, therefore, the compounded and constantly changing forms of nature preach thusness from moment to moment, and the supposedly inert materials of the monastic compound actually function as unique vehicles for awakening. One just has to develop the True Dharma Eye (J. *shōbōgen* 正法眼) through the discipline of Zen practice in order to perceive the self and the world in this way.

As a result, Dōgen concretely invokes the most advanced material theory of his day to literally build up the architectural and anatomical bodies of a new Song-style Sōtō Zen monastery in Japan, which he calls establishing the bodhi-mind. Dōgen thus masterfully deploys Chinese material theory in the service of his fundraising and recruitment efforts to establish his new monastic enterprise at Kōshōji.

Conclusion

The material turn of religious studies demonstrates the fundamentally inseparable nature of concrete particulars with all our abstract ideas about the universe, enlightenment, and mind. The notion of a "material religion" collapses the long-standing genealogical inheritance of a vertically oriented split cosmology and a substance ontology that neutralizes any kind of embodied epistemology. It deflates ideas of a sui generis ineffable and ethereal realm above and a mucky, murky material realm below, which privileges mind over matter. Instead, non-dualistic religious traditions such as Japanese esoteric and Zen Buddhism offer alternative models for envisioning a horizontal cosmology, where mind and matter are inseparable, as they co-condition one another and everything else in the universe precisely because they are empty of fixed essence, can change, and karmically impact other forms. This gives rise to unique combinations of factors and agents "such as they are," whether theorized along the Indian or Chinese models.

In Indian esoteric Buddhism, which Kūkai imported into Japan via China in the early ninth century, the sixth element of mind runs through the five elements of earth, water, fire, air, and space. This is evidenced by *bija* inscriptions on the *gorintō* five-element stupa, the buddhas within Kōyasan's fundamental great pagoda, and the elements and enlightened wisdoms associated with each of the five Buddhas in the Diamond and Womb World mandalas. Alternately, in Chinese Zen Buddhism, which is heavily influenced by Daoism, the five phases of earth, water, fire, wood, and metal are subtly invoked and equated with the bodhi-mind itself. This is evidenced most clearly in Dōgen's first text, the *Bendōwa* (1231), which repeats a series of two-character compounds that roughly line up with the five agents—and which, he insists, are tantamount to establishing the bodhi-mind in and as the Zen monastery.

What do these Buddhist examples tell us about our own material and mental makeup? What do they say about the world around us? They indicate that the self and the world are empty of fixed essence on the ultimate level, but that on the conventional level they can and do exist as amalgamated real, unique, and impactful forms that are already enlightened but need practice to be realized. The genealogical legacy of this non-dualistic outlook, which views the phenomenal realm as always and already inherently enlightened, has had profound ramifications—not only in Japan and East Asia, but also increasingly throughout the world today.

Notes

1 The concept of "zero" originated in Sumeria was adopted by the Babylonians, and was transmitted to India via the Greeks. See Robert Kaplan, "What is the origin of zero?," *Scientific American*, October 4, 2001, accessed August 1, 2021, https://www.scientificamerican.com/article/what-is-the-origin-of-zer/.

2 For more on how the five/six aggregates reconstitute to form a new embryo, see Sanford 1997: 1–38. See also numerous works by Anna Andreeva, accessed August 1, 2021, http://www.asia-europe.uni-heidelberg.de/en/people/person/persdetail/andreeva.html.

3 *Taishō Shinshū Daizōkyō*, T18:9a. This six-fold explanation also correlates with Kūkai's citation of the *Vajraśekhara Sūtra* that says, "All things are originally unborn; their intrinsic nature is beyond any verbal expression; it is pure and clean, being free from defilements and causality; it is equal to empty space" (T18:331a; Hakeda 1972: 229).

4 Nanyō's statement means that the monastic compound itself is both an enlightened space and an enlightening catalyst, as the sound of shattering roof tiles, for example, had triggered other famous cases of awakening.

References

Davidson, Ronald. 2002. *Indian Esoteric Buddhism: A Social History of the Tantric Movement*. New York: Columbia University Press.

Dōgen Kigen. 1994. *Master Dōgen's Shōbōgenzō*. Translated by Gudo Nishijima and Chodo Cross. London: Windbell Publications.

Glassman, Hank. 2018. *The Five-Element Pagoda, the Mantra of Light, and the Six Paths: Tantric Elements in Medieval Japanese Funerary Practice*. Paper presented at the Woodenfish Foundation Conference: The Ultimate Concern—Death and Afterlife. Guangzhou, PRC, June 7–10.

Hakeda, Yoshito S. 1972. *Kūkai: Major Works*. New York: Columbia University Press.

Harvey, Peter. 2012. *Introduction to Buddhism: Teachings, History, and Practices*. 2nd ed. New York: Cambridge University Press.

Kaplan, Robert. 1999. *The Nothing That Is: A Natural History of Zero*. New York: Oxford University Press.

Kōbō Daishi (Kūkai). 1983–85. *Kōbō Daishi Kūkai Zenshū* (The Complete Works of Kōbō Daishi Kūkai). Edited by Miyasaka Yūshō et al. 8 Vols. Tokyo: Chikuma Shobō.

Sanford, James H. 1997. "Wind, Waters, Stupas, Mandalas: Fetal Buddhahood in Shingon." *Japanese Journal of Religious Studies* 24, nos. 1–2 (Spring): 1–38. Accessed August 1, 2021. https://doi.org/10.18874/JJRS.24.1-2.1997.

Taishō Shinshū Daizōkyō (the Taishō Buddhist canon). 85 Vols. *The SAT Daizōkyō Text Database*. Japan: University of Tokyo. Last modified June 11, 2012. Accessed August 1, 2021. http://21dzk.l.u-tokyo.ac.jp/SAT/index_en.html.

Wilson, Jeff. 2014. *Mindful America: The Mutual Transformation of Buddhist Meditation and American Culture*. New York: Oxford University Press.

Winfield, Pamela D. 2019. "The Philosophy of the Mandala." In *The Dao Companion to Japanese Buddhist Philosophy*, edited by Gereon Kopf, 235–253. Dordecht, Netherlands: Springer.

1.3

GENDER, RITUAL, AND DANCING IMAGES

Jane E. Harrison's Aesthetic Approaches to the Materiality of Religion

Ulrike Brunotte

This chapter introduces the archaeologist and Hellenist Jane E. Harrison (1850–1928) as a scholar who made an important intellectual contribution to a performative and material approach in religious studies. The chapter thus discusses a neglected strand in the genealogy of material religion and an "aesthetics of religion" (Grieser and Johnston 2017) by presenting Harrison's work as an example of a radical epistemological shift from the linguistic paradigm to images, artifacts, rituals, and dancing bodies as "aesthetic formations" (Meyer 2009) of religious communication. Around 1900, Harrison came to the conclusion that rituals preceded myths—and she did this independently of William Robertson Smith (1846–1894) (see Schlesier 1994: 147; Brunotte 2017b). Previous to this shift toward a materialization of religion in media like images and artifacts, researchers pursued an Idealist-classicist or Protestant understanding of religion. Harrison described the then hegemonic valorization of belief, doctrines, and scriptures in the study of religion in this way: "Religion, we have seen, was in the last century regarded mainly in its theoretical aspect as a doctrine. Greek religion, for example, meant to most educated persons Greek mythology" (Harrison 1915: 151–152; [1909] 2009: 506). Her thinking progressed through a turn to a ritualist understanding of religion, whose point of departure was cultural and religious practices:

> Yet even a cursory examination shows that neither Greek nor Roman religion had any creed or dogma, any hard and fast formulation of belief. In the Greek Mysteries only we find what we should call a *Confiteor*; and this is not a confession of faith, but an avowal of rites performed. When the religion of primitive peoples came to be examined it was speedily seen that though vague beliefs necessarily abound, definite creeds are practically non-existent. Ritual is dominant and imperative. . . . In examining religion as envisaged to-day it would therefore be more correct to begin with the practice of religion, i.e., ritual, and then pass to its theory—theology or mythology.
>
> *(Harrison 1915: 152; [1909] 2009: 498–499)*

These few sentences already demonstrate Harrison's progressive approach. The "discovery" of ritual and the revaluation of rituals in the formation of knowledge, science, and culture around 1900, and the establishment of comparative anthropology in Cambridge at the same

DOI: 10.4324/9781351176231-5

time, would certainly not have been possible without the knowledge transfer that had taken place from the British colonies (Brunotte 2013a: 45). Harrison used the then widespread comparison of ancient Greek religious cults to anthropological examples of "primitive people" to argue that rituals are not mere containers of an inward idea or meaning, or the mere recitation or adherence to a script (of a creed or belief system), but are, rather, dynamic cultural-religious forces. Further, as will be shown, her pioneering work on the analysis of ritual scenes in vase paintings drew "a direct genealogical connection between ritual and theater, emphasizing the pre-eminence of performance over text" (Fischer-Lichte 2008: 31). Her innovative aesthetic approach to ancient Greek religion was further inspired by the cultural enthusiasm for Dionysian aesthetics (see Brunotte 2013) and a pronounced female or heretical Hellenism (Fiske 2008; Prins 2017). Like Charlotte Brontë, Virginia Woolf, George Eliot, and Isadora Duncan, Harrison attempted a different sort of appropriation of ancient Greek tradition, one conveyed by non-linguistic as well as linguistic means. Contemporaries were fascinated (and shocked) by Harrison's radical modern openness to topical questions and the dynamics of her time, such as innovative tendencies in the sociology of religion (Durkheim, see Schüler 2017), literature (see Phillips 1991, Carpentier 1998), theater (see Peters 2008), philosophy (Nietzsche, Bergson), and psychology. She was especially inspired by the performative repertoire of the modern dance movement:

> All her life Harrison acted as an intermediary between the scholarly world of Cambridge and the artistic circles of the London metropolis. In doing so, ritual dance represented for her the decisive link between scholarship and art and between art and ritual: "We shall find in these dances," Harrison wrote in 1913, "the meeting-point between art and ritual."
>
> *(Brunotte 2017a: 174)*

This chapter will touch on the intertwining of Harrison's feminist commitment with her radical research innovations. The following dynamic novelties and upheavals of her time particularly shaped the context of her work: the archaeological discovery of a presumably matrilineal or even matriarchal archaic Greek culture in Crete; the admission of women to the study of ancient Greek history; and the artistic and political appropriations of ancient Greek visual and ritual culture in female Hellenism, dance, and the suffrage campaign. Not only (female) artists, writers, and dancers, but also the suffragettes "often borrowed from the art of classical antiquity" (Comentale 2001: 479).

"Material Culture": Archaeological and Anthropological Beginnings

Harrison was one of the first women to give university lectures on the Greek classics. In addition, as Robert Ackerman has observed, "she was the first female British classical scholar to achieve international recognition" (Ackermann 1991: 3). Her scholarly point of departure was archaeology and studies in the visual arts. Her ritualist and pictorial approach to "lived religion" (Hall 1997; McGuire 2008) has therefore to be contextualized within the then emerging field of archaeology. Archaeology was taught at Cambridge from around 1880 onwards. In 1888 the courses and topics for the "Classical Tripos" examinations, the tests that students were required "to pass to receive an honors degree in their field" (Fiske 2008: 199), were reformed: the traditional predominance of linguistics and philology shifted toward an integration of archaeology. Greater importance was attached to material objects, artifacts, and religious customs. Striking, too, was the amount of space religion, rituals, and culture took up in the new exams. As Mary Beard has noted: "late nineteenth-century subject definitions at least in Cambridge saw religion, mythology, art, and antiquities as constituent parts of the same subdiscipline, classical archaeology" (Beard 2000: 127). In this context, the introductory sentences of the once famous lecture delivered in 1850 by the archaeologist Charles Newton (1816–1894), the keeper of Greek and Roman Antiquities at the British Museum, sound peculiarly topical to us: "The record of the Human Past is not at all contained in printed books. Man's history has been graven on the rock in Egypt, stamped on the brick of Assyria. . . . [I]t is embodied in all heirlooms of religions" (Newton 1880: 1). At the end of his speech, Newton programmatically defines the purpose of archaeology: "[T]o collect, to classify, and to interpret all the evidence of man's history not already incorporated in Printed Literature" (Newton 1880: 2). In light of these remarks, it is not surprising that Peter Bräunlein's historical overview of the "material turn" in the study of religion locates the institutional-academic starting point of early British and American "material culture studies" in the then emerging fields of anthropology and archaeology. "Both disciplines were born in museums of the nineteenth century, and the engagement with artefacts was essential for their identity formation" (Bräunlein 2016: 368).

In 1874, the twenty-four-year-old Harrison, then a student at Newnham College—a newly founded Cambridge women's college—became acquainted with the academic field of archaeology. Her fascination with material and visual culture and the artifacts of ancient Greek religion was already growing when she became a student of Sir Charles Newton in London. From 1879 to 1897, Harrison studied and later taught classical archaeology at the British Museum. She used objects from the museum for her maverick and methodologically innovative lectures on Greek art, religion, and visual culture. She furthermore made use of her theatrical talents and of diverse innovative media. In addition to her own voice and eccentric, antique clothes, she employed a kind of *laterna magica* to produce special light and pictorial effects and even used a reconstructed bull-roarer for certain "authentic" ritual sound effects (Beard 2000: 47, 9; Robinson 2002: 60–65; Brunotte 2013a: 169–171). In one of her early publications, *Myth of the Odyssey in Art and Literature* (1882), Harrison expressed greater appreciation for the *aesthetic* and sensual skills of archaeologists than for their positivist accumulation of facts:

> I believe the educational value of a study of archaeology to consist far more in the discipline of taste and feeling it affords than in the gain of definite information it has to offer . . . the best gifts of archaeology, —the trained eye, quick instinct, pure taste, well-balanced emotion.
>
> *(Harrison 1882: xii–xiii)*

Harrison's approach goes beyond the pure aesthetic "connoisseurship" of her time because she refers to the "corporeal capability on the basis of a power given in our psyche to perceive objects in the world via our five different sensorial modes" (Meyer and Verrips 2008: 21). It is worth noting that Harrison's sensual approach to the perception and study of religion was also inspired by Henri Bergson's *Philosophy of Life* (see Harrison 1912; 1970).

Ritual-Image-Myth: Aesthetics of Religion

In Harrison's first book (1882) there are already hints of the central innovations in her approach to the study of Greek religion and culture: first, the anthropological comparison of Greek myths and rituals to those of "primitive people" and indigenous cultures, inspired by Edward Tyler's (1871) *Primitive Culture*; second, a strong interest in the interaction of rituals and myths; and third, her commitment to images as energetic media for the expression and embodiment of myth. Most important for a genealogy of material religion, however, was Harrison's thesis that visual expressions and artifacts are active producers of mythological meaning. In the introduction to *Myths of the Odyssey* (1882), she urged that artistic material visualizations in vase paintings, sculptures, or gems are not mere decorations of a myth, but

> [W]e shall see again and again that the ancient artist was no *illustrator* in the modern sense of the term. Frequently we have plain evidence that it is not the artist who is borrowing from Homer, but that both Homer and the artist drew their inspiration from one common source, local cultic and national tradition.
>
> *(Harrison 1882: ix, emphasis in original; see also Schlesier 1994: 126)*

Harrison expanded the concept of the image (sculpture, figurine), which had hitherto been fixed to individual works of art and artists, to include the function of the image as active medium in cultural religious traditions. Moreover, she drew attention to habitual ritual actions and visual materializations as aesthetic vehicles of emotion and knowledge. Vase paintings or ancient figurines were no longer treated as individual artistic masterpieces deposited in museums, but as independent sources for exploring rituals and myths. In *Myths of the Odyssey in Art and Literature*, Harrison explains:

> Nothing perhaps makes us realise so vividly that the epics of Homer are *embodiments*, not creations, of national Sagas, as this free and variant treatment of his mythology by the artists.
>
> *(Harrison 1982: ix, emphasis added)*

Archaeological findings and artifacts were analyzed not only as illustrations of literature but also as part of "aesthetic formations." Birgit Meyer developed the term "aesthetic formations" (2009) to emphasize the tangible, emotional, and sensual elements in religious mediations, to "better grasp the ways in which religious mediations address and mobilize people and form them aesthetically" (13). Sonia Hazard has suggested connecting the material-religion concept of "aesthetic formations" with the Deleuzian concept of "assemblages" (Deleuze and Guattari 1987). "[A]esthetic formations," she maintains, "may be described as assemblages of bodies, senses, media, things, practices, attitudes, and ideas" (Hazard 2013: 65). Harrison started from a comparison of visual expressions and literary embodiments of mythical tradition. With the shift to the Dionysian mystery cults in her groundbreaking monograph *Prolegomena to the Study of Greek Religion* (1902), she came to emphasize the sensual collective dance experience in local cults as a medium and part of aesthetic formations. In *Myth of the Odyssey* (1882), it was (still) mainly visual expressions that functioned for her as an archive of local and national cultural memory, but even her notion of cultural memory focused less on texts and monuments than on oral, visual, and ritual repertoires of local cults and traditions.

It was the field of memory studies that recently developed a performative approach to remembrance. In her book *The Archive and the Repertoire. Performative Cultural Memory in the Americas* (Taylor 2003), the Mexican theorist of performance studies Diana Taylor redefined the terms "repertoire" and "archive" to first describe a "preponderance of writing in Western epistemologies," and second to "suggest [that] writing has paradoxically come to stand in for and against embodiment" (2003: 16). However, "[t]he rift does not lie between the written and the spoken word, but between the *archive* of supposedly enduring materials (i.e., texts, documents, buildings, bones) and the so-called ephemeral *repertoire* of embodied practice/knowledge (i.e., spoken language, dance, sports, ritual)" (2003: 19, emphases in original). If we want to analyze the performative as well as mnemonic potential of mediated embodied acts, she argues, we shall have to change our methodologies. "Performance, for me, functions as an episteme, a way of knowing, not simply an object of analysis" (2003: xvi). This proposal resonates with Harrison's radical shift to rituals and material religion, which included a new concept of (academic) knowledge. Harrison's emphasis on collective ritual actions, affects in local cultic songs, and gestures was inspired by the work of the German classical scholar and founding father of German archaeology, Karl Ortfried Müller (1797–1840), whose influential books she read easily in German. She often discovered ritual scenes or unknown versions of myths on vases. These discoveries indicate that Harrison was one of the very first female archaeologists (a minority to this day) who recognized myths or variants of myths in these discrete commentaries (Schlesier 1994).

Monstrous Materiality: Beyond Mythical Anthropomorphism

Harrison devoted her first monograph, *Prolegomena to the Study of Greek Religion* (1903), to the study of monsters, spirits, and Greek daemons, and she was indeed the first scholar in religious studies to write a whole book on these hybrid mythical figures, their chthonic rituals, and the mythic underworld (see Brunotte 2013). She discovered what Eric Robertson Dodds (1951) would later define as *irrational* ecstasy, fear, and (cultic) madness. Her anti-classicist approach moved beyond the classical image of heroic Greek antiquity and the anthropomorphic forms of the beautiful Olympian gods. It was not she, however, who would reap the glory of pioneering research on Greek irrationality, but Dodds, who had been inspired by her work. Dodds succeeded Gilbert Murray as Professor of Greek at Oxford University and gained fame with his book *The Greeks and the Irrational* (1951).

In *Prolegomena*, Harrison summarized her critical view on the popular opinion among researchers that Antique Greek religion developed in a linear progression that culminated in the anthropomorphism of the Olympian gods. For her, this approach to religion had never been neutral, and had always been a colonizing and gendered discourse of power. It suppressed older, often mater-material (relating to the "mother" and relating to the maternal line) and hybrid layers of archaic Greek religion, making its goddesses and gods invisible or transforming them into underworld demons. To give voice to the material knowledge of demons (Brunotte 2013a), Harrison focused on specific embodiments, chthonic cults, and myths of predominantly female-animal hybrids like Harpies, Erinyes, Sirens, and, above all, Medusa. These monstrous figures were part of an archaic religious world in which Hera and Athena were not daughters or subordinate wives of the Olympic Zeus but goddesses in their own right. "These primitive goddesses reflect another condition of things, a relationship traced through the mother, the state of society known by the *awkward* term matriarchal" ([1903] 1991: 260, emphasis added). Her skepticism about the phantasies of an early matriarchy shows, however, in her choice of the adjective "awkward." Another pioneering aspect of Harrison's work was her emphasis on the gendered connotations of matter/(mater)/ otherness versus spirituality/(father)/logos in ancient Greek religion and philosophy (see Braidotti 2002). In the field of recent feminist philosophy (see Brunotte 2013b), the classical philosophical association of femininity with materiality was traced back to Plato (Timaios), Aristotle, and neo-Platonic appropriations (Butler [1993] 2011; Braidotti 2002). The same applies to the "metonymic link between women and these other Other" (Butler [1993] 2011: 3–28, 22). In a chapter of *Prolegomena* with the title "The Making of a Goddess," Harrison reconstructed the cultural process of abstraction, violation, and "forming" of the local mother goddess(es) "from ghost and snake to Olympian" (Harrison [1903] 1991: 321). Yet for Harrison, the hegemonic Olympic anthropomorphism also implied a more general reduction. She particularly emphasized the loss of (creative, daemonic) *formlessness*:

> We are apt to regard the advance to anthropomorphism as necessarily a clear religious gain. A gain it is in so far as a certain element of barbarity is softened or extruded, but with this gain comes loss, *the loss of the element of formless*, monstrous mystery. The ram-headed Knum of the Egyptians is to the mystic more religious than any of the beautiful divine humanities of the Greek. Anthropomorphism provides a store of lovely motives for art, but that spirit is scarcely religious.
>
> *(Harrison 1991: 258, emphasis added)*

Inspired by the studies of William Robertson Smith and James George Frazer, Harrison integrated ethnographic material and objects into the analysis of Greek myths and rituals and made use of the evolutionary comparative method prevalent in British anthropology. As David Chidester has shown, early *comparative religion* was based on and reproduced the colonialist world view of the British Empire. It was located in the context of colonial frontier discourses. In *Savage Systems*, Chidester argued that "comparative religion was at the forefront of the production of knowledge within these new power relations" (Chidester 1996: 1). As shown previously, Harrison critically opposed the colonial perspective and evolutionist rationalism of Tylor and Frazer (see Brunotte 2013 and Schlesier 1994). She focused instead on marginalized traditions, colonized indigenous groups, and expressive religious behavior in local cults.

Performative Speech Act and Ritual Materialization

After returning home in 1888 from her first trip to Greece, Harrison developed her initial theory of ritual and myth, which "was to inspire religious studies for decades" (Kippenberg 1997: 154). In *Mythology and Monuments of Ancient Athens* (1890), which combines an English translation and a commentary on Pausanias's work, she stated her program:

> I have tried everywhere to get at, where possible, the cult as the explanation of the legend. . . . Some of the loveliest stories the Greeks have left us will be seen to have taken their rise, not in poetic imagination, but in primitive, often savage, and I think, always practical ritual.
>
> *(Harrison 1890: iii)*

Together with her colleagues, Gilbert Murray and Francis Macdonald Cornford, Harrison established the circle of the Cambridge Ritualists, later joined by Arthur Bernhard Cook (Ackermann 1990: 3). Robert Segal explains that "for them, myth-ritualism is likely the earliest stage of religion" (Ackermann 1990: 108). Harrison developed her later, much more complex myth-ritual theory in her second main book, *Themis: A Study of the Social Origin of Greek Religion* ([1912] 1963). In *Themis*, she argued that myths, even collective beliefs, stemmed from ritual dance; they were not a mythical idea, but rather "a projection of group unity" (Harrison [1912] 1963: 48), an embodiment of collective affects. Here, in her second theory of ritual, myths and rituals are no longer hierarchically or causally ordered; they are, rather, an expression of the same social-affective process. This understanding of myth and ritual informed Harrison's development of a performative theory that she presented in a nutshell in her interpretation of the *Hymn of the Kouretes*, to which I turn in the next section.

Ulrike Brunotte

The term "performative" was coined by John L. Austin (1911–1960), a British philosopher of language, in his book *How to Do Things with Words* (1962). He introduced his new philosophy of ordinary language in his Harvard lectures of 1952–1955. Current theories of performativity link Austin's theory of *speech acts* with the concept of *performance* in theater studies (Fischer-Lichte 2008) and with Victor Turner's anthropological theories of *social drama* and *liminality* (Turner 1969; 1974). Common to all these approaches is a special connection between speaking and acting that hints at the power of the performative speech act to *do* something (see Kreinath 2009: 230–231). In his first two lectures, Austin draws a distinction between utterances that state something and *performative utterances* that not only "say" something but also perform a certain kind of action and, thereby, constitute something new. Although Austin did not explicitly incorporate religious and legal traditions into his theory, it is striking that many of the performative utterances he examines in his lecture are connected to rituals or ritual phrases. On the one hand, Austin recognizes performative utterances as a form of social communication with "magic" qualities. On the other hand, as Sybille Krämer (2003) has stressed, he completely excludes from his theoretical considerations the obvious and strong link between the power of those performative speech acts and non-verbal, mostly repetitive, and highly formalized social practices like ceremonies and rituals. Yet, it is exactly such ritualized frames that enable the performative speech act to constitute or even transform reality. The problem here, to which Krämer points with the question "What does Austin do when he talks about the performative?" (Krämer 2003: 51), is the curious tension between what he says systematically and what he does performatively in his examples but does not bring to express statement. For even in these early lectures, performativity was not merely a linguistic phenomenon but also went beyond "pure language."

The Performative Approach to Ritual: The Initiation Paradigm

It is no coincidence that one of the most important initiators of the *performative turn*, the anthropologist Victor Turner, mentioned Harrison's preliminary work in 1964 (see Brunotte 2017a, 2017b). Like Harrison, Turner considers rituals, in contrast to ceremonies, to be *transformative* processes. Based on Arnold van Gennep's three-phase model of *Rites de Passage* (van Gennep, [1908] 1987), Turner focuses on the liminal period of initiation rituals to elaborate his performative approach to ritual. Similarly, one of Harrison's innovative contributions to the study of Greek religion is the analysis of the initiation complex and the ritualist approach to the Dionysian mystery cults. As Walter Burkert stated: "Harrison makes this important theoretical progress in a 'solo run'" (Burkert 1979: 175).

In *Themis*, she interpreted the myths of the tortured, slain, dismembered, and reborn Dionysus Zagreus as an expression of the symbolic death and social rebirth of the neophyte during the initiation ritual. Her focus on the initiation complex was prompted by an archaeological finding in Eastern Crete: the fragments of the *Hymn of the Kouretes*. Discovered on an excavated stele, the engraved text presented, according to Harrison, a "ritual hymn commemorating the birth of the infant Zeus." She proposed that the text "embodies very early material, material so primitive that we seem at last to get back to the very beginnings of Greek religion. . . . It lets us see myth as well as ritual in the making" (Harrison [1912] 1963: 1). The hymn is said to praise the *Megistos Kouros*, the greatest youth of all. He is identified as the young Zeus and is invited to head a group of dancers and to "rejoice in dance and song," to "leap for full jars, and leap for fleecy flocks, and leap for fields of fruit, and for our cities, . . . and for goodly Themis" (Harrison [1912] 1963: 8). The collectively felt emotions, the longing for the invoked god—according to Harrison—provoked the *epiphany* of the god. The performative power to constitute something new and to open up a virtual space of collective imagination creates the presence of the god as co-dancer. The ritual/hymn *did* what it *said*:

> [T]he god invoked is not present, not there in a temple ready waiting to be worshipped; he is bidden to come, and apparently his coming, as well as, we shall later see, his very existence, depends on the ritual that invokes him. . . . Strangest of all, the god it would seem performs the same ritual as his worshippers, and it is by performing that ritual that he is able to confer his blessings.
>
> *(Harrison [1912] 1963: 10)*

Harrison argues that the hymn and the dance of the mythical Kouretes were the mythical expression of the real orgiastic dance, the dance of youths during the ritual of initiation. At the same time, as Henrik Versnel notes, these dancers could be interpreted as the "mythical Kouretes, who perform a war dance at the birth of the Cretan Zeus" (Versnel 1993: 27–28). It was evident to her that "the worshippers in the Hymn invoke[d] a Kouros who [was] obviously but a reflection or impersonation of the [real] body of Kouretes" (Harrison 1912: 27). As the Kouros and the Kouretes "belong[ed] to the cultus," Harrison concluded, "[w]e are face to face with the fact . . . that these religious figures arise . . . *straight out of the social custom*" (Harrison 1912: 27–28, emphasis in original). In resonance with Durkheim's social theory of religion, she wrote in her *Epilegomena to the Study of Greek Religion* (1921): "Rituals not only procure the means of life but they are the means whereby the social group periodically reaffirms itself" (Harrison [1921] 1962: xxx).

Aesthetics of Religion: Role of Emotions and Form

To elaborate on the relation between ritual deeds and mythical utterances, Harrison looked for the *tertium comparationis*, the connections among mythical utterances, songs and ritual acts, music, rhythm, and gestures. She considered rituals and myths as having developed from collectively felt and gesturally formed emotions. Thus, in her second theory of myth and ritual, there was no priority of ritual over myth, of the rhythmic action of dance over the narrative lines of the song. "They probably arose together," she conjectured. "Ritual is the utterance of an emotion, a thing felt in *action,* myth in words or thoughts. They arise *pari passu*" (Harrison [1912] 1963: 16). Later, in *Themis*, she writes: "Myth is the spoken correlative of the acted rite, the thing done; it is *to legomenon* as contrasted with or rather as related to *to drômenon*" (Harrison [1912] 1963: 328).

In its linking of myth to the enactment of the cult, to song and dance, Harrison's second myth-ritual theory approximates the performative theory of ritual *avant la lettre*. In Harrison's view, rituals can express emotions, generate knowledge, and transmit meaning in their own manner. However, she acknowledged that repetition, rhythm, and gesture are also media of formalization and distancing. Even the ecstatic dance of the intoxicated followers of Dionysus was not a mere chaotic expression of emotions, not a spontaneous and immediate acting out or "dancing out" of feelings, but a symbolic gestural activity. Here, Birgit Meyer's concept of "sensational forms" affords a helpful analytical tool to expand upon Harrison's material and performative theory of myth-ritual dance. The idea of "sensational forms" accents the importance of both the senses *and* simultaneously at the same time the role of form. Addressing "the paradox of mediation and immediacy requires developing a new synthesis of approaches that stress the importance of the senses and experience with those stressing the forms and codes that are at the basis of cultural and religious systems" (Meyer 2011: 29–30; 2013). For Harrison, ritual distancing and ritual-gestural formalization allowed the cultural production of form: repertoires, images, and symbols. Formalized gestural acts, songs, and rhythm, she maintained, opened up a cultural and psychological space of remembrance and imagination between the heightened collective affects and their direct realization. This in-between space made symbol formation possible:

> If an impulse finds instantly its appropriate satisfaction, there is no representation. . . .
> It is out of the delay, just the space between the impulse and the reaction that all our mental life, our images, ideas, . . . most of all our religion, arise.
>
> *(Harrison 1977: 44)*

In *Themis*, Harrison combined *dromenon* and *drama* and summarized her complex theory of religious ritual as follows:

> A high emotional tension is best caused and maintained by a thing felt socially. . . . If . . .
> [the] whole tribe dances together . . . emotion will mount to passion, to ecstasy. . . .
> [A *dromenon*] is a thing *re*-done or *pre*-done, a thing enacted or represented. It is sometimes *re*-done, commemorative, sometimes *pre*-done, anticipatory, and both elements seem to go to its religiousness. . . . [T]he drama or *dromenon* [the thing done] here is a sort of precipitated desire; a discharge of pent-up emotion. . . . [The desire] breaks out into mimetic, anticipatory action. Mimetic, not of what you see done by another, but of what you desire to do yourself.
>
> *(Harrison 1977: 43–45)*

Ritual was a kind of proto-drama, based on specific collectively felt emotions and making use of symbolic gestures to perform mimetic dances and create a virtual space of shared imagination. This element was based on the desire to re-live, to re-present."[I]t was a conjunction of acting, making, and doing that was essentially performative: a magic invocation of the object of desire, a creation of the event its pre-enactment. . . . It was *methexis* more than *mimesis*; participation more than imitation" (Peters 2008: 16). In this context it is necessary to mention that, since the beginning of her work on ritual, art, and theater, Harrison had followed Friedrich Nietzsche, whom she admired. She was greatly inspired by the Dionysian psychology of transgression he developed in his *Birth of Tragedy* (1872). Harrison first learned about Nietzsche's theory through the scholar Erwin Rohde, who restored the central role of the maenads (made invisible by Nietzsche) in the cultic experience of dance and intoxication. In an early review from 1894 of Rohde's book *Psyche: The Cult of Souls and the Belief in Immortality Among the Greeks* (Rohde [1925] 2000), Harrison formulated her aesthetic approach to religion and argued that an aesthetic knowledge (of the god) is both physical and spiritual. She described the dance of the maenads in enthusiastic words: "And what a madness it must have seemed! . . . To dance till we are dizzy, to toss our heads in ecstasy" (Harrison 1894: 165). Harrison admittedly qualified her description by raising doubts that this might "not seem to us the best means of promoting spirituality" (Harrison 1894: 165), but she maintained that Dionysus is experienced best through the muscles and the senses. "According to Harrison, the women who follow Dionysus have greater access to the truth, even though it is dubbed 'dangerous, disreputable, immoral, a peril to hearth and home'" (Prins 1999: 63, citing Harrison 1894: 165).

Female Appropriations of Greek Antiquity: Performative Acts

Following Walter Pater's essays on Dionysus (see Brunotte 2013: 187–190), Harrison "came to understand Dionysian ritual as a primal aesthetic impulse at the origin of all religious experience" (Prins 2017: 211). In *Prolegomena*, she called herself a follower of Dionysus and argued that "the constant shift from the physical to spiritual . . . [was] of the essence of the religion of Dionysos" (Harrison 1903: 452). As a prominent and influential representative of a feminist Hellenism (see Fiske 2008; Prins 2017), Harrison ascribed to the female worshippers, the dancing chorus of maenads, a central performative power in the Dionysian cult and in tragedy. She stressed the dynamics of the expressive potential inherent in the gestural patterns and visual forms of Dionysian ecstasy, and demonstrated how religious representation could arise from collective action and emotion (Harrison 1912). Linking emotion and motion with the cry and song of the chorus, Harrison stated that the god was produced by and in the ritual dance: "Dionysos is but his thiasos [group of followers] incarnate" (1912; 1977: 38).

In Victorian times, female authors, dancers, and artists had already taken up Euripides's tragedy *Bacchae* to re-image the bacchante or maenads as ecstatic female figures in motion. "Their imaginative identification with maenads took different forms in prose and poetry, in dance and drama, to incorporate an idea of rhythm into a moving body, both individual and collective" (Prins 2017: 33). The American dancer Isadora Duncan, whom Harrison helped in developing her choreographies, sought inspiration for her dance experiments in images of Dionysian scenes in European museums (Brandstetter 1995: 72).

Dionysus and his train of intoxicated female worshippers thus partly served as a means to project female desires for emancipation and change of gender roles onto ancient Greece. Representing an imaginary alternative to Victorian family life and spinsterhood, the dancing community of maenads and their "new" god were performative inventions driven by collective desire and aesthetic impulse. At the same time, there was another female form of appropriating the gestural and symbolic repertoire of (presumably) ancient Greek religion, one much more explicitly political: the suffrage movement.

These female activists' "turn to antiquity, however, also implies awareness that militant protest. . . recalled ancient transformative rites" (Comentale 2001: 479). In her essay "Homo Sum. Being a letter to an anti-suffragist from an anthropologist" (Harrison 1915: 80–115), Harrison wrote that the idea of a ritual revival in her time was related to the struggle for suffrage, which was primarily conducted in symbolic acts. She was not, she claimed, really a political person, yet her studies of primitive and ancient rituals led her to the suffragettes (Harrison 1915: 4).

Archaeology Again: Excavations of the "Great Mother" and a Matrilineal Culture

As doyenne of the Cambridge Ritualists, Harrison remained an archaeologist interested in visual material culture. The corroboration even of Harrison's thesis concerning the origin of the mystery god Dionysus and her interpretation of rituals is "founded in visual evidence: more than one hundred and fifty 'figures' (from a modern African initiation dance to ancient coins, Minoan seal stones to Attic vase paintings) are analyzed and compared" (Beard 2000: 106). As Harrison argued in *Themis*, the Greek mystery cult of Dionysus was a *revival* of an archaic religion of the "Mother":

> The mystery—god arises out of those instincts, emotions, desires which attend express life; . . . the form taken by the divinity reflects the social structure of the group to

which the divinity belongs. Dionysos is the Son of his Mother because he issues from a matrilinear-group.

(Harrison 1912: xiii)

Harrison was influenced by archaeological excavations of and associated speculation about an early culture of mother goddesses (see Hutton 1999). Most of all, she was inspired by the excavation of the Minoan-Mycenaean civilization that was taking place in Crete. In the English archaeologist Sir Arthur Evans, who spent almost his entire fortune in order to bring to light the remains of the palace of Knossos, Harrison found an important kindred spirit. It was above all a still-famous clay seal from the time around 1700 BC—which showed the "Great Mother" as "Mistress of the Beasts" on her cult hill surrounded by two lionesses—that proved a revelation for Harrison, who was present at the site:

> I shall never forget the moment when Mr. Arthur Evans first showed it to me. It seemed too good to be true. It represented the Great Mother standing on her mountain with her attendant lions, and before her a worshipper in ecstasy. . . . Here was the ancient cult of the Mother which long preceded the worship of the Olympians: here were the true *Prolegomena*.

(Harrison 1925: 72)

Harrison also took part in the then current speculations about matriarchy, but she remained skeptical. For example, in *Prolegomena* she mentions only once Johann Jacob Bachofen's famous study of matriarchy (1861). However, Harrison pointed out the gender connotation of the religious and later philosophical dichotomy of the mother-material demonic and father-symbolic logos in Ancient Greek culture (Heinrich 1982; Schlesier 1994; Vernant 1974). She was thus one of the earliest researchers in religious studies to discuss the role of gender in the production and representation of (religious) knowledge. Her scholarly project to reconstruct the suppressed Mycenaean cultural world, "characterized by an intense materialism, immanent deities, and sensual rites" (Comentale 2001: 480), was highly political. Harrison's work moved away from a classicist view of antiquity in order to explore the material activity of ancient local and often female communities.

This chapter has placed Harrison in the genealogy of the emerging fields of "material religion" (Meyer 2013) and the "aesthetics of religion" (Grieser and Johnston 2017). And finally it has tracked the intertwining of her methodological engagement with image, material objects, and ritual with her feminist approach to religion, materiality, and culture.

References

Ackermann, R. 1990. *The Myth and Ritual School.* New York: Garland.
Ackermann, R. 1991. "The Cambridge Group: Origins and Composition." In *The Cambridge Ritualists Reconsidered*, edited by W. M. Calder III, 1–19. Atlanta, GA: Scholars Press.
Austin, J. L. 1962. *How to Do Things with Words.* Cambridge, MA: Harvard University Press.
Beard, M. 2000. *The Invention of Jane Ellen Harrison.* Cambridge, MA: Harvard University Press.
Braidotti, R. 2002. *Metamorphosis. Towards a Materialist Theory of Becoming.* Cambridge, MA: Polity.
Brandstetter, G. 1995. *Tanz-Lektüren. Körperbilder und Raumfiguren der Avantgarde.* Frankfurt: Fischer.
Bräunlein, P. J. 2016. "Thinking Religion Through Things. Reflections on the Material Turn in the Scientific Study of Religion\s." *Methods and Theories in the Study of Religion* 28 (4–5): 365–399.
Brunotte, U. 2013a. *Dämonen des Wissens. Gender Performativität und Materielle Kultur im Werk von Jane Ellen Harrison.* Würzburg, Germany: Ergon Verlag.

Brunotte, U. 2013b. "'A Body that Matters?' Jane E. Harrisons Epistemologische Ontdekking Van de 'Grote Moeder' en de Rol van de Chôra." *Tijdschrift Voor Genderstudies* 16 (3): 66–80.

Brunotte, U. 2017a. "The Performative Knowledge of Ecstasy: Jane E. Harrison's 1850–1928 Early Contestations of the Textual Paradigm in Religious Studies." In *Aesthetics of Religion. A Connective Concept,* edited by A. K. Grieser and J. Johnston, 161–188. Berlin: de Gruyter.

Brunotte, U. 2017b. "The Myth-Ritual Debate." In *Religion, Theory, Critique. Classic and Contemporary Approaches and Methodologies,* edited by R. King, 362–376. New York: Columbia University Press.

Burkert, W. 1979. "Griechische Mythologie und die Geistesgeschichte der Moderne." In *Les Études Classiques aux XIX et XX Siècles: Leur Place dans L'histoire des Idées,* edited by O. Reverdin and B. Grange, 159–207. Vandoeuvres-Geneva: Hardt.

Butler, J. (1993) 2011. *Bodies that Matter.* London: Routledge.

Carpentier, M. C. 1998. *Ritual, Myth, and the Modernist Text: The Influence of Jane Ellen Harrison on Joyce, Eliot, and Woolf.* Amsterdam: Gordon and Breach.

Chidester, D. 1996. *Savage Systems: Colonialism and Comparative Religion in Southern Africa.* Charlottesville, VA: University of Virginia Press.

Comentale, E. P. 2001. "Thesmophoria: Suffragettes, Sympathetic Magic, and H. D.'s Ritual Poetics." *Modernism/Modernity* 8 (3): 471–492.

Deleuze, G., and F. Guattari. 1987. *A Thousand Plateaus.* Translated by Brian Massumi. Minneapolis, MN: University of Minnesota Press.

Dodds, E. R. 1951. *The Greeks and the Irrational.* Berkeley, CA: University of California Press.

Fischer-Lichte, E. 2008. *The Transformative Power of Performance: A New Aesthetics.* Translated by I. J. Saskya. New York: Routledge.

Fiske, S. 2008. *Heretical Hellenism: Women Writers, Ancient Greece, and the Victorian Popular Imagination.* Athens, OH: Ohio University Press.

Grieser, A. K., and J. Johnston, eds. 2017. *Aesthetics of Religion. A Connective Concept.* Berlin: de Gruyter.

Hall, D. 1997. *Lived Religion in America: Towards a History of Practice.* Princeton, NJ: Princeton University Press.

Harrison, Jane E. 1882. *Myths of the Odyssey in Art and Literature.* London: Rivingtons.

Harrison, Jane E. (1885) 2009. *Introductory Studies in Greek Art.* London: Unwin repr., Cambridge: Cambridge University Press.

Harrison, Jane E. 1890. "Preface." In *Mythology and Monuments of Ancient Athens: Being a Translation of a Portion of the "Attica" of Pausanias,* edited by Jane E. Harrison and Margaret G. de Verrall, i–xiv. London: Macmillan.

Harrison, Jane E. 1894. "Review of Erwin Rohde's Psyche. Seelenkult und Unsterblichkeitsglaube der Griechen." *Classical Review* 8: 165–166.

Harrison, Jane E. (1903) 1991. *Prolegomena to the Study of Greek Religion.* Princeton, NJ: Princeton University Press.

Harrison, Jane E. (1909) 2009. "The Influence of Darwinism on the Study of Religions." In *Darwin and Modern Science Essays in Commemoration of the Centenary of the Birth of Charles Darwin,* edited by C. N. Seward, 494–511. Cambridge: Cambridge University Press.

Harrison, Jane E. (1912) 1977 repr. of 1963 edition. *Themis: A Study of the Social Origins of Greek Religion.* London: Merlin Press.

Harrison, Jane E. (1913) 1951. *Ancient Art and Ritual.* London: Williams and Norgate.

Harrison, Jane E. 1915. ""Homo Sum": Being a Letter to an Anti-Suffragist from an Anthropologist." In Harrison, Jane E. *Alpha and Omega,* 80–115. London: Sidgwick & Jackson, Ltd.

Harrison, Jane E. 1921. *Epilegomena to the Study of Greek Religion.* Cambridge: Cambridge University Press.

Harrison, Jane E., and Margaret G. de Verrall. 1890. *Mythology and Monuments of Ancient Athens: Being a Translation of a Portion of the "Attica" of Pausanias.* London: MacMillan.

Hazard, S. 2013. "The Material Turn in the Study of Religion." *Religion and Society: Advances in Research* 4: 58–78.

Heinrich, K., 1982. *Parmenides und Jona. Vier Studien über das Verhältnis von Philosophie und Religion.* Frankfurt/M.: Roter Stern.

Hutton, R. 1999. *The Triumph of the Moon. A History of Modern Pagan Witchcraft.* Oxford: Oxford University Press.

Kippenberg, H. G. 1997. *Die Entdeckung der Religionsgeschichte. Religionswissenschaft und Moderne.* Munich: Beck.

Krämer, S. 2003. "Was tut Austin, Indem er Über das Performative spricht?. Ein anderer Blick auf die Anfänge der Sprechakttheorie." In *Reserve der Form. Theorie*, edited by A. Fritz and K. Stattmann, 51–63. Frankfurt/M.: Künsterhaus Wien.

Kreinath, J. 2009. "Virtuality and Mimesis: Toward an Aesthetics of Ritual Performances as Embodied Forms of Religious Practice." In *Religion, Ritual, Theatre,* edited by B. Holm, B. F. Nielsen and K. Vedel, 229–259. Frankfurt/M.: Peter Lang.

McGuire, M. 2008. *Lived Religion: Faith and Practice in Everyday Life.* New York: Oxford University Press.

Meyer, B. 2009. "Introduction: From Imagined Communities to Aesthetic Formations: Religious Mediations, Sensational Forms and Styles of Binding." In *Aesthetic Formations: Media, Religion and the Senses,* edited by B. Meyer, 1–30. New York: Palgrave Macmillan.

Meyer, B. 2011. "Mediation and Immediacy: Sensational Forms, Semiotic Ideologies and the Question of the Medium." *Social Anthropology* 19 (1): 23–39.

Meyer, B. 2013. "Material Mediations and Religious Practices of World-Making." In *Religion Across Media: From Early Antiquity to Late Modernity,* edited by L. Lundby, 1–19. New York: Peter Lang.

Meyer, Birgit, David Morgan, Crispin Paine, and S. Brent Plate, eds. 2011. "Introduction: Key Words in Material Religion." *Material Religion* 7, no. 1 (April): 4–8. Accessed August 1, 2021.

Meyer, B., and J. Verrips. 2008. "Aesthetics." In *Key Words in Religion, Media, and Culture,* edited by D. Morgan, 20–30. New York: Routledge.

Nietzsche, F. (1872) 1909. *The Birth of Tragedy: Out of the Spirit of Music.* Translated by William A. Haussmann. London: Unwin.

Newton, C. T. 1880. *Essays on Art and Archaeology.* London: Macmillan.

Peters, J. S. 2008. "Jane Harrison and the Savage Dionysus: Archaeological Voyages, Ritual Origins, Anthropology, and the Modern Theatre." *Modern Drama* 51 (1): 1–41.

Phillips, K. J. 1991. "Jane Harrison and Modernism." *Journal of Modern Literature* 17 (4): 465–476.

Prins, Y. 1999. "Greek Maenads, Victorian Spinsters." In *Victorian Sexual Dissidence,* edited by R. Dellamore, 43–81. Chicago, IL: Chicago University Press.

Prins, Y. 2017. *Lady's Greek. Victorian Translations of Tragedy.* Princeton, NJ: Princeton University Press.

Robinson, A. 2002. *The Life and Work of Jane Ellen Harrison.* Oxford: Oxford University Press.

Rohde, E. (1925) 2000. *Psyche: The Cult of Souls and the Belief in Immortality Among the Greeks.* Translated by W. B. Hillis. Abingdon: Routledge.

Schlesier, R. 1994. *Kulte, Mythen und Gelehrte. Anthropologie der Antike seit 1800.* Frankfurt/M.: Fischer.

Schüler, S. 2017. Aesthetics of Immersion: Collective Effervescence, Bodily Synchronisation and the Sensory Navigation of the Sacred." In Aesthetics of Religion. A connective Concept, edited by Grieser, A. K., and J. Johnston. Berlin/Boston: de Gruyter, 367–387.

Taylor, D. 2003. *Archive and Repertoire: Performing Cultural Memory in the Americas.* Durham, NC: Duke University Press.

Turner, V. 1969. *Ritual Process: Structure and Anti-Structure.* New York: Aldine P. Company.

Turner, V. 1974. *Dramas, Fields and Metaphors.* Ithaca, NY: Cornell University Press.

Van Gennep, A. (1908) 1987. *Les Rites de Passage (Übergangsriten).* Frankfurt/M.: Campus.

Vernant, J.-P. (1987). *Mythos und Gesellschaft im alten Griechenland.* Frankfurt/M.: Suhrkamp.

Versnel, H. 1993. *Transition and Reversal in Myth and Ritual, Inconsistencies in Greek and Roman Religion II.* Leiden: Brill.

1.4

THE PHILOSOPHY OF UBUNTU AND MATERIAL RELIGION IN AFRICA

Engaging Henry Rowley's Mid-Nineteenth-Century Perspective on the Materiality of Religion

Kapya J. Kaoma

But I believe the conversion of an African . . . will be found to be an easier work—humanly speaking—than that of the Hindu or Chinese. He is dark, barbarous and degraded; but they have a system of religion, a regular philosophy for which they think no problem in life too hard. . . . [T]hey can give you no reason for what they do beyond this; 'it is the custom of our country.'

(Rowley 1867: 229)

In 1860, Henry Rowley was among the first Church of England missionaries sent to Nyasaland (today's Malawi), under the leadership of Bishop Charles Mackenzie. The mission was spearheaded by David Livingstone's 1858 emotional appeal to the British people at the University of Cambridge to send missionaries to "Central Africa" (which in fact was Southern Africa). On January 1, 1861, Mackenzie was consecrated as the first Church of England Missionary bishop under the Universities' Mission to Central Africa (UMCA)—indeed, as the bishop "to the tribes dwelling in the neighbourhood of the Lake Nyasa and River Shire" (Wilson 1936: 5). On July 8, 1861, the Bishop and his party arrived in Nyasaland.

The formal mission did not last long: the missionaries got entangled in wars against slave traders. The bishop exchanged his crozier for a gun, and the missionaries rescued thousands of slaves, partnered with local people to fight Portuguese slave raiders, and declared slavery illegal in most of Nyasaland. "I had myself in my left hand a loaded gun, in my right hand the crozier," the Bishop wrote. "I thought of the contrast between my weapon and my staff, the one like Jacob, the other like Abraham, who armed his . . . servants to rescue Lot" (Harvey 1864: 283). Sadly, the bishop and three missionaries subsequently died from illnesses such as malaria and dysentery. Bishop Mackenzie succumbed to dysentery on February 22, 1862. In addition, the mission station lost more than fifty liberated women and children in less than three months. Their involvement in violent wars against slave traders, however, did not go well with UMCA funders in England.

DOI: 10.4324/9781351176231-6

Mackenzie's replacement, Bishop William George Tozer, disavowed the wars and moved the mission to Mozambique. He later abandoned the entire project for the Island of Zanzibar, which ironically was one of the central markets of captured slaves.

Rowley and African Philosophy and Religion

Given that Henry Rowley was an official recorder to Bishop Mackenzie, his works on African philosophy and religions are abundant—but they are rarely found in academic studies on Africa. This erasure is due in part to the way the abandoned mission was received in the Church of England. Yet, his writings on Bantu religion, rituals, and philosophy are informative to the study of early African traditional beliefs, culture, and rituals. Rowley's methodologies were planted in the African lifeworld; he was a participant observer of the very people he lived with and studied. Unlike the authors of similar African works, whose minds were already formed and informed by European perceptions of Africans, Rowley had an openness to African cosmologies that afforded him insights that contradicted most of the findings of previous European scholars of his time. This is another reason why his works were sidelined in the study of Africa.

Bantu religion, Rowley rightly observed, was earthly centered. It dealt with life issues here on Earth. The Bantu "idea of God was that of a benevolent deity. . . . If they were in trouble or distress, they would all meet together and offer up a prayer to God to deliver them from that trouble or distress, whatever it was" (Rowley 1867: 201). People interact with spiritual forces to obtain a good life in the here and now. In times of community crisis, Rowley rightly observed, the Bantu communally supplicate God at sacred shrines. Like the Mwari of Zimbabwe (Daneel 1970) and Chisumpi cults (Schoffeeleers 1978), women controlled the Mang'anja Mbona cult (see also Mandala 1984: 143). For example, Rowley witnessed how, following the long drought shortly after missionaries settled at Magomero, the Mang'anja supplicated to God for rain. And though the chief led the community procession to the shrine, once all had entered the enclosure, it was the priestess who presided over the ritual. After entering the sacred hut, she placed the basket of corn flour and the pot of native beer on either side and then supplicated God

> In a high-pitched voice, "Imva Mpambi! Adza mvula!" (Hear thou, God, and send rain!) and the assembled people responded by clapping their hands softly and intoning—they always intone their prayers—"Imva Mpambi!" (Hear thou, God!). This was done again and again until the meal was expended, and then, after arranging it in the form of a sugarloaf, the beer was poured, as a libation, round about it.
>
> *(Rowley 1867: 269; 1877: 17)*

Thereafter, the whole community was invited to participate in the sacred ritual. Rowley explains:

> The supplications ceased, Mbudzi [*sic*] came out of the hut, fastened up the door, sat on the ground, threw herself on her back; all the people followed her example, and while in this position they clapped their hands and repeated their supplication for several minutes. This over, they stood up, clapped hands again, bowing themselves to the earth repeatedly while doing so; then marched to where Chigunda [*sic*] was sitting, and danced round about him like mad things. The dance ceased, a large jar of water was brought and placed before the chief; first Mbudzi washed her hands, arms, and face; then

water was poured over her by another woman; then all the women rushed forward with calabashes in their hands, and dipping them into the jar threw the water into the air with loud cries and wild gesticulations.

(Rowley 1867: 269)

After the ceremony, Rowley noted, "the thunder-cloud passed over Magomer[o]," the land "had an abundant shower of rain."

The employment of cornmeal, native beer, water, the throwing of water into the air, and the clapping, the dancing, and gesticulations in the supplication of God do not only illustrate the material expression of Bantu religion; they also confirm the ecological nature of Bantu lifeworld—the universe exists as a web.

But the lying on the ground in this ritual signifies the value of land in *ubuntu* philosophy. In this philosophy, landlessness constitutes non-being—it is on par with non-existence. Until colonialism, land was a community common not to be sold (Rowley 1867: 111, 265). Almost all African rituals are connected to the land. The chief is only a living custodian; ancestors, spirits, and high gods are the default owners and guardians of the land (Kaoma 2013). This belief is central to *ubuntu* philosophy—the material world is connected to the spiritual world.

Ubuntu philosophy seeks answers to earthly problems. As in the ritual above, people materially supplicate the deity or spiritual beings for rain using material objects—water, corn flour, native beers—with clapping and dancing. These acts are part of religious expressions and practices. Birgit Meyer et al. (2011: 6) write, "A materialized study of religion begins with the assumption that things, their use, their valuation, and their appeal are not something added to a religion, but rather inextricable from it."

The materialization of *ubuntu* might appear unsophisticated; yet, it is informed by a well-thought-out philosophy of life in which humanity, non-humans, nature, and culture are materially, spiritually, and ecologically interconnected. In *The Religion of Africans*, Rowley observes that Africans believe that spiritual forces

People the darkness with hideous shapes, poison the light with their presence, sweep over the plains in the forms of wild beasts, fill the forests, inhabit trees, live on the tops of the mountains, and in the secluded recesses of caves and valleys; make their homes in the sea, the lakes, and the rivers; the air is full of them, the earth teems with them, fire is not free from their presence, and human beings are possessed by them.

(Rowley 1877: 54)

The African materiality of religion is cosmic. The human, non-human, and spiritual forces influence how religion occurs (Bräunlein 2016: 377–382). Since Bantu lifeworld is ontologically interconnected, the philosophy of *ubuntu* centers around the morality of respect for elders/ancestors, adherence to the guidance of spirits and gods, and harmonious relationships in the cosmos. For this reason, *ubuntu* is a critical aspect to identity formation—it is the loci of faith, security, and ethical life (Bhengu 2006; Chasi and Ndlovu-Gatsheni 2021; Ntarangwi 2011; Tutu 2004).

Yet, scholarship on *ubuntu* philosophy as it relates to material religion hardly exists. Partially this is because it has been examined in opposition to Western philosophy. This is equally true with religion and other fields of studies: Western thought is the frame within which it is examined, which thereby leads to the materialization of *ubuntu* being overlooked. Birgit Meyer et al. (2011: 6) argue that any examination "of religion that fails to consider bodies is guilty of ignoring the materiality of religions." If that argument holds, then African rituals, customs, and culture bring new insights to the understanding of African religious expressions in the postcolonial, global, and highly material religious sociopolitical contexts. Though the theological concepts of enculturation and contextualization seem to capture some elements of the materialization of African religions, an examination of the philosophical materiality of African rituals, cults, ceremonies, and rites has been lacking. Partially this is due to the fact that most scholars of religion are affiliated with organized religion—hence, *probing beyond established dogma can be threatening.* This fear has limited the study of materiality of religion.

An Attempt to Define Ubuntu: A Challenge or Opportunity?

Bénézet Bujo (1940–)—who is a Roman Catholic priest of the Democratic Republic of the Congo and professor emeritus of moral theology at the University of Fribourg, Switzerland— confirmed some of Rowley's findings more than a century later: at the heart of an African soul is the traditional philosophy of life as experienced by ancestors (*mizimu*). In *The Ethical Dimension of Community*, Bujo writes:

> In existentially critical situations, even the intellectual elite and the loyal church-goers return to their [ancestors'] practices. Apparently, to them the challenges to existential problems cannot be solved within the technologically oriented society or within the churches of foreign origin. Considering this, it seems right to admit that the ancestral tradition still influences the African down to his very roots. If this is true, ancestral tradition is indispensable for the announcement of the Christian message as well as for coping with conflicts that result from the modern world of technology.
>
> *(Bujo 1998: 15; 1992: 23–27)*

Bantu Africanists have identified Bujo's "ancestral tradition" and Rowley's "regular philosophy" as *ubuntu*, the concept that continues to attract attention from religious scholars, political scientists, economists, international relations experts, and anthropologists—among many other disciplines. This African system of thought has been identified as critical to the study of Africa and its place in the world. Bujo (2012) writes, *ubuntu* "sees one's own full humanity as inextricably tied to one's relatedness with others and the environment."

Peter J. Bräunlein (2016: 1) attributes the growing interest in the study of material religion to "fundamental doubts about hierarchical and binary modes of thinking that invoke the mind-body, subject-object, nature-culture, and human-non-human divides that have dominated the history of Western philosophy." Although *ubuntu* philosophy respects the hierarchical order of human relations—the young are expected to respect the elders; it does not share the binary modes of thinking—nonetheless, one being encompasses all aspects of human life (Mafunisa 2008: 116; Tutu 1999: 31–32). Central to it is the perception of life as materially interconnected; the distinctions between the secular and the spiritual are highly pronounced in Christianity, but African traditional religions hardly make such distinctions. The sacred encompasses all aspects of life—nothing can exist in isolation from the whole.

Ubuntu is equally a secular and religious philosophy. African rituals are material expressions of African morality, religion, and life. For example, humanity is linked to nature just as nature is linked to humanity. Similarly, as a spiritual being, humanity is linked to the ancestors just as the ancestors are linked to gods and the natural world. And this relationship is visibly expressed in various rituals and ceremonies. For instance, among the Bemba as in other Bantu cultures, the burying of the dead must follow laid-down traditions; doing otherwise would disqualify one from being human (*umuntu*), even in death. The same with marriage, planting, and even eating. In short, this traditional philosophy applies across all aspects of life. Desmond Tutu writes:

> *Ubuntu* is very difficult to render into a Western language. It speaks of the very essence of being human. When we want to give high praise to someone we say, "*yu, u nobuntu*" ("Hey, so-and-so has ubuntu"). Then you are generous, you are hospitable, you are friendly and caring and compassionate. You share what you have. It is to say, "My humanity is caught up, is inextricably bound up, in yours." We belong in a bundle of life.
>
> *(Tutu 1999: 31–32)*

Justice Yvonne Mokgoro (1998: 2) also writes: "Group solidarity, conformity, compassion, respect, human dignity, humanistic orientation and collective unity have, among others, been defined as key social values of *ubuntu*." Again, the values of *ubuntu* are embodied—they are duties and obligations, which are anticipated from every community member. But they are equally performances—in daily greetings, naming ceremonies, weddings, planting ceremonies, funerals, etc. All these activities are meant to unify, bless, and heal the community or the land—by which they mean the living, the living dead, and the future generations of life.

Ubuntu philosophy does not share Eliade's and Durkheim's binary of "the sacred and the profane." For instance, when South Africa's Constitutional Court employed "*ubuntu*" in the interpretation of the law, Ilze Keevy (2009: 84) objected to its application to secular law. Keevy argued that *ubuntu*'s values and beliefs "are derived from African Religion"—thus, employing it in secular law imposes religious belief on secular jurisdictions. Such an accusation, however, is misleading since *ubuntu* is not only hardly undefinable, but also an expansive concept (Mokgoro 1998; Kaoma 2013; Tamale 2014). It applies to material religion just as to law, ethics, and other academic disciplines.

The marriage between African religion and philosophy exists—the two cannot be studied aside from the other. The word is impossible to translate into English without losing some of its original meaning and application. To possess it is to be virtuous; it is to live in constant harmony with all of Earth's community, ancestors, spirits, and of course, the Supreme Being (God). Since African material religion is community-centered (Magesa 1997; 48, 65–71; Mbiti 1969: 175), social unity of the living, ancestors, the yet-to-be-born, and the natural world are the loci of *ubuntu*.

Whereas *ubuntu* is highly associated with South Africa, it is part of the wider frame of indigenous lifeworld across Bantu cultures (Kaoma 2015; Ntarangwi 2011; Samkange and Samkange 1980). In these cultures, sharing; solidarity and interdependence; and respect for elders are treasured aspects of life. Young persons must kneel before elders, known or unknown. The living must respect ancestors just as the ancestors must respect spirits and gods. Like Rowley's account above, among the Tonga of Zambia, the annual Lwiindi Ceremony, usually held in November, is one occasion when the community supplicates royal ancestors for rains and good harvests at the *malende* (royal graves) (Kaoma 2013).

In this cosmology, *ubuntu* cannot be divorced from holiness and vice versa. As Magesa observes, whereas "holiness" in the Hebrew Bible is associated with God, "holiness" in African religion "is the normal way of preserving communion and therefore guarding and promoting personal and communal wholeness, *ubuntu*" (Magesa 2004: 158). When Bembas say, "*ubu e buntu*" (this is being human), they mean someone is carrying out community obligations as opposed to mere personal interests. Desmond Tutu asserts, "We can tell when *ubuntu* is there and when it is absent. It has to do with what it means to be truly human, to know that you are bound up with others in the bundle of life" (Tutu 2004: 27). Rowley, for example, documents the encounter with Mankokwe, the first chief in whose land they sought to settle. After deliberations, the missionaries showered Mankokwe with many gifts. Following the community meeting, however, their gifts were returned with the message that his land could not be bought. Had he allowed missionaries in his land against his people's interests—(Bembas would say, *"uyu te muntu,"* this one is not human)—he would have lost his humanity. Acting against the common good means losing one's humanity.

Another difference between Western philosophy and *ubuntu* resurfaces. Working from the Western assumptions, the missionaries could have assumed that their gifts were meant for the chief as an individual. In *ubuntu* philosophy, however, sharing is a higher virtue—as such, those gifts were meant for the community, not just the chief. For example, in 1861 Rowley encountered a man who had the great fortune of securing a fowl to eat—most of which he gave to his friends. To Rowley's puzzled inquiry, the man replied: "It is our custom. We don't eat fowl every day. And when we do eat it, we share it with others who do not" (Rowley 1867: 214).

What is telling in this encounter is the fact that, though in some cultures scarcity invites greediness, in Bantu culture it invites generosity. Though globalization and capitalism may continually threaten *ubuntu*, sharing is a virtue that continues to inform Bantu spirituality. It is expected that people share material things: food, salt, clothes, shoes, plates, pots, etc. Those who don't share are evil; witches. This ethic may trouble Westerners when they visit the Bantu—people are ready to kill their last remaining animal to feed a visitor. Since *ubuntu* emphasizes sharing, it is a curse for an elder to return your gift—since a rejected gift is indicative of bad relationships, as was the case with the chief above. What is important here is the greater attention this philosophy invites to the material world in the perception, interpretation, and understanding of religion. In *Africa Unveiled*, Rowley recounts one expression of this value when he spent an unplanned night at a village:

> It was some distance from our station, and out of the common route. But the people of this place had heard good things of the "Anglesi," and learning that I was one of them, they made me unreservedly welcome. A good hut was placed at my service; wood, water, and food were brought to me. The men and women clustered about me in perfect confidence, and the children played with me without fear. By - and - by the chief visited me.
>
> *(Rowley 1876: 48)*

Rowley was later invited to the chief's palace, where he was entertained with music and special events. Such a reception was not exceptional—it was simply the standard. He writes, "I have no wish to appear in the light of a special pleader for the brighter side of the African's life, but it is right that it should be known" (Rowley 1876: 49). Similarly, the Bantu share in suffering. The funeral affects all. Thus, when one dies, the whole community is expected to contribute to the costs of the funeral too.

Understanding the Philosophy of Ubuntu

Given the vastness of the continent of Africa, it cannot be reduced to one homogenic unit. And so, although *ubuntu* philosophy is present in many Bantu community cultures, each ethnic group has its own heritage, customs, and material culture. Nonetheless, broad themes and concepts exist on which the study of material religion can be based. Ugandan Law Professor Sylvia Tamale (2014: 151) identifies *ubuntu* as a shared theme.

From Southern to Eastern to Central Africa, many African community cultures identify as Bantu. Some of these cultural groups are patriarchal, while others are matrilineal. Apart from some easily identified linguistic phrases and words, most of these groups do not share a common language. Thus, as John Gunther writes:

> [M]ost Bantu languages have similar qualities, and the roots of many words are the same, or approximately the same, all the way from [Cameroon] to the Cape. The word for [person] is *umu-ntu* in Zulu, *um-tu* in Xhosa, *oma-ntu* in Luganda, and *m-tu* in Swahili. The plural form, *aba-ntu*, is the same in a number of languages, and from this comes the word "Bantu" itself, meaning "Human Being." [African] languages on the other flank of Africa are totally dissimilar. They differ from Bantu almost as much as English does from Japanese.
>
> *(Gunther 1953: 287)*

This observation is to the point. Bantu communities share many words that are easily identifiable. Whereas *ubuntu* philosophy is found among all Bantu cultures, University of KwaZulu-Natal South African professor Nhlanhla Mkhize argues that the word *ubuntu* is derived from the Nguni prefix *ubu-* and the stem *-ntu*. The prefix *ubu-*, he contends, applies to the class of nouns that denote a process of perpetual becoming, while *-ntu* is reserved "for human beings. Thus, the whole word ubuntu points to a being that is oriented towards becoming; it refers to an ongoing process that never attains finality" (Mkhize 2008: 41). This observation, however, is hard to defend across Bantu cultures. Aside from failing to acknowledge the wider application of this ethical system in Bantu communities, Mkhize ignores that Bembas, Shonas, and other Bantu languages can make similar claims to the linguistic origin of *ubuntu*. As I explain below, to argue that the stem *-ntu* is reserved for "humanity" ignores how the stem *-ntu* is used in most Bantu languages, including Nguni dialects such as Ndebeles of Zimbabwe and Ngoni of Zambia.

On the contrary, *ubuntu* deals with how a person (*umuntu*) behaves toward other material objects/beings. This is self-evident in similar words for non-humans: *icintu* in Bemba, *chinhu* in Shona, and *kinto* in Tswana—all mean "non-human objects." Rather than following the daily usage of these words in Bantu contexts, philosophers limit the discussion of *ubuntu* to apply to only human beings—thereby isolating it from its application to non-human objects/ beings. Unfortunately, this Western prism is the lens through which *ubuntu* has been analyzed and studied.

However, a closer look at the word *umuntu* reveals that *mu* refers to human, while *ntu* points to "being," hence human being. Likewise, *icintu*, while translated as "thing," can be broken into two parts: *ici* points to non-human, while *ntu* refers to "being." Linguistically, *umuntu* and *icintu* suggest cosmic interconnectedness. What *umuntu* and *icintu* have in common is *ntu*. Humans and non-humans are not only intrinsically interlinked, but also ontologically interdependent. Ecologically, both nonhumans and humans are products of the common material origin of *NTU*—the vital force that holds the universe together (Kaoma 2013).

On the other hand, German scholar Janheinz Jahn divided Bantu ontology into four material categories based on the stem *ntu*. Unlike Mkhize, Jahn notes that *-ntu* is the universal force manifested in *muntu* (human being), *kintu* (thing), *hantu* (place and time), and *kuntu* (modality). Jahn argues that *ntu* expresses the being of forces, and hence "*NTU* is what *Muntu, Kintu, Hantu* and *Kuntu* all equally are (material elements). Force and matter are not being united in this conception; on the contrary, they have never been apart" (Jahn 1961: 101). As intelligent beings, God, spirits, ancestors, and certain trees are accorded the status of *umuntu*, while *kintu* is reserved to forces that act on *Muntu*'s command—among them plants, animals, minerals, etc. Whereas *hantu* refers to time and space, *kantu* defines modality, beauty, laughter, and other material expressions. In part quoting Paul Klee care of Werner Haftmann (1950: 96), Jahn writes:

> NTU is that . . . "far off point from which creation flows, where I suspect there is a formula for man, beast, plant, earth, fire, water, air and all circling forces at once.". . .
> NTU expresses, not the effect of these forces, but their being. But the forces act continually, and are constantly effective. Only if one could call a halt to the whole universe, if life suddenly stood still, would NTU be revealed.
>
> *(Jahn 1961: 101)*

Substantial differences between Bantu and Western philosophies are easily identifiable. In much of Western philosophy, humanity is at the apex of creation—whereas in Bantu philosophy non-humans are. Thus, humanity does not solely control the world—an assertion that contradicts Jahn's argument that *kintu* includes all beings that act under human command. The Bantu don't differentiate between humans and non-humans solely based on intelligence. If this were the case, Jahn's observation that certain trees, rivers, and animals can be termed *umuntu* does not hold. Neither can it explain the divinity and sacredness associated with certain human-made objects, natural objects, animals, rivers, and waterfalls. If *NTU* is what both humans and non-humans hold in common, African scholars who associate *ubuntu* with the image of God impose Western thought on Bantu philosophy. Gabriel Setiloane (1986: 13), for example, argues that Motho (*muntu*) "is that Energy or Force, that is Modimo—Divinity. The word used to describe the human person . . . is the same as employed to describe the mysterious, all-pervasive Energy-Force which is in fact the source of life." John M. Mafunisa (2008: 116) also writes, "[U]buntu is the essence of God's presence within humanity and God's manifestation to humanity." Setiloane and Mafunisa seem to follow Thomas Aquinas in placing reason at the center of the human–God relationship. Nonetheless, their argument is hard to defend. *In African religion, gods, spirits, and ancestors manifest in material objects; rarely are high gods manifested in humanity.* Exceptions include Mwari of the Matopo Hills in Zimbabwe and Mbona in Malawi, where the high gods communicate through females (Daneel 1971; 2001; Ranger 1999; 1973; Rowley 1867: 266; Schoffeleers 1978). But in most cases, gods, spirits, and ancestors manifest in natural phenomena. Hence, *ubuntu* respects humanity—but, etymologically, every material being is imbued with this divine being, NTU. For this reason, *ubuntu* objectifies ideas, values, histories, myths, rituals, and cultic spaces in which religion is expressed and communally lived and re-lived from generation to generation (Kaoma 2015; Nyamiti 1984; Shoko 2007).

The Philosophy of Ubuntu and Vital Force

The philosophy of *ubuntu* has been linked to Placide Tempels's theory of *vital force* (Tempels 1952). While Tempels did not address material religion, he nevertheless asserted that everything is imbued with the vital force. *Umuntu* (person) signifies the vital force endowed with intelligence and will. *Bintu* refers to "things." Thus, "It is because all being is force and exists only in that it is force, that the category 'force' includes of necessity all 'beings': God, [humanity] living and departed, animals, plants, and minerals" (Tempels 1952: 36). In other words, all material beings are linked to the life force, or what Nkafu M. Nkemnkia (1999) terms "African vitalogy." Edwin W. Smith (1946: 200–201) noted that Tempels's theory upheld the belief that nothing exists in isolation. "Every created thing is in rapport with every other creature according to a law of hierarchy. This world is like a spider's web of which you cannot touch one thread without disturbing the whole."

Tempels's observations received pushback from African scholars of religion and philosophy. John S. Mbiti, for example, called the work too ambitious and open to great criticism since "the theory of 'vital force' could not be applied to other African peoples with whose life and ideas [Mbiti was] familiar" (1969: 10–11). Mbiti was right—the work was limited in application, which, according to Edwin Smith (1946: 200), Tempels also acknowledged.

Critiquing Janheinz Jahn's emphasis on *Ntu* (action and force), however, J. N. K. Mugambi argues that Tempels's theory of vital force influenced Jahn's examination of Bantu philosophy. Mugambi (1987: 23) writes: "To claim, therefore, that Vital Force is the fundamental concept of African religions and philosophy, is to project the personal thoughts and beliefs of Tempels, which developed from a different heritage, on to an actual African situation which is different both in tradition and presupposition." Mugambi's observation, however, only holds if *NTU* is limited to action as opposed to "Being," by which Tempels meant God—the point Mugambi himself acknowledged (Mugambi 1987: 23; Kaoma 2013).

Stephen O. Okafor equally critiqued Tempels's work. Despite accepting the key elements of Tempels's analysis, he observed that the center of Bantu philosophy is *life* as opposed to vital force. He identifies three important aspects: the meaning and the meaningfulness of the universe is nothing else than the meaningfulness of life; the conviction that the goodness of life is only reflected in the philosophy of commensality; and the conviction that every phenomenon emits an aura particular to it. All these are not only inseparable but also intricately linked (Okafor 1982: 91–92).

Okafor's observation is shared by Magesa (2010: 54), who writes: "All reality has a sacred dimension." In this philosophical frame, religion is materially experienced and understood. Moreover, *all life is a dance of vital forces*—God, spirits, clan founders, ancestors, humanity, animate, and inanimate objects are in what can be termed "perichoresis" (to borrow the word from Trinitarian Theology)—that is, co-indwelling, co-participation, equal-inhering, and mutual interpenetration of existence. All these beings, objects, and forces exist in a perfect symphony of cosmic interconnectedness. Hence, the philosophy is essentially material; high Gods, gods, spirits, and ancestors and every creature in the cosmos exist in material harmony. For this reason, Bantu religion is earthly as opposed to heavenly or otherworldly. This belief does not deny the spiritual realm—rather, it interconnects them. Humanity is ecologically linked to the sacred web of life from which it cannot be disconnected without being destroyed.

Materialization of Religion in Nature—Case of Snakes

The snake may carry negative implications in Western Christianity, but not in African religions, in which spirits, ancestors, and gods are associated with snakes (Kaoma 2016: 163–178; Olupona 2009: 60–65). The Tonga, Shona, Zulu, Xhosa, Chewa, Lamba, Nguni, and Bemba, for example, are among the many community cultures that associate sacredness with certain snakes. In *Religion in Africa*, Rowley writes: "But though inhabitants of a spirit world, the dead are not supposed to be always excluded from the earth; it is thought that some continue to inhabit it, occasionally in human form, but more frequently in the form of an inferior animal" (Rowley 1877: 112). Similarly, Magesa (1997: 35–36) asserts, "[S]pirits are active beings who are either disincarnate human persons or powers residing in natural phenomena such as trees, rocks, rivers, or lakes." Thus, the Bantu consider several animals—snakes, lions, hyenas, crocodiles, etc.—as sacred. Rowley writes:

> One of my colleagues, while accompanied by a native, saw a large snake crossing his path just ahead of him, and raised his gun to shoot it. His attendant, however, in great alarm, besought him not to do so. The snake was well known, he said, he was a spirit snake, and the chief of all the spirit snakes in the country; if let alone, no harm would come of it; but if killed, his children all round about would come together and revenge their father's death by killing many men, women, and children.
>
> *(Rowley 1877: 135)*

While spiritual forces are readily present in the natural environment and humanity interacts with them, special rituals are held to commune with, and to maintain the active connection between gods, ancestors, spirits, the cosmos, as well as to seek guidance from spiritual forces. About the Chisumpi Cult, Schoffeleers writes: "[T]he central cult object was conceived of as a snake, called 'tunga,' which was associated both with the shrine hut and with the sacred pool. . . . The snake spirit was visibly represented by the senior Mbewe official, who was himself known as 'tunga' and who acted as the spirit wife's ritual consort" (1999: 153). Traditionally, the sexual relationship between Thunga (male) and Makewana the priestess of the shrine did not only symbolize fertility rites, but also spoke to the cosmic elements of this cult. In *The Creator's Symphony*, I write:

> Although Chiuta (God) represented in the "Nile monitor" lives above the clouds, it is the python that is treated with uttermost respect. Known as nsato, the python represents the Deity and ancestral spirits—hence it is a taboo to kill it. Killing the python would attract severe environmental consequences ranging from drought to famines, so it is believed. Thus, many rain shrines are dedicated to Thunga, who is believed to move between sacred pools and sacred mountains. Hunting is forbidden around Thunga's shrines.
>
> *(Kaoma 2015: 63)*

The priest dresses and paints his body as a python for the rituals when the community seeks rain, community guidance, and other blessings from Chiuta.

African scholars acknowledge materialization of the sacred in snakes, but they dismiss such expressions as being of little value to the study and application of religion. Yet, the manifestation and representation of ancestors and spirits in non-human beings and objects remain an important aspect of Bantu religious expressions. The appearance of monkeys, lions, birds, and many other animals during certain festivals can signify ancestral or spiritual presence.

Materialization of Religion in Human Objects—Case of Spirit Mediums

The Bantu believe that humanity can impart power to certain objects through diviners or mediums. Anchored in "the belief in the existence of a vast spiritual agency" (Rowley 1876: 116), traditional doctors or *in'ganga* act as a bridge between the two worlds—of the living and that of the living dead.

Bantu philosophy does not discount the manifestation of ancestors in human persons. In addition to dreams, ancestors can embody any living person. Such a person carries the authority of the living dead—either in the family or in the locality. Whenever the person is possessed by the spirit, people would ask questions and seek answers. The Bantu, however, believe in different mediums.

Not all mediums claim to speak for the entire community—only privileged ones do. The high God mediums—that is, mediums who speak for God at specific Shrines, like the Mwari Shrine in Zimbabwe, the Chisumpi Cult, and Mbona Shrine in Malawi—are extremely rare and held in very high regard (Daneel 1971; 2001; Kaoma 2014: 57–84; Ranger 1999; 1973). Communities and chiefs go to them for guidance—but they only speak after entering the spiritual state. Prophetic figures, such as Mbuya Nehanda and Sekuru Kaguvi of the first Chimurenga (war of liberation) in Colonial Zimbabwe, Nongqawuse of the Xhosa Cattle Killing Movement in South Africa, and Kinjikitile Ngwale of the Maji Maji rebellion in Colonial Tanzania (Ranger and Kimambo 1972), are among the many Bantu prophets who exploited this element of Bantu religion to build social movements that threatened colonial rule. Aside from mediums who claimed to be possessed by these prophets playing key roles in liberation struggles, to some extent their actions remain in the consciousness of their respective nations. The Mwari and Chisumpi cults have also been involved in contemporary politics by opposing dictatorial rule from the shrines.

The second group is the most common—the mediums who can block the powers of witches (*indoshi*) or restore social harmony in the community. They have the abilities to impart power "for good, or for evil to objects either animate or inanimate," and as Rowley (1867: 258) rightly noted, the Bantu have "an implicit faith in or a dread of such objects." In addition to rain calling and healing, an example of manipulating natural objects "for good" involves using certain potions called *ifishimba* (power enhancers) to protect oneself from spiritual and physical harm. "Potions from leopards, dangerous snakes, lions, certain parts of specific animals, and many rare creatures are considered important to tap the power of the universe. Kings, diviners, and hunters receive the help of the natural world by using *ifishimba* for most of their endeavors" (Kaoma 2013: 99). Such objects are not only worn or carried "but are also set up in [people's] fields, their villages, and in their houses as a protection against harm of those who seek their harm" (Rowley 1876: 140).

The assumption was that Western education and Christianization would erase such beliefs among the Bantu, but the opposite has proven to be true. What Rowley wrote more than a century ago is just as true today:

> I have no doubt that many of these professors of magic firmly believed in their own power; and cases came under our notice where, when put on their trial for having com-passed the death of someone by their supernatural acts, they vauntingly owned they had done so. A man was struck dead by lightning in a village a few miles from Magomer[o]; people came forward and testified that they had seen a certain professor of witchcraft go up into the clouds and bring the lightning down upon the man. It was proved that he had threatened to do so, and, when on his trial, he boasted that he had done it.
>
> *(Rowley 1867: 261; 119)*

This material emphasis of African religions brought Western Christians to conclude that Africans are "animistic" in their beliefs (a negative term in Christian circles). What Western Christians missed and still miss is that in the African lifeworld, the sacred cannot be divorced from the material world. Magesa notes:

> The world is the manifestation of God, God's power, and benevolence. Accordingly, a big rock where people go to sacrifice is not just a big rock, but it incorporates, shows,

and for that reason is, in fact, some supernatural quality of the Divine. The same can be said . . . of practically anything that inspires awe: mountains, trees, snakes, certain animals, and so on. While African Religion understands . . . that these elements are by no means God but creatures . . . it also recognizes that they have divinity in them because they exist by the will and through the power of the divinity. In a sense they "represent" the Divinity and surely demonstrate God's will and power to humanity.

(Magesa 1997: 59)

Accordingly, Charles Nyamiti concludes, "[T]he universe is conceived as a sort of organic whole composed of supra-sensible or mystical correlations and participations" (1973: 21). The ancestors/elders are key to this view.

Ubuntu Morality as Respect for Ancestral Tradition

Respect for tradition is critical to the philosophy of *ubuntu*, hence the emphasis placed on respect for the hierarchy in the community. Ancestors/elders come just after spirits and gods in this hierarchy (Driberg 1936; Fortes 1961; Kaoma 2015; 2013; Kopytoff 1971; Rowley 139). In Bantu ontology, however, the term "elder" can refer to living elders or ancestors (living dead) (Driberg 1936; Fortes 1961; Kaoma 2015). Either way, the elders/ancestors are appealed to for help in times of social crises. Anthropologist Igor Kopytoff explains: "If I am young, I go to my elders who happen to be alive. The old people go to their elders; but since these are dead, they are to be found at the grave or at the cross-roads at night" (1971: 131). Although the Supreme Being is the ontological source and guardian of norms, elders/ ancestors are the guardians of morality. Tempels writes:

> [The Bantu] have a notion of what we may call immanent justice, which they would translate to mean that to violate nature incurs her vengeance and that misfortune springs from her. They know that he who does not respect the laws of nature becomes . . . a person whose inmost being is pregnant with misfortune. . . . This ethical conscience of theirs is at once philosophical, moral and juridical.

(Tempels 1952: 88)

Here, observing ancestral tradition is life; disregarding it is death and at par with disparaging God's moral laws. Magesa (2014: 112) writes, "What happens to living humanity and the universe in general flows through the ancestors from God and back to God. Life—in both positive and negative aspects—cannot therefore be conceived apart from ancestors." Since morality is upholding ancestral norms (Kalu 1993: 15), upholding *ubuntu* ensures ancestral protection, land productivity, good rains, good health, and other social and economic blessings. Thus,

> African Religion's conception of morality is steeped in tradition; it comes from and flows from God into the ancestors of the people. God is seen as the Great Ancestor, the first Founder and Progenitor, the Giver of life, the Power beyond everything that is. God is the first Initiator of a people's way of life, its tradition. However, the ancestors ... are the custodians of this tradition.

(Magesa 1997: 35)

As a result, *ubuntu* emphasizes rites of passage. From birth to naming to puberty to marriage to pregnancy to death to burial, among many others, *umuntu* (a person) passes through various rituals to attain authentic personhood. Key among them is the passing from childhood into adulthood. For example, the girl's puberty rite of Chisungu among the Bemba, and Chinamwali among the Chewa/Nyanja, does not only signify the passage into womanhood but connects initiates to the spiritual and natural world (Kaoma 2017; Mandala 1984: 146; Richard 1956). The religious value of this ceremony is evident. In 1861, Rowley documented Chinamwali held by liberated slaves at the mission station. Being a female-only initiation ritual, Rowley confessed ignorance of what happened to the girls before the public procession. He explains:

> After this they were washed and oiled, and invested with a profusion of beads; the entire procession, in fact, of our whole community in the bead line, was hung about the necks and bodies of the girls, who seemed to be principally operated upon, and who submitted to everything with depressed heads, arms hanging listlessly by their sides, and as though for ever deprived of power of speech. The women then formed themselves into a procession, and with hand-clapping and singing conducted their charge beyond the village to a place in the bush where the grass had been cleared away, and boughs of trees were so arranged as to form a fence and bower.
>
> *(Rowley 1867: 248)*

This ritual was accompanied by songs, dances, and sexual lessons, and lasted three days and nights. Thereafter, "the girls were re-washed, re-oiled, and reconducted into the village, amid the songs and shouts of the assembly" (Rowley 1867: 249). Despite his positive presentation of Bantu culture, on this material culture Rowley writes, "I felt that this Niamwali (*sic*) has so much wrong in it that I presented to the bishop the advisability of preventing it for the future" (1867: 210).

What Rowley missed is the religious and material significance of this ritual. Initiates go through it with grand pride—it makes them authentic human beings. Without being initiated, one is disconnected from the shared community identity—something that explains the persistence of this ritual to this day. Zambian feminist and religion scholar Mutale Mulenga Kaunda (2016) documents the similar female initiation Bemba rite of *imbusa*, which though traditional is practiced among professional women in Zambia. In cities, families are paying *bana chimbusa/balangazi* (traditional initiators) to have their young go through these traditional material rituals. And the music of these rituals populates the streets (Kaunda and Kaunda 2016; Lwanda and Kanjo 2013; Kaoma 2018). Arguably, the Bantu women are returning to traditional roots in search of cultural identity.

The Philosophy of *Ubuntu* in Wider Context

Ubuntu philosophy upholds the interconnectedness of vital forces/objects in the universe in which religion occurs. But its cosmic bias proposes an ecological approach to the study of material religion; Bantu religion is earthly—high God cults, ancestor cults, and all life rituals are land-centered (Daneel 2001; Kaoma 2015; Muzorewa 1988; Ranger 1999; 1973). This observation has huge implications for environmental ethics and theology. The 2021 United Nations Report, *Code Red for Humanity*, made it clear: there is a need to act to arrest the ongoing ecological disaster. The damage is already done, and some damages will take centuries to reverse. This philosophy, however, allows us to see ourselves as capable of making choices with moral responsibilities to future generations. Appealing to *ubuntu* in rituals of honoring the ancestors and Gods in relation to the land and other creatures, for example, can lead to ecological resilience informed by *ubuntu*—such as Marthinus Daneel's African

Earthkeepers' tree planting movement in Zimbabwe and Wangari Maathai's Green Belt Movement in Kenya, which collectively and independently planted millions of trees. The success of these movements could be attributed to applied *ubuntu* beliefs—such as, "[humanity] lives in a religious universe, so that the natural phenomena and objects are intimately associated with God" (Mbiti 1969: 48).

African American theologian Michael Battle adds that, in *ubuntu* theology, true human identity is discovered through "our common imago Dei" (1997: 40). Fully realized *ubuntu*, he argues, can "overthrow all forms of exploitation and, in the context of South Africa, the residue effects of apartheid" (Battle 1997: 40). Yet *ubuntu's* transformative potential goes beyond Africa—it can direct global relations as well. Accepting *ubuntu* implies acknowledging our common global vulnerability. It recognizes the humanity of each individual while insisting that the distinctiveness of each person depends on one's connection to other forces. We are born with the potential of *ubuntu*, but this potential can only be fully realized through relationships. So, to possess *ubuntu* is to proactively seek the transformation of human communities into welcoming, hospitable, and caring societies. Here, the success of one is celebrated by the greater whole, and the diminishment of one's humanity affects the whole.

Although Battle and many African scholars ignore the ecological potential of *ubuntu*, I argued that any African thought, theology, or ethics that ignores the cosmological, material, and ecological interdependence of Bantu ontology misrepresents *ubuntu* philosophy (Kaoma 2013). For this reason, we must revisit the popular Xhosa saying "*umuntu ngubuntu ngabantu*" (a person is a person through other people), since humanity is related to other material objects—something Janheinz Jahn noted above. The relatedness of humanity to the land, animals, trees, totems, and rituals embodies meaning beyond the human person. It speaks to what I have termed the "*missio Creatoris*"—that is, the Creator's mission of caring for all the Creation to which all humanity is invited. In this case, the interpretation and application of *ubuntu* suggest a wider cultural and material religious meaning.

An individual exists in a web of eco-social *ubuntu* obligations. In material terms, corruption and greed do not just undermine human well-being; they undermine the whole created order—something this philosophy condemns. Here, when people demonstrate against climate change, oppression, and immigration reform, they are practicing *ubuntu*. In this regard, the Xhosa, Sotho, and Shona sayings "*umuntu ngubuntu ngabantu, motho ke motho ka batho*" and "*munhu munhu nekuda kwevanhu*" (a human being is only human through other people), or even the Bemba saying "*icalo bantu*" (Earth is people) attest to the interconnectedness of human relationships—something that is central to *ubuntu* (Kaoma 2013).

But the Bemba saying adds the material aspect to human interconnectedness. Authentic humanity is only realized in relationship with the Earth. The word "*icalo*" can be rendered as the world, country, land, ecosystems, or simply planet Earth. The Earth accords meaning to people in this worldview, and to think otherwise is a fallacy. Arguably, anthropocentric interpretations of these sayings dominate African philosophy due to the Western individualistic philosophical thought African scholars seek to oppose. The ecological application of *ubuntu*—and, by expansion, material religion—together suggest that humanity experiences humanness within the material environment in which meaning is informed and reformed by material culture.

A person becomes a person through material interactions with other beings and objects—forming identity, values, and norms in communion with other people and the ecosystem. In a community where religion and material culture are one and the same, one's identity is married to that of others in holistic ways. The interpretation of *umuntu ngumuntu ngabantu* should be informed by the African material culture, traditional lifestyles, and the cosmos.

Moreover, the ecological element of *ubuntu* is explicitly expressed in the metaphors of "pollution" and "cleansing" of the land. For instance, killing another person or a sacred snake, or eating the first fruits before the elders have sacrificed to the ancestors, spirits, and gods, is said to pollute the land. Depending on the severity of the case, an individual or the entire community is expected to participate in the earth cleansing ritual. It is believed that failure to do so leads to the ancestors and gods withholding community blessings—chiefly rains and good harvest. The importance of high God cults, ancestor cults, and rain-making rituals (Daneel 1970; Ranger 1973; Rowley 1867; Schoffeeleers 1978) speaks to the ecological applications of *ubuntu*.

Africa should accept that some of the wisdom it received had some flaws, and the ecological age demands that we right them. If *ubuntu* encourages caring and compassion for humans alone, then the adage *umuntu ngubuntu ngabantu* is only limited to the interdependence of human life. In this regard, it can be said to be environmentally bankrupt. Yet, if Bantu ontology is based on material interconnectedness of all forces in the universe, the ecological and all material culture in which humanity exists constitutes *ubuntu* (Kaoma 2013).

Concluding Observations

In Bantu lifeworld, life exists in material embodiment—thus, examining *ubuntu* ought to interact with people's material cultures. Partially, this is the reason behind the failure to define "*ubuntu*"—it remains a mystery to be experienced within the human bodies in eco-social locations and environments. *Ubuntu* unites the sacred, humanity, and all creatures in the universe. Snakes, trees, rivers, stars, waterfalls, animals, birds, and many other material beings and objects are infused with divine essence—they are cosmic symbols through which humanity communes with the divine.

The philosophy of *ubuntu* informs and forms the religious practices and cultural identity of the Bantu. How one worships; how one supplicates God, spirits, and ancestors; how one behaves and acts toward others and the natural world—all are directed by *ubuntu*. It was the community's duty to ensure that the young are instructed and oriented into this philosophy through material culture for the sake of tradition, community identity, and, of course, upholding *ubuntu*. Thus, prayer is not a private affair; it is a communal act in which the community partakes ritualistically—an important element that explains the Africanization of both Christianity and Islam. Moreover, gods, spirits, and ancestors are encountered in material bodies through rituals and the use of specific physical objects—natural and human-made (Kaoma 2015; Muzorewa 1988). In some cases, communities are allowed access to such rituals—while, in others, access is limited to select groups.

The use of Henry Rowley's nineteenth-century works shows the resilience of this philosophy amidst various sociopolitical and economic phases of African history. Nonetheless, there is a danger in presenting *ubuntu* as fixed. Whereas some of its elements remain the same over the century, globalization and capitalism are slowly eroding some sociopolitical, religious, economic, and eco-social values of this philosophical system. Contemporary Africa continues to experience corruption, bad governance, individualism, and other social ills—while masses languish in poverty (Kaoma 2015; Ntarangwi 2011). With the continent leading the world with the youngest population—as well as the highest birth rate, and the highest unemployment rate and poverty—it remains to be seen how *ubuntu* would engage democratic capitalism: the Western, donor-heralded, and donor-promoted economic theory imposed on Africa.

Amidst the imminent ecological disaster, *ubuntu* reconnects humanity to Earth and the entire creation; humanity is materially connected to the sacred web of *NTU*, from which all creatures originate. As a conceptual tool, *ubuntu* can hold global leaders accountable to eco-justice, ensuring policies for a resilient environment. Likewise, it can also hold Western leaders accountable to African and poor majority world nations to past and present ecological injustices; right them; and then together forge a better and resilient future for all humanity. Dollars, euros, pounds, yen, and yuan are not all there is to life; *ubuntu* is life!

The expansiveness of this philosophy continues to provoke new questions as to how *ubuntu* should be understood aside from Western thought. Accepting that much is written on the subject, there is a need to (re)position *ubuntu* within material religion if we are to appreciate the unsaid elements of Bantu community cultures. Centering on material religion allows for the liberty to expose the limitations of Western-informed lenses in the study of African religions and philosophy to which most of us are exposed—and then to provoke new questions about the interpretation of early missionary documents about African religions and experiences.

Reading Rowley's works allows one to see how Africans materialized religion long before the Christianization project—as well as what has changed, and what remains the same. A further examination of *ubuntu* and material religion, however, may demand studying the link between corruption and pictures and images of poverty in Africa. Such studies would provide new insights as to how this important philosophy is being employed by ordinary people to negotiate economic oppression in the changing sociopolitical, economic, and political environments.

References

Battle, Michael. 1997. *Reconciliation: The Ubuntu Theology of Desmond Tutu*. Cleveland, OH: Pilgrim Press.

Bhengu, Mfuniselwa J. 2006. *The Global Philosophy for Humankind*. Cape Town: Lotsha Publications.

Bräunlein, Peter J. 2016. "Thinking Religion Through Things: Reflections on the Material Turn in the Scientific Study of Religion\s." *Method & Theory in the Study of Religion* 28 (4-5): 365–399.

Bujo, Bénézet. 1992. *African Theology in Its Social Context*. Maryknoll, NY: Orbis Books.

Bujo, Bénézet. 1998. *The Ethical Dimension of Community: The African Model and the Dialogue Between North and South*. Nairobi: Paulines Publications.

Bujo, Bénézet. 2012. "Understanding and Responding to AIDS in Africa." *U.S. Catholic*, October 13, 2012. https://uscatholic.org/articles/201210/understanding-and-responding-to-aids-in-africa/.

Chasi, Colin. 2021. *Ubuntu for Warriors*. Trenton, NJ: Africa World Press.

Daneel, Marthinus L. 1970. *The God of the Matopo Hills: An Essay on the Mwari Cult in Rhodesia*. The Hague and Paris: Mouton.

Daneel, Marthinus L. 2001. *African Earthkeepers: Wholistic Interfaith Mission*. Maryknoll, NY: Orbis Books.

Driberg, J. H. 1936. "The Secular Aspect of Ancestor-Worship in Africa." *Journal of the Royal African Society* 35 (138): 1–21.

Fortes, Meyer. 1961. "Pietas in Ancestor Worship: The Henry Myers Lecture, 1960." *Journal of the Royal Anthropological Institute of Great Britain and Ireland* 91 (2): 166–191.

Gunther, John. 1953. *Inside Africa*. New York: Harper.

Haftmann, Werner. 1950. *Paul Klee: Wege bildnerischen Denkens*. Munich: Prestel.

Harvey, Goodwin. 1864. *Memoir of Bishop Mackenzie*. Cambridge: Deighton, Bell and Co.

Idowu, Bolaji E. 1973. *African Traditional Religion: A Definition*. London: SCM Press.

Jahn, Janheinz. 1961. *Muntu: An Outline of the New African Culture*. Translated by Marjorie Grene. New York: Grove Press.

Kalu, Ogbu U. 1993. "Gods as Policemen: Religion and Social Control in Igboland." In *Religious Plurality in Africa: Essays in Honor of John Mbiti*, edited by Olupona K. Jacob and Sulayman S. Nyang, 111–131. Berlin: Mouton de Gruyter.

Kaoma, Kapya J. 2013. *God's Family, God's Earth: Christian Ecological Ethics of Ubuntu.* (Foreword from President Joyce Banda and endorsed by Desmond Tutu). Zomba: University of Malawi Kachere Press.

Kaoma, Kapya J. 2015. *The Creator's Symphony: African Christianity, The Plight of Earth and the Poor.* Dorpspruit, South Africa: Cluster Publications.

Kaoma, Kapya J. 2016. "African Religion and Colonial Rebellion: The Contestation of Power in Colonial Zimbabwe's Chimurenga of 1896–1897." *Journal for the Study of Religion* 29 (1): 57–84.

Kaoma, Kapya J. 2016. "The Serpent in Eden and in Africa: Religions and Ecology." In *The Wiley Blackwell Companion to Religion and Ecology*, edited by John Hart, 163–178. Hoboken, NJ: John Wiley & Sons.

Kaoma Kapya J. 2018. *Christianity Globalization and Protective Homophobia: Democratic Contestation of Sexuality in Sub-Saharan Africa.* Cham, Switzerland: Palgrave Macmillan.

Kaunda, Mutale M. 2016. *Negotiated Feminism: A Study of Married Bemba Women Appropriating the Imbusa Pre-marital 'Curriculum' at Home and Workplace.* PhD Dissertation, University of KwaZulu-Natal, Pietermaritzburg, South Africa. https://researchspace.ukzn.ac.za/xmlui/handle/10413/15811.

Kaunda M. M., and C. J. Kaunda. 2016. "Infunkutu—The Bemba Sexual Dance as Women's Sexual Agency." *Journal of Theology for Southern Africa* 155 (July): 159–175.

Keevy, Ilze. 2009. "The Constitutional Court and Ubuntu's 'Inseparable Trinity.'" *Journal for Juridical Science* 34 (1): 61–88.

Kopytoff, Igor. 1971. "Ancestors as Elders in Africa." *Africa: Journal of the International African Institute* 41 (2): 129–142.

Lwanda, John, and Chipo Kanjo. 2013. "Computers, Culture and Music: The History of the Recording Industry in Malawi." *Society of Malawi Journal* 66 (1): 23–42.

Mafunisa, John M. 2008. "Ethics, African Societal Values and the Workplace." In *Persons in Community: African Ethics in a Global Culture*, edited by Ronald Nicolson, 111–124. Scottsville, South Africa: University of KwaZulu-Natal Press.

Magesa, Laurenti. 1997. *African Religion: The Moral Traditions of Abundant Life.* Maryknoll, NY: Orbis Books.

Magesa, Laurenti. 2014. *Anatomy of Inculturation; Transforming the Church in Africa.* Maryknoll, NY: Orbis Books.

Mandala, Elias. 1984. "Capitalism, Kinship and Gender in the Lower Tchiri (Shire) Valley of Malawi, 1860–1960: An Alternative Theoretical Framework." *African Economic History* 13: 137–169.

Mbiti, John S. 1969. *African Religions and Philosophy.* London: Heinemann.

Meyer, Birgit, et al. 2011. "Introduction: Key Words in Material Religion." *Material Religion: The Journal of Objects, Art and Belief* 7 (1): 4–8.

Mkhize, Nhlanhla. 2008. "Ubuntu and Harmony: An African Approach to Morality and Ethics." In *Persons in Community: African Ethics in a Global Culture*, edited by Ronald Nicolson, 35–44. Scottsville, South Africa: University of KwaZulu-Natal Press.

Mokgoro, Y. 1998. "Ubuntu and the Law in South Africa." *Potchefstroom Electronic Law Journal/Potchefstroomse Elektroniese Regsblad* 1 (1): 16–32.

Mugambi, J. N. K. 1987. *God, Humanity and Nature in Relation to Justice and Peace.* Geneva: World Council of Churches, Programme Unit on Faith and Witness, Sub-unit on Church and Society.

Mugambi, J. N. K. 1989. "Christological Paradigms in African Christianity." In *Jesus in African Christianity: Experimentation and Diversity in African Christology*, edited by J. N. K. Mugambi and Laurenti Magesa, 136–161. Nairobi: Initiatives Ltd.

Muzorewa, Gwinyai H. 1988. "Christ as Our Ancestor: Christology from an African Perspective." *Africa Theological Journal* 17 (2): 255–264.

Nkemnkia, Nkafu Martin. 1999. *African Vitality: A Step Forward in African Thinking.* Nairobi: Paulines Publications.

Ntarangwi, Mwenda, ed. 2011. *Jesus and Ubuntu: Exploring the Social Impact of Christianity in Africa.* Trenton, NJ: Africa World Press.

Nyamiti, Charles. 1984. *Christ as Our Ancestor: Christology from an African Perspective.* Gweru, Zimbabwe: Mambo Press.

Nyamiti, Charles. 1990. "The Church as Christ's Ancestral Mediation: An Essay on African Ecclesiology." In *The Church in African Christianity*, edited by J. N. K. Mugambi and Laurenti Magesa, 129–177. Nairobi: African Initiatives.

Okafor, Stephen O. 1982. "'Bantu Philosophy': Placide Tempels Revisited." *Journal of Religion in Africa* 13 (2): 83–100.

Olupona, Jacob. 2009. "Comments on the Encyclopedia of Religion and Nature." *Journal of the American Academy of Religion* 77 (1): 60–65.

Pew Research Center 2011. *Global Christianity: A Report on the Size and Distribution of the World's Christian Population.* December 19, 2011. www.pewforum.org/files/2011/12/Christianity-fullreport-web.pdf.

Ranger, Terence O. 1973. "Territorial Cults in the History of Central Africa." *The Journal of African History* 14 (4): 581–597.

Ranger, Terence O. 1999. *Voices from the Rocks: Nature, Culture and History in the Matopos Hills of Zimbabwe.* Indiana, IN: Indiana University Press.

Ranger, Terrance O., and I. N. Kimambo, eds. 1972. *Religious Symbols in East and Central Africa: Historical Study of African Religion.* Los Angeles, CA: University of California Press.

Richards, Audrey I. 1956. *Chisungu: A Girls' Initiation Ceremony Among the Bemba of Zambia.* London: Tavistock.

Rowley, Henry. 1867. *The Story of the Universities' Mission to Central Africa; from its Commencement Under Bishop Mackenzie, to its Withdrawal from the Zambesi.* Saunders: Otley and Co.

Rowley, Henry. 1876. *Africa Unveiled. With Map and Illustrations.* London: Christian Knowledge Society.

Rowley, Henry. 1877. *The Religion of the Africans.* London: W. Wells Gardner.

Samkange, Stanlake, and Tommie M. Samkange. 1980. *Hunhuism or Ubuntuism: A Zimbabwe Indigenous Political Philosophy.* Salisbury: Graham.

Schoffeeleers, Mathew J., ed. 1978. *Guardians of the Land: Essays on Central African Territorial Cults.* Gweru, Zimbabwe: Mambo Press.

Setiloane, Gabriel M. 1986. *African Theology: An Introduction.* Johannesburg: Skotaville Publishers.

Shoko, Tabona. 2007. *Karanga Indigenous Religion in Zimbabwe: Health and Wellbeing.* Surrey, UK: Ashgate Publishing.

Smith, Edwin W. 1946. "La Philosophie Bantoue." *Journal of the International African Institute* 16 (3): 199–203.

Tamale, Sylvia. 2014. "Exploring the Contours of African Sexualities: Religion, Law and Power." *African Human Rights Law Journal* 14 (1): 150–177.

Tempels, Placide. 1952. *Bantu Philosophy.* Translated from *La Philosophie Bantu* by A. Rubbens. Paris: Presence Africaine.

Tutu, Desmond. 1999. *No Future Without Forgiveness: A Personal Overview of South Africa's Truth and Reconciliation Commission.* London: Rider.

Tutu, Desmond. 2004. *God Has a Dream: A Vision of Hope for Our Time.* New York: Doubleday.

Wilson, George Herbert. 1936. *The History of the Universities' Mission to Central Africa.* Westminster: Universities' Mission to Central Africa.

1.5

MESOAMERICAN NIGHTLIFE AND THE QUEER MATERIALITIES OF RELIGION

Xiomara Verenice Cervantes-Gómez

For many Mexicans, Sunday afternoons after church are traditionally reserved for quality "family time." Grandparents, parents, and children gather at someone's house, joined by aunts, uncles, and extended cousins—all forming parts of a cross-generational space and time known across the heteronormative topologies of Mexican family structures. For many of us, we are all too familiar with the soundtrack of this scene: children screaming and crying, dogs barking, men yelling at the soccer game, beer cans cracking open, and the women laughing in loud crescendo. Yet in this chapter on the queer materialities of religion, we do not find ourselves in the *sala* (living room) with our mothers and *tías* listening to the latest gossip—though an argument could certainly be made for the queerness of those spaces to be explored elsewhere. Rather, where we find ourselves on this proverbial Sunday is away from our families (at least in the "traditional" sense of that term). Instead, we find ourselves at a nightclub, but one unlike any other. The sounds are remixed into a playlist of crashing reggaetón, house, and *baile* funk. The big ass of the deity San Polencho on the wall watches how the packed crowd moves to the deep bass propelling from the DJ booth. Then, suddenly, the music quiets. All eyes are fixed upon an artist moving to the center of the dance floor, almost as if to take the center of a theater's stage. We eagerly wait in anticipation and arousal. What is going to happen? What occurs is a politically charged, queer performance art that is hard to convey in words. The artist contorts their body in uncomfortable positions, posing in ways that made their exhaustion visibly aestheticized. The once *perreando* dancers have been converted into spectators, bystanders, perhaps even participants in this ritual-like production, the dance club instantly repurposed into a gallery performance space. When the piece is complete the artist exits the stage, and the music slowly transitions back to maintaining the pulse of those moving to its every thump. "Did that just happen?" we might ask ourselves. Yet, we just keep dancing.

This chapter positions us within the spaces of what I call "Mesoamerican nightlife": within the theological and theoretical frameworks of a postmodernity defined by the lingering of the past in the present. Though, to be specific, we find ourselves at Mexico City's latest queer pop-up party that combines nightlife with art and religious ritual. In the wake of the 2016 mass shooting on Latin Night at Pulse Nightclub in Orlando, Florida, the significance and importance of gay nightclubs as sacred spaces became knowable to most larger audiences beyond LGBTQ+ folx. In short, these spaces provide safety and community for those who

DOI: 10.4324/9781351176231-7

cannot find them elsewhere. To therefore have these spaces violated with the tragedy of a mass killing jeopardizes their very sanctity. This jeopardy reflects an act of desecration— as opposed to blasphemy or sacrilege. The queerness of these spaces transcends dogmatic practices; if anything, these queer spaces are blasphemous in and of themselves. Etymologically, the word "sacrilege" stems from the Latin *sacrilegus*, a noun signifying "stealer of sacred objects," which is a capital crime under theocratic juridical law. Rather, "desecration" describes an act of removing that which is sacred. That is, to unplug the DJ booth. To stop the music. To remove that sacred charge. Moreover, desecration permits us to also think more heterogeneously about what we define or refer to as "sacred." The term invites us to redefine and rethink who or what is "the sacred."

The fact that the Pulse nightclub shooting occurred on Latin Night adds an imperatively necessary racialized and postcolonial lens through which to read just how these spaces are converted into ceremonial centers. In the afternoon following the shooting, I published a brief piece meditating on these themes from the perspective of a queer Latina theologian:

> Surely, gay nightclubs become religious spaces amidst the *communitas* of queer bodies inhabiting space together in kinship, but our people, Latin@s and Latin Americans, have a long history of creating ceremonial centers when our own homes became violent landscapes. And just so, Latin@ queer spaces were always spaces of healing—migratory spaces we journeyed to, to be in solidarity with one another in our shared pain and suffering, but also in our shared joy and triumph.
>
> (Cervantes-Gómez 2016)

Maintaining this perspective of queer Latinx and Latin American nightlife as the emergence of ceremonial centers that structure and restructure movement, bodies, and affects, I approach a reading of the queer materialities of religion through how these ritual spaces of Mesoamerican nightlife are necessarily (re)imagined in contrast or resistance to the cisheteronormativity of the categories of "family" and "nation." As such, these spaces create objects of attachment that orient and embody the divine for those who come *to be*, that is to come into existence in these ceremonial centers. In what follows, I trace a queerness about the theological and ecclesiastical contours of queer nightlife that sanctify the materiality of the *sexual* body to be at the *center* of a queer cosmovision that becomes realized through ritual and new understandings of what constitutes religious materialities.

In this chapter, I think through and from Traición, a monthly *sexo diverso* party (translating to "sexually diverse" or "diverse sex") that combines queer politics, performance, music, art, and nightlife. Founders Pepe Romero (a self-described "postdramatic" actor-director)[1] and Alberto Bustamante, a.k.a. Mexican Jihad (a Oaxacan DJ, architect, and creative director for the queer record label NAAFI), sought an event that would capture the evolution of contemporary sexual cultures while at the same time "betraying" the homonationalist and reactive organizations that have dominated LGBT activism in Mexico City—organizations and independent movements really began to take shape in the 1990s through countercultural movements.[2] With the help of influential Mexico City-based local nightlife promoters and club owners to bring this vision into reality, Traición was born under the rubric of *sexo diverso*. In an interview with *Remezcla*, Romero explains, "The term speaks to performativity." That is,

> It's about the *act of being with someone*—that's a concept that more people identify with, rather than '*diversidad sexual*,' which has more to do with gender and fixed categories of

sexuality. We celebrate *sex* as an action, sharing. It's not about which genders it takes place between.

(Donohue 2016, emphasis added)

The "*diversidad sexual*" (sexual diversity) that Romero describes is a term associated with social capital campaigns in Mexico City and other large metropolitan and touristy areas, like Guadalajara and Puerto Vallarta, to portray a flattened image of inclusivity across all sexual orientations. Yet, the term breeds with nationalist and neoliberal rhetorics that promise political and social access to all, because sexual differences become replaced by a banner term that permits the erasure of queer sexualities through a process of reduction and homogenization of sexuality.[3] In fact, "Gay" Pride in Mexico City is named *Festival por la Diversidad Sexual* (Festival for Sexual Diversity), fully accompanied by rainbow banners in the Zona Rosa (the local gay neighborhood) bearing the official seal of the capital and rainbow-painted sidewalks. While this may be the goal and vision of dominating LGBT activism groups in Mexico City—to participate within the nation-building project—this is certainly not the aim of Traición. The name "Traición" appropriately translates to both "treason" and "betrayal," and the event simultaneously straddles both definitions as part of its brand: to betray those LGBTs auditioning for a role within the nationalist theater, and to thus commit treasonous acts against the nation in which they would never even be able to participate.

What further sets Traición apart from other queer nightlife spaces is the presiding presence of a very special deity: San Polencho. The figure of San Polencho is a "fictional" anal deity from the memoir of Mexican writer Salvador Novo, *Estatua de sal* ([1945] 2008). In the text, Novo recalls hosting sex parties in his apartment with San Polencho presiding over these sexual encounters:

A large-assed idol, who we called San Polencho, hung at the headboard of the couch, or the 'sacrificial stone,' to preside over our scenes. And, an extreme nationalism induced me to purpose a small gourd as the vessel most appropriate for the Vaseline needed for our rituals.

(Novo 2008: 166)

Accordingly, in this bodily crossing of sex and "extreme nationalism," the Traición parties anchor San Polencho as the religious center and imago of their own queer rites. A new visual artist is commissioned for each party to design a new image of the Polencho that will preside over the scenes of that night's *sexo diverso* party.

Thinking through and alongside Traición as both a queer ritual and national space, I approach the question of queer materialities by way of the party's attachment to the figure of an anal deity that I argue is not so "fictional." Given that "Traición" is an always already nationalistic term, the club Traición's theological attachment to anality through the figure of San Polencho converts the space into a divergent act of national belonging—even through its disavowal. Traición is a ritualistic and ceremonial space wherein the sexual body engages in a performative dialogue between anal politics and narratives about national belonging. This chapter begins with and departs from material religion discourses in Latin America to blend out the theological contours that would constitute a space grounded in the ritual imaginary of the body and its interactions with a deity of anal sex. By caressing the historicity of anality in Mesoamerican religions, what is revealed is a genealogical trajectory of the promiscuity of embodiment in religious and theological terms as they relate to any concept of nation. I intentionally invoke an anachronistic reading, in favor of the nonlinear, to blur those lines between what is defined as "past" and "present" in relation to how and when those stories are told and retold. And, finally, this chapter argues that a critical engagement with Mexican sexual culture begins with queer negativity, addressing the theological significance of attaching anality and space to a deity figure. At stake in this reading is the development of new approaches to transnational engagement with the materialities of queerness, politics, and religion—and an account for divergent or alternative of genealogical praxis.

Aztec Anal Theologies and Their Promiscuous Genealogies

Though San Polencho is only mentioned once in Salvador Novo's brief autobiographical memoir *Estatua de sal*, the legacy and trace of the anal deity are conjured as a sacred object to preside over the *sexo diverso* party Traición. The name "San Polencho" bears no significant translation or etymological history. Novo doesn't even tell us why he and his friends selected that name. He just describes him as *un idolillo nalgón*: a small idol with a big ass (2008: 166). In a recent English translation of *Estatua de sal*, Marguerite Feitlowitz translates "San Polen-cho" to "Saint Bollocks." In fact, she doesn't even use the word "ass" anywhere. Instead, she opts for "buttocks" to translate *nalgón* into English (2014: 129). Admittedly, I find these translations to be disappointingly conservative, sanitized, and clinical. "Buttocks" does not capture the sexually crude Mexican tongue as the mouth says "*nalgón*." If anything, *la pompis* would be the Spanish equivalent of "buttocks," which in the Spanish-speaking context is very clinical—laughably so. The origins of the term "bollocks" from Middle English were to signify not the "ass" but "testicles"—and even then it is also antiquated. Rather, the significance of the Traición parties is to reassure that these qualities of sex do *not* become unnecessarily hygienic and neatly packaged so as to be digestible by the neoliberal machine of homonationalism. Rather, San Polencho's necessarily dirty, raunchy qualities need to be preserved. After all, Novo did say the deity presided over their orgies and bore the vessel for the Vaseline needed for their "rituals."

As noted above, for each of Traición's parties, a new artist is commissioned to design their own incarnation of San Polencho (Figures 1.5.1–1.5.6). A common motif among these designs is a nod toward Aztec and Nahua deities. As for the creators of Traición, they too read San Polencho as an incarnation of the Nahua celestial beings. But before offering a sustained reading of Polencho, I want to tug at the threads of an incarnational theology being exposed in this discussion. This gesture enables us to arrive at the promiscuity of these incarnational cosmologies that combine the divine, the body, and materiality, or what Laurel Schneider has described as "promiscuous incarnation" (2010). The origins of the term "promiscuity" describe an essential mixing of the body and identities, derived from the Latin *promiscuus* (*pro-* "forward" + *miscere-* "to mix"). While *promiscuous*, with its contemporary meaning of "sexual excess," may sexualize material religion as expected, I deploy *promiscuity* as a necessary framework for analysis by calling upon the multiplicity of meanings lingering in the term—since it is braided with my assessment of a queer materiality of religion. Through this invocation, *promiscuity*'s more primary meaning, "mixture"—and even in rare occurrences, "third gender"—are allowed to come into focus. In other words, *promiscuity* offers more to religion and theology than just sex alone. By taking the risk of embracing pro-miscuity, I engage in a task that should not be taken lightly, and nor should it be considered a task functioning solely out of contradictions, or even a frivolous act of mere provocation. It is through the discretion and decorum of all its variants that I shape this reading of the queer materialities of religion.

Figures 1.5.1–1.5.6 Various artist commissions of the San Polencho for Traición. Reproduced with permission.

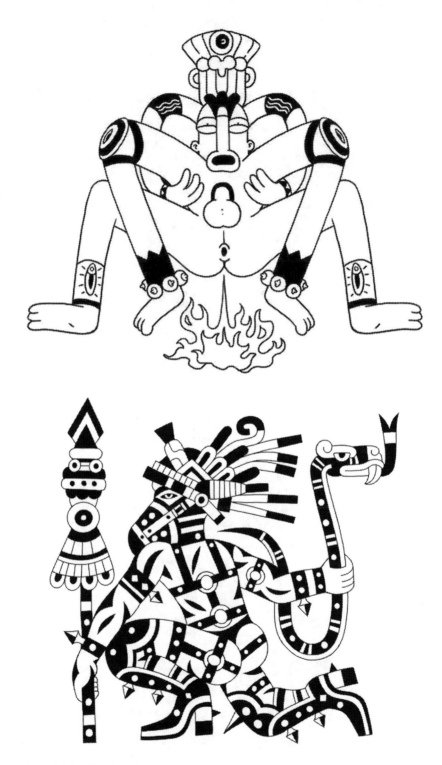

Figures 1.5.1–1.5.6 (Continued).

NOV
0 2
HALLO
QUEER

Kim Ann Foxman **MikeQ** Mexican Jihad **Pucha Empellejada** Priest Transmutaciones Pornírikas (Maria Perkances Ft. La Chacala) Julio Láudano Fafa Ext Paco Santander **Gvajardo Cadena Nacional** Concurso de disfraces: Runway Bizarre $$$ Exfábrica de harina / PRE $300 / Taquilla $400 / Sin disfraz $500

TRAICIÓN

Figures 1.5.1–1.5.6 (Continued).

San Polencho and his parties guide followers to what Schneider describes as a "mutable and utterly unexchangeable world of bodies" (2010: 232)—that is, toward the materialization of a queer theology of multiplicity, mixing, and in excess within Mesoamerican nightlife. Given Mexico's very intimate relationship with Christianity, namely Catholicism, my reading of theology thus speaks with the vernacular of these traditions, while allowing Mesoamerican cosmovisions to expose themselves to this theology—as it has been for centuries—to problematize and extend these categories. Moreover, if we think about San Polencho's name itself: he is both of sainthood and of Mesoamerican origins. His name invites a necessary Christian theological interlocution—a queer one, of course, that underscores how the body and its desires are captured and converted into a politically religious structure.

That being said, I contend that the use of the term "promiscuous" represents the refusal of divine exclusivity in God's flesh. Schneider explains that promiscuity "suggests intercourse and multiplicity, a posture of generosity toward change and of ambiguity toward identity, any of which goes a long way actually to describing the character of Jesus' interactions in the narratives of his life" (2010: 233). She continues by arguing, "Promiscuous incarnation suggests excess and indiscrimination in divine love" (245). If Christian theology accepts that God so loved the world that Christ was sent into the world for those to experience and believe in him, so that they may not perish but have an eternal life, *then* incarnation not only becomes a distinctive feature of Christian theology but also unveils an intimate and passionate divine love—one requiring the sacrificial flesh for the sake of other bodies.[4] That is, the necessity for the body to become undone—to be used, and yet, intimately taken. This begs the question, then: does this expression of love in relation to the desire for an experience with the divine through flesh stop at Christ?

Thinking in the spirit of *sexo diverso*, which San Polencho represents and embodies, through the practice of an indiscriminate and excess expression of selfless love and pleasure *through* the flesh, there is an act of community building that leads his followers: at *sexo diverso* parties. Sex is a shared experience. Everyone becomes participatory in one form or another, thus all becoming one flesh.[5] Laurel Schneider proposes thinking about theology, and specifically incarnational theology, through the lens of multiplicity. In doing so, she suggests a theology whereby people learn to imitate God's promiscuous pursuit of lovers. "Love," here, means *being present* to and in the multiplicity that *is* the material world. She makes clear that such love "is grown-up, and it is not cheap" (2008: 205). It is a kind of differential repetition of incarnation—for what love demands is a being present in the world in its excesses, making divinity inseparable from the cultural fabrics of the world. Therefore, as Schneider so elegantly articulates:

> As the conceptual shape of divinity, multiplicity is therefore the embodiment of love. And love is what divinity is because love cannot *be* One, as Augustine realized. Love, necessitating the existence of others, of difference, gravity, and encounter, is the divine reality of heterogeneity even among those usually classed as "same." And love is the only commandment that is possible in a logic of multiplicity, because at its simplest level, ethical "love" is the actualized recognition of the presence of others, acceptance of the dangerous gift of the world itself.
>
> *(Schneider 2008: 205)*

The sexual theological frameworks captured and proposed by Schneider and Marcella Althaus-Reid convince me that San Polencho, most especially through his promiscuous constitution, gestures toward space in which to understand and read into a queer materiality of religion in the world through sex, love, and desire, rooting itself in the body.[6]

I turn us back to San Polencho, who in his constitution can be many things. I read San Polencho as a figure capturing a Mexico painted by religions in contact, wherein these indigenous rituals and myths still play intimate roles in quotidian life. I argue that the *mestizaje* of the Americas of both race and religions are significant contours of San Polencho's constitution. That is, a figure always already made out the mixing of semen, sweat, Vaseline, and possibly excrement. His portrayal within *sexo diverso* parties is on a messianic level, as if to have a statue of a blessed Saint to look over your home—as many Mexican households do. However, the creators of Traición and the media surrounding their parties always refer to San Polencho as a "fictional" Aztec deity. (Thankfully they never use "bollocks," nor "buttocks.") In Latinx popular culture media reporting on these parties, or even from the creators and founders, there is little to no talk about the Aztec cosmology surrounding the figure of San Polencho. As I describe above, Novo's memoir effectively omits an origin story. But in the interest of a promiscuous incarnational theology, it is only necessary to discuss the Aztec theology of sex and desire.

Much of what is known about the Aztec religious myths and rituals comes from the writings of the conquistadors and priests, codices, and illustrated manuscripts, and the field has certainly come very far in learning how best to interpret these materials. Among the more popular, the *Codex Borgia* is dated back to circa 1,400 AD, and was found in the southern central highlands of Mexico (modern-day Puebla or Oaxaca). The *Codex* is a 260-day ritual calendar (Nah. *tonalpohualli*) on the material aspects of Tlāhuizcalpantecuhtli (The Morning Star Venus) and the numerological prognostication of marital couples. That is, it may be read as a 260-day cycle linked to the female body and its pregnancy terms, beginning with the day of a missed menstrual cycle. The *Codex Borgia* is arguably the most important text that gives the most visual access, with its limitations, to the *cemanahuac* (the Aztec world).

On Plate 74 of the *Codex Borgia* (Figure 1.5.7), we encounter the gods of sensuality: Ahuiatēotl (male) and Tlazōtētotl (female).[7] I want to focus most of our attention on Ahuiatēotl, who is a god of voluptuousness and one of the Auiateteo (Nah. *macuitonaleque*), a group of five Aztec gods of excess and pleasure. Yet, they also represent the dangers associated with these pleasures. Among the Auiateteo, Ahuiatēotl is considered to be one the most important: Macuilxōchitl (Nah. *macuilli* [five] + *xōchitl* [flower]). Appropriately, in the *Codex Borgia*, we find our male god with an erect flower as his penis. In the frame, we also see Tlazōtētotl mounting a flower. Continuing to follow this genealogical trajectory, Macuilxōchtil is considered an aspect of Xōchipilli (Prince of Flowers).

Xōchipilli has often been co-opted and referred to within LGBTQ+ circles as the patron "queer" deity among the Aztec gods, with his reign over summer, flowers, pleasure, love, dancing, creativity, and souls. Xōchipilli is considered a manifestation of Pilzitecuhtli, the young sun god who was himself a manifestation of Tōnatiuh—the supreme sun god of Mesoamerica who is believed to be the central figure of the infamous Aztec Sun Stone (Figure 1.5.8). Now, returning to the *Codex Borgia*, if we pay close attention to the details of the frame with Ahuiatēotl, we see him bending over. His long flower penis is erect, but not penetrating anything in the same scene. *Rather*, it is Ahuiatēotl who is being penetrated. By Tōnatiuh (represented through the Day Sign of Rain). Up his ass. Of course, we might ask ourselves (I know I do): Why is the male god of sensuality being fucked in the ass by the supreme sun god? In the frame above, we have Tlazōtētotl's sensual and voluptuous body as she straddles and rides the flower penis. Yet, similar to Ahuiatēotl, there is no other partner

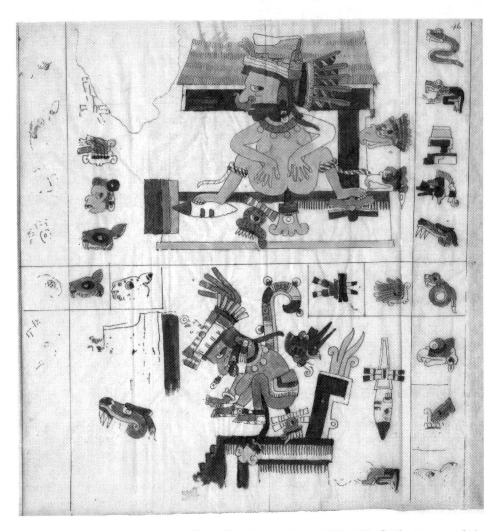

Figure 1.5.7 Plate 74 of *Codex Borgia* (facsimile). Vatican City (c. 1825–1831). © The Trustees of The British Museum. Reproduced with permission.

in the scene. Could this flower penis be a dildo of sorts? Or is Ahuiatēotl's penis so big that it carries on to the next frame? But, even then, she is straddling that dick and taking the power role of being on top. Does she represent the top and he a bottomness inherent to Aztec theological understandings of pleasure?

Perhaps some answers might be found in Plate 73 (Figure 1.5.9), the presentation of the gods of death and life with twenty-six days and the twenty-day signs. In the Díaz and Rodgers restoration, these plates face one another. Of course, the pages of the *Codex Borgia* are constructed to be an accordion-style document, so it would be easy to position these plates to face one another with the original codex. Plate 73 presents us with Mictlāntēcutli, god of the dead and ruler of underworld Mictlán (Nah. *chiconauhmictlān*); and Quetzalcōātl, here represented as god of creation. In other words, Plate 73 captures the cyclical parts of life and death. Positioning Plates 73 and 74 in dialogue with one another, we can begin to think about the

Figure 1.5.8 Mexica Sun Stone. Mēxihco Tenōchtitlan (c. 1500). Photograph by Juan Carlos Fonseca Mata. Museo Nacional de Antropología, México.

relationship among sex, death, life, and religion. I argue that in Plate 74, we witness the promiscuous acts of life and death through pleasure and sex through the *bodies* of the gods. In other words, Plate 74 reveals how sex is both life-giving and death-dealing. Since the focus of this chapter is on San Polencho, I want to challenge the idea of fictionality through Ahuiatēotl. I argue there is nothing fictional about San Polencho; rather, Novo introduces a figure that already fits within an Aztec celestial genealogy. Ahuiatēotl is an Aztec anal god.

Why is he penetrated by Tōnatiuh? There is power surrounding the representations of this frame. One interpretation would be that this is an image of subjugation in which the supreme sun god wields his power over Ahuiatēotl through anal sex. Another, and what I propose to be most productive, is that I do not disagree with the prior reading, but I would add that there is a power that is *assumed* through the act of bottoming.[8] Ahuiatēotl absorbs power into his rectal walls to represent a nonprocreative form of sensuality through his bottomness. Much like Tlazōtētotl, who invokes a bottomness by not being physically at the bottom with a male god on top of her; rather, she straddles and rides the penis. The power downloaded rectally from Tōnatiuh into the rectal walls of Ahuiatēotl is also therefore transferred through the penetration of Tlazōtētotl. She rides with a sense of pride and power—she is after all a manifestation of Teteoinnan (Mother of the Gods). In sum, I posit that San Polencho is indeed an aspect of Ahuiatēotl.

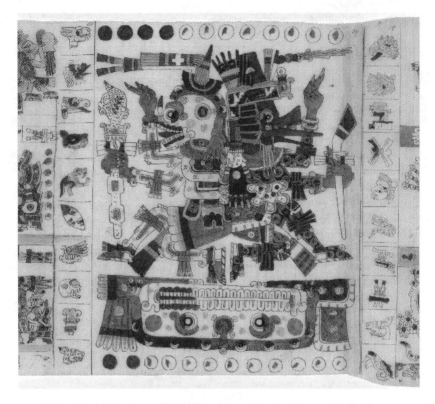

Figure 1.5.9 Plate 73 of *Codex Borgia* (facsimile). Vatican City (c. 1825–1831). © The Trustees of The British Museum. Reproduced with permission.

Looking for Queer Material Religion in Mesoamerica

Let's return to 1519 with Hernán Cortés and his cronies of Spanish conquistadors. After defeating the Chontal Maya and receiving corn, gold, and twenty women as "gifts" for their victory, including Mexico's first *traidora* (traitor), Malinche, the historically infamous translator and concubine to Cortés. Together they traveled 263 miles from the Yucatán peninsula, where the Spanish had erected the town of Veracruz, up and over the Sierra Madre Oriental, passing Mexico's highest peak, to Moctezuma's empire at Tenōchtitlan.[9] Upon arriving to the breathtaking Templo Mayor (Nah. *Huēyi Teōcalli*), Cortés and his men were splendored and taken aback by the rich and beautiful art, façades, structures, and the overall complexity of the city's infrastructure itself. It was like nothing they expected or had even seen thus far in their colonization of the Americas.

Dedicated to Aztec god of war Huītzilōpōchtli, *Huēyi Teōcalli* is historically understood to have had a huge pyramidal base that supported two major shrines (Figures 1.5.10–1.5.12). Two stairways lead up to the shrines of the Aztec gods Tlāloc and Huītzilōpōchtli. The south side of the pyramid represents the historic and legendary Coatepetl, the mountain birthday of the war god Huītzilōpōchtli and the dismemberment of the moon goddess Coyolxāuhqui. The north side of the Templo represents the Mountain of Sustenance linked to Tlāloc's paradise, which provides the sacred rains and moisture that regenerated the agricultural cycles of the Mexica-Nahua capital. We can thus imagine the profound impact this great architecture

Figures 1.5.10–1.5.11   North side of Huēyi Teōcalli, Mēxihco Tenōchtitlan. Photograph by author (2014).

Figure 1.5.12   West side of Huēyi Teōcalli, Mēxihco Tenōchtitlan. Photograph by author (2014).

had on not only the Spanish but also the populace whose quotidian affairs revolve around this ceremonial center, which structured the movement and flow of the city of Tenōchtitlan like great mythical mountains at the urban center. It is also important to account for this great city as one of sacrifice, as Davíd Carrasco describes (2000), in which human sacrifice remains at the center of urban culture. I would push this a step further to argue that central to Tenōchtitlan is a city of bodies in which the materiality of the body possesses its own sacred resonance that (re)structures the surrounding material world.

It is my contention that material religion in Latin America begins with these Meso-american ceremonial centers. These spaces serve multiple purposes in the daily lives and practices of individuals. These are *urban* centers, advanced in their development and imple-mentation, that organize the infrastructure of cities, movement, politics, and civil affairs. In this regard, religious and public life are not so easily disimbricated because quotidian affairs revolve around these religiously tinged spaces. In other words, religious practices and cosmic worldviews regulated and organized daily life, trade affairs, warfare, and every other significant aspect of existence. As Davíd Carrasco aptly argues, "The ceremonial precincts of Mesoamerica were the centers and theaters for the acting out of religious and social life." In other words:

> These ceremonial centers showed people where the *axis mundi*, or "sacred focal point of the world," stood, thus providing them with a solid sense of orientation and the location

for communicating with gods, ancestors, and other transcendental forces who were imminent in their landscapes.

(Carrasco 2013: 14)

The human and celestial spheres blended and blurred one another through the ways these structures recreated what "structure" looks like when thinking in terms of social religious practices. This cosmovision, I posit, accentuates spatiality as a vital category of material religion. That is, the body's orientation toward or by these spaces bears religious significance that redefines the parameters of what becomes a religious experience or affective feeling. The Templo Mayor is decorated with great shrines of Aztec gods that are religiously charged in the sense that the gods themselves are embodied within these structures, filling the gap between the celestial and human worlds. But these shrines—thought of through celestial embodiment—and their interactions with the human body occupy space in ways that embolden that spatiality with sacred constitution, experience, and attachment.

Central to my reading of the queer materialities of religion is a preoccupation with the affective experiences encountered within certain spaces that would seem unorthodox to the exegetical and hermeneutical reading practices of Christian imperialism that articulate a very cisgender and heteronormative reading of the body and *eros*. I propose the "unorthodox" approaches of turning to *how* queer materiality accounts for the mutual imbrication and contamination of body and space within religious and theological discourses. Mesoamerican ceremonial centers certainly throw the results of this nexus into sharp relief. In her theorization on religious affect and the Cristo Aparecido in Mexico, Jennifer Scheper Hughes rightfully argues that "the transmission of religious affect does not only move person to person as if by contagion . . . but is also communicated from one generation to the next." She continues, "This sentiment of affection emerges from the Mesoamerican belief that the sacred permeated and penetrated the material world: the ordinary objects and things of everyday life and common use were perceived to be 'alive with the sacred'" (2010: 78–79). I propose, then, that the material world itself imbues this liveliness of the sacred by way of affective experiences rooted within the body's core and the occupation of and movement with those spaces of the material world in which other texts and cosmologies also cross.

The material relationship between bodies and space is always already at the center of the *ethos* of queer theory. As I look for this relationship in Latin America, I find it could not be more apparent than when we account for the myths and rituals of Mesoamerican religious life. The study of material religion in Latin America affirms my preoccupation with the queerness of embodiment and spatiality. In their introduction to *Material Religion*'s special issue on "Material Religion in Latin America," Jennifer Scheper Hughes and Jalane Schmidt remind us:

Quite distinct from the USA, Latin American theories of religion are fundamentally materialist in their orientation—attentive to bodies, structures of power, and constraint. The most critical and rigorous discourses about religion from Latin America have often been theological ones. In its non-reductive appropriation of critical social science (including its rejection of dialectical materialism), Latin American liberation theology contains within it a well-elaborated materialist theory of religion.

(Hughes and Schmidt 2017: 410)

As a Latina theologian and queer and trans theorist, I find this astute observation to flow into the same currents of my own approach to studying the queer materialities of religion. "Queer," in this chapter, refers to the capture and conversion of sexual bodies into religious and political structures. It is certainly fitting then that I argue Traición is a material-theological project of Tenōchtitlan, popping up and erecting itself in contemporary Mexico City. In an interview, Pepe Romero describes how the Traición space is always a ceremonial center—with queerness as its primary subject that reveals a subculture (a spiritually serving community even) that is only known to the historicity of Mexico City's pre-Columbian past:

> To be diverse in Mexico City is a great opportunity that affords the concrete, the infrastructure, and culture that exists here, it's a privilege in comparison to other places, including the outskirts of the city that are many barriers to cross.
>
> *(Nájera 2018)*

Traición as a pop-up queer party thus rejects—in its own act of treasonous betrayal—the colonial conditions of contemporary Mexico City and reclaims the spatiality of the great Tenōchtitlan *through* the body. Taking the history of Mesoamerican religion into account, it is important to underscore the body's centrality to Aztec cosmology. The human body is always already at the center of the Aztec cosmovision. Carrasco rightfully describes the "the sacrality of the human body and its potential to return its energy to the celestial forces that created it" as a defining detail of Aztec religion (2013: 84). He continues:

> We have seen that Mesoamerican religions were most vividly expressed in ceremonial centers. The most pervasive type of sacred space where elaborate ceremonies were carried out was the human body. The human body was considered a potent receptacle of cosmological forces, a living, moving center of the world.
>
> *(86)*

As such, the body's own matter is weighted with sacred and celestial potency. This was most notable in rituals of bloodletting and human sacrifice. The central role of the materiality of body at the center of the cosmos is beautifully captured within the illustrated manuscripts of the time, such as the *Codex Fejérváry-Mayer* and the *Codex Borgia*. I call this orientation between the celestial world and the human body "queer"—that is, the desire to engage in a sacred and intimate experience with the body through an act of mixing. This promiscuity is captured and converted into a political and religious structure—to return us to how *queer* operates throughout this current work.

It would be appropriate to pause and elaborate upon this term "queer" and its variations I have used thus far as they relate to material religion and also to promise to diffuse the borders between sexual spaces and urban ones as we see in Traición. As the creators of Traición rightfully describe, *queer* sexualities refer to a resistance to any normative trajectories of sexual and gender identities, including sexual practices that are extramarital, group-oriented, and outside the "privacy" of the bedroom. Yet, viewing queer sexualities as a theoretical framework and lens through which to read the body and space, I push toward the rhetoric wherein *queer* exposes and resists the established power structures that attempt to regulate the body and its desires.[10] I thus return to my definition of "queer" as described above, as the capture and conversion of sexual practices and identities into political and religious structures.

As a theological category, *queer* lends itself to explaining and interpreting the world around us through the traditions, narratives, and experiences of queer persons. If theology is "talk about the divine," then, following the trajectory of the aforementioned meanings of "queer" I have described, queer theology offers a way of speaking about the divine in nonnormative terms, or as Patrick Cheng describes:

> In light of the definition of "queer" as transgression, queer theology can be understood as a theological method that is self-consciously transgressive, especially by challenging societal norms about sexuality and gender. Thus queer theology refers to a way of doing theology, in the words of the *Magnificat*, brings down the powerful and lifts up the lowly. In particular, this theology seeks to unearth silenced voices or hidden perspectives.
>
> *(Cheng 2011: 9)*

Spaces and bodies representing a public transgressive sexuality remain in the margins of mainstream society. Yet, I position the event of Traición's mission, and most especially San Polencho as a deity, as one to be read through a theological lens to consider how that symbiotic relationship experiences the Aztec cosmological vision that propels itself into the twenty-first century: precisely through the body's affective encounters and experiences. Cheng reminds us: "Queer theology draws upon experience as a source for theology." As is the case for other contextual forms of theological reflection, "queer theology is premised upon the belief that God acts within the specific contexts of our lives and experiences, despite the fact that LGBTQ+ lives and experiences have been excluded from traditional theological discourses" (2011: 18). The affective experiences with bodies and spaces are foregrounded as queer in the context of those theological events.

To look for the *queer* in material religion from the vantage point of theology, we must take seriously Traición's self-description of being *sexo diverso*. We need to linger in the folds of indecency—indeed, the queerness—of the sexual experience. As the late Argentine queer theologian Marcella Althaus-Reid argues, "Indecent theologies are sexual theologies without pages cut from the books of our sexual experiences" (2000: 146). The genesis of my conceptualization of the queer materialities of religion is indebted to Althaus-Reid's liberationist theological project, which is thought through, from, and against the assemblage of sex, gender, and politics. Althaus-Reid suggests that theology begins to understand the sacred through human sexuality and human experience. In other words, queer theology is a first-person theology: self-disclosing and autobiographical (2003: 8). Arguably one of Althaus-Reid's most significant contributions to queer theological discourse is her epistemological grounding of divine incarnation into human erotic longings and passionate intimacies, while invoking a queer praxis to the approach of the sex, gender, and desire continuum and the exclusion of queer desire in liberation theologies.[11] Queer sexual theologies differ from idealistic processes because they start from the sexual actions of people. She notes that sexual theology is doing theology from one's own experiences and from their sexual stories. Such a contextual queer location reveals the falsity of constructions between the material and divine dimensions of human lives (2000: 146–148). Althaus-Reid keeps us accountable for the sexual poverty present in our communities while dismantling the hegemonic discourses in place that neglect queer experiences.

My interest in Traición resides at the center of the bodily experience within this space, but more pressingly how these bodies and the event itself are oriented around and toward the deity of San Polencho. Polencho's history emerges from the autobiographical sexual stories of Salvador Novo; he was created to preside—I would argue to participate in—the orgies Novo hosted in his apartment. The evolution of San Polencho is an act of sexual storytelling: stories told to remind of us of the sexual material of the body. Yet, why sexual stories, especially those of a fictional deity? Sexual stories are incarnational stories (which I discuss further in the subsequent section). That is, Polencho's presence at Traición is a theological celebration of sexual desire—*sexo diverso*—and a revelation of the divine in people's sexual experiences, which may help facilitate the liberation of the sexually and racially oppressed, thus disrupting the normative trajectories of dominant, heterosexist discourses in theology. Riffing off of Althaus-Reid, I argue that all theology is a sexual act: an act of desiring a relationship with the divine, a desire to experience the flesh. Sexual stories, sexual theologies even, are transgressive stories that disrupt orthodox readings of Christian doctrine. Althaus-Reid writes:

> Transgressions have always been with us. Sexual theologies are the opposite of idealistic processes. They are *materialist theologies* which have their starting points in people's actions, or sexual acts without polarising the social from the symbolic. It is from human sexuality that theology starts to search and understand the sacred, and not vice versa.
>
> *(Althaus-Reid 2000: 146, emphasis added)*

By reading sexual stories as an essential contour of San Polencho, the queer nature of religious materialities can be viewed as the disruption of all forms of sexual and theological normativity. Traición takes this one step further by positioning an anal deity within the semantical space of "treason" and "betrayal"—terms that are always already political and nationalistic. These stories are paramount to undo orthodox and normative understandings of incarnation by gesturing toward an understanding of the divine encounter through sexually deviant spaces.

Conclusion: For the Queer Materialities of Religion

I bring us back to our sexual-historical present—over five hundred years after the fall of the Aztecs—in which we find this aspect of Ahuiatēotl. San Polencho, proudly displayed over *sexo diverso* parties, be they Salvador Novo's orgiastic events or the queer pop-up party Traición. To bring together the themes discussed in this chapter, I rethink nightlife through queer theory, performance studies, and theology. I propose an understanding of San Polencho as a Mesoamerican anal deity experienced through nightlife's performative aspects of sex and the political. Here, I use nightlife to refer to both the orgies and Traición's *sexo diverso* parties. I refer to the nightlife pantheon of sexual possibilities that San Polencho/Ahuiatēotl embody.

In an interview for *Coolhuntermx*, Pepe Romero explains the history of these Traición parties and how he understands who San Polencho is, stating:

> From the Polencho, we have developed a party poetic and we've created distinction stories around him. Each edition of Traición commissions a different illustrator to create a new Polencho. Tración creates a cult for this demigod of intersexuality, that some have affirmed could be Cuilioni or Xochipilli in ancient Mexican culture.
>
> *(Nájera 2018)*

While I come to a different conclusion about San Polencho's Aztec genealogy, we find ourselves nonetheless in the semantic space of the Mesoamericanness of nightlife discourse he and his cofounders sought to create by centering a god of anality as their "patron saint" of sorts. Yet, San Polencho is so much more than that. San Polencho brings an "electrifying" charge of sexual rawness, as Aisha Beliso-De Jesús (2015) would describe in relation to Santería, a rawness that travels across temporal planes but is still rooted in Mesoamerican religion. The performative act of *sexo diverso* is a queer ritual to conjure the spirits of the Mesoamerican past that is never past. Rather, the past continues to live and find movement within spaces that represent a hemispheric Latinidad that captures those in Mexico and Latinxs in the diaspora. Regarding contemporary Latinx ritual practices of the Mesoamerican past, Davíd Carrasco comments:

> It is a special gift of the religious imagination that allows a people, after 500 years of colonialism, dependency, oppression, and resistance, to turn to the ancient Mesoamerican past for symbols, stories, and message that help make a world meaningful, give it a standing center, and provide for social and spiritual renewal.
>
> *(Carrasco 2013: 187)*

It is within that religious imaginary that queer Latinxs experience sex and one another. In that space, we find a continuity of the divine that incarnates itself in an anal deity to preside over their rituals. Leticia Alvarado rightfully argues, "Latinidad emerges here as a performative utterance that gestures at once to an affective state shared by a diverse community of individuals of Latin American dissent and the challenges of finite denotation" (2018: 5). I propose that performance in the aspect of the religious nightlife being discussed here is a shared affective experience with the divine.

Thinking alongside and with a promiscuous incarnational theology, we will recall a desire to experience desire through the flesh. As Laurel Schneider described, "promiscuous" signifies a type of mixing of theologies, histories, and identities. How we practice that is through the indiscriminate intimacy of the body with other bodies. Accordingly, the realm of contemporary queer nightlife has begun to combine immersive experimental art with the nightclub experience and pop-up culture. The best way to describe this—and especially how San Polencho becomes an aspect of an anal deity who has survived over five hundred years of temporal memories—is through performance.

A primary feature of Traición's parties is that they are pop-ups. Each in a different location, each presided over by a different Polencho icon portrayed by a different artist. When a Traición crosses borders into the United States and Europe, Polencho experiences different geographies and different patrons. No two parties are the same. Similarly, no two Catholic Masses are the same, no two rituals are the same, no two orgies are the same. But yet, there is something that threads all these episodic events into a defining tapestry we call a religious experience. I thus turn to performance theory to access a lexicon with which to discuss both the ephemerality of the event and also the traces left behind that lead to an ancient time. In her canonical text *Unmarked: The Politics of Performance*, Peggy Phelan vehemently argues, "Performance's only life is in the present. Performance cannot be saved, recorded, documented, or otherwise participate in the circulation *of* representations: once it does so, it becomes something other than performance" (1993: 146). For Phelan, performance is only the instant of the event. There is no afterlife to the performance. Performance is only in the ephemera. She continues:

> Performance[s] implicate the real through the presence of living bodies. . . . Without a copy, live performance plunges into visibility—in a maniacally charged present—and disappears into memory, into the realm of invisibility and the unconscious where it eludes regulation and control.
>
> *(Phelan 1993: 148)*

Traición's parties to some extent do follow the trajectory of Phelan's argument, but only infrastructurally. As a pop-up that distinguishes each party from one another, the event cannot be saved. But what lingers is a shared affective encounter and experience with San

Polencho as he presides over their *sexo diverso* parties, just as he voyeuristically absorbed the sex scenes of Novo's apartment.

Yet, we have to account for the cum stains, sweat, and other remnants of the body left behind. Rebecca Schneider counters Phelan by arguing, "Performance does remain, does leave 'residue.' Indeed the place of residue is arguably *flesh* in a network of body-to-body transmission of affect and enactment—evidence, across generations, of impact" (2011: 100, emphasis in original). For me, performance is ephemeral, but leaves behind the stickiness of the residues of the body's presence that then themselves create their own affective experiences and encounters, with even more remains in those afterlives. Religion and theology grant us the ability to think through the afterlives of the sexual body. The necessary anachronistic reading of Mesoamerican sexuality performed in this chapter propels the study of the queer materialities into those unlikely and unjourneyed channels of the afterlives of the past.

The stories produced by San Polencho (in his many afterlives) represent what the late queer of color theorist José Esteban Muñoz describes as "a testimony to a queer lifeworld in which the transformative potential of queer sex and public manifestations of such sexuality were both a respite from the abjection of homosexuality and a reformatting of that very abjection" (2009: 34). Muñoz describes the ghosts of performance that he reads in public sexuality:

> I see the ghosted materiality of the work as having a primary relation to emotions, queer memories, and structures of feeling that haunt gay men on both sides of a generational divide that is formed by and through the catastrophe of AIDS.
>
> *(Muñoz 2009: 41)*

In other words, these ghosts "bring to life a lost experience, a temporally situated picture of social experience, that needs to be read in photo images, gaps, auras, residues, and negations" (42). Both Novo's orgies and the *sexo diverso* parties are acts of a worldmaking anew. Even further, they are the ceremonial centers of the anal deity San Polencho/Ahuiatēotl, with whom a desire to experience the flesh and its pleasures is always already part of the religious experience. These icons possess the divine that becomes material through our sexual bodies.

Queer materiality is sex. To discuss the queer materialities of religion is to account for sex's afterlives in the hieroglyphics of a past sexual experience that is not yet passed. San Polencho is very real. He has a traceable Aztec genealogy. Novo never said he was fictional, so should we believe otherwise? Perhaps this was never about Polencho to begin with. Rather, it has always been about the materiality of the body. San Polencho embodies only the spirit of anality, but it is the electrical charge that arouses our bodies to commit ritual acts of anality that best captures what could be read as part of the queer materialities of religion. Perhaps, we locate the divine in the material performative utterances of our sexual desires and practices. A queer approach to material religion is an approach that resists being defined, translatable, or holistic. Yet, as I hope to have demonstrated throughout this chapter, queer theory opens the body to be read by religion and theology—but also for religion and theology to be read through, from, and against the body in all its sexualities.

Notes

All translations from Nahuatl and Spanish are my own unless indicated otherwise.

1 "Postdramatic" may describe performance beyond the normative confines and strictures of theater and art writ large. Rather, this term favors the undefinable plethoric qualities of what performance is or could be.

2 "Homonationalism" refers to the alignment of both nationalist ideologies and LGBTQ+ persons, wherein LGBTs are able to fully participate within the normative structures of the nation-building project. The term was made popular by queer theorist Jasbir Puar—though it long preceded her work. Puar contends *homonationalism* refers to the processes by which some powers align with the claims of the LGBTQ+ community in order to justify racism, xenophobia, and aporophobia, basing these beliefs on the assumption that those outside of Western society are homophobic (Puar 2007: 83). My occasional use of "LGBT" in lieu of "LGBTQ+" is to account for the differences among homonormative-seeking gays and lesbians (LGBT) and the nonnormative (LGBTQ+) outsiders who seek something queerer.

3 The term "*diversidad sexual*" replaces the acronym "LGBTQ+" in the interest of thinking about sexuality and sexual orientation more holistically. In other words, there are gay people and there are straight people—we're just all part of this thing called "sexual diversity." One of the biggest critiques of this category is that it effectively erases the existence of there being such a thing as "gay" or any sexual orientation other than heterosexuality. Moreover, it eliminates inherent differences among nonheterosexuals that are unique to those individuals. In other words, it disallows the productivity of speaking through, from, and against queer lexicons in order to try to untangle the messiness of human sexuality. Finally, if a term can eliminate homosexuality, then homophobia is in effect eliminated as well—there can't be homophobia if there's no such thing as homosexuality. These are the critiques associated with such a reductive term.

4 This, of course, can be followed in Catholic dogma regarding transubstantiation and the Eucharist (see Catholic Church 2006), in which the belief is that the wine and the communion wafer representing bread are *actually* the blood and body of Jesus Christ. In other words, even the act of receiving communion is a desire to consume the body and flesh of Christ.

5 Here, I am also thinking with Paul the Apostle, who writes, "So in Christ, we who are many form one body and each member belongs to all the others" (Romans 12:5). That is, "Just as a body, though one, has many parts, but all its many parts form one body, so it is with Christ" (1 Corinthians 1:12).

6 Let me be clear that I do not consider the terms "love" and "sex" to be synonymous. Rather, I still allow the semiotics of "love" into my citational practices by identifying a congruency regarding the pretext of intimacy: exposure. Both terms describe that moment in which the body appears as other in its bareness or basic nudity before the subject. What becomes clear in both terms is an intimate encounter that is best captured by thinking about how the body must necessarily expose itself before either love or sex may take place.

7 My reading of the *Codex Borgia* is through the full-color restoration of the illustrated manuscript conducted by Gisele Díaz and Alan Rodgers (1993) with commentary by Bruce Byland. Regarding the gods of sensuality on Plate 74, Byland remarks: "The original of the *Codex Borgia* has been very badly damaged on this page through burning and the less of the white lime surface that underlies the paintings. As a result much of this page is reconstructed by Díaz and Rodgers following a drawing of the page made for Lord Kingsborough in the nineteenth century" (1993: xxxi). As such, note that my readings of the codex stem from the restoration of a very heavily destroyed Plate from the *Codex Borgia*.

8 In the gay male vernacular, "top" and "bottom" refer to sexual positionalities. The top is the penetrator and the bottom is the one being penetrated.

9 According to historians, since the indigenous women were considered "property" by the Spanish, Malinche walked all of this journey by foot, alongside Cortés as he rode on horseback to Tenochtitlán. For the most comprehensive and well-respected historical studies of Malinche, see Camilla Townsend's *Malintzin's Choices: An Indian Woman in the Conquest of Mexico* (2006).

10 This follows the Foucauldian trajectory of the "biopolitical" in which the labor of the State depends on the regulation of sexual desires, in which only procreative heterosexual sex can contribute to the political sphere of the State. In other words, the biological imperative of survival (in which the solution is to have procreative sex) becomes a central political issue. The State itself thus becomes sexualized (see Foucault 1988).

11 By the "sex-gender-desire continuum," I refer to what Judith Butler has described as a cultural matrix through which hegemonic heterosexist discourse makes itself intelligible: gender follows from a specific sexual configuration and desires the opposite of that assignation (see Butler 2006).

97

References

Althaus-Reid, Marcella. 2000. *Indecent Theology: Theological Perversions in Sex, Gender and Politics.* London: Routledge.

Althaus-Reid, Marcella. 2003. *The Queer God.* London and New York: Routledge.

Alvarado, Leticia. 2018. *Abject Performances: Aesthetic Strategies in Latino Cultural Production.* Durham, NC: Duke University Press.

Beliso-De Jesús, Aisha M. 2015. *Electric Santería: Racial and Sexual Assemblages of Transnational Religion.* New York: Columbia University Press.

Butler, Judith. 2006. *Gender Trouble: Feminism and the Subversion of Identity.* 1st ed. New York: Routledge.

Carrasco, Davíd. 2000. *City of Sacrifice: The Aztec Empire and the Role of Violence in Civilization.* Boston, MA: Beacon Press.

Carrasco, Davíd. 2013. *Religions of Mesoamerica: Second Edition.* Long Grove, IL: Waveland Press.

Catholic Church 2006. *Compendium of the Catechism of the Catholic Church.* Washington, DC: United States Conference of Catholic Bishops.

Cervantes-Gómez, Xiomara Verenice. 2016. "Sacred Geography: A Queer Latino Theological Response to Orlando." *Religion Dispatches.* June 13, 2016. https://religiondispatches.org/sacred-geography-a-queer-latino-theological-response-to-orlando/.

Cheng, Patrick S. 2011. *Radical Love: Introduction to Queer Theology.* New York: Seabury Books.

Díaz, Gisele, Alan Rodgers, and Bruce E. Byland, eds. 1993. *The Codex Borgia: A Full-Color Restoration of the Ancient Mexican Manuscript.* New York: Dover Publications.

Donohue, Caitlin. 2016. "Guided by a Patron Saint of Nalgas, Party Traición Explores the Future of Queerness in Mexico City." *Remezcla* (blog). September 20, 2016. https://remezcla.com/features/culture/mexico-city-queer-party-traicion/.

Foucault, Michel. 1988. *The History of Sexuality. Volume 1: An Introduction.* Translated by Robert Hurley. New York: Vintage Books.

Hughes, Jennifer Scheper. 2010. *Biography of a Mexican Crucifix: Lived Religion and Local Faith from the Conquest to the Present.* Oxford and New York: Oxford University Press.

Hughes, Jennifer Scheper, and Jalane Schmidt. 2017. "Introduction: Material Religion in Latin America." *Material Religion* 13 (4): 409–213.

Muñoz, José Esteban. 2009. *Cruising Utopia: The Then and There of Queer Futurity.* Sexual Cultures. New York: New York University Press.

Nájera, María. 2018. "Traición, Fiestas de Experimentación Sin Prejuicios." *Coolhuntermx* (blog). June 18, 2018. https://coolhuntermx.com/trend-junio-traicion-fiestas-pepe-romero/.

Novo, Salvador. 2008. *La Estatua de Sal.* 1st ed. Vida y pensamiento de Mexico. México, DF: Fondo de Cultura Económica.

Novo, Salvador. 2014. *Pillar of Salt: An Autobiography, with 19 Erotic Sonnets.* Translated by Marguerite Feitlowitz. 1st ed. Texas Pan American Literature in Translation Series. Austin, TX: University of Texas Press.

Phelan, Peggy. 1993. *Unmarked: The Politics of Performance.* London and New York: Routledge.

Puar, Jasbir K. 2007. *Terrorist Assemblages: Homonationalism in Queer Times.* Next Wave. Durham, NC: Duke University Press.

Schneider, Laurel C. 2008. *Beyond Monotheism: A Theology of Multiplicity.* London and New York: Routledge.

Schneider, Laurel C. 2010. "Promiscuous Incarnation." In *The Embrace of Eros: Bodies, Desires, and Sexuality in Christianity,* edited by Margaret D. Kamitsuka, 231–246. Minneapolis, MN: Fortress Press.

Schneider, Rebecca. 2011. *Performing Remains: Art and War in Times of Theatrical Reenactment.* New York: Routledge.

Townsend, Camilla. 2006. *Malintzin's Choices: An Indian Woman in the Conquest of Mexico.* Albuquerque, NM: University of New Mexico Press.

1.6

COMPARISON AFTER MATERIALITY

Johan Strijdom

The use of "after" in the title of this chapter plays intentionally on the double sense of the preposition. In a temporal sense, it anticipates that comparison—indeed, comparative religion—might look different *after* the entrance of the material turn in the study of religion. The use of "after" also invites us to compare religious phenomena *in accordance with* the tenets of the material turn.

Structurally, the first half of this chapter offers a reflection on the way in which analytical categories are constructed by way of comparison, with particular attention to the categories "religion" and "material religion," along with their subcategories. The second half compares two approaches to "sacred place" as a material concept: namely, the phenomenological approach of Gerardus van der Leeuw (an important ancestor of the material approach to religion) and the critical approach of David Chidester (a prominent contemporary exponent of the material study of religion).

Comparison and Categories: Religion and Materiality

The comparison of religious phenomena has been a fundamental strategy in the academic study of religion since its emergence in the second half of the nineteenth century. It remains fundamental in at least two respects: first, the definition of categories and subcategories is based on similarities and differences; and second, case studies illustrating a category must be compared and contrasted in a manner that is both systematic and historically nuanced in order to shed new light on each other—as well as on the category itself. "The end of comparison," as Jonathan Z. Smith (2004: 29–30, 197) insists, "cannot be the act of comparison itself." Instead, he argues, the purpose of comparison should be to provoke thought that would enable us to "see things in a new, and frequently unexpected light." It would be appropriate to think of this process as a hermeneutical spiral, wherein our initial understanding merges with new horizons and results in new insights.

The first part of the thesis holds that categories are constructed on the basis of similarities. Smith's practice in comparison took root during his early training in the biological classification of grasses; taxonomies remained of primary interest even after he embarked on the academic study of religion. He posits that if the term "religion" is the *genus*, the term "religions" is the *species*. This means that the researcher's definition of the generic term "religion"—on

DOI: 10.4324/9781351176231-8

the basis of shared characteristics of a certain class of phenomena—would be applicable to the *species* or religions, which might, in turn, be divided into types of religion on the basis of arguments of shared features among the respective subcategories.

One of the best-known sociological definitions of religion is by Émile Durkheim ([1912] 2008): "religion," as a category constructed for analytical purposes, refers to beliefs and practices relative to the sacred that serve to unite adherents into a group. Each of the constituent parts or subcategories in the definition might be further defined: "sacred" as that which is "set apart" from the ordinary; "beliefs" as including myths and doctrines; "practices" as entailing rituals and ways of life; and "sacred beliefs and practices" as fulfilling the function of uniting adherents into a group. Although Durkheim assumed like the founders of the academic study of religion that religion evolved from primitive to advanced, he disagreed with their judgment of the earliest form of religion as inferior. Instead, he argued that if one can isolate the earliest form of religion, one would be able to identify the basic elements of all religions—hence his definition that takes all religions seriously as social facts with the same social function. Informed by critical theories, we may adapt Durkheim's functionalist definition by situating religious phenomena politically and economically, thereby foregrounding asymmetrical relations of gender, class, and race that are created, maintained, and subverted.

I underline two general points on categories that are constructed on the basis of comparison. First, for Smith (1995; 2004: 134, 204, 221), "etic" or second-order categories, in order to do the work of analysis, necessarily do not coincide with emic or first-order categories. By constructing and filling them with content and giving them theoretical depth, analytical categories provide us with a map to interpret our territory.

Second, we need to be relentlessly self-conscious of the genealogy or history of the analytical terms we employ. Using terms such as "religion" or "fetishism" today for analytical purposes requires from us an awareness of their colonial and imperial uses in order to employ them with self-critical circumspection. Smith (2004) poignantly insists that the dehumanizing classification of persons (notably according to race) by imperial political systems, in which the founders of the academic study of religion were complicit through their evolutionary classifications of religions, is no reason to abolish comparison and categories. Instead, our task is rather to constantly reconsider our comparisons and accordingly adapt the categories or maps that we construct for analytical purposes (Strijdom 2018a).

The key category for analysis in this *Handbook* is "material religion." What does this category convey? Which characteristics define the term? Which subcategories can be included under this term?

If a Protestant bias has led scholars of religion to prioritize the texts and the interior beliefs of individuals, the material turn emphasizes the need to correct this bias by focusing attention on the fact that religion is necessarily *materially* mediated (Houtman and Meyer 2012). David Chidester (2018) credits Ludwig Feuerbach and Karl Marx as being eminent ancestors of this awareness of the material base of everything, including religion. For Feuerbach, "human consciousness is not an independent spiritual essence, aloof from the material world of objects." "Against any idealist rendering of humanity," Chidester (2018: 79–80) continues, "Feuerbach argued that human beings were constituted by their reciprocal engagements with material objects." For Marx (1976), building on Feuerbach, the "spiritual intercourse" of human beings must be conceived as an "efflux of their material condition" (Chidester 2018: 10).

Accepting this material base as the defining feature of a study of material religion, which elements or subcategories can we include under the category of "material religion"?

If Durkheim ([1912] 2008) identified "sacred beliefs and practices that unify a group" as defining the category "religion," which elements does the category "material religion" entail? Although Chidester (2018: 209) holds that its scope is so vast as to include everything—"Everything is material, including beliefs that arise within material conditions and texts that have material consequences in the world"—the following subcategories of the category "material religion" seem to be foregrounded in this redirection of the academic study of religion:

- objects like relics, amulets, painted or sculpted images, dress codes, food, written words, architectural and natural spaces;
- feelings and sensory experiences like seeing, hearing, smelling, tasting, and touching, including their metaphorical uses, the interior experiences of visions and dreams, and their extended uses in media technologies; and
- bodily performances in specific gestures, rituals, ceremonies, and festivals.

To elucidate the reasoning behind this clustering of subcategories, let us briefly compare Brent Plate's subcategories in his working definition of "material religion" in the introduction to *Key Terms in Material Religion* (2015) with David Chidester's clusters in *Religion: Material Dynamics* (2018) which Chidester himself considers a kind of Handbook intended to capture what he has learned about religion in his academic career of the past forty years.

Plate's working definition of "material religion" consists of five constituent parts. Although he states that a phenomenon does not need to have all five of these features in order to qualify as material religion, the listed features nonetheless identify common elements that help to define the category of "material religion." These features or subcategories in his working definition comprise, to simplify:

1 Objects
2 Senses
3 Time and place
4 Community and individual
5 Tradition

In his discussion and illustrations of these parts or subcategories of the category "material religion," he emphasizes the *intersection* between them: objects are engaged through the senses in time and place by groups and individuals, whose bodies are trained by authorities to behave in accordance with tradition. This five-part conceptualization of material religion, he holds, does not assume that a belief or idea is expressed or manifests in the material world, but to the contrary forces us to recognize the material foundation or base of religious beliefs and thought. He further argues that his working definition of material religion is not limited to conventional forms of religion, but also includes forms of popular culture (such as sports events), to the extent that the latter *shares* the same five characteristics with the former.

How does Chidester's definition of material religion as an analytical category compare with Plate's five-part definition? Which subcategories does he distinguish in defining the category? In *Religion: Material Dynamics* (2018), he includes an essay—earlier published as "Material Culture" in Segal and Von Stuckrad's *Vocabulary for the Study of Religion* (Chidester 2016)—in which he, as we have seen and like Plate, insists that religion is necessarily materially mediated. Under the analytical or etic category "material religion," Chidester (2018) includes objects, the senses, and media as aspects of material religion, and gives the following further content to these subcategories:

1   Objects: Chidester argues that anything—from hair to the vuvuzela at the 2010 World Cup in South Africa—can be made sacred by intense interpretation and regular ritualization. (Chidester accepts Durkheim's definition of the sacred here.) As examples, he analyzes medieval relics and icons as well as cargo and the fetish as objects that emerged under modern colonial and imperial capitalist conditions. To these portable objects, he adds sacred buildings and natural environments. He embeds these objects historically, and underlines the political and economic contestations around them. For example, by tracing the genealogy of the concept of the fetish, he shows how, though it was invented by seventeenth-century Portuguese traders to denigrate indigenous people on the West Coast of Africa, it was later turned against Western modernity by Marx and Freud, when they used the concept to criticize modern capitalist or sexual fixations on objects. Thus, it is possible to use the term today to critically assess how human beings engage with objects. Like Plate, Chidester (2005) notes how objects from popular culture can function as religious objects—notably in his analysis of Coca-Cola and Tupperware in *Authentic Fakes*.

2   The senses: Chidester begins his definition with the five conventional senses, but broadens it to include sensory metaphors as well as visions and dreams. In his doctoral thesis, revised and extended in *Word and Light: Seeing, Hearing, and Religious Discourse* (Chidester 1992), he argues that sensory metaphors are based on theories of the bodily senses. In *Christianity: A Global History*, Chidester (2000a) shows how medieval intellectuals theorized visions of Christian believers as being interior; in *Wild Religion* (Chidester 2012), he analyzes colonial and imperial theories of Zulu dreams as being interior senses, and proposes his own interpretation of dreams by shamans and neo-shamans within a post-apartheid context.

3   Media: As extension of the senses, Chidester (2018) includes under this subcategory of material religion communication technologies—from handwritten word through printed text to audio-visual technologies.

Chidester's and Plate's definitions of the category material religion and its subcategories broadly overlap, although Chidester arguably discusses the last three parts in Plate's definition already under his discussion of objects and the senses. Like Plate, Chidester considers it of crucial importance that the subcategories not be conceived as separate, but that their *intersection* consciously be explored.

Chidester's *Religion: Material Dynamics* (2018) extends the discussion of the material terms used in analyzing religion. His book is organized by fifteen terms in groups of five divided into three parts: categories, formations, and circulations. In the introduction and conclusion to the book, as well the introduction to each of the three parts, he provides the rationale for this organization, emphasizing the intersectionality of the terms.

He begins "Part One: Categories" with a definition of the term "category" itself: "a class of things or people with *shared* characteristics" (Chidester 2018: 19; emphasis added), considering it a necessary condition of thinking, but simultaneously emphasizing the need to trace the genealogies of our categories in order to understand what we do when we apply them to analyze specific case studies. If the material study of religion is more about a *shared approach* among several academic disciplines than it is about scope, this material approach has forced us to rethink the following basic categories in the academic study of religion:

1   the dichotomy of and hierarchy between *matter* and *spirit*, underscored in E. B. Tylor's concept of animism, has been challenged by action network theorists and new materialists who argue for the agency of material objects;

2   the strict separation between *sacred* and *profane* in Durkheim's definition is elaborated when we realize that anything in everyday life—notably objects, people, and events in popular culture—can be rendered sacred by means of intense interpretation, ritualization, and contestation over ownership;

3–4 sacred *time* and sacred *space* are not merely conditions of thought—as in Aristotle's and Kant's categories—but are orientations that are *constructed* under contingent historical conditions, and are culturally, politically, and economically *contested*;

5   *incongruity* between categories opens up space for laughter and thinking as our best hope to produce new insights into material religion.

In "Part 2: Formations," Chidester (2018) focuses on five terms to highlight cultural, economic, and political forces that have shaped both religious formations and the academic study of religion. Rather than seeing these forces as separate entities, he emphasizes that religion is always contextually embedded and thoroughly entangled with cultural, economic, and political forces:

1   Under cultural forces that have shaped religious formations and the academic study of religion, he engages the material culture of objects—such as relics and icons, the fetish and cargo, as well as the senses and media (the chapter discussed in more detail above).

2   Under economic forces that have shaped religious formations and the academic study of religion, he explores the intersection between cultural and economic forces, proposing that the inversion of the relationship *economy of religion* (after Bourdieu's (1977) analysis of the economy of cultural and religious symbols) and *religion of economy* (after Benjamin's ([1921] 1996) capitalism as religion) might produce surprising insights into the future study of material religion. Not only has capitalism as a material force shaped religion. Capitalism itself also functions like a religion.

3–5 Under political forces, he discusses colonialism, imperialism, and apartheid as political forces that have profoundly shaped and transformed both religious formations and the academic study of religion. Central to his argument is that, if dominant religions and religious studies under these conditions have systematically dehumanized colonized people, the latter have simultaneously also been creative agents in their interactions with colonizers.

In "Part 3: Circulations," Chidester (2018) includes terms that draw the analyst's attention to change, mobility, and diffusion as being crucial in the material study of religion:

1   Shamanism is in material religion not simply studied as indigenous techniques of ecstasy (as in the phenomenology of Mircea Eliade [1958]), but also as a modern phenomenon that has become part of activist networks on behalf of the environment and indigenous land rights—as well as commercialized in the tourism market.

2   Change itself (after Walter Capps [1995]) is theorized as tradition that is taken up and transformed by agents in surprising and discontinuous ways—rather than simply as tradition that is handed down (as in the phenomenology of C. J. Bleeker [1959, 1979]).

3   The diffusion of religion in popular culture, which itself functions like religion, is explored in the material study of religion.

4   Touch as the most fundamental sense of modernity—both in reality and as metaphor—has been theorized by Levinas (1989) as embrace and by Benjamin ([1939] 2008) as concussion, in both cases involving the movement of bodily parts.

5   Lastly, objects have moved across oceans—of which the fetish and cargo are the most important under modern conditions of colonialism and imperialism.

If we realize that everything, including religion, is materially grounded, and that anything can be studied under material religion, what makes the material turn in religious studies different? Chidester (2018: 209) maintains it has to do with *approach*: "[T]he question is: What do we do with all this stuff?" He continues to maintain that the answer has to do with studying the *dynamics* of materiality (hence the subtitle of his book *Religion: Material Dynamics*): "[E]verything rides on how we pursue the material dynamics and the dynamic materiality of religion," taking "the material dynamics of categories, formations, and circulations" and their intersection as "different dimensions" of Marx's insight in the material base of religion.

Accepting that *approach* is crucial in the study of *material* mediations of religion, I compare in the second half of this chapter two theories and approaches to "sacred place" as a subcategory in the study of material religion: the phenomenology of Gerardus van der Leeuw and the critical phenomenology of David Chidester. To illustrate these theories and approaches to "sacred place" and their relevance to a comparison of case studies, I take as case studies two monuments in Pretoria, the capital city of South Africa. As one enters the capital from Johannesburg or its international airport, one is confronted with the Voortrekker Monument on one hill, and Freedom Park on the opposite hill. I will, in conclusion, ask to what extent Chidester has succeeded in adequately analyzing the material *dynamics* of these monuments comparatively and critically in order to suggest a way forward in the comparative study of religion after the material turn.

Two Approaches to "Sacred Place" as a Material Concept: Comparing Gerardus van der Leeuw's Phenomenology with David Chidester's Critical Phenomenology

The second part of the thesis with which we began this chapter posits that by comparing in a disciplined and systematic way two *exempla* or case studies that illustrate a category, we should be able to see in a new light the one in terms of the other, as well as the category itself. If the analytical categories provide us with the broad brush strokes, whose intersection we need to consciously explore, the application of the categories to specific case studies demands a detailed grounding of the case studies within their historical and political-economic contexts. It is only after analyzing each case study in this way, Smith (2004) proposes, that we can legitimately compare them and ask ourselves in which respect we consequently better understand the analytical category—and even redescribe its definition.

How can "sacred place" as analytical subcategory of "material religion" be defined, theorized, and approached? Like "religion," "sacred place" has been theorized in two major ways in religious studies: in an essentialist way by phenomenologists, and in a historical and critical way by social anthropologists. If Gerardus van der Leeuw ([1924] 1948; [1933] 1956; [1938] 1963]) exemplifies the first approach, David Chidester (1994; 1996; 2000b; [2000] 2009; 2014; 2018) might be taken to illustrate the second approach.

Phenomenologists typically consider a place *essentially* sacred or holy wherever a transcendental "Wholly Other" (*das Ganz Andere*) has revealed or manifested itself to adherents, who experience the overwhelming presence of this "transcendental power" with awe and trembling (following Rudolf Otto's [[1917] 1958] *mysterium tremendum et fascinans*). Acknowledging this as the absolute essence of religion and sacred place, the phenomenologist then proceeds, on the basis of a comparison of holy places, to identify *recurring patterns*.

Gerardus van der Leeuw (1890–1950), one of the major phenomenologists in the first part of the twentieth century, posited on the basis of comparison that, if a sacred place (*heiliger Ort/heilige plaats*) marks a special location within the extension of space (*Raum/ruimte*) where adherents have experienced the revelation of the Wholly Other, humans can in the case of human-made structures then decide on the positioning and orientation of the sacred place—typically to the rising sun in the east or a star. He also discerned a further recurrent pattern in the sense that each sacred place typically has an even more sacred spot: the hearth of the home, the altar of the temple or church, the sanctuary of the settlement, the shrine at the end of the pilgrimage, or, finally, in mysticism the heart of the human body (Van der Leeuw [1924] 1948: 114–117).

Take, for example, two sites in Pretoria, South Africa. The most sacred center of the massive Voortrekker Monument is the cenotaph with the words "Ons vir jou Suid-Afrika" (literally "We for you South Africa"), on which the sun shines through a strategically placed opening in the roof every December 16 at noon. And the most sacred center of Freedom Park is *isivivane* (isiZulu for "shrine"), an encircled area with rocks and indigenous plants. Leading to this most sacred center is a memorial (*sikhumbuto* in siSwati) consisting of a wall with the names of fallen heroes in the struggle for justice and against oppression, a sanctuary with a hall of heroes, a gathering for public events (the amphitheater), and a stylized sculpture of stainless steel poles symbolizing reeds from Zulu indigenous creation myths. Finally, a museum (the *//hapo* after the San word for "dream") traces the history of South Africa since primordial times (Strijdom 2012: 29).

If these two examples illustrate the way in which phenomenologists typically describe sacred places in terms of recurrent structural patterns, and if we assume that such places are manifestations of a transcendent religious essence, how might such a phenomenological approach be problematized and adapted? In his critical assessment of van der Leeuw's "poetics" of sacred place, Chidester (1994) argued that scholars of religion need to move from a phenomenological description to a critical phenomenology. Although a phenomenological description of architectural designs should be appreciated for insight into the typical structure of sacred places, that phenomenological description is often simply blind to the power relations at work in the myths and rituals that make a particular place sacred.

In our postcolonial era, we now need to foreground the "politics" of sacred place by both historically contextualizing case studies and exposing the political and economic power relations at work. Who is included and who is excluded? Which hierarchies are established? Who owns the sacred place? These are critical questions to ask when analyzing sacred objects and sacred places. Too often, Chidester holds, did van der Leeuw's phenomenology of sacred place "mystify political relations of power" and "remythologize power from the vantage point of the conqueror" by appealing to "the mythology of place and person," that "might deny the legitimacy of any resistance to the conquest that had established a sacred place." Instead, Chidester insists, "power and resistance go together defining in practice the *contested* process of positioning a sacred place" (1994: 215–217).

This point is illustrated by the speech that van der Leeuw, as delegate of the Dutch government, gave at the inauguration of the Voortrekker Monument on December 16, 1949—a year after the introduction of apartheid under the National Party—where he shared the podium with the first apartheid prime minister D. F. Malan. That speech simply echoed the myths of Afrikaner nationalism. With the Afrikaner *volk*, van der Leeuw said, the Dutch *volk* celebrated at the joyful festival their victory over the Zulu king Dingane a century earlier, which marked the birth of a new nation under the guidance of God, who had led them like Abraham to a new fatherland to live in freedom and justice. Though his speech can be taken to illustrate his phenomenological approach, this assessment must be considered in relation to, specifically, his writings from his two visits to South Africa and, more generally, his blindness to the history of black protest movements in the first half of the twentieth century in South Africa (cf. Strijdom 2018b for an analysis of the speech and other primary documents of his visits to South Africa). What should, however, be clear is the need to historically understand and politically critique the Voortrekker Monument as mediator of a racist ideology underpinned by Afrikaner Calvinist nationalism.

What to make of Freedom Park? How do we move in this case from a phenomenological description that echoes its founding myth and ritual enactments to a critical assessment of this monumental object as sacred place?

The construction at the turn of this century of Freedom Park, which followed on South Africa's post-apartheid Truth and Reconciliation Committee, was the most ambitious heritage project of Thabo Mbeki's presidency. Its foundation myth tells the story of humanity's struggle for freedom from the beginning of human evolution—as backed by scientific evidence in early fossil records—through the struggle of Khoisan and Bantu speakers against colonial and apartheid oppression, to the liberating vision of a multicultural and multireligious future, which was ritually enacted by representatives of different religions performing purifications throughout South Africa.

Situating its genesis historically and politically must include a consideration of the history of its design, which was the result of a competition. The designs that embodied universality were widely preferred by international jurors on the 2003 adjudicating panel, but they were declined by South African jurors. The committee—headed by Wally Serote, CEO of Freedom Park as of 2004, and inspired by president Thabo Mbeki's Afrocentric ideals—eventually decided that the Freedom Park complex would include three main sections: a shrine (*isivivane*), a memorial (*sikhumbuto*), and a museum (*//hapo*), which foreground *indigenous* designs and objects considered *authentically African*.

Faced with the problem that the museum is a Western colonial construct, the committee consulted Credo Mutwa, a Zulu sangoma or diviner, in the Northern Cape for assistance in selecting authentically African indigenous elements for the complex. His advice regarding the primacy of rocks in African indigenous creation myths led the committee to decide that the museum be constructed in the form of seven connected boulders around an Indigenous Knowledge Systems garden.

Within the most sacred encircled area of *isivivane*, stones were placed symbolizing the final burial site (*lesaka* in seTswana) of ancestral spirits who had died in the struggle for human freedom. Before entering this most sacred area in the complex, with mist being emitted from the floor of the *lesaka* to create a sense of aura, visitors are expected to remove their shoes.

Jonathan Noble, a scholar of architecture at the University of the Witwatersrand in Johannesburg, aptly captures the essentializing use of indigenous myths by the ANC government under Mbeki and the Freedom Park committee:

> The crucial point here is to note how the discourses that produced Freedom Park have wished to determine the essence of things. The Park has wished to promote the authenticity of indigenous forms to document and thereby to fix—through commissioned research—the significance of indigenous myths and practices, and ultimately to use this material as a motivation for the design of the Park.
>
> *(Noble 2011: 252)*

Note that this essentializing use of indigenous African symbols by the ANC government ironically coincided with their simultaneous limiting of the role of indigenous rulers to cultural matters (Settler 2010).

Freedom Park as a sacred place has indeed been contested on several fronts: from conservative Afrikaners and Christian groups (for example, the African Christian Democratic Party and black members from Pentecostal churches) to liberal writers. Among the latter, the writer Ivan Vladislavic characterized the state initiative of Freedom Park as "propaganda by monuments" that promoted uniformity and stifled debate from diverse perspectives. A better model, one could argue, would enable artists to commemorate the past in diverse ways at pertinent sites throughout South Africa, such as was done by the decentralized heritage project of the *Sunday Times*.

In comparing these "sacred places" as examples of "material religion," we can appreciate the common structural design that van der Leeuw's phenomenology has taught us. We can also appreciate Chidester's point that these large objects have been made sacred places through intense interpretation and regular ritualization, binding together particular groups (with a nod to Durkheim). But, as Chidester insists, we also need to critically assess these sacred sites as politically and economically embedded places that have provoked conflict, created hierarchies between insiders and outsiders, and entailed the contestation of ownership (which is particularly evident within contexts of conquest). Chidester (1994) holds that, although van der Leeuw's poetics of "sacred place" hints at a consciousness of political power relations, it often mystifies the latter, which should now be foregrounded in our analysis of "sacred place."

Ways Forward in Material Comparisons

Has Chidester been consistent in his critical assessment of the power relations that are at work around the Voortrekker Monument and Freedom Park as "sacred places"? On the one hand, Chidester (2012: 11) characterizes the Voortrekker Monument as "monumental fascist architecture." On the other hand, his assessment of Freedom Park as being an initiative of both the post-apartheid Truth and Reconciliation Commission and Thabo Mbeki's African Renaissance program is more benign, even within his point that the "sacrality" of the site has been contested. It can, however, be argued that, as an extension of the classroom, Freedom Park's prioritization of indigenous religious symbols and practices in the most sacred spot of *isivivane* contradicts the South African *National Policy on Religion and Education*, according to which the state is not to promote any religion above others, but to educate citizens to respect and value cultural and religious diversity as a resource for national unity (Strijdom 2012).

My first suggestion is that comparisons after materiality make explicit the normative frameworks underlying the analysis in order to prevent inconsistencies in critical judgment. One may, for example, make one's own ethical stance clear by taking as a framework Martha Nussbaum's list of capabilities for a fulfilled life, and then arguing to what extent these posited universal values should be applied or adapted according to specific cultural traditions. Nussbaum herself illustrates this approach in her work on women in India's Kerala (see, among her numerous works, Nussbaum 2011).

There is also a second suggestion to take material comparisons forward. If we agree with Chidester that it is the foregrounding of the *dynamics* of materiality that makes the difference in the recent material turn in the study of religion, how has he theorized change and mobility, and to what extent has he sufficiently illustrated the material dynamics in his analysis of our two case studies?

In a chapter on mobility in *Religion: Material Dynamics*, Chidester (2018: 152–165) engages with theories of change by contrasting the approaches of C. J. Bleeker (1959, 1979), the

Dutch historian and phenomenologist of religion, and Walter Capps (1995), the American theorist of religion and historian of theory in the study of religion. Whereas Bleeker, influenced by van der Leeuw, used the image of a snapshot to argue conservatively that identity and the identification of recurrent patterns should remain the focus, Capps used the image of moving pictures in film to argue for a revolution in method that would highlight disruption and surprising innovation in the academic study of religion.

In that same chapter on mobility, Chidester elaborates on Capps's theory of change as propelled by contrariness and his imagining of new flexible ways of retelling the history of religious studies from diverse locations—a second-order tradition that has indeed had a profound impact on his own analysis of both the material *dynamics* of religion and the retelling of the history of the academic study of religion from a South African location. His innovative approach is, for example, evident from his tracing of the genealogy of the concept of the "fetish"—from a category used by early modern European colonial capitalists to denigrate Africans, via Marx's appropriation of the term to critique Western capitalist modernity—to his own use of the category to analyze popular objects such as Tupperware and Coca-Cola that function like sacred objects. But has he in his analysis done justice to the material *dynamics* of the Voortrekker Monument and Freedom Park?

In the case of the Voortrekker Monument, Chidester (2012: 102) notes that in postapartheid South Africa, this site, which was constructed as a "sacred site" to celebrate "a militant white Afrikaner nationalism," has become "a monument to a failed nationalism, but also . . . a privatized (although partially state-subsidized) tourist attraction." Much more is surely needed to analyze contestations around the changing and diverse functions of the Voortrekker Monument after 1994. In the case of Freedom Park, Chidester's analysis similarly needs a more elaborate historical analysis that traces its origin from the competing design contests (cf. Noble 2011) to its changing roles within changing post-apartheid contexts in South Africa (cf. Strijdom 2012 and Jethro 2015).

In summarizing his most persistent interests in the study of religion in debate with the phenomenology of Mircea Eliade, J. Z. Smith (2004) considers the integration of synchronic and diachronic perspectives in the comparison of religious phenomena a noble aspiration—but one that is actually quite difficult to achieve. If a synchronic synopsis of data helps us to see connections, similarities, and patterns on the one hand, diachronic analyses let us see surprising transformations of the data on the other hand.

Chidester's (2018: 13) introduction of the term "boundary object" might in the future be helpful in integrating these analytical perspectives in the study of material religion. "The boundary object," he says, "is flexible in that it is subject to multiple interpretations, but its materiality, as an object, sustains continuity through . . . multiple engagements." Since no object is a "single bedrock object," but always a "discursive object," what is at stake is "an argument about the meaning and value of all objects," or "flashpoints around which competing communities of interpretation contend," as he has illustrated for the fetish and cargo, relics and icons, as pertinent religious objects (Chidester 2018: 207). He concludes that it is precisely the contestation over not only the meaning, but also the economic ownership of the matter, embedded within contested political power relations, that has generated the *dynamics* of these material mediations of religion.

The above case studies of the two monuments show to what extent the comparative analysis of material mediations of religion as a necessary second-order discourse has a challenging task ahead in both making explicit normative frameworks for critique and integrating snapshot comparisons with an emphasis on surprising historical changes in religious phenomena and the academic study of religion.

References

Benjamin, Walter. (1921) 1996. "Capitalism as Religion." In *Walter Benjamin: Selected Writings, Vol. 1: 1913–1926,* edited by Marcus Bullock and Michael W. Jennings, 288–291. Cambridge, MA: Harvard University Press.

Benjamin, Walter. (1939) 2008. *The Work of Art in the Age of Its Technological Reproducibility, and Other Writings on Media.* Cambridge, MA: Harvard University Press.

Bleeker, C. Jouco. 1959. "The Phenomenological Method." *Numen* 6(2): 96–111. Accessed August 1, 2021.

Bleeker, C. Jouco. 1979. "Commentary." In *Science of Religion: Studies in Methodology,* edited by Lauri Honko, 173–176. The Hague: Mouton.

Bourdieu, Pierre. 1977. *Outline of a Theory of Practice.* Cambridge: Cambridge University Press.

Capps, Walter. 1995. *Religious Studies: The Making of a Discipline.* Minneapolis, MN: Fortress.

Chidester, David. 1992. *Word and Light: Seeing, Hearing, and Religious Discourse.* Urbana and Chicago, IL: University of Illinois Press.

Chidester, David. 1994. "The Poetics and Politics of Sacred Space: Towards a Critical Phenomenology of Religion." In *Analecta Husserliana* 43, edited by Anna-Teresa Tymieniecka, 211–231. Dordrecht: Springer.

Chidester, David. 1996. *Savage Systems: Colonialism and Comparative Religion in Southern Africa.* Charlottesville, VA: University Press of Virginia.

Chidester, David. 2000a. *Christianity: A Global History.* London: Penguin; San Francisco, CA: HarperCollins.

Chidester, David. 2000b. "Colonialism." In *Guide to the Study of Religion,* edited by Willi Braun and Russell McCutcheon, 423–437. London and New York: Continuum.

Chidester, David. 2005. *Authentic Fakes: Religion and American Popular Culture.* Berkeley, CA: University of California Press.

Chidester, David. (2000) 2009. "Situating the Programmatic Interests in the History of Religions in South Africa." In *History of Religions: Origins and Visions. Proceedings of the 18th IAHR World Congress, Durban, August 5–12, 2000,* edited by Rosalind Hackett and Michael Pye, 298–326. Cambridge: Roots and Branches.

Chidester, David. 2012. *Wild Religion: Tracking the Sacred in South Africa.* Berkeley, CA: University of California Press.

Chidester, David. 2014. *Empire of Religion: Imperialism and Comparative Religion.* Chicago, IL: University of Chicago Press.

Chidester, David. 2016. "Material Culture." In *Vocabulary for the Study of Religion,* edited by Robert A. Segal and Kocku von Stuckrad. Leiden: Brill. Accessed October 18, 2021.

Chidester, David. 2018. *Religion: Material Dynamics.* Oakland, CA: University of California Press.

Durkheim, Emile. (1912) 2008. *The Elementary Forms of Religious Life.* Abridged translation by Carol Cosman. Oxford: Oxford University Press.

Eliade, Mircea. (1949) 1958. *Patterns in Comparative Religion.* New York: Sheed and Ward.

Houtman, Dick, and Birgit Meyer, eds. 2012. *Things: Religion and the Question of Materiality.* New York: Fordham University Press.

Jethro, Duane. 2015. *Aesthetics of Power: Heritage Formation and the Senses in Post-apartheid South Africa.* PhD Dissertation, University of Utrecht.

Levinas, Emmanuel. 1989. "Ethics as First Philosophy." In *The Levinas Reader,* edited by Séan Hand, 75–87. Oxford: Oxford University Press.

Marx, Karl. (1867–1894) 1976. *Capital,* 3 volumes. New York: International Publishers.

Noble, Jonathan. 2011. *African Identity in Post-apartheid Public Architecture: White Skin, Black Masks.* Surrey, UK: Ashgate.

Nussbaum, Martha. 2011. *Creating Capabilities: The Human Development Approach.* Cambridge, MA: Harvard University Press.

Otto, Rudolf. (1917) 1958. *The Idea of the Holy.* Oxford: Oxford University Press.

Plate, S. Brent. 2015. "Material Religion: An Introduction." In *Key Terms in Material Religion,* edited by S. Brent Plate, 1–8. London: Bloomsbury.

Settler, Federico. 2010. Indigenous Authorities and the Post-Colonial State: The Domestication of Indigeneity and African Nationalism in South Africa. *Social Dynamics* 36 (1): 52–64.

Smith, Jonathan Z. 1995. "Emic/Etic." In *The HarperCollins Dictionary of Religion,* edited by Jonathan Z. Smith. San Francisco, CA: HarperSanFrancisco.

Smith, Jonathan Z. 2004. *Relating Religion: Essays in the Study of Religion*. Chicago, IL: University of Chicago Press.

Strijdom, Johan. 2012. "Problems with Indigeneity: Fragmentation, Discrimination and Exclusion in Post-Colonial African States." *Image and Text: A Journal for Design* 19: 24–32.

Strijdom, Johan. 2018a. "Comparison and Classification in Religious Studies: Indigenous Discourses as Case Study." In *Similarity: A Paradigm for Culture Theory*, edited by Anil Bhatti and Dorothee Kimmich, 255–272. Delhi: Tulika Books.

Strijdom, Johan. 2018b. "Gerardus van der Leeuw at the Voortrekker Monument: A Postcolonial Critique of his Concept of Sacred Place." *NTT Journal for Theology and the Study of Religion* 72 (3): 243–251.

Van der Leeuw, Gerardus. (1924) 1948. *Inleiding tot de Phaenomenologie Van den Godsdienst*. Haarlem, Netherlands: Bohn.

Van der Leeuw, Gerardus. 1950. "Boodschap Voortrekkersmonument." *Zuid Afrika* 27, no. 1 (January 1950): 11.

Van der Leeuw, Gerardus. (1933) 1956. *Phänomenologie der Religion*. Tübingen, Germany: Mohr.

Van der Leeuw, Gerardus. (1938) 1963. *Religion in Essence and Manifestation*. Translated by J. E. Turner. London: George Allen and Unwin.

PART II

Materializing the Terms of the Study of Religion

2.1

BOOKS IN RELIGIOUS STUDIES

From Relentless Textualism to Embodied Practices

Katja Rakow

Religious studies scholars have dealt with books since the inception of their discipline. The philologist and orientalist Friedrich Max Müller (1823–1900), often hailed as one of the founding figures of the discipline, regarded books to be of fundamental importance to what he called "the new science of religion" (Molendijk 2016: 93). Müller envisioned the study of religion as the comparative study of the sacred texts of religious traditions, and his enormous publishing project *The Sacred Books of the East* (1879–1910) provided the material base for such an academic endeavor. As editor in chief, Müller oversaw the translation, editing, and publishing of forty-nine volumes of religious texts from "the East."[1] Müller's gigantic book project promoted and popularized interest in the comparative study of religions in academic circles and among the larger public (Girardot 2002). Together with other similarly large encyclopedic publishing projects of that time, *The Sacred Books of the East* literally built the material foundation for the new science of religion (Molendijk 2016: 168).

Given the importance that Müller and later generations of scholars assigned to books and, more specifically, to "sacred books" in the study of religion, it is surprising that "book" did not become one of the discipline's conceptual key terms. Handbooks, companions, and dictionaries for the study of religion often refer to related categories, such as "text" (Blackburn 2011), "texts/textuality" (Kort 2016), "scripture" (Graham 2005), "writing" (Tracy 1998; Kubota 2006), or "words" (Plate 2015b), but seldom to "book" (Reichert 2006)—although these entries often address sacred books at some point. Entries such as text, scripture, or words are an indicator for the persistent textualism that is concerned with the content of books but not so much with the material container.

This chapter is about the book as a material object and the materiality of text and text-related practices. The first section will briefly retrace the role of books in the early history of the discipline and show how the focus on written sources resulted in a strong textualism that shaped the study of religion for many generations. The second section focuses on developments in the last three decades, where scholars began to focus on the book as a material object and ritual device to overcome the dominant textual orientation of religious studies. Such research highlights the role of sacred books in mediating the divine in religious practices. The third section discusses this chapter's central terms—"book," "texts," and "words"—and their material dimension. The fourth section looks at "scripture" as the most prominent category of religious texts and discusses how we can move from a predominantly mentalist

DOI: 10.4324/9781351176231-10

and textualist understanding of scripture to a materially grounded conceptualization. To that end, I will make three conceptual suggestions in the fifth and final part of the essay: (1) scriptures are transmedial objects dispersed across various media formats; (2) scriptures are transtextual objects related to other non-scriptural texts and popular textual products, which need to be included in the study of religious texts; and (3) all text-related practices— from reading to ritually handling texts—involve body and mind when engaged with a material text. Throughout this chapter, I will use examples from my research on the use of printed and digital Bibles and from my fieldwork at Lakewood Church, an evangelical and neo-Pentecostal megachurch in Houston, Texas.[2]

Books and the Emergent Study of Religion

Max Müller's *Sacred Books* project played a major role in what scholars have called the "textualization of religions" (Molendijk 2016: 168–173). In the process of selecting, translating, and publishing the *Sacred Books*, a variety of oriental religions—lived and practiced traditions in past and present times—were turned into translated texts that scholars could read, study, dissect, interpret, and compare.[3] Published and distributed by Oxford University Press, the volumes were readily available for scholarly attention and consumption. The book series cemented an already existing emphasis on the "sacred texts" of a religious tradition based on the assumption that the "core" or "essence" of a religion is to be found in its foundational authoritative texts. Such "reductive textualism" is the result of the confluence of two historical developments—in other words, historical philology and Protestant approaches to texts and religious history (Blackburn 2011: 152), both of which are embodied in the person of Max Müller. His new science of religion could be characterized as the "history of master texts," where the ultimate authority lies with textual sources assembled, translated, curated, published, and mastered by Western scholars (Lopez 1995: 7). The assigned authority of these texts overrides not only observable religious practices as a legitimate source of knowledge about a religious tradition, but also material, epigraphic, or archeological evidence that might contradict the ideal-typical account of authoritative texts and canonical sources (Schopen 1997). In addition, a primary focus on written sources categorized as foundational authoritative texts tends to neglect all other kinds of textual products that fall outside the strict boundaries of scripture, such as commentaries, handbooks, prayer books, storybooks, hymn books, and the like. Such books are nevertheless important resources in the context of everyday religion and devotional practices of religious experts and laypeople alike.

From Textualism to the Materiality of Books

Müller's *Sacred Books of the East* have shaped the study of religion in lasting ways. Müller's most enduring influences can be seen in the "'relentless textuality' of sacred books and a particular grouping of 'world religions,' a concern for the importance and authority of the earliest written scriptures of a tradition if not the tradition's ultimate origins" (Girardot 2002: 220). Such "relentless textuality," which characterized the study of religion until a few decades ago, has led to a countermovement that Anne Blackburn describes as an "apologetic retreat from the study of religious texts" (Blackburn 2011: 155). Scholars were "seeking an end to the primary text" (Sullivan 1990: 58) by forgoing the recourse to authoritative sources in order to understand and explain religion. Instead, they directed their attention toward the study of religious practices and lived religion to analyze and explain religion and its role in the life of religious practitioners (e.g., McGuire 2008; Orsi 2013).

The study of lived religion often revealed a certain incongruence between what is officially written in the sacred books of a tradition and what religious people believe and do in their everyday lives (McGuire 2008). Such incongruence demonstrated the limitations of studying religious traditions solely based on officially codified and canonized texts. At the same time, the focus on practices showed that religious practitioners used their sacred texts in many ways. Reading and interpreting these texts was just one way of engaging scriptures and was often confined to specific groups—such as scribes, religious experts, and religious elites able to read and to afford manuscripts or printed books. For the majority of religious practitioners, reciting, displaying, performing, venerating, or ritually manipulating sacred texts were often more important than the study of texts and their contents (Graham 1989; Griffiths 1999). The academic shift to religious practices as witnessed in lived religion approaches is, therefore, one toward religious books' users. Religious books and texts became known as more than mere semantic resources, but also as ritual or devotional objects actively engaged by religious readers and practitioners (cf. the collection of essays in Watts 2015a, 2018).

The new focus on religious books as objects used in rituals fitted well with material approaches emerging in the study of religion since the 1990s. Material religion scholars view "religion as a practice of mediation between humans and the professed transcendent that necessarily requires specific material media, that is, authorized forms through which the transcendent is being generated and becomes somehow tangible" (Meyer 2013: 8). The practice of mediation depends on material media—such as images, objects, clothes, food, incense, liquids, spaces—but also on the acting, sensing, and experiencing human body's engagement with the material world the religious actors inhabit. All these media are used to render the sacred tangible to the human senses and to bring religious practitioners into contact with the divine by making it "sense-able" in official religious rituals as well as in the context of everyday life (Meyer 2015: 141). Scholars studying religion through the framework of its materiality work with a broad notion of media, encompassing every form of materiality that is employed to mediate religion. Thus, media are broadly understood to range from the world of objects to less solid substances such as sound and smell, and media include the human body, practices, performances, and spaces. Books, texts, and words are important media in that they are able to render the sacred tangible and are actively engaged in religious worldmaking.

An example from my research on the use of printed and digital Bibles in evangelical and neo-Pentecostal circles illustrates not only the role of religious books as mediators of the divine but also how concrete material properties of a book impact religious practices.[4] Evangelical Christians often use the terms "the Word of God," "His Word," or "Scripture" to reference the Bible as words to be read or heard and interpreted. They regard the Bible as a text to be explored to discern God's will and to enable an encounter with God through His Word. As anthropologist Matthew Engelke (2009: 151) points out, many Christians perceive the Bible as "a material text with immaterial qualities, the latter of which are revealed as signs of God's presence in the act of reading." Evangelical and neo-Pentecostal Christians combine the perceived immateriality of their scripture with the idea that God's Word is timeless and unchanging. The perceived immateriality and timelessness of the Bible often go hand in hand with the assumption that a Bible is a Bible regardless of the concrete translation or material form of the biblical text.

Yet, occasionally, when there occurs a change in either medium or the established mediating practices, the materiality of the Bible suddenly becomes an issue for Christian practitioners even when they insist on the immaterial quality of God's Word. Most recently, the new ubiquity of smartphones and tablets both in church and at home led to discussions of the appropriateness of digital Bibles for religious practices. The ensuing discussions across the North American Christian landscape revealed that the issue at hand was the concrete materiality of the Bible—printed book or e-book—and its suitability for religious uses. Many Christians voiced a preference for digital versions (online or a Bible app) in Bible study because of the many practical advantages. A digital Bible contains many different translations and editions of the text, but often also supplementary material that enriches the Bible text for further studies (annotations, maps, commentaries, and other explanatory resources). Bible apps offer structured reading plans and daily reminders with push notifications that helped some readers to establish a devotional reading practice and thus to fulfill the Protestant imperative to regularly read the Bible.

What some perceived as technological and practical advantages of electronic versions was contested as impractical and unreliable by others. Digital Bibles depend on a material interface such as a computer screen, e-reader, or smartphone. Usually, displaying the Bible text is neither the only nor the primary function of such devices because these are also used to read other reading material, watch TV, check emails, play games, etc. Moreover, smartphones and apps become outdated fast and need to be replaced by upgraded versions. It is often the specific properties of electronic devices that render digital Bibles unsuitable for liturgical or ritual use in churches. Thus, some Christians have expressed a preference for the printed Bible, which they regard as offering direct—in other words, what they perceive as unmediated—access to God's Word. In their view, a book can be opened and read at any time. To be read, a book is not dependent on battery power or a digital screen. As Carl Lentz, former pastor of Hillsong Church NYC, once said to his audience, "Your Bible needs to have pages" (Lentz cited in Rakow 2020: 415). With its unity of pages, printed words, and binding, a book is perceived as a "real" thing that can be touched, its heft weighing heavily in the hands of its reader. Compared to the concrete materiality of a book, the electronic text seems rather intangible. Here, the image of the printed Bible as a durable and reliable material container for the immaterial Word of God is pitched against a rather ephemeral digital Bible to which the reader has access only through an electronic device dependent on battery power, hardware, and software. To Christians who share Lentz's sentiment toward the printed Bible and thus share a similar "semiotic ideology" when it comes to accessing God's Word, digital versions are a materially insufficient medium to make God present via the act of reading (Engelke 2009: 155–156; Keane 2018).[5] To conclude, the concrete material form of a book matters for reading as well as for ritual, liturgical, or devotional practices. A book's material properties come with specific "affordances" (Hodder 2012: 49), which enable and support some uses better than others.

The Material Dimension of Books, Texts, and Words

The example of printed and digital Bibles showed that the concrete materiality of the book mattered for its users. In the following, I will extend the focus on materiality beyond the object itself—the book—to the components that make up a book: texts and words. Although we might easily acknowledge the book as a physical object, we still have a strong tendency to think of texts and words as immaterial carriers of meaning decoded in the act of reading.

What, then, is a book, and how do book, text, and word relate to each other? We usually think of a book as a portable object made of bound pages either of blank sheets of paper or covered with script, print, or images and glued or sewn together at one side. Book historians handle a much broader view of what counts as a book. To them the term "book" refers to a broad variety of written or printed texts on different materials (such as clay tablets, papyrus, parchment, or palm leaves) and in various formats (such as scrolls, plates, leaves, or pages), which do not resemble the codex format of the book in the narrow sense (Howsam 2015).[6] Some book historians apply the term to "virtually any piece of written or printed text that has been multiplied, distributed, or in some way made public" (Eliot and Rose 2007: 2). The latter understanding of the term "book" indicates not only a concrete object—in other words, text in whatever format and material quality—but also the processes of production, publication, and distribution. A book in its widest sense then is a human-made artifact, even a "technology" that involves human agency and interaction with text at every stage of a book's making and usage (McKenzie 1999: 4, 15). Leslie Howsam (2015: 4–6) suggests thinking of the term "book" as a concept that references a text and a material object as well as a "cultural transaction" and an "experience," indicating that books are embedded in a larger network of human activities and cultural practices.

If we follow this conceptualization of book, then book and text are interrelated but not synonymous, because not every text has to take the written or printed form of a book. Invoking the Latin origin of the English term "text" (Lat. *textere*, to construct, plait, or weave together), anthropologist Karin Barber describes text "as a tissue of words," and the act of producing a text accordingly as "weaving or fabricating with words," which can be done orally or in writing (Barber 2007: 1–2). Thus, text can be verbal if it exists only in oral form, or an originally verbal text can become a written text once it has been committed to writing (Griffiths 1999: 21–28). A written text can be read aloud or recited and thus temporarily turned again into verbal form. Books are written texts, but not "verbal texts" in the sense of Barber (2007: 2). In short, books are text, but not all kinds of texts are books.

The notion of written texts as silent and the act of consuming books—reading—as an individual and silent activity is a relatively recent development (Saenger 1997). For most of human cultural history, texts have functioned as an "oral-aural text" even when existing in written form (Graham 1989: 130). The Qur'an, for example, exists for many Muslims primarily as an oral-aural text in the form of recitations, while the *mushaf*—the written/printed material object that mediates the Qur'anic message—plays a secondary but nevertheless important role in religious practices (Suit 2020: 1–11). In terms of the materiality of texts, the visual and the oral-aural dimensions are the most obvious, but some texts also have a tactile dimension (such as engraved, embossed, or punched text). Texts are the product of human bodily labor—not just of human minds that compose or reproduce. Mouth and voice are needed to speak; hands, writing instruments, and a suitable surface are required to weave words into written texts. In turn, texts are encountered by listeners and readers in two primary ways: aurally via the ears and visually through the eyes.

Written texts are made of written words that, in turn, are composed of letters. Readers might notice the actual shape of printed letters when these take strange and unfamiliar forms or are heavily embellished. In such cases, they need to make an extra effort to decipher the letters to make out the words and thus the meaning of what is written. But in most cases of contemporary printed texts, the singular letters and words of a text tend to be relatively unseen in the actual act of reading. The eyes scan the lines of text, swiftly process the content, and fly over the pages. The semantic content mediated through printed words stay with the reader and transport them, moving along a storyline or argument, while the image of the words just read is already forgotten. The ephemerality of the words in the process of reading is an effect of modern typography. Modern typefaces have been developed to reduce the distance between text and reader and to enhance legibility and readability to make the process of (silent) reading smoother. As a result, the process of reading erases words, renders them into "words unseen" (Plate 2015a: 121). The erasure of the materiality of words is further supported by a modernist understanding of words heavily influenced by Protestantism. In Protestantism, words are rated higher than images, the mind higher than the body, and interiority higher than exteriority. Words are understood as "silent, individual, immediate (i.e., 'without media'), of the spirit"; the assumed immediacy of words is pitched against images, which in contrast are regarded as external, material, and visible and thereby available to a collective (McDannell 1995: 2–15; Plate 2015a: 121). Protestantism's strong emphasis on religious reading led to the advent of individual (silent) reading practices and with it to a significant increase in literacy within the broader population (Furedi 2015: 57–80). It shaped our modern understanding of reading as a rational practice of moral (re)formation (Nord 2004) with an emphasis on the solitary reader and reading and interpreting as purely internal, mental activities (Kort 1996; Griffiths 1999). Contesting such an immaterial, mentalist notion of words, S. Brent Plate (2015a: 119) reminds us that, "regardless of their semantic meaning, words exist in and through their mediated forms and do not exist apart from their materiality." The visual design of text, if it is handwritten, printed, or electronically displayed, is not neutral but affects the emotional interaction with text as well as the cognitive interpretation of words. Visual design processes are therefore not only decorative adornments that could be disregarded; they also "impact engagement with a text, well before readers grasp its semantic meanings" (Plate 2015a: 129). Both the physical form of texts and typographical conventions affect readers and how they read. Not only what is written in a text but also *how* the text is displayed influences the constitution of meaning and the process of interpretation (Bell 2002; Acheson 2020).

The example of the Red-Letter Bible, an invention of the late nineteenth century, will illustrate how the materiality of a text influences the engagement with it. The convention of using red ink to mark the words of Jesus in the Bible or the New Testament is traced back to Louis Klopsch, a Christian journalist and publisher. In line with his evangelical convictions, Klopsch wanted to emphasize the importance of Jesus's message, and using red ink for the words of Christ translated his intent into a visual form. Verses printed in red helped to distinguish Christ's words from the surrounding text set in black (Eng 1986). Text marked in red—so-called rubrics—is a classical paratextual feature that helps to structure a text. It has been used in medieval manuscripts or in liturgical texts to mark, for example, the beginning or end of a passage, to emphasize specific sections, or to visually distinguish different text and/or musical genres (Brown-Grant et al. 2020: 4). Klopsch's typographical innovation of the biblical text quickly became popular, and red-letter editions are still in print today. To a reader familiar with the typographical convention, biblical text printed in red signals that Jesus is speaking. The reader can arrive at that conclusion solely by visual cues before having read any of the printed words on the page. The example of the red-letter Bible illustrates that what is relevant is not only what is written on a page but also *how* it is written in material terms.

Scripture: From Master Text to Performance

The Bible and other authoritative religious texts, often categorized as "scripture," have long been the central focus of scholars of religion. Scriptures are often described as powerful and authoritative religious texts with implied sacrality that can be distinguished from other religious texts (such as commentaries and prayer books), cultural classics (such as *The Odyssey* and the Harry Potter books), and other documents of iconic status (such as the Constitution and the Declaration of Independence). In their endeavors to define the category, several scholars have pointed out that "scripture" is a relational term, indicating that scripture does not simply exist in itself but only in relation to religious communities who make and use authoritative religious texts (Graham 1989; Smith 1989). Such an understanding turns the object-oriented question—"What is scripture?"—into a process-oriented question—"How does a text become scripture?"—by extending the focus from the text as such to the human activities and relations pertaining to texts considered scripture. It indicates a shift from the study of scriptures as "master texts" to a study of religious texts and their use in religious practices.

James Watts (2015b) developed a three-dimensional model to further unpack the process of how a text becomes scripture. According to Watts, religious communities ritualize scriptures along three different dimensions: semantic, performative, and iconic. The semantic dimension pertains to questions of meaning, interpretation, and commentary—and appeals to the content of the text. The performative dimension encompasses two modes of performance: the performance of the words of a text (such as ritualized forms of reading, recitations, memorization, calligraphy, and the like) and the performance of scriptural content (such as dramatization or artistic illustrations). Watts consciously extends the notion of the performance of scriptures to include not only oral recitations in the narrow sense but also artistic and popular performances like dramatizations of the Indian epic *Ramayana* or movies such as *The Passion of the Christ* (2004). The iconic dimension relates to the physical form of the text and the way the text is handled in rituals and devotional practices as well as how the text is publicly displayed, venerated, or addressed in artistic representations. According to Watts, the religious significance and persuasive power of scriptures are not primarily warranted by exegesis and interpretation, but by their dramatic performance and iconicity. Although all three dimensions are to a greater or lesser degree relevant to any kind of text, it is only scriptures that have been ritualized in all three dimensions.

Observations from my fieldwork at Lakewood Church, an evangelical megachurch in Houston, Texas, serve as an example to explore the advantages and limits of Watts's three-dimensional model for a material analysis of scripture.[7] During a typical Sunday service at Lakewood Church, pastor Joel Osteen enters the stage of the capacious auditorium with his Bible in hand. Before delivering his message, he engages his congregation (and his audience in front of the TV screen) in a small ritual of declaration. Holding up his Bible, Osteen speaks the following words:

> This is my Bible. I am what it says I am. I can do what it says I can do. Today, I will be taught the Word of God. I boldly confess, my mind is alert, my heart is receptive. I will never be the same. I am about to receive the incorruptible, indestructible, ever-living seed of the Word of God. I will never be the same. Never, never, never. I will never be the same. In Jesus's name. Amen.

Many of the worship attendees assembled in the sixteen-thousand-seat auditorium follow along. They hold up their Bibles (either in the classical and instantly recognizable book format or on their smartphones) and speak the declaration in unison with Osteen. After the declaration, he places his Bible (usually unopened) on the pulpit on stage and proceeds to deliver his carefully crafted and memorized message. Osteen's sermons are a blend of prosperity theology and positive thinking interspersed with anecdotes and various Bible quotes. When Osteen quotes from the Bible, the relevant quote (alongside information on the translation from which the quote is taken) is temporarily displayed on the large LED screens on the stage (as well as at the bottom of the screen for the TV viewers). Throughout, the Bible that Osteen brought on stage remains closed on top of the pulpit. The service ends with an altar call and a final prayer before Osteen leaves the stage, taking his Bible with him.

All three dimensions of scripture are relevant to the scene I have just described. The semantic dimension is present in Osteen's appeals to the content of the Bible to which his message provides commentary and interpretation. Spoken quotations from the Bible (either read or produced from memory) illustrate the performative dimension. And, finally, the physical Bible brought on stage, held high during the ritual of declaration and later placed on the pulpit, is an enactment of the iconic dimension. The material Bible signals the Bible-centeredness of the speaker and the congregation in whose midst it is displayed. Together, all three instantiations of the dimensions demonstrate the relevance of the Bible and its status as scripture for the pastor and the Lakewood Church community.

Watts's three-dimensional model is indeed helpful to discern scripture from religious texts not considered sacred or authoritative. Joel Osteen, like many other popular TV pastors, regularly publishes Christian inspirational books based on his messages delivered at Lakewood Church. When a new book is going to be published, Osteen announces his new publication during a service at Lakewood Church and displays the cover on the LED screens or the webpage of Lakewood Church and Joel Osteen ministries. Once the new book is published, he brings a copy on stage and shows it to his congregation. I observed similar scenes whenever a popular guest pastor was preaching at Lakewood Church. For example, when T. D. Jakes (bishop of the megachurch Potter's House in Dallas, Texas) published his book *Let It Go: Forgive So You Can Be Forgiven* (New York: Atria Books, 2012), he went on a preaching/book promotion tour with a stop at Lakewood Church. In March 2012, Jakes preached for three consecutive days to a full auditorium. Every time, Jakes was introduced by Osteen and the new book was held high before the assembled audience. Of course, the books were on sale after each service, and many attendees bought several copies. When I asked why they bought so many, they explained that they wanted to share bishop Jakes's message of God's forgiveness and planned to give the books to friends and family. Sharing Jakes's message of "God's forgiveness" by gifting his books was—by extension—sharing God's message. Of course, none of my interlocutors would claim that such books are scripture or comparable to the Bible, but these popular texts are a conduit through which people come in contact with what they regard as a Bible-centered message. To conclude, although Osteen's or Jakes's books were brought on stage, displayed, and referenced in sermons, none of these texts would count as scripture in the narrow sense because none of these books were ritualized along all three dimensions.

Watts's model might help distinguish scripture from non-scripture, but it cannot sufficiently account for the role that materiality plays in all three dimensions. Materiality is most prominent in the iconic dimension where the physical object and its handling, manipulation, display, and artistic representation are central. The performative and semantic dimensions address materiality only implicitly as both dimensions require human agents that bodily interact with scripture in their practices of reading and interpreting (semantic dimension), and the recitation and performance of scriptural words and contents (performative dimension).

Rethinking Scripture, Religious Books, and Text-Related Practices

To emphasize the role of materiality in thinking about scripture, Plate (2017) suggested adding the aesthetic dimension as the fourth dimension to Watts's model. For Plate, the aesthetic dimension is not simply an additional dimension, but one that intersects with each of the other three dimensions. Plate's choice of terminology refers to the role of the senses in interacting with scripture, whether in reading, oral performance, or ritual display. I understand his suggestion as an invitation to rethink scripture—and, in extension, religious books and the engagement with texts more generally—in fundamentally material terms. It will not suffice to simply focus on texts as material objects if we do not simultaneously study what people do with them and how their uses relate to the materiality of texts. For a thorough reconceptualization of the study of religious texts that accounts for the materiality of texts in all aspects, I suggest a three-fold intervention. First, to fully understand the materiality of scripture, we need to not only regard them as written and/or oral-aural texts but also as transmedial objects often dispersed across various media formats. Second, to account for the role and uses of religious books in the life of religious practitioners, we need to extend our focus beyond the narrow category of scripture and include other religious texts—be they established commentaries on scriptures or popular religious books. Third, we need to think of *any* engagement with religious texts—from handling texts in rituals to reading and studying them—as embodied practices and, thus, as more than mental activities. In the remainder of this chapter, I will address each intervention in turn.

Scripture as Transmedial Object

My examples of printed and digital Bibles illustrated the fact that a book can take various forms, and that the material properties influence what religious actors can do and what they feel is appropriate to do with a sacred book. Keeping in mind the question of different book formats and their material affordances, I would like to return to my earlier example of the Sunday service at Lakewood Church. A closer look reveals that the "Bible" as an instantiation of the category "scripture" is present in various translations and in different media formats, which all come with their affordances. First, there are printed Bibles on display, most prominently Osteen's Bible on stage, and the many Bibles visible in the audience during the declaration. Looking around, one can discern a multiplicity of Bibles—old and new; classical versions in dark brown or black covers; colorful versions embellished with flowers; branded Bibles such as Osteen's *Hope for Today Bible*; and many others.[8] Second, there are electronic Bibles in the form of Bible Apps on smartphones, which again are most visible during the declaration but also during the service, when attendees use their smartphone to look up the Bible quotes referenced in Osteen's message. Third, there are what one could regard as partial Bibles in the form of Bible quotes displayed on screen. Having attended countless services, I observed that Osteen often uses different quotes from different translations within one sermon. His first quote might come from the New Living Translation, another verse is taken from the Amplified Bible, and yet another comes from the New International Version. He chooses the translation whose choice of words best fits into his narrative and can be most seamlessly integrated into his message. Often that cannot be done by using one translation only. It might also explain why Osteen rarely reads a verse from the Bible he brings on stage, because that particular Bible contains only one translation of the Bible text—whereas he needs to reference several translations to make his message work. As mentioned earlier, the limitation of the printed book is easily overcome by electronic Bible versions, which allow access to various translations. At the same time, digital Bibles on smartphones do not *look* like Bibles; individual quotes displayed on screens and read out aloud mediate and represent the idea of the "Bible" without invoking its iconic form, the printed book. Within the described scene, it is the presence of physical Bibles on stage and in the auditorium that warrants the "Bibleness" of the digital text and the spoken discourse of the pastor (Beal 2015; Rakow 2017).

To conclude, the term the "Bible" in the singular invokes uniformity, the idea that whatever is called a Bible essentially contains the same message independent of its concrete material container or translation. But behind this assumed uniformity lies a veritable multiplicity of translations and material formats. The Bible and other scriptures are thus best understood as transmedial objects dispersed over various media formats, whether print, digital, scripted, or audiobooks. These material forms come with their affordances, shape practices, and impact "semiotic ideologies" (Keane 2018). We saw one example where the semiotic ideology of the immediacy of God's Word was suddenly questioned when the Bible moved from print medium to digital device.

Popular Religious Texts

To further unpack the transmedial and transtextual qualities of scripture, we need to move beyond the narrow category of scripture and related texts that carry religious authority or the sanction of tradition (such as theological commentaries, catechisms, prayer books, and the like). In addition to such established commentaries, the study of religious texts should include popular religious texts such as tracts and pamphlets, biographies and hagiographies, broadsides and newspapers, passion plays and poems, spiritual novels, and best-selling advice books. These texts can have the form of printed text, audiobook, or digital application. Such a broad notion of religious texts allows us to include and study the largely underestimated but important role these popular textual sources spread over various media formats play in the everyday life of religious practitioners.

During my fieldwork in evangelical megachurches, I could observe the important role that popular religious bestsellers such as the earlier mentioned T. D. Jakes's *Let It Go* (2012) or Joel Osteen's *Every Day a Friday: How to Be Happier 7 Days a Week* (New York: FaithWords, 2011) play in the life of religious practitioners. The books of popular TV pastors usually present the themes, examples, and anecdotes of their sermons in written format. New books are often accompanied by other related textual products or activities—for example, the *Let It Go Workbook* (Jakes) or *Daily Readings from Every Day a Friday: 90 Devotions to Be Happier 7 Days a Week* (Osteen). Such companion materials contain passages from the original publication, Bible quotes, and invitations for reflection and application to the reader's own life.[9] In conversation with Lakewood Church attendees, I realized that many of my interlocutors regarded reading Osteen's books and discussing or referencing them in Bible study as a way to engage with the Bible and its message. Next to sermons and Bible study, such popular books were the main medium through which these Christians learned to make sense of the Bible, and how to apply the insights to their everyday lives. The phrase "reading the Bible" thus often implies not only reading the biblical text but also different kinds of companion materials, such as Bible study manuals, workbooks, or best-selling Christian advice books (cf. Bielo 2009). Such popular books often mediate a specific Bible discourse. Osteen and Jakes merge evangelical Bible-centrism with emotional overtones, prosperity gospel, and positive thinking packaged in an accessible writing style for a broad readership. What Lakewood Church attendees know about God's Word is not necessarily or solely based on Bible reading in the narrow sense but on what they have learned in Bible study groups or from sermons, Osteen's TV program, or his books. Because of the transtextual nature of popular religious texts and their relation to authoritative texts, I argue that such texts are relevant for the acquisition of religious knowledge, the shaping of religious subjectivities, and their enactment in everyday religious practices within private as well as institutional religious settings. If one wants to understand how these Christians engage with and encounter the Bible, and integrate and make sense of God's Word in their daily lives, one needs to include these other popular texts.

We need to study how such texts are produced, used, and experienced and how users relate them to authoritative texts.

Practicing Texts

Of course, reading, writing, memorizing, reciting, and circulating religious texts are not just prominent practices within the different streams of Christianity; they are practiced in many other religions as well. Such textual practices intersect with other text-related practices where texts are ritually manipulated, paraded, displayed, and venerated. Sikhs treat their sacred scripture as a living guru. The Guru Granth Sahib is installed on a throne, treated like a king, and attended to with prayers, food, clothes, and offerings. The scripture is placed in a bed at night and its words recited and listened to "as if the guru continues to give verbal instructions to disciples" (Myrvold 2015: 265). In Egypt, Muslims use saffron or honey to write Qur'anic verses, which are subsequently dissolved in water and drunk as healing potions (Suit 2020: 153). In Singapore, the diasporic Hindu community celebrates Gita Jayanti, a birthday party for the *Bhagavad Gita*. It is an annual ritual in which the *Gita* takes birth as a divine *murti* (Waghorne 2015). Thus, texts are used as protective or divinatory devices, as a healing charm, or as a powerful marker of status and social identity. In many religious contexts, the handling of physical texts in the form of books, scrolls, or amulets is a central religious practice within institutional as well as non-institutional religious contexts. Therefore, the study of scripture and religious texts as material and cultural products needs to include the study of textual practices. I refer to the nexus of texts and the entire spectrum of text-related practices as "practicing texts." The phrase emphasizes that human agents are not just passive recipients of their contents—they actively engage books and texts in many ways. Further, the phrase avoids isolating the material object—the text—from its actual bodily engagement by religious practitioners, and allows us to think of text in relation to its users and their use of the text. And, finally, the phrase "practicing texts" helps us to sidestep otherwise immediate associations of seeing reading as the primary way to engage with texts; reading is just *one* among *many* ways of practicing texts.

My understanding of practicing texts is guided by practice theories, which regard practices "as materially mediated nexuses of activity" (Schatzki 2001: 20). Andreas Reckwitz (2002) describes practices as routinized actions that encompass various interconnected elements such as bodily and mental activities, artifacts and their use, movement in and perception of spaces, different forms of knowledge (understanding, practical know-how), as well as emotions and motivations of social actors. From a praxeological perspective, humans are conceptualized not as actors with certain mental qualities but as bodied agents with embodied capacities (know-how, skills, tacit understanding, and dispositions). Practices are materially anchored in human bodies and non-human artifacts (Schatzki 2001). Such a praxeological perspective provides a useful link between the materiality of texts and the embodied engagement of texts. My notion of practicing texts is based on two fundamental assumptions. First, textual practices always engage the human body's sensorium and cognitive capacities. Second, textual practices never stand on their own but are embedded within a network of practices relating to the production, circulation, and consumption of textual products and the related discourses on meaning, interpretation, and authority. Such a broad understanding of practicing texts can overcome narrow approaches to scripture and religious texts, which focus on reading and interpretation as a disembodied process of decoding meaning. It reminds us that textual practices are socially embedded practices influenced by and thus changing according to socio-historical contexts, practice settings, and embedded technologies (Saenger 1997; Griffiths 1999; Fischer 2003).

Conclusion

Tracing the role of texts in the study of religion—and, more specifically, that of scriptures—we saw a move from "relentless textualism" to a focus on the materiality of practicing texts in lived religion. This chapter discussed central concepts—"book" and "scripture" as well as the related terms "texts" and "words"—and their material dimension. Over the years, different scholars went beyond a focus on semantic content and the history of sacred texts and emphasized the sensual and material dimensions of scripture. They developed ways to account for the materiality of scripture—more so in performative practices and the ritual handling of the material text, less so in actual engagement with the semantic content. But text and words are material as well, and they influence the act of reading and interpretation. I suggested a three-fold reconceptualization of scripture and religious texts to more broadly put the study of texts onto a material foundation: (1) I proposed to view scriptures as trans-medial objects dispersed across various media formats; (2) I regard scriptures as transtextual objects related to other popular textual products, which need to be included in the study of religious texts; and (3) I conceptualized all text-related practices—from reading to ritually handling texts—as not just a mental but also a bodily engagement with a material text. Such a materialization of the study of religious texts and their use allows us to see not just the ritual uses of texts as material, but also the practices that are primarily concerned with the semantic content of a book (reading, interpreting, commenting, etc.). Echoing Engelke's (2012: 209) statement that "all religion is material religion," I argued that all texts are material, and every engagement with text is material. From reading to performing or ritually venerating texts—all text-related practices are embodied practices engaging the sensorium of the human body and its cognitive capacities while encountering text as a material object. Thinking of texts and related practices in material terms allows us to bring together textualist studies and practice-centered approaches so as to fully explore the importance of all kinds of religious texts as sematic-material artifacts in the lives of religious practitioners.

Notes

1 All in all, the series contains fifty volumes: forty-nine translations of religious texts published between 1879 and 1894 and one index published many years after Müller's death in 1910.

2 I conducted two periods of fieldwork at Lakewood Church: from February to March 2011 and from February to April 2012. My research on the use of printed and digital Bibles is based on field-work observations at megachurches in the United States and Singapore and at various Evangelical and neo-Pentecostal conferences and events in Europe and Australia (2011–2015 and 2019)—as well as on the analysis of various Christian media, ranging from opinion pieces to newspaper articles and blog posts.

3 The *Sacred Books* contain twenty-one Vedic-Brahmanic volumes, ten volumes from the Buddhist tradition (mostly Indian Buddhism), two volumes from the Jain tradition, eight volumes of Persian-Zoroastrian texts, six volumes from Chinese traditions (Confucianism and Daoism), and two volumes of Qur'an translations (Girardot 2002: 226).

4 The example provides a brief summary of some of my findings, which I have published in a more extensive form elsewhere (Rakow 2017, 2020).

5 According to Keane, "semiotic ideologies" refer "to people's underlying assumptions about what signs are, what functions signs do or do not serve, and what consequences they might or might not produce." This includes all possible signs, their material carriers, and the sensory perception they might trigger (2018: 65).

6 The codex format was first used in antiquity, and its emergence coincided with the move from papyrus to parchment (which was cheaper and more durable). The codex gradually replaced the scroll format between 100 and 600 CE. Interestingly, it was the material properties of the codex that made it especially attractive for early Christian usage: it was compact and portable, which allowed for small formats and easy referencing; it was durable, and so could survive extensive handling; and it was economical, since it allowed for writing on both sides (Fischer 2003: 82–86).

7 I provide a more extended analysis of Lakewood Church worship services and Osteen's messages in another article (Rakow 2015).

8 Many popular TV pastors have published branded Bibles, which provide the biblical text packed in a way that resonates with their specific message. Osteen's *Hope For Today Bible* was published by Howard Books in 2009 and contains the Bible text in the New Living Translation (red-letter edition). The branded Bible provides specially written introductions to the Bible books and so-called "Hope Notes" and illustrations that apply Osteen's characteristic positive-thinking framework to topics and verses in the Bible. Such material-paratextual features help to establish a specific framework for reading the Bible text, a framework that resonates with the content and aesthetics of Osteen's so-called "message of hope" (Rakow 2015).

9 Osteen publishes a new book every one or two years. The TV program, his books, and other products of the Joel Osteen brand are part of a larger production and marketing machinery employed by many popular evangelical pastors and churches. Jessica Johnson (2017) has termed this phenomenon the evangelical-industrial complex.

References

Acheson, Katherine. 2020. "Visual Form and Reading Communities: The Example of Early Modern Broadside Elegies." In *The Edinburgh History of Reading: Early Readers*, edited by M. Hammond, 135–159. Edinburgh: Edinburgh University Press.

Barber, Karin. 2007. *The Anthropology of Texts, Persons and Publics: Oral and Written Culture in Africa and Beyond.* Cambridge: Cambridge University Press.

Beal, Timothy. K. 2015. "The End of the Word as We Know It: The Cultural Iconicity of the Bible in the Twilight of Print Culture." In *Iconic Books and Texts*, edited by J. W. Watts, 207–24. Sheffield, UK: Equinox.

Bell, Maureen. 2002. "Mise-En-Page, Illustration, Expressive Form: Introduction." In *Cambridge History of the Book in Britain Vol. 4, 1557–1695*, edited by J. Barnard and D. F. McKenzie, 632–635. Cambridge: Cambridge University Press.

Bielo, James S. 2009. *Words Upon the Word: An Ethnography of Evangelical Group Bible Study.* New York: New York University Press.

Blackburn, Anne M. 2011. "The Text and The World." In *The Cambridge Companion to Religious Studies*, edited by Robert A. Orsi, 151–167. Cambridge: Cambridge University Press.

Brown-Grant, Rosalind. 2020. "Introduction." In *Inscribing Knowledge in the Medieval Book: The Power of Paratexts,* edited by Rosalind Brown-Grant, Patrizia Carmassi, Gisela Drossbach, Anne D. Hedeman, Victoria Turner and Iolanda Ventur, 1–17. Berlin: Walter de Gruyter.

Eliot, Simon, and Jonathan Rose. 2007. "Introduction." In *A Companion to the History of the Book*, edited by Simon Eliot and Jonathan Rose, 1–6. Malden, MA: Blackwell.

Eng, Steve. 1986. "The Story Behind: Red Letter Bible Editions." *International Society of Bible Collectors*, n.d. Originally published by Bible Collectors' World, Triads Quarterly, January/March 1986. http://www.biblecollectors.org/articles/red_letter_bible.htm.

Engelke, Matthew. 2009. "Reading and Time: Two Approaches to the Materiality of Scripture." *Ethnos* 74 (2): 151–174.

Engelke, Matthew. 2012. "Material Religion." In *The Cambridge Companion to Religious Studies*, edited by Robert A. Orsi, 209–229. Cambridge: Cambridge University Press.

Fischer, Steven Roger. 2003. *A History of Reading.* London: Reaktion Books.

Furedi, Frank. 2015. *Power of Reading: From Socrates to Twitter.* London: Bloomsbury Continuum.

Girardot, Norman J. 2002. "Max Müller's 'Sacred Books' and the Nineteenth-Century Production of the Comparative Science of Religions." *History of Religions* 41 (3): 213–250.

Graham, W. A. 1989. "Scripture as Spoken Word." In *Rethinking Scripture: Essays from a Comparative Perspective*, edited by Miriam Levering, 129–169. Albany, NY: State University of New York Press.

Graham, William A. 2005. "Scripture." In *Encyclopedia of Religion*, Vol. 12, 2nd ed., edited by Lindsay Jones, 8194–8205. Detroit, MI: Macmillan Reference USA.

Griffiths, Paul J. 1999. *Religious Reading: The Place of Reading in The Practice of Religion.* New York: Oxford University Press.

Hodder, Ian. 2012. *Entangled: An Archaeology of the Relationships Between Humans and Things.* Hoboken, NJ: John Wiley.

Howsam, Leslie. 2015. "The Study of Book History." In *The Cambridge Companion to the History of the Book*, edited by Leslie Howsam, 1–13. Cambridge: Cambridge University Press.

Johnson, Jessica. 2017. "Megachurches, Celebrity Pastors, and the Evangelical Industrial Complex." In *Religion and Popular Culture in America*, edited by Bruce David Forbes and Jeffrey H. Mahan, 159–176. Oakland, CA: University of California Press.

Keane, Webb. 2018. "On Semiotic Ideology." *Signs and Society* 6 (1): 64–87.

Kort, Wesley A. 1996. *"Take, Read": Scripture, Textuality, and Cultural Practice.* University Park, PA: Pennsylvania State University Press.

Kort, Wesley A. 2016. "Texts/Textuality." In *Vocabulary for the Study of Religion*, Vol. 3, edited by Robert Alan Segal and Kocku von Stuckrad. Leiden: Brill. Also available at Brill.com.

Kubota, Hiroshi. 2006. "Writing." In *The Brill Dictionary of Religion*, edited by Kocku von Stuckrad. Leiden: Brill. Also available at Brill.com.

Lopez, Donald S. Jr. 1995. "Introduction." In *Curators of the Buddha: The Study of Buddhism under Colonialism*, edited by Donald S. Lopez Jr., 1–29. Chicago, IL: University of Chicago Press.

McDannell, Colleen. 1995. *Material Christianity: Religion and Popular Culture in America.* New Haven, CT: Yale University Press.

McGuire, Meredith B. 2008. *Lived Religion: Faith and Practice in Everyday Life.* Oxford: Oxford University Press.

McKenzie, D. F. 1999. *Bibliography and the Sociology of Texts.* Cambridge: Cambridge University Press.

Meyer, Birgit. 2013. "Material Mediations and Religious Practices of World-making." In *Religion Across Media: From Early Antiquity to Late Modernity*, edited by Knut Lundby, 1–19. New York: Peter Lang International.

Meyer, Birgit. 2015. "Medium." In *Key Terms in Material Religion*, edited by S. Brent Plate, 139–144. London: Bloomsbury Academic.

Molendijk, Arie L. 2016. *Friedrich Max Müller and The Sacred Books of the East.* New York: Oxford University Press.

Myrvold, Kristina. 2015. "Engaging with the Guru: Sikh Beliefs and Practices of Guru Granth Sahib." In *Iconic Books and Texts*, edited by James W. Watts, 261–281. Sheffield: Equinox Publishing.

Nord, David Paul. 2004. *Faith in Reading: Religious Publishing and the Birth of Mass Media in America.* Oxford: Oxford University Press.

Orsi, Robert A. 2013. *Between Heaven and Earth: The Religious Worlds People Make and the Scholars Who Study Them.* Princeton, NJ: Princeton University Press.

Plate, S. Brent. 2015a. "Looking at Words: The Iconicity of the Page." In *Iconic Books and Texts*, edited by James W. Watts, 119–133. Sheffield: Equinox.

Plate, S. Brent. 2015b. "Words." In *Key Terms in Material Religion*, edited by S. Brent Plate, 275–280. London: Bloomsbury Academic.

Plate, S. Brent. 2017. "What the Book Arts Can Teach Us About Sacred Texts: The Aesthetic Dimension of Scripture." In *Sensing Sacred Texts*, edited by James W. Watts, 5–26. Sheffield: Equinox.

Rakow, Katja. 2015. "Religious Branding and the Quest to Meet Consumer Needs: Joel Osteen's 'Message of Hope.'" In *Religion and the Marketplace in the United States*, edited by Jan Stievermann, Philip Goff and Detlef Junker, 215–239. Oxford: Oxford University Press.

Rakow, Katja. 2017. "The Bible in the Digital Age: Negotiating the Limits of 'Bibleness' of Different Bible Media." In *Christianity and the Limits of Materiality*, edited by Minna Opas and Anna Haapalainen, 101–121. London: Bloomsbury Academic.

Rakow, Katja. 2020. "The Material Dimension of the Bible from Print to Digital Text." In *The Oxford Handbook of the Bible and American Popular Culture*, edited by Dan W. Clanton Jr. and Terry R. Clark, 414–432. Oxford: Oxford University Press.

Reckwitz, Andreas. 2002. "Toward a Theory of Social Practices: A Development in Culturalist Theorizing." *European Journal of Social Theory* 5 (2): 243–263.

Reichert, Andreas. 2006. "Book." In *The Brill Dictionary of Religion*, edited by Kocku von Stuckrad. Leiden: Brill. Also available at Brill.com.

Saenger, Paul. 1997. *Space Between Words: The Origins of Silent Reading.* Stanford, CA: Stanford University Press.

Schatzki, Theodore. R. 2001. "Introduction: Practice Theories." In *The Practice Turn in Contemporary Theory,* edited by Theodore R. Schatzki, Karin Knorr Cetina and Eike von Savigny, 10–23. London: Routledge.

Schopen, Gregory. 1997. "Archaeology and Protestant Presuppositions in the Study of Indian Buddhism." In *Bones, Stones, and Buddhist Monks: Collected Papers on the Archaeology, Epigraphy, and Texts of Monastic Buddhism in India,* edited by Gregory Schopen, 1–22. Honolulu, HI: University of Hawai'i Press.

Smith, Wilfred Cantwell. 1989. "Scripture as Form and Concept: Their Emergence for the Western World." In *Rethinking Scripture: Essays from a Comparative Perspective,* edited by Miriam Levering, 29–57. Albany, NY: State University of New York Press.

Suit, Natalia K. 2020. *Qur'anic Matters: Material Mediations and Religious Practice in Egypt.* London: Bloomsbury Academic.

Sullivan, Lawrence E. 1990. "'Seeking an End to the Primary Text' or 'Putting an End to the Text as Primary.'" In *Beyond the Classics? Essays in Religious Studies and Liberal Education,* edited by Sheryl Burkhalter and Frank Reynolds, 41–59. Atlanta, GA: Scholars Press.

Tracy, David. 1998. "Writing." In *Critical Terms for Religious Studies,* edited by Mark C. Taylor, 383–393. Chicago, IL: University of Chicago Press.

Waghorne, Joanne. P. 2015. "A Birthday Party for a Sacred Text: The Gita Jayanti and the Embodiment of God as the Book and the Book as God." In *Iconic Books and Texts,* edited by James W. Watts, 283–298. Sheffield: Equinox.

Watts, James W., ed. 2015a. *Iconic Books and Texts.* Sheffield: Equinox.

Watts, James W. 2015b. "The Three Dimensions of Scriptures." In *Iconic Books and Texts,* edited by James W. Watts, 9–32. Sheffield: Equinox.

Watts, James W., ed. 2018. *Sensing Sacred Texts.* Sheffield: Equinox.

2.2

OF MANUSCRIPTS THAT CAN'T BE READ AND ROADS THAT CAN'T BE SEEN

Historical Matters among Chams in Cambodia

Emiko Stock[1]

His hand caresses the page as if to dust it off. It's brown, thick, torn, rough at the edges, and burnt out. Then his fingers stop. His mind is somewhere else, I can tell. We are moving away, falling into another conversation: people we know in common between here and there, across the country and beyond, still around or gone. I can't quite figure out if he is still here, in this moment. His mind away, maybe? His hands holding on certainly. Fingers stilling the final lines of the last page of the manuscript. A manuscript that I am finally offered to see after years looking for it. A manuscript that many Chams—the Muslim minority of Cambodia, a vastly Buddhist country—redirect me to whenever I ask about history: "You have to look for that manuscript. That is [our] history," I am told. Or, "Go find it, and then. You will see history."

This history is one often placed under erasure, the result of a diasporic trajectory. What the historiography written in the Cham, Khmer, and French colonial archives have left for us to see from this diasporic history is that Chams used to live in today's Vietnam. This was before they left, under the pressure of the Viet armies, and took refuge between the fifteenth and nineteenth centuries in today's Cambodia.[2] Chams now compose most of the Cambodian Muslim minority, itself a mere 5 percent of the nation's population.

Among Cambodian Chams, with whom this ethnography takes place, the manuscript in front of me is referred to as "history" by many of my correspondents: old and young, history buffs and casual curious. Some of them have witnessed the manuscript with their own eyes. Some have dreamed it as they envision its once-upon-a-time existence. I am not sure what the manuscript is actually about. And that's why finding it and its owner today fills me with such long-awaited excitement: I expect Ong-Angry-Not-So[3] to leave the lines traveled by hand and to come share this excitement by venturing into some reading and explanations. But Ong-Angry-Not-So, a retired farmer and Imam, knows Cham just as most other Cambodian Chams do: as a spoken language, but not necessarily as one consigned in writing. Cham literacy, or knowing how to read Cham script, is, in this diasporic context, a complex and rare affair.[4] Ong-Angry-Not-So holds on to the manuscript but can't read any of it. As he tells me: there is nothing to be said about it, and so the excitement for history falls through. Except. . .

DOI: 10.4324/9781351176231-11

This chapter is not about what a more-expected ethnographic or historical documentation of the manuscript might have to tell us. I could discuss the facts that this archive contains since, after all, I could read and analyze the manuscript in conversation with Cham studies colleagues working on similar texts (Po Dharma 1987; Weber 2014). I could also develop observations around the manuscript's care to discuss how a material study of books is needed to go beyond content and language matters, as other anthropologists have done elsewhere (Bacigalupo 2016; Cohen & Mottier 2016; Diemberger & Hugh-Jones 2012). Instead, what I have at heart, here, is to let go of the palpability of social sciences (the archival impulse, the elaboration of facts and data, the conclusions of participant observation), and instead suggest to stay with the most subdued moments that open up in our various research endeavors. What I am wondering is whether material matters are not best understood in the absence, silence, and erasure of materiality.

In other words, I suggest to look at material things (here a manuscript) not for what they seem to gesture to as content (the specific historical information contained in the writing of this manuscript) or as symbol (the kind of history that such a book might recall) but as the thing itself. What I am offering is to let go of a thinking in which the manuscript acts "like" history, or "represents" history: rather, I take the manuscript to *be* history itself. What I am asking, then, is what to make of moments when something begging erasure and silences (a history which cannot be told, written, or seen) seems to be all so omnipresent (everything *is* history). What I am attempting here is to envision a way in which anthropologists of history and historians of anthropological bending might attune themselves to this apparent contradiction: rather than solve it (with answers, a quest to fill the gaps), could we let such contradiction do its own work in its own terms? I wonder: can we present history by herself, for herself, and on her own ground?

To start this conversation, I follow Ong-Angry-Not-So and other Chams who have offered me to rethink what history *is* or *could be*, in bringing our attention back to the materiality of the thing on the one hand (it is the materiality of the manuscript that matters, its existence somewhere, more than the history actually contained in its writing); and, on the other hand, the lack of materiality or the ethereal quality of theories made in the world[5] (the theories of history that are brought by and on to the manuscript rely, as we will see, on the assertion of the absence of its very material matters).

To do so, let's go back to Ong-Angry-Not-So and the manuscript in this stilling moment: his fingers are holding on to the last lines of the last page of the manuscript. Those are intricate lines: there are notes in Cham script enclosing the manuscript. But that's not what Ong-Angry-Not-So is following: lines of periods pick up where the writing ends, it seems. Those are handwritten lines made of dots,[6] meshed in knots, drawn in an old strong and thick ink, tracing in curves and pending in openings in a manner reminiscent of those described by the anthropologist Tim Ingold.[7] The lines meet the text in its conclusion as if they were leading it to finish the story. As if they were going into an end that isn't quite ready to stop just yet.

It's the end of the manuscript. And yet it is still holding on to us beyond the story its writing set out to tell. A story that, we are told, is one of history: this is how the manuscript is renowned unanimously among various Cham communities across the country, beyond variations of religious practices and orientations, beyond variations in genealogical and geographical affiliations. And yet, most of the Chams referring to the manuscript have actually never seen it. They just know *of* it. Most of the few who have seen it cannot read it. So that the manuscript cannot be read (to), cannot be (re)written, cannot be (made) seen. This, as we will see, matters. After all, Ong-Angry-Not-So himself, just like many other Chams, cannot read Cham.[8] As he gestures toward the lines, what Ong offers is to look for another reading of history: one that goes beyond writing, which might be to say: one that goes beyond regimes of hypervisibility and tracing. This might have profound implications for the ways we position the fields of anthropology and history through their methods and objects: the observable of the participant observation, and the track record of the documentation.

Rethinking History

This might be the conundrum that (Cham) history sets out for us: on the one hand, history is always omnipresent, people conjuring it to explain quite a lot, from marriage preferences to regional migrations, from religious contrasts to personal objects' locations, from genealogies to positions of political or economic power. And yet, when prompted, history always slips away, the narrator retracting to a variation on the recurrent Cham saying, "[This] cannot be told|read, cannot be copied|written, cannot be seen|shown."[9] The conundrum then is as follows: if history cannot be told, written, or seen, how does the researcher tell, write, or show history? The answer might lie in a re-orientation of how we generally think of history. This re-orientation requires us to ponder the two following questions:

> 1/ How can history be observed beyond its facts, in a way that echoes Benjamin's "flashing" image (Benjamin 1969)? How does history show itself to us with a strength that might not fall too far from the religious? A strength that overtakes and goes beyond what social scientists—or humanists—usually attend to in their descriptions and reflections. Another way to ask is this: If Ong sees history in a manuscript that he cannot read, then what is the image of history that comes to him? Which is really to ask, quite simply: *How do we see history?*
>
> 2/ But this first question itself bears the assumption of a sensorial spectrum perceived across divisions: seeing is not hearing—we assume—just as we believe that images come to our eyes before they can hit the heart and raise the goosebumps out of our skin.[10] The poet knows otherwise. So do historians, more often than not.[11] To our question, then: How do we see beyond sight if the image of history exceeds what we look at? If the manuscript cannot be read and if "all" that Ong can hold on to are lines of dots filled with blanks, what is there to see? Or, let's wonder: If not much, if nothing, *how do we see with more than our eyes?*

In this chapter, I shall call upon Ong and others who have led me again and again on that road of common wonderment: What, then, is history? I do not offer, in response, any definition, for I am never given one. The researcher's work might be humbling in just this: rather than prompt for the extraction, to stay *in* and *with* the guesswork. I invite you, reader, into that guesswork. Employing similar about-and-around devices that have been used by Ong and other Cham interlocutors, I will attempt to conjure an image of history through and beyond its very own materiality.

Lines for History

The lines of the manuscript that Ong is holding on to, beyond scripture, do not seem to do the work of archiving or documenting history. They refract mainly—although never exclusively—three instances of being in history: roads, lineages, and threads. Such interpretations are, however, never offered as such when the lines come up during fieldwork. The lines of the manuscript resonate with other lines that keep on repeating themselves, threading themselves back into the research somehow: in casual interviews, free-floating hanging outs, graveyards' visits, and in landscapes that refuse to show themselves. Lines come as roads of deportations, as lineages always threatening to be lost, and as networks threading the way to the (Khmer) royal palace.

When I first got acquainted with lines, I had to first get what "lines" imply, despite not knowing much about them. (The lines were not made of precise facts I could hold on to.) This was a form of "education": to get the lines while never actually being "taught" about them.[12]

This education, though, didn't come in distinct ways: I wasn't told that lines are essential. I wasn't trained to stop, take note, document, and acknowledge the lines. One doesn't sit to study lines so to get history. Yet, it seems to me that it is just how many Chams—or, at the very least, many of the very few I got to spend time with—do history. History, I am led to see, is not a specific place one goes to when one is in the mood for it (or when school forces it into us all). History is a path, a line that some Chams may take on, to live. Moving along the lines and knowing them go hand in hand (Ingold 2007). Hitting the road often echoes a remembering of it. Knowing your lineage cannot be done by merely reciting names and reading out life stories: you have to touch the ground so that ancestors and future little ones can keep you in touch.

Such an endeavor is necessary if we are to capture the image of history in all its uncertainty. The uncertainty is not located in the image of the lines: that image is clear and accrues its sense as we learn how to see the lines. What remains productively inscrutable is the meaning of the lines. Because they shall not be read, the lines do not give us data or information. We have to let them in and let go of facts, just as we hold on to the "formulas of silences" (Trouillot 2012) that Chams' history imposes.

Michel-Rolph Trouillot groups under "erasures of silence" all tropes that attempt either the direct erasure of historical events (formulas of erasure) or the emptying of meaning and political power (formulas of banalization) (Trouillot 2012: 96). As he further elaborates: "The joint effect of these two types of formulas is a powerful silencing: whatever has not been canceled out in the generalities dies in the cumulative irrelevance of a heap of details" (96). This resonates profoundly with Cham historiography, or at least the manners of historiography that I have been familiarized with. Stories of history never come full circle, are never completed, are always left open by the sentence putting an end to it: "This cannot be told|read, cannot be written|copied, cannot be seen|made seen." The sentence, one that Ong-Angry-Not-So puts into practice, leaves uncertainty for sole companion, an empty question filling the air, a pending for more, an attending left in suspension. The sentence is not just something people say; it doesn't work like that, and it doesn't come with the convenient repetition and diffusion that adages and maxims might carry for study and citation. The sentence is something that might come at the end of the conversation, and so everything sort of stops or moves on. The sentence directs us toward what a theory of history could be, but also toward the kind of practice that silenced histories can engender.

This may be where our seeing history with Chams finally begins. If things cannot be told, read, written, or seen, what is it that the manuscript and its dotted lines have to tell, write, or make see? If history cannot be told, read, or seen, what is the image of history that the lines lead us to watch with? As I mentioned previously, most of the times the lines come into some form of explanation; they come into the materiality of roads, lineages, and threads. In order to limit this chapter to one case study, I shall focus on the idea that lines are roads—and what that means for our understanding of (Cham) history.

Roads: Of Returns and Repetitions

In the following pages, I will make use of field notes taken from my own observations, and elements of interviews, life stories, and day-to-day apparently random conversations. Those field notes are separated from the body of the text. This is not to reinforce the fetishization of field notes as the source of ethnographic authority and knowledge—since I do not believe in the strict verbatim that field notes often claim. My goal here is mainly to ease the unfamiliar reader into some pacing. The field notes you are about to read might sound literate: this is a reminder that field notes are always a literature of sorts, even when the genre of choice is the distant academic voice. To begin, we travel back to the early 2000s, as Imam-Full-of-Stories-History-Buff recalls Cham history:

> It was a long road.
> Very long. . .
> From there to here.
> And then from here to there.
> Back and forth.
> Strewn with bodies | ghosts.
> The bodies | ghosts of Chams.
> The bodies | ghosts of ancestors.
> Just there, on the road, right there, all over.
> . . .
> You go yourself, you see. The road, the bodies | ghosts.
> That road, you know . . .
> Over there.
> Right here.
> That road . . .
> Our history.
> *This* is history.
>   —Early 2000s. Imam-Full-of-Stories-History-Buff recalling Cham history,
>   recalling his grandmother's[13] testimony of "the road."

The road is still there, I am told. And yet I was never to find it. Go for yourself and look for it, you won't see it. Open a map, and it won't be drawn. Walk through the tombs and find no graveyard. You step back. You ask for more. Less and less it gives. No more road in the story. No more road to history.

The road is one of the images Cham history throws at us. When silence takes on the "too difficult" of history.[14] The road is Cham history: very real, right here it seems, and yet it can't be seized, it can't be grasped. You don't see it. Maybe because you just can't take it. Just like Cham history, the road is everywhere and nowhere at the same time. If the road is (Cham) history, if the road is an image of history, and if that image cannot be seen, what are the implications for Cham history—as well as for broader theories of history? How do we learn to see the road as we practice watching with the lines of the manuscript?

Here, I would like to insist that, when it comes to "the road," the real isn't to be opposed to the image. Seeing the road as an image doesn't necessarily imply that it is not real; or that it is "just" an image (it is not that, since there is no road in the landscape, the road doesn't exist anywhere and that it is therefore "just" an idea). To the reverse, precise actual roads might just be stand-ins confirming the reality of the image (it is not that since there is a road in the landscape here, this very road is "just" the one road we are currently talking about).

The road, therefore, does exist, but it cannot be seen. This is different from a metaphor since a metaphor relies on its image to exist. While a metaphor requires a suspension of "the thing" to replace it by "another," the image can be sustained not in contrast, opposition, or superposition to reality but along with it. The image is, therefore, not separated from reality since it feeds on a truth that may not be accessible in that flashing instant but is nonetheless tangible. When you see the road, its concreteness doesn't matter. It matters that you see it. What is left of the road, here and now, is the image we are left with: it doesn't mean that the road does not have a potential reality somewhere, elsewhere, in another time. When people mention in passing "the road(s)," they often have very vivid pictures in mind; they describe it as if they had seen that particular road, as if they had been there. Sometimes, it doesn't even matter that they may not have seen it or been there. They still have seen it; they still have been there, in a certain way.

Through the evocation of his grandmother's testimony, Imam-Full-of-Stories-History-Buff tells of his ancestor's recalling of the road generations ago, in another region. This is a road he hasn't lived, and which, we may say, doesn't hold any reality for him. Yet, this road is still felt, lived again, in a very affective way, not only as he tells it but also, we could venture, probably every time he thinks about the road. In its uncanny historical repetition, the road becomes truer than reality. The road is in the systematic company of Chams' diasporic history: a pattern of loyalty turned treason, unfairness turned injustice, displacements turned deportations—all leaving tenuous traces in the French, Khmer, and Cham nineteenth-century archives (Aymonier 1891; Mak Phoeun 1987, 1990, 1994; Moura 1883; Po Dharma 1982, 1987, 1998; Weber 2014).

The facts may be too thin to establish what, where, when, and how the road was. But the sense that the road keeps on coming back (along with its repressions), that you keep on hitting it again and again across history, makes it more real than any reality. The road comes with such a certainty that the actuality of its facts, the concreteness of its reality, somehow feels like superfluous fluff. This way, it materializes more than if it were given any actual materiality. It matters little to know which king launched the repression, which itinerary did the displacements follow, and how many were lost in the deportations. It matters little to get to know the when/where/what/how of the road. It matters that the road asserts with conviction its historical repetition. The truth is that the road keeps on happening, one way or another. *That* we can rely on. *That* is the truth.

In a way, truth is stronger than what you would take reality to be. The road that Imam-Full-of-Stories-History-Buff tells of is the one of his great-grandmothers, who did experience the nineteenth-century forced deportations across Cambodia survived by *some* Chams (more on this below). Still, Imam-Full-of-Stories-History-Buff talks of the road as if he had lived it—through glimpses transmitted by his own grandmother—but also, as if he had been there and then himself. This might be because Imam-Full-of-Stories-History-Buff has lived another road himself: that of the long 1970s forced deportations all across the country survived by *some* Cambodians (more on this below). The road then is not a metaphor as much as it is an image that wears various realities across time and place. Let me now venture into what this image of the road actually conjures for both Imam-Full-of-Stories-History-Buff and his ancestor.

The actual roads taken by Imam-Full-of-Stories-History-Buff and his grandmother are inherently different: to her, the road of history most probably marks the conflicts, repressions, and displacements of the 1858 Cham uprisings that will be crushed by the Khmer royal palace, the remaining survivors being deported under brutal surveillance (Weber 2014). The accusation of rebellions waved by the royal palace against the population and the erasures to follow are neither unique nor isolated. The pattern of revolt + conflict + repression + displacement actually comes back with such an uncanny familiarity in Cham history that it anchors the image of "the road(s)" as exemplary of this repetition. For the grandmother, the road is one of those repetitions located in a long, very long, 1858.

For Imam-Full-of-Stories-History-Buff, the road of history is, therefore, the one imprinted by the grandmother. But it is also probably one re-imprinted by the war(s) of the long, very long, 1970s. In his region, as in others, the war(s) started at the dawn of 1970 to end in the mid-1990s. Conflicts opposing the Republican Army to the yet-to-be-Khmer Rouge forces were then soon to be followed by waves of displacements of families looking for shelter in supposedly safer areas of the country (such as the capital Phnom Penh). At the fall of the US-supported Republican government and its country-wide bombings, those relocations were to be followed by the Khmer Rouge's massive deportations. The new regime's goal was to create a "new society," one "emancipated" of its ties to any past and any previous life. The goal was nothing but erasure. The roads of Imam-Full-of-Stories-History-Buff and his ancestor then are drastically different: in global tensions, in regional locations, in moments in time, in periods and pauses. And yet, none of that really matters—what matters, again, is "the road" itself.

What Imam-Full-of-Stories-History-Buff and his gone grandmother build together is a theory of history inscribed in the method that the road can be. What their lines gesture toward is the uncanny ink of repetitions that Cham history has been dipped in. After all, much before either the grandmother or the grandson were born, Chams had already followed roads from various areas of today's Vietnam to Cambodia. From then on (and much before) the repressions and deportations lived by the grandmother, Chams had to follow roads of forced migrations, under—yet again—other accusations of agitation against rulers in place, kings in legitimation, and history-as-it-is (Weber 2014). The road is a compact of roads' multiplicity, a reminder that diasporas have to move along in their histories so to be.

Now, if the road has a multiple reality but no concrete body that we can see or touch, it would be very easy to discard the road's image as being just that: a convenient image for storytelling. A picture for illustration, a metaphor to play with. Yet, that would be quite unfair: the image plays a role in telling the truth of history that facts, information, data, and numbers can never quite fully reveal. Archives do not account for flashing images that leave traces with a stronger imprint than any account coated with details might do.

It makes sense, then, that even when directions came, the finding of "the road" never happened. I was given names of places, explanations very much layered with the "heaps of details" of Trouillot. South or north, left or right. And still: no road. I was coming back empty-eyed. The landscape had swallowed the road. Because the road is such a line in Cham history, it just had to become invisible as a way to become untraceable. For you to see it, it has to become inscrutable. For us to realize its omnipresence, it has to look and feel absent. Or, as per the method of the ancestors: "never even leave footprints" (more on that later).

The traces of ancestors vanish, and so does the road to history. Yet, not seeing your ancestors' footprints doesn't mean that they didn't pass through here. Not seeing the road doesn't mean the road doesn't exist. There may be something of a disappointment for the historian in us: like Trouillot, who, upon his arrival at the Sacred Well of Chichén Itza, in Maya Land, couldn't find any tangible proof of history. "I had missed a vital connection to the present," says Trouillot contemplating the Maya lake, "I had honored the past, but the past was not history" (Trouillot 2012: 143).

Down the road, I went.

I, too, aimed to honor the past—but like Trouillot, I was to miss the vital connection to the present. Rather than staring at the road, it is an encounter with an old lady of history that would educate me into watching the road. She is the one who will bring this vital connection to the present.

Roads: On Enduring

Toh-the-Gigantic:[15] Where are you going after that?

The ethnographer: I am thinking of heading to X's house, you know, daughter of Y and cousin of Z.

Toh-the-Gigantic: Sure, I know. They live right here in Bobor Village.

The ethnographer (embarrassed):. . . Well. . . Uh. . . No. . . Not exactly. . .

[Obviously, Toh-the-Gigantic got it all wrong]:

Toh . . . You know the Xs, they live just across the road.

Toh-the-Gigantic: Yes, Bobor village. Across-the-road-Bobor.

The ethnographer (confused): But you mean. . . Bobor village, right? In the Province-of-the-Plantations, a hundred miles away?

[Ethnographer concerned: her old partner-in-crime has been growing into forgetfulness lately]: Toh, you do know we are here in the Village-of-the-Enduring, right? In the District-by-the-Lake? Bobor is an entire day of travel away. . . I was just planning to stick around for today and go to that house of X before night falls.

Toh-the-Gigantic (mumbling something like "you, young fool"): Uuuuuuh . . . !!!!! Of course, the house of X in our very own Village-of-the-Enduring!! But in the Bobor part of Village-of-the-Enduring.

The ethnographer (lost): ". . ." [Finally put to silence].

Toh-the-Gigantic—growing impatient: Our village, here, Village-of-the-Enduring. But our very own Village-of-the-Enduring has a Bobor village in it. Across the road. Just like we have a Phum Bo village and a Kambor village, get it?

The ethnographer (now completely lost): You mean the Phum Bo and Kambor of the Province-of-the-Plantations?

Toh-the-Gigantic concluding, exhausted: You don't know anything, now do you?!

—Early 2000s. Toh-the-Gigantic tending to my education.

I knew a lot. That much, I thought I knew.

Years I had been on the road. Back and forth between the capital where I lived and the District-by-the-Lake where Village-of-the-Enduring is located and where, with time, I was to become something of a "stranger of ours" as the expression would have it. At the time, I was also going around the country where I was trying to untangle meshes of kinship relations and collect patches of history. Notebooks full of stories, memories full of encounters, 5 am phone calls echoing relatedness. And surely a lot of facts.

The fact here is that Bobor, Phum Bor, and Kambor are villages located in the Province-of-the-Plantations, upward on the Mekong, not in the District-by-the-Lake where Toh lives in the Village-of-the-Enduring. Much before those villages became the center of my dissertation fieldwork, I had visited quite a few times, and the road confirmed that no confusion could be made: they were far, far, far away. The roads leave marks on you, and sometimes they scratch maps on your skin to follow through. The villages of Bobor, Phum Bor, and Kambor are indeed nowhere close to Toh-the-Gigantic's actual and current physical location. She doesn't live anywhere nearby the circle that those villages could draw on the map. Her Village-of-the-Enduring is a hundred miles away.

What I am trying to say is this that I know for sure: when Toh-the-Gigantic talks about Bobor minutes away, right across the road on the other side of the village, there must be some kind of misunderstanding. For this is what I know: Village-of-the-Enduring is here; Bobor is there. Way over there. But Toh-the-Gigantic doesn't think of here and there. She sits, truly gigantic, ruling atop the surrounding world, with her age, her charisma, and also . . . Well, people just say she is a queen. I squeeze my tiny seated self, nice and tight, I look up to her, and I tend to agree.

Toh-the-Gigantic doesn't think of here and there. And what is more: she doesn't think of now and then. It is not that she doesn't know the difference. She does. It is that the difference doesn't matter, that it makes really very little sense. It is not that she lives in a timeless present and all that. She doesn't. She is coming to an end anytime soon, and of that too, she is sure. Toh-the-Gigantic does have an acute sense of time and feels quite strongly about past, present, and future. But for her and some other Chams, those timelines all invite themselves in each other's moment constantly. And maybe, just maybe, something similar happens for locations: it's not that she confuses here and there; it is just that time makes them layer over each other. Toh-the-Gigantic knows all that. I don't. So now I realize: I know nothing indeed.

What Toh-the-Gigantic is about to educate us into, in a way that I believe Trouillot would appreciate, is that *the past is not history*. She is about to teach us how to *honor the past while maintaining a vital connection to the present*. Maybe that is what Toh-the-Gigantic was redirecting me to. Yet, I couldn't get much more out of her, either that day or any time after that. Strong and steady in her massive seating, she always seemed in no hurry to go anywhere until she hurried to leave life for good. To understand why Toh-the-Gigantic would refer to this here as a somewhere else, to ask how could this place be also one located hundreds of miles away, and to wonder how could the past double the present, I had to slowly take in Cham history and its many lines again, without her, in her absence. For Toh-the-Gigantic had left us, on the road, leaving us to watch for her, maybe forever. Watching matters.

Bobor, Kambor, and Phum Bor come up sometimes when Cham history is mentioned in pieces through oral accounts, random conversations, rituals, and more. Those places, which I have named otherwise, come up under different names in chronicles entangling Cham and Cambodian historiographies. That tight neighborhood of hamlets acquires peculiar *lettres de noblesse* in the seventeenth- and nineteenth-century narratives: Chams from that area are strong, independent, loyal to the end, and ready to die for a king to defend. We are also told that they might be just about ready to murder a king for no good reason at all (Khin Sok 1991; Mak Phoeun 1987, 1995; Weber 2014).

During the Cambodian Middle-Period,[16] movements and uprisings within the Khmer Royal Palace were frequent: reigns were tumultuous; successions often opened to debates and interpretations (Chandler 2000; Mikaelian 2009). Chams carrying a reputation of military knowhow became the convenient missing link to support a conquest or brutally end it (Mak Phoeun 1994; Po Dharma 1982, 1996, 1997; Weber 2014). Their strength was used to support one opponent against another. One against another: a prince against another, and along yet another prince, one Cham community against another. So that it would be too simple, if not just impossible, to summarize everything as the struggle of a marginalized minority against a ryuling majority.

Chams took different roads to reach the royal palace: either attempting to murder the ruler or trying to offer protective services. When the princes, supported by a significant number of those Chams, lost access to their thrones, the Khmer royal chronicles and colonial archives spoke of "Chams agitators" and "Muslim rebellions" (Aymonier 1891; Khin Sok 1991; Mak Phoeun 1994; Moura 1883; Weber 2014). The villages of Bobor, Kambor, and Phum Bor became entangled in those movements, inscribed as the center of the fire.

Those villages now flash as an image of struggle for both Chams and Khmers from nearby and afar. The image endures across time and across place: the villages may have been geographically displaced, the few survivors and descendants may have been relocated, the origins of those movements may have been erased, but the villages' names leave the imprint of history along their roads. A sense of something "difficult," carried away and carried on.

Rulers did away with their Cham opponents the way Imam-Full-of-Stories-History-Buff and his grandmother relate: through forced displacements that left little traces but roads; through massacres that left too many ghosts to care for; through things "too difficult" to tell and listen, to read and write, to see and make see (see Stock 2019).

Those displacements aimed to bring potential future rebels—Chams from the Province-of-the-Plantations—under stricter surveillance of the royal palace, then located in the District-by-the-Lake. "So, the king asked us to come," says Toh-the-Gigantic in a fragmented telling: "Closer to the royal palace He said, closer to Him. What were we to do? Not come?! Of course, we came! We had to. So, we came closer. Closer to the royal palace. Closer to Him."

Here we are: on the road.

The king(s) did know how to put an end to the circle of "uprisings": out of the worst enemy, Chams had to be disciplined into the best ally . . . or be gone. So, the king sent his army to the Province-of-the-Plantations. And the rest followed. The road: of all of those who stayed over there—Bobor, Kambor, and Phum O—not many survived the battles. Of all of those who went on the roads into the deportations, not many survived the repressions. Not many survived the exhaustion, the pain, the separations, the sorrows: it was *difficult*. This was the road *strewn with dead bodies. The bodies of Chams. The bodies of ancestors* of Imam-Full-of-Stories-History-Buff.

For those who had stayed alive and finally given up into an alliance with the king, weapons had to be dropped, swords confiscated, families bound around the capital. Once closer to the king, Chams would be placed under his protection, under his control. Some found it just a little too close: "The sand here is too dirty for our hands O king. Please let us walk further O king," echoes the halted whisper of Toh-the-Gigantic. And so, they would go further. Further down the road. "The soil here is not proper to grow rice O king. Please let us go further, O king." And so, they would go further still. Further down the road. Till a string of Cham villages spread along the road: from the former Khmer royal capital to Village-of-the-Enduring and beyond. But what to make of the string of villages of Bobor, Kambor, and Phum O? A string here, in the Village-of-the-Enduring, a string there in the afar, way deep into The-Province-of-the-Plantations. One hiding under the then thick forest; the other shining over the lake. One: centuries ago; the other: now. Toh-the-Gigantic offers a conclusion:

> We used to be from there.
> From the Bobor, the Kambor, the Phum O, over there.
> We came here.
> It may seem just like one village over here [the Village-of-the-Enduring] because those names are hidden under one single name.
> So, to . . . [pause] forget.
> But this village, it has many insides.
> Many small villages within one.
> Just like back there, back then.
> Toh-the-Gigantic takes a deep breath. She pulls her sarong back over her chest, and stops. She stops history right here.

Roads: On Bearing the Absence in Watching

"So to . . . Forget . . ." as Toh-the-Gigantic offers to ponder.

It might be tempting to characterize all refusals of historiography, all stories of history starting and ending in silence, as markers of specific trauma. One cannot, after all, speak the unspeakable. But I think there is something to be said about those silent repetitions, those evocative re-orientations to an eternal "something else." We don't exactly know what Toh-the-Gigantic means with "so to . . . forget." She doesn't educate us in any of the facts that have to be forgotten: What happened exactly? What was the itinerary? How many died and how many survived? When did that all happen? Is it still 1858 we are talking about or are the long 1970s coming back haunting? Toh-the-Gigantic doesn't provide us with any of those details. This may be because she doesn't herself hold any of the answers we long for. But she holds something else: a sense that things covered by the "so to . . . forget" are too difficult to be uncovered. A sense that writing history, sometimes, requires the ink of absence. This forgetting is, therefore, an erasure that conceals as much as it reveals. It is a form of respect given to history, one where what really matters is to get a sense for it, one that will stand the suppression of facts, one that will stand the absence of witness, one that will stand the impossibility of trials. A history that will stand the forgetting that is required each time we remember.

The notion of absence as a form of remembering itself is not proper to Chams. It can be found in Cambodia at various periods, as demonstrated in the works of historian Ashley Thompson and anthropologist Fabienne Luco. In Cambodian's contemporary writing and art, Thompson shows how external observers often read the lack of commemoration or remembrance of the Khmer Rouge's exactions as a refusal to remember or a will to forget. In contrast to this position, Thompson reads such an absence as a form of "re-membering" (Thompson 2013). This forgetting as re-membering can be better seen, she suggests, if we pay careful attention to the "approximate care for relics" consisting of "apparent neglect" and "abandon" in the Cambodian countryside funeral sites (Thompson 2013: 89). Luco also works against the trope of "amnesia" and shows how memory cannot be seen when what we look for are commemorative traces: the kind of memory lived by Khmers inhabiting the historical site of Angkor has little to do with monuments or archives. It is about locating history in the landscape, situating oneself in space, and inhabiting temporalities on-site (Luco 2016). When Toh-the-Gigantic drops "so to . . . forget" in a conversation that she is about to leave, what she may ask us to do is to stay put, at that moment, so that we too can re-member. Her making of history leads us to re-member the road despite its apparent absence, or even despite its overwhelming repetition and multiplicity, despite the *heaps of details* threatening of erasure at all times.

History Matters

What then do those many roads contained in the single image of "The Road" tell us about the image that history can be? What does it say about the history that Chams see with, when its image is conjured as a line of dots? This might tell us that there wasn't *a* road. Singular. There were many roads to make this history. Histories. Plural. There were many roads taken by the Chams in their migrations to Cambodia: they took boats on rivers, they crossed forests and jungles, they went over the top, over the hills up north. And in the end, they arrived at different times and different places. Because they had left at different times and different places, those moments fuse into one single image to re-member: *a very long road*. Many generations were part of the process. Some left this place we tend to call Champa so long ago that it seems like no one was Muslim just yet.[17] Some left only a few ancestors ago: recently, there was still a great-grandmother or a great-grandfather alive to remember it (Mak Phoeun 1987; Po Dharma 1983; Weber 2014). A multitude of roads, an entanglement of lines.

The lines of Ong-Angry-Not-So's manuscript are not straight. Neither were the roads of the deportations: people left the Province-of-the-Plantation to relocate in the District-by-the-Lake, but in doing so, they didn't stop the line. They just curved it around, picked it up yet again, paused in the blank, starting all over not from nothing, but by following traces left by ancestors. Some of them later went back to the Province-of-the-Plantation, attempting to find what was left of their beloved ones, dots at best. Some of them went away yet another way, all the way back to what is now Vietnam, leading us to the end of the blank page to know more.

In thinking the image of roads to tell lines, Imam-Full-of-Stories-History-Buff and Toh-the-Gigantic are sketching for us a theory, an image of history. But again, the road is not "just" an image. It is lived repeatedly as it is told—hence an economy of telling, reading, and writing. Images come to us. They take us in, yet a little too far into *the difficult*. Ancestors had to walk those roads. They left traces. Actual traces with many bodies left on the side: "She was a tiny little kid. She was too little to see. Her father was closing her eyes with his hands so she wouldn't see the bodies | ghosts all over the road. She told me so," adds Imam-Full-of-Stories-History-Buff about his grandmother. *She was too little to see. And yet she saw.*

History to come to us in full materiality, even in the absence of concrete: we have to hold on, despite having nothing to hold on to. We have to see, even if there is nothing to see, even if we are too little to see, even if it is *too difficult* to do so. No paper marks, no road to follow, no explicit storyline. And yet an insistence from ancestors to follow them. And yet their persistence in leaving no traces. Imam-Full-of-Stories-History-Buff once completed his telling of the road with the least amount of history, it seems. And yet truth as only history knows it. The field notes below weave in the ethnographer contextualizing, doing the work of journaling as an introspective process required by her profession, allowing her to pause before she goes into citation:

> He paused.
> And that pause was a long one.
> He turned his face to me.
> Looked.
> Then he sided away and said:
> The "lines."
> [the term here can imply roads, lineages, or ancestors all at once] . . .
> They didn't leave any trace.
> Their foot didn't leave any print on the floor.
> So they couldn't be followed.
> And like that . . .
> They're gone.

They didn't leave footprints on the road. They left no traces on their way. They are gone. Unread, unwritten, unseen. But that unreading, unwriting, and unseeing cannot merely be categorized as disappearance. It is an absence that makes history present. The kind of presence that is always on the edge of vanishing. Or, as my ethnographic field notes recall, echoing what I am told (in passing) again and again, over time and by quite a few:

> Read that manuscript
> You cannot
> It is burnt out
> Dig that sword

> You shall not
> It is buried
> Check out that photograph
> You won't
> It's lost.

History can never be touched, for it is always, in essence, burnt out, buried, or lost. And yet, it always comes back, haunting in its most touching way. Just as lines ghost us because they are never mentioned while still lurking around, history is continuously placed under erasure the moment it reveals itself: "This cannot be told|read, cannot be written|copied, cannot be seen|made seen." Just as roads and lines of ancestors are "difficult" to picture, so is history. The lines of history are not just metaphors one thinks with: they have a haptic, affective reality. They knock you out as you grapple with them.

History cannot be told because it can upset the dead. Leave them alone already. Let them leave you too. It cannot be read because it can be just too much: it will hold on to you, that's for sure, but are you certain you can hold it? The reading out loud will move you, physically, emotionally. There is no other way, they say. That's what it is to move along history, to follow her way. The image of history that Chams are after might be one of blank lines and discontinued dots, just as those inscribed on the manuscript of Ong-Angry-Not-So.

People may have never seen the manuscript itself and yet still understand what the lines may be about: roads and ancestors. But they may also be unknown at the same time: the manuscript and its lines go into a certain death every time the manuscript is packed back into its black plastic bag. The lines are also about something and about nothing at the same time: they can be read as roads, lineages, and threads, but mostly they are not read, or nothing is read off them. The lines are inscribed on paper, dot after dot, and yet the last dot seems to be a footprint that does not leave trace. The last dot appears to be ours to inscribe, in the blank of the page, out in the open left for us tell, read, write . . . see. Something Ingold (2007) also calls us to do.

Just because we cannot see the road doesn't mean it doesn't exist; just because lineages can't be inscribed doesn't mean they shouldn't be followed; just because history can't be voiced doesn't mean we shouldn't listen. *Carefully. Attentively.*

History defines herself by the traces she leaves for you to present her. You cannot see the road: you have to live it. You have to move along the road. As ancestors move along the road of history, they show us the way. They inscribe traces to be followed in repetition, movement, and attention (Ingold 2007). They move along those roads so that history can move us. They care enough to watch the road for us who are unable to see with our eyes. They look for the road, they look *with* the road, and in doing so, they do more than merely see it. They are "watching the road": an expression that, in Khmer,[18] indicates a caring, a longing, a protective attention. While seeing implies a distance, this watching brings you to a close: watching the road is to look with history and with lines. Those are lines of affection, as this process is always one of profound care.

I am leaving this conclusion, reader, to some ethnographic field notes, something completely different, we might think, with someone else, much somewhere else. Something an old, caring teacher once—or was it so many times—said. Something with very little relevance, it may seem, and yet . . . It is a field note taken from very early attempts in fieldwork, in endeavors that had nothing to do with my research on Cham history and its image. This particular quote is from Ong-Old-and-Cranky, with whom I was studying magic and divination in a much too casual manner and irregularity for his taste. The first lines in each paragraph of the extract to follow indicate that they would be actually spoken out; or, rather, they are the most standard translation into English from Khmer. The lines following them, contained in brackets, offer additional interpretations, layering the poetics of translation that often go unacknowledged in our research reports. In doing so, they provide the ultimate reminder in history—as in most things: that watching, in the end, right from the beginning does indeed matter (Figure 2.2.1).

Where have you been?!! It's been so long . . . I've watched the road for you . . .
[*Which in English could also translate as:*
I've cared for the road to bring you back
I have missed you on this road empty of you
I have longed for you, hoping you would come]
You know, one day I will be gone, and then nobody will be here to watch the road for you.
[*Which in English could also translate as:*
nobody will be here to care for you
nobody will be here to miss you
nobody will be here to long for you]
Oh well, who cares, nobody ever watches the road [for me] anyway.
　　　—Early 2000s. Ong-Old-and-Cranky.

Old, cranky, caring teacher, now gone off the road.
I am watching Ong. Constantly. Still. I watch for You . . . Very much.

Figure 2.2.1　A page of the manuscript of Ong-Angry-Not-So, 2007, Cambodia. Photo by the author.

Notes

1 I wish to thank Erick White, Nicolas Weber, and Alberto Perez Pereiro for their views and comments on some of the preliminary drafts of this chapter. During the early workings of this chapter, I benefited from the comments and advices of Magnus Fiskesjo (through his seminar Making History on the Margins: The China-Southeast Asia Borderlands), Paul Nadasdy (through the Cornell Anthropology Proseminar) and Aaron Sachs (through the informal gatherings of Historians are Writers!). I am grateful to all the suggestions through which this piece grew.

2 The narrative of collapse of a centralized Cham kingdom (Champa) set as the source of origins, and of Cambodia set as the "final" destination, has been revised by both historians (Vickery 2005) and anthropologists alike (Taylor 2007) to show more complex and varied dynamics within a more diverse diaspora. Taking into account a reader unfamiliar with Cambodian and Cham histories, I am keeping the trope of origins and destinations here for the sake of simplicity. It also serves to note that this narrative is pervasive among a majority of Cambodians, and even among a number of Chams.

3 All names of individuals and places have been modified. I have chosen pseudonyms such as "Auntie-So-and-So" and "Village-Here-and-There," as a process more hospitable to conveying a sense of who my correspondents are than would the mere substitution of one name for another. This naming process also feels closer to the way we recall relations among many Chams, among many inhabitants of Southeast Asia, and surely in many other places of the world: we address individuals and refer to them by family terms such as "Auntie" or "Little Brother," coupled with idiosyncrasies and personal characteristics to recall them. Those made-up names carry the multidimensional and affective relationships that we develop with each other better than any other pseudonym could. *Ong* here implies the respect given to an elder and can roughly translate as "grandfather."

4 In other places, I explore how "Cham Script" is defined differently by the scholar of Cham studies and the reader-writer of Cham. While scholars (whether Chams or foreigners) generally consider "Cham script" to be solely the alphabet of Devanagari import, a majority of Chams often consider Jawi and other forms of Arabic transcriptions to be "Cham script." Here, for the sake of simplicity, I take "Cham script" to be the one emphasized in the manuscript—"the script of the ancients" as many refer to it, today read and written by a very small minority of Chams in Cambodia.

5 I am borrowing here from Tim Ingold, for whom the anthropologist is "a correspondent observer at large [who] does his or her thinking in the world" (Ingold 2014: 391).

6 Those dotted lines also appear as connecting text to image in some Malay manuscripts, as shown in a few examples from Kelantana and Patani, as well as Bali where they are known as "rows of ants" (Yahya 2016: 75). I am grateful to Farouk Yahya for pointing out those references to me.

7 While the ethnographic materials and conclusions exposed in this chapter are my own, I found support, encouragement, and a sense of correspondence in Ingold's anthropology of lines (2007). Ingold encourages us to consider an anthropology of lines to understand relations in human life and experience among movement, knowledge, and description. The learning with lines that Ingold puts into practice does not separate locomotion from cognition, something that will come to resonance with how Cham history and roads are entangled.

8 Cambodian Chams often fluently read Khmer, the language taught in public primary school, and have in addition a variable reading command of Arabic or Jawi through religious education. Cham, the language primarily spoken at home, is read or written by only a very small and localized minority in what is referred to as "Cham script" or "Ka-Kha" (after the first two letters of the alphabet).

9 Resisting the temptation of unequivocal translations, I layer the multiplicity of meanings and interpretations that both Cham and Khmer can carry in English by halting the reading with the graphic "|." The symbol aims to remind the reader of the choices that I make, or that I do not make, as a translator.

10 Scholars of what is often referred to as "the sensory turn" show that the division of senses is both a historical and cultural product—one far from being ubiquitous—on how humans approach perception and experience (Classen 1997, 2012; Geurts 2002, Howes 2003; Stoller 1995).

11 The idea that historians rely on "facts" is one long deconstructed within the field of history itself: from Carr's "imaginative understanding" (Carr 1961) to the more recent calls to writing history

as literature (Jablonka 2018) and the contribution of feminist and queer history to the reconsideration of the archives (Arondekar et al. 2015; Stoler 2010).

12 I echo Ingold's definition of education here as a process akin to anthropology since both are forms of *correspondence* requiring a "patient experimentation" working "more by intuition than by reason" (Ingold 2018: 41).

13 The term that Imam-Full-of-Stories-History-Buff uses translates as "grandmother" but could very well be "great-grandmother" or any female ancestor in time.

14 Stories of history are often stopped short, in their telling, by the narrator retreating into an end since things become "too difficult" (to tell, read, write, see, and make seen). Often, a switch to a completely different topic is generated by this moment: an invitation to a neighbor's wedding, an instruction to eat, a redirection in the conversation toward the ethnographer's life and news.

15 *Toh* here implies the respect given to an elder and can roughly translate as "grandmother."

16 The Middle-Period refers in both linguistics and history to the interval between Angkor's collapse (fifteenth century) and the French Protectorate (nineteenth century).

17 There has long been, among Cham studies scholars, a debate as to whether Chams arrived in Cambodia already Muslim (the "conversion" event taking place before the departure from Champa/Vietnam), or actually became Muslim at a later stage, within Cambodia, as they settled along communities of Malays.

18 My interlocutors speak in both Cham and Khmer on a daily basis, some of them more comfortable with the former, some with the latter. The notes that I use in this chapter are taken from conversations mostly in Khmer, since my command of Cham early in my research didn't allow me to conduct full discussions.

References

Arondekar, Anjali, Ann Cvetkovich, Christina B. Hanhardt, Regina Kunzel, Tavia Nyong'o, Juana María Rodríguez, Susan Stryker, Daniel Marshall, Kevin P. Murphy, and Zeb Tortorici. 2015. "Queering Archives: A Roundtable Discussion." *Radical History Review* (2015) 122: 211–231.

Aymonier, E. (Etienne). 1891. *Les Tchames et Leurs Religions*. Paris: E. Leroux.

Bacigalupo, Ana Mariella. 2016. *Thunder Shaman: Making History with Mapuche Spirits in Chile and Patagonia*. 1st ed. Austin, TX: University of Texas Press.

Benjamin, Walter. 1969. "Thesis on the Philosophy of History." In *Illuminations: Essays and Reflections*, edited by Hannah Arendt, 253–265. New York: Schocken.

Chandler, David P. 2000. *A History of Cambodia*. 3rd ed. Boulder, CO: Westview Press.

Classen, Constance. 1997. "Foundations for an Anthropology of the Senses." *International Social Science Journal* 49 (153): 401–412.

Classen, Constance. 2012. *The Deepest Sense: A Cultural History of Touch*. Urbana, IL: University of Illinois Press.

Cohen, Anouk, and Damien Mottier. 2016. "Pour une Anthropologie des Matérialités Religieuses." *Archives de Sciences Sociales des Religions* 174 (April–June): 349–368.

Geurts, Kathryn Linn. 2002. *Culture and the Senses: Bodily Ways of Knowing in an African Community*. Berkeley, CA: University of California Press.

Howes, David. 2003. *Sensual Relations: Engaging the Senses in Culture and Social Theory*. Ann Arbor: University of Michigan Press.

Hugh-Jones, Stephen, and Hildegard Diemberger. 2012. "L'objet Livre." In *L'objet Livre, Terrain: Anthropologie and Sciences Humaines* 59: 4–17. Paris: Maison des sciences de l'homme: Ministère de la Culture et de la Communication.

Ingold, Tim. 2007. *Lines: A Brief History*. London and New York: Routledge.

Ingold, Tim. 2008. "Anthropology Is Not Ethnography." *Proceedings of the British Academy* 154: 69–92.

Ingold, Tim. 2018. *Anthropology and/as Education*. Abingdon, UK: Routledge, an imprint of the Taylor & Francis Group.

Jablonka, Ivan. 2018. *History Is a Contemporary Literature: Manifesto for the Social Sciences*. Translated by Nathan Bracher. Ithaca, NY: Cornell University Press.

Khin Sok. 1991. *Le Cambodge Entre le Siam et le Viêtnam: de 1775 à 1860*. Paris: EFEO (École française d'Extrême-Orient); Adrien-Maisonneuve [distributor].

Luco, Fabienne. 2016. *Les Habitants d'Angkor: Une Lecture dans L'espace et dans le Temps des Inscriptions Sociales de Populations Villageoises Installées dans un Territoire Ancien*. Thesis, EHESS, Paris. https://tel. archives-ouvertes.fr/tel-01706247/document

Mak Phoeun. 1984. *Chroniques Royales du Cambodge: Des Origines Légendaires Jusqu'à Paramaja Ier*. Vol. I. Paris: EFEO (École française d'Extrême-Orient); Adrien-Maisonneuve [distributor].

Mak Phoeun. 1990. "La Communaute Malaise Musulmane au Cambodge (de la fin du XVIe siecle Jusqu'au roi Musulman Ramadhipati Ier)." In *Le Monde Indochinois et la Péninsule Malaise*, 47–68. Kuala Lumpur: Malaysia. Kementerian Kebudayaan dan Pelancongan, Ambassade de la France en Malaisie.

Mak Phoeun.1994. "La Communauté Cam au Cambodge du Xve au Xixe Siècle." In *Proceedings of the Seminar on Champa: Held at the University of Copenhagen on May 23, 1987*. Copenhagen: Southeast Asia Community Resource Center.

Mikaelian, Grégory. 2009. *La Royauté d'Oudong. Réformes Institutionnelles et Crise Du Pouvoir Dans Le Royaume Khmer Du XVIIe Siècle*. Paris: Presses Universitaires de la Sorbonne (PUPS).

Moura, Jean. 1883. *Le Royaume du Cambodge*. Paris: E. Leroux.

Po Dharma. 1982. "Note sur les Cam du Cambodge: Religion et Organisation." *Seksar Khmer* V: 103–116.

Po Dharma. 1987. *Le Pāṇḍuraṅga (Campā) 1802–1835: Ses Rapports Avec le Vietnam*. Paris: Ecole française d'Extrême-Orient.

Po Dharma. 1998. "Les Cam et Malais au Cambodge: Organisation Socio-Religieuse." In *International Conference on Khmer Studies: Knowledge of the Past and its Contributions to the Rehabilitation and Reconstruction of Cambodia*, edited by Sorn Samnang. Phnom Penh: Royal University of Phnom Penh.

Stock, Emiko. 2019. "Archiving the Difficult to Picture," *Southeast Of Now: Directions in Contemporary and Modern Art in Asia*, 3(2), National University of Singapore, Singapore, 131–148.

Stoler, Ann Laura. 2010. *Along the Archival Grain: Epistemic Anxieties and Colonial Common Sense*. Princeton, NJ: Princeton University Press.

Stoller, Paul. 1995. *Embodying Colonial Memories: Spirit Possession, Power, and the Hauka in West Africa*. New York: Routledge.

Taylor, Philip. 2007. *Cham Muslims of the Mekong Delta: Place and Mobility in the Cosmopolitan Periphery*. Edited by Asian Studies Association of Australia. Honolulu, HI: Asian Studies Association of Australia, in association with University of Hawai'i Press.

Thompson, Ashley. 2013. "Forgetting to Remember, Again: On Curatorial Practice and 'Cambodian Art' in the Wake of Genocide." *Diacritics* 41 (2): 82–109. https://www.jstor.org/stable/43305657.

Trouillot, Michel-Rolph. 2012. *Silencing the Past: Power and the Production of History*. Boston, MA: Beacon Press.

Vickery, Michael. 2005. "Champa Revised." *ARI Working Paper*, No. 37, March 2005. https://cupdf. com/document/wps-37-champa-revised.html.

Weber, Nicolas. 2014. *Histoire de la Diaspora Cam*. Paris: Les Indes savantes.

Yahya, Farouk. 2016. *Magic and Divination in Malay Illustrated Manuscripts*. Oxford: Barakat.

2.3

THE RECURSIVITY OF THE FETISH

Roger Sansi

The fetish keeps on coming back. In the last few years, at least two new monographs on the fetish have been published (Morris 2017; Matory 2018), and the problem of the fetish has been the focus of an open debate between two major figures in anthropology (Graeber 2015; Viveiros de Castro 2015). So much has been written about the fetish in the last few centuries, especially in the last thirty years; in particular, after the publication of William Pietz's seminal set of essays "Problem of the Fetish," numbered I, II, and IIIa. Pietz inspired many authors to try to solve the problem, such as "The Problem of the Fetish, IIIb" (Graeber 2005). If Pietz's work was so authoritative, did it need a supplement, a IIIb?

Perhaps the supplement, the constant addition, variation, repetition of the theme, is part of the very problem of the fetish. The fetish always draws back to itself, in its infinite recursion. The constitutive incompleteness of the fetish, as a thing, as a concept, invites constant iterations, additions, returns to the thing. By attempting to close the circle, we add more and more layers to this very indeterminacy. In the context of this *Handbook of Material Religion*, the return to the fetish is inevitable (a curse? a fixation?). The problem of the fetish, a thing, a concept, a text (or a set of texts, unfinished) is at the origin, and end, of many of the discussions on religion and materiality in the last few decades. The fetish is the epitome of material religion (Meyer 2012). The focus on the materiality of religion does not only imply a shift from research in immaterial ideas, myths, symbols, spirits, or gods toward the physical objects that represent them. It has also implied a deeper questioning of the very distinctions between the immaterial and the material sides of religion: ideas and matter, signifier and signified, gods and things. At the base of this questioning lies the irreducible problem of the fetish. This chapter will not pretend to close the circle of the fetish, but to reflect on its recursive constitution, exploring the different iterations of the concept. Starting as usual, by the origin of the problem.

The Birth of the Fetish

"Fetishism" was a term invented by Charles De Brosses in 1760 to identify the adoration of objects and natural events. The "fetish" was the very object of adoration: not just the representation or image of a divinity, but a material object or natural event that is worshiped as a divinity itself. These terms originally make reference to religious worship, but they have

DOI: 10.4324/9781351176231-12

also been applied to other domains in which things acquire the qualities of persons—as in Marxist commodity fetishism or Freudian sexual fetishism.

Fetish and *fetishism* are two of the most controversial and contradictory terms in the social sciences. They have been explicitly rejected as anthropological concepts since the late nineteenth century; for Marcel Mauss, they revealed an "enormous misunderstanding" (Iacono 1992: 116). Yet, in recent decades, there has been a growing interest in this very misunderstanding, this "problem of the fetish" (Pietz 1985, 1987, 1988). The "problem" of the fetish touches upon some of the basic distinctions of Western thought: people and things, action and event, subject and object, culture and nature, religion and economy. The questioning of these very distinctions—not just in material religion, but also in recent social theory in general—has inevitably brought the problem of the fetish back to the center of attention.

We should start by addressing the original "misunderstanding" that gave birth to "the problem of the fetish." As Pietz says (1985: 5), the "fetish" is a cross-cultural and historical event: it was born in the writings of European travelers to West Africa in the seventeenth century to identify a supposedly African phenomenon. This is the first misunderstanding: the term "fetish" does not come from any African language, but from the Portuguese word *feitiço*. And yet, there is a significant shift between "*feitiço*" and "fetish." The Portuguese *feitiço* is a magical event—a spell or charm, an act of sorcery; not exactly a divinity, but a magical action. The term itself has a long and interesting etymology: it comes from the Latin "*factitius*" (Bohme 2006), which connotes "made up" or "artificial"; from there comes the Medieval Latin "*maleficium*," something said or done for or with magical effect. In fact, in Portuguese "*coisa feita*" ("something done") is synonymous with "*feitiço*" (Sansi 2007, 2011). The *feitiço* was persecuted not only because it was evil, but also because it was a trick, a falsification. Originally, *feitiçaria* was more an object of law than of theology (Pietz 1987: 31). *Feitiçaria* is always an accusation; no one would admit to being a *feiticeiro*: it was not an organized religion, but a false practice and perception. This introduced a considerable ambiguity in its persecution.

The discourse of the *feitiço* arrived to the coasts of West Africa with the Portuguese in the fifteenth century. The Portuguese addressed the pagan practices of the Africans as "idolatries and sorceries" (*Idolatrias e feitiçarias*) (Sansi 2007, 2011). Idolatry would be a form of organized religion but with false images of gods or "idols" (Bernand and Gruzinski 1988); *feitiçaria*, on the other hand, would not be organized religion, but individual practices of sorcery. Where does "fetishism" fit into this picture? The discourse of the fetish and fetishism emerges in the seventeenth and eighteenth centuries not in the writings of the Portuguese but in those of other European travelers (Morris 2017), essentially Dutch and Protestant ones like De Marees (1602), Dapper (1686), and Bosman (1705). For these travelers, the *fetissos* were the gods of the Africans, and the *fetisseiros* were their priests. The reference to the Portuguese term is anecdotal—or, better, misrecognized. Misrecognition and disavowal are in fact central to the "problem" of the fetish (Morris 2017). As opposed to a discourse of idolatry, these travelers understood that Africans worshiped the *objects* as gods—not as images (idols) of the gods. This was the novelty of the discourse of fetishism in relationship to idolatry: its "untranscended materiality," in Pietz's terms; the object does not represent a god, but it is a god itself.

The Dutch tradesman Bosman made one of the more accurate accounts of the fetish. According to him, Africans worshiped objects, like stones, trees, even animals and artifacts. What was more surprising was that Africans recognized that they were "found" by chance, that they made them with their own hands, and that they had as many as they wished (they were uncountable).

In other terms, they recognized that their gods were artifices made by them. The priests of these *fetissos* were the *fetisseiros,* inevitably defined as greedy, power-mongering, and treacherous, manipulating the fear of the people for their own benefit. Bosman was not just scandalized by what he identified as the hypocrisy of the priests; he also thought that most people were quite aware of the fatuousness of their beliefs, but still they believed in the *fetissos.*

In Bosman's argument, we can identify some of the core issues of the problem of the fetish. First is the "confusion" of creation and the creator: Africans, for Bosman, worship things of their own making, instead of worshiping the creator who made the Africans. Second, African religion is described as a form of trade and exploitation by a priestly elite who manipulates the masses. Still, Bosman is adamant to make clear that these masses are fully aware of their exploitation and yet still accept it—again, the theme of misrecognition. Ultimately, Bosman's reading is also full of misrecognition; behind the construction of an "African" other, it seems clear that the model he is attacking is much closer in space and time: the Papism of the Portuguese who preceded Bosman and the Dutch in the African trade, and who still were their main enemies and competitors in the Atlantic world.

In fact, the problem of the fetish was not just one of religion but also one of commerce. For Bosman, the difficulty of trading with Africans was that they valued things irrationally, according to "caprice." The issue, then, was how to establish the terms of exchange between two different systems of value. Protestant European traders were particularly annoyed when they were obliged to make "fetish-oaths" on the objects that Africans worshipped. The objects of trade themselves were also subject to this ambiguity and artificiality: European traders were particularly wary of "fetish-gold" (Atkins 1735: 183)—gold mixed with other metals.

Fetishism

In the end, this is more a story of misrecognitions than of misunderstandings. The theory of fetishism that emerged was built on these misrecognitions, but it nonetheless had crucial importance in the history of social thought. In *Du Culte des Dieux Fétiches,* Charles De Brosses (1760) finally developed a full-fledged theory of the fetish and invented the term "fetishism." For De Brosses, the African fetish is not just a curiosity but also a general model at the origin of all religions—starting with Egypt. For De Brosses, the origins of religion are fear and need: "savages" would worship unexpected events and beings that they couldn't understand and control, addressing them as persons with a will and power superior to those of humans—indeed, addressing them as gods. This is not a naturalism, or a religion of nature, since fetishism does not have a notion of "nature" as opposed to the social or the supernatural. Fetishism confuses people with things, events with actions, the given with the made, and immanence with transcendence.

With his theory of fetishism, De Brosses organized the most powerful argument against religion in a century of skepticism. By identifying the worship of things as the first step of religion, it was finally possible to integrate the criticism of religion to a general theory of progress, which would see the Enlightenment as the last, logical end of human achievement. In modern Europe, people had finally managed to relate to things just in the terms of science (as objects of natural law), or in the terms of the economy (as commodities with a market value)—separate from any religious prejudices and fears. Religion, science, and economy would be finally separated in what Bruno Latour (1993) has called a process of "purification," separating their religious beliefs from material things altogether.

By the same token, the African fetishists would be seen as the more primitive and abject of humans. For Immanuel Kant,

> [The cult of fetishes] is so disgraceful that it seems to contradict human nature. A feather, a horn, a shellfish or any common thing, just being consecrated with some words, becomes an object of veneration invoked in oaths. The Blacks are extremely vain, and so loud that they have to be dispersed with a stick.
>
> *(Kant 1960: 111)*

G. W. F. Hegel thought that Africans arbitrarily "adored the first thing that comes their way." This was the reason why, for Hegel, fetishism was not even a form of religion, since the fetish was not even an object of religious worship. Africans lived in a moment prior to history, since they lacked "the principle which naturally accompanies all our ideas—the category of Universality" (Hegel 1956: 93). They were slaves of chaotic contingency, or, better, of the false priests who mediated this chaos. The "purification" of religion from science, and of people from things, was also a geopolitical process of the separation of "modern" Europe from fetishist Africa. As a matter of fact, the development of a theory of the fetish was essential for the very construction of this very model of European modernity since it offered a perfect model of what an "impure" humanity would look like. In these terms, the theory of fetishism in the social sciences as an elementary, and mistaken, form of materialism persisted during most of the nineteenth century. Auguste Comte (2001) defined fetishism as the first stage of religious worship, before polytheism and monotheism.

But by the end of the nineteenth century, the use of the term started to be questioned and replaced by other theories. Tylor (1874) subsumed fetishism under his own theory of animism, stating that the object of worship of the fetish was a *spirit* contained in the object, not the object itself. In other terms, he basically questioned the very notion of the fetish as an essentially material entity. Rather than viewing his conclusions as based on specific empirical evidence, we should understand Tylor's questioning of the notion as an attempt to redeem the "primitive" from their banishment outside history and human nature. For the Western tradition, the very distinction between body and spirit, and between object and subject, is at the basis of human reason; and Edward Burnett Tylor, as the founding father of anthropology, was keen to demonstrate on these grounds the psychic unity of humankind, as well as the basic evolutionary capacities of all humans. Fetishism, in these terms, is not just irrational but also outside of reason itself. To recognize the irredeemable materiality of the fetish would question the whole enterprise of a unified description of humanity based on shared reason.

Mauss's rejection of the fetish as an enormous misunderstanding follows Tylor's humanistic approach, denying the very possibility of fetishism and the accusations of irrationality—and even inhumanity—addressed to non-Western peoples. The explicit rejection of fetishism has been central to most of the anthropology of religion since Tylor and Mauss. Jean Pouillon (1975) acknowledged that there was room to discuss ethnographically the question of the fetish, or the material god, but not in the framework of a theory of fetishism. Contemporary cognitive theories of religion, following evolutionary psychology, identify the origin of religion in similar phenomena to the classical theory of fetishism: for example, the abduction of agency in inanimate beings. Still, these phenomena are seen as exceptional and counter-intuitive, or counter-ontological, based on the assumption that all humans share a common rationality and intuitive naturalist ontology (Boyer 2001). Hence, the origin of religion would not be seen as an irrational, generalized belief in the agency of inanimate beings, or fetishism, but the opposite, the surprise produced by the possibility of phenomena that contradict basic ontological assumptions that are universal. It is interesting to note that in this literature, the term "fetishism" is rarely mentioned.

Fetishism as Critique

Paradoxically, by the time that anthropology was rejecting fetishism, the very notion had also been used critically by some of its major contemporary thinkers, Karl Marx and Sigmund Freud. Marx's brief but powerful parable of "commodity fetishism" reverts to the basic parallelisms between religion and commerce that were at the center of the Dutch traders' questioning of the African fetish. For Marx, instead, it was the very Western form of commodity value that could be defined as fetishism (Marx 1992). Marx noticed the same mechanism the European travelers had attributed to African fetishists: people in capitalism make commodities with their own hands, but then misrecognized that the value of these commodities was the result of their own making; in contrast, it is thought that commodities have value in themselves. Freud's use of the notion of the fetish (Freud 1927) would also impinge on the question of misrecognition, or, in more psychoanalytical terms, disavowal. For Freud, the sexual fetish is a thing that becomes a surrogate object of desire, a replacement for the actual object of desire, which is repressed. This object emerges out of the event of an encounter that the fetishist tries to recreate in his or her fantasies. The temporality of the fetish is central to this argument: the fetishist is bound to return to an event in the past and unable to move forward.

Marx's and Freud's approaches involve a clear emphasis on misrecognition and the repression or hiding of the truth of interpersonal relations behind objects, which are falsely endowed with a power they don't have. The combined influence of these two thinkers has been crucial in the twentieth century, and the critical theory of the fetish has been a tool for many modern authors, if in very different ways—from Pierre Bourdieu (1992) to Michael Taussig (1980).

The Irreducible Fetish

As I mentioned, Pietz made a major contribution to the literature of the fetish in a series of articles published in the late 1980s, each with the title "The Problem of the Fetish" (Pietz 1985, 1987, 1988). Pietz offered an encompassing historical account of the term, emphasizing that it was the result of a very specific space and time. According to this author, the "problem" could be defined around four fundamental questions: personification, territoriality, historicity, and reification, which we should address with some detail.

First is personification. Fetishes are intensely personal objects (Pietz 1985: 11): they add to the person, as, for example, in the case of wearing an amulet as protection from assault. By the same token, parts of a person—when stolen or found by enemies—can also be used in sorcery. This is a form of distributed personhood, as Gell notes (1998), although it is based on negative reciprocity: a distributed person has to avoid leaving dispersed pieces of his or her self to avoid the risk of sorcery, and has to add to the body elements that can act as shields. But of course, to make these shields work, one has to give a part of one's self to them, as an offering in a mediated exchange between person and thing; the fetishes have to become a part of the person, not just instruments or technological devices. That is why other people cannot use a person's own fetish: because they are a part of the self.

The life and the value of the fetish, however, cannot be solely understood as an extension of the personhood of humans: it is also a result of its territoriality and historicity. On the one hand, the "untranscended" materiality of the fetish, which is not just a symbol or icon of a divinity but also a "self-contained entity" with an active force, introduces the question of the position of the object in space and time as a "territorialized" object (Pietz 1985:

12). The "life" of the fetish is conditioned by material constraints, in space and in time: its inability to move physically, which makes it strictly dependent on its human associates; and its inscription in a concrete and specific place where it is protected, like an altar or a body. But these are not the only ways in which materiality influences processes of value. In contrast, Pietz notes that "the fetish is always a meaningful fixation of a singular event; it is above all a 'historical' object, the enduring material form and force of an unrepeatable event" (1985: 12). This is what defines the historicity of the fetish: that is, emerges from a unique, specific, and unrepeatable event. It is not only a material object but a historical object. What was interpreted as "caprice" or "arbitrary" choice is, in fact, the recognition of the singular values generated by events, which cannot be explained by the list of elements that make a part of the situation before they happen (Latour 2001: 131). Finding a fetish is an event that cannot be planned: it just happens. But, paradoxically, this unexpected event is recognized as meaningful: those who found the fetish recognize in this event something that is a part of themselves, something that becomes personified. Pietz explains this point wonderfully by making reference to Michel Leiris and the surrealist notion of the objet trouvé: "these crisis moments of singular encounter and indefinable transaction between the life of the self and that of the world become fixed, in both places and things, as personal memories that retain a peculiar power to move one profoundly" (Pietz 1985: 12).

The historicity of the fetish founded in events is different from Hegelian notions of history as teleology, where historical events have a finality, driving in one direction. The historicity of the fetish is apparently chaotic: it does not come from any previous event, nor does it lead anywhere. It stands on its own. And yet the event in which the fetish is found is not perceived by the person as arbitrary and random, but as necessary: it *had* to happen. It has a meaning. The value that the person finds in the object is not random, but it is seen as an immanent value of the object, something inchoate that was already there, waiting for this particular person to recognize it. It is as if the thing was offering itself to the person to reveal its true nature; and as if they always belonged together. This point is key to the Freudian discussion of fetishism: the problem of the fetish is that fetishists are obsessed with a traumatic event they try to recreate through an object that, in their mind, embodies the trauma (Freud 1927). This return to the original event, however, is always unsuccessful because the event belongs to the past, not to the present. This circular return entraps fetishists with their objects in an always incomplete circular time.

The last point that Pietz raises is "reification." The fetish, for Protestant European travelers and Enlightenment philosophers, raised the question of the relative value of objects: values were not universal, but dependent on a "particular order of social relations, that in turn, they reinforce" (Pietz 1987: 24). This leads to a questioning of contextualization, or, as Pietz puts it, of reification: how values attributed to objects are in fact constructed by humans. Of course, reification is always an accusation: it is the others who reify, who think, through a process of disavowal, that objects have intrinsic values. Thus, the identification of a system of value with fetishism is an accusation of a false ideological projection, a false consciousness. Stemming from the critical and skeptical definition of De Brosses, the accusation of fetishism became an extreme form of criticism of ideology.

The first three questions that Pietz identifies—personification, territoriality, historicity— are relatively independent from the problem of reification. They are central to the formation of the notion of the fetish in early colonial West Africa, whereas the problem of reification was raised later, in the criticism of the fetish by Enlightenment philosophers in the formation of a theory of fetishism. There is a fundamental difference between the two moments. The first is a moment of intercultural mediation, in which the notion of the fetish emerges in a sphere of exchange; the second is a moment of differentiation and alienation, when enlightened Europeans try to clarify what makes them different from and superior to Africans (and, by the same token, the Portuguese).

Pietz's work inspired a revival of literature on the fetish, developing some of the different lines of his argument. Some were closer to a more conventional reading of fetishism as cultural critique (Apter and Pietz 1993). This strand of literature on critical fetishism has endured and reproduced itself, most recently with, as previously noted, two more volumes addressing "return" and "revisitation" (Morris 2017; Matory 2018). But Pietz also inspired a new strand of literature more interested in the historicity of the fetish as an object of cultural exchange (Spyer 1998). In his work on Protestant missions in Indonesia, Webb Keane (2007) describes the encounter of semiotic ideologies, different sets of semiotic assumptions about agency, and the relations among words, things, and people. For Protestant missionaries, fetishism involved "mistaken" assumptions concerning agency that they encountered among natives. The contradictory ways of approaching the problem of the fetish are exemplified by two very different readings of Pietz: by David Graeber (2005) and Bruno Latour (2010).

Graeber: Fetishism as Social Creativity

The central argument in Graeber's reading of Pietz is a defense of fetishism as social creativity. If fetishism, at root, is our tendency to see our own actions and creations as having power over us, how can we treat it as an intellectual mistake? The bad reputation of fetishism is a result of a misunderstanding. Africans would "make" fetishes as a means of creating social relations. They would not hide the fact that the objects, like the social relations that depended on them, were "made up" and thus were, in a way, arbitrary. The Europeans, however, would not recognize that the value they gave to objects was the result of a social relation: it would be the Europeans who would misrecognize (or disavow) the social construction of reality, as it were, giving it a bad name—fetishism. In Graeber's reading, Europeans and Africans share a certain existential pessimism: both see society and its institutions as necessary evils that have to be institutionalized to prevent chaos. The Europeans and the Africans were not that different, but in fact were all too similar. For Graeber, "it was the underlying affinity, I suspect, which accounted for the common European reaction of shocked revulsion and dismay on being exposed to so many aspects of African ritual: a desperate denial or recognition" (Graeber 2005: 415).

Graeber is underscoring one of the four problems identified by Pietz: the problem of reification—how social values are a social construction. Graeber insists upon the fact that there is nothing abnormal or stupid in using objects as the objectification of social relations, and that this process of objectification is ultimately arbitrary. It is not the object, but the action made upon it, that gives it social power. For Graeber,

> [Objects are] only the medium. Hence what they are is ultimately somewhat arbitrary: one can use valuable objects from faraway lands, or one can, in fact, use pretty much any random object one lays one's hands on, "a Lion's Tail . . . a Bird's Feather . . . a Pebble, a Bit of Rag." In this, Pietz's sources had a point, because this is exactly the moment where the arbitrariness of value comes fully into focus. Because, really, creativity is not an aspect of the objects at all, it's a dimension of action. In this sense, the new does in fact emerge from the old, and the numinous, alien nature of the object is really the degree to which it reflects on that aspect of our own actions that is, in a sense, alien to ourselves.
>
> (Graeber 2005: 425)

In this sense, for Graeber, the object does not actually have any power; the power we attribute to the object is only the result of human actions upon it. But, paradoxically, the problem of the fetish is that humans ignore, misrecognize, or disavow these actions: and hence the power of the object appears as radically alien.

The first question to ask here is if these "Africans" whom Graeber, Pietz, and their sources invoke would actually agree with this idea of creativity. Would they say that, really, the power they recognize in objects is of their own making? It seems like Graeber falls back into the European understanding of the problem of the fetish. The power of objects is not just the result of a process of reification, of imposition of human value. The power of the fetish, or these objects that Europeans identified as fetishes, is not arbitrary but necessary. The power of the fetish is not arbitrarily attributed by the person who finds it, but is recognized by this person as inherent to the object. This power, however, is only revealed in the encounter of the object and that person. In that sense, we could say, it emerges in and by this encounter. It is not "any random object one lays one's hands on, 'a Lion's Tail, a Bird's Feather, a Pebble, a Bit of Rag,'" but it must be, and it could only be, that particular lion's tail, bird's feather, pebble, or bit of rag—found at that specific moment and at that specific place—that unveils the power of the fetish over the subject.

It is not irrelevant, in this sense, that this object has an "alien nature." It is precisely its alien nature—its radical alterity—that awakes the shock of recognition. That connection of subject and object, and of space and time, is not just an action by which the subject infuses the object with his or her creativity, but is an event of encounter that brings about something else, something that was not present before the encounter. This encounter, in other terms, has a historicity. Historicity, as we have seen, is one of the central questions that the problem of the fetish creates for Pietz; and, in many ways, historicity is irreducible to reification.

Latour and the Factish

Latour's *On the Modern Cult of the Factish Gods* (2010) was also written as a follow-up to Pietz. But we should also read it as a follow-up to his now classic pamphlet *We Have Never Been Modern* (1993), where he takes on the question of the great divides of modernity—the "purification" of society from nature, and of people from things. The emergence of the problem of the fetish is crucial in this process of purification—as a first instance when European traders and slave mongers explicitly accused Africans of confusing nature with culture, cause with consequence, people with things, and the producer with the product. Latour argues that it was the construction of this African counterexample that actually helped the Enlightenment objectify these distinctions: essentially the distinctions between nature and culture, between natural law and human convention, and between fact and fetish.

According to the European slave mongers, Africans worshiped the things they made with their own hands. That would not be such a surprise for a cynical, Western, freethinking slave monger who would not necessarily believe in God or religion: all religions were made by men, since gods don't really exist in nature; they are not facts. But still, all religions would hide the construction of the gods: priests would keep the masses in ignorance of this construction. Africans, on the other hand, as Graeber says, were explicit about this construction. In these terms, religions would be described basically as mechanisms of social power, using fetishes as puppets through which they could control the ignorant masses. This, in the long run, became a general theory of society as opposed to nature. Nature would be based on facts—given things that happen in the world—and would respond to natural laws independent of the intentions of humans. Society, however, would not be based on facts but on fetishes, made-up things that happened only within humans responding to human intentions—their will to power. Fetishes, as opposed to facts, would not exist autonomously from humans; they would be just intermediary entities used to veil the agency of humans.

It could be said that Latour is caricaturizing Western thought, which is historically much more polyphonic and diverse than this radical dualism is (Meyer 2019), and yet Latour's caricature is a tool for counteracting this central tradition of Western thought—an extremely powerful discourse that has endured for three hundred years to the present day. This is what Latour (1993) calls the "anti-fetishist" tradition, which sees social institutions as fictions hiding the facts: in general terms, the social domination of some humans over others. Latour wonders if it is possible to overcome this distinction between social fictions and real facts, going back to the roots of the problem of the fetish, to overcome theories that reduce processes of objectification to fetishism, alienation, disavowal, and misrecognition. This is an important point: saying that values are attributed to objects through processes of objectification, and that these processes are culturally relative, is not the same as saying that all attribution of value to objects is a false projection that hides a will to power. This is a point on which Pietz is not clear when he reduces objectification to reification.

After all, the so-called African fetishes inspired the foundations of a great deal of modern European social theory—anti-fetishism. Still, what was shocking for Europeans about Africans was not so much that they believed in fetishes, since this was the very essence of social life everywhere. What was shocking is that they did not hide their fetishism! They acknowledged they made their fetishes with their own hands, and they recognized they were artifacts. But for Latour, as opposed to Graeber, this doesn't mean that Africans were explicit fetishists. In contrast, it means that they did not really make a distinction between facts and fetishes, real and invented things: fetishes were autonomous entities with their own agency, not just because the Africans had had made them. We could say that if Graeber stresses the Pietz argument on reification, Latour stresses the argument on historicity: the recognition of the emergence of new agencies generated by events, which cannot be reduced to the list of elements that make up situations before they happen (Latour 2001: 131). Latour called this hybrid of fact and fetish the "factish."

Latour proposed to reverse social theory from this point. What if Africans were right? What if it does not make sense to distinguish between fact and fetish, things given and things made, natural reproduction and human production, and nature and culture? What if it is all these distinctions that are counterintuitive, strange, and irrational, and not the confusion between these distinctions? Starting from here, Latour's program for a social science is not to reveal the hidden truth of the artifice of social life dissecting fact from fetish, looking for the dark secrets of human nature, but to follow the factish, as it were, to see how things are made into autonomous entities with their own agency.

Is Latour, then, rehabilitating the much-criticized notion of the fetish? His position is quite ambiguous in developing a third, hybrid term—factish. The basic point that Latour was making is that we have to acknowledge the possibility of thinking about agency beyond the human, beyond classical Western distinctions between nature and society and between people and things, and beyond all the oppositions we have inherited from the tradition of Western thought since the Enlightenment. But then why do we need a third term—factish—to bring together fact and fetish if the central argument is that we have to question the oppositions they are premised upon? Isn't the fetish itself the term he is looking for since it brings together facts and fictions, objects and subjects—the fundamental oppositions of Western thought? Latour seems to accept the separation between African fetishists and European anti-fetishists, when in fact this separation is more a result of the emergence of the fetish than a result of its premise. Latour is pointing to the ontological affordance of the fetish, both as thing and as concept: how it emerged, as a new thing and concept that was instrumental to the elaboration of the whole ontological apparatus of modernity. Without the fetish, a myriad of new entities—from the economy and the commodity to the subject, desire, art, facts, and fictions—would not have existed in the way we know them now.

The fetish helped the Europeans in "purifying" moderns from Africans—and nature from society—precisely by showing a counter-model in opposition to which the whole edifice of modern naturalism could be constructed. In fact, Latour's argument is more powerful when read together with cognitive theories of religion. In opposition to theories that defend the existence of a universal, intuitive, naturalist ontology—which is only occasionally contradicted by counter-ontological events—what Latour is proposing is precisely that these "counter-ontological" events show the possibility of other ontologies that question the "naturality," or givenness, of naturalism as the only possible framework. In the same way that the fetish was built as a counter-model to construct naturalism, Latour is proposing to use it to show its gaps as well as the multiplicity of modes of existence it can afford.

The Recursivity of the Fetish

The fetish is an object and term, without authorship or origin, that emerges in an ambiguous borderland of peoples, places, and languages, a concept that is immediately misrecognized, disavowed, and repressed, an idea that has been denounced and withdrawn and ridiculed. And yet, we keep coming back to it. Like the object of fetishist obsession described by psychoanalysis, we keep going back to the (misrecognized) original event, telling the same stories, again and again, hoping that, once and for all, we will be able to close the circle, know what the fetish really is, and break the spell. But each time, the spell seems to grow more powerful, more entangled.

Latour's and Graeber's takes on the fetish go in different directions: one stresses the radical alterity of the fetish, while the other proposes its universality. To develop this point more thoroughly, I will refer to a third author, Eduardo Viveiros de Castro, who has made a direct criticism of Graeber's argument while taking a position similar to Latour's. According to Viveiros de Castro (2015), Graeber reduces the problem of the fetish to a projection of human value. Graeber wants to find an underlining universal human condition through a dialectical method. In opposition to Graeber's argument, Viveiros de Castro approaches the problem of the fetish through a "symmetrical anthropology" (Latour 2017): stating that, rather than demonstrating a shared humanity, the fetish can help us problematize our own assumptions by exposing them to a radical alterity. If Graeber accuses Viveiros of relativism, Viveiros accuses Graeber of reductionism. But neither Graeber nor Viveiros de Castro seems to consider a third possibility that is, in fact, implicit in both Pietz's and Latour's arguments: the fetish is not African, or European, or universal; it is neither "ours" (as in a pre-existing, universal human thought) or "theirs" (as in a pre-existing different ontology or nature-culture). The fetish is neither one nor the other, but an emergent third part. The fetish happens; it is an event, an unexpected outcome of encounter; it performs a new truth, producing a new possible entity that escapes these distinctions. The fetish is not a token of a general type, an iteration of an already existing entity; it does not represent anything previous, but it is always new. It has a specific historicity.

How is it always new? We can go back to the paradox of the fetish in Freud: the fetishist wishes to return to the original event of the fetish—but that is not possible, because the event is in the past. Every enactment or recreation will inevitably be different. This difference can be perceived in terms of lack or desire: what is left wanting for the event to happen. This difference, however, can also be seen in opposite terms: there is always something slightly different, something new, in each enactment, in each performance. Perhaps then, rather than as a trap, a circle that never manages to close, we can see it as an always expanding spiral.

What if we look at the ontology of the fetish beyond dialectics and symmetry, but in terms of recursivity? Recursivity is the act of drawing upon itself. Let me explain what I mean by "recursion" through a metaphor. A classical image of the incommensurability of cultures is opposing mirrors. Both stand in direct contraposition to each other, backward, reflecting the culture that produced them (Western culture on the one hand, "Other" cultures on the other hand). But what happens if we turn the mirrors toward each other, looking into each other? The problem is reversed. The mirrors no longer reflect opposing worlds, but they create a world within themselves, a world that is infinitely recursive.

The self-reflecting mirror can be a quite apt image of the problem of the fetish. Psychoanalysis would describe the constant return to the original event of the fetish as a loop that keeps the subject of desire bound to an object that, in fact, is part of herself; a mirror in the mirror, in which we disavow our own image. But what if we look at the mirror not as an illusion—a limit and a bond—but as an infinity within, a door to a new possible world? What if instead of trying to close the circle of the fetish, always unsuccessfully, we look at the layers and layers, the supplements that we add to it, to its affordances, to its potential, to the worlds that have been built within it? Then, the indeterminacy of the fetish is not its problem, but its power.

References

Apter, Emily, and William Pietz, eds. 1993. *Fetishism as Cultural Discourse*. Ithaca, NY: Cornell University Press.

Atkins, John. 1735. *A Voyage to Guinea, Brasil and the West Indies*. London: Ward and Chandler.

Bernand, Carmen, and Serge Gruzinski. 1988. *De L'idôlatrie: Une Archéologie des Sciences Religieuses*. Paris: Seuil.

Böhme, Hartmut. 2006. *Fetischmus und Kultur. Eine Andere Theorie der Moderne*. Reinbek bei Hamburg: Rowohlt Taschenbuch Verlag.

Bosman, Willem. 1705. *A New and Accurate Description of the Coast of Guinea*. London: J. Knapton.

Bourdieu, Pierre. 1992. *Les Règles de l' Art. Gènese et Structure du Camp Literaire*. Paris: Seuil.

Boyer, Pascal. 2001. *Religion Explained: The Evolutionary Origins of Religious Thought*. New York: Basic Books.

Brosses, Charles de. (1760) 1988. *Du Culte des Dieux Fétiches ou Parallèle de l' Ancienne Religion de l' Egypte Avec la Religion Actuelle de Nigritie*. Paris: Fayard.

Comte, Auguste. 2001. *Cours de Philosophie Positive*. Paris: Book Surge Publishing.

Dapper, Olfert. 1686. *Description de l' Afrique*. Amsterdam: W. Waesberge, Boom et Van Someren.

De Marees, Pieter. (1602) 1987. *Description and Historical Account of the Gold Kingdom of Guinea*. Oxford: Oxford University Press.

Freud, Sigmund. [1927] 2001. "Fetishism." In *The Standard Edition of the Complete Psychological Works of Sigmund Freud*, vol. 21, edited and translated by James Strachey et al., 147–157. New York: Vintage.

Gell, Alfred. 1998. *Art and Agency*. London: Carendon Press.

Graeber, David. 2005. "Fetishism as Social Creativity, or, Fetishes Are Gods in the Process of Construction." *Anthropological Theory* 5 (4): 40738.

Graeber, David. 2015. "Radical Alterity Is Just Another Way of Saying 'Reality': A Reply to Eduardo Viveiros de Castro." *Hau: Journal of Ethnographic Theory* 5 (2): 1–41.

Hegel, Friedrich. 1956. *The Philosophy of History*. New York: Dover.

Iacono, Alfonso M. 1992. *Le Fétichisme. Historie d' un Concept*. Paris: Presses Universitaires de France.

Kant, Immanuel 1960. *Observations on the Nature of the Beautiful and the Sublime*. Berkeley, CA: University of California Press.

Latour, Bruno. 1993. *We Have Never Been Modern*. Cambridge, MA: Harvard University Press.

Latour, Bruno. 2001. *L'Espoir de Pandore*. Paris: Éditions de La Découverte.

Latour, Bruno. 2010. *On the Modern Cult of the Factish Gods*. Durham, NC: Duke University Press.

Latour, Bruno. 2017. "A Dialog About a New Meaning of Symmetric Anthropology (with Carolina Miranda)." In *Comparative Metaphysics—Ontology After Anthropology*, edited by Pierre Charbonnier, Gildas Salmon and Peter Skafish, 327–345. London: Rowman & Littlefield.

Marx, Karl. 1992. *Capital: Volume 1: A Critique of Political Economy*. London: Penguin.

Matory, J. Lorand. 2018. *The Fetish Revisited: Marx, Freud, and the Gods Black People Make*. Durham, NC: Duke University Press.

Meyer, Birgit. 2012. *Mediation and the Genesis of Presence. Towards a Material Approach to Religion*. Utrecht: University of Utrecht.

Meyer, Birgit. 2019. "Idolatry beyond the Second Commandment: Conflicting Figurations and Sensations of the Unseen." In *Figurations and Sensations of the Unseen in Judaism, Christianity and Islam: Contested Desires*, edited by Birgit Meyer and Terje Stordalen, 77–96. London: Bloomsbury.

Morris, Rosalind C., Daniel H. Leonard, and Charles de Brosses. 2017. *The Returns of Fetishism: Charles de Brosses and the Afterlives of an Idea*. Chicago, IL: University of Chicago Press.

Pietz, William. 1985. "The Problem of the Fetish, I." *Res, Anthropology and Esthetics* 9 (Spring): 5–17.

Pietz, William. 1987. "The Problem of the Fetish, II: The Origin of the Fetish." *Res, Anthropology and Esthetics* 13 (Spring): 23–45.

Pietz, William. 1988. "The Problem of the Fetish, IIIa: Bosman's Guinaea and the Enlightenment Theory of Fetishism." *Res, Anthropology and Esthetics* 16 (Fall): 106–123.

Pouillon, Jean. 1975. *Fétiches Sans Fetichisme*. Paris: Maspero.

Sansi, Roger. 2007. "The Fetish in the Lusophone Atlantic." In *Cultures of the Lusophone Atlantic*, edited by Nancy Priscilla Naro, Roger Sansi-Roca and David Treece, 19–40. London: Palgrave MacMillan.

Sansi, Roger. 2011. "Sorcery and Fetishism in the Modern Atlantic." In *Sorcery in the Black Atlantic*, edited by Luis Nicolau Parés and Roger Sansi, 19–40. Chicago, IL: University of Chicago Press.

Spyer, Patricia, ed. 1998. *Border Fetishisms*. London: Routledge.

Taussig, Michael. 1980. *The Devil and Commodity Fetishism in South America*. Chapel Hill, NC: University of North Carolina Press.

Tylor, Edward. 1874. *Primitive Culture*. London: H. Holt and Company.

Viveiros de Castro, Eduardo. 2015. "Who's Afraid of the Ontological Wolf: Some Comments on an Ongoing Anthropological Debate." *Cambridge Anthropology* 33 (1): 2–17.

2.4

ANIMISM? ANIMATED? ENSOULED? THE ACTIVE LIVES OF BALINESE MASKS

Laurel Kendall and Ni Wayan Pasek Ariati

Anthropologist Jane Belo describes how, sometime in the 1930s, devotees from Tegaltamu Village carried their powerful Rangda mask to a temple festival in a neighboring community, a common practice then as now. With the god displayed in a basket on the head of a devotee, the returning procession was nearing Tegaltamu when "villagers who were subjects of the god but who had not gone on the excursion fell in trance spontaneously as the Rangda [mask] passed." As villagers subsequently described these events to Belo,

> There was a man working upon a culvert, and when he saw the Rangda arriving from Padangdawa [a temple site] he ran home, his body still covered with mud, and took up his Kris [keris], and did *ngoerek* [*ngurek*, chest-stabbing] before the Rangda. And there was another man who was climbing a coconut tree, and in the same way, when he saw the people coming from Padangdawa, he came down from the tree and took a kris and did *ngoerek*. There was also a woman cooking in her kitchen, and when she saw the Rangda arriving she ran and took a Kris and began to *ngoerek* before the Rangda.

There were other, equally dramatic examples of arrested labors diverted into spontaneous chest-stabbing, "Many were the people who went in trance. ...All the women cried and were afraid to see the people doing *ngoerek*" (Belo 1960: 73).[1]

A temple mask carried in procession radiates a sufficient force field to throw villagers into spontaneous and violent trance, a ferocious abduction of agency (Gell 1998). There was no doubt in Tegaltamu that something powerful operated through the mask. Such things happen; Wayan Ariati recalls a grandmother who, in recent times, ran topless to a temple festival heeding a similar compulsion. But Belo also records how, while some villagers held that the intervention was appropriately divine, others contended that demonic forces were operating through the mask (Belo 1960: 72–74). As a Balinese temple mask, the Rangda had been carefully carved and ritually enlivened through processes similar to those we will describe below. The mask's behavior, inducing violent trance, was not unusual within Balinese expectations for such a mask; indeed, in some contexts it would be expected. That the villagers were thrown into trance in broad daylight, villagers dirty from work and in need of a bath, was problematic—and perhaps not even possible for a divine presence. As such, the incident provoked extended debate in Tegaltamu. We begin with this local example of

DOI: 10.4324/9781351176231-13

social and religious phenomena sometimes described as "animation" or "ensoulment"—and sometimes, more problematically, bundled into the broad category of "animism" as an old idea now revenant.

"Animation" or "ensoulment" as action verbs describe work intended to make seemingly inanimate matter agentive in the context of religious practice. While authors of the "new animism" have sensitized us to ontologies that account for the agentive behavior of things, enabling a larger dialogue, in the imperfect process of translation, and the false security of thinking we know what we are talking about, a generalizing terminology can also elide some of the richness and complexity of the object at hand, in this instance a Balinese mask. After considering these concepts and their contemporary use, we will return to Bali, where masks sometimes disappoint and sometimes exceed Balinese expectations for them, encouraging us to think both with and beyond our generalizing terminology. We will argue that if, as Alfred Gell suggested, we study human relationships with things as anthropologists study other human relationships, we need also be attuned to social actors who sometimes act out of type and be willing to pursue them through new apertures of understanding.

Animism, Animated Object, Ensoulment

"Animism" is a legacy from anthropology's Victorian forebears. Sir Edward Burnett Tylor described humanity's earliest religious consciousness as a "doctrine of souls"; animists regard humans, animals, and seemingly inert matter as containers for energizing souls or spirits. Tylor's animism was "essentially rational, though working in a mental condition of intense and inveterate ignorance." It was also, for Tylor, a tenacious way of seeing that persisted "into the midst of our own modern thought" (Tylor [1871] 1958: 23). Sir James Frazer, less tolerant, described the animistic-seeming beliefs of "Siamese Buddhists" and similar phenomena as "common savage dogma incorporated in the system of a historical religion" (Frazer [1922] 1996: 135). Both Tyler and Frazer regarded animism stratigraphically as primitive patterns of thinking and doing that sometimes erupted into more evolved modes of religious practice. Twentieth-century anthropologists tended to eschew the word "animism" and its prejudicial baggage. Nevertheless, non-Muslim, non-Hindu, and non-Buddhist populations are still often categorized as "animist" for want of another generalization. The idea of a primordial substratum of animist religious consciousness bubbling up into contemporary practice is sometimes also evoked to account for such seemingly anomalous activities as powerful masks throwing otherwise decorous Hindu Balinese into spontaneous and violent trance (cf. C. Geertz 1973). Sometime in the late twentieth century, religious studies breached the once well-policed boundary between textual orthodoxies and the things people actually do. What had been regarded as animistic survivals came to be understood and written about as lived religion. The explanatory value of "animism" as a historicizing construct would seem to have disappeared.

New directions in Amazonian ethnography would return "animism" to the anthropological conversation. By the new millennium, it had "escaped from its cage," in Graham Harvey's words (2006: 11), but to a new explanatory purpose. In Harvey's characterization of an animistic ontology, "the world is full of persons, only some of whom are human, and life is always lived in relationship with others" (xi). In recent works, animism appears not as mistaken perception but as a fully realized ontological practice that recognizes spirits, humans, animals, and plants as being endowed with more or less equivalent souls, a condition that enables interspecies communication, including hunting magic (Costa and Fausto 2010). In an animistic ontology, common soul stuff can migrate among people, animals, and features of the landscape, such that—as in Eduardo Viveiros de Castro's memorable description—the shaman as jaguar craves blood with an appetite that matches the shaman as man's craving for manioc beer (Viveiros de Castro 2004). Philippe Descola ([2004] 2014) uses an animist ontology to destabilize the seeming universalism of the nature/culture divide, arguing for a typology of animisms that is both geographically broad and historically deep.

A world "full of persons, only some of whom are human" also resonates with Alfred Gell's notion of "agency"—his once-radical suggestion that people commonly abduct acts of thought, will, or intention to things—as well as with his recommendation that the relationship between people and things be studied in the manner that anthropologists analyze other kinds of human relationships: defined by rights, obligations, and legitimate mutual expectations (Gell 1998: 16, 17–18). A Hindu temple, ritually ensouled and enlivened through processes not unlike those used in Bali, becomes "a locus for person-to-person encounters with divinities" (125). In this context, "idols are 'social others' to the extent that, and because, they obey the social rules laid down for idols as co-present others (gods) in idol-form" (128). Where Gell's work and the animism conversation allow us to study relationships between temple images and people as anthropologists have commonly studied relationships between human subjects, our Balinese examples also suggest equivalents of the kinds of deviations from ideal behavior—domestic quarrels, postponed funerals, witchcraft accusations—that anthropologists have plumbed to better understand the messy complexity of lived experiences.

Characterizing relationships between people and, say, temple masks as "anim*ism*" is not without potential hazard. The "*ism*" of "animism," like the "*ism*" of "shamanism," invites overgeneralization, whereas animism's ontological possibilities are multiple. Important works from the Mongolian Steppe (Pedersen 2011), the far north (Cruikshank 2005; Ingold 1998), or Aboriginal communities in Australia (Provinelli 1996) offer a fruitful parsing of different animist ontologies in excess of Descola's ambitious global typology. Bali is yet another kind of place, a majority Hindu island province in the Muslim-majority Indonesian state with a complex history of rivalrous kingdoms, irrigated rice farming, Hinduism, Tantrism, Dutch colonialism, nationalism, Balinism, and several decades of intensive tourism that traffics in Bali's long reputation as a site of exquisite artistic production. Temple masks are produced by master carvers—and this was true long before Jane Belo studied Bali. While empowered Balinese masks breach the nature/culture, person/thing divide, not all Balinese masks carry an animating soul or energy, and those that do come into being through human labor as works of both craft and magic. Following Peter Pels's distinction between the fetish as "matter that strikes back on its own terms," and the animated thing, installed with a soul, spirit, or other empowering substance through the hand of an external agent (Pels 1998: 91–92, 94–95, 112), Balinese masks are animated things, with "animation" as an action verb—although possibly not the best verb.

"Animation" is no more easily generalized than "animism," "religion," "shamans," or "magic." Teri Silvio defines animation as "the construction of social others through the projection of qualities perceived as human—life, soul, power, agency, intentionality, personality, and so on—outside the self and into the sensory environment, through acts of creation, perception, and interaction" (Silvio 2019: 19). But while Silvio's Taiwan material includes both temple images and puppets, the "animation" of images functions differently from "animation" as the life-simulation of puppets and masks—and, in modern media, from animated cartoons, game avatars, and social media personas (Silvio 2019). The latter are caused to act through reassuringly mechanistic operations, the former through processes that are not reducible to mechanistic understanding and may not, in the physical sense, move at all. In Gell's words,

> When particular statues bleed, or perspire, or move about, these are 'miracles.' But such happenings would not be miracles if the expectation was that all idols should behave in this way; in fact, they are generally expected not to. Idols may be animate without, in other words, being endowed with animal life or activity…. It follows that 'ritual' animacy and the possession of 'life' in a biological sense are far from being the same thing.
>
> *(Gell 1998: 122)*

The Balinese temple mask draws on both possibilities, ritually "animated" with invisible forces and mechanistically animated when it appears in a ritual performance on the shoulders of an entranced medium (*pemundut*). With respect to the former, Fernando Santos-Granero's characterization of an "ensouled" object "amenable to some kind of subjectivation" (Santos-Granero 2009) may be the most apt characterization, implying both a condition of presence and the work undertaken to make it so.

Ensoulment as an Action Verb

In both Catholic Europe and Hindu and Buddhist Asia, religious images have long been produced in specialized workshops, their production subsidized by patrons or communities of worshippers as acts of devotion. Heir to a tradition of image veneration in the ancient Mediterranean and Abrahamic iconoclasm, Catholicism keeps the image as an inspiration to piety but rejects the specter of presence as irreligious "idolatry." Rare and contested historic instances of "miraculous images" are the kinds of exceptions that Gell described (cf. Belting 1994). In Hindu, Buddhist, and related popular practice, much to the contrary, the commissioning and crafting of an image happen in anticipation of ensoulment, the expectation that an image will acquire a life of its own as the desired culmination of a material and ritual process. A growing body of literature on image production across the map of Asia describes broadly recognizable practices and resonant themes.[2] The image is made according to an established protocol with respect to size, proportion, and appearance. Wood is cut and metal cast on an appropriate day by a ritually clean artisan, and the entire production process is marked with offerings and austerities. The craftsman's skill and the quality of his materials, the most mechanistic aspects of the operation, are not without magical intention in making an effective container. Once the image is complete, enlivening materials—five-colored metals to hold the power of the five cardinal deities—are inserted into a prepared cavity in the image. A ritual specialist, on an auspicious day and hour, draws on well-traveled textual knowledge to perform the incantations and gestures that bring the image to life, awakening its senses and opening its eyes, fully enlivening it. While "animation" or "ensoulment" refers most explicitly to the image's awakening, the work began well in advance of this moment.

And now, to Bali.

Bali: Becoming *Tenget*

In Bali, the combined presence of the ensouled mask (*tapel*), the enlivening presence within it (*sesuhunan*), and the purified, entranced body of the medium who wears the mask (*pemundut*) participate in what Hildred Geertz characterizes as the basic work of all Balinese rituals: "Propitiations of potentially destructive spiritual beings; these propitiations are followed by rituals of gratitude to the beings and forces that have accepted propitiation and are willing to desist from hurting their people and actively protecting them" (H. Geertz 2004: 73). The temple mask channels divine energies in the cyclical work of drawing forth and transforming demonic forces, usually through the ritual contestation between Rangda, the mistress of black magic, and the lion-like healing Barong in the Calon Arang play featuring Rangda.[3] To do this work, efficacious masks are *hidup* (enlivened), *berwibawa/wibawa* (charismatic, exalted), and especially *tenget* (charged with a magical and potentially dangerous power analogous to an electrical current). Bali scholars describe the maker of masks and other potent objects as necessarily a man of deep spiritual power "to insure that these forces do not inadvertently get out of hand and create imbalance" (Eiseman 1990: 207), and because "the potency of such objects" as *keris* blades and masks "depends in part on the spiritual power of their creators. Throughout the process of manufacturing such things, offerings rest at the artisan's side, and at various stages he invokes invisible forces with mantras, sacred syllables, seeking to join their power with that of his creation" (Wiener 1995: 55–56). Such "work" (*karya*) is, in part, "service and homage paid to *niskala* beings who pervade village." By means of such labor, "the constant threat of destructive anger on the part of *niskala* beings—which could release not only all sorts of natural disasters but also the malevolence of local human sorcerers—may be dispelled" (H. Geertz 2004: 242–243).

In the first instance, the community's decision to make or refurbish a temple mask is prompted by a divine message (*pewisik*) received from trancers or heard in dreams or during meditation, then subsequently deliberated by the community as a matter of consequence, expense, and possible danger.[4] Decorative masks, souvenir masks, and masks intended for secular performance are carved from commercial lots of wood, but the wood for a temple mask is extracted with ceremonious caution from a pregnant (*beling*) swelling on a *pulé* tree that has been struck by lightning or has absorbed a ball of light seen in a priest's vision—and sometimes confirmed with other tests. The ritual for cutting wood (*ngepel*) occurs on an auspicious day (*dwasa ayu*) by the Balinese calendar. The priest wraps the trunk of the tree in a white cloth and makes offerings requesting permission from the Lord of the Forest (Banaspati Raja) to extract the wood so that the community can use it for a particular mask, then chants appropriate mantras and removes the tree's spirit/soul substance to a temporary bamboo shrine [*sanggah cucuk*]. When he works the wood, the carver maintains the tree's orientation (as some carvers of images do in other places), so that the base of the piece becomes the bottom of the mask.

When the wood is properly seasoned, the carving begins with another ritual (*ngendag*) on another auspicious day, performed in the purified precinct of a temple by a Brahmin priest (*pedanda*). The cut wood rests for three days in the temple while the priest meditates, joined by some members of the community who focus collectively and intensely on their intentions for the mask, sometimes receiving a waking vision or sign that the spirit (*bayu*) in the wood is compatible with their project. The carver has prepared himself with a ritual purification (*mewinten*) and another for his tools (*melaspas, mlaspasin/masupatin*). He does not touch the mask until after he has bathed and works in peaceful seclusion, ideally in a state of intense concentration that enables him to infuse the mask with something of his own soul/spirit/vital energy (*bayu*, Ind. *jiwa*), becoming one with it (Ind. *satu pikiran*). One Balinese carver illustrated for us how he worked his chisel from a yoga-like posture—bending his hand in a mudra-like gesture toward the mask—and said that when he can work this way, holding the uncomfortable posture from morning until night, he knows he is producing a good mask. Another carver told us that he (and very likely other carvers) would not work on the inauspicious first day (*pasah*) of the three-day Balinese week. Attention to all of these details has a positive impact on the outcome, and inattention can have bad consequence—such as one carver described for a Barong mask inhabited by "something else," some ominous presence that might ask for "human sacrifice," as in the death of one or more community members after a performance.

The completed mask is ritually purified and then ensouled (*pasupati*). A Brahman priest installs five sacred elements (Skt. *panca dathu*)—gold, silver, bronze, iron, diamond—in the mask as conductors for the forces that charge a mask and render it *tenget,* makes appropriate offerings (*upakara*), and recites the appropriate mantra (*doa-doa*) to activate the process. One of our conversation partners, a priest who performs these rituals himself, described the *pasupati* as equivalent to the gas needed to make the motor bike run through an accurately connected cable: the gasoline is the offering, the priest is the cable that makes the connection between the mask and the divine, and the priest's performance of the correct mantra is the charge that brings the engine to life. But elements of the fantastic also accompany the enlivening of a Balinese temple mask in a graveyard night-keeping ceremony (*ngeréh*). Amid chanting priests and anticipatory community, the tutelary god or *sesuhunan* gives dramatic evidence of presence when, at the midnight hour, the mask is seen to explode in a ball of flame, emit a strange sound, or move of its own accord. Someone, chosen by the *sesuhunan,* falls into deep trance and takes on the mask. A veteran of many such events described a particularly memorable occasion when, meditating in the cemetery with his eyes closed, he saw with his mind's eye a burst of light irradiating the Rangda mask, then felt the mask jump onto his face and propel him back to the temple. Scholar performer I Wayan Dibia describes how, as a young and newly initiated Barong dancer, he was asked to carry a new mask to the cemetery for this culminating ritual. As he approached, he felt a strange lightening of what had theretofore been an extremely heavy mask and a sense of his own body floating on the verge of trance. He was unready, he thought, and handed the mask to another dancer who immediately fell into trance. Dibia recalls this uncanny lightening as

> The sign that an object was transformed into a sacred object: 'Before that, when I was on my way to the cemetery, the Barong was just a puppet, just a costume, but the spirit was not there yet. It was already blessed but the spirit was not there yet, the body was there but the soul was not there yet'.
>
> *(Dibia 2012)*

On these occasions, the graveyard becomes a force field of potentially dangerous energy and a site of black magic whose practitioners are challenged by the *tenget* forces of the deity empowering the mask. This is serious business, and any observer can be thrown into spontaneous and violent trance. Two of our conversation partners, traditional healers (*balian*) who are regarded as having the power or force (*sakti*) to repel black magic, find themselves in demand on these occasions. "Tales are told of high priests, *pedandas*, actually falling dead while bringing an especially important and sacred mask to life" (Eiseman 1990: 208); others spoke of the designated human vehicle dying shortly after the encounter (Belo 1960: 98). But not all midnight empowerments are equally graphic, and some occurrences are more spectacular than others. Belo, writing of events in the 1930s, records a woman in Tegaltamu enthusiastically describing the relative illuminations of newly made masks commissioned by rival communities: flames small as a finger and shooting up to the sky, fire large as a fist, and, most impressively, fire the size of a cock basket confirming the *tenget* qualities of Tegaltamu's own Rangda mask. Since one mask showed no fire at all, "it was not *tenget.*" Another of Belo's conversation partners described a mask that failed to perform and had to be destroyed (Belo 1960: 75–76). In the experience of a healer by the name of Balian A., a reddish light infuses Rangda and Barong masks; he considers a small, gentle, and refined (Ind. *alus*) light flickering like fireflies as indicating greater power than the big explosions, which to him are invisible forces "showing off." A carver/priest sees different colored lights identified with different directions and their associated deities. Such stakes—both the danger of engaging with *tenget* forces and the possibility of a community investing effort and resources in a dud mask—make temple mask production a matter of much consequence; ensoulment is a complicated and by no means certain process.

Masks that Bend the Rules

Not all masks are made to be enlivened. In well-touristed Bali, inexpensive masks are knocked out in workshops to satisfy the souvenir market, and respected carvers also produce masks for secular performers, collectors, and museums. In conversations, the boundaries between enlivened temple masks and secular masks are well policed; a mask that has not been equipped with the *panca-dathu* and subsequently enlivened in a night-keeping ritual remains a decorative object made of wood. And yet, Bali scholars note the potentiality of material forms to become abodes of invisible (*niskala*) beings depending on how they are regarded and treated. A secular mask that receives offerings in small acts of devotion might absorb sacredness over time and eventually become something else. Even ordinary souvenir masks have been known to rattle on the walls of craft shops. We heard stories of a mask given as a wedding gift, or in some retellings purchased in a shop, and taken to North America, where it rattled on the wall, crunched its jaws at mealtime, disturbed dreams, and threw small children into hysterical fits. The owner returned the mask to Bali, where it was received by the former ruling family of Ubud. After more uncanny mask behavior, the palace (*puri*) community recognized the mask as being energized by a protective *sesuhunan,* and subsequently enshrined and venerated it. Known as "Jero Amerika," the mask appears at local festivals on the head of an entranced human vehicle and runs through and beyond Ubud exposing practitioners (*leyak*) of black magic (*pengiwa*) (Kendall and Ariati 2020). In our interviews with mask-makers, mask-venders, and dancers, our queries about "the mask that went to America" elicited an outpouring of stories about other masks that had also proven themselves to be *tenget*—counter to the intentions of those who had made or subsequently acquired them. In the words of scholar/performer I Wayan Dibia, such masks became "sacred by accident" (2012).

When Balian A. was a student going to pray in a temple, a mysterious stranger gifted him with a Rangda mask that he hung on the wall of his boarding house as decoration. When his roommates playfully tossed it to one another, and they all got diarrhea. After graduation, he gifted the mask to the priest of the Pura Dalem in his village who hung it, also decoratively, in his home compound, but the mask came alive and hovered over the priest while he slept. When Balian A.'s father went to retrieve the mask, it was too heavy for him to lift—but Balian A. could carry it with no difficulty. After Balian A. placed the mask in the temple in his family's garden, the shrine caught on fire and the mask's hair burned, though the mask itself was unscathed—as has happened to some other *tenget* masks in other accounts. During a festival, a woman in trance told Balian A. that he should have the mask consecrated as a first step in his becoming a *balian* (healer). Although Balian A. deferred the calling, the mask now hangs as a source of power in his personal shrine (*kamar suci*).

The director of a performing arts troupe bought two inexpensive masks in the Badung market, "ordinary things" she carried in her backpack. But when a student danced with one of these masks, she fell into a deep trance and could not stop dancing until the mask was forcibly pulled from her face, leaving her in near-hysterical tears. The director marked the mask container DO NOT USE, but another dancer put it on by mistake and similarly fell into trance. After this the dancers took the mask back to their home temple.

I Wayan Dibia described a village in Bangli Regency where, in the early 1960s, a bull Barong had been made to enact the National Party's logo at rallies, which was a campaign stunt and not a religious act. Retired from political work after the 1965 coup, the bull Barong hung in a private house. Weirdly, the house began to shake. After the owner moved the Barong to the community hall, that building shook as well. The members of the community (*banjar*) decided that the Barong was very strong, that something was empowering it, and installed it in a temple as a source of protective power. The bull Barong now performs in temple festivals to contest demonic forces and to encourage good crops. To safeguard their health and strength, cattle and horses are sprinkled with holy water that has passed through the Barong's beard (Dibia 2012, 2018).

Mask-makers described how masks they had made for secular purposes struck back on their own terms. A carver in Singapadu made an oversized mask as a novelty for handicraft exhibitions; he also hung it by his gate to advertise his skill. A paranormal from Java who was passing by in the night screamed and shouted that he wanted to worship the mask. After that, no gallery would exhibit the mask, deeming it no longer a neutral, secular novelty, and so the mask-maker moved it into his family shrine. Down the street from that shrine, another well-respected mask-maker carved a Rangda mask for the Art Institute in Denpasar for student performances. On *kajeng kliwon* days when Balinese make periodic offerings, the Rangda would come out from storage and walk around, terrifying the sleeping security guard. After this the mask was ritually enshrined and the students made offerings on appropriate days, ending the Rangda's nocturnal wandering.

As in the case of Jero Amerika, some masks that have been taken away from Bali give unsettling evidence of their desire to return. We heard of other cases: a mask bought by a visiting Javanese academic and precipitously sent back to a Balinese colleague; a Rangda mask stored in a closet of the Indonesian Embassy in Washington, DC, that emitted mysterious light and peals of laughter in the dead of night. As in the case of Jero Amerika and the campaign bull, at least some of these unexpectedly enlivened masks that made trouble overseas enter new careers as local protectors. "Jero California" passed through multiple hands on a transpacific journey until reaching her current residence in a priest's family shrine—when not performing in local temple festivals. A carver in Bali presented a retired Barong that had been used in tourist performances to a French collector, J., who after experiencing domestic unease with it, returned the mask to the carver. The carver assumed that the Barong had been enlivened by years of offerings set out at the start of each tourist performance. When he later received a commission for a temple mask, he offered J.'s Barong, since it had already proven itself.

Sacred by Accident

Many Balinese speculate that the buzzing noises emanating from a mask are invasive insects, or that "flying" masks are moved by the wind, and that at least some uncanny things are "all in the mind"—in the words of one master mask-carver regarding Jero Amerika. Nonetheless, most of our interlocutors comfortably abducted agency to temple masks that had been ritually ensouled as well as some masks that showed themselves to be *tenget* outside the expected Balinese procedures for making and ensouling a temple mask. When we asked carvers and other knowledgeable Balinese how such a mask could become "sacred by accident," most began with the wood. A mask-maker explained, "The wood must have been taken from a really special place. The carver bought the wood from someone [in a commercial lot], [so] he didn't know." But the source could have been a particularly charged and powerful *pulé* tree with an enlivening spirit/soul (*bayu*) already present in the wood. Or the carver might have used wood left over from a sacred commission, and therefore the wood was already the beneficiary of sacred protocols for making a *tenget* mask. The carver of the Art Institute mask noted earlier still remembered the strangely forked wood he had used for that commission, wood from a *pulé* tree that had been cut to widen a road. Even if the wood-cutter had paid no attention to the calendar, and although there was no ceremony, the tree could have been cut on a lucky day just by chance. The carver, similarly oblivious, may have begun his work in a good hour on a good day. The carver and his tools may have been in a state of purity for other reasons, and he may have worked in a properly meditative frame of mind owing to personal temperament and work practice. In other words, protocols could be performed by accident.

Some communities that perform for tourists use a substitute Barong (Barong *serep*), which is made without ritual protocol to be deployed when the community is in a state of pollution and thus cannot use the temple Barong. But because offerings are always made for the success of the performance and the well-being of the dancers, the *serep* may absorb this sacredness cumulatively over time—as did J.'s Barong. And so, just as an understudy can be promoted to primary performer, a substitute Barong might become sufficiently *tenget* to replace the original Barong when it retires.

A final means by which a mask can become sacred by accident is if the *sesuhunan* that enlivens the mask exerts its own agency in choosing a vehicle. This happened in a village in Gianyar Regency that separated into two; we will call the original village Village A. Village B became wealthy making handicrafts. Though Village B retained the original Rangda mask— Ratu Anom—it commissioned a new mask—Ratu Ayu—to replace it and thus erase the former tie. But when Village B tried to burn the now-deconsecrated original mask, a woman in trance grabbed Ratu Anom back from the flames and said, "Since you ignore me, I'm not here anymore." The community kept the unburned mask in a basket in the temple, but no longer made offerings to the mask. Meanwhile, a trancer in Village A, speaking for the abandoned Ratu Anom mask, announced that he had been abused in Village B and had returned to Village A. This was allegedly the first knowledge Village A had of Ratu Anom having been abandoned. After due deliberation and further entranced confirmation of Ratu Anom's desires, Village A commissioned a new mask and Ratu Anom was invited, with full ceremony, to inhabit it—leaving the original mask in Village B as an empty shell, "just wood."

Another mask-maker, living near Ubud, made a set of new masks for a temple in Peliatan. When, following protocol, the old masks were to be cremated (*pralina*), the carver asked if he could keep one of them—the mask of Celuluk, the comic old woman practitioner of black magic—to use as a prototype. Because this mask's enlivening presence had been moved to the newly made mask, this Celuluk should have been nothing more than a mask. But when the mask-maker hung it in a corner of his studio, it began to show signs of life, knocking against the wall. The mask-maker was skeptical but consulted a *balian* friend, who immediately asked, "Where did you get that mask in the corner?" The *balian* had never seen the mask the mask-maker was asking about, but he could visualize it clearly and discerned that it was now inhabited by the spirit of the sacred *lontar* texts the mask-maker's uncle had studied in the family shrine just east of the mask-maker's studio. And so the mask was placed in a basket and venerated with daily offerings. This migration was plausible; *tenget* masks, *lontar* texts, and *keris* blades are imbued with energizing forces that can also depart from them (Wiener 1995), and mask types are not always consistent with the deities who appear when the masks are borne on the head of a human host (Belo 1960: 3; Hobart 2003: 31; Kendall and Ariati 2020). And so it would appear that Jero Amerika, Ratu Anom from Village B, and the *lontar* spirit in the mask-maker's Celuluk chose their own habitations—all remarkable circumstances that are read as attributes of their power.

Conclusion

By now, dear reader, you may be groaning from an excess of ethnographic detail, but example and variation are exactly the point of it. That a mask becomes *tenget* is an active process, either by conventional means (that are not always adequate) or when parsed in unconventional circumstances. Making a *tenget* mask involves a concatenation of materials, some more powerfully energized than others; ritual and workshop procedures, some more scrupulously adhered to than others, and some a matter of habit; auspicious timing, sometimes as a matter of happenstance; craftsmen—some more skilled, knowing, and meditative than others; and, finally, a battery of elaborate and potentially dangerous rituals that might, in rare instances, not even be necessary, given that some masks can become sacred "by accident." These are conditions of doing and making as much as of being and becoming. Words like "animated" or "ensouled," or even "animism" enable broad conversations, but they must be deployed with caution lest they elide the sometimes messy and variable processes they are intended to define. If, as Gell suggested, the relationship between people and things is to be studied in the manner of other human relationships, then we must also be attuned to the possibility of bent rules and things acting out of type or expectation just as human subjects do. These departures may be as revealing for the study of material religion as were their human-human equivalents in more conventional ethnography.

Notes

1 Quote marks are in Belo's original text to indicate direct citations from her interviews.
2 Bentor (1996) for Tibet, Brinker (2011) for China; Davis (1997) for India, Horton (2007) for Japan, Kendall, Vū, and Nguyễn (2010) for Vietnam, Swearer (2004) for Thailand, and Kendall 2021 for four complementary cases, among other examples.
3 Belo (1960), Bandem and deBoer (1995: 102–126); H. Geertz (1994: 65–81); Hobart (2003: 123–205); and many others.
4 Accounts of mask production and mask behavior appear in Eiseman (1990: 207–219), Hobart (2003: 132–149), and Slattum and Schraub (2003: 23–27) and elsewhere. We have also drawn on conversations with mask-makers Tjokorda Raka Tisnu, Ida Bagus Anom Alit, Ida Bagus Anom Suryawan, I Wayan Candra, I Ketut Kodi, Wayan Lalar ("Kak Dalang"), and the late Ida Bagus Anom and I Wayan Tangguh.

References

Bandem, I. Madé, and Frederik E. De Boer. 1995. *Balinese Dance in Transition: Kaja and Kelod*. Oxford: Oxford University Press.
Belo, Jane. 1960. *Trance in Bali*. New York: Columbia University Press.
Belting, Hans. 1994. *Likeness and Presence: A History of the Image Before the Era of Art*. Chicago, IL: University of Chicago Press.
Bentor, Yael. 1996. *Consecration of Images and Stupas in Indo-Tibetan Trantric Buddhism*. Leiden: Brill Publishers.
Brinker, Helmut. 2011. *Secrets of the Sacred: Empowering Buddhist Images in Clear, in Code, and in Cache*. Seattle, WA: University of Washington Press.
Costa, Luiz, and Carlos Fausto. 2010. "The Return of the Animists: Recent Studies of Amazonian Ontologies." *Religion and Society* 1 (1): 89–109.
Cruikshank, Julie. 2005. *Do Glaciers Listen? Local Knowledge, Colonial Encounters, and Social Imagination*. Vancouver and Toronto: University of British Columbia Press.

Davis, Richard H. 1997. *The Lives of Indian Images.* Princeton, NJ: Princeton University Press.

Descola, Philippe. (2004) 2014. *Beyond Nature and Culture.* Chicago, IL: University of Chicago Press.

Dibia, I Wayan. 2012. *Personal Communication with the Author,* April 4, 2012.

Dibia, I Wayan. 2018. *Personal Communication with the Author,* April 23, 2018.

Eiseman, Fred B. Jr. 1990. *Bali: Sekala & Niskala: Essays in Religion, Ritual, and Art.* Vols. I and II. Singapore: Periplus Editions.

Frazer, James G. (1922) 1996. *The Golden Bough: A Study in Magic and Religion, Abridged Edition.* London: Penguin Books.

Geertz, Clifford. 1973. "Person, Time, and Conduct in Bali." In *The Interpretation of Cultures: Selected Essays by Clifford Geertz,* 360–411. New York: Basic Books. https://chairoflogicphiloscult.files. wordpress.com/2013/02/clifford-geertz-the-interpretation-of-cultures.pdf.

Geertz, Hildred. 1994. *Images of Power: Balinese Paintings Made for Gregory Bateson and Margaret Mead.* Honolulu, HI: University of Hawai'i Press.

Geertz, Hildred. 2004. *The Life of a Balinese Temple: Artistry, Imagination, and History in a Peasant Village.* Honolulu, HI: University of Hawai'i Press.

Gell, Alfred. 1998. *Art and Agency: An Anthropological Theory.* Oxford: Clarendon Press.

Harvey, Graham. 2006. *Animism: Respecting the Living World.* New York: Columbia University Press.

Hobart, Angela. 2003. *Healing Performances of Bali: Between Darkness and Light.* New York: Berghahn Books.

Horton, Sarah H. 2007. *Living Buddhist Statues in Early Medieval and Modern Japan.* New York: Palgrave MacMillan.

Ingold, Tim. 1998. "Totemism, Animism, and the Depiction of Animals." In *Animals, Anima, Animus,* edited by Marketta Seppala, Jari-Pekka Vanhala, and Linda Weintraub, 181–207. Pori, Finland: Pori Art Museum.

Kendall, Laurel. 2021. *Mediums and Magical Things: Statues, Paintings, and Masks in Asian Places.* Oakland, CA: University of California Press.

Kendall, Laurel, and Wayan Pasek Ariati. 2020. "Scary Mask/Balinese Local Protector: The Curious History of Jero Amerika." *Anthropology and Humanism* 45 (2): 279–308.

Kendall, Laurel, Vũ Thị Thanh Tâm, and Nguyễn Thị Thu Hương. 2010. "Beautiful and Efficacious Statues: Magic, Commodities, Agency, and the Production of Sacred Objects in Popular Religion in Vietnam." *Material Religion: The Journal of Objects, Art and Belief* 6 (1): 60–85.

Pedersen, Morten A. 2011. *Not Quite Shamans: Spirit Worlds and Political Lives in Northern Mongolia.* Ithaca, NY: Cornell University Press.

Pels, Peter. 1998. "The Spirit of Matter: On Fetish, Rarity, Fact, and Fancy." In *Border Fetishisms: Material Objects in Unstable Spaces,* edited by Patricia Spyer, 91–121. New York and London: Routledge.

Provinelli, Elizabeth A. 1996. "Do Rocks Listen? The Cultural Politics of Apprehending Australian Aboriginal Labor." *American Anthropologist, New Series* 97 (3): 505–518.

Santos-Granero, Fernando. 2009. "Introduction: Amerindian Constructional Views of the World." In *The Occult Life of Things: Native Amazonian Theories of Materiality and Personhood,* edited by Fernando Santos-Granero, 1–29. Tucson, AZ: University of Arizona Press.

Silvio, Teri. 2019. *Puppets, Gods, and Brands: Theorizing the Age of Animation from Taiwan.* Honolulu, HI: University of Hawai'i Press.

Swearer, Donald K. 2004. *Becoming the Buddha: The Ritual of Image Consecration in Thailand.* Princeton, NJ: Princeton University Press.

Slattum, Judy, and Paul Schraub. 2003. *Balinese Masks: Spirits of an Ancient Drama.* Singapore: Periplus.

Tylor, Edward B. (1871) 1958. *Religion in Primitive Culture.* New York: Harper and Row.

Viveiros de Castro, Eduardo B. 2004. "Exchanging Perspectives: The Transformation of Objects into Subjects in Amerindian Ontologies." *Common Knowledge* 10 (3): 463–484.

Wiener, Margaret J. 1995. *Visible and Invisible Realms: Power, Magic, and Colonial Conquest in Bali.* Chicago, IL: University of Chicago Press.

2.5

"BRAINSMITHING" AFRICAN MATERIAL RELIGION

Allen F. Roberts and Mary "Polly" Nooter Roberts[1]

In "An Artist's Life of Perseverance" (2021), Yinka Elujoba presents the African American artist Lonnie Holley's evocative works created from salvaged materials. Born in 1950 as the seventh of his mother's twenty-seven children, Holley's growing up was difficult indeed. A poignant revelation led to his current practice: "I had been thrown away as a child, and here I was building something out of unwanted things."[2] Holley holds that "art saved my life. It was a lifeline I found. It was my floatation device" (Tepper 2019), and his "positive existence" is "a living testament to the power of faith and redemption. The work he creates is shaped by memories as much as it is a form of catharsis, and behind it all the drive of the true artist gives the work life. His message seems to be, 'If Lonnie can make it'"—if he can persevere—"'you can too'" (Sloan 2015: 7). As he has "discovered art as service" to others, Holley further asserts: "I want that when all of these—all my work—are presented, people can say, 'Oh that Lonnie, he took it all, his hands took the spirit, the things they don't want us to have, and *boom*, brought it together'" (Elujoba 2021).

Just one example of this sort of bringing together can be seen in the work *Memorial at Friendship Church* (see Figure 2.5.1). Holley found some of the materials for the sculpture discarded in the parish graveyard of Friendship Church in Gee's Bend (Boykin), Alabama, including the artificial flowers. The piece honors those living and those who have been lost in Gee's Bend. As Holley holds, "African Americans' first schooling was in those churches. I'm proud of the churches in that humans can go to them and learn something" (quoted in N. Brown 2015).

Materials that Holley repurposes "'speak'" to him (Sloan 2015: 7). He states that "'art is the language that all people speak. I feel like I can speak back to my ancestors through my art'" (Tepper 2019). The "furious curiosity" that Holley manifests in his works created from found materials responds to "the oldest tradition of African American sculpture," and one must assume that African influences are so implied.[3] He is also an accomplished improvisational musician, and in reflecting upon his art-making, Holley holds that "it's about the brain—same brain that produces music produces visual art. I call it *brainsmithing*" (Elujoba 2021, emphasis added). Given the artist's fusing of scrap metal with other detritus, one has to imagine that "brainsmithing" is Holley's riff on "blacksmithing," undoubtedly with added nuance should the blacksmith be Black.[4] An ambitious exhibition and book program at the UCLA Fowler Museum called *Striking Iron: The Art of African Blacksmiths* (2019) suggests

DOI: 10.4324/9781351176231-14

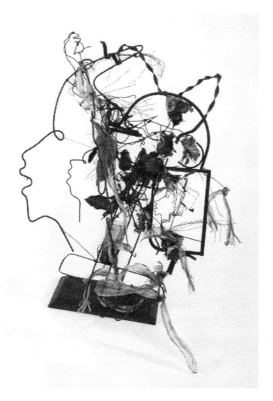

Figure 2.5.1   *Memorial at Friendship Church*, 2006, by Lonnie Holley, USA. Repurposed metal, artificial flowers, ribbon, wood, glass. 96.5 cm. Artist's collection. Photo by John Bentham with permission.

associations that may inform extension of Holley's wonder-word to other circumstances in the pages to follow.[5]

African blacksmiths have long been masters of transformation—especially in precolonial times when their roles complemented those of men smelting iron from local ores. The latter process requires contained and controlled temperatures of 2,200° Fahrenheit (1,200° Celsius). What a staggering achievement it was that such ends were achieved in hand-crafted earthen furnaces via technologies independently invented in several widely distant regions across sub-Saharan Africa. A combination of keen observational sciences, practical technologies, carefully coordinated taskscapes, and sympoietic division of labor constituted brainsmithing of the first order.[6]

Once iron ore was smelted, earlier African blacksmiths forged the resulting metal into all manner of useful tools, weapons, currency tokens, sacred paraphernalia, accouterments, jewelry, and gadgets. Such work requires precise skills matched by keen intellect guided by ancestral wisdom and intercession (see McNaughton 1988; Dougnan 2019). In these regards one recalls how, in his "Images of the Smithy," philosopher Gaston Bachelard suggests that "dreamed hypotheses . . . [are] at the root of even the clearest of technical processes" (1991: 133). Indeed, African iron-working required "enchanted technologies" (Gell 1994) that marshaled arcane medicines and spiritual relationships as "the craft of ritual made faith physical" (Sennett 2008: 12).

Complexities of an African blacksmith's taskscape and the sympoietic coordination of his assistants are illustrated by a Gelede headpiece realized by a Yoruba artist in the Republic of Bénin (Joyce and Drewal 2019; see Figure 2.5.2). Gelede masks depict calm female faces

169

to invoke and praise "Our Mothers" for their generative powers (Lawal 1997). An upper register often comments upon community affairs, here depicting blacksmiths forging useful and significant iron objects. The men are guided by Ogun, the Yoruba divinity responsible for such cutting-edge brainsmithing (Abiodun and Drewal 2019). The headpiece would have been an element of complex costuming, choreography, and music composed for a single performance event. An audience drawn to such creativity was offered an opportunity to reflect upon spiritual and practical aspects of blacksmiths' work so essential to community life.

The transformational capacities of forging iron were of such fundamental importance that some central African societies associated blacksmiths with semi-divine royalty, while smiths' hammers and anvils might bear their own powers as animated beings (Dewey and Roberts 2019). Furthermore, as blacksmiths then and now "participate in the world of materials, the properties of materials are not attributes but histories" that are "processual and relational" (Ingold 2007: 14–15). "Every property is a condensed story," and such recognition leads Tim Ingold to propose a "radical . . . ontology that assigns primacy to the processes of formation as against . . . final products." That is, iron and what is crafted from it "give shape to the forms of thought" as often as "the mind imposes its forms on material objects" (2010: 91, 95).

All these intersections, all these inputs constitute what contemporary sculptor Alison Saar has termed the "wisdom" of materials: where they have been, what they have "seen," what has happened in their presence, and the memories they hold and instigate that then contribute

Figure 2.5.2   Gelede mask, Yoruba peoples, mid-twentieth century. Attributed to Alaiye Adeisa Et-
uobe, Ketu region of southeastern Republic of Bénin. Wood, laundry bluing, pigment.
62 cm. Fowler Museum at UCLA, X70.990. Gift of Mr. and Mrs. Harry Hughes. Photo
by Don Cole printed with permission.

to what is made from them next.[7] As Victoria Rovine might add, "reused products . . . project *facture*—the traces, visible or implied, of the artists' hands. These implied narratives of people interacting with materials provide the space for imagining how objects connect to cultures" (2014: 253, emphasis added). Such creative relationships inform what we understand Lonnie Holley to mean by brainsmithing, for "every feature [of his works]—each bend of wire, piece of string, empty bottle, or metal rod—is imbued with meaning" (N. Brown 2015), all based upon the "condensed stories" and "wisdom" of the varied materials he finds, combines, and repurposes through his own inspired and inspiring *facture*.

Resonant with such reasoning is Houston Baker's suggestion that "there are no arrested *things*, only myriad relations in the making" (1994: 186). Indeed, a brainsmith's works may seem static, yet they never sit still. As Jane Bennett suggests, "the desire of the craftsperson to see what a metal can *do* . . . enables him to discern a life in metal and thus, eventually, to collaborate more productively with it" (2010: 60). Notice Bennett's term "collaborate": such materials afford their own efficacies as they are worked, their own "incipient tendencies and propensities" that lead to a "vibrant materiality . . . that is *itself* heterogeneous, itself a differential of intensities, itself a life" (56–57).

Vital materials become what a brainsmith can and will create from them. Yet what is so produced is informed by what might have been crafted but was not, leaving an "*otherwise* that remains unrealized," a "might make" to be executed on another occasion, as Susan Stewart suggests (2011: 16–17). A completed work "comes to dominate as all of the possible 'otherwises' in the artist's choices fall away and the work emerges as what it is as being as well as happening—the outcome of a series of decisions that are dense with the possibilities of what was not chosen, what was not actualized" (118). The efficacies of objects are informed by such potential.

Brainsmiths' imaginative but intensely hard work characterizes the pluck of disadvantaged people everywhere, throughout time. Senegalese and other French-speaking Africans often jokingly refer to such abilities as "System D" via the common exhortation *Débrouille-toi*: be resourceful, figure it out, make do with what is available when so much is not.[8] Ironies include that there can be nothing systematic about System D. In defying others' expectations of what materials are and what can be produced from them, "we do things contrary to their sense," as a young Senegalese recycler put it. Meaning is upended, new courses charted (A. Roberts 1992, 1995). Such abilities are so essential that success—as measured in being able to feed and clothe one's family—is deemed divinely inspired. One is reminded of how, in his improvisations, Lonnie Holley "[takes] it all, his hands [take] the spirit" (Holley in Elujoba 2021).

Brainsmithing entails ever-evolving processes as circumstances change and new necessities arise. Mundane materials may be transformed to meet emerging spiritual needs, as when Assane Faye cut up and spot-soldered food and beverage cans, fashioning the metal into model boats.[9] Although his primary market was expatriate tourists buying clever toys to bring home to their children, to Faye's initial surprise, elderly Senegalese Muslim men occasionally purchased his miniature craft. As a venerable gentleman explained, the talismans that they wear—often holy texts held in amulets—must remain unsullied and so they must be removed before a couple engages in conjugal relations. Faye's vessels serve as ideal repositories for such sacred scripts—especially since the vast ocean on which boats venture forth from Senegalese shores is the essence of God's purity. When he learned this, Faye sought ways to attract just such local customers in addition to his usual clientele. To him, though, this new outlet was not so much a stroke of "luck" or a manifestation of his own creative genius; instead, Faye knew that his every innovation was a blessing. Indeed, it would be hubristic to take credit for any such inventions.[10]

Then there are shrines composed of recycled materials associated with quotidian practice that may be understood as "repositories of history" (K. Brown 1989: 72). For example, a blacksmith named Alomadin Robert Adjovi who maintained a forge in the ancient city of Ouidah, Republic of Bénin, composed an altar of metal snippets from his various projects that he deemed too small or irregular for further use (A. Roberts 1995: 99–100). Adjovi was devoted to the powerful god Gu (Ogun), as are peoples of the Vodun religious complex of southwestern Nigeria, coastal Bénin and Togo, and throughout the African Americas. Metals and innovation are Gu's province as "Lord of the Cutting Edge"—with the pun as apposite in local languages as in English (Thompson 1984: 53; cf. Abiodun and Drewal 2019). When Adjovi's forged works were directed to everyday needs, they possessed and generated *ase* (pronounced "ah-shay") vital force and "performative power" (Abiodun 2014: 53–87). As the blacksmith repurposed detritus, potential was accumulated in his shrine and *ase* instigated his ongoing creativity. Furthermore, as "an apocalypse of iron" and the "face" of Gu (Thompson 1993: 184), Adjovi's shrine was nourished with palm oil and other sacralizing substances to sustain its vitality as a source of inspiration and empowerment.

Brainsmithing in Contemporary Senegalese Arts

For decades now, Senegalese artists have realized engaging works from repurposed materials.[11] Like Lonnie Holley, such artists are "prophets of ordinary stuff" (Young 2001: 5, cited in Umberger 2015: 30). Reflecting upon his own repurposing of materials, Viyé Diba has asserted that "my problem is not representation as usual. It is another vision that reveals but is not at the disposition of everyone. . . . I am in the ideology of the least known."[12] Such a purposefully obscure philosophy is at play in the paintings, sculptures, and other creations of many Senegalese contemporary artists. While their works attract through evident genius of color and composition, and while the artists certainly hope for exhibitions and sales, sacred secrets are nonetheless often in the mix.

Zahir and *batin* are Arabic terms borrowed into Wolof and other languages of Muslim worlds to articulate a dialectic between that which is evident in life (*zahir*) and the hidden, secret side of things (*batin*). *Batin* is at the disposition of those whose mystical training permits them to perceive such revelations.[13] The *work* of such works of art—their efficacies, that is—is realized through blessing energies called *baraka*. In a way, then, Diba's ideology may remain "least known" to many, for it is not necessary to plumb the esoteric depths of his sculpted paintings to enjoy their beauty at the superficial levels of *zahir*. Yet, if one *does* know something of his works' *batin*, the *baraka* that is thus conveyed makes their aesthetic impact all the greater. Indeed, for some, owning or simply viewing such paintings and sculptures may bring the sacred to bear upon even the most mundane of circumstances.

Most Senegalese are Muslims and follow Sufi Ways (*tariqa*) which are either local or were introduced to what is now their nation-state (Mbacké 2005). Among these, material arts and practices are far more pronounced in a movement known as the Mourides (Muridiyya) than in other Senegalese *tariqa*. Mourides are inspired by the writings and life lessons of Sheikh Amadu Bamba (1853–1927), a pacifist, poet, and Senegalese Sufi saint. They especially recall his celebrated exhortation: "Work as if you'll never die, Pray as if you'll die tomorrow," as complemented by rousingly euphonious Wolof exclamations such as *Ligey ci topp, Yalla la bokk* ("Work is among the ways to adore God") and *Yall, Yall, bey sap tool* ("Call upon God, Call upon God, but farm your field!") (Anon. 1999). Indeed, Mourides are known for their sustained labor, and none more so than Baye Falls, who are a subset of the *tariqa* named for their dedication to Sheikh Ibra Fall (c. 1858–1930), Bamba's first and most fervent follower (Roberts and Roberts 2003a: 109–121). Baye Falls are often ascetic in their deep commitment to work as prayer, to the extent that some must be beseeched or instructed to cease their toils lest they collapse in exhaustion.

The power and practicality of Bamba's messages have enabled Mourides to thrive within the harsh contexts of their ever-expanding diaspora. As the renowned Mouride vocalist Youssou NDour asserts in his anthem "Mame Bamba" (1994): "Do you hear me Father Bamba? . . . Now I can go anywhere, 'cause I know you'll be there. . . . Your prayers, our prayers, oh no they will not be ignored" (cf. Babou 2021). The need for such succor is especially acute in the inner cities of Senegal's fast-growing urban complexes, where Bamba's blessings help people to "create work where there is none," as Viyé Diba holds. And more than a few Mourides express the depth of their devotional commitment by making art, for "they do not draw a distinction among art making, work and prayer. Rather, they see all three as conjoined aspects of service" (Kart 2020: 48). Like Lonnie Holley, then, Mouride artists can be most *purposeful*, inspired brainsmiths.

Several renowned contemporary artists have considered themselves to be Baye Falls first and foremost, and so are dedicated to work as prayer. The late Moustapha Dimé (d. 1998) was one such. He often created anthropomorphic sculptures from jetsam he discovered on the rocky shores of Gorée Island, an infamous entrepot of the trans-Atlantic slave trade.[14] There Dimé maintained a studio perched like an aerie on a cliff below ruined French battlements that protected the harbor of colonial Dakar.[15] Both his artwork and his studio can be seen in Figure 2.5.3, wherein an unnamed, two-part anthropomorphic sculpture hewn from driftwood stands to either side of the studio's staircase leading to a turret. The work had been featured in the 1993 Venice Biennale (McEvilly 1993). Another anthropomorphic work hanging from the side of the staircase includes sections of wooden pestles with which women grind staple grains. As evocative as Dimé's constructions remain, Susan Kart suggests that his "ultimate achievement . . . was his adoption of process over product. Making the [art] object was no longer quotidian, it was spiritual; the finished product was simply a phase in a larger, ongoing process of harvesting from nature, work, service, and transformation" (2020: 48, 53, echoing Ingold 2010: 91, 95, as cited above).

Dimé held that "for me, sculpture is a form of practicing Islam. . . . God created visual beauty in the world. And there is nothing more beautiful than a work of art, so the work of art is very close to God" (cited in McEvilly 1993: 40, 51–52; cf. Sotiaux 1997: 13). Following such reasoning, the artist told us that

> I don't separate the artist in me from the *taalibé* [devotee] because it is the artist who is a *taalibé*. And I think that, fundamentally, what permits me to understand that I live the Creation is that, really, it is the life of a *taalibé* which has given me this strength. I work just as other Mourides do [recycling materials] in places like the Colobane junkyard of Dakar. . . . It's the same thing, except that I work through artistic expression. I work with my sentiments and my emotions. . . . For me, work is even a prayer. . . . I divinely transcend myself through my work.[16]

The artist then explained that, as a Baye Fall, he was particularly devoted to Ibra "Lampe" Fall, who

> had a way of life that surpassed spirituality in space and time. He was not interested in the material world. Sheikh Ibra was nothing but Light. He metamorphosed into Light through *fana*.[17] He has the ability to speak with the ocean, the wind, to see angels, and

Figure 2.5.3   Studio of the late Moustapha Dimé, Gorée Island, Dakar Harbor, Senegal. Photo by the
authors (2001).

to intervene with people from very far away. This is *batin*. *Batin* is an interior Light. You
can read on a person's forehead that he is a Mouride. This is a capacity to go where one
must that belongs neither to the rich nor the poor but to the person who takes the time
to develop the Light of *batin*.

As was Dimé, Moussa Tine is motivated by profoundly mystical thoughts shared by Senegalese Sufis that he makes manifest in many of his works of art.[18] In particular, his "Elevations"
and "Rythme Baye Fall" sculptural paintings of the late 1990s exemplify how his sense of
purpose is based upon the uplifting messages and practices of Senegalese Sufism in the lives
of devotees of Sheikh Ibra Fall (Roberts and Roberts 2003a: 204–211). For example, we
see in Figure 2.5.4 the abstracted forms of two hardworking Baye Fall followers of Sheikh
Amadu Bamba. The figures are fashioned from muffler metal painted shades of ochre and
tooled to suggest details of anatomy and clothing. Tine depicts the Baye Falls as uplifted in
ecstasy. As the artist explained, the frame, clad in colorful recycled metal sheeting and wire,
is to be mounted away from the wall so that the Baye Falls throw shadows.

   Tine began his career in humble circumstances as a boy taking fares from passengers
riding a *car-rapide* mini-bus. *Car-rapides* are often brightly decorated, and while young, Tine
painted his vehicle with action-packed portraits of Ibra Fall and other Mouride devotional
imagery. His work was so admired that he was paid to decorate other buses. Later in life,
Tine studied contemporary art at the National School of Fine Arts of Dakar where he

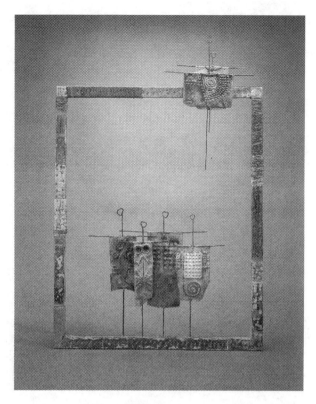

Figure 2.5.4   Altitude, 2001, from the *Elevations* series, by Moussa Tine, Dakar, Senegal. Scrap metal, wood, paint. 100.5 cm. Fowler Museum at UCLA, X2007.12.3. Gift of Doran H. Ross. Photo by Don Cole printed with permission.

learned to paint with acrylics and often explored spiritual themes such as when portraying Baye Fall families. In the late 1990s, Tine created evocative figures of paint-soaked rags attached to canvases covered with earth-tone acrylics stressed with sand and other abrasives. More frequently during this period, the artist fashioned thin sheets of recycled plywood into anthropomorphic figures.

In such work, Tine presented essential qualities of Baye Fall life from a perspective that art theorist Kobena Mercer might term "discrepant abstraction." Postcolonial understanding of the world's "multiple modernities" can be understood through such approaches as "creative dynamics . . . set in motion when different visual languages are brought into dialogue" (2006: 7). In other words, the works of Tine and other Senegalese contemporary artists do not strictly exemplify Modernist "abstraction" as understood through Eurocentric models—although, superficially, such a reading may be possible given the artists' beaux-art training and, of course, the fact that those beholding such works are free to interpret them as they will. Complementing such aspects of Tine's artistry, however, are secrets of *batin* that may reveal what making art can mean to artists and their knowledgeable clients. Rather than being "reduced" to the seeming simplicities of abstraction, artists like Tine who participate in Diba's "ideology of the least known" present esoteric nuances and efficacies. As a result, many contemporary works by Senegalese artists are far more profound than may meet the eye.

In the late 1990s, Tine began experimenting with tooled, highly abstracted, repurposed-metal figures bolted to underlying painted surfaces. The figures' colorful tunics are stippled and punctured in allusion to patchwork or patterned textiles, and lower extensions are attached with woven wire. Their positioning evokes Baye Fall rhythms—that is, the slow circling that Mourides perform to loudly intoned devotional music as dancers become entranced (Roberts and Roberts 2003b). "There are specific symbols" in such works, Tine asserts:

> I see an *elevation* in the Baye Fall. . . . It is a spiritual elevation, and an elevation of the person. . . . In Africa, the grouping of individuals is very important. The family is one kind of group and Islam another, and people praying together create a certain atmosphere of forgiveness which in turn allows an individual to reach a state of bliss more easily. The group facilitates this process. This is why there are always masses of Mourides in my works. And groupings of people produce rhythm, but an innocence has been discovered as well. I am always trying to interpret the grouping of people, a grouping which will lead to the ideal.

Tine's work with recycled metal has added further spiritual dimensions to his creations. As he explains:

> I look for metal in my environment, and this is why it takes a long time to make these works. I studied the elements, and I pulled apart a discarded automobile muffler to find this metal. It comes to me already slightly bronze-colored because of the heat it has known, and it is very strong metal. My choice relates to my earlier work with *car rapides*: these things are connected through an existence that is mine. You can always feel the metal, the iron, the thread in my work.

As Tine emphasized in a different conversation with us, he chooses muffler metal because it "has taken the heat"—it has proven itself, it has resisted its own destruction, it has continued to function despite the dire challenges it has endured. By analogy, so have the Baye Falls to whom he alludes. Such careful consideration of materials means that the "wisdom" and "vibrant materiality" of repurposed muffler metal are given participatory places in Tine's brainsmithed works.[19]

Like Moussa Tine, Viyé Diba acknowledges the *ontology* of his materials as he "interrogates" them—as he puts it. From the earliest stages of his artistic career, Diba has sought to dialogue with recycled materials as a means of interrogating urban environments.[20] When "African artists *aggress* wood, as one aggresses the human body with scarifications, tattoos, and the like," he asserts, "the body reacts. There is a dialog, a total communication between the medium and the person who creates. . . . It is a matter of seeing through my artistic pre-occupations how I can recuperate materials and valorize them, elevate them to the dignity of a work of art"(cited in Huchard 1994: 24). For example, many of Diba's works feature locally strip-woven textiles of the sort most often used for shrouds these days. He sews the strips together and covers them with paint mixed with sand to make the surface more tactile and so an object in its own right. His canvases are then mounted on recycled wood that he gouges and wrenches and pulls and twists to test the expressive limits of his media. By such means, he engages and—indeed, as Jane Bennett (2010: 60) might put it—he "collaborates" with the substances to unlock their expressive potentialities. That is, Diba permits wood, cloth, and pigment to *prove* what they can do in resisting his "aggressions." In this, he honors the materials' resilience while moving a step closer to understanding and revealing their *batin*—their mysteries.

Diba's works possess several signature motifs. One, often carved into or painted upon the surface of his paintings, is a vertically oriented rectangle with an inverted V-shaped bottom. Such forms refer to humanity, Diba explains, and he situates them in his works to emphasize intimate environmental relationships. Another repeated sign is a knotted strip of fabric on the lower edge of his compositions and/or a piece of wood wrapped in cloth and suspended from the border of the work as if pulling it downward. These anchoring elements underscore the importance of "weight" for Diba, suggesting gravity, closeness to the earth, and a sense of having one's feet firmly planted.

Among the most suggestive elements of Diba's works are cloth-covered pockets that bulge from the surface of his canvases. They recall those of Senegalese men's robes that may hold sacred talismanic texts as well as practical items; but for Diba, pockets also allude to *batin*, the hidden side of every visible reality that permeates Sufi thought and spiritual quest. Consider the sculpted painting seen in Figure 2.5.5. A pocket holds secrets, and one is escaping its confinement.

Through such practices, Diba hopes to develop a relationship between his work and "the spirit of Mouridism," as he puts it. For instance, he visits tailors who produce the strikingly fashionable clothing of Dakarois and, especially, Dakaroises (see Heath 1990; Mustafa 2001). Some tailors also assemble scraps of fabric to produce the patchwork clothing of Baye Falls called *njaxas*, a name for assembling things once separate and so standing for the solidarity that Baye Falls demonstrate through their hard work together as a form of prayer. Diba obtains such odds and ends from tailors because, as he notes: "These scraps will not be isolated and unable to communicate. They play an essential role, for they provoke volume and they release another dimension of my painting" when they are stuffed into pockets sometimes sewn onto his painted surfaces. The contents of these pockets may spill forth to "reveal what is hidden. Therefore I think it is a dialectic between the secret, which constitutes the pockets in my work, and their outburst in a kind of revelation, a discovery of Light, truth, and knowledge." Indeed, Mouridism itself "is also *batin*, or hidden knowledge, a kind of avant-garde knowledge" that Diba seeks to "interrogate" and vitalize through his works.

Ndary Lo (or Lô, 1961–2017) was another contemporary artist whom we were fortunate enough to interview before his untimely demise. Lo garnered international acclaim during

Figure 2.5.5 *Suspension*, 2001, by Viyé Diba, Dakar, Senegal. Cotton, wood, acrylic paint, fiber bindings. 99 cm. Smithsonian Institute, National Museum of African Art, 2018–21–6. Gift of Allen F. Roberts and family in loving memory of Dr. Mary (Polly) Nooter Roberts. Photo by Don Cole printed with permission.

his last years. From the start, his larger-than-life, impossibly stretched figures welded from recycled iron rebar have been celebrated for a dynamism informed by mystical profundity. As the Senegalese art critic Sylvain Sankalé has suggested, "the driving force of Ndary Lo's work resided in his spirituality." Yet, as the same critic continued with acerbic hyperbole, Lo's approach was

> not one of those spiritualities of shoddy quality (*de pacotille*) exhibited like indecent wounds by the fatuous hypocrites (*cagots*) that our new century discovers and reveres. Instead, his spirituality was an intimate fusion, lived, a way of seeing and a way of life, a way of being. And he did not seek exotic, esoteric, and grotesquely abstruse sources, nor was his work the return of a paganism of uncertain origins. Nor was it one of those "ready-to-use" or "one-use-only" concepts of which our time without a soul repays itself as victim of the eternal money-changers of the Temple. Lo's work was all the more attractive for never taking on the discourse of an artist, . . . [and it still] reads like a watermark for the initiate who knows how to see, read, and decipher the messages deliberately sown into his codes and signs.[21]

Among Lo's best-known works are taut figures that stride forth with evident purpose. The artist often created configurations that defined meaningful places all too often anonymous and anomic. Yet his sculptures "occupy space in a surprising manner, like a compass tracing a curve into infinity" (Sankalé 2004: 29). Even more expressive are tall, mostly female figures looking upward and raising their open palms in Muslim postures of prayerful supplication that seem to "remain there, for an instant, perhaps for eternity" (Falgayrettes-Leveau 2002: 5). For example, in the foreground of Figure 2.5.6, a five-foot-tall *Walking Man* is caulked in white. Behind are two praying figures of rusted rebar, one partially covered with white pigment. To the left is a blackened figure wearing a loosely realized dress of yellow, green, and red strings. To the right is the breast of a large figure of rusted rebar standing outside the frame of the picture. Lo kept a host of such sculptures packed into a narrow courtyard at his studio in Dakar. Although convenient storage was undoubtedly his first-order goal, such a fervent collectivity deeply affected us when we visited the artist in 2006.

Lo took a different path at the 2006 Dak'Art Bienniale of Contemporary African Art for which he created a complex installation in memory of Rosa Parks who had died the previous fall (M. Roberts 2006; Wade 2006: 224–225). Lo's "The Refusal of Rosa Parks" referred to the signal moment in 1955 when the then-young African American woman defied the racial segregation of public busing in Montgomery, Alabama. Lo's work consisted of banks of sepia-toned photo-realist paintings of Parks and many other heroes of human rights struggles worldwide, including Sheikh Amadu Bamba. The portraits were set in an environment framed by chains of sliced bovine bones linked with thick circlets of recycled iron recalling the fetters of enslaved Africans.

In the course of painting and then constructing his installation, Lo had a revelation. As he explained to us in his impeccable English,

> the work I made for Rosa Parks was very important for me because she was the first Black woman who refused to give up her place to a White man, and I took this idea and wanted to make a major tribute to her. And then I thought of all the Rosa Parkses in the world, [and] Sheikh Amadu Bamba is one of them. . . . The work I want to do on Sheikh Amadu Bamba is really important for me, because when I was doing "The Refusal of Rosa Parks" I said to myself, "I have something more than Rosa Parks here

Figure 2.5.6   Sculptures in repurposed iron rebar by Ndary Lo, Dakar, Senegal. Photo by the authors (2006).

in my own country." Bamba was deported to Gabon, but he escaped [death] every time. Now I wanted to consider those who were in the contemporary time of Sheikh Amadu Bamba, and all the things he endured, with the ship [of exile to Gabon], and with the bull [that Bamba miraculously escaped in a murderous colonial conspiracy], and now I am doing something like this to have ideas of how to represent all these things.[22] It will be just like the Rosa Parks, a wall piece, different elements composing the work, paintings, sculptures, found objects. All will be in one room. . . .

What interests me first . . . is Black people, all the Blacks who have given Blackness a good name. . . . When you have something in front of you, you do not see it, you do not pay attention. But really, Rosa Parks made me aware of all the responsibilities that Sheikh Amadu Bamba has, she is the one who made me realize all the intentions of Bamba. Things are getting in order in my mind. . . . And talking about Black people, work like this is for us to do, we Black people, because if we don't do it no one will do it for us. This is our responsibility. . . . I will do it for myself, and it is my responsibility to do this for everyone.

Through such sentiments, brainsmiths Ndary Lo and Lonnie Holley share(d) a sense of "art as service" (Holley cited in Elujoba 2021).

The ease with which Ndary Lo, Mustapha Dimé, Moussa Tine, Viyé Diba, and other Senegalese contemporary artists who are mystically inclined Muslims navigate among global aspirations and local inspirations is mirrored in the interactions of universal Islamic principles and focused devotions. The tensions between such positions are the fabric of Mouride daily life. Contemporary artworks may be read as superficially evident (*zahir*) to global audiences, but also for their hidden inspiration (*batin*) available to those engaged in Sufi profundities. Indeed, the Senegalese artists presented here would be unlikely to find any contradiction between the *zahir* and *batin* of their oeuvres, for the *work* of such works includes reflection of just such meaningful dimensions and dialectics.

Envoi

The processual brainsmithing of certain Senegalese artists may be based upon Sufi precepts deserving even deeper exploration. The savant Souleymane Bachir Diagne has reflected upon Islam's "open, dynamic, ever-changing cosmology" of "a world continuously making itself"—as in the Quranic verses "[God] adds to creation as He will" (Sura 35: 1) and "Every day [God] attends to some task" (Sura 55: 29). Following such logic, Diagne continues, "we are poles apart here from the notion of a completed, finite world: a world to be contemplated." Instead, "cosmology as an open world, an unfinished world . . . leads to a philosophy of time perceived as creativity" and "an élan vital . . . to renew and revive society" (2020: 75). From a "Sufi perspective in Islam, particular emphasis lies on the notion that *the human being is not a state but a task*" (84, emphasis added).

Never-finished processes of *making* material religion—including the "facture" of objects that bear "the traces, visible or implied, of . . . artists' hands" (Rovine 2014: 253)—often outweigh the significance of end products. Indeed, brainsmithing of the sort may be "the oldest tradition of African American sculpture" (Holley 2018), linked as such work is to African "radical ontologies assigning primacy to processes of formation as against final products" (paraphrasing Ingold 2010: 91). Furthermore, it is in bringing together recycled materials from first-purposed items "*they* don't want us to have" that "hands may take the spirit" inhering within such things to redirect to persons and communities in need (paraphrasing Lonnie Holley in Elujoba 2021). As the celebrated Los-Angeles-based African American brainsmith Betye Saar might add, "The chanciest thing is to put spirituality in art . . . because people don't understand it. . . . They're scared of it, so they ignore it. But if there's going to be any universal consciousness-raising, you have to deal with it."[23] And such is precisely what many artistic brainsmiths aspire to bring into being as gifts to humanity.

Notes

1 Contributions of Polly Roberts are posthumous, as she passed away in 2018 when our work toward this paper was already underway. Her research, writing, teaching, and museum exhibitions inform every word of the present essay, which is dedicated to Polly's memory. Thanks are extended to the many Senegalese friends who made our years of work together so joyous.

2 See Elujoba 2021. See Rosengarten 2015 for Holley's detailed exposition of his difficult upbringing and how he became an artist.

3 Quotations from Holley 2018 (www.lonnieholley.com, viewed 2021); "brainsmithing" is not mentioned on the site. Thanks to Matt Arnett for discussing these matters on behalf of Lonnie Holley via email in December 2021. On African roots of African American arts, see Thompson 1984.

4 "Brainsmithing" also resonates with "brainstorming" but offers creative nuances different from the potentially destructive ambiguities of "storm." A Google search in summer 2021 only brought up "brainsmith" as the name of an Indian manufacturer of innovative learning materials for children.

5 The *Striking Iron* book offers sixteen essays by anthropologists, archaeologists, art historians, historians, an astronomer, and a blacksmith. A. Roberts 2019 is an overview and introduction to the project; A. Roberts and M. Berns 2018 reviews the *Striking Iron* traveling exhibition.

6 See A. Roberts 2019 for an explanation of "taskscape" as the layout of skilled labor (from Ingold 2010: 97–98) and "sympoeisis," from the Greek, as the coordinated complexities of "making [something] together."

7 Lonnie Holley's works are consciously mnemonic in similar ways; see Umberger 2015. Saar's sense of material wisdom grew from her discovery of patterned Victorian ceiling tin discarded during the rehabilitation of Harlem brownstones in the early 1980s. "I'd find the stuff and . . . realize it . . . [had seen] babies being born and people making love and people dying. And so it had this wisdom." Covering her wooden figures with recovered tin was "sort of putting a skin on them . . . [that] contains these spirits and holds all these things . . . [and] gives the works a strength" (M. Roberts and Saar 2000: 41).

8 One is reminded of Tomás Ybarra-Frausto's compelling exposition of *rasquachismo* in Chicano expressive culture as "whatever coping strategies one uses to gain time, to make options, to retain hope" by "making do with what is at hand" (1991: 133).

9 See A. Roberts 1995: 89–90. This and the example of Mr. Adjovi's shrine in the next paragraph should be understood as particular to the place, moment, and persons named as interlocutors; the "ethnographic present" of these cases is the mid-1990s. Permission to use the artists' names was explicitly granted during A. Roberts's 1994 research in Senegal and Bénin.

10 "Creativity" as a cultural construction was among topics of Polly Roberts's studies of Luba art in the Democratic Republic of the Congo (M. Roberts 1998). While artists' identities are remembered and may be revered in some African societies (e.g., Yoruba; see Abiodun 2014), Assane Faye, as an ardent member of the Mouride Sufi movement of Senegal, attributed his success to the intercessions of Sheikh Amadu Bamba (1853–1927), founder of the Mourides; see Roberts and Roberts 2003a.

11 In discussing such matters, one must keep in mind how ethnocentric biases sometimes know no bounds, for African artists may be stigmatized for their very creativity simply because they are African. Holland Cotter (2013, cited in Rovine 2014: 259) has written of the Ghanaian artist El Anatsui's magisterial, captured cascades composed of colorful bits of detritus. He notes that, when some observers realize that the artist uses scrap, "clichés click into place: Africa = Recycling"—as though such choices indicate poverty of minds as well as means. Quite the contrary.

12 Our conversations with Viyé Diba, Moustapha Dimé, Moussa Tine, and Ndary Lo offered in the following paragraphs have been published at greater length (Roberts and Roberts 2003a, 2012) but are thoroughly recontextualized here.

13 See Nooter 1993 on how African arts more generally conceal and reveal through secrecy.

14 Gruber 2019 provides a discussion of contemporary Muslim approaches to depiction of living beings.

15 Dimé's studio has been converted to a non-profit atelier offering artist residencies (Kart 2020: 57); see "C.I.F.R.A (Atelier Moustapha DIME)" at the Sudplanète/South Planet "multilingual database" and portal, viewed January 27, 2022, http://www.spla.pro/en/file.organization.c-i-f-r-a-atelier-moustapha-dime.11285.html.

16 See Moustapha Dimé, personal communications 1996, 1997; Roberts and Roberts 2003a: 208–11. On recycling in the former junkyard of the Colobane neighborhood of Dakar, see A. Roberts 1995.

17 *Fana* is mystical effacement into the Word of God; see Ngom 2016: 47–48. The present tense of the next sentence of Dimé's transcribed conversation with us reflects the living presence of "Lampe" Fall, though long deceased.

18 Artists are obviously not "stuck in time," and although we assume that the thinking of Senegalese artists presented here continues to inform their more recent and ongoing works, the thoughts they shared with us were specific to the late 1990s and early 2000s, when we were working toward our *A Saint in the City: Sufi Arts of Urban Senegal* exhibition program. In the following paragraphs, our transcribed conversations with Moussa Tine date to this period.

19 One is reminded of Lonnie Holley's sculptures of repurposed materials: "To the extent that many Southern, vernacular African American artists respond visually and emotionally to objects that have traveled a hard road or [that] embody, materially or metaphorically, the place they come from, it is an affinity both poignant and logical" (Umberger 2015: 12).

20 Viyé Diba holds degrees from the Senegalese National Institute of the Arts and the National School of Art Education, where he has taught since 1986. He also holds a doctoral degree in Urban Geography from the University of Nice. See M. Roberts 2009, from which the following paragraph is adapted; cf. Harney 2004: 192–93, Grabski 2015.

21 See Sankalé 2004: 29–30, our translation from the French. Here and in the next paragraph, Sankalé's words are changed to the past tense because of Ndary Lo's death in 2017.

22 On the persecution of Amadu Bamba by French colonial authorities and the saint's miraculous responses, see Ngom 2016; Roberts and Roberts 2019.

23 Quoted in Cotter 2019. Betye Saar and Lonnie Holley have collaborated, and their evocative assemblages of found materials have sometimes been exhibited together—as in the Los Angeles County Museum of Art's *View from Here: Recent Acquisitions* exhibition of 2021 (Gonzalez 2021).

References

Abiodun, Rowland. 2014. *Yoruba Art and Language: Seeking the African in African Arts*. New York: Cambridge University Press.

Abiodun, Rowland, and Henry J. Drewal. 2019. "Ògún's Resonance in Yorùbá, Edo, and Fon Worlds." In *Striking Iron: The Art of African Blacksmiths*, edited by A. F. Roberts et al., 278–315. Los Angeles, CA: UCLA Fowler Museum.

Anonymous. 1999. "*Ligey ci Yopp, Yalla la Bokk*: Le Travail est une Dimension Élevée de L'adoration de Dieu." *Touba: Mensuel Islamique D'informations Générals, D'analyses et de Reflexions* 1: 30–31.

Babou, Cheikh Anta. 2021. *The Muridiyya on the Move: Islam, Migration, and Place Making*. Athens, OH: Ohio University Press.

Bachelard, Gaston. 1991. "Earth, Fire, and Water: Images of the Smithy." In *Gaston Bachelard, Subversive Humanist: Texts and Readings*, compiled by Mary McAllester Jones, 129–134. Madison, WI: University of Wisconsin Press.

Baker, Houston. 1994. "Beyond Artifacts: Cultural Studies and the New Hybridity of Rap." In *Cultural Artifacts and the Production of Meaning: The Page, the Image, and the Body*, edited by Margaret Ezell and Katherine O'Brien O'Keeffe, 183–197. Ann Arbor, MI: University of Michigan Press.

Bennett, Jane. 2010. *Vibrant Matter: A Political Ecology of Things*. Durham, NC: Duke University Press.

Brown, Karen. 1989. "Systematic Remembering, Systematic Forgetting: Ogou in Haiti." In *Africa's Ogun, Old World and New*, edited by Sandra T. Barnes, 65–89. Bloomington, IN: Indiana University Press.

Brown, Nic. 2015. "Southern Masters: Lonnie Holley." *Garden & Gun,* October/November. https://gardenandgun.com/feature/southern-masters-lonnie-holley/. See also "From the Mind of Lonnie Holley: A Brief Retrospective with Comments from the Artist," October/November 2015. https://gardenandgun.com/slideshow/from-the-mind-of-lonnie-holley/.

Cotter, Holland. 2013. "A Million Pieces of Home." *New York Times*, February 10, 2013. https://www.nytimes.com/2013/02/10/arts/design/a-million-pieces-of-home-el-anatsui-at-brooklyn-museum.html.

Cotter, Holland. 2019. "'It's About Time!' Betye Saar Takes the Summit." *New York Times*, September 15, 2019. https://www.nytimes.com/2019/09/04/arts/design/betye-saar.html.

Dewey, William J., and Allen F. Roberts. 2019. "Of Blacksmiths and Kings: A Central Bantu World." In *Striking Iron: The Art of African Blacksmiths*, edited by A. F. Roberts et al., 366–387. Los Angeles, CA: UCLA Fowler Museum.

Diagne, Souleyman Bachir. 2020. "On Philosophy in Islam and on the Question of a 'West African Islam.'" In *In Search of Africa(s): Universalism and Decolonial Thought* by Souleyman Bachir Diagne and Jean-Loup Amselle, translated by Andrew Brown, 71–86. Medford, MA: Polity Press.

Dougnan, Isaie. 2019. "Forged in the Marketplace: Migrant Blacksmiths' Identities in Bamako." In *Striking Iron: The Art of African Blacksmiths*, edited by A. F. Roberts et al., 448–455. Los Angeles, CA: UCLA Fowler Museum.

Elujoba, Yinka. 2021. "An Artist's Life of Perseverance." *New York Times,* May 7, 2021. https://www.nytimes.com/2021/05/06/arts/design/lonnie-holley.html.

Falgayrettes-Leveau, Christiane. 2002. *L'art en Marche de Ndary Lo*. Paris: Éditions Dapper.

Gell, Alfred. 1994. "The Technology of Enchantment and the Enchantment of Technology." In *Anthropology, Art, and Aesthetics*, edited by J. Coote and A. Shelton, 40–63. New York: Oxford University Press.

Gonzalez, Rita. 2021. "View from Here—Responding to the Present through LACMA's Evolving Collection." *LACMA Unframed*, February 18, 2021. https://unframed.lacma.org/2021/02/18/view-here%E2%80%94responding-present-through-lacma%E2%80%99s-evolving-collection.

Grabski, Joanna. 2015. "Viyé Diba's *Tout Se Sait* and the Affective Experience of Urban Life." *Nka: Journal of Contemporary African Art* 36: 94–106.

Gruber, Christiane, ed. 2019. *The Image Debate: Figural Representation in Islam and Across the World.* London: Gingko Library Press.

Harney, Elizabeth. 2004. *In Senghor's Shadow: Art, Politics, and the Avant-Garde in Senegal, 1960–1995.* Durham, NC: Duke University Press.

Heath, Debora. 1990. "Fashion, Anti-Fashion, and Heteroglossia in Urban Senegal." *American Ethnologist* 19 (1): 19–33.

Holley, Lonnie. 2018. Viewed January 26, 2022. https://www.lonnieholley.com/.

Huchard, Ousmane. 1994. *Viyé Diba, "Plasticien de L'environnement."* Dakar, Senegal: SEPIA.

Ingold, Tim. 2007. "Materials against Materiality." *Archaeological Dialogues* 14 (1): 1–16.

Ingold, Tim. 2010. "The Textility of Making." *Cambridge Journal of Economics* 34: 91–102.

Joyce, Tom, and Henry J. Drewal. 2019. "Gelede Mask Honoring Blacksmiths." In *Striking Iron: The Art of African Blacksmiths*, edited by A. F. Roberts et al., 100–103. Los Angeles, CA: UCLA Fowler Museum.

Kart, Susan. 2020. "Murid Methodology: Moustapha Dimé's Figurative Sculptures." *African Arts* 53 (4): 46–57.

Lawal, Babatunde. 1997. *The Gelede Spectacle: Art, Gender, and Social Harmony in an African Culture.* Seattle, WA: University of Washington Press.

Mbacké, Khadim. 2005. *Sufism and Religious Brotherhoods in Senegal.* Princeton, NJ: Marcus Wiener.

McEvilly, Thomas. 1993. *Fusion: West African Artists at the Venice Biennale.* Munich: Prestel for the Museum for African Art, New York.

McNaughton, Patrick. 1988. *The Mande Blacksmiths: Knowledge, Power, and Art in West Africa.* Bloomington: Indiana University Press.

Mercer, Kobena. 2006. "Introduction." In *Discrepant Abstraction*, edited by Kobena Mercer, 6–29. Cambridge, MA: MIT Press.

Mustafa, Hudita. 2001. "Ruins and Spectacles: Fashion and City Life in Contemporary Senegal." *Nka: Journal of Contemporary African Art* 15 (Winter): 47–53.

N'Dour, Youssou. 1994. "Mame Bamba." In *The Guide (Wommat)* CD. New York: Chaos Recordings, Columbia Records, Sony Music Entertainment.

Ngom, Fallou. 2016. *Muslims Beyond the Arab World: The Odyssey of 'Ajami and the Muridiyya.* New York: Oxford University Press.

Nooter, Mary H., ed. 1993. *Secrecy: African Art that Conceals and Reveals.* Munich: Prestel for the Museum for African Art, New York.

Roberts, Allen F. 1992. "Chance Encounters, Ironic Collage." *African Arts* 25 (2): 54–63, 97–98.

Roberts, Allen F. 1995. "The Ironies of System D." In *Recycled Reseen: Folk Art from the Global Scrap Heap*, edited by C. Cerny and S. Seriff, 82–101. New York: Harry Abrams for the Museum of International Folk Art, Santa Fe.

Roberts, Allen F. 2019. "Introduction." In *Striking Iron: The Art of African Blacksmiths*, edited by A. F. Roberts et al., 42–49. Los Angeles, CA: UCLA Fowler Museum.

Roberts, Allen F., and Marla C. Berns. 2018. "Exhibition Preview: 'Striking Iron: The Art of African Blacksmiths.'" *African Arts* 51 (1): cover, 65–85.

Roberts, Allen F., and Mary Nooter Roberts. 2003a. *A Saint in the City: Sufi Arts of Urban Senegal.* Los Angeles, CA: UCLA Fowler Museum of Cultural History.

Roberts, Allen F., and Mary Nooter Roberts. 2003b. "Music and 'Ontological Memory' Among Senegalese Sufis." In *The Interrelatedness of Music, Religion, and Ritual in African Performance Practice*, edited by Daniel K. Avorgbedor, 347–368. *African Studies* vol. 68. Lewiston, NY: Edwin Mellen Press.

Roberts, Allen F., and Mary Nooter Roberts. 2012. "Sufi Arts: Engaging Islam through Works of Contemporary Art in Senegal." In *The Wiley-Blackwell Companion to African Religions*, edited by Elias Kwifon Bongmba, 417–429. Oxford: Blackwell.

Roberts, Allen F., and Mary Nooter Roberts. 2019. "Enigma and Purpose: Visual Hagiographies of Urban Senegal." In *The Image Debate: Figural Representation in Islamic and Global Cultural Contexts*, edited by Christiane Gruber, 194–211. London: Gingko Library Press.

Roberts, Mary Nooter. 1998. "The Naming Game: Ideologies of Luba Artistic Identity." *African Arts* 31 (4): 56–73, 90–92.

Roberts, Mary Nooter. 2006. "DAK'ART 2006: Positions and Perspectives." *African Arts* 39 (4): 54–67.

Roberts, Mary Nooter. 2009. "Viyé Diba." In *The Dictionary of African Biography*, edited by E. Akyeampong and H. L. Gates, Vol. 2 of 6, 196–197. New York: Oxford University Press.

Roberts, Mary Nooter, and Alison Saar. 2000. *Body Politics: The Female Image in Luba Art and the Sculpture of Alison Saar.* Los Angeles, CA: UCLA Fowler Museum of Cultural History.

Rosengarten, Theodore. 2015. "Blackbirds: Lonnie Holley as Told to Theodore Rosengarten." In *Something to Take My Place: The Art of Lonnie Holley*, edited by Mark Sloan, 18–207. Charleston, SC: Halsey Institute of Contemporary Art, College of Charleston.

Rovine, Victoria. 2014. "'Africa = Recycling': Continuities and Discontinuities in the Reception of African Contemporary Art." In *Double Desire: Transculturation and Indigenous Contemporary Art*, edited by Ian Mclean, 245–263. Cambridge: Cambridge Scholars Publishing.

Sankalé, Sylvain. 2004. "Où Allons-Nous?" In *Ndary Lo, Verticales*, edited by Ndary Lo and M. Massamba, 26–30. Villeneuve d'Ascq, France: Éditions Périplans.

Sennett, Richard. 2008. *The Craftsman.* New Haven, CT: Yale University Press.

Sloan, Mark. 2015. "A Thought into a Thing." In *Something to Take My Place: The Art of Lonnie Holley*, edited by Mark Sloan, 6–9. Charleston, SC: Halsey Institute of Contemporary Art, College of Charleston.

Sotiaux, Daniel. 1997. *Viyé Diba/Moustapha Dimé.* Brussels: Centre d'Art Contemporain.

Stewart, Susan. 2011. *The Poet's Freedom: A Notebook on Making.* Chicago, IL: University of Chicago Press.

Tepper, Allie. 2019. "Drawn Out of the Muck of America: Lonnie Holley Interviewed by Allie Tepper." *Bomb Magazine*, August 26, 2019. https://bombmagazine.org/articles/drawn-out-of-the-muck-of-america-lonnie-holley-interviewed/.

Thompson, Robert Farris. 1984. *Flash of the Spirit: African and Afro-American Art and Philosophy.* New York: Vintage.

Thompson, Robert Farris. 1993. *Face of the Gods: Art and Altars of Africa and the African Americas.* Munich: Prestel for the Museum for African Art, New York.

Umberger, Leslie. 2015. "In Memory of the Blood." In *Something to Take My Place: The Art of Lonnie Holley*, edited by Mark Sloan, 10–33. Charleston, SC: Halsey Institute of Contemporary Art, College of Charleston.

Wade, Ousseynou. 2006. "Lo Ndary, Sénégal." In *DAK'ART 2006: 7ème Biennale de L'art Africain Contemporain*, edited by Ousseynou Wade, 224–225. Dakar: Biennale de l'Art africain contemporain de Dakar.

Ybarra-Frausto, Tomás. 1991. "The Chicano Movement/The Movement of Chicano Art." In *Exhibiting Cultures: The Poetics and Politics of Museum Display*, edited by Ivan Karp and Steven Lavine, 128–150. Washington, DC: Smithsonian Institution Press.

Young, Andrew. 2001. "Life Behind the Wall: A Call to Respond." In *Souls Grown Deep: African American Vernacular Art of the South*, 2 vols., edited by Paul Arnett and William Arnett. Atlanta, GA: Tinwood Books.

2.6

CROSSING HERITAGE

Material Religion at the Humboldt Forum

Duane Jethro

The Prussian Cultural Heritage Foundation triggered a furor in May 2017 when it announced that the Berlin City Palace, a monumental reconstruction project on the Museum Island housing the Humboldt Forum complex, would be decorated with a golden Christian cross. The public, politicians, scholars, religious figures, and heritage professionals were surprised and confounded by the idea that an iconic Christian religious symbol would top Germany's ambitious €600 million cultural heritage project. Complaining in the press, the Foundation for the Future of Berlin laid out one strand of the consternation, saying, "The Humboldt Forum is a place of worldwide dialogue, where the cultures of the world should be at home and on an equal footing without hierarchies. . . .[But] under a cross?" (Förderverein Berliner Schloss 2017).[1] Sigrid Hupach, the cultural policy spokesperson for the Left Party, similarly argued, "The Federal Government always asserts that the Humboldt Forum should become a museum complex of a new type for the entire world community. But how can such an open dialogue between cultures succeed if a cross on top of the dome already sets the tone?" For these critics, the cross interfered with Humboldt Forum's public character as a museum of world cultures because it symbolically elevated Christianity above the other cultures represented inside the building's exhibition halls, and thus framed intercultural dialogue in unequal terms. Or, as Sigrid Hupach bluntly put it, "Such a hierarchization of cultures is absurd." Rather than establishing cultural hierarchies or elevating Christian culture, the cross was also problematic, according to the spokesperson for the Green Party, because it "Redu[ced] the Humboldt Forum to a religion," which did "not correspond to basic humanist principles. . . . The new Berlin City Palace should serve the exchange of all cultures" (Wiegelmann 2017a). It seemed the cross blocked rather than brokered cultural exchange (Figure 2.6.1).

Evidently, the real problem with the cross was that it structured problematic relationships among religion, religious culture, and cultural heritage in the public domain. Religion conflicted with basic humanism and obstructed free cultural exchange, and the Humboldt Forum was a public heritage institution associated with secular humanism, cultural education, dialogue, tolerance, openness, and equality. The announcement about the Berlin City Palace's Christian cross therefore did not merely bring the Humboldt Forum into public conflict. It also threw the idea of the museum, and the concept of heritage as a secular notion, into relief.

DOI: 10.4324/9781351176231-15

Figure 2.6.1   Cross being prepared for installation. May 29, 2020. Photo by the author.

While critics could confidently adjudicate the secular properties of the museum as containing heritage, as opposed to the religious symbolism of the cross erected above, scholars were unsure about how and where heritage shaded into religion more generally. If heritage is assumed to refer to a shared past manifest in material form, that is consciously recalled and honored by a defined group or people, then it bears the hallmarks of many definitions of religion. Artifacts of high-cultural and aesthetic value, such as rare, iconic works of art, are curated and treated with the kind of reverence that borders on religious devotion (Duncan 1995). Contemporary museums of all kinds often invoke religious architectural styles to draw on the awesome, iconic power associated with sacred sites and places of religious devotion (Britton 2010; Alba 2015; Buggeln 2017). Acts of collecting, storing, and displaying objects in museums, premier temples of heritage, could be said to confer a sense of enchantment that approximates a sense of the holy (Côté 2003; Macdonald 2005; Hooper 2014). The popularity of heritage as a discourse and institutional practice, managed by authoritative regional, national, and international bodies, has even led the historian of heritage David Lowenthal to suggest that heritage itself is a religion. "The world rejoices in a newly popular faith: the cult of heritage," he says, and, "devotion to heritage is a spiritual calling." As a "revealed faith," it "awakens piety the world over," that requires that "we elect and exalt our legacy not by weighing its claims to truth, but in feeling that it must be right." Indeed, he posits, heritage has eclipsed religion as a devotional substitute in the contemporary West: "The creed of heritage answers the need for ritual devotion" (Lowenthal 1997: 1–2).

Scholars of religion have, however, not been so easily persuaded: the debate about heritage's secular or religious status remains unresolved. The opening paragraphs here show some of the conflated, implied uses of heritage that scholars of religion struggle with. Part of the issue here is that the concept heritage invoked in museum settings bundles up associations of material culture, art, science, and cultural difference, that together assumes a notion of the secular that is at once definitive and decidedly unstable. Talal Asad has shown that the secular is not opposed to the sacred or religion, but is instead "an ordering principle that brings together certain 'behaviors, knowledges, and sensibilities in modern life.' Saba Mahmood goes a step further by pointing out that the notion of "the secular" is far from a neutral separation of religion and state, but should be seen as an extension of an ideological view, secularism, in which a normative bias toward Christianity is palpable" (Balkenhol et al. 2020: 6, citing Asad 2003 and Mahmood 2009). These subtle operations of signification and power are at work in the ways heritage is used in the debate about the cross at the Berlin City Palace. This chapter pulls out and illustrates these unclear, overlapping ascriptions by profiling the strategic uses of heritage in the debate about the appropriateness of the cross. Tracking these associative, calculated references, I contribute to research that takes the formative and functional associations of heritage with religion and the sacred as a point of departure for sustained analysis.

The Berlin City Palace's dualism—of a Royal Palace with religious decorations housing museums with heritage artifacts—presents an exemplary but also extraordinary illustrative case for observing the conceptual transactions that the term heritage brokers. That is to say, religious associations accrued to the Palace building outside and secular, cultural heritage associations accrued to the museum within in ways that led to an apparent conflict of values that stakeholders struggled to resolve. It is worth noting that the historic Berlin City Palace was never a museum, but a Royal Palace that had been imbued with Christian religious significance (Burchard 2016). The primary home of the Hohenzollern Royal dynasty between 1443 and 1918, the Berlin City Palace was a stately royal residence that had undergone significant baroque renovations in the eighteenth century (Ellrich 2008). Religious decorations, including the cross and Christian religious inscriptions, were added in the mid-nineteenth century, when Fredrick William IV sought to arrogate religious authority to the royal throne at a time of democratic political change. The building was, however, severely damaged during WWII and then demolished by the East German government. The latter built another palace on the site, the Palace of the Republic, which housed the East German Parliament and doubled as a bustling cultural and entertainment venue. In the early 1990s following German reunification, West German citizen movements mobilized to recall and rebuild the original Berlin City Palace (see Boddien and Engel 2000).[2] The Palace of the Republic was later stripped and demolished under the auspices of the discovery of asbestos contamination to make way for the Berlin City Palace reconstruction (Ledanff 2003; Buttlar 2007; Colomb 2007; Ekici 2007; Bach 2017; Costabile-Heming 2017).

Fred von Bose, curator and ethnographer of the Humboldt Forum's planning, points out that the 2002 decision by the German Federal Parliament to demolish the Palace of the Republic and rebuild the Berlin City Palace turned on the successful proposal to relocate the collections of the Ethnology Museum and the Museum of Asian Art, both located in the district of Dahlem, to the site (von Bose 2013).[3] The new institution was framed as a Humboldt Forum, a "place for dialogue, of civic participation and coequal contemporaneity of the world cultures" (as cited in von Bose 2013). Three partner institutions were identified as best supporting the venture, the Prussian Cultural Heritage Foundation and Berlin Library and the Humboldt University. The non-European collections were profiled

Figure 2.6.2 Cross being installed. May 29, 2020. Photo by the author.

as complementing the European collections held by the Neues, Altes and Bode Museums, also located on the Museum Island (see von Bose 2016). As its official title "The Humboldt Forum inside the Berlin City Palace" suggests, the reconstructed Palace building and the heritage institution inside are often awkwardly distinguished, as distinct yet encapsulated entities in promotional language (see Flierl and Parzinger 2009; Bredekamp and Eissenhauer 2013; Bredekamp 2019) (Figure 2.6.2).

This chapter unpacks the controversy over the inclusion of a Christian cross on the Berlin City Palace in which the Humboldt Forum is located. It maps the arguments made for and against its inclusion according to three dominant scholarly ways of theorizing heritage; that is, the notion of heritage as related to the nation and national identity; the notion of heritage as the sacred; and the notion of Christianity as heritage. In the first section, I review some of the current leading literature in the area of material religion that takes heritage broadly construed as a focus both to highlight the term's significance for the study of religion and to situate my discussion of the cross. The second section illustrates how the Berlin Palace stands as an example of the theory of heritage and the nation as indicative of the historical process of the revolutionary seizure and transformation of royal and Christian religious material culture into the collective possession of citizens for collective enjoyment, preservation, and bequest as national heritage. The third section draws on examples of contentious ethnographic objects from the Ethnological Museum inside the Humboldt Forum show how their incorporation, curation, preservation, and display not only domesticated them as museum objects but also sacralized them, thus illustrating the theory of heritage as the sacred. The fourth section discusses the counter-claim made that the cross was not a purely Christian symbol but rather also signified

German cultural heritage. Here, I show how the Palace was drawn into a political project of the culturalization of Christianity as national heritage and the reformulation of heritage for the regulation of social and cultural difference. Showing up the complicated, contradictory, and unfinished entanglements of heritage with Christianity at the Berlin City Palace, I argue that, ultimately, it should be embraced as a material religious term.

Heritage, Religion, and the Sacred

It is worth briefly reviewing some of the current literature on heritage and museums in the study of religion to illustrate the academic context in which the debate about the cross is situated. The distinction between religion and heritage has been explored in literature that focuses on the status of objects in museum settings. What kind of practice is curation, and what meaning does it confer on cultural objects in museum collections? How does museum curation affect the social and cultural significance of religious objects in museums? For example, in *Godly Things: Museums, Objects and Religion* (2000), Crispin Paine and others initiated early, focused research into the place of religion in museum settings that went beyond formative comparisons of museums as, say, churches. They advanced substantive analysis of how religion was being curated, managed, and displayed that illustrated its vibrance and dynamism in this cultural setting. The essays that comprise the special issue on *Museums and Material Religion* (2012) edited by Crispin Paine took this line of inquiry further by illustrating how "through its material forms," religion "can help museums fulfil their mission to change and enrich their visitors' lives" (Paine 2012: 6). Taking a global and multi-perspective approach to the same set of questions, the book *Religion in Museums*, edited by Gretchen Buggeln, Crispin Paine, and S. Brent Plate (2017), illustrates the multi-sited significance of religion for museums of all kinds, from architecture through curation to visitor experience. This literature shows that religion appears in different ways in museums and requires careful yet considered attention by museum practitioners, who may harness it for lively, inclusive visitor engagement. A sub-theme here is literature that addresses religious and spiritual objects in museum settings. Crispin Paine's book *Religious Objects in Museums* (2013), for example, reflects on the vitality, life, and work of religious objects in museums and how practitioners can work with them in enriching ways. Bruce M. Sullivan's edited volume *Sacred Objects in Secular Spaces* (2015) examines the effects of Asian religious objects on museums, as well as the museums' effects on the museum visitors, the objects themselves, and the religious traditions with which they were associated. These texts therefore attend to the charged, ambivalent status of objects as being both religious and museological—as well as how those different modes of objecthood are enacted and how they can be effectively managed.

Scholars have also extensively theorized religion and heritage through the notion of the sacred. For example, Birgit Meyer and Marleen de Witte, editors of the special *Material Religion* issue "Heritage and the Sacred" (2013), argue that heritage formation is a sacralizing practice that is inherently fraught with uncertainty and that requires dynamic aesthetic practices to stage its persuasiveness.[4] This emphasis on aesthetics and mediation of heritage as drawing an adjacency with religion is elaborated upon on in *Sense and Essence: The Cultural Production of the Real*, edited by Birgit Meyer and Mattijs van de Port (2018: 6), which stresses that cultural heritage is "a construction subject to dynamic processes of (re)inventing culture within particular social formations and bound to particular forms of mediation." As such, heritage requires but also denies its own fabrication. The Berlin City Palace lends itself well to arguments about how heritage is made and staged. The Palace is caught up in debates about the "politics of authentication" as a reconstruction, as well as the "aesthetics of persuasion" in that it is designed explicitly as a compelling material heritage site (Meyer and van de Port 2018). It is the "politics of authentication" that the cross embroiled the project in that most intrigues me—more specifically, how the controversy serves as an arena for the renegotiation of the terms religion, the secular, publicness, and heritage.

The secular has been an important entry point for research on the interchange between religion and heritage. In the book *The Secular Sacred* (2020), Markus Balkenhol, Ernst van den Hemel, and Irene Stengs take the importance of this overlap further, emphasizing that the "ways in which sacrality and secularity inform, enforce and spill over into each other" should be taken as an analytical starting point. Asserting their case, they argue for a conceptual compounding—that is, arguing for the notion of the secular-sacred: "a person, object, image, representation or place in which secular and sacred ideas, feelings, emotions, motivations, experiences, perceptions, intertwine, conflate and conflict." Heritage forms, such as statues, mark out one example of "the intertwining processes of secularization and sacralization" (Balkenhol et al. 2020: 5).

More recent research looks at how heritage marks a special point of overlap between religion, the religious, and the secular in institutional settings and the public domain, and its ties into the development of national cultures and the regulation of religious diversity. For example, in their edited volume *The Religious Heritage Complex,* Cyril Isnart and Nathalie Cerezales argue that we should abandon "the separation of religious sacredness and the artistic aura of cultural heritage," and instead pay attention to "continuity between the *habitus* of the conservation of the past within religious traditions and a conscious *policy* regarding the care of the past in heritage contexts." They propose the religious heritage complex as "a theoretical tool to capture the coexistence of two different layers of values attributed to religious practices and materiality" to address this conceptual interweaving (2020: 6–8). Emphasizing the incorporation of religion as heritage, Marian Burchardt (2020: 3) argues instead for the notion of the religious heritage assemblage, or the "totality of heterogenous discourses, sites and places in which claims to religion as a national culture are articulated, authorized and institutionalized" and its role in regulating religious diversity. I will show that stakeholders' vigorous claims and counter-claims made in the Berlin Palace cross debate illustrate very well these struggles over the kind of institutionalization of religion as heritage and questions of social diversity.

Intertwining secularization and sacralization—in complicated yet generative ways— heritage, the literature shows, has extensive conceptual and substantive entanglements with religion. In other words, heritage is a crucial term in the study of religion.

Heritage and the Nation

The reconstructed Berlin City Palace was a flagship national cultural heritage project intended to not only restore the architectural integrity of inner city Berlin. Hailing from the eighteenth and nineteenth centuries, the royal architectural and cultural legacy out of which the building arose was promoted as a period of great cultural and scientific flourishing worth celebrating. Untrammeled by the disasters of the twentieth century, this was a period in which most Germans could take pride. The Humboldt Forum, housed inside the palace, also explicitly anchored itself in the scientific and cultural heritage of the eighteenth and nineteenth centuries. As Hermann Parzinger, the then president of the Prussian Cultural Heritage Foundation, explained at the laying of the foundation stone for the Palace building—that great secular ritual of architectural consecration—it was no accident that the Humboldt Forum was returning to the castle, since the collections of the Ethnological Museum, the Museum of Islamic Art, and the Humboldt University had "their origins in the Kunstkammer in the historic castle." A visit to the Humboldt Forum would allow visitors to "experience what the Kunstkammer means for us and for Europe in terms of the history of the humanities and the history of science" (see also Mairesse 2019a). The Humboldt Forum marked a return to the tradition of Prussian royal collecting, ordering, and displaying objects. "Particularly in view of our difficult history in the twentieth century," he said, "there is something very positive about this return. It is the return to the great tradition of Prussia as an educational and cultural state (Stiftung Preußischer Kulturbesitz 2013)." The great traditions of the Prussian educational and cultural states were synthesized in the Kunstkammer, which, in future, would be greatly expanded as the Humboldt Forum.

This claiming of a historic age as a materialized representation of a national past very well represents one of the more common definitions of heritage. Here it appears as the material and cultural legacy that belongs to a distinct group from a bounded territory that has been passed on from the generation before to be preserved for that to come. It "is considered the rightful legacy of every distinct people"; "bonding us with precursors and progenitors and our own earlier selves, and with our promised successors" (Lowenthal 1994: 41, 43). This definition of heritage, as the shared property of citizens who are members of a nation, is anchored in a European notion of modernity, the emergence of the nation-state, and the sometimes violent revolutionary separation between church and state that accompanied these processes in countries like Germany and France in the eighteenth and nineteenth centuries. The cross on the Berlin City Palace symbolizes and acutely focuses the tensions of political revolt against monarchical claims to divine rule and the church's holy authority that shadow this definition of heritage.

The Prussian Royal age that Hermann Parzinger made reference to was more complicated and problematic than was suggested by his celebratory pronouncements. Alfred Hagemann, the site historian for the Humboldt Forum, explains that the religious decorations that adorn the reconstructed palace—such as the cupola, the Christian inscription, and the cross—were added to the Palace in the mid-nineteenth century by Frederick William IV following his ascension to the throne in 1840. The cupola "was to house the palace chapel and therefore place the entire palace in a sacral context," and to cement symbolic relations between "God, throne and church." Featuring images of members of the House of Hohenzollern royal dynasty, the chapel stood as "a monument to the dynasty's Christian rule." The religious decorations on the exterior were meant to convey the symbolism of "absolute faith in God's divine rule to the public." A gilded Christian inscription, personally drafted by Frederick William IV, adorned the base of the cupola. It read, "Neither is there salvation in any other: for there is no other name under heaven given to men, than the name of Jesus, to the glory of God the Father, that at the name of Jesus every knee should bow, of things in heaven, and things in earth, and things under the earth" (Hagemann 2020). Unveiled on October 14, 1848, the day before the king's birthday, the cross arrogated royal authority to Frederick William IV as king. The year 1848 was, however, also a time of significant, bloody democratic revolutionary upheaval, which the king fiercely resisted by shoring up a claim to ultimate authority through deferring to a royal Christian faith (Robertson 1952; Hahn 2001). For example, speaking at the Confederation's first Parliament sitting in 1847, the king said, "No power on Earth shall succeed in persuading me to transform the natural relationship between ruler and populace into a conventional constitutional one" (Hagemann 2020). The Christian decorations, such as the inscription and the cross, were therefore purposefully added as a political symbol of the divine authority to rule at a time when democratic reforms increasingly challenged Prussian royal authority.

After the inclusion of the cross was announced in 2017, critics of the Palace reconstruction were quick to cite this bloody political history. The journalist Christian Schröder writing in the *Tagesspiegel* argued that the cross was not a religious but a "political symbol" marking "an unfortunate alliance of crown and church and for the suppression of the first German democracy movement with military dictatorial means" (C. Schröder 2017). The art historian and critic Kia Vahland added that, "This cross . . . refers to the Prussian authoritarian state. It was only built after the Prussian king had crushed the liberal revolution of 1848 and hundreds of rebels died in the Berlin barricade fight" (Vahland 2017). This criticism drew out the monarchy's revival of Christian religious authority for the violent suppression of democratic revolutionary change.

Religious histories of monarchies resisting democratic change through claims to the authority of God and the church cross into the definition of national heritage. For example, the folklorist and heritage theorist Regina Bendix asks, "Is heritage an effort to claim some of the sacredness lost with the advent of democracy and the political downfall of monarchy?" (2018: 111). If traced through the French term *patromonie*, heritage is related to the sacred power of royal and religious collections—that is, if we limit our understanding of its emergence as a Western, European concept arising out of the seizure of material from royal palaces and Christian churches. French Historians Jean-Pierre Babelon and André Chastel (1994) argue that, in France, cultural heritage has roots in "the Christian idea of the sacred inheritance of faith" and Roman Catholic clergy's conservation of relics (cited in Isnart and Cerezales 2020: 1). The power of these Christian ideas, remains, and symbols was violently seized and transformed during the French Revolution into the collective possession of citizens. "The historic record shows," the art historian Brenda Schildgen points out, "that in 1793 in France, revolutionary decrees had ordered the destruction of all the signs and symbols of the Christian religion and the feudal order" (2008: 140). The "dechristianizing" impulses of the French Revolution, therefore, aimed at transforming "religious collective memory into national cultural memory when art and artefacts were wrenched from their erstwhile places in churches, castles, and private collections to find a new home in the national museum" (Schildgen 2008: 128; see also Gliozzo 1971; Aston 2000; van Kley 2003; McPhee 2013: 153–155). The historian Dominique Poulot writes that "heritage was identified with a new, carefully demarcated cultural foundation and not with 'natural,' hereditary transmission" (1988: 40). The transformation of the Pantheon in Paris into a national necropolis is one example of this "cultural conversion" of royal and religious sites (Mcclellan 1999; Bresc-Bautier 2003; Clarke 2007).

This decidedly French European history provides the basis for a genealogy that has to some extent come to explain how national cultures all over the world are enshrined in monuments, memorials, and museums. It conveys the idea that heritage is imbued with power as a narrative of transfer of political authority from monarchies and the church to "the people" at a time of democratic revolution. By ceding authority over heritage to the people and the state, heritage in some sense neatly shores up distinctions among religion, the religious, and the secular.

Yet the Berlin City Palace is an outlier in this history of heritage. The German democratic revolution had complicated ties with the Protestant church; for example, when national Parliament first sat in 1848–1849, it chose to convene at St. Paul's Church in Frankfurt rather than in Berlin. And though the streets of Berlin saw violence, none was directed at the historic palace or its possessions.

The Palace was, however, the one source of museum development in the city. The art historian Hans-Joachim Koloss explains that the Berlin Ethnological Museum "can trace its beginnings to the sixteenth century with the Elector Joachim II of Brandenburg who began collecting objects for his *Kunstkammer* or cabinet of curiosities" (1990: 16). Indeed, in Europe, the cabinet of curiosities was widely employed as a means of displaying ethnographica (Olmi and Macgregor 1985; Gundestrup 1988). The Berlin Palace *Kunstkammer* was gradually built up as a space for the accumulation, storage, and display of artifacts of culture and nature, which were held under the divine authority of the king and largely for the consumption and appreciation of nobility (Theuerkauff 1985; Dolezal 2017). In the early eighteenth century, Frederick William I transferred to the Society of Science what today would be called natural history collections; a further apportioning of the collections occurred again at the end of the eighteenth century. The division and distribution of the *Kunstkammer* collection seeded major heritage and research institutions in Berlin, including the collections of the Humboldt University, the Neues Museum, and the Museum für Völkerkunde (the forunner of the Berlin Ethnological Museum; see Penny 2002; Zimmerman 2010). In being transfered from royal holdings, the collections were thus differentiated as part of the formalization of distinct sciences in Berlin. Moreover, objects and artifacts were incorporated into museums dedicated to different scientific fields through practices of documentation, preservation, and display that effectively musealised them as specimens of research and education. As I show in the following section, these practices of setting apart heritage matter and treating it with a heightened sense of care have troubled scholars of religion, heritage, and museums since these practices introduce ideas of sacralization and the sacred in spaces theretofore considered profane.

Heritage and the Sacred

Thus, centuries of cultural artifacts and objects from Africa, Asia, Oceania, and South and North America were assembled as non-European ethnological collections in the Ethnological Museum inside the Humboldt Forum (Figure 2.6.3). As such, they were incorporated as material scientific data. Yet, in 2017, it was announced that the building they would be located in, the Berlin City Palace would be adorned with a Christian cross. Two persistent criticisms were raised. First, this elevation of the cross projected the dominance of Christianity over the ethnographic collections, which would establish a hierarchy of cultures—as has been discussed. The second concern was that this hierarchy negated the historic links between the German colonial enterprise (Perraudin and Zimmerer 2010; Conrad 2011), ethnographic collecting in colonial contexts, the establishment of the Berlin Ethnological Museum, and Christian missionary work (van der Heyden 2011; Best 2012).

In the 1880s, Christian missionaries held propaganda campaigns in Germany that facilitated the expansion of the colonial frontier in different parts of Africa (van der Heyden 2011). In southern Africa, missionary work conducted by German Protestant Churches complemented the colonial enterprise (see Lessing et al. 2012), that in Namibia, contributed to the genocide of the Nama and Herero people. In 2017, the Evangelical Church in Germany officially apologized for being silently complicit in that genocide (see Jethro 2019; Förster 2020). A special memorial service was held in 2019 in the Friedrichstadkirche, Berlin, during which it officiated over the return of human remains to a Namibian delegation of descendent affected communities and made an official apology for its contribution to the Nama and Hero Genocide (EDK 2017).

Consequently, the Ethnological Museum, a museum within the Humboldt Forum, in time came to hold African artifacts assembled from heterogenous sources, some with

Figure 2.6.3 Street renaming fest and demonstration in front of the Berlin City Palace, with the cross in the background. August 23, 2020. Photo by the author.

explicitly Christian missionary ties (König 2007). For example, art historian Koloss (1990: 16) notes that, "the first West African objects emerged in the collection in 1844, when the museum purchased 148 pieces made in Dhomey, Old Calabar Cameroon, Sierra Leone, and the Gold Coast from a German missionary named Halleur." During the 1840s, Hermann Halleur was a missionary working on behalf of the Basel Evangelical Missionary Society based in the British Colony of the Gold Coast (Quartey 2007; Miller 2014).

Koloss continues: "With the acquisition of colonies, the flow of material into the Berlin museum increased substantially" (1990: 21). Ethnographic collections were assessed accord-ing to scientific principles by leading scholars such as Felix von Luschan and Leo Frobenius, both avid, complex, but also dubious collectors of ethnographic artifacts and human remains. At their hands, some items remained ethnographic objects, while others were reclassified as art. They "had come to appreciate African works as art, an almost unheard of perspective at the time, writing as early as 1898 about the 'treasures' in ethnological collections and speak-ing perceptively of their greatness" (Koloss 1990: 21). What is particularly significant are the fields of classification that African objects traveled through as they moved from the colonial periphery into museums in the metropolitan center. When African art came into vogue in the first decades of the twentieth century, "We find [Frobenius] marveling at Africa's 'rav-ishing splendors' and describing the artistic sensibility of the peoples of Zaire [present-day Democratic Republic of Congo] with utmost enthusiasm: 'Every cup, every pipe, every spoon a work of art, altogether deserving of comparison with productions of the Roman-esque style in Europe'" (cited in Koloss 1990: 22). Beyond individual missionary contribu-tions, European mission societies also sanctioned and organized the collection of objects for museum-like purposes. For example, as David Morgan [2011, 2018] shows, the London Mission society was systematic in its collecting work during the nineteenth century—later founding its own museum of objects gathered by missionaries. After the collection was later deaccessioned, much of it ended up at the Pitt Rivers Museum in Oxford.

What I mean to show is that African objects—collected by missionaries spreading the gospel and analyzed by anthropologists building problematic science of race and civilizational progress—were not only incorporated as data, as art or material culture; they also formed the basis of scientific and aesthetic systems of knowledge about culture and race and difference. This complicated relationship connecting Christian missionary work, the colonial enterprise, African material culture, and ethnographic collecting prompts more careful reading of religious—and especially Christian—influences behind contemporary ethnographic collections. It is worth noting that, in contemporary Germany, curators and museum officials working with the African collections have grappled extensively with these difficult histories in pursuing provenance research, staging exhibitions, and producing publications to shed light on their history as an attempt to undo some of their painful legacies (Ivanov 2000; Chapuis et al. 2017).

The historic inclusion of African objects in the Ethnological Museum and its predecesors was in effect a secular practice of stripping them of their original spiritual and religious significance and sacralizing them through practices of curation and display. How, specifically, have scholars of religion approximated heritage and the sacred, especially in regard to curatorial practice in museums? Drawing on Ronald Grimes's (1992) notion of "singularization," or the oversignification of objects of cultural worth in museums, Crispin Paine observes that "Museumification—the entry of an object into a museum—has a striking parallel with 'sacralization'—the making of an object sacred," since "once [museum or sacred objects] have been accessioned or consecrated they can not be commercially exchanged" (2013: 2). Further, he suggests that once a religious object becomes "a museum object," it effectively acquires "a new meaning, a new value, a new personality" that reinscribes it as exemplary material culture or as art. There is an unresolved tension here—of museumification as a process of both sacralization and desacralization. This generative conflation carries through cultural definitions of "heritage." Heritage, according to cultural studies theory, is not found but produced. Contemporary definitions of "heritage" by leading scholars highlight how sites, objects, and things are ascribed with special significance as heritage through practices of focused attention in the present that calls attention to the past (Smith 2006; Macdonald 2013; Bendix 2020). Barbara Kirshenblatt-Gimblett's widely cited definition of heritage captures this turn in scholarship. She defines *heritage* as "a new mode of cultural production in the present that has recourse to the past" (1998: 149). Heritage is intelligible as a practice of cultural engagement with the past relative to significant material things that are singled out as a focus of attention. Yet it presents a conceptual tension—as part of the secular, yet also sacred—which necessarily also complicates the status of religious objects in museums.

Perhaps one way through this debate is to pay heed to the conceptual heritage of the notion of the sacred, which has been associated with French sociologist Emile Durkheim. The sacred, according to Durkheim, sits at the heart of religion as the opposite of profane or ordinary things, as both a part of and essential for social order.[5] Durkheim famously emphasized that anything could gather sacred significance, saying "a rock, a tree, a spring, a pebble, a piece of wood, a house, in a word, anything can be sacred" (1995: 37). Focused, purposeful, socially engaged ritual action set things apart as meaningful—as sacred—and bonded a group through such systematic repetition. Highlighting how material things are set apart as sacred at the center of social relations through focused ritual action with commemorative functions, one could argue that Durkheim was ahead of his time as a scholar of religion theorizing heritage. As a heritage theorist, Durkheim reformulates Paine's vexing problem. By situating ritual attention "relative to sacred things" at the center of religion itself, heritage and religion can be seen as similar rather than diametrically opposed processes of signification. Sacred things are taboo, dangerous—but, due to their esteem, they are also highly valued and therefore highly desirable for their earthly and spiritual powers. Sacred things are often subject to competition, and sometimes even conflict, as different groups compete for ownership over it. David Chidester calls this the "political economy of the sacred," which describes how "the immediate and infinite availability of materiality for interpretation and reinterpretation, for ritualization and consecration, but also for desecration, creates a surplus of signification" that is highly valued. The sacred is valued because of its scarcity, and hence, "generates struggles over position, power, and . . . ownership" (Chidester 2012: 18).

The ethnographic collections within the Humboldt Forum were a site of fierce struggles over position, power, and ownership. As an assemblage of sacred heritage, it can be seen as a theater of the political economy of the sacred. For example, the conceptual vagary of heritage and/as the sacred was explicitly drawn upon for mobilizing political activism against the Humboldt Forum. In October 2017, a transnational conference titled "Prussian Colonial Heritage—Sacred Objects and Human Remains in Berlin's Museums," was held in Berlin. Scholars, artists, and indigenous activists—from Cameroon, Germany, Japan, New Zealand, several South American countries, Tanzania, and the United States—spoke about the violent conditions in which objects and human remains were historically acquired; the pain caused by the dispossession; and the frustration, denial, and dismissal the activist experienced in appealing for their return. For example, Gad Samai Shiynyuy spoke about his attempt to recover a sacred object violently taken by German colonial officials from his hometown in Cameroon in 1909. In relating his story, journalist Gouri Sharma writes, quoting Shiynyuy: "Ngonnso—a statue considered to be a goddess in his community—was stolen. 'In my tradition, no one can give Ngonnso away, so people fought to take it.' 'We still think about this loss every day. . . . We believe that this object has divine powers and it's the same object that our forefathers used to perform rituals to cleanse our land" (Sharma 2018). This was no mere object, but an ancestor, a living being vital to the life of a community in Cameroon, which was now being held—indeed, imprisoned—in the storage rooms of Berlin's ethnographic collections ready for display in the Humboldt Forum. Critics of the Prussian Cultural Heritage Foundation, who founded the Humboldt Forum, were questioning the legitimacy of the possession of such objects and the terms under which they were being held. The critics called attention to the various inflexions of the power used to violently take possession of objects of subordinated others, to reinscribe their significance as cultural or scientific, and then to claim them as national heritage. Competition over these collections were contested in competing notions of materiality and the sacred.

Religion as Heritage

The cross had its defenders. Monika Grütters, then Federal Government Commissioner for Culture and the Media and a member of the Christian Democratic Party, argued, for example, that by rooting the Humboldt Forum in the Christian image of man, the cross anchored the institution in authentic German religious and cultural values: "Our culture of openness, freedom, and mercy has its roots in our Christian image of man. . . . Only those who are sure of their identity can give the other space without feeling threatened. That's what the cross stands for" (Wiegelmann 2017a). Religious figures from different faiths also supported the decision, Aiman Mazyek, then Chair of the Central Council of Muslims, said, "Crosses are part of our cultural and historical heritage in Germany." He elaborated, saying, "The building has a historical context, and this historical context has to do with Christianity and Christian symbolism" (Wiegelmann 2017b). The then Bishop of the Evangelical Church Markus Dröge also welcomed the announcement, saying: "The cross [is] a sign of reconciliation and remembrance [that] can and should inspire discussions," and can stand as a model for shaping "how our society wants to behave to their historical Christian roots and to their current Christianity" (Evangelisch Kirche 2017). The cross was roundly defended on the grounds that Christianity and Christian symbols were German cultural heritage.

In some ways it is easy to see how the cross's defenders could arrive at this rather counter-intuitive conclusion. The crucifix is a Christian aesthetic form that also reads as a cultural historical sign—one that, when adorning churches, forms part of the historic architectural landscape in cities across Germany. And, across Europe, Christian material culture and religious life are steeped in heritage. Churches and cathedrals are important sites of sometimes dynamic, heritage-like engagement around questions of building conversion and iconicity (Beekers and Tamimi Arab 2016), religious building use, ritual, replication, and the heritagization of Christianity (Bowman and Sepp 2019; Coleman and Bowman 2019; Coleman 2019). Christian festivals and holidays have become mainstreamed as popular festivals, as Ernst van den Hemel (2017) shows in his discussion of public display and ritual treatment of the Christian cross in hugely popular Easter Passion plays in the Netherlands. As Birgit Meyer (2020) shows, the cross has also been thoroughly commercialized in the Netherlands; decorations acquired from decommissioned churches are desacralized and resold as part of a cultural recycling of the Christian past. While Christianity is the main focus here, this heritagization applies to sacred sites, practices, and material of all religions (Shackley 2001; Mairesse 2018). It demonstrates how, as noted by Isnart and Cerezales (2020: 7), "religious buildings, rituals, and objects" of all kinds "do not always lose their religious values and powers when they enter the heritage realm." Indeed, "heritage is a valued field of action for religious people who attempt to restore and maintain continuity between their own past and their current material legacy" (Ibid).

But the prevalence and ambiguity of the crucifix have especially, and quite easily, encroached upon and crossed both commonly held and legal distinctions concerning religion, the secular public sphere, and cultural heritage in Europe and beyond. In *Landscapes of the Secular*, Nicolas Howe (2016) documents the protracted church–state legal dispute about a cross displayed on Mount Soledad in La Jolla, California, with religious supporters arguing for its status as a secular war memorial and secular opponents arguing it was a hurtful Christian religious symbol. In this debate about religious freedom, the cross brokered a struggle over the definition of religion, memorialization, and the secular. As David Chidester argues, "As these conflicting interpretations move through the courts, the cross becomes simultaneously more sacred and more profane." The cross was a definitive juncture where "the secular struggles to define the religious and the religious struggles to define the secular" (Chidester 2018: 4).

Similar legal cases have been contested in Europe. In 1995, for example, the Federal Constitutional Court in Germany overruled a Bavarian regulation that mandated a crucifix be mounted inside every primary school classroom—triggering a national debate about federal and state laws, majoritarian Christianity, and religion as heritage. In that case, the Bavarian state "asserted that the cross represented shared 'Western' values, specifically, tolerance and brotherly love," while the Court "argued that though the cross did express these values, it expressed a 'definite religious conviction'" (Caldwell 1996: 260). Similar appeals to Christianity as cultural heritage won favor with the European Court of Human Rights (ECHR) in 2011 when it ruled on the status of crucifixes mounted on walls of Italian schools. Effectively crossing normative distinctions between religion and the secular in public by privileging majority religious rights, the court ruled "that the symbol corresponded to a tradition which [the Italian government] considered important to perpetuate," and that "Beyond its religious meaning, the crucifix symbolised the principles and values which formed the foundation of democracy and western civilization" (cited in Oliphant 2012: 10; see also Auslander 2000). The ECHR judgment set a precedent for a blanket reading of Christianity as cultural heritage in majority Christian contexts. Whether appearing on the walls of schools in Bavaria or classrooms in Italy, the Christian crucifix has been at the forefront of groundbreaking legal judgments that have profoundly reconfigured the terms in which Christianity, religion, heritage, and the secular can be understood.

Christianity as heritage is intuitive but also confusing. Religious studies scholars have struggled to pin it down, calling it the "culturalization of Christianity" (Joppke 2018), "folklorized religion" (Laniel 2016, 2018), or "culturalized religion" (Astor and Mayrl 2020). The increasing significance of heritage as a term for working out predominantly Christian heritage dynamics has led scholars to identify the moment as marking either a major turn, as with Marian Burchardt's argument about "the religious heritage assemblage" (2020) or an epistemic regime of sorts, as in Isnart and Cerezales's notion of a "religious heritage complex" (2020). Whatever it is termed, the reconfigured legal and conceptual intersections the Christian cross sets up among religion, heritage, and the public sphere have been to the detriment of minority religious groups, especially Muslims. Public symbols of Islamic faith—from the visual appearance of minarets (Langer 2010), the sound of the call to prayer (Tamimi Arab 2017), and religious attire (Nanwani 2011)—have been prohibited or policed precisely on the basis of appeals to majority religious and cultural norms such as cultural heritage.

Returning to arguments made in defense of the Humboldt Forum cross, Christianity as cultural heritage is mobilized to cast a long shadow of Eurocentrism that was also mobilized to close off, rather than open up, intersections of cultural difference. Take the remarks of the theologian Richard Schröder, who said the contradiction between the Humboldt Forum and the cross was "quite easily" resolved if you followed the reasoning that "if the wealth of humanity is the totality of their cultures, then our European contribution to it is undoubtedly Christian" (R. Schröder 2017). Or those of the Reverend Ben Johnson, who added similarly saying the cross symbolized the extent to which European culture and "Western civilization [are] inconceivable apart from Christianity" (Johnson 2017). These formulations collapse ideas of Christianity, Europeanness, Enlightenment, and Western civilization into each other in problematic ways. Such formulations assign "culture and heritage" to a particular group, namely Europeans, homogenizing them as being distinctly the same, and then bring in "heritage" as justification for "ownership over" ideas of Enlightenment and civilization. Implicitly, this formulation of Christianity as heritage excludes cultural, religious, and group expressions that fall outside of this narrow frame; Islam and Muslims, for example, are excluded from being enjoined into it. Clearly, as Elayne Oliphant presaged, "There are unsettling implications in attributing versatility to the sign of the crucifix" (2012: 10). Christian cultural heritage therefore creates possibilities for political crusades aimed at the denigration of the Other under the sign of the cross as culture and heritage. Regina Bendix flagged this problem when she remarked that "the opposite of valuing is devaluation, and cultural scholarship has perhaps been . . . reluctant in giving prominence in analyzing the ways in which culture and folklore are marked to denigrate" (2018: 11). The cross and Christianity have drawn scholars of religion and heritage into a convergence in assessing the regulatory role heritage plays in framing culture and religion in contemporary European society. In its guise as Christian cultural heritage, the cross on the Humboldt Forum signifies the ever-more-crucial significance of "heritage" used as a term for grasping the significance of religion, and for marking the boundaries of inclusion in secular public life.

Conclusion

Even as Christian heritage, the Berlin City Palace cross posed problems for its religious defenders. Bishop Heiner Koch complained about the debate in the German press, saying, "The cross must under no circumstances become a subject of struggle. In the cross is salvation and hope and life, so we Christians believe. Struggle and strife would rob it of its meaning" (katholisch.de 2017). The struggle and strife of vociferous public debate, I have tried to show, instead generated rather than detracted from a set of meanings about the nature of heritage in Berlin, Germany, Europe—and indeed the world. That debate surfaced the cross's intrusions into the history of the term heritage as a symbol of the Christian faith and a religious sign encroaching on its largely secular definitions. This surfacing is evidenced by how the cross's erection was tied to significant political upheaval and royal resistance in Germany in the nineteenth century, a time in which the concept of heritage was emerging as a term for designating valued national culture. It also included interference in the ontological status of the collections that would be displayed in the museums inside the Humboldt Forum: I showed how, as heritage, the cultural significance of collections were attributed with a heightened, fuzzy sense of value as sacred but also secular. Finally, the cross's defenders reformulation of Christianity as cultural heritage aimed to redraw the terms in which the secular could be understood in Germany—in step with wider developments in religious theorizing of the significance of heritage in Europe. Given the complicated, contradictory, and unfinished entanglements heritage has with the religious at the Berlin City Palace, I argue that, ultimately, heritage should be embraced as a material religious term.

The debate over the cross on the Berlin City Palace was about much more than the appropriateness of a potent symbol of the Christian religion standing atop a new heritage institution in Berlin. The cross linked to, and was illustrative of, crucial shifts in formulations of Christianity, religion, and heritage. Mapping these shifts—from heritage as national culture, heritage as the secular and sacred, to heritage as Christian culture—I have tried to trouble the very terms structuring the original argument about the cross; namely, that the cross was a purely Christian religious symbol and the Humboldt Forum was a secular institution trading in the business of culture. Close analysis reveals that this set of basic assumptions was fundamentally inverted, reversed, or contradictory: the original Royal Palace was imbued with Christian religious significance, the contemporary cross was claimed to be a symbol of Christian heritage, and the Humboldt Forum's ethnographic collections were construed as sacred material culture. This was the crossing of heritage. By that I mean to say, as a Western term for material representations of pasts meaningful for collectives, the term heritage itself has a religious heritage, a Christian religious heritage specifically. It is for these reasons, that it makes an announcement like the plan for the cross seem both starkly strange yet also comfortingly familiar. And it is for this reason that we try to make better sense of the conditions in which, and in what ways specifically, heritage is recruited for staking claims to and about the secular in drawing boundaries of difference and inclusion.

Acknowledgments

Many thanks to David Chidester, Fred von Bose and Birgit Meyer for their generous, sharp comments on earlier drafts of this chapter. Thanks to the editors for their robust editorship, and to Harriet Merrow for earlier editorial assistance. Research for this chapter was funded by the Alexander von Humboldt Foundation as part of the research award for Sharon Macdonald's Alexander von Humboldt professorship and was carried out at CARMAH at the Institute for European Ethnology, Humboldt University, Berlin.

Notes

1 All quotes here and following in German translated by the author.
2 The Palace of the Republic, they argued, disrupted the historic symmetry and aesthetic beauty of the Unter den Linden Boulevard and the Museum Island with its iconic museums. Special emphasis was placed on the Berlin City Palace's richly decorated baroque facades as crucial for historic urban aesthetic restoration.
3 In a move remarkably out of step with both the current global museological trend of critical interrogation of colonial legacies of ethnographic museums and the thoroughgoing research of the provenance of ethnographic collections of non-European Others, the Prussian Cultural Heritage Foundation decided to relocate its vast collections to a reconstructed Prussian Palace.
4 See also the International Committee for Museology's special collection of essays *The Sacred in the Prism of Museology*, edited by François Mairesse (2019a), produced in the context of the ICOFOM forty-first symposium held in Tehran in October 2018.
5 Durkheim's complete definition of religion reads, "Religion is a unified system of beliefs and practices relative to sacred things, that is to say, things set apart and forbidden—beliefs and practices which unite into one single moral community called a Church all those who adhere to them" (Durkheim 1995: 44).

References

Alba, Avril. 2015. *Holocaust Memorial Museums: Sacred Secular Space*. London: Palgrave Macmillan.
Asad, Talal. 2003. *Formations of the Secular: Christianity, Islam, Modernity*. Stanford, CA: Stanford University Press.
Aston, Nigel. 2000. *Religion and Revolution in France, 1780–1804*. Washington, DC: Catholic University of America Press.
Astor, Avi, and Damon Mayrl. 2020. "Culturalized Religion: A Synthetic Review and Agenda for Research." *Journal for the Scientific Study of Religion* 59 (2): 209–226.
Auslander, Leora. 2000. "Bavarian Crucifixes and French Headscarves: Religious Signs and the Postmodern European State." *Cultural Dynamics* 12 (3): 283–309.
Babelon, Jean-Pierre, and André Chastel. 1994. *La Notion de Patrimoine*. Paris: Liana Levi.
Bach, Jonathan. 2017. *What Remains: Everyday Encounters with the Socialist Past in Germany*. New York: Columbia University Press.
Balkenhol, Markus. 2020. "Colonial Heritage and the Sacred: Contesting the Statue of Jan Pieterszoon Coen in the Netherlands." In *The Secular Sacred: Emotions of Belonging and the Perils of Nation and Religion*, edited by Markus Balkenhol, Ernst van den Hemel and Irene Stengs, 195–216. London: Palgrave Macmillan.
Balkenhol, Markus, Ernst van den Hemel, and Irene Stengs, eds. 2020. *The Secular Sacred: Emotions of Belonging and the Perils of Nation and Religion*. London: Palgrave Macmillan.
Barrie, Thomas, Julio Bermudez, and Phillip James Tabb, eds. 2015. *Architecture, Culture, and Spirituality*. London: Ashgate.
BBC 2018. "Germany's Bavaria Orders Christian Crosses in All State Buildings." *BBC*, April 25, 2018. https://www.bbc.com/news/world-europe-43892329.
Beekers, Daan, and Pooyan Tamimi Arab. 2016. "Dreams of an Iconic Mosque: Spatial and Temporal Entanglements of a Converted Church in Amsterdam." *Material Religion* 12 (2): 137–164.
Bendix, Regina. 2020. *Culture and Value: Tourism, Heritage and Property*. Bloomington, IN: Indiana University Press.
Best, Jeremy. 2012. *Founding a Heavenly Empire: Protestant Missionaries and German Colonialism, 1860–1919*. PhD Dissertation, University of Maryland.

Bowman, Marion, and Tiina Sepp. 2019. "Caminoisation and Cathedrals: Replication, the Heritagisation of Religion, and the Spiritualisation of Heritage." *Religion* 49 (1): 74–98.

Bredekamp, Horst. 2019. "Vom Berliner Schloss zum Humboldt Forum: Ein Paradigma Deutscher Konfliktgeschichte." *Artium Quaestiones* 30: 279–304.

Bredekamp, Horst, and Michael Eissenhauer. 2013. *Das Humboldt-Forum im Berliner Schloss: Planungen, Prozesse, Perspektiven.* Berlin: Hirmer.

Bresc-Bautier, Geneviève. 2003. "The Louvre: A National Museum in a Royal Palace." *Museum International* 55 (1): 61–67.

Britton, Karla, ed. 2010. *Constructing the Ineffable: Contemporary Sacred Architecture.* New Haven, CT: Yale School of Architecture.

Buggeln, Gretchen, Crispin Paine, and S. Brent Plate, eds. 2017. *Religion in Museums: Global and Multidisciplinary Perspectives.* London: Bloomsbury.

Burchardt, Marian. 2020. *Regulating Difference: Religious Diversity and Nationhood in the Secular West.* New Brunswick, NJ: Rutgers University Press.

Burchard, Wolf. 2016. "Royal Remains: As Berlin's Humboldt Forum Is Being Constructed on the Site of the Former Stadtschloss, It Raises the Question—Often a Fraught One in the Post-War Period—of What Rebuilding a German Palace Means Today." *Apollo* 183 (640): 146–153.

Caldwell, Peter. 1996. "The Crucifix and German Constitutional Culture." *Cultural Anthropology* 11 (2): 259–273.

Chapuis, Julien, Jonathan Fine, and Paola Ivanov, eds. 2017. *Beyond Compare: Art from Africa in the Bode Museum.* Berlin: Staatliche Museen zu Berlin.

Chidester, David. 2012. *Wild Religion: Tracking the Sacred in South Africa.* Berkeley, CA: University of California Press.

Chidester, David. 2018. *Religion: Material Dynamics.* Berkeley, CA: University of California Press.

Clarke, Joseph. 2007. *Commemorating the Dead in Revolutionary France: Revolution and Remembrance, 1789–1799.* Cambridge: Cambridge University Press.

Coleman, Simon. 2019. "On Praying in an Old Country: Ritual, Replication, Heritage, and Powers of Adjacency in English Cathedrals." *Religion* 49 (1): 120–141.

Coleman, Simon, and Marion Bowman. 2019. "Religion in Cathedrals: Pilgrimage, Heritage, Adjacency, and the Politics of Replication in Northern Europe." *Religion* 49 (1): 1–23.

Colomb, Claire. 2007. "Requiem for a Lost Palast. 'Revanchist Urban Planning' and 'Burdened Landscapes' of the German Democratic Republic in the New Berlin." *Planning Perspectives* 22 (3): 283–323.

Conrad, Sebastian. 2011. *German Colonialism: A Short History.* Cambridge: Cambridge University Press.

Costabile-Heming, Carol. 2017. "The Reconstructed City Palace and Humboldt Forum in Berlin: Restoring Architectural Identity or Distorting the Memory of Historic Spaces?" *Journal of Contemporary European Studies* 25 (4): 441–454.

Côté, Michel. 2003. "From Masterpiece to Artefact: the Sacred and the Profane in Museums." *Museum International* 55 (20): 32–37.

Deutsche Welle 2018. "Catholic Cardinal Rebukes Bavaria for Ordering Crosses in State Buildings." *Deutsche Welle*, April 30, 2018. https://p.dw.com/p/2wsqK.

Dolezal, Eva. 2017. "Der erste Berliner Museumsstreit: Nutzungskonzepte im Umfeld der Berliner Kunstkammer." In *Ein öffentlicher Ort: Berliner Schloss—Palast der Republik—Humboldt Forum: Beiträge des Fünften Colloquiums in der Reihe Kulturgeschichte Preußens–Colloquien vom 3. und 4. November 2016*, edited by Jürgen Luh. Berlin-Brandenburg: Prussian Palaces and Gardens Foundation.

Duncan, Carol. 1995. *Civilizing Rituals: Inside Public Art Museums.* London: Routledge.

Durkheim, Emile. 1995. *The Elementary Forms of the Religious Life.* Translated by Karen E. Fields. New York: Macmillan Company.

Ellrich, Hartmut. 2008. *Das Berliner Schloss. Geschichte und Wiederaufbau.* Petersberg, Germany: Imhoff.

EKD 2017. *'Forgive us our Sins'": EKD Asks for Forgiveness from Descendents of Genocide in Former German South West Africa.* April 24, 2017. Accessed at https://www.ekd.de/en/pr_2017_04_24_ekd_statement_genocide_german_south_west.htm.

Ekici, Didem. 2007. "The Surfaces of Memory in Berlin. Rebuilding the Schloß." *Journal of Architectural Education* 61 (2): 25–34.

Evangelisch Kirche 2017. "Berliner Stadtschloss Bekommt Kuppelkreuz." *Evangelisch Kirche,* June 22, 2017. https://www.ekbo.de/themen/detail/nachricht/berliner-stadtschloss-bekommt-kuppelkreuz.html?tx_ttnews%5BbackPid%5D=1011&cHash=e5114548e70f239c63afa9aceb789e69.

Flierl, Thomas, and Hermann Parzinger, eds. 2009. *Humboldt Forum Berlin. Das Projekt*. Berlin: Theatre der Zeit.

Förderverein Berliner Schloss 2017."Stiftung Zukunft Berlin Will Kein Kreuz auf dem Schloss." *Förderverein Berliner Schloss* e.V. May 18, 2017. https://berliner-schloss.de/blog/pressespiegel/stiftung-zukunft-berlin-will-kein-kreuz-auf-dem-schloss/.

Förster, Larissa. 2020. "The Face of Genocide: Returning Human Remains from German Institutions to Namibia." In *The Routledge Companion to Indigenous Repatriation*, edited by Fforde, Cressida, C. Timothy McKeown, and Honor Keeler, 101–127. London: Routledge.

Gliozzo, Charles. 1971. "The Philosophes and Religion: Intellectual Origins of the Dechristianization Movement in the French Revolution." *Church History* 40 (3): 273–283.

Grimes, Ronald. 1992. "Sacred Objects in Museum Spaces." *Studies in Religion* 21 (4): 419–30.

Gundestrup, Bente. 1988. "The Royal Danish Kunstkammer." *Museum International* 40 (4): 186–189.

Hagemann, Alfred. 2020. *Symbolism Politics: Friedrich Wilhelm IV's Cupola for the Berlin Palace*. May 25, 2020. https://www.humboldtforum.org/en/magazin/artikel/symbolism-politics/?dossier=1.

Hahn, Hans Joachim. 2001. *The 1848 Revolutions in German-Speaking Europe*. Harlow: Pearson.

Hooper, Steven. 2014. "A Cross-Cultural Theory of Relics: On Understanding Religion, Bodies, Artefacts, Images and Art." *World Art* (4) 2: 175–207.

Howe, Nicolas. 2016. *Landscapes of the Secular: Law, Religion and American Sacred Space*. Chicago, IL: University of Chicago Press.

Impey, Oliver and Arthur Macgregor, eds. 1985. *The Origins of Museums: The Cabinet of Curiosities in Sixteenth and Seventeenth-Century Europe*. Oxford: Clarendon Press.

Isnart, Cyril, and Nathalie Cerezales. 2020. *The Religious Heritage Complex: Legacy, Conservation, and Christianity*. London: Bloomsbury.

Ivanov, Paola. 2000. "African Art in the Ethnologisches Museum in Berlin." *African Arts* 33 (3): 18–39.

Jethro, Duane. 2019. "The Commemoration Service on the Occasion of the Third Repatriation of Human Remains from former German South-West Africa on the 29th of August 2018 at Franzosische Friedrichstadtkirche, Berlin." *Material Religion* 15 (4): 522–526.

Johnson, Reverend Ben. 2017. "Erasing the Cross: Public vs. Private Sector." *Acton Institute*, September 12, 2017. https://www.acton.org/publications/transatlantic/2017/09/12/erasing-cross-public-vs-private-sector

Joppke, Christian. 2018. "Culturalizing Religion in Western Europe: Patterns and Puzzles". *Social Compass*, 65 (2): 234–246.

katholisch.de. 2017. "Koch: Kreuz Darf Nicht zum Kampfthema Werden." *katholisch.de*. May 20, 2017. https://www.katholisch.de/artikel/13383-berliner-schloss-kreuz-kein-kampfthema.

Kirshenblatt-Gimblett, Barbara. 1998. *Destination Culture: Tourism, Museums, and Heritage*. Berkeley, CA: University of California Press.

Knight, Ben. 2018. *German State Orders Crosses Mounted in Government Buildings*. April 25, 2018. https://p.dw.com/p/2wbQ5.

Koloss, Hans-Joachim. 1990. *Art of Central Africa: Masterpieces from the Berlin Museum Für Völkerkunde*. New York: Metropolitan Museum of Art.

König, Viola. 2007. "Zeitgeist and Early Ethnographic Collecting in Berlin: Implications and Perspectives for the Future." *RES: Anthropology and Aesthetics* 52 (1): 51–58.

Laniel, Jean-François. 2016. "What 'cultural religion' says about secularization and national identity: A neglected religio-political configuration." *Social Compass* 63 (3): 372–388.

Laniel, Jean-François. 2018. "Religion and national identity in Catholic societies: The quarrel between religion and culture." In *The Changing Faces of Catholicism*, edited by Solange Lefebvre and Alfonso Perez-Agote, 21–42. Leiden: Brill.

Langer, Lorenz. 2010. "Panacea or Pathetic Fallacy: The Swiss Born on Minarets." *Vanderbilt Journal of Transnational Law* 43: 863–951.

Ledanff, Susanne. 2003. "The Palace of the Republic Versus the Stadtschloß: The Dilemmas of Planning in the Heart of Berlin." *German Politics & Society* 21 (4): 30–73.

Hanns Lessing, Julia Besten, Tilman Dedering, Christian Hohmann and Lize Kriel, eds. 2012. *The German Protestant Church in Colonial Southern Africa The Impact of Overseas Work from the Beginnings until the 1920s*. Wiesbaden: Harrassowitz Verlag.

Lowenthal, David. 1994. "Identity, Heritage and History." In *Commemorations: the Politics of National Identity*, edited by John Gillis, 41–60. Princeton, NJ: Princeton University Press.

Lowenthal, David. 1997. *The Heritage Crusade and the Spoils of History.* Cambridge: Cambridge University Press.

Macdonald, Sharon. 2005. "Enchantment and its Dilemmas: The Museum as a Ritual Site." In *Science, Magic and Religion: The Ritual Processes of Museum Magic,* edited by Mary Bouquet and Nuno Porto, 209–227. London: Berghahn.

Macdonald, Sharon. 2013. *Memorylands: Heritage and Identity in Europe Today.* London: Routledge.

Mahmood, Saba. 2009. "Religious Reason and Secular Affect: An Incommensurable Divide?" In *Is Critique Secular? Blasphemy, Injury, and Free Speech,* edited by Talal Asad, Wendy Brown, Judith Butler and Saba Mahmood, 58–94. Berkeley, CA: Townsend Center for the Humanities.

Mairesse, François. 2018. *Museology and the Sacred: Materials for a Discussion.* Papers from the ICOFOM 41th symposium held in Tehran (Iran), 15-19 October 2018. Paris: ICOM.

Mairesse, François. 2019a. "The Sacred in the Prism of Museology." ICOFOM Study Series. *Museology and the Sacred* 47 (1–2): 15–22.

Mairesse, François. 2019b. "Museology and the Sacred." *Material Religion* 15 (5): 651–653.

McClellan, Andrew. 1999. *Inventing the Louvre: Art, Politics, and the Origins of the Modern Museum in Eighteenth-Century Paris.* Berkeley, CA: University of California Press.

McPhee, Peter, ed. 2013. *A Companion to the French Revolution.* London: Wiley-Blackwell.

Meyer, Birgit. 2020. "Recycling the Christian Past: The Heritagization of Christianity and National Identity in the Netherlands." In *Cultures, Citizenship and Human Rights,* edited by Rosemarie Buikema, Antoine Buyse and Antonius G. M. Robben, 64–88. London: Routledge.

Meyer, Birgit, and Marleen de Witte. 2013. "Heritage and the Sacred: Introduction." *Material Religion* 9 (3): 274–280.

Miller, Jon. 2014. *Missionary Zeal and Institutional Control: Organizational Contradictions in the Basel Mission on the Gold Coast 1828–1917.* London: Routledge.

Morgan, David. 2011. "Thing." *Material Religion* 7 (1): 140–146.

Morgan, David. 2018. "Museum Collection and the History of Interpretation." In *Religion in Museums: Global and Multidisciplinary Perspectives,* edited by Gretchen Buggeln, Crispin Paine and S. Brent Plate, 109–114. London: Bloomsbury.

Nanwani, Shaira. 2011. "The Burqa Ban: An Unreasonable Limitation on Religious Freedom or a Justifiable Restriction?" *Emory International Literature Review* 25 (3): 1431–1476.

Oliphant, Elayne. 2012. "The Crucifix as a Symbol of Secular Europe: The Surprising Semiotics of the European Court of Human Rights". *Anthropology Today* 28 (2): 10–12.

Paine, Crispin. 2012. "Introduction: Museums and Material Religion." *Material Religion* 8 (1): 4–8.

Paine, Crispin Paine. 2013. *Religious Objects in Museums: Private Lives and Public Duties.* London: A&C Black.

Paine, Crispin. 2000. *Godly Things: Museums, Objects and Religion.* London: Bloomsbury.

Penny, H. Glenn. 2002. *Objects of Culture: Ethnology and Ethnographic Museums in Imperial Germany.* Chapel Hill, NC: University of North Carolina Press.

Perraudin, Michael, and Jürgen Zimmerer, eds. 2010. *German Colonialism and National Identity.* London: Routledge.

Poulot, Dominique. 1988. "Revolutionary Vandalism and the Birth of the Museum: The Effects of a Representation of Modern Cultural Terror.'" In *Art in Museums,* edited by Susan Pearce, 192–214. London: Bloomsbury.

Quartey, Seth. 2007. *Missionary Practices on the Gold Coast, 1832–1895.* Youngstown, NJ: Cambria Press.

Robertson, Priscilla Smith. 1952. *Revolutions of 1848: A Social History.* Princeton, NJ: Princeton University Press.

Schildgen, Brenda. 2008. *Heritage or Heresy: Preservation and Destruction of Religious Art and Architecture in Europe.* New York: Palgrave Macmillan.

Schröder, Christian. 2017. "Ein Symbol der Staatsgewalt." *Der Tagesspiegel,* May 27, 2017. https://www.tagesspiegel.de/kultur/debatte-um-kreuz-auf-berliner-schloss-ein-symbol-der-staatsgewalt/19857596.html.

Schröder, Richard. 2017. "Warum das Kreuz auf Berlins Schlosskuppel gehört." *Welt,* May 31, 2017. https://www.welt.de/debatte/kommentare/article165110920/Warum-das-Kreuz-auf-Berlins-Schlosskuppel-gehoert.html.

Shackley, Myra. 2001."Sacred World Heritage Sites: Balancing Meaning with Management." *Tourism Recreation Research* 26 (1): 5–10.

Sharma, Gouri. 2018. "An Inconvenient Truth of Berlin's New Cultural Centre." *TRT World*, January 12, 2018. https://www.trtworld.com/magazine/the-inconvenient-truth-of-berlin-s-new-cultural-centre-14093.

Smith, Laurajane. 2006. *Uses of Heritage*. London: Routledge.

Stiftung Preußischer Kulturbesitz. 2013. *Rede von Hermann Parzinger, Präsident der Stiftung Preußischer Kulturbesitz, Anlässlich der Grundsteinlegung für das Humboldt-Forum*. December 6, 2013. https://www.preussischer-kulturbesitz.de/en/karriere/freie-stellen/alle-news-stiftung-preussischer-kulturbesitz/news-detail-stiftung-preussischer-kulturbesitz/article/2013/06/12/rede-von-hermann-parzinger-praesident-der-stiftung-preussischer-kulturbesitz-anlaesslich-der-grundsteinlegung-fuer-das-humboldt-forum.html.

Sullivan, Bruce M., ed. 2015. *Sacred Objects in Secular Spaces: Exhibiting Asian Religions in Museums*. London: Bloomsbury.

Tamimi Arab, Pooyan. 2017. *Amplifying Islam in the European Soundscape: Religious Pluralism and Secularism in the Netherlands*. London: Bloomsbury.

Theuerkauff, Christian. 1985. "The Brandenburg Kunstkammer in Berlin." In *The Origins of Museums: the Cabinet of Curiosities in Sixteenth and Seventeenth-Century Europe*, edited by Oliver Impey and Arthur Macgregor, 110–114. Oxford: Clarendon Press.

Vahland, Kia. 2017. "Kreuz auf Berliner Stadtschloss Symbol der Unterdrükung." *Süddeutsche Zeitung*, June 7, 2017. https://www.sueddeutsche.de/kultur/diskussion-um-kreuz-auf-berliner-stadtschloss-symbol-der-unterdrueckung-1.3535836.

Van den Hemel, Ernst. 2017. "The Dutch War on Easter: Secular Passion for Religious Culture & National Rituals." *Yearbook for Ritual and Liturgical Studies* 33: 1–19.

Van der Heyden, Ulrich. 2011. "Christian Missionary Societies in the German Colonies, 1884/85–1914/15." In *German Colonialism: Race, the Holocaust, and Postwar Germany*, edited by Volker Langbehn and Mohammad Salama, 215–253. New York: Columbia University Press.

Van Kley, Dale. 2003. "Christianity as Casualty and Chrysalis of Modernity: The Problem of Dechristianization in the French Revolution." *American Historical Review* 108 (4): 1081–1104.

Von Boddien, Wilhelm, and Helmut Engel. 2000. *Die Berliner Schlossdebatte: Pro und Contra*. Berlin: Spitz.

Von Bose, Friedrich. 2013. "The Making of Berlin's Humboldt-Forum: Negotiating History and the Cultural Politics of Place." *Darkmatter Journal* 11 (November 2013). https://s3.amazonaws.com/arena-attachments/480616/015783aec7fd1429edce1a72a7821030.pdf.

von Bose, Friedrich. 2016. *Das Humboldt-Forum: Eine Ethnographie Seiner Plannung*. Berlin: Kulturverlag Kadmos.

Von Buttlar, Adrian. 2007. "Berlin's Castle Versus Palace: A Proper Past for Germany's Future?" *Future Anterior* 4 (1): 13–29.

Wiegelmann, Lucas. 2017a. "Grüne und Linke wollen Kreuz auf Kuppel Verhindern." *Welt*, May 20, 2017. https://www.welt.de/kultur/kunst-und-architektur/article164759558/Gruene-und-Linke-wollen-Kreuz-auf-Kuppel-verhindern.html.

Wiegelmann, Lucas. 2017b. "Zentralrat der Muslime Befürwortet Kreuz auf Kuppel." *Welt*, May 31, 2017. https://www.welt.de/kultur/kunst-und-architektur/article165114080/Zentralrat-der-Muslime-befuerwortet-Kreuz-auf-Kuppel.html.

Zimmerman, Andrew. 2010. *Anthropology and Antihumanism in Imperial Germany*. Chicago, IL: University of Chicago Press.

2.7

MATERIAL GOD *MENGDU*

A Symbol and Real Presence

Yohan Yoo

Mengdu, which is the main set of ritual instruments of Jeju shamans (*simbang*), is also believed to be their tutelary deity (Hyeon 1986: 50; Kang 2012: 3). In Jeju-*do* (Jeju), the largest island of Korea and also one of South Korea's nine provinces,[1] Jeju shamans use *mengdu* in *gut* (shamanic rituals) for practicing divination as well as for propitiating deities and rebuking evil spirits. In this chapter, I illuminate both the materiality and the divinity of *mengdu*. The shamans keep these utensils in *dangju*, closet-shaped domestic shrines installed in their homes, where they also worship it and dedicate offerings to it.

A set of *mengdu* includes three kinds of shamanic instruments made of brass: *sinkal*, which are two divine knives; *sanpan*, which refer to a set of divination tools consisting of two *cheonmun* (coins) and two *sangjan* (flat cups); and *yoryeong*, which is a shamanic bell. This set of material instruments is also a deity who helps *simbang* at the closest hand. In Jeju, *mengdu* is believed to be both the representative of the shamanic ancestor gods and an independent deity that belongs to the divine world. The *simbang* seeks to invite the gods to the ritual place in this world from the other world in order to perform *gut*. Community deities, who are believed to live in their shrines in or around villages, and household deities, who are in charge of the specific places of each house, are also invited through a ritual process to cross over to the human realm. Likewise, the *simbang* should ask the deity *mengdu* to come out of the shrine and go to the ritual place with him or her.

Some scholars argue that Jeju *simbang,* unlike some shamans of other areas in Korea who are thought to be possessed by spirits, do not try to directly contact the gods in performing *gut*; these scholars think that *simbang* conduct divination by using *mengdu* as a set of instruments. It is true that *simbang* toss *sinkal* or *sanpan* and determine the divine will depending on the way the instruments fall. However, *simbang* clearly say that they always keep in touch with the divine being *mengdu*, which reveals its will directly to them. It is believed that sometimes *mengdu* manifests itself to the persons it chooses. To become a shaman in Jeju, he or she must have a set of *mengdu*. Parents or teachers can give them to new shamans. In rare instances, a person becomes a shaman because he or she has been chosen by *mengdu*. *Simbang* say that they do not use *mengdu* but are guided by *mengdu*.

In the following, I suggest that the existing explanation of the relationship between symbols and signified deities should be rethought. The classical notion of "hierophany" as conceived by Mircea Eliade, the idea of "inherently efficacious" natural objects of Kimberly

DOI: 10.4324/9781351176231-16

Patton, and the notion of the "real presence" of Robert Orsi will be critically examined and re-described. Next, I will explore the divine and the material characteristics of *mengdu*. In the third and fourth sections, I will demonstrate the materiality and divinity of *mengdu* of Jeju in detail, articulating that materiality and divinity are not separated in Jeju religion. Finally, I will conclude that the real and the symbolic are resolved in *mengdu*—and that materiality and divinity can be experienced as one.

Materiality and Divinity in Conceptions of Symbols

Mircea Eliade suggested the term "hierophany" "to designate the act of manifestation of the sacred" (1987: 11). Though this sounds totally theological, he was focusing on human thoughts and activities by articulating "a manifestation of the sacred in the mental world of those who believed in it" (1996: 10). This manifestation has a dialectic structure, which he called "the dialectic of the hierophanies" (1996: 13). The sacred, "something of a wholly different order, a reality that does not belong to our world," is manifested "in objects that are an integral part of our natural 'profane' world" (1987: 11), which Eliade also summarized as being "the manifestation of the sacred in material things" (1996: 29). He clearly emphasizes the necessity of material things in the dialectic of the hierophanies. But these material things are recognized as totally other things in human experience. For those to whom a material thing manifests itself as sacred, "its immediate reality is transmuted into a supernatural reality" (1987: 12). For instance,

> The sacred tree, the sacred stone are not adored as stone or tree; they are worshipped precisely because they are *hierophanies*, because they show something that is no longer stone or tree but the sacred, the *ganz andere*.
>
> *(Eliade 1987: 12)*

Namely, when a material thing reveals the sacred, it becomes a symbol. By a symbol, Eliade means that which "signifies something other than itself" (1996: 324). A symbol remains itself but at the same time "becomes something else" (1987: 12). The thing that becomes sacred is "separated in regard to itself . . . stopping to be a mere profane something" (1996: 13).

Eliade clearly recognized that a material symbol, which is regarded as something other than itself, is often identified with the divinity. However, he did not consider this identification as universal, but reduced it to elementary, primordial, or primitive phenomena (1996: 24–28; 229–231). According to Eliade, "The confusion between sign and divinity" is "the primitive conception, identifying the divinity with matter and adoring it in whatever form of place it appeared" (1996: 230). Though he was aware that material things are accepted as divine beings, his focus was on symbols. By emphasizing the symbolic hierophany, he consequently made light of the divinity of a material thing.

Kimberly Patton has criticized Eliade's idea of hierophany. While Patton appreciates the category of hierophany in that it acknowledges the importance of a natural object, she also points out that it is inadequate for articulating the sacredness of the object itself. She agrees with Eliade that certain features of natural elements lend themselves consistently to the idea of the sacred, and that direct experience of natural objects is fundamental to the formation of this idea (2007: 15–17). But she raises an objection to Eliade's emphasis on the structure of symbolism because it can obstruct our view of the sacredness of the natural object itself. "The Eliadian category of 'hierophany,' in so far as it implies the expression of something uncanny in something ordinary, is, in a sense, undermined by the nature" of a natural object itself, especially the sea, which is her focus in her book *The Sea Can Wash Away All Evils* (2007: 53). The category of hierophany prevents us from recognizing the inherent efficaciousness of the natural object by overemphasizing "a foreign, hierophanic force that does not belong to this world" (2007: 53). In most religious traditions other than the monotheistic traditions, she asserts, "the sea does not index something greater than itself" (2007: 54).

Patton properly shows that a natural object that is experienced as sacred may not stand for something else but manifests only itself. But by focusing on the sea and natural elements, she neglects and never mentions material things other than natural objects. Though she calls Eliade "a religious phenomenologist of natural objects" (2007: 14), Eliade actually dealt with many artificial material things—such as temples, towers, houses, stone works, and metal tools—along with natural objects. Though it is true that Eliade emphasized the consistent features and natural characteristics of natural objects, he did not limit material things only to natural objects.

Orsi expands Patton's scope of sacred objects by including not only natural objects—such as spring water, dirt, or dead bodies—but also human-made things like artificial rocks, printed images or words, and the cross, which all can be experienced as "real presence." He points out that modern Western society, both inside and outside of scholarship, has ignored people "who lived with the gods really present to them," often deeming such people "savage and primitive" (2016: 3). Orsi criticizes theories of religion in which "the gods really present"—namely, "all the special suprahuman beings with whom humans have been in relationship in different times and places" have been regarded as "symbols, signs, metaphors, functions, and abstractions" (2016: 4). In other words, he objects to reducing the sacred beings in the experience of religious people to symbols or signs. According to Orsi, this real presence should not be thought to be transcendent: "The gods are not transcendent but immanently present," and this presence is in "the material and political circumstances of everyday life" (2016: 69).

However, his strict separation between the real and the symbolic should be reconsidered. Orsi himself is aware that "the divide . . . between the real and the symbolic" also "defines the modern temperament" (2016: 37). But he sticks to the modern, narrow meaning of the symbol. Though he says "the symbol is not an experience of something, but a sign or a representation of it" (2016: 38), for many religious people, representing is an important way of experiencing. Louis Dupré points out that symbols represent the signified object "in the double sense of making present and taking the place of" (2000: 1). Hierophanies as symbols of the sacred make it possible for religious people to experience the sacred, as Clifford Geertz puts it, "by formulating conceptions of a general order of existence and clothing those conceptions with such an aura of factuality that the moods and motivations seem uniquely realistic" (Geertz 1973: 90). That is the reason a material object that is experienced as sacred remains itself and at the same time becomes something else. Actually, some of the examples that Orsi presents imply that sacred material objects can be both symbolic and real to religious people. For instance, Catholic pilgrims in the Bronx go to a human-made reproduction of the Lourdes grotto, which is a focus of devotion to the Blessed Mother Mary and is believed to hold "the power of the Blessed Mother's presence." The water flowing from plumbing in the artificial rocks "is both ordinary and extraordinary; it is identical and not to the water at Lourdes" (Orsi 2016: 54). The water from the Bronx artificial grotto is ordinary water and at once becomes identical to the sacred water. A symbol, which makes the signified present and takes the place of it, can be an experience of something and simultaneously a representation of it. In brief, though Orsi maintains a notion of "real presence" but not a "symbol," religious experiences are often related to "a symbol and at once real presence itself."

As I have shown, therefore, the three scholars' theories on the sacred and the symbolic should be elaborated further. I will carefully examine divine and material characteristics of the material god *mengdu*, which will lead us to a clearer view on the relationship between the symbolic and the real.

Mengdu as Both an Instrument Used in *Gut* and a Deity Leading *Gut*

As described above, a set of *mengdu* includes three kinds of shamanic instruments made of brass, which are *sinkal*, *sanpan*, and *yoryeong*. For this reason, it is often called "*sam-mengdu*," meaning three *mengdu*. *Sinkal* (divine knives) consists of a pair of dull knives that are 20 to 22 centimeters long with paper tassels that are 55 to 60 centimeters long. These tassels are called "divine skirts." Shamans use *sinkal* in performing *gut* mainly for the purpose of inviting gods to the ritual place, demonstrating the authority of gods for whom they act, expelling evil spirits, and asking the will of gods. *Sanpan* refers to a set of divination tools consisting of two brass coins (*cheonmun*: 5–6 centimeters in diameter) on which Chinese characters such as "heaven," "earth," "gate," or "sun" and "moon" are engraved and two flat brass cups (*sangjan*: about 4 centimeters in diameter and 1–2 centimeters in depth); these are stored in a kind of tray (*sandae*). *Yoryeong* is a brass bell, 6–7 centimeters in diameter and 4–5 centimeters high, to which five to seven pieces of 60-centimeter-long colorful cloths, which are also called "divine skirt," are attached. Divine skirts attached to *sinkal* and *yoryeong* resemble jackets and skirts put on *myeongdu*, a brass or bronze mirror, which is a shamanic instrument of the mainland. *Simbang* sometimes ring the bell in order to open the door to the other world and invite deities; they also use the bell as a musical instrument while they perform *gut* (Figures 2.7.1 and 2.7.2).

Though *mengdu* is composed of three different instruments, *simbang* think of a set of *mengdu* as a single entity. According to the shamanic narratives of the *Chogong bonpuri*, the ancestor gods of shamans—three brothers known as *Jetbugi* (errand boys)—were the first users of *mengdu* in mythic times, and their names correspond to the three *mengdu* (Hyeon 2005: 36–63; 2007: 126–150). Before performing a *gut*, the *simbang* should set a table with food for the three brothers. On this table a set of *mengdu* is placed, representing the ancestor gods.

Chogong bonpuri presents *mengdu* as the representative of the three brother gods remaining in this world. First of all, the childhood names of three brothers are Bon-mengdu, Sin-mengdu, and Sam-mengdu. Though the meanings of these names are not obvious, it is noteworthy that all three names include *mengdu* in them. According to the myth, the name of the instrument set originated from the names of the gods. Each *simbang*'s *mengdu*, which is modeled after the first *mengdu* of the three brothers, is their symbol in this world.

However, *mengdu* is not just the representative or symbol of the shamanic ancestor gods, but is also regarded as an independent deity. Hyeon asserts that "*mengdu* as a basic shamanic instrument is the symbol of a *simbang*'s tutelary god or the selfsame god itself" (1986: 52, 437). Though Hyeon argues that *mengdu* is the symbol of the god *or* the god itself, *mengdu* is the god itself *and* at once its symbol. In Jeju shamanic religion, as is in many other indigenous religions, the gods and their symbols are not often distinguished (see Eliade 1949: 24–28, 230–231). To adherents, both are sacred beings. Some *simbang,* when their shamanic ability and skills have improved, are said to "be taught by *mengdu* directly" (Kang 2012: 86).

The divinity of *mengdu*, both as the symbol of the gods in the myths and as an independent deity in its own right, can be seen in *dangjuje*—which literally means a ritual for *dangju* (Gungnip munhwajae yeonguso 2008: 357; Kang 2012: 31). The word *dangju* designates

Figures 2.7.1–2.7.2 *Mengdu* enshrined in *dangju* of *Simbang* Kim Yeongcheol's house. Photos by the author.

domestic shrines for *mengdu* in a *simbang*'s house and is sometimes used as a nickname of *mengdu* itself. *Dangjuje* is carried out on the birthdays of the three mythic brother gods, who according to *Chogong bonpuri* were born on the eighth, the eighteenth, and the twenty-eighth days of September by the lunar calendar. Though most *simbang* today no longer perform this ritual, some do so on the twenty-eighth day of September when the third brother was born—and as such when all three brothers began to exist.[2] But this ritual is dedicated to the specific *mengdu* that a *simbang* has chosen to enshrine in his or her home rather than the archetypical *mengdu* used by the brothers in the myth. While the family hosting shamanic rituals usually prepare food and serve the community, *dangjuje* is the only ritual in which *simbang* provide food for *mengdu* and community members, offering them free shamanic ritual services by using or with the help of *mengdu*—such as divination or *neokdeurim,* which is performed to heal and reintegrate damaged human souls (for *neokdeurim,* see Yoo 2018).

Each *mengdu* is an independent deity that has its own history. In the opening part of the *gut,* one of the *simbang* who conduct the ritual, usually the one who is in charge, recites the history of the *mengdu* while holding it in his or her hands. The *mengdu* is then placed on the table. The table, therefore, is dedicated to *mengdu* itself, as well as to the three brothers. This ritual recitation is called *gongsi puri.* Though the three progenitor brothers are mentioned during the recitation, the main part of *gongsi puri* is the genealogy of all the shamans who have taught or influenced the reciting *simbang* as well as the genealogy of all the shamans who have ever owned and served this particular *mengdu.* Even the shamans who have used older sets of *mengdu* after which the *mengdu* in question is modeled are mentioned as its ancestors (Hyeon 2007: 127, 150, 738; Kang 2012: 153–155). The spirits of the predecessors are invited by the enumeration of their names, titles, or relations to the reciter.

Furthermore, though the *mengdu* is kept in a shrine in their house, shamans are clearly aware that the *mengdu*—just like the other 18,000 Jeju gods and goddesses—belongs to the divine world, which is different and separate from that of human beings. *Dangju,* the domestic shrine in the *simbang*'s house, is dedicated only to *mengdu,* not to any other gods (Gungnip munhwajae yeonguso 2008: 357). *Dangju* is not only a sacred place in the *simbang*'s house, which is strictly distinguished from the other areas of the house, but also the divine local office in this world. But Jeju *simbang* say that it is not good for *mengdu* to just stay in *dangju.* It should go to the ritual place to perform *gut.* When *simbang* invite all the deities in the Jeju pantheon to the ritual place, the *simbang* should invite *mengdu* to come out of the shrine and go to the ritual place with him or her. In *gut,* divine will is revealed by divination. *Simbang* cast a pair of *sinkal* or *sanpan* (*cheonmun* and *sangjan*), then discern the divine will by interpreting the shapes in which they land on the ground. (For the way *simbang* interpret the shapes, see Hyeon 1986: 424–434.) *Simbang* is the person who interprets the revelation given by *mengdu.*

Some scholars argue that Jeju *simbang* do not try to directly contact the gods in performing *gut,* unlike some shamans of other areas in Korea who are thought to be possessed by spirits, but instead conduct divination by using *mengdu* as a set of instruments (see Cho et al. 2003: 213; Hyeon 1986: 49). It is true that *simbang* cast *sinkal* or *sanpan* and judge the divine will depending on the way the instruments fall down to the ground. However, all the four *simbang* I interviewed for this research clearly said that they always keep in touch with the divine being *mengdu,* which reveals its will directly to them.

I am not denying the active role of *simbang,* not only in rituals but also in the relationship with the deity *mengdu. Simbang* are human beings who are the closest to deities. Though the meaning of the word "*simbang*" is not agreed upon among scholars, they call themselves "*sinui-seongbang*"—petty officials of the gods—when they recite myths in performing *gut.*

The official can converse with or make suggestions to the gods, as well as dedicate offerings to them. If the officials think a god's repeated ominous signs indicate that it is unnecessarily upset, they try to coax or even rebuke the god (Hyeon 1986: 51–52). It may seem as if *simbang* try to accomplish their goal by both appropriating the material *mengdu* and manipulating the divine *mengdu*; but in truth most *simbang* have steadfast loyalty to and complete confidence in *mengdu* and other gods. Thus, borrowing the insight from Orsi, it can be said that "a density of relationships" and "a certain kind of intersubjective receptivity and recognition" had been established between the official and the god (2016: 66–67). In this dense relationship, *simbang* are very cautious to disclose only the divine will, not their own intention. Even if they can feel what the god wants to say, they abstain from expressing it. Only after the divine will has been shown by the casting of the *mengdu* will they deliver what they perceived. *Simbang* say that sometimes the god shows firm proof before exercising miraculous power. For instance, one of my interviewees told me that one time when he was performing *gut* so as to heal a cancer patient, the god showed an auspicious sign by having the knives, *sinkal*, that were cast on the ground land on their edges. He added that, in fact, the patient had been cured of cancer.

In this chapter, I have used the expression that "*mengdu* are used," as scholars usually do in talking about shamanic instruments. This expression articulates the materiality of *mengdu*. However, for Jeju people participating in *gut*, the divinity of *mengdu* is also taken for granted. As Patton rightly puts it, "in the view of its adherents, practiced religion may belong to the sphere of, and have its source in, the divine. The gods practice religion because religion in essence belongs to them" (2009: 17). In the view of Jeju people, it is *mengdu* that conduct *gut* and reveal the divine will—through *simbang*. In the Jeju shamanic indigenous religion, the divinity is confirmed by what the material god shows.

Mengdu is obviously a god who is present among Jeju people—and yet, it is also simultaneously symbolic in that it takes the place of and makes present the ancestor gods who are believed to be in the invisible divine world. The divine material *mengdu* is a clear example of *a symbol and at once real presence itself*, rather than a *real presence that is not a symbol* (see Orsi 2016: 37–38).

Obtaining and Celebrating *Mengdu*

In this section, I will first demonstrate the divine characteristics of material *mengdu*, which can be seen in the process of new shamans preparing a set of *mengdu*. Then, I will describe two Jeju shamanic rituals directly related to *mengdu* to illuminate the divine characteristics of the material god *mengdu*. The first ritual is *singut*, which is performed when a person acquires a set of *mengdu* and begins to work as a *simbang*.

There are several ways for novices to obtain *mengdu*, which are closely related to the way they become *simbang* (Hyeon 1986: 88–110). First, in Jeju, just as in the southern part of the mainland, many shamans pass on their work—along with the village or area of which they have been in charge—to their children or other family members, often bequeathing their *mengdu* at the same time. Some *simbang* adopt one of their disciples for the same purpose. It is said that the new shaman can begin to work smoothly if he or she inherits *mengdu* that have a long history and are known for their divine power. Second, some Jeju people become *simbang* because they are told to do so. Although it is not common, Jeju *simbang* may prescribe that a certain client should become *simbang*—mostly when he or she gets *sinbyeong*, meaning "the disease from the gods," the cause of which doctors cannot explain; or if he or she has consecutive unfortunate experiences such as failures in business or loss of family members.

This person first tries to find a *simbang* willing to hand over his or her *mengdu*. If this is not successful, a new set of *mengdu* should be made. Ideally, a new set should be modeled after a preexisting set of senior *simbang*. But if no *simbang* is willing to lend his or her own *mengdu* for that purpose, new *mengdu* must be made without a prototype model. This new *mengdu* is called "*mengdu* without a genealogy," and is often disrespected (Kang 2012: 122). Third, there are several *simbang* in Jeju who say that *mengdu* chose them: they came upon a *mengdu* by chance—such as that of a deceased shaman—and therefore became *simbang* (Kang 2012: 59–62). If a person happens to see or pick up a *mengdu*, for instance, around the graves in which it is buried with a deceased shaman, he or she is believed to be destined to become a shaman because the person is chosen by *mengdu*. The chosen person is usually said to have mysterious experiences, including the disease from the gods.

This variety of ways novice *simbang* can acquire *mengdu* demonstrates how the divinity and the materiality of *mengdu* are not separated. To recap: first, a person can become *simbang* only if he or she possesses the material set of *mengdu*. Second, revered *mengdu* has material genealogy—if not derived from those who have used it before, then at least derived from the preexisting set it is molded from. Third, the material god *mengdu* may choose its official in person by revealing its material body to the person. The divinity of *mengdu* is based on its materiality.

Once a person has acquired *mengdu*, the person may well satisfy the necessary condition to become *simbang*. To do this, the person must perform *chosinjil singut*, the *gut* for (or of) the gods for the shaman who "goes the gods' way"—namely, the main or leading shaman. In this ritual, the *simbang* accepts and resolves to serve *mengdu*, while *mengdu* also accepts the *simbang* as its official and gives him or her divine ability. (For the details of this ritual, see Hyeon 2002: 142–143; Kang 2012: 139–151.) For the *simbang* to accept *mengdu* as his or her tutelary deity, the procedure of *dangjumaji*—also called "*samsiwangmaji*"—is most important. In this procedure, assistant *simbang*—usually a few seniors who have carried out this ritual before—place a morsel of food from the offering table into the mouth of the main *simbang*, stating that it is food offered by Samsiwang, the three brother gods. Then they put *cheonmun* (coins) and *sangjan* (flat cups) on the initiate *simbang*'s shoulder, stating those are also from Samsiwang. Next, they cast *cheonmun* and *sangjan* to the floor to ask *mengdu* if the shaman is qualified for the position of the official of the gods and, if so, how he or she conduct his or her mission as *simbang*.

As I wrote above, *dangju* is another name for *mengdu,* and "Samsiwang" is the name of the Jetbugi brothers, deities of the other world. A shaman accepting the material *mengdu* as one's own deity is equated with following the way of the deities who first performed shamanic work during the mythic time. This *dangjumaji* procedure clearly demonstrates the double identity of *mengdu*, both as an independent deity and as the representative of the mythic gods.

After *dangjumaji* has been conducted, the new shaman performs *gobunjilchim*, which is a procedure for straightening and cleaning the crooked ways (*gobunjil*) he or she has trod; essentially, the new *simbang* must have a shrine for the *mengdu* in his or her home—for which it is necessary to sweep away all the old evils. To begin, an assistant shaman cleans up part of the floor that is thought to be the way from the offering tables to *dangju,* then puts cotton cloth on the route; this prepares the path on which Samsiwang are to come. Then, the main shaman performs a ritual drama in which he or she loses *mengdu*. The loss is set up by Samsiwang, who are angry at the wrongdoings of the *simbang* and decide to take it back. To earn back the *mengdu,* the *simbang* then prays for the gods' pardon. Then, the *simbang* wraps *mengdu* in a cotton cloth that has been laid on the floor, binds it to his or her body, carries it to the *dangju,* the closet-shaped sacred space in which it is enshrined. In other words, possessing the material *mengdu* amounts to inviting and thereafter serving the god *mengdu*. *Mengdu* simultaneously possesses the characteristics of both material things and divine being.

Mengdu gain their divinity in part from the other important ritual directly related to *mengdu*—*mengdu-gosa*, a ritual performed by the smith who manufactures both the material and divine *mengdu*. The *mengdu-gosa* is conducted in two stages: at the beginning and again at the end of the manufacturing process (for *mengdu-gosa*, see Kang 2012: 121–128). The first stage of the ritual is performed before melting the brass from which *mengdu* will be made. A table placed in front of the bellows in the workshop is laden with cooked rice (or other grain), rice cakes, raw rice, fruit, boiled eggs, and refined grain wine. Next, pork is prepared on this table in order to make the *mengdu* appropriate for use by gods partaking of pork (for the taboo on pork in Jeju, see Yoo and Watts 2021: 75–98). Then, the smith and the *simbang*, who ordered the *mengdu*, together bow down to the ground to the god of the forge and the god Jeongyeongnok, asking them to ensure the quality of the new *mengdu*. According to *Chogong bonpuri*, Jeongyeongnok is a heavenly god who successfully cast the first *mengdu* for the three brothers after the god Shuecheoriadeul from the East Sea failed to do it. On the basis of this myth, it is believed that the divinity of *mengdu* comes from heaven, and the *mengdu-gosa* ritual is dedicated to the heavenly god and the god of the forge (Kang 2012: 126).

Once the manufacturing process is complete, the second stage of the ritual is carried out. After taking the *mengdu* out of the mold, the smith douses it three times: first in water in which (usually) sprigs of a juniper tree have been boiled, then in a sweet rice drink, and finally in distilled spirits. Then, the smith dresses *mengdu* by attaching paper tassels (divine skirts) to a pair of *sinkal* (divine knives). Then, the smith, not the *simbang*, performs a *neok-deurim* ritual to integrate the *mengdu* and its soul. Then, the smith conducts a divination by tossing *sinkal* and *sanpan*—again, two *cheonmun* (coins) and two *sangjan* (flat cups)—to ask the *mengdu* if the *simbang* would be a good shaman.

It has been said that smiths were regarded as sacred in many cultures because they were thought to "collaborate in the work of nature" to help "the transformation of the matter" which is "at once alive and sacred" (Eliade 1978: 8–9). However, in Jeju, smiths are sacred because they produce the god *mengdu*. Making the material *mengdu* is making the divine being *mengdu*, in which *simbang* cannot interfere because they are petty officials of the completely made *mengdu*. The *mengdu-gosa* ritual again demonstrates that materiality and divinity are not separated in Jeju.

Mengdu as a Symbol and as a Real Presence

On the basis of the divine status and material characteristics that have been explained, I will now return to the three scholars' ideas of symbols introduced earlier.

Mircea Eliade's classical theory of hierophany suitably explains the characteristic of *mengdu* as both material things and a deity. For Eliade, and for some of his contemporaries who delved into religious symbolism, a profane thing can become a hierophany because a symbol can replace the signified—which is the sacred—and make it exist (Dupré 2000: 1). According to Clifford's Geertz's phrasing in *The Interpretation of Cultures*, a religion as a system of symbols "acts to establish powerful, pervasive, and long-lasting moods in men by formulating conceptions of a general order of existence and clothing those conceptions with such an aura of factuality that the moods and motivations seem uniquely realistic" (Geertz 1973: 90). By emphasizing the symbolic hierophany, Eliade made light of the divinity of a material thing. If we apply his theory as it is to the understanding of Jeju *mengdu*, *mengdu* as the deity itself is not to be seen clearly, but its symbolic function and status alone become remarkable.

Kimberly Patton does not agree with Eliade's conception of symbolism; in her view, it ignores the sacredness of the natural object itself. She adeptly shows that a sacred natural object may manifest itself without standing for something else. But Patton does not include in her study material things other than natural objects, whereas Eliade took notice of the importance of artificial material things. Since *mengdu* are explicitly artificial things, they do not apply to Patton's interpretation.

On the other hand, Robert Orsi's sacred objects include human-made things, such as artificial rocks, printed images or words, and the cross. Furthermore, he points out that religious people do not reduce sacred things to mere symbols. Using Orsi's language, *mengdu* is believed to be the god who is really present among Jeju people, not just a symbol of the gods of the other world. This real presence should not be thought to be transcendent because it exists in the material circumstances of people. *Mengdu* is obviously present as material things in houses of *simbang* and other ritual spaces.

Orsi's theory includes a problematically strict separation between the real and the symbolic. According to him, a symbol, which is a representation of something, cannot also be an experience of that thing. However, as I demonstrated in the second section on materiality and divinity, a symbol can be an experience of something and simultaneously a representation of it.

These theories of three scholars on sacred objects help expand our view on the relationship between materiality of *mengdu* and its divinity. But new light should be shed on the three theories on the basis of *mengdu*'s ambivalent characteristics. *Mengdu* is a set of brass instruments and at the same time something else, as is the characteristic of symbols. Jeju people know that *mengdu* is a physical item, one that will eventually need to be replaced by a new set made by a smith in its form. And yet they also believe *mengdu* to be extraordinary, to hold the power of a deity. *Mengdu* represents the first tool used by the three brother gods Samsiwang, takes the place of Samsiwang of the other world, and makes them present in the ritual space. As the symbol of the first tool used by the three brother gods in the mythic time, *mengdu* is the symbol of the mythic gods. At the same time, it is also an independent deity who is enshrined at the *simbang*'s house and to whom offering is dedicated. *Mengdu* should be understood as *a symbol and at once real presence itself*, rather than as *real presence not a symbol*. As scholars, we should not reduce material gods to just symbols. But we also should not ignore functions and roles of symbols that take the place of the signified, and that are honored by some as being sacred.

In conclusion, while *mengdu*, which is a material object and a divine being, is a good example of the dialectic of hierophany, it is not confined to the structure of symbols in that it is an independent deity itself. *Mengdu* demonstrates that materiality and divinity are not separated, but experienced as one—which ultimately allows us to better understand the sacred.

Notes

1 The Korean word "*do*" can mean both "province" and "island"; therefore, "Jeju-*do*" refers to Jeju Island as well as Jeju Province. When the word Jeju-do is used to designate Jeju Province, it includes the main island, namely Jeju Island, which is located south of the mainland, and 63 smaller nearby islands, eight of which are inhabited (for information on religions in Jeju, see Yoo 2012).

2 I interviewed four *simbang* for this research (Sunsil Seo on May 19 2017; Sundeok Sin and Yeonhui Kim on October 20 2017; Yeongcheol Kim on December 14 2018). Among them, only *Simbang* Yeongcheol Kim keeps performing this ritual and is very proud that he maintains it when most *simbang* nowadays do not. My interviewees were aware that their interview will be used for academic publication.

References

Cho, Seongyun, Sangcheol Lee, and Sunae Ha. 2003. *Jeju Jiyeok Mingan Sinang-ui Gujo-wa Byeonyong* (The Structure and Changes of Popular Belief of Jeju Region). Seoul: Baiksanseodang.

Dupré, Louis. 2000. *Symbols of the Sacred*. Grand Rapids, MI: Eerdmans Publishing.

Eliade, Mircea. (1956) 1978. *The Forge and the Crucible: The Origins of Structures of Alchemy*. Translated by Stephen Corrin. Chicago, IL: University of Chicago Press.

Eliade, Mircea. (1957) 1987. *The Sacred and the Profane: The Nature of Religion*. Translated by Willard R. Trask. New York: Harcourt.

Eliade, Mircea. (1949) 1996. *Patterns in Comparative Religion*. Translated by Rosemary Seed. Lincoln, NE: University of Nebraska Press.

Geertz, Clifford. 1973. *The Interpretation of Cultures*. New York: Basic Books.

Gungnip munhwajae yeonguso (National Research Institute of Cultural Heritage) ed. 2008. *Ingan-gwa Sillyeong-eul Inneun Sangjing, Mugu: Jeollanamdo, Jeollabukdo, Jejudo* (Shaman's Instruments, Symbols that Relate Humans and Spirits). Seoul: Minsokwon.

Hyeon, Yongjun. 1986. *Jejudo Musok Yeongu* (A Study of Shamanism in Jeju-Do). Seoul: Jipmundang.

Hyeon, Yongjun. 2002. *Jejudo Musok-Gwa Geu Jubyeon* (Jeju Shamanism and Its Surroundings). Seoul: Jimmundang.

Hyeon, Yongjun. (1976) 2005. *Jejudo Sinhwa* (Myths of Jeju-Do). Seoul: Seomoondang.

Hyeon, Yongjun. (1980) 2007. *Jejudo Musok Jaryo Sajeon* (Dictionary of Sources on Jeju Shamanism). Jeju, Korea: Gak.

Kang, Sojeon. 2012. *Jejudo Simbangui Mengdu Yeongu: Giwon, Jeonseung, Uirye-leul Jungsimeuro* (A Research on Jeju Shamans Mengdu: Focusing on Origin, Transmission, and Ritual). PhD Dissertation, Jeju National University.

Orsi, Robert A. 2016. *History and Presence*. Cambridge, MA: Harvard University Press.

Patton, Kimberley C. 2007. *The Sea Can Wash Away All Evils: Modern Marine Pollution and the Ancient Cathartic Ocean*. New York: Columbia University Press.

Patton, Kimberley C. 2009. *Religion of the Gods: Ritual, Paradox, and Reflexivity*. Oxford: Oxford University Press.

Yoo, Yohan. 2012. "Jeju Tochakjonggyo-wa Oeraejonggyo-ui Galdeung-gwa Jilseohyeongseong Gwajeong-e Gwanhan Yeongu" (Conflicts and Coexistence of Native Religion with Imported Religions in Jeju Island). *Jonggyo-wa Munhwa* 22: 1–36.

Yoo, Yohan. 2018. "View of the Soul in the Jeju Shamanistic Religion as Evident in the Neokdeurim Ritual." *Seoul Journal of Korean Studies* 31 (2): 219–234.

Yoo, Yohan and James W. Watts. 2021. *Cosmologies of Pure Realms and the Rhetoric of Pollution*. New York: Routledge.

2.8

THREE SACRED MOUTHFULS

Transformed and Transformative Materiality of Sacred Food in Hindu Publics

Tulasi Srinivas

On the cold morning of January 20, 1999, Babu Bhattar, the chief priest of a temple dedicated to the great god Krishna in Malleshwaram, Bangalore, recounted to me a popular myth of friendship between Krishna and a poor man called Sudhama. He said:

> Sudhama was a childhood friend of Krishna, but as they grew to adulthood, they drifted apart. Sudhama was poor and lived in a one-room shack with his wife and children in a small village, whereas Krishna lived in a palace in the royal city. One day, Sudhama decided to visit his friend Krishna. Sudhama had no money with which to buy him a gift, and so, after some thought, he took with him a small bag of parched rice which he knew Krishna enjoyed.
>
> Sudhama walked for days and arrived at the palace. Krishna recognized him and welcomed him, offering him a perfumed bath, a tasty meal, and soft silken clothes. Sudhama shyly took out the small bag with the parched rice and offered it to Krishna. Krishna was delighted that Sudhama remembered his favorite snack, and he greedily ate three mouthfuls. After the third mouthful, Krishna's wife, Rukmini, gently suggested that he had eaten enough.
>
> After a week visiting Krishna, Sudhama decided to return home. As he neared his village he realized it had been transformed into a beautiful town. Sudhama found his little thatched hut was replaced with a glittering palace and an overflowing treasury. His wife and children came out happily clothed in silks and jewelry. Sudhama understood in an instant that Lord Krishna, in his infinite generosity, had gifted him three lifelong blessings of happiness, wealth and freedom from anxiety, in exchange for the three mouthfuls of parched rice.

Krishna Bhattar looked at me meaningfully and offered the takeaway moral of the story. He said:

> Whatever object is offered to God it should be offered with bhakti (devotion), with the rasa[1] of love, then even parched rice will be transformed into the greatest ruchich[2] blessings!" He added emphatically, "Three mouthfuls! That's all it takes."

DOI: 10.4324/9781351176231-17

Babu Bhattar's "three mouthfuls" story made me realize that *prasadam* as sacred food offered first to the deity, as Sudhama did to Krishna, and then distributed among devotees, is considered transformational in life as in myth. *Prasadam*, or "the sacred share" as Andrea Pinkney rightly translates it, is a central concept in Hinduism that has both abstract and material dimensions (2008). Though dominated by the sacred and ritualistic, the practice of *prasadam*, as well as conversations about it in my hometown of Bangalore, often slipped into the pragmatic and the mundane, running through personal, social, spiritual, and ideal domains. Pinkney notes that, grammatically, the term "*prasada*" stands both for what is instantiated as well as for the ineffable, a linguistic and ideological connection between material worlds and abstract intangibles (2008: 415). So *prasadam* is understood in two main senses: as a material substance imbued with the divine through ritual activity, and as an ineffable state of benevolence associated with deities, gurus, or other extraordinary beings.

Partaking of *prasadam* is material practice and experience that stamps one as being and becoming Hindu.[3] In Hinduism, the consumption of *prasadam* is venerated and considered to have "automatic and immediate soteriological benefit" (Pinkney 2008: 351), and its many forms (cooked and uncooked) reflect myriad sensibilities—from sectarian-specific aesthetics to supposed specific divine taste preference, and from the sub-local to the pan-South Asian. Underlying practices of material religion, the abstract senses of *prasadam* and the logics and technologies of its exchange provides a structure for other sacred and secular material exchanges in Hindu South Asia.

The Sudhama story echoes this braiding of the invisible and the material—the material (food) transforms into the immaterial (blessings) and back again into material gifts (a palace and treasury) through the sheer power of divine consumption. For the duration of the offering "a union is established between god and man" (Yalman 1969: 93). Moreno extends Yalman's theory of union to state that it is "restorative" for the individual devotee to consume *prasadam*, as doing so makes the devotee's body "more like the body of the god" itself (1992: 149)—for, as devotees consume the *prasadam*, the food is transformed yet again from material object on the plate into part of their subjective fleshly bodies.

So *prasadam* is clearly a "comprehensive discourse" in itself (Ricoeur 1981) with manifold meanings not only in the sacred realm, as is traditionally understood, but, as I hope to demonstrate, also in its contemporary forms. *Prasadam* is a material evocation of an explicit religious ideology (devotion, purity, hospitality) or an impugned logic of hierarchy (power, status). All these constituents are ethnographically visible in its preparation and distribution (Appadurai 1981). But contemporary *prasadam* in Bangalore is, I suggest, more than this. I argue that it is an experimental material space in which contemporary meanings are constantly emergent and traditional meanings are ruptured, which invites a reworking of ritual and everyday worlds.

In the following pages, I use Babu Bhattar's story to explore the contemporary making, unmaking and remaking of *prasadam* in three Hindu temples—variously dedicated to Krishna, to the elephant-headed god Ganesha, and to the Muslim fakir-saint Shirdi Sai Baba, who has been absorbed into the Hindu pantheon—in my hometown of Bangalore. They offer a window into transformational and transformed material worlds that interdigitize object and subject, material and transcendent, and ingredients to ritual substance— inviting us to interrogate the various discourses that surround ritual material culture.

Material culture, as this volume suggests, has illuminated our understandings of the biography of things (Appadurai 1986; Kopytoff 1986) to reflect upon the quiddity of things themselves. Kopytoff underscores that investigating the biography of things can "make salient what otherwise might remain obscure" (1986: 67) and how, in a lived religion like

Hinduism, these obscurities often gesture to the larger meanings of religious traditions and their possibilities—infilling what was thought to be the "decisive conflict" between the material and the transcendent that define religion in its essence (Pintchman in Dempsey and Pintchman 2016).

Let me note that this chapter is not comprehensive in the consideration of *prasadam*; rather, I argue that shifts in *prasadam*—in the materials offered, the manner of offering, and the distribution—that occur in temples in my hometown in Bangalore—signal larger creative shifts in the practice of ritual itself. I suggest, as I have suggested before, that these shifts are not simply a mistake, or a singular innovation of the moment; they coalesce into a practice of ritual creativity in the pursuit of wonder (T. Srinivas 2018, 2020) that indicates an emergent regime of what I have termed, along with Antoinette DeNapoli, "experimental Hinduism" (De Napoli). Indeed, I remain convinced that such a fuller consideration of experiments in *prasadam* making and sharing allows for a more inclusive appreciation of the many textures of Hinduism as it is lived, practiced, and experienced, compelling us to consider the limitations of our interpretive paradigms.

Materiality and Abstraction: The Many Worlds of Sacred Food

Andrea Pinkney, an expert on *prasadam*, states that *prasadam*'s empirical range of material forms is infinite, seemingly "limitless in its possibility" (Pinkney 2008: 7)—including leaves, fruit, flowers, ash, turmeric, rice, milk and other forms of dairy, snacks, and sweets. Whatever its material form, through the deity's partaking of the offering, either consuming it or taking of its essence, it is made consecrated, pure, and sacred.

For Pinkney then, *prasadam* though limitless in material forms, is undeniably relational, allowing for a connection among the natural, the social, and cosmological worlds: "In their creation, consumption and exchange, prasada items are integrated into a network of human relationships involving individual devotees, communities of religious practitioners, religious professionals, shopkeepers and of course divine beings" (2008: 8). In Pinkney's understanding *prasadam* is a sort of connective tissue *within* a social and theological "regime of value" (Appadurai 1988:15).

In everyday life, ordinary food was transformed into *prasadam* through the ritual act of *naivedhyam* (offering of food to the deity) and the deity's consumption of it (Toomey in Lynch 1990, Pinkney 2008). The deity is perceived as actually consuming the food—by seeing it, smelling it, tasting it, imbibing it, or receiving it. The deity's partaking of the offering materially changes the substance of the *bhogam*, transvaluing it and rendering it sacred (Khare 1980: 295; Pinkney 2013), and this makes *prasadam* a *tirtha* or "bridge" (Khare 1992: 10) between this-worldly and the other-worldly spheres. *Prasadam* is made "heavier" as it leaves the deity, weighted as it is with love and sacredness (Toomey 1986: 164 note 10) or "the quality of sanctity and the capacity to sanctify" (Pinkney 2008: 62).

It is this ineffable quality of divine love that makes *prasadam* valuable in devotees' eyes as a comestible blessing. *Prasadam* is what Joyce Flueckiger might call "a material act," a material object that speaks of a relation, and holds agentive properties in an ability to act in the world through the addition of divine love (2020). The act of consuming *prasadam* confirms devotees' spiritual connection to the god and acceptance of the love and blessing, thereby reifying their identity *as* devotees.[4] While Lawrence Babb argues that *prasadam* exchanges affirm the deity's superior transactional ranking above mere humans, as it is exchanged in ways that restore hierarchical social or ideological structures (Babb 1970: 298), C. J. Fuller observes that the consumption of *prasadam*, its internalization by the devotee, completes the cycle of identification between worshippers and worshipped. For devotees on the other hand, the grace of the deity invests the edible material substance:

> During *puja* [worship], different substances—ash, water, flowers, food, or other items—have been transferred to the deity, so that they have been in contact with the images or, as with food, have been symbolically consumed by the deity in its image form. As a result, these substances have been ritually transmuted to become *prasada* imbued with divine power and grace, which are absorbed or internalized when the *prasada* is placed on the devotee's body or swallowed. Whenever *puja* is concluded by waving the camphor flame, taking in the *prasada* is a process that replicates and consolidates the transfer of divine power and grace through the immaterial medium of the flame.
>
> *(Fuller 2018: 74–75)*

Thus, *prasadam* is and has been understood to be discursive, manifold in sacred meanings, and processually transformative for the devotee. But in the contemporary moment in Bangalore, *prasadam* is imbued with unfamiliar and often contradictory meanings evidenced in its aesthetic form, its visual appearance, and its distributive technologies.

The First Mouthful: The Aesthetics of *Prasadam*

January 2006 at the Krishna temple. Two elderly male devotees watched Babu Bhattar, the chief priest, ladling out the prasadam. *They asked other devotees, "What is the dish? Is it good? Sweet? Does it smell like it has enough ghee?" Their curiosity regarding the* prasadam, *its smell and taste, seemed similar to a gourmand's interest in the complex culinary processes leading to good taste.*

Narasimha, one of the temple's resident cooks, stood at the door of the temple kitchen (Madepalli) and grumbled loudly about the lack of proper ingredients, the stinting of ghee, the few cardamom pods he could buy because the "budget" (as decided by Babu Bhattar) wouldn't allow it. He wanted to ensure the devotees did not blame him if the prasadam *did not taste rich enough. All the devotees reassuringly complimented him on the "divine" taste of the prasadam, regardless of the stinting of ingredients.*

As we ate the prasadam, I mentioned to some of my friends among the devotees that I was planning to go to the new Sai Baba temple a few blocks away that was dedicated to a Muslim saint who had been incorporated into the Hindu pantheon.

They shrugged in dismay: "You know what they serve you there for prasadam? Bread! And then they do not even get the bread themselves. They make some poor bhaktha (devotee) get it. Then they make it into small pieces and give it to people. What madness! They do not know who made it, what is in it, what it is . . . Bread?!" Their disappointment and disapproval was clear.

I made my way to the Sai Baba temple and found that indeed, as the Krishna temple devotees suggested, pieces of baked bread were being distributed to waiting devotees.

> *One devotee waiting in the queue for the bread prasadam, explained to me the rationale of bread distribution, "Sai Baba used to make rotis (unleavened bread) on the chulah (in Hindi) in the mosque where he lived. When people came to him as a sant (saint) he distributed what he had—small pieces of dry chapati and the ash from the fire. It was not about taste but about sharing what he had as blessing. Now we cannot make roti for so many people . . . so we have bakery bread."*

I found that the cooking and the eating of the *prasadam* was seen by temple ritualists not solely as a communicative experience with the divine, but also as a primary sensual and aesthetic experience. Whether of negation and control as in the Shaivite ascetic tradition, or one of culinary excess as in the Vaishnavite tradition,[5] there was an underlying aesthetic to *prasadam* creation, distribution, and eating that all the devotees seemed to share.

As the devotees in the Krishna and Sai Baba temples pointed out, the sense of taste (*rasa*[6]), as in an aesthetic distinction, played an important role in conceptualizing the experience of belief whether by presence or absence (Toomey in Lynch 1992)—making sensual aesthetics, a sense of enjoyment and of connoisseurship, a primary plank in the experience of devotion[7]. And so, in both classical Hindu aesthetic theory and the medieval devotional theory patterned after it, the terms *rasa*—*ruci* (taste or liking), used in this context to refer to a person's spiritual inclination)—and *rasika* (meaning both gourmet and a sensitive person, a connoisseur) indicate that sensuality of the religious experience is key to devotion.

The bread *prasadam* at the Sai Baba temple posed a ritual, caste, and aesthetic problem for the devotees of the Krishna temple. Not only did it not conform to the rules of aesthetics, but it introduced several problematic "modern" elements. A particularly significant challenge was the industrial production of *prasadam* outside the temple precincts, where one could not be sure of the ingredients used, the process of cooking, or the caste of the cook. Though a critique of establishment religion was the essence of the Sai philosophy, in the everyday world of *prasadam* distribution it seemed to be elided. Every time I went to the Sai temple, the person distributing the bread was particular to tell me that they bought the bread from an "Iyengar bakery"—a type of popular neighborhood bakery in Bangalore run by a sub caste of Sri Vaishnavite Brahmins—so as to indicate to me the purity of both the bread and the cook.

The Krishna temple devotees warned me of an even more significant problem with the ingredients used in the bread. Baked bread contained yeast (which was considered animalistic in its capacity to grow) and white flour (known as "American flour," and considered a "foreign" food)—both made popular by the yeasted breads of British colonists. The Krishna temples devotees' disgust with bread was therefore an indigenous critique of both "foreign" popular foods, and the possible pollution inherently carried based on the known caste of the cook.

But this rejection of foreign food was merely a moment in time in the early 1990s. Returning to Bangalore over the following two decades, I saw that the opposition to the Sai Baba temple's bread *prasadam* grew weaker and weaker; by 2010, it was no longer considered worthy of comment and it no longer drew the ire of the Krishna temple devotees.

Unlike the Sai temple devotees, devotees in the Krishna temple were socialized into expecting excess, both in the variety of dishes offered as *prasadam* and in the ingredients. Krishna temples were known for their distinctive food, and their devotees prided themselves over their sophisticated palates. Audrey Hayley and Paul Toomey for Vaishnavas in Assam and in Braj, centers of Krishna devotion, speak of this sense of Krishna devotion being allied with food appreciation (Hayler 1980; Toomey 1990). Similarly, the famous Krishna temple at Udupi in Karnataka, the state of which Bangalore is the capital, is known for its incredibly tasty meals of more than a hundred courses offered to the deity before being distributed to devotees underlying this connection of excessive food consumption and appreciation by the deity and his devotees.[8]

Devotees at the Krishna temple acted like restaurant critics or gourmands, developing the skills of *rasikas*, comparing the *prasadam* available at each temple—the freshness and seasonality of the ingredients, the tastiness of the offering and how traditional the flavors seemed, the cleanliness of the cook, the aesthetics of the cutting of the vegetables, the amount of ghee or other rich ingredients used, and other such metrics. The type and tastiness of the *prasadam* played a part in deciding which temple devotees would visit. My informants gave me "tips" on which temples I should study based on the quality of their *prasadam*. On certain Vaish-navite festival days (such as Krishna Jayanthi celebrating the birth of Lord Krishna), Hindus of different sectarian stripes arrived at the Krishna temple for the festival worship because they knew that "good," i.e. tasty and well-cooked *prasadam* would be offered to the deity and distributed afterward. The tastiness and richness of the *prasadam* was also seen as a metric of the value of the deity. According to Khare, only "good" deities produce edible leftovers that human beings covet, and they may be propitiated with different flavored foods according to two distinct categories: regular foods for everyday eating and special foods for presents and sacrifices (1970: 93–94).

Regular devotees are expected to be experts on how to evaluate which "dishes" of the prasadam were made well in each temple. Familiar with the daily and calendrical schedule of food preparation in each temple, ritual insiders knew what *prasadam* would be served at spe-cific temples, and they time their visits to coincide with the distribution of the food. I heard one of my interlocutors tell another: "We must go on Karthike to the Krishna temple; we will be sure to get good *prasadam*."

Mr. Rangachari, one of my friends and interlocutors, who had grown up in the shadow of the Krishna temple but was not overtly religious, told me he made a point of going to the temple during Dhanurmasa (the winter months).

> During that month they serve the Pongal for early morning *prasadam*. It is divine (*divyam*). No matter how we cook Pongal at home it is not that tasty. So I go to the temple in Dhanurmasa during early morning for the *prasadam*.

Then, he became lyrical about the *prasadam* in a Lakshmi temple close by.

> You know their *prasadam* is very good. I really enjoy it. Everyone who goes to that tem-ple says that their *prasadam* is the best. I know the cook there. He is really a good cook. We were planning to do a *puja* at another temple and we asked him if he could cook for that but he said no. He is not supposed to do "private work." His food is so fresh and it is cooked in full ghee.[9]

When a respected devotee like Mr. Rangachari claimed the *prasadam* at a particular tem-ple was good, then the temple profited considerably from the patronage of his extensive network of kin and friends. Conversely, if there was a hint that the *prasadam* in a temple was inferior, and there was no compensatory element, then attendance at that temple fell, especially on ritual days. Competition was therefore fierce among the temples to provide good *prasadam*.

This is not only true of the contemporary temple publics. My father, the anthropologist M. N. Srinivas, recounted to me that in his boyhood (some eighty years prior) he and a cou-ple of his friends had evaluated the local temples in a hierarchy dependent upon the type and quality of the *prasadam* that they distributed. He said:

> The temple down the street from our home, a Vishnu temple, was noted for the quality of *prasadam* but they were mean in their portions. Other temples that we visited gave lots of *prasadam* but it was not good. My father had a hereditary share at the Varaha temple in the Mysore Palace and on certain ritual days they gave three small *dosas* that had tiny pieces of a local truffle called Mustafchurna. They were delicious and we would all go

to that temple on those festival days and try to repeatedly stand in the queue to get more shares of the *prasadam*[10].

I found this discernment about the taste and aesthetics of *prasadam* to be true of contemporary devotees as well. Devotees in all the temples I visited would constantly compare the cuisine in competitor temples. Regular devotees were the most publicly critical of the *prasadam* from a competitor temple—just as Krishna temple devotees were about the bread in the Sai Baba temple. Obvious and public denigration of the rival temple *prasadam* continued to be seen as a sign of loyalty to one's own temple. For example, one day I had eaten what I thought was tasty *prasadam* in the Krishna temple, and I happened to share some with a lady friend of mine who did not worship at that temple. Though she ate it her reception of it was lukewarm. I was surprised, since sharing of *prasadam* is both a sign of friendship and a sharing of divine benevolence—something usually received with pleasure and reverence. After eating all of the *prasadam*, she told me, "You know, in my temple, they make better *prasadam* than this." I was offended by what I saw as boorish behavior, but I later learned that this was a standard practice of demonstrating one's affiliation and loyalty to one's "own" temple.

The Second Mouthful: The Visual Appearance of *Prasadam*

Sometimes, on festival days, the *prasadam* consisted of edibles and non-edibles with which the deity had been decorated for the day—fruits, herbs, dairy products, and snacks. In the Ganesha temple in Malleshwaram—where the deity was the elephant-headed god of protection, Ganesha—indigenous fruit such as bananas, coconuts, and wild figs; and flowers such as the lotus, jasmine, Tulasi leaves, and wild cactus, were often used in the *alankara* or decoration of the deity before being distributed as *prasadam* to waiting devotees as the liturgical rules demanded.

But the Ganesha temple knew that the nearby Krishna temple served very attractive cooked *prasadam*. So Dandu Shastri, the chief priest of the Ganesha temple, began experimenting using "new" and potentially exciting ingredients to attract devotees who enjoy the spirit of innovation and gastronomic adventure. For example, in early 1998, I noticed that an apple and orange had been used in the decoration of the Ganesha deity, fruits that had not been used before. I asked Dandu Shastri how these fruits had been included. He told me that devotees offered them regularly to the deity, and "after all, oranges come from Nagpur and apples come from Kashmir." This was a plausible explanation of indigeneity.

In December 2002, I noticed yet another new fruit had crept into the fruit *alankara*—a kiwi. Glistening bright green slices of kiwi, dotted with their black seeds, adorned the stomach of the deity along with bright red slices of apple and plum. I asked Dandu Shastri how the kiwi fruit could be offered to the deity. He ignored my implicit critique of the fruit as not being indigenous. "Yes, yes, they have newly come from Australia," he said in answer to my question. "They are so pretty, no?" When I pressed Dandu Shastri about these new "exotic fruit" that were not in any agamic texts that I knew, he had a complex answer prepared: "First, it is not as though they are not Indian. You see this is before India or even before Bharath. It was in a time long ago. I read that India was joined to all these foreign countries (Gondwanaland) and at that time maybe these fruits were Indian. He added, "God accepts anything if given with love . . . even foreign fruits. And also they are very expensive since they come from 'foreign.'" And by way of a final explanation he said, "For Ganesha kiwi is okay because in the Ganesha Stotram it is said he likes fruit with many seeds."

The fruit was then distributed as *prasadam,* eliciting much curiosity and commentary about its texture, color, and taste. Thus, this was an example of how the emergent economies of taste and aesthetics can overcome heritage tastes in cases where the new food or ingredient has high value due to its "exotic" or scarce nature.

The priest's claim was supported by more than just an emphasis on antecedents—such as the origin of kiwi fruit from an ancient Gondwanaland (linked fictively to the nation state of India) but also on experimentation and myths about the deity's supposed preferences. His claims not only significantly expanded the geographical space of Hindu India beyond the modern (smaller) geography of the nation state of India, gesturing to the longer historical continuity of geo-morphology that slipped into cultural and theological continuity.[11] So here, in an experimental genre of innovations in *prasadam*, emerged a discursive "oscillation" between the traditional and the radically new: between the historically and traditionally focused indigenous foods for offering of the agamic texts and the aesthetic, progressive new fruits of the modern global economy; between the old value of patronage and the new status of affording expensive foreign fruit. Following the rationale that the kiwi fruit both indicated a longer Hindu tradition much vaunted in conservative Hindu circles and served as a "new" and tasty innovation for the more liberal devotees, the Ganesha temple regularly began to experiment with *alankara* using unusual fruit—including mangosteens imported from New Zealand and Australia.

One of the traditional *alankaram* decorations that became *prasadam* at the Ganesha temple was a coat of white glistening butter smeared onto the deity known as a Vennaialankaram in Tamil. One day, Dandu Shastri decorated the buttered surface of the deity with a bottle of red maraschino cherries, studding the white butter at regular intervals with the red cherries, creating what looked like a suit of glistening red armor. I was surprised by the aesthetics of the deity clad in a polka dot red and white suit. Dandu Shastri was pleased by my evident interest, saying, "Oh, looks nice, no? It glitters like rubies. Ganesha looks like the sun in his red coat!" According to Dandu Shastri, Ganesha dazzled like the red sun, "*suryan polle*": a cosmological metaphor overflowing with wonderment and beauty. Indeed, the closely studded cherries did glitter, so much so that devotees commented on its divine radiance and shimmer.

The power of the light captured in such shimmery objects has a mesmeric quality for devotees. Sparkling gemstones, or glittering fruit and tinsel, are deemed marvelous not only for their market value but for their aesthetic brilliance and visual resonance as well (Greenblatt 1991: 11–15). What Marcia Pointon calls the "contradictions between the transcendent and the material" break down as the gemstones and cherries are seen as encapsulating the radiance (*ujjwala, hiranaya*) of the deity. As in Vedic alchemy, shininess is illuminating and cosmic; it radiates divine energy and power. The fact that the cherries were industrially produced and bottled seem to bother no one. Again, like the kiwi fruit, when distributed as *prasadam* the cherries were enjoyed for their novelty, their taste, as well as for their visual aesthetic qualities both drawing the eye of the devotee and representing the divine radiance of the deity.

The Third Mouthful: The Distribution of *Prasadam*

On December 20, 1998, I arrived at the Krishna temple as the prasadam was being distributed to waiting devotees.

The temple cook, Narasimha, stood at the door of the smoky temple kitchen ladling the prasadam *into enormous vats as Babu Bhattar with a huge spoon doled out the* prasadam *on to each devotee's waiting banana leaf.*

There was hierarchy of distribution indicated by the spaces where devotees sat. Elderly male goshtis (ritual honorifics) sat closest to the sanctum and expect the first serving after the ritualized offering. Next were a few elderly lady volunteers who held positions of responsibility within the temple taking care of the lamps and flowers and such. Further down the line were the devotees recognized as "regulars" because they visit the temple several times a week or even daily. Last in line were the devotees who visit the temple only occasionally.

Babu Bhattar walked down the line, dropping spoonfuls of the delectable rice offering into the leaf plates held out for him. The distribution was orderly until raised voices at the other end of the line could be heard. Mr. Venugopal, an erudite and respected goshti *(senior devotee) who held hereditary rights at the temple, was very upset. Apparently, his seat had been usurped by an upstart youngster. Babu Bhattar settled the dispute by asking the young gentleman to move to another spot. The upstart moved reluctantly. It was clear he did not realize the ramifications of his jumping the line.*

The next week I was at the Ganesha temple at the time of prasadam *distribution. Unexpectedly, no priest handed out food. Rather, devotees were asked to head in an orderly queue to a desk where a temple official, clad in business attire of shirt and pants, handed each devotee a woven carry bag. The bag had the image of the deity and the text "Om Shri Ganesha namaha" (we bow to you, O Ganesha) emblazoned on it in bright yellow text.*

The bag I was handed contained a bit of turmeric for auspiciousness, a coconut, a banana, a small coin, one kiwi fruit, one keychain, and two plastic tubs with transparent lids rather like restaurant takeaway containers; these bore the insignia of the temple and were filled with cold rice prasadam*, one sweet and one savory. The turmeric, banana, and coconut were all traditional, but the rest was new and intriguing.*

I asked the official about the takeaway containers. He smiled and said, "They are good, no? Everyone likes them. My grandson eats from restaurants and I suggested to the caterer that he bring the prasadam *in these boxes. They are much neater and cleaner." He was clearly proud of his idea and the cleanliness, modernity, and the sophistication implied by the containers and the contents of the bag.*

As Arjun Appadurai has argued in his magisterial study of the historic disputes over *prasadam* distribution at the Sri Parthasarthi temple (1981), all *prasadam* rituals performed in the temple are offerings to the sovereign deity of the temple, which is determined by the specific Agamic code that governs that particular temple. Appadurai reads the distribution of *prasadam* as processes of redistribution where a wealthy patron offers food in the name of the deity that then gets redistributed in the community. Appadurai argues that the offering of the sacrifice of *prasadam* is a "transaction" between devotee and deity, where the deity accepts the transaction through the *naivedyam*, and the *prasadam* is then "redistributed" (drawing from Sahlins) as "leavings" to devotees. The deity in this reading is a "sovereign lord" who oversaw a system of economic redistribution.

This distribution of the divine leftovers marks a hierarchy of devotion and status among devotees based on their timely access to the leavings—those higher in the hierarchy received more of the leavings, and earlier—and those lower in the hierarchy, including women and children, got less of the leavings, and later. Therefore, for Appadurai, *prasadam* distribution merely reinforced hierarchy between supplicant and lord as well as among supplicants themselves; this was thus a divine manifestation of the human social structure of kingship, where king/deity was overlord, and nobles in the court disputed the right to serve the king (1981: 35).

Following this logic, Lawrence A. Babb has concluded that such a transaction implies that the devotee is inferior to the deity:

> The transaction is a reciprocal one: the worshippers give food to the god and the food is taken back and consumed. In the initial offering god is given superior food, whereas the worshippers receive the symbolic leftovers or jutha [literally "spittle"], of the god. The retrieval of God's jutha enables the God to be 'paid' for the past and future favors and at the same time establishes a hierarchical opposition between the God and the worshippers as a group.
>
> (Babb 1970: 302–303)

The category of food known as *jutha* or *ucchista*, meaning "left-over" or "remainder" in princi- ple is a neutral category conveying the simple fact of food being left over from prior consump- tion. But in a food system dominated by pollution norms like in Hindu India, *ucchista* tends in practice to have negative connotations. Treating *ucchista* as *prasadam* is a rationalized transgres- sion of typical Hindu food norms intended to express a special relationship between the creator and consumer of leftover food. Quoting Babb (1986: 72), Pinkney (2020: 415) notes that "upon consumption of leftovers deemed to be *prasada*, the devotee enjoys an intimate, yet transient, identification with the divine, which 'strikingly symbolizes human internalization of divine qualities and the physiological engagement between deity and devotee.'" But C. J. Fuller dis- agrees with this purely political reading of *prasadam* distribution as a polluted leftover, and of the function of the redistribution to distinguish individuals within a hierarchical system. He states:

> [I]n placing so much emphasis on honour and kingship, this school of writers comes perilously close to reducing puja to its political component, as if it were a ritual whose primary function is to constitute rank and authority among powerful men.
>
> *(Fuller 2018: 81)*

For Fuller, as for me, the idea of "leavings" or of the "remainder" fails to adequately capture the sacredness the "heaviness" of divine love that invests the consecrated *prasadam* for the devotee that I referred to earlier. The transaction model removes one essential component of *prasadam*—the transformative power of divine consumption.

All my interlocutors at the temples emphatically expressed the idea that when the deity consumed the food offered to them, the acceptance of the food exalted the *prasadam* to *amritham* (nectar). Through divine consumption (whether the deity consumes the whole, a part, or the essence) the deity raised the food to the plane of the sacred. These interlocutors confirmed Pinkney's reading that the leftovers were seen to have been transvalued by some portion of divine substance of the deity that partakes of the food, making it sacred (2008: 108). This metaphysical flow of the potency of the deity (*tejas* or radiance) into the *bhogam* that occurs during the *naivedhyam* ritual exalts the *bhogam* into *prasadam*. So, unlike human leftovers, which are polluted and reduced, divine leftovers are made more sacred by this potency transfer (Khare 1980: 109). As such, they become transvalued, transcending the classification of pure or impure, making *prasadam* more valued and its consumption a divine right. So the closer one was to the moment of *naivedhyam* or transvaluation, the greater one's merit and one's status and honor in the eyes of other devotees. Hence, devotees fought over their position of hereditary honors in the Krishna temple to receive *pradasam* as their right to receive and consume the divine. Their unique position in this reception indicated to the devotees one's virtue and standing in the community.

So the democratization of the process of *prasadam* distribution and the new technologies used in the Ganesha temple for its distribution irrevocably changed the redistribution pro- cess, allowing for the interrogation of the notion that redistribution is a political act that reinforced hierarchies between the god and human, and also among the devotees.

The takeaway containers shifted the single patronage model of "deity to status devotee" to a democratic and neoliberal customer-based model of "temple to all devotees," flattening the previous hierarchy. In fact, when someone in the queue started pushing to get the *prasa- dam*, one of the younger priests shouted, "First come, first served, sir!"

Furthermore, the question of individual virtue and status was moot, since everyone queued up to receive the *prasadam* and it was not the priest who served the consecrated food. Virtuous or not, everyone received *prasadam* based on how quickly they joined the line.

These shifts in the distributive economy, though seemingly merely an imitation of a successful modern marketplace model, change both the symbolic capital as well as the moral economics of *prasadam*. The practice of packaging the offering in the restaurant-inspired plastic "takeaway" containers with the temple logo mimic a consumption economy in which the devotees are recast as "customers." This practice erases the connection joining the cook, the priest, and the devotee, and puts the devotee at a distance from the *naivedyam* but at the center of the *prasadam* distribution.

Devotees were impressed by the "takeaway" containers for *prasadam*; they especially liked that the containers were divided into small compartments for different dishes. Devotees found them "neat," "clean," "super"—all terms indicating appreciation of their modern hygienic quality. Usha, a regular devotee, said:

> They are so convenient. Now I don't have to bring my stainless steel tiffin box. Also they don't leak, so I don't have to worry. I wash them after and use them to send my grandson his lunch to school.

Familiarity with international packaging standards for food products were made manifest in conversation. Another devotee, Mr. Sivan, gestured to a pile of temple takeout containers: "You see these plastic *dubbas*? Soon, I'm telling you we will have *prasadam* in plastic sachets with nutritional information on them like you do in the US!" Another elderly lady also laughed and said, "Heat in microwave and serve, is it?" But an elderly male devotee was disapproving of this hilarity and said quellingly:

> We can all laugh and say nice things about the boxes, but what about the *prasadam* in-side? Are we sure it had been offered to the deity? How do we know that this fellow didn't simply bring some food in nice boxes and give us?

This literal "repackaging" of the *prasadam* subversively challenges traditional notions of belonging located in caste and seniority, or the structures of position within a hierarchy. This new form of distribution purports to allow for alternative potentialities of social existence—including democracy, inclusion, and equity—through the context of new capitalist consumption practices of restaurant takeout boxes. New ideas of democracy, inclusion, and equity bleed into temple publics, interweaving traditional sectarian divides with modern political identity struggles around caste and nation. Here, innovations in distribution gesture to the shift from the purity of the *prasadam* as consecrated food of high ritual symbolic value to simply food of a different marketplace symbolic value of hygiene and convenience. The material form of the package interrogates the immaterial content of a symbolic comestible blessing from the deity, even throwing into question what *prasadam* is, and what it is meant to be.

Conclusion: The Discursive Worlds of *Prasadam* Re-Formed

In the complex ritual gastro-worlds in Hindu temples in contemporary Bangalore, *prasadam* has always been a multistranded semiotic instrument layered with the idea of communication between divinity and humanity, the idea of consuming a transformative blessing from the deity, and the purity of the cook and servers. But contemporary *prasadam* is innovative in many ways, and it hosts intermingling and often contradictory ideas about authenticity of food practices, hygienic preparation and presentation, and the aesthetics of the offering and its distribution. Simply put, *prasadam* in contemporary Hindu ritual worlds is transformative of the tradition and of individual life worlds—while also being transformed in itself.

Whatever progression we may see in history, its material reality is layered and textured. So, as the previous pages demonstrate, *prasadam*—its form, distribution, and meanings—are never fully foreclosed, but are constantly reworked, causing "moments of instability, ambiguity, and contradiction" that hold the "potential for interventions that might destabilize a field" (Kondo 1997: 151); an experimental ethos central to ritual creativity. In contemporary ritual worlds the discursive worlds of *prasadam* are constantly re-emergent.

In sum, contemporary prasadam is an emergent experimental space, a stage for ritual creativity in which meanings of things are constantly re-formed and reworked, possibly throwing into question the very constitutive logic of sacred food and of materiality in religion as a whole.

Notes

1 *Rasa* literally translates in Sanskrit and Tamil as "juice" but in Hindu performance literature, such as Abhinava's Navasara and Bhakti devotional literature, the term indicates an emotional performance that calls out a response in the devotee known as *bhava.*

2 *Ruchi* in Tamil translates as "tasty."

3 This makes particular sense for a lived religion like Hinduism that comes in the form of practices: of seeing, speaking, eating, and singing; and a broad variety of rituals—formal and informal, public and private, prescribed, and improvised.

4 As Andrea Pinkney points out, building on the work on Diana Eck, *prasadam* is, like *darshan*, an "extrusive process" (2008: 55).

5 In most Vaishnavite temples like the Krishna temple, the basic prasadam is rice (called *anna*, "life's breath," that on which life depends), which is given high moral evaluation and is the food offering par excellence.

6 In the broad semantic sense, *rasa* refers to the flavor, taste, or essence of something that can be extracted and experienced in various ways.

7 Though for the Shirdi Sai devotees the experience of devotion was in negating most expectations of prasadam being tasty and for the gourmand and pivoting to the moral value of prasadam as shared consecrated blessing.

8 This expertise of cooking many different *prasadam* in large quantities led to many Udupis going into the restaurant business. In fact, most south Indian restaurants in India are Udupi restaurants.

9 Cooking in "full ghee"—as in cooking with ghee as the medium—was seen as the appropriate richness and purity for temple food, as it indicated that the ingredients were of the highest quality and that there was no adulteration.

10 Personal conversation with the author, September 8, 1998.

11 This fictive cultural continuity, known by the popular term "heritage" in Bangalore, allows for a nostalgia for "ancient times." It legitimates newer traditions as "ancient" and therefore valuable, allowing for conservative cultural and political readings, a twisting of modern Hindu cultural and religious practice.

References

Appadurai, Arjun. 1981. *Worship and Conflict Under Colonial Rule: A South Indian Case.* Cambridge South Asian Studies, 27. New York: Cambridge University Press.

Appadurai, Arjun. 1988. "How to Make a National Cuisine: Cookbooks in Contemporary India." *Comparative Studies in Society and History* 30 (1): 3–24.

Appadurai, Arjun, ed. 1986. The Social Life of Things: Commodities in Cultural Perspective. Cambridge: Cambridge University Press.

Babb, Lawrence A. 1970. "The Food of the Gods in Chhattisgarh: Some Structural Features of Hindu Ritual." *Southwestern Journal of Anthropology* 26 (3): 287–304.

Babb, Lawrence A. 1986. "Spiritual Recognition and the Radhasoami Faith." In *Redemptive Encounters: Three Modern Styles in the Hindu Tradition*, 15–92. Berkeley, CA: University of California Press.

Breckenridge, Carol Appadurai. 1986. "Food, Politics, and Pilgrimage in South India, 1350–1650 a.d." In *Food, Society, and Culture: Aspects in South Asian Food Systems,* edited by R. S. Khare and M. S. A. Rao, 21–53. Durham, NC: Carolina Academic Press.

DeNapoli, Antoinette Elizabeth. 2017. "'*Dharm* Is Technology': The Theologizing of Technology in the Experimental Hinduism of Renouncers in Contemporary North India." *International Journal of Dharma Studies* 5 (18): 1–36.

DeNapoli, Antoinette Elizabeth and Tulasi Srinivas. eds. 2016. "Special Issue, The Moralizing of Dharma in Everyday Hinduisms." *Nidan: The International Journal for Indian Studies* 28 (2): 1–14.

Eck, Diana L. 1998. *Darśan: Seeing the Divine Image in India.* New York: Columbia University Press.

Fuller, Christopher J. 1979. "Gods, Priests and Purity: On the Relation Between Hinduism and the Caste System." *Man* 14 (3): 459–476.

Fuller, Christopher. J. 2018. *The Camphor Flame: Popular Hinduism and Society in India—Revised and Expanded Edition.* Princeton, NJ: Princeton University Press.

Gold, Ann Grodzins. 1998. "Grains of Truth: Shifting Hierarchies of Food and Grace in Three Rajasthani Tales." *History of Religions* 38 (2): 150–171.

Khare, Ravinder S. 1976b. *Culture and Reality: Essays on the Hindu System of Managing Foods.* Simla: Indian Institute of Advanced Study.

Khare. R.S. 1980. "Food as Nutrition and Culture: Notes Towards an Anthropological Methodology." *Social Science Information* 19 (3): 519–542. London, Delhi: Sage publications.

Khare, R. S. ed., 1992. *The Eternal Food. Gastronomic Ideas and Experiences of Hindus and Buddhists.* Albany, NY: State University of New York Press.

Kopytoff, Igor. 1986. "The Cultural Biography of Things: Commoditization as Process." In *The Social life of Things: Commodities in Cultural Perspective,* edited by Arjun Appadurai, 64–92. Cambridge: Cambridge University Press.

Olivelle, Patrick. 2002a. *Food for Thought: Dietary Rules and Social Organization in Ancient India.* Amsterdam: Royal Netherlands Academy of Arts and Sciences.

Parry, Jonathan. 1986. "The Gift, the Indian Gift and the 'Indian Gift.'" *Man* 21 (3): 453–473.

Pinkney, Andrea Marion. 2008. *Prasada: The Sacred Share.* PhD Dissertation, New York: Columbia University.

Pinkney, Andrea Marion. 2013. "Prasāda, the Gracious Gift, in Contemporary and Classical South Asia." *Journal of the American Academy of Religion* 81 (3): 734–756.

Pinkney, Andrea Marion. 2020. "*Prasāda,* Grace as Sustenance, and the Relational Self." In *The Wiley Blackwell Companion to Religion and Materiality,* edited by Vasudha Narayanan, 414–432. Hoboken, NJ: Wiley Blackwell.

Pintchman, Tracy. 2016. "Fruitful Austerity: Paradigms of Embodiment in Hindu Women's Vrat Performances." In *Refiguring the Body: Embodiment in South Asian Religions,* edited by Barbara A. Holdrege and Karen Pechilis, 301–320. Albany: State University of New York Press.

Raheja, Gloria Goodwin. 1988. *The Poison in the Gift: Ritual, Prestation, and the Dominant Caste in a North Indian Village.* Chicago, IL: University of Chicago Press.

Smith, B. K. 1990. "Eaters, Food, and Social Hierarchy in Ancient India: A Dietary Guide to a Revolution of Values." *Journal of the American Academy of Religion* 58 (2): 177–205.

Srinivas, Tulasi. 2018. *The Cow in the Elevator: An Anthropology of Wonder.* Durham, NC: Duke University Press.

Srinivas, Tulasi. 2020. "Of Kiwi Fruit and Kewpie Dolls: The Wonder of Modern Alankara in Bangalore." *The Jugaad Project,* 2 December 2020, thejugaadproject.pub/home/kiwi-fruit-and-kewpie-dolls [last accessed, September 15, 2022]

Toomey, Paul. M. 1986. "Food From the Mouth of Krishna: Socio-Religious Aspects of Sacred Food in Two Krishnaite Sects." In *Food, Society, and Culture: Aspects in South Asian Food Systems,* edited by R. S. Khare and M. S. A. Rao, 55–83. Durham, NC: Carolina Academic Press.

Toomey, Paul. M. 1992. "Mountain of Food, Mountain of Love: Ritual Inversion in the Annakūṭa Feast at Mount Govardhan." In *The Eternal Food: Gastronomic Experiences of Buddhists and Hindus,* edited by R. S. Khare, 117–145. Delhi: Sri Satguru Publications.

Yalman, Nur. 1969. "De Tocqueville in India: An Essay on the Caste System." *Man: Journal of The Royal Anthropological Institute* 4 (1): 123–131.

2.9

DARK MIRRORING

The Satanic Temple's Queer Material Religion

Sharday C. Mosurinjohn

This chapter will analyze the activities of The Satanic Temple (TST) as a queering of the moral and aesthetic norms belonging to hegemonically Christian public life in North America (particularly the United States) as they act on bodies, specifically the bodies of women and queer folx. These activities include private ceremonies for members within TST chapters, as well as public volunteerism and activism. This chapter discusses TST's after-school programming, lobbying for reproductive rights and the rights of LGBTQIA2+ people, as well as volunteer activities, such as adopting a stretch of Arizona highway and its "Menstruatin' With Satan" menstrual supplies drive. It also covers TST's most famous public action: the display of its eight-foot-tall bronze Baphomet monument. Satanist aesthetics, drawing from occult, metal, goth, and BDSM scenes, fundamentally shape the material character of TST rituals, as do tropes from the 1980s Satanic Panic. The spectacle generated by these actions provides a platform for TST to reclaim Satan to symbolize the possibility of a queer future for religion in public life.

TST is queer on several levels. I am using "queer" in the sense of the writer Maggie Nelson (2015), who emphasizes the term's connotation of "in betweenness"—between an identity; a speech act; a behavior having to do with gender, sex, and sexuality; and a form of social resistance that has nothing to do with sexuality. The broadest and most fundamental sense of TST's queerness is the way it materializes a "counter-myth to the idea of America as a Christian nation" (Laycock 2020: 189). The TST community is constituted around a spectacular refusal of the traditional moral order and the centering of freedom for sexual minorities, women and nonbinary folx, and religious practitioners of all kinds.[1] But the energy that unites the motley crew of Satanists comes from the subversive way it wields material religion.

A variety of affective-aesthetic modes can be found among TST's public actions. For example, TST opted for low-budget theatrics in a stunt in January 2013, when it hired actors to rally at the Florida State Capitol wearing black cloaks and horns and carrying banners praising the Republican Senator Rick Scott for allowing prayer in US schools—that is, allowing presumably Satanic as well as Christian prayer ("Fake Satanists rally" 2013). In the name of religious pluralism, in 2014 TST commissioned (via $20,000 crowdfunding) a stately eight-foot-tall bronze monument of the goat-headed Baphomet—seated with two small children—to "complement and contrast the 10 Commandments monument" at the Oklahoma State Capitol (TST n.d.). In displays of support for social causes—such as a

DOI: 10.4324/9781351176231-18

the Australia chapter's menstrual supplies drive ("Menstruatin' with Satan"), or after-school reading clubs ("After-School Satan")—the Baphomet or similarly horned and goateed figures are rendered more cartoonishly. At other times, the cartoonish turns into the grotesque. Graphics on TST's website draw clichés from the Christian horrific imagination, weaving the Baphomet—with imagery of roses, skulls, candles, and chalices—into the bordered format of a tarot card. Body horror has been the aesthetic strategy of many TST protests, such as counter-protests against anti-abortion groups. In one event held by the Detroit chapter, men dressed as priests have drenched kneeling women with milk to represent "forced motherhood" (Burns 2015). At a separate Detroit event, members dressed in bondage fetish wear, baby masks, and diapers engaged in group flagellation (Stone 2016)—recalling the abjection of performance artist Paul McCarthy's 1976 "Class Fool." In contrast, when TST performs for itself, it does not engage the abject, as in the threatened breakdown in meaning caused by the loss of the distinction between subject and object or between self and other—so as to traumatically remind us of our own materiality (Kristeva 1982). Instead, TST embraces ritual acts of pain, fear, and bodily exposure in order to affirm one's own humanness, autonomy, and capacity to come together in collective action.

The sensory elements of TST's ritual practices involve getting campy with this society's cult stereotypes and opening to bodily pleasures. Opposing the conservative Christian scorn of the body that has informed legal practices of regulating the body—especially sexuality and reproduction—TST members revel in the physical and the physiological as the ground of their atheist religion.

TST emerged in the early 2010s[2] thanks to two cultural precedents: the lineage of modern religious Satanisms, and the Satanic Panic of the 1980s. In the former case the timeline looks essentially like this. Starting in 1966, organized Satanism emerged out of the occult subculture with the formation of Anton LaVey's atheistic and hedonistic Church of Satan (CoS) (see Figure 2.9.1). Next, in 1975, there was a breakaway from CoS led by former military intelligence officer Michael Aquino, who founded the much more esoteric Temple of Set (ToS). The next major shift dates to around 1997 with the Internet boom (and also the death of LaVey). In his 2004 essay "Modern Satanism," Jesper Aagaard Petersen periodizes modern religious Satanisms into three major phases, leaving off at the 2000s advent of online democratization of Satanisms. We could say, then, that TST represents the fourth phase.

It was in the second phase that the second cultural precedent occurred: the Satanic Panic in the 1980s. Indeed, TST grows directly out of the experience of cofounders Lucien Greaves and Malcolm Jarry[3] living through the Satanic Panic as teenagers. The Satanic Panic started when false allegations concerning the ritual abuse of children were made against daycare centers in the United States and Canada (Victor 1993). These hideous fantasies bound together fears about youth vulnerability in the context of working women and paid childcare, on the one hand, and conservative evangelical fears about a changing culture on the other—linked with the realities of actual Satanisms and other new religious movements ("cults") as well as now-discredited practices such as "memory recovery" of repressed past trauma and the use of child testimony. The Satanic Panic spread across the United States, tainting anyone perceived to be part of occult culture: such as people who liked heavy metal music, people who played Dungeons and Dragons, people involved with new religious movements. The actually existing but politically apathetic Satanisms of CoS and ToS likewise fueled the fire of the moral panic (Figure 2.9.2).

Today, TST wields all of this controversy for its own activist ends, converting social problems into social possibilities (see Feltmate 2016). Jarry explains: "Once you realize how

Figure 2.9.1   The satanic baptism of Zeena, daughter of the church of Satan's cofounders Anton LaVey and Diane Hegarty, May 23, 1967. © Walter Fischer, courtesy of Alf Wahlgren.

Figure 2.9.2   The Satanic Panic was widely spread in the media. Advertisement for the Oprah Winfrey Show, 1980s. Image circulating online without original reference.

the media is constructed, it becomes incredibly easy to manipulate" (quoted in Lane 2019). In other words, TST uses the fear and ignorance fomented by the Satanic Panic and other anti-cult "witch hunts" (Greaves, quoted in Lane 2019) to induce outrage that ultimately leads to media coverage, thus amplifying the organization's message and attracting more membership.

However, TST wasn't originally supposed to be a large organization. Originally, Greaves and Jarry thought that it could make its point simply by existing at all—as long as it was a thing that could be physically pointed to and turned into a media spectacle. In a 2015 interview, Jarry said:

> The first conception was in response to George W. Bush's creation of the White House Office of Faith-Based and Community Initiatives. I thought, "There should be some kind of counter." Imagine if a Satanic organization applied for funds. It would sink the whole program.
>
> *(Quoted in Oppenheimer 2015)*

Accordingly, the first public action TST took was much more cynical than many of its subsequent ones: ironically supporting an existing piece of conservative legislation. In 2012, Florida governor Rick Scott was pushing a bill to allow voluntary prayer at public school functions. After the bill passed, Greaves and Jarry traveled to Florida to capitalize on a small media event happening around the issue.

In January 2013, the two held a mock rally in support of Rick Scott where, as Jarry put it, "we were coming out to say how happy we were because now our Satanic children could pray to Satan in school" (quoted in Oppenheimer 2015). Greaves stood on the steps of the Florida State Capitol behind a banner proclaiming, Hail Satan! Hail Rick Scott! A paid actor adorned in a long black cape and spindly Baphomet horns delivered a speech praising Rick Scott for providing religious freedom to Satanist schoolchildren. To the TV cameras, they insisted they were completely sincere, though they were dismissed by some as merely trolls. Such was a plausible interpretation of TST in 2013; at the time of the event, TST didn't have much of its own identity to express. It was really the newborn brainchild of Jarry and Greaves, not the lived religion it also is today. In 2015, however, TST "attracted hoards of new followers . . . when it unveiled its eight-foot-tall bronze statue of Baphomet" (Browne 2019).

In late 2021, Malcolm Jarry counted the number of registered members at 500,416, stipulating that a registered member is a member who has gone to TST's website, entered their name and email address, and clicked a box affirming that they believe in TST's seven fundamental tenets (Laycock, personal communication 2022). But this number requires some further breaking down. Laycock suspects that some of these members' involvement ends there, consisting of official membership with no participation in either activism or rituals through their local congregations, and that some members are probably from various media organizations, churches, and other Satanic organizations who have only registered in order to monitor what TST is up to (Laycock, personal communication 2022). At the same time, Jarry attests that TST has "many members who are not officially registered presumably because they do not want to be on a list, even one that is private" (qtd. in Laycock, personal communication 2022).

Satanic Temple Demographics

Judging by the news headlines, TST has remained ambiguous in its political intentions and religious sincerity. The question mark in the title of Penny Lane's 2019 documentary *Hail Satan?* reflects the fact that TST has enough moral ambiguity to trade on for shock value. Its still-taboo dimension manifests in shocking public displays of queer bodies and sexuality, mixed with symbols of death, evil, and darkness (Ryan 2017). Thus, despite the fact that Greaves and other leaders explicitly articulate an atheistic understanding of Satan as a *symbol* for freedom, public uncertainty remains around TST's political intentions and the nature of its religious commitment to Satan. To some extent, the uncertainty is a function of the fact that general religious literacy levels are low (Prothero 2007; Gallagher 2009), and so TST can capitalize on surprise and ambiguity in order to be sensational. Emphasizing its noncon-formist attitude, TST, like most modern Satanisms, "repeatedly reorients itself along a scale of respectability and outrage" (Petersen 2004: 434).

Because of its nonconformity, TST attracts interest from those who are already cast out from the conservative social order.[4] As Joseph Laycock reports, "chapter heads from Albany and Chicago estimated that as many as 75 percent of their membership identifies as LGBTQ" (2020: 78). TST's queerness actually contrasts with that of previous Satanic groups. Lay-cock contrasts TST's demographics with those found in the survey work of James R. Lewis between 2000 and 2011, which showed a sizable majority of Satanists to be white, hetero-sexual males (77). In TST, the female/male split is more even, among both leadership and membership. White people are also overrepresented for at least three reasons: the aesthetic dimensions of TST, like the heavy metal music scene, tends to interpellate White people more than people of color. Another is the social and cultural importance of Christianity within Black and Latinx communities. And another is that the social stigma of being pub-licly seen as a Satanist burdens racialized minorities heavier than it does those with white privilege.

Nonetheless, for some, including some Satanists of color, participation does get around what Cathy Cohen (1997) calls the limitations of a political agenda based on assimilation into, and replication of, dominant institutions. While TST piggybacks on the way conser-vative religious interests exploit hegemonic power to achieve their goals, it ultimately hopes to remake those institutions in the image of Satan the adversary. One of its tenets is that "The struggle for justice is an ongoing and necessary pursuit that should prevail over laws and institutions" (The Satanic Temple, "Tenets"). Yet by some accounts, TST has failed to materialize this ideal.

In 2018, a "substantial" number of chapters, as Joseph Laycock puts it, "had either defected, dissolved or lost the bulk of their membership" (2020: 61). This was due primar-ily to two factors. One was TST's decision to work with controversial free-speech lawyer Marc Randazza, and the other was, as TST-Los Angeles put it, "the complete lack of racial diversity within leadership" (quoted in Laycock 2020: 67). In the case of TST-Los Angeles, which later became HelLA, they preferred to put their work not into fixing TST, but into "fighting bigotry and promoting community engagement" (HelLA website). Meanwhile, TST itself remains more focused on giving "a civics lesson" (Greaves, quoted in Vu 2019) to government, with the aim of extracting its legislative claws from the bodies of women and LGBTQIA2+ people.

TST activism involves a range of physical demonstrations, from lawsuits to performance to counter-protests to volunteering in schools. Whenever TST perceives a threat to the sepa-ration of church and state, it responds with ironic and darkly funny public performances that stake a spot for itself alongside the (usually Evangelical Christian) religion being privileged.[5] And though not all TST actions are solely focused on properly situating public and religious agencies vis-à-vis one another, all of their actions have some kind of civic character. TST devotes volunteer time to conspicuously model civic values, such as holding a blood drive in Seattle, and cleaning up a stretch of highway in Arizona and beach in Santa Cruz using pitchforks ("'Highway to Hell' Has Roadside Cleanup in Southern Arizona," *Tucson News Now* 2018). In all of these, Satanist aesthetics, drawing from occult, metal, goth, and BDSM scenes, fundamentally shape the material character of TST's performative interventions on the landscape of their communities.

For instance, the "Menstruatin' With Satan" menstrual supplies drive helps shelters and underfunded public schools (whose menstrual products often come from school nurses' personal funds). For promotional materials, the Baphomet's head provides the perfect geometry on which to superimpose a drawing of the ovaries, fallopian tubes, uterus, and vagina. A pentagram—blood red, of course—ties the whole composition together. The gynecological Baphomet visually unites the taboos of satanic imagery and menstrual blood with the "sanitary" ethical values of respecting bodily autonomy and acting with compassion and empathy.

Where appropriate (i.e., not in TST's "After School Satan" clubs), TST events also use nudity (often male), sexuality (often kinky and/or same-sex), and bodily fluids or simulations thereof (milk, wine). In the first year of its existence, TST held a "Pink Mass" at the gravesite of the mother of Fred Phelps, founder of the Westboro Baptist Church (WBC), which is known for its anti-gay hate speech. The queering ceremony, "to make her gay in the afterlife," was simultaneously a play on the Mormon practice of baptizing the dead and a response to WBC's claims in the wake of the 2013 bombing of the Boston Marathon. Two hours after the first explosion, WBC tweeted: "Westboro Baptist Church to picket funerals of those dead by Boston Bombs! GOD SENT THE BOMBS IN FURY OVER FAG MARRIAGE! #PraiseGod" (quoted in Chasmar 2013). Lucien Greaves officiated the Pink Mass while wearing horned headgear, and capped it off by putting his genitals on the gravestone. Same-sex couples performed a ritual kiss over the grave. Afterward, Greaves issued the following statement:

> Fred Phelps is obligated to believe that his mother is now gay . . . [and] if beliefs are inviolable rights, nobody has the right to challenge our right to believe that Fred Phelps believes that his mother is now gay.
>
> *(quoted in Smith 2013)*

Greaves's statement emphasizes the way TST was playing with both WBC's theological logic and the legal logic of American religious freedom. The exhibitionist play—the couple making out and Greaves taking out his genitals—was TST's way of playing with WBC and American Christocentrism.

The Pink Mass playfully blasphemed the traditional liturgy with stigmatized sexuality, occult ritual garb, and its setting on consecrated ground. In such a ritual it is clear to see how TST weaponizes its own misrepresentation by aesthetically leveraging cult stereotypes. The publicity these actions generate provides a platform for TST to reclaim Satan as a symbol for rebellion, and to reclaim religion itself as a practice with which people give meaning to their lives. In this, TST offers a queer future for religion in public life—one that refuses to reproduce normative social institutions by insisting that, whenever you publicly open the door to God, you open it to Satan too, or else you close it to both.

TST as a Materialist Religion

Generally speaking, we could say there are two (linked) dimensions of this queer "counter" energy: one being political (for the good of the body politic) and the other being sensational (for the spiritual nourishment of the Satanists themselves). TST's external and internal dimensions mutually shape each other and contribute to each other's vital materialities and practices.

TST is a religion that is both materialist and materializing. Since it is atheist and secular, it does not believe in transcendent forces or transcendent deities; it is scientifically materialist and immanent. TST is expressly atheist and essentially secularist; properly separating "church and state" is its *raison d'etre*.

TST materializes religion in its practice: it treats bodies as things that matter; it wants to bring about physical changes to its environment through the bodily labor of its members in their activist practices. Sometimes, the bodies of its members are also changed and united physically; at one Black Mass a group of women were bound to one another by piercings on their necks and faces. Though TST is a growing reservoir of subversive and queer *cultural* repertoires, it is first and foremost politically and socially activist. It acts on and in the civic spheres it fights to change.

In both content and practice, TST departs meaningfully from what religion scholar Kim Knott (2005: 61) calls the "common sense" notion of religion—that is, a theistic cultural tradition. Building on Knott's common sense notion of religion, Lois Lee's *Recognizing Non-religion: Reimagining the Secular* (2015) introduces a vocabulary to describe all things that are relational to religion. This relational taxonomy is helpful for thinking about TST's queer and material religiosity.

Let's begin with Lee's concept of "nonreligion," which is that which gets its identity primarily in contrast to religion (though not necessarily in *opposition* to religion in an ideological sense). TST fits this bill insofar as the organization materialized only because public assertions of conservative Christian values called it into being. TST takes seriously the image of Satan-as-adversary, in the tradition of Milton and literary figures like Blake, Byron, Shelley, Baudelaire, and Huysmans. As the devil's advocate, TST is the adversary that publicly forces those conservative Christian actors to face the hypocrisy of their stated beliefs versus their actual practices. TST exposes the weakness of their apologetics and the implications for the liberties that must be accorded to the symbols and rituals of others.

Yet TST maintains a meaningful likeness to the religion it is mirroring darkly, and in this sense does not fulfill Lee's other criterion of "nonreligion," which is that nonreligion is meaningfully unlike the phenomena to which it self-contrasts. In fact, TST's public challenges hinge directly on its religiosity. So TST is not "nonreligion"; it is queerly religious. TST's status as a religion is what allows it to make claims to public space in parallel—and as provocations—to the ones made by certain brands of conservative Christianity. The most famous of these provocations was TST's proposal to erect a Baphomet statue beside the Ten Commandments monument on the Oklahoma State Capitol. After an ACLU court victory led to the subsequent removal of that Ten Commandments monument, the proposal was redirected to the Ten Commandments monument at the Arkansas State Capitol.

In the Arkansas case, an eight-foot-six-inch bronze Baphomet statue was driven on a flatbed truck from TST headquarters in Salem, Massachusetts, to Little Rock, Arkansas, to anchor a rally for religious liberty. Leaders representing groups of "atheists, mainline Protestants, evangelicals, and Satanists spoke on the importance of the establishment clause" (Laycock 2020: 13). The assembled Satanists dressed for the occasion, their aesthetic animating the sinister and transgressive elements that from the outset made Satanism shocking to the mainstream and appealing to outsiders.

The rally is depicted at length in the final scenes of Penny Lane's 2019 documentary *Hail Satan?* Despite the amount of black clothing, it is a vibrant composition in the Southern sun, much of it coming from colorfully dyed hair and intricately tattooed skin. There are bustiers, boots, fishnets, chains, pentagram jewelry, BDSM harnesses, capes, trenches, and masks—one a bubblegum-pink goat face mask with long, sinuous horns and pink/blonde ombre goatee. The sartorial permutations and combinations run along a spectrum of gender expressions, including drag and high femme.

In the background of the shots, Baphomet itself embodies an uncanny union of opposites. Historically, in the design of nineteenth-century ceremonial magician Eliphas Lévi (1810–1875, civil name Alphonse Louis Constant), Baphomet represented good and evil, dark and light, human and animal, earth and heaven (with its goat head and feathery wings), male and female. The chest and lap of TST's Baphomet were sanitized of sexual characteristics so that the government could not reject the monument proposal on those grounds. The material asexuality also made space for the possibility that visitors—even young ones like the cherubic children flanking Baphomet—might sit on its lap for a moment of contemplation.

Importantly, Baphomet is *not Satan*. (Though Baphomet does come out of the same milieu of radical Romantic socialist writings of the 1830s and 1840s that featured the tragic figure of Lucifer and the notion of the redemption of Satan.) There are very many etymologies for the name "Baphomet," as well as interpretations of its significance to esoteric groups. As imagined by Lévi, Baphomet symbolizes the notion of the "Astral Light," his best-known concept from his magical theory of the equilibrium of opposites. Lévi thought that the Astral Light had been known to the Kabbalists, the Chaldean magi, the alchemists, and "the Gnostics," [6] and was the force behind magnetism and therefore the ultimate cause of magical operations. Since Lévi was drawing from "spiritualistic magnetism," Spiritism, and Catholicism, for him magical operations were supposed to be of public significance. Historian Julian Strube (2016: 75) writes that Lévi,

> As one of many socialists who had been disillusioned by the failed revolution of 1848 . . . developed his occultism in distinct opposition to 'false' socialism and 'false' Catholicism. . . . The monstrous figure of the Baphomet is an embodiment of all those aspects: the final synthesis of science, religion, philosophy, and politics, which would be realized through the progressive decryption of the tradition of 'true' religion and the creation of the Kingdom of God on Earth.

The fact that Lévi's Baphomet represents "a pantheistic and magical figure of the absolute" (Lévi 1861: 83–84) is deeply at odds with TST's scientific atheism, while the fact that stands for what Lévi imagined as the one "true" form of religion is at odds with TST's secularism. Yet the fact that Baphomet expresses a historical-political tradition of seeking social equilibrium and synthesis of religion and science make it apropos for TST's vision of an inclusive public. In this, the iconic Satanic artifact models a form of negotiation and reconciliation.[7] In its material culture TST reminds us that incorporating difference into the body politic means accepting and expecting that difference isn't just going to even out smoothly in the average; there will be spots of bright pink that don't fade and sharp points of pentagrams that don't dull.

TST as a Secular Project

The idea that the political type of religious rights is inseparable from the cultural type points us from the concept of "nonreligion" to an adjacent node in Lee's relational vocabulary, "secularism."

Lee defines *secularism* as "a theory or ideology that demarcates parts of a whole as secular, notably but not only as stipulated or enacted by the state" (204). *Secular* means "a condition in which religion is a subordinate cultural or political authority" (204). For TST, no religion in the public sphere should be dominant over or subordinate to any other. It is important to emphasize that TST does not wish to see the public sphere become absent of religion ("areligious" [Lee 203]), but rather properly pluralist. In this, they align better with a post-secularist position Lee defines as "a critical stance towards a religious and anti-religious modes of secularity" (204). TST's vision of secularism is unusual because, while a lot of religions have adjusted to secularism (or variously seek to dominate, or embrace, or reject it), such comes after their formation. TST, on the other hand, is a new religious movement that hardwires secularism into the beginning, broadly thematizing the unconscious of new religious movements in general.

The secularism of the TST, rather than being a- or anti-religiosity, instead revels in a material religious culture encompassing objects, clothing, public space, monuments, and media. It is this complex of material-aesthetic-ethical dispositions that most sets TST apart from other atheisms (see, for instance, Amarasingam and Brewster 2016). In fact, you could say that TST tapped into the same market that made a social movement of sorts out of New Atheism, but captured only the segment of those who found New Atheism aesthetically and morally unsatisfying: supercilious, devoid of its own positive cultural forms like iconography and ritual, and willfully ignorant of religion's many prosocial dimensions.

At the same time, some observers will draw more comparisons than contrasts with the New Atheists. One *Hail Satan?* reviewer describes Greaves as wearing a "permanently smug expression" and characterizes TST as touting, at its "stuffiest," something "like Dawkins-style atheism meets hashtag resistance" (Vu 2019).[8] TST is not immune to sometimes veering toward a "faith" in its contrarianism, a bit like the way the New Atheists seem to be enamoured of how their skepticism and scientific "*knowledge feels*" (Schaefer 2018: 70, emphasis in original; see also Sacco 2018 on organized skepticism). Yet by comparison, TST is not only far less certain that any one worldview is correct, but, unlike the New Atheists, it does not aim critiques at faith-based groups themselves; TST is friendly to religion *per se*. After all, it sees itself as one. Where TST aims its critiques is at the way conservative religion is wielded in matters of public deliberation about whose bodies and whose practices get to be welcomed, to be represented, and to be free. TST's ethic-aesthetic is not one of elite entitlement, but rather a both/and kind of underdog plenitude. As TST staff member Ash Astaroth (2017) has said, "Queer is an extra layer on top of being gay just like Satan is an extra layer on top of being an atheist. You can be both."

Their first-line tactic is not to fight other religions' symbols and speech out of the public sphere, but to add their own to it. Using the ritual of protest to détourn the Christian heteropatriarchal status quo, TST aims to materially constitute an alternative, queerly religious public sphere. The latter dimension describes TST's outward-looking activism, while the former dimension describes the way TST's ritual life gives its own members something aesthetically rich to enjoy as a community.

As a communal celebration of personal liberty, TST's rituals like the Black Mass[9] perform freedom by enacting taboos, often including the blaspheming of Christian symbolism. One particularly well-attended Black Mass held by the former LA Chapter included a lecture (on demonic cats) by art historian Paul Koudounaris; a concert by the bands Lumerians, Author + Punisher, and 3Teeth; and a bloodletting ritual performed by Coven of Ashes. Another example can be found in an Unbaptism, which is described in this 2015 account of prominent one-time member Jex Blackmore[10]:

> The ritual featured seven participants and included use of holy water or a relic from the participant's baptizing church. Celebrants extinguished baptismal water into fire when called to "cast your chains into the dust of hell." Following the extinguishing, participants were given an apple by a man and woman adorned with live snakes and

prompted to "savor the fruit of knowledge and disobedience." At the close of the ritual, the audience demonstrated their support through call and response. When asked "Do you humble yourself before god? Do you apologize for your sins?" the crowd shouted "No!" . . . Now "Unbaptised, in the name of Satan, the Light-Bearer, the Adversary, and the Animal," . . . the crowd erupted in "Hail Satan" and devolved into a wild death-rock dance party.

(Blackmore 2015)

In Unbaptism, participants renounce superstitions that may have been imposed upon them without their consent as a child. But TST is clearly not about renouncing a sense of mystery, awe, or wonder—nor about publicly purging religious spectacle generally, or Christian symbolism specifically. TST's interest in Christian symbolism is to the extent that it participates in oppressive institutional and discursive regimes at the level of the nation. Comparing TST rituals to "gory" religious iconography, William Morrison (cofounder of what is now HelLA) quips: "Let's take the pentagram and paste that on a wall, then let's take the [crucifix] and put that on a wall. Which one is scarier? This [star] shape or this bleeding hippy dude nailed to a cross?" (quoted in Swann 2017) (Figure 2.9.3).

Thus, Black Masses and Unbaptisms are not held primarily to create the spectacle of "a topsy-turvy Christianity" (Petersen 2004: 433). As Jesper Aagaard Petersen has demonstrated, modern Satanism is not the same as "the popular model of Satanism," consisting of "inverted Christianity, Devil worship, and rebellion" (2004: 443). The Unbaptism ceremony, for instance, literally undoes a Christian sacrament, but it is crucial to realize how it is not actually just a blasphemous reworking of Christian visual symbols and bodily gestures, but more precisely a *material queering* of hegemonically Christian cultural norms. In this

Figure 2.9.3 2015 Unbaptism ritual with Jex Blackmore at the podium. Photo credit Chris Switzer and Matt Anderson.

sense, Christianity *is* the religion that gets re-presented in the public sphere, and in the ritual lives of Satanists. And though TST draws on Western esoteric aesthetics, these are also tied to Christianity; early Christians instituted three ontological categories—Christians, Jews, and Pagans—and to draw ritual and symbolic life from the history of Western esotericism is to identify with that Christian-defined catch-all category.

TST rituals seek a religious antidote for the nation's suffering "from Americana nervosa, a compulsive self-gorging on ritual images" (Berlant and Freeman 1997: 147). In the diagnosis of Lauren Berlant and Elizabeth Freeman, "the struggle to secure national discursive propriety . . . is now . . . over proper public submission to national iconicity and over the nation's relation to gender, to sexuality, and to death" (147). In this struggle, TST's blasphemy is a refusal to self-censor and a bid to publicly express embodied rituals of subversion. It is a ritual manifestation of an alternative public, whose imagination is enchanted with the compassionate pulse of the erotic and visceral. TST's religious imagination materially queers the public sphere, using sundry sexual, spoken, and visual taboo or blasphemy to animate personal agency in spaces where the political agency of marginalized bodies has been constrained. Aesthetically and affectively powerful spells, incantations, and ceremonies are meant to be the ritual speech acts and performances that bring about the changes that laws and norms have not.

Toward a Queerly Religious Public Sphere

Yet while TST says it wants the best of religion's collective effervescence and aesthetic power, the best of religion might be whatever vestige it still has of a way of thinking that is pre-capitalist secularism. Since the esoteric rituals and concepts TST borrows have to conform to the structure of liberal democracy, which is necessarily and rightfully structurally boring, these symbols may become enervated, too. As the organization goes on, it will be interesting to observe whether TST Satanists produce much of their own music, poetry, and art.

From my perspective as a Canadian observer, it appears to me that the heart of TST is performatively queering both America's worship of itself and its approach to religion in the public sphere. The religious situation in other national contexts,[11] even hegemonically Christian ones, is, of course, different. Yet, at the same time, there is no place where matters of gender identity, sexuality, and bodily autonomy are not morally valent. In this way, TST's ritual mixing of sex and death necessarily challenges the politics of the sacred—that is, "what can and cannot be and what should and should not be tolerated and accepted in the community, based on its relation to that which is sacred for that community" (Squiers 2018: 20).

Yet TST's approach may be insufficiently intersectional[12] to achieve real transformation, except insofar as it attracted critical masses of people who then broke with TST over their disappointment and regrouped to start new Satanic organizations. These organizations will likely succeed to the extent that they can be built on a coalitional politics among those united not by "some homogenized identity" (Cohen 1997: 438), but by their participants' relation to power. That struggle with power is, to borrow Berlant and Freeman's phrasing, "over proper public submission to national iconicity and over the nation's relation to gender, to sexuality, and to death," via religion (1997: 147).

Nevertheless, TST at least proposes a queer form of public material religion. It is, on the one hand, a religion that ritually confers on its own members their own libidinal pleasures, and on the other, a religion that makes a spectacle of its rituals in order to provoke public deliberation over the politics of the sacred.

Notes

1 I am indebted here to the phrasing of Will Clark's 2018 characterization of the "relational school" of queer thought—that of "[José] Muñoz, Jack Halberstam, David L. Eng, and others, [which] posits that queerness is all about constituting communities through the refusal of the social order. Understanding the traumas and pleasures of others, in their view, could help build a new social world removed from the violence of the present."

2 TST is new even in "new religious movements" terms—it dates only from 2012. Yet already it has changed the way we talk about Satanism, evil, pluralism, and religion itself. This is the claim recently made by Joseph Laycock in *Speak of the Devil*, the first book-length work to be published on TST (2020). In it, Laycock gives the first comprehensive history of the movement and characterizes it with respect to the way he and other scholars writing about modern religious Satanisms (Petersen 2009; Faxneld and Petersen 2012; Dyrendal, Lewis, and Petersen 2015) have characterized Satanism in general: as "a reaction to a Christian establishment and frequently an indictment of it" (187).

3 Professional pseudonyms.

4 Additionally, at least in some chapters that have tracked it, people with disabilities tend to become involved with TST at a higher rate to that of the general American public (25 percent in TST versus 12.6 percent nationally [Bialik 2017]).

5 This rhetorical framework of "church–state separation" reflects the fact that TST originated in the United States, but a few chapters and affiliates have organized in Canada, and around the world. (And organizing a group whose membership rose steeply [Browne 2019] in less than a decade has posed a lot of problems, with rather bureaucratic, apparently unsatanic solutions.)

6 The groups conventionally classified as "gnostic" did not constitute a unified movement, and the designation is not an emic one but either a heresiological term or a scholarly one. Groups referred to under this label often include the Valentinians, Marcionites, Sethians, and the many other movements within the ambit of the early Jesus Movement. Their texts tend to advance the idea of a secret, salvific knowledge of demiurgy—the creation of the world by a god who is lower than the primary god. See Williams 1999.

7 Number three of TST's Seven Fundamental Tenets is one clear representation of this negotiation between the bodily/material and the principle/abstract, the claim that "One's body is inviolable, subject to one's own will alone." Likewise, Lucien Greaves has expressed the way material culture and political principles are always in negotiation together. In a 2013 interview with *Vice*, he said: "Religion can and should be a metaphorical narrative construct by which we give meaning and direction to our lives and works. . . . Nonbelievers have just as much right to religion—and any exemptions and privileges being part of a religion brings—as anybody else." And as a religion, one of TST's seven fundamental tenets is that "The freedoms of others should be respected, including the freedom to offend. To willfully and unjustly encroach upon the freedoms of another is to forgo one's own."

8 Rather than advocating, as Dawkins did, to accord religion less respect, TST's tenets include a statement of their own belief that "Beliefs should conform to one's best scientific understanding of the world. One should take care never to distort scientific facts to fit one's beliefs" (TST website, "Tenets"). It is significant that this statement is codified as it is: as a religious tenet applicable to its own self-selected adherents, and inviolable to the same extent as the religious tenets of others, which is precisely to the extent that it would "willfully and unjustly encroach upon the freedoms of another" (TST website, "Tenets").

9 The Black Mass can include other rituals, like the destruction ritual (participants destroy an object they own that symbolizes a source of pain in their lives), the defiance ritual (signifying a pledge to challenge the status quo in a way that is personally meaningful), as well as invocation rituals (a statement of the Seven Tenets, plus a call to stand up to racial, gender, and other inequalities) (TST website, "FAQ").

10 In a 2018 incident that epitomizes the challenges of simultaneously embodying rebellion and running a unified organization, Greaves and Jarry asked Blackmore to resign over apparently calling for Satanists to, among other things, murder President Donald Trump.

11 It will therefore be interesting to see what national character TST takes on in Canada if its Ottawa chapter and its unofficial affiliates (waiting for designation of official status) continue to be active, and how this may happen elsewhere in the world where TST exists.

12 The most recent example of which I am aware where intersectionality is noticeably absent from TST official communications is when, on April 6, 2021, Lucien Greaves tweeted the *ABC News* headline "Rapper Lil Nas X causes 'satanic panic' with new music video." The tweet linked to a blog post Greaves wrote and published to his Patreon page, titled "The Lil Nas X Controversy is not a Satanic Panic . . . the Satanic Panic had already arrived." Greaves does not characterize or explore Lil Nas X's positionality in this controversy as a queer black man. His only purpose is to "distinguish 'Satanic Panic' from mere flare-ups of righteous indignation against Satanists and Satanic imagery," which is what he thought the Lil Nas X controversy was: the controversy being how the video for the song "Montero (Call Me By Your Name)" depicts "the artist giving a homoerotic lapdance to Satan." Greaves limits his take on the situation by saying: "It may be a bit less annoying to hear a Satanist opine to the media on the merits of the Montero video than it is to hear Christian prigs—who actively fight for the religious freedom to discriminate against homosexuals—cry about their feelings of persecution at learning of a gay man's art that does not fit their prescribed narrative, but it is still a bit annoying nonetheless."

References

Amarasingam, Amarnath, and Melanie Brewster. 2016. "The Rise and Fall of the New Atheism: Identity Politics and Tensions Within US Nonbelievers." In *Annual Review of the Sociology of Religion: Sociology of Atheism*, edited by Roberto Cipriani and Franco Garelli, vol. 7, 118–136. Leiden: Brill.

Berlant, Lauren, and Elizabeth Freeman. 1997. "Queering Nationality." In *The Queen of America Goes to Washington City: Essays on Sex and Citizenship*, edited by Lauren Berlant, 145–173. Durham, NC: Duke University Press.

Bialik, Kristen. 2017. "7 Facts About Americans with Disabilities." *Pew Research Center*. July 27, 2017. https://www.pewresearch.org/fact-tank/2017/07/27/7-facts-about-americans-with-disabilities/.

Blackmore, Jex. 2015. "The Satanic Temple of Detroit performs 'Unbaptism Ritual' on Devil's Night." *Daily Kos*. November 4, 2015. https://www.dailykos.com/stories/2015/11/4/1444849/-The-Satanic-Temple-of-Detroit-performs-Unbaptism-Ritual-on-Devil-s-Night.

Browne, Rachel. 2019. "The Rise of the Satanic Temple in Canada." *Global News*. July 20, 2019. https://globalnews.ca/news/5488632/satanic-temple-canada/.

Burns, Gus. 2015. "Detroit-Area Satanists Doused with Milk at Planned Parenthood Protest." *MLive Media Group*. https://www.mlive.com/news/detroit/2015/08/detroit-area_satanists_doused.html.

Chasmar, Jessica. 2013. "Westboro Baptist Church to Picket Funeral of Woman Killed in Boston Bombings." *Washington Times*. April 21, 2013. https://www.washingtontimes.com/news/2013/apr/21/westboro-baptist-church-picket-funeral-woman-kille/.

Clark, Will. 2018. "Queer Desires, Queer Disagreements." *Los Angeles Review of Books*. February 16, 2018. https://lareviewofbooks.org/article/queer-desires-queer-disagreements/.

Cohen, Cathy, J. 1997. "Punks, Bulldaggers, and Welfare Queens: The Radical Potential of Queer Politics?" *GLQ* 3, no. 4 (May): 437–465.

Dyrendal, Asbjørn, James R. Lewis, and Jesper Aagaard Petersen. 2015. *The Invention of Satanism*. Oxford: Oxford University Press.

Faxneld, Per, and Jesper Aagaard Petersen, eds. 2012. *The Devil's Party: Satanism in Modernity*. Oxford: Oxford University Press.

Feltmate, David. 2016. "Rethinking New Religious Movements Beyond a Social Problems Paradigm." *Nova Religio: Journal of Alternative and Emergent Religions* 20 (2): 82–96.

Gallagher, Eugene V. 2009. "Teaching for Religious Literacy." *Teaching Theology and Religion* 12 (3): 208–221.

Greaves, Lucien. 2021. "The Lil Nas X Controversy Is Not a Satanic Panic … the Satanic Panic Had Already Arrived." Patreon. April 6, 2021. https://www.patreon.com/posts/lil-nas-x-is-not-49717911.

Knott, Kim. 2005. *The Location of Religion: A Spatial Analysis*. London: Equinox.

Kristeva, Julia. 1982. *The Powers of Horror: An Essay on Abjection*. Translated by Leon S. Roudiez. New York: Columbia University Press.

Laycock, Joseph. 2020. *Speak of the Devil: How The Satanic Temple Is Changing The Way We Talk About Religion*. Oxford: Oxford University Press.

Lee, Lois. 2015. *Recognizing Nonreligion: Reimagining the Secular*. Oxford: Oxford University Press.

Lévi, Eliphas. 1861. *Dogme et Rituel de la Haute Magie*. Translated by Arthur Waite. Paris: G. Baillière.

Nelson, Maggie. 2015. *The Argonauts*. Minneapolis, MN: Graywolf Press.

News Service of Florida 2013. "Fake Satanists 'Rally' for Scott." *Herald-Tribune*. http://politics.heraldtribune.com/2013/01/25/fake-satanists-rally-for-scott/.

Oppenheimer, Mark. 2015. "A Mischievous Thorn in the Side of Conservative Christianity." *New York Times*. July 10, 2015. https://www.nytimes.com/2015/07/11/us/a-mischievous-thorn-in-the-side-of-conservative-christianity.html.

Petersen, Jesper Aagaard. 2004. "Modern Satanism." In *Controversial New Religions*, edited by James R. Lewis and Jesper Aagaard Petersen, 423–458. Oxford: Oxford University Press.

Petersen, Jesper Aagaard, ed. 2009. *Contemporary Religious Satanism: A Critical Anthology*. Farnham, UK: Ashgate.

Prothero, Stephen. 2007. *Religious Literacy: What Every American Needs to Know—and Doesn't*. San Francisco, CA: HarperCollins.

Ryan, Kate. 2017. "How the Satanic Temple Became a Queer Haven." *Vice*. July 24, 2017. https://www.vice.com/en_us/article/zmv7my/how-the-satanic-temple-became-a-queer-haven.

Schaefer, Donovan O. 2018. "Beautiful Facts: Science, Secularism, and Affect." In *Feeling Religion*, edited by John Corrigan, 68–91. Durham, NC: Duke University Press.

Smith, Jonathan. 2013. "Satanists Turned the Founder of the Westboro Baptist Church's Dead Mom Gay." *Vice*. July 17, 2013. https://www.vice.com/en_au/article/5gwnj8/satanists-turned-the-founder-of-the-westboro-baptist-churchs-mom-gay.

Squiers, Anthony. 2018. *The Politics of the Sacred in America: The Role of Civil Religion in Political Practice*. Cham, Switzerland: Springer.

Stone, Michael. 2016. "'Fetal Idolatry': Satanic Temple Mocks Planned Parenthood Protest." *Patheos*. April 26, 2016. https://www.patheos.com/blogs/progressivesecularhumanist/2016/04/fetal-idolatry-satanic-temple-mocks-planned-parenthood-protest/.

Strube, Julian. 2016. "The 'Baphomet' of Eliphas Lévi: Its Meaning and Historical Context." *Correspondences* 4 (February): 37–79.

Swann, Jennifer. 2017. "Is a Trump Presidency the Satanic Temple's Chance to Go Mainstream?" *LA Weekly*. February 27, 2017. https://www.laweekly.com/is-a-trump-presidency-the-satanic-temples-chance-to-go-mainstream/.

The Satanic Temple n.d. *FAQ*. https://thesatanictemple.com/pages/faq.

The Satanic Temple n.d. "Put a Satanic Monument at OK Capitol." *IndieGoGo Campaign*. https://www.indiegogo.com/projects/put-a-satanic-monument-at-ok-capitol#/.

The Satanic Temple n.d. *Tenets*. https://thesatanictemple.com/pages/tenets.

Tucson News Now. 2018. "'Highway to Hell' Has Roadside Cleanup in Arizona." *KOLD News*. https://www.kold.com/story/37408653/highway-to-hell-has-roadside-cleanup-in-southern-arizona/.

Victor, Jeffrey S. 1993. *Satanic Panic: The Creation of a Contemporary Legend*. Chicago, IL: Open Court.

Williams, Michael. 1999. *Rethinking Gnosticism: An Argument for Dismantling a Dubious Category*. Princeton, NJ: Princeton University Press.

Vu, Ryan. 2019. "Something Spiritual Simmers Beneath Satanism's Media-Baiting Pranks." *Indy Week*. May 15, 2019. https://indyweek.com/culture/screen/Hail-Satan-documentary-Satanic-Temple/.

PART III

Entanglements, Entrapments, Escaping

3.1

THE ENTANGLEMENTS OF RELIGION AND THINGS

Ian Hodder

I intend in this chapter to make some general points about the relationships between religion and things, using the example of Çatalhöyük, a 9,000-year-old Neolithic (New Stone Age, 10,000–4,500 BCE) site I have been excavating in central Turkey for the past twenty-five years (see Figure 3.1.1 and, for example, Hodder 2006 and www.catalhoyuk. com). One way of talking about Çatalhöyük is to say that it consists of houses tightly packed together into a town (Figure 3.1.2), and that people buried their dead beneath the floors of houses. In this perspective, houses (secular) contain burials (religion). But, in fact, there are grounds for arguing that burial was a pre-requisite for the house. In a number of instances, small burial cemeteries had houses built upon them—as if a prime function of the house was to "house" the dead. In the construction of many houses, a burial—sometimes of a child—is placed in the foundation and leveling deposits (as in the case of Building 53). So, it can be said that the house at Çatalhöyük was always already religious. Certainly many daily tasks took place in the house—from tool manufacture to food preparation and consumption—but the house was also the focus of much symbolism and ritual, including bull's heads and wall paintings showing the hunting of wild animals. Thus it is impossible to separate secular and religious at the site. Within each house there was a separation between the north and south parts of the main rooms, with the northern areas generally having cleaner floors and more burial and art, while in the south parts of main rooms there is often more evidence of hearths, ovens, and tool manufacture. But it is difficult to argue for a strict divide, since some burials (of children) have been found in the southern parts of main rooms, and there is much situational variation regarding where hearths and ovens are located; for example, in some early houses ovens occur in the north of main rooms.

It is difficult to separate secular and religious at early farming sites in the Middle East such as Çatalhöyük. Religion is brought close to daily life at these sites. Indeed, most religions are brought close through materializations; in this way, religious or spiritual forces can be manipulated and managed. And certainly at Çatalhöyük material things were continually and purposefully drawn into the processes of objectification and manipulation. For example, the houses at the site were apparently always in a continual process of collapse. Built of

DOI: 10.4324/9781351176231-20

Figure 3.1.1   Excavations underway in the South Area of Çatalhöyük.
Source: Çatalhöyük Research Project and Jason Quinlan.

unfired mudbrick, the walls expanded and contracted in the changing seasonal round. There is much evidence of slumping and leaning of walls, and much evidence that the inhabitants tried to stop the decay of walls. They did this by doubling walls, making sandier bricks, and building thicker walls as well as walls with buttresses. But they also called upon the spirit world to sustain and protect the house. This was partly achieved by burying ancestors beneath floors and in foundation deposits. A specific example was found in Building 89. Heads of the ancestors were often kept and circulated for some time before being deposited into the foundation; sometimes, they were painted, the human features replastered onto the skull. In Building 89, a skull was found placed at the base of one of the posts that held up the house and its upper story.

But, of course, a limitation of most symbolic devices is that their force tends to decline over time, as was the case with Building 89. Maurice Bloch (2010) is one of many who have argued that the house at Çatalhöyük, which tended to lose its efficacy over time, had to be continually re-animated to keep it from falling and crumbling. Even the vibrant nature of matter, such as has been described by authors such as Jane Bennett (2010), declines over time; vibrancy must be continually renewed. In the case of Çatalhöyük, this is done most clearly in two ways. First, there is the harnessing of the power of wild animals. Most of the bull horn and other animal installations in the houses (see Figures 3.1.3 and 3.1.4) were taken from wild animals. (Although the inhabitants of Çatalhöyük depended very heavily on domesticated sheep for their livelihood, depictions of sheep in the site's symbolism are rare, even non-existent.) Bloch (2010) argues that the power of wild animals was harnessed to help sustain the settlement and its houses. Second, as we have already seen, the ancestors played their role too, by both helping to hold up the house posts and infusing the house with their presence and memory. Sixty-two such ancestors were buried under Building 1. Indeed, there are correlations between the number of people buried in a house and the degree of symbolic and ritual elaboration (Hodder 2016a)—both the dead and various ritual paraphernalia helped to animate the house.

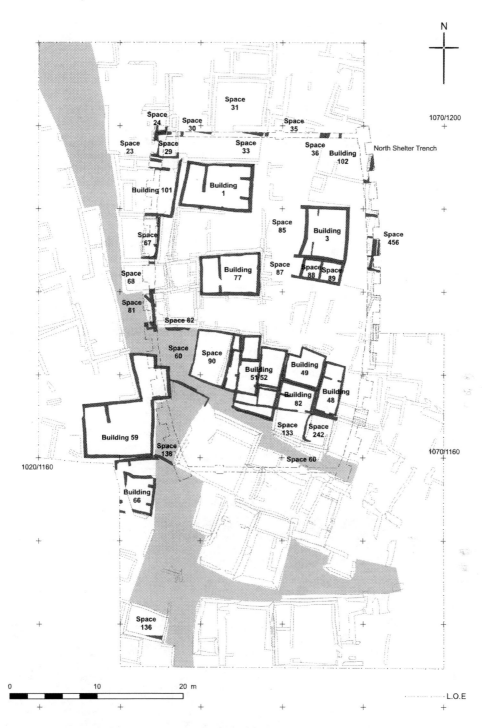

Figure 3.1.2   Houses excavated in the North Area of Çatalhöyük, indicating some of the buildings mentioned in the text: Buildings 1, 52, and 77.

Source: Çatalhöyük Research Project and Camilla Mazzucato.

Figure 3.1.3 A stack of wild bull horns placed in a niche in Building 52.
Source: Çatalhöyük Research Project and Jason Quinlan.

Figure 3.1.4 Wild bull horns set around a burial platform in Building 77.
Source: Çatalhöyük Research Project and Jason Quinlan.

Things as Waves

Houses at Çatalhöyük were built on top of each other in a continual process. A house was lived in for perhaps 50 to 100 years—after which the upper walls and roof were knocked down and the materials used to carefully fill the lower part. A solid platform was thereby created for a new house to be built on top of the old. As such, it becomes very difficult for excavators to know where an earlier house ends and a later one begins. The layout of a later building is often presaged in the layout of an earlier building, and the filling in (ending) of one building can also be seen as the start of a new building—thus the continual process of rebuilding on much the same footprint over time.

In this tradition we can see a continual process of becoming. It is as if the house is not a thing but a column of matter that is continually re-animated and given force. The sequence of houses is like a force, such as an electro-magnetic force, that flows through time and joins with other forces to create continuity and change. The sequence of houses can be seen as a wave of energy that produces the pulses of individual buildings. But since the pulses lose their energy, they need to be continually revived.

There are many forces that run through and animate a single house site at Çatalhöyük. We have already seen the religious and spiritual forces of human burials and wild animals. There are also social forces, such as the drive towards aggrandizement as houses vie with each other for dominance. There are also physical forces, such as the force of gravity that holds unfired mud bricks on top of each other on a wall, and that holds the roofs on houses. Numerous electro-chemical interactions prevent entities such as bricks from falling apart.

These heterogeneous forces run through the conduit of the house—producing and reproducing it, generating and regenerating it. Each new house, each new artifact brought into the house, each new person or skeleton, created a new pulse of onward-goingness. We can follow Alfred North Whitehead in arguing that "an actual entity is a process, and is not describable in terms of the morphology of a 'stuff'" (Whitehead in Sherburne 1981: 8). Similar concepts of things as flows and forces are found in the work of Ingold (2015) and Deleuze and Guattari (1987). For the latter, the question of philosophy is not "What is it?" (the question of being) but "In which direction is it going?" and "Along with what else?" and "What can become of it?" (the question of becoming). In their discussion of nomad science, Deleuze and Guattari foreground fluids rather than solids, and becoming and heterogeneity rather than stability. They see lines or flows that interact to either increase their forces or to constrain each other.

While the flows of the house are animated by other forces—from the religious to the physical—the house itself becomes a force in its own right, with its own momentum. Once constructed, the house affords potentials (powers) that can be exploited and turned in multiple possible directions. Its weight presses down on the layers of soil beneath it, causing slumping and buckling of walls—which will draw humans to tend to its maintenance. The house affords cooking around the hearth, but the cooking produces smoke and soot that darken the interiors—which will draw humans into the labor of whitening the walls with a fine clay. The house affords burial, as we have seen—but as the burials increase, a new house must be constructed to create more space.

Entanglement and Religion

I have tried to build an image of strings or threads along which forces or flows run. These different forces intersect and are tied up with each other. In a recent definition of entanglement (Hodder 2020), I have argued that this image is a metaphor to capture the contradictory messiness of the heterogeneous flows and counter-flows that produce, enchain, and encompass entities (humans, animals, things, ideas, social institutions). In much the same way, Barad (2007: 33) describes "intra-action" as the "mutual constitution of entangled agencies." However, I will below place particular emphasis on the contradictory nature of flows and the frictions between them that lead to change.

Why is religion a component of human-thing entanglements? I have argued (Hodder 2016b) that entanglements are unbounded—they are open systems. Their threads stretch out over space as well as through time, such that many aspects of our lives derive from the descent of actions and events that have historical, and often prehistoric, sources. (For example, cars today are indebted to the invention of the wheel in Eurasia around 4,000 BCE.) Spatially, too, a car is made of over 20,000 components that have global biographies. As such, small events in distant places and times can have long-term effects that are impossible to tease apart given the complexity and messiness of entanglements. Causal relations are in truth often unknowable; we have to accept that there is a beyond to which we have little access. Religion too is about the beyond, and, indeed, it can be defined in those terms—as well as in terms of the actions taken to influence what is beyond our immediate agency. So, for me, one of the things that religion does is to help humans gain access to the beyond, to try to control and regulate its stretchiness and uncertainty (whether the "beyond" be death or the future or the wild). Religion in this sense is like science; both involve reaching into the unknown to understand and control it.

So when at Çatalhöyük the dead and wild animals were brought into the house, attempts were being made to control and manage unknown forces. Bull horns were placed within a regulated spatial structure within the house, where they could be painted, managed, watched, honored, and cared for. And the forces such as the bull heads could also be used to animate the house, to protect it from unknown forces and harms, to protect the crops and grains and their processing and storage, to protect the herds of sheep managed from the house, as well as the platforms, beams, and benches of the house.

But if religion is part of what it means to be an entangled human as just described, why does religion have to be materialized? Why do we need to have material bull horns, material dead, material figurines, material symbols? Is it not enough to call upon the unknown forces through prayer and incantation, or though meditation and trance (Lewis-Williams and Pearce 2005)? More generally, why do even the most ascetic of religions seem so often to use material things as part of devotional practices? At sites such as Çatalhöyük the question may seem fruitless, since there was so little separation and specialization of different aspects of life. In these early farming societies, there was a remarkable holism—such that the house at Çatalhöyük contained the religious, the domestic, the cemetery, the industrial all in the same space. There was little differentiation overall, so it is unsurprising that the religious was engrained in the material. In many societies, the religious is made manifest in matter. Why is this?

I have previously discussed (2017) how Meyer (2012: 23) has argued that materiality is a key component of religious practice. "As practices and materials are indispensable for religion's existence in the world as a social, cultural, and political phenomenon, they need our utmost theoretical and empirical attention." Meyer provides an example from the Ewe from Ghana and Togo:

> According to Ewe cosmology, in principle all gods—trōwo or vodu—by necessity require some material vessel in order to be present and enact their power, and humans can access, and partake in, this power through certain religious acts. These acts begin with the actual carving or moulding of a figure, its subsequent animation through

spitting alcohol and saliva, its regular maintenance through sacrifices and feeding, its worship through repeated incantations, body movements, and so on. Here, human action was indispensable for the gods to be present and act on people.

(Meyer 2012: 23)

There are numerous examples of external powers and agencies being made present in religious practices. The Orthodox or Catholic icon itself becomes a being that is kissed, carried around, prayed to. Saints and prophets were made present in the form of circulated body parts. The body and blood of Christ are made present (in different ways) in the Catholic and Protestant churches. Why does the supernatural have to be made material to be experienced? I have argued (Hodder 2016b) this is precisely because religious practice is about "getting a hold on" the beyond, the divine. One gets a hold on the divine partly by making it human and anthropomorphic. As noted above, the practice of seeing human agency in things is found in all areas of life, but it is also used as a technology to intervene in the beyond. More generally, manipulating things allows the practitioner a sense of agency in relation to the beyond; it allows a connection to be made and interventions to occur. Material things are central to religion because they allow us to participate in the divine—as well as enable us to use religion as a technology to manage the beyond of the world in which we live. Placing religion in matter allows humans to gain some sense of being able to participate in the divine, influence outcomes, handle solutions. Matter matters, and so, by manipulating things of import, there is a real handle on that which is distant and unknown.

At a deeper level, the dependence between religion and matter is simply an example of the wider human dependence on objectification. As Heidegger argued, we can only think *of* something in the same way that we can only feel if we feel something, and only see or smell if we see or smell something. As humans we cannot get very far without things—including words, images, smells—even before we consider the human dependence on technologies. We are designed to be thingly. In the same way, we cannot have religious feeling, spiritual awakening, or divine experience without reference to something or to some experience. The divine may be abstract and distant, but it also needs to be concrete and near, to be emotional and embodied. We need the icon to kiss, the incense to smell, the bells to hear. Even the most ascetic of religions involve material practices (Buchli 2015).

Religious Entanglement and Entrapment

Human-thing entanglement always involves some degree of entrapment (Hodder 2012, 2016b). This is because of the double bind by which humans depend on things that depend on other things that depend on humans. Humans thus get drawn into the care of things and the multitude of threads in which they are produced. Put another way, things are but pulses along threads or strings of energy, or nodes within force fields. They are thus dependent on the strings with which they are entangled. Humans thus get forced to work along the radiating strings in the attempt to manage the energy flows.

In the case of religious energies at Çatalhöyük, a clear example is provided by the wild bulls that are the foci of feasts and that furnish the horns that are the main installations in the houses. Recent research has shown that throughout the eleven-hundred-year span of occupation at the Çatalhöyük settlement there is a gradual process of greater human intervention in the management of cattle (Wolfhagen et al. 2021). There is a gradual diminution in the size of the cattle as they were brought into closer relationships with humans, leading ultimately to the appearance of domestic forms. Why does this process of greater human investment in cattle occur? Though domestic sheep outnumber cattle in the settlement, little evidence suggests they played a significant role in ritual—whereas cattle played a prominent role. It is possible that the increased management of cattle resulted from the need to provision feasts and ritual events and installations with bulls and their horns. In Building 52 of the site, thirteen horns were stacked above a bucranium in a niche in the main room (Figure 3.1.3). This was a substantial amassing of resources. Certainly, it seems possible that humans depended on cattle for religious rituals, and that over time humans were drawn into the increased management of cattle in order to provision religious events.

Entrapment of this kind is often associated with path dependency (Hodder 2012). Humans often invest in things down certain pathways, and it becomes more and more difficult to change paths as the entanglements increase in complexity. Certainly at Çatalhöyük there is good evidence that managing cattle, and especially bulls, became entangled with many aspects of life, from food production and feasting to rituals and installations. It seems possible that the killing of bulls and the providing of meat in feasts was a key part of the social fabric of the town, and the type of aggrandizement just referred to in Building 52 may have been one of the main routes to increasing social standing. The inhabitants of Çatalhöyük were very late to adopt fully domestic cattle—in comparison to other parts of Anatolia in the seventh millennium BCE. Arbuckle (2013) has suggested that the delayed adoption at Çatalhöyük may have been because cattle were so thoroughly entangled in social and ritual life in the town. This is a prime example of path dependency in relation to religious practices. It might be argued that path dependency is particularly prevalent with regard to religion because the religious deals with ultimate questions of being and becoming. The emotional involvement is thus profound and deeply embodied. Because religion deals with the ineffable beyond, it is entangled with our deepest fears and our ultimate goals. The entrapment is especially dangerous because the religious engagement with things comes to define what it means to be human, to underpin deeply held convictions, and to pit different groups against each other from the ground up. Religious forces thus transform as the entanglements with which they are entwined change, but the path dependency often results in very long-term threads that manage to persist in the face of radical change. For example, as we shall see below, there is much evidence for change during the occupation at Çatalhöyük, and yet the symbol of the bull earlier associated with installations in houses becomes used as a motif on painted pottery on the adjacent site of Çatalhöyük West during the *ensuing* Chalcolithic era, at the start of the sixth millennium BCE. Indeed, Hodder and Meskell (2011) have shown how many of the distinctive attributes of the iconography of the Neolithic of the Middle East, including the wild bull, have enormous life spans, continuing for at least three millennia. This is path dependency taken to an extreme, and it shows the ability of religious forces to re-invigorate themselves as they come into new conjunctions. The example also shows the ways in which humans get "stuck" into managing key religious components.

Religious Entanglement and Change

It is important to recognize that the various forces that become entangled with religion may not be cooperative with one another. Indeed, the different forces may often by discordant and contradictory. So it is not that the different strands are co-constitutive in some symmetrical way. Rather, the strands are semi-autonomous with different forces; there is no reason why the forces of gravity and religious zeal should always work in the same direction. They are not co-constitutive but entangled—working for and against each other. It is the frictions between these different forces that often lead to change. At Çatalhöyük the aggrandizement that was described above with reference to Building 52 occurred toward the end of the Middle phase that lasts from 6,700 to 6,500 BCE, when there is much other evidence of large amounts of bull horns being deposited (for example in Building 77—see Figure 3.1.4), as well as more installations in houses such as leopard reliefs on walls, more burials in houses, more physical stress and disease on the body, and high fertility. There are probably many reasons for these changes, but one seems to be that during the Middle phase cooking pottery was introduced to the settlement. This had positive effects in that cooking with pottery rather than with clay balls (the previous cooking method) was more efficient and allowed the cook to undertake other tasks. The use of cooking pottery in the houses contributed to the expansion of house size and the range of activities carried out in houses. Ultimately, however, as the house became more a center of production and consumption, a contradiction emerged with regard to the focus on wild bull paraphernalia. The expansion of domestic activities changed the nature of the house so that the house became more like a productive farm, leaving less space, time, energy, and purpose for religious practices. The house came to be defined in terms of production rather than through the control of ritual and the dead. Burial in houses declined, ceasing altogether by the time of the West Mound in the early sixth millennium BCE. Ritual symbolism continued, but shifted from the house walls to pottery, which was sometimes decorated with bull heads and painted horns. So, altogether, the introduction of cooking pottery contributed to an increased focus on production in the house that contradicted the house as a ritual space, leading to change in the nature of the house.

Another type of contradiction that we see through this period concerns the role of cattle. In the Early (7,100–6,700 BCE) and Middle phases of occupation, large wild bulls played a key role in religious ritual practices. But through the Middle phase there is evidence of aggrandizement such as we have seen in Building 52. Another interpretation of the increased focus on wild bull and other wild animal installations in the Middle phase is that greater investment in wild animals was needed in order to counter any decline in symbolic and religious efficacy. But the increased dependence on wild bulls in an increasingly large settlement would have put pressure on local stocks of wild animals and would have encouraged humans to invest in the management and perhaps breeding of wild cattle. An unintended product of such management would have been a decrease in the size of wild cattle, as we see in the measurements studied by Wolfhagen et al. (2021). Management of cattle would also have come into contradiction with the farming of arable crops near the site, since both humans and cattle would be vying for the same food source. The protection of those crops would have led to further pressures on cattle management, and thus to size diminution, since smaller cattle would be more easily manageable and thus do less harm to crops. Humans also started depending on cattle for milk and on cattle dung for fuel. In all these ways the availability of large, fierce, impressive wild bulls would have declined. This may be part of the reason that the role of cattle in animating the house declined over time.

Another example of the ways in which the entanglements of religion with material things leads to friction, contradiction, and change is provided by the treatment of the dead at Çatalhöyük. As noted, throughout most of the occupation of the site, the dead were buried beneath the floors of houses. At times large numbers of people were crammed beneath the platforms in the northern parts of the main room of the house. Regardless of the symbolic intention at work here, in practical terms this would have led to disease, odor, and the slumping of floors as flesh decayed beneath them. Recent research has shown that these problems were averted by a process of delayed burial (Haddow et al. 2021). Bodies were initially dried or smoked but also carefully wrapped in cloths and skins. These tightly flexed bundles took up less space and caused fewer problems than did fully fleshed bodies. As later bundles were added, earlier bodies were pushed aside. When the time came to tear down a house and build anew, the walls and roof were dismantled and the clay material from them densely packed to for the foundation of a new house. It seems likely that this infill platform raised the floors enough for a new phase of burial. Indeed, as burial declined in houses in the Final phase (6,300–6,000 BCE) of occupation, less emphasis was placed on filling earlier houses with soil before constructing a new house. So, in this example, humans were drawn into further labor in order to bury their dead beneath house floors. They were drawn into lengthy and complex drying or smoking of bodies in the period between death and burial. And they were drawn into labor-intensive filling of houses with large amounts of sterile soil that was carefully compacted. But, as the number of burials increased into the Middle phase of occupation, the contradictions between burying the dead and all the labor required to sustain that burial seem to have reached unacceptable levels. In the Late occupation (6,500–6,300 BCE) of the mound there is a shift to more secondary burial in which bodies are moved after primary burial. Then, in the Final phase, burial in houses declines, finally disappearing in the sixth millennium. So here religious practices change in response to frictions between the different pathways—biological bodily decay, religious burial practices, and material house building.

Conclusion

All things are forces. They act like magnetic attractors or repulsers. This is because, as argued above, human being is thingly and depends on the world. Humans need things to think with, feel with, and be with—within whatever ontological frame. But there is an asymmetry between humans and things because things are not themselves passive constructs of human beings; rather, they have their own lives and forces, which are often in contradiction with human needs and desires. It is the contradictions in the heterogeneity of forces that lead to change.

Religious things often carry the strongest of forces. What creates the aura—the electric charge—in religious things? In this chapter, I have argued that the charge, the wave, is created because religion deals with deep emotions and ultimate questions, such as death and the wild. The religious deals with the beyond, the unfathomable, the mysterious. It deals with questions of suffering and being. It promises answers to deep questions. It looks into the past and the future. And so religious objects are embedded in concerns that are highly charged and ultimate. It is not that religion produces anger, nationalism, belonging, hatred—but that these characteristics are central to its endurance. Religious things feed off ultimate questions and draw them in.

In this chapter, I have been using the 9,000-year-old site of Çatalhöyük to illustrate my argument. In the case of Çatalhöyük, as well as the earlier site of Göbekli Tepe in southeast Turkey (Schmidt 2006), religious practices act as attractors for wild dangerous animals. At both sites there are hybrid forms such as human-animal or human-bird beings, as well as horns, fangs, and claws. And at Çatalhöyük there is a particular concern with death. Questions of ultimate concern draw together different strands that reinforce and revitalize each other. All forces decline over time, and so much human ingenuity is required to re-animate. Work is needed to sustain the power of religious things. New cattle and new dead have to be found, the house has to be rebuilt. In its entanglements with the world, religion draws in other things in order to re-animate itself; it has to be continually performed and worked at—drawing humans into further entanglements.

The house at Çatalhöyük is not a thing in itself, but a pulse within a force field or flow. As an active force it attracts and repels other forces. Taking a long-term view of the Neolithic of the Middle East (Hodder 2018), the burial of humans in or below houses began before the Neolithic period. So from early on the house acted as a religious attractor. And through the early Holocene (from 10,000 to 5,000 BCE) it is remarkable how more and more was drawn into the house. Symbolism and ritual are increasingly found, but also cooking and various forms of production were gradually brought in, as well as the storage of grain and other foodstuffs.

Religion is a powerful force because it deals with ultimate questions, but the force can only be made manifest through things. Religious things are charged, and they attract other forces to them. The result is a heterogeneous set of strands that are entwined around each other. In these bundled strands there emerge frictions and contradictions that lead to change. Religious things, by virtue of being material and biological, are tangled up with other forces that have their own trajectories, and it is this entanglement that leads to change. But religious things also have a strong tendency to path dependence. This is mainly because religion is tied up with so many other forces, many of them material and biological. But since religion deals with ultimate questions and the beyond, this path dependence also occurs because there is the possibility of a separation from daily life—so re-interpretation is always possible. But, equally, the fact that religion deals with ultimate questions leads to deep emotions, strongly held beliefs, and repetitive and thoroughly embodied practices; all this reinforces path dependence.

Thus, religious forces have a tendency to endure, however much they might be buffeted by change. But the force of all things tends to diminish through time. There is always a need for new sources of energy that can be dragooned in to sustain religious imperatives. At Çatalhöyük, wild bulls and the dead played their animation role—whether through animism, totemism, or doctrine (Descola 1994). At Göbekli Tepe, the power of religion was re-animated through magnificent and towering temples (Schmidt 2006). And in the modern world, too, a new massive mosque is seen as revitalizing religious devotion. There is an ever-present need to sustain and manage religious things. Our religious dependence on things leads inevitably to a greater entanglement with things, greater labor investment, increased expenditure and management, and so on. Religious forces are an important component in the overall process of increasing human-thing entanglement (Hodder 2020).

References

Arbuckle, B.S. 2013. "The Late Adoption of Cattle and Pig Husbandry in Neolithic Central Turkey." *Journal of Archaeological Science* 40 (4): 1805–1815.

Barad, K. 2007. *Meeting the Universe Halfway: Quantum Physics and the Entanglement of Matter and Meaning.* Durham, NC, and London: Duke University Press.

Bennett, J. 2010. *Vibrant Matter: A Political Ecology of Things.* Durham, NC: Duke University Press.

Bloch, M. 2010. "Is There Religion at Çatalhöyük … or Are There Just Houses?" In *Religion in the Emergence of Civilization. Çatalhöyük as a Case Study,* edited by Ian Hodder, 146–162. Cambridge: Cambridge University Press.

Buchli, V. 2015. *An Archaeology of the Immaterial.* London: Routledge.

Deleuze, Gilles, and Félix Guattari. 1987. *Capitalism and Schizophrenia, Volume 2: A Thousand Plateaus.* Minneapolis, MN: University of Minnesota Press.

Descola, P. 1994. *In the Society of Nature: A Native Ecology in Amazonia.* Cambridge: Cambridge University Press.

Haddow, S.D., E.M.J., Schotsmans, M. Milella, M.A. Pilloud, B. Tibbetts, B. Betz, and C.J. Knüsel. 2021. "Funerary Practices at Çatalhöyük. Body Treatment and Deposition." In *Peopling the Landscape of Çatalhöyük: Reports from the 2009–2017 Seasons,* edited by Ian Holder, 281–314. London: British Institute at Ankara.

Hodder, I. 2006. *The Leopard's Tale: Revealing the Mysteries of Çatalhöyük.* London: Thames and Hudson.

Hodder, I. 2012. *Entangled. An Archaeology of the Relationships between Humans and Things*. Oxford: Wiley Blackwell.

Hodder, I. 2016a. "More on History Houses at Çatalhöyük: A Response to Carleton et al." *Journal of Archaeological Science* 67 (March): 1–6.

Hodder, I. 2016b. *Studies in Human-Thing Entanglement*. http://www.ian-hodder.com/books/studies-human-thing-entanglement

Hodder, Ian. 2017. "Religion as a Technology of Entanglement." In *Human Origins and the Image of God: Essays in Honor of J. Wentzel Van Huyssteen*, edited by Christopher Lilley and Daniel J. Pedersen, 52–53. Grand Rapids, MI: William B. Eerdmans Publishing.

Hodder, I. 2018. "Things and the Slow Neolithic: The Middle Eastern Transformation." *Journal of Archaeological Method and Theory* 25 (1): 155–177.

Hodder, I. 2020. "The Paradox of the Long Term: Human Evolution and Entanglement." *Journal of the Royal Anthropological Institute* 26 (2): 389–411.

Hodder, I., and L. Meskell. 2011. "A Curious and Sometimes a Trifle Macabre Artistry." *Current Anthropology* 52 (2): 235–263.

Ingold, T. 2015. *The Life of Lines*. Abingdon and New York: Routledge.

Lewis-Williams, David, and David Pearce. 2005. *Inside the Neolithic Mind: Consciousness, Cosmos, and the Realm of the Gods*. London: Thames & Hudson.

Meyer, B. 2012. "Mediation and the Genesis of Presence. Towards a Material Approach to Religion." Inaugural Lecture, Utrecht, Utrecht University.

Schmidt, K. 2006. *Sie bauten die ersten Tempel: das rätselhafte Heiligtum der Steinzeitjäger: die archäologische Entdeckung am Göbekli Tepe*. Munich: C. H. Beck.

Sherburne, D.W. 1981. *A Key to Whitehead's Process and Reality*. Chicago, IL: University of Chicago Press.

Wolfhagen, J., K.C. Twiss, J.A. Mulville and G.A. Demirergi. 2021. "Examining Caprine Management and Cattle Domestication through Biometric Analyses at Çatalhöyük East (North and South Areas)." In *Peopling the Landscape of Çatalhöyük: Reports from the 2009–2017 Seasons*, edited by Ian Hodder, 181–198. London: British Institute at Ankara.

3.2

MEASURING ENTANGLEMENT IN MATERIAL TRACES OF RITUALIZED INTERACTION

Preferential Attachment in a Prehistoric Petroglyph Distribution

Tom Froese and Emiliano Gallaga Murrieta

Rock art distributions are often puzzling. Imagine you are part of an archaeological survey expedition to record petroglyphs in a large desert valley. You are on your way to a rock outcrop that once could have served as a highly visible landmark, and that you know from aerial photos was also in an area that served as a source of water. As you arrive with the morning sun rising into the sky behind you, you notice that a couple of its boulders are dotted with a few petroglyphs (Figure 3.2.1b). But as you walk around to the other side, you suddenly find yourself confronted with a large number of rock art panels, including a few with exceptionally dense concentrations of petroglyphs, to the point that they overlap and occlude each other (Figure 3.2.1a).

Why did their creators not take advantage of all the highly suitable surfaces on the other side of the rock outcrop? And even if they strongly preferred the western side, why did they not make more homogeneous use of that side's surfaces, rather than leaving some otherwise perfectly fine surfaces completely untouched while overcrowding others with petroglyphs?

This is a brief description of the rock art site called *El Peñón del Diablo*, located in the northern Mexican state of Chihuahua, which had its heyday in archaic times. But the site's uneven distribution of rock art motifs is just one illustrative and accessible example of a more general phenomenon: in many sites around the world the choices of where to make rock art seemed to have had little to do with a concern for leaving visual representations for the benefit of other observers. For example, the same phenomenon has been observed in the context of rock art from Ice Age Europe. In the words of prominent French archaeologist Clottes:

> In Chauvet cave, the first chamber (Chamber of the Bear Wallows) is the largest in the cave and its walls, smooth and white, would seem a priori to be highly suitable. But paintings are present only right at the back. This came as such a surprise to me that, at the beginning of our research in the cave, I asked the geologists on the team whether

DOI: 10.4324/9781351176231-21

Figure 3.2.1   Comparison of petroglyph manifestation on the west and east sides: (a) The west side of the *El Peñón del Diablo* has several densely clustered panels on it; the arrow shows an inexplicable empty space between two of them; (b) The east side with only two panels, #70 and #72, indicated by arrows. Photographs by Emiliano Gallaga.

some form of superficial degradation caused by natural phenomena (air currents, water flow, superficial calcification) might have occurred that could have destroyed any artwork. Their response ruled this out.

(Clottes 2016: 116)

Clottes suggests that the absence of images in the first chamber could be explained in terms of two principles. First, the artists might have preferred locations far away from the light of day, because the first paintings in Chauvet cave are found exactly at the edge of daylight, where one is already entering the permanent darkness of the cave but can still weakly perceive the light from the entranceway. Interestingly, this transition between light and darkness could have also played a role at *El Peñon*, given that the petroglyphs are concentrated on the western side of the outcrop, and thereby remain in the shadow of the first rays of the rising sun and, at the end of the day, receive the last rays of the setting sun.

Second, Clottes contends that the artists were not so much concerned with the technical suitability of a surface for producing a public image, but whether it personally attracted them or not: "The artist needed to know whether this particular wall was suitable—not physically, but spiritually—for affixing an image and for what kind of image, or whether, on the contrary, the wall refused it or was devoid of power" (Clottes 2016: 117). This materially mediated experience of what we may call a power spot would have been shaped by natural phenomena, for example, Clottes highlights the role of enhanced acoustics and the presence of natural reliefs. But there will also surely have been a social dimension to the selection process, and particularly the presence of rock art left behind from previous cave visitors. Moreover, as Clottes's account indicates, such a power spot may have been perceived as having some kind of agency of its own, either attracting or refusing material engagement. This perspective may seem strange to us, but other cultures saw rock as potentially animate, sentient, and sacred (Dean 2010). So, could it be that, rather than viewing the primary aim of such prehistoric rock art as the creation of images meant for public consumption, it is more appropriate to treat them as traces of materially mediated ritual interaction?

These two competing approaches have been actively debated over the last couple of decades in cognitive archaeology (for example, Hodgson and Pettitt 2018; Lewis-Williams 2002; Malafouris 2007). The field of cognitive archaeology tries to reconstruct the nature of the human mind in the deep past (Abramiuk 2012), and two broad orientations can be distinguished in that field, which to a large extent mirror the divisions of philosophy of mind and cognitive science more broadly (Clark 2014). We will refer to the traditional, dominant orientation as the *representational* approach, which holds that cognition essentially consists in the generation and manipulation of mental representations, such as updating internal world models—a process that is typically cashed out in computational, information-processing terms (Frith 2007). Traditionally, the underlying operational basis of the mind is spatiotemporally restricted to the brain, and in this sense the representational approach is at the same time also an *internalist* approach; it limits the boundaries of the mind to the brain (Hohwy 2013). In the context of cognitive archaeology, this approach is consequently interested in explaining the origins of the specifically human mind in terms of cognitive changes primarily driven by genetic evolution of the brain (for example, Henshilwood and Dubreuil 2011), with the implication that the archaeological artifactual record is relegated to a secondary role of being only an external cultural expression of these internal biological changes.

Here we will adopt an alternative, still relatively minor theoretical orientation called the *enactive* approach. This approach started as a way of integrating phenomenology of embodiment into cognitive science (Thompson 2007; Varela, Thompson, and Rosch 2017), but its scope includes research of our situatedness in a sociocultural environment, including work in archaeology (for example, Durt, Fuchs, and Tewes 2017; Hutto 2008; Malafouris 2013). The foundational assumption of this approach is that embodied action in the world is both a product of and a constitutive part of cognitive processes—and that this is also the case for culturally patterned forms of behavior (Di Paolo, Cuffari, and De Jaegher 2018; Hutchins 1995; Kirchhoff and Kiverstein 2019). In other words, the basis of the mind is not restricted to an individual's brain; rather, it consists in the complex, self-organizing interactions of the individual's brain, body, and world—including of course interactions with artifacts and other agents (Di Paolo, Buhrmann, and Barandiaran 2017). In this sense, the enactive approach is at the same time also an *externalist*—or, perhaps, more adequately a *relational* approach that adopts a systems perspective.

According to this approach, the origins of representations should not be explained by appealing only to a genetically primed brain, as if representations were biologically prebuilt inside the brain, only waiting to be externalized after the emergence of an appropriate sociocultural context. Instead, representations are enacted during the course of people's embodied interactions within a suitable sociocultural environment (Hutchins 2010). In the context of cognitive archaeology, this approach is therefore interested in explaining how representational practices could have emerged from people's material engagement, as well as how the resulting representational practices could have, in turn, shaped the evolution of the human mind (Froese 2019; Iliopoulos and Garofoli 2016; Malafouris 2007), eventually giving rise to the full range of symbolic cognition, including writing (Overmann 2020; Stewart 2010). Given that the starting point of the enactive approach is that the mind is, at its core, a self-organizing process of embodied interaction, it has found a natural ally in the *material engagement theory* developed in cognitive archaeology (Malafouris 2013; Renfrew 2004), which holds that our interaction with things shapes our mind. This integration of theoretical perspectives provides the background for this chapter's analysis of rock art. When applied to the origins of rock art in the Paleolithic (Old Stone Age) period for example, it becomes possible to argue that, when people's material engagement with cave walls left traces, these could then serve as the basis for the emergence of new forms of culturally mediated interaction, eventually scaffolding the development of specifically representational practices (Froese 2019).

Yet it may be necessary for the enactive approach to zoom out its perspective even further: as this approach continues to develop outward from its theoretical roots in the biology of the organism-environment system, and hence to cast a broader view over all the complex networks of interactions that humans engage in, it seems fruitful for it to also ally with recent archaeological work on *material entanglement* (Hodder 2012, 2018). This line of work has already attracted the interest of researchers in embedded, extended, and distributed cognition (Sutton 2020; Wheeler 2020), and there are potentially fruitful points of contact with the enactive approach to be explored as well. For instance, there is the key insight that spontaneously unfolding interactions can both enable and constrain further actions, potentially resulting in "entrapment" (Hodder 2012) or "bad habits" (Ramírez-Vizcaya and Froese 2019). And there is also the hypothesis that, over the long term, complex networks of these interaction processes can add up to irreversible, self-amplifying processes that shape human evolution (Froese 2018; Hodder 2020). We hope that this chapter's contribution to research in material religion can serve as a step toward a deeper dialogue among these approaches.

Toward an Enactive Approach to Rock Art

The enactive approach has developed a distinct interpretive framework for the archaeological record of prehistoric artifacts (Garofoli 2017; Malafouris 2008), including rock art (Froese 2019; Malafouris 2007). Before we develop our case study of rock art, it is useful to get a better understanding of this approach to rock art by considering how it differs from the default assumptions of the representational approach.

The representational approach, as the name suggests, tends to interpret the significance of rock art in representational terms. Thus, the intention of figurative imagery is often taken to be the creation of pictorial signs—of things perceived or imagined—while non-figurative imagery tends to be treated as abstract signs. It is therefore not surprising that from this perspective the study of rock art is treated akin to the decipherment or reading of a prehistoric "text": "Researchers are readers of the art that has been left behind, those visual cues in many ways presenting themselves like graphic 'texts' made of strange, unknown signs" (David 2017: 11). Moreover, analysis of the intentions and significance of the rock art is thereby *product*-oriented—in other words, biased to the static signs—while the active *process* of creating them is relegated to being just a contingent means of achieving that end goal. Consequently, in this traditional view rock art is also sharply distinguished from other forms of contingent substrate manipulation, such as the undulating lines found in some caves that were created by dragging fingers along a clay wall (cf. Clottes 2016). And, finally, the end goal of rock art is conceived of in the context of potential observers, who could in principle "read" these signs. This representational approach to rock art as "graphic texts" comes quite naturally to us modern observers, especially to literate academics, but it may over-intellectualize some forms of rock art.

The enactive approach does not rule out that some rock art was created for specifically representational purposes, but it questions the validity of generalizing that purpose. Moreover, the metaphor of a graphic text does not fit very well with the archaeological record, especially regarding rock art from Paleolithic caves and certain hunter-gatherer contexts. We know that in many cases observability by others was not a primary concern of the artists, whereas a lot of attention was paid to the affordances for material engagement (Robert 2017). This is reflected by a preference for suggestive rock forms, suitable substrates, and strenuous and messy access routes (Clottes 2016; Hodgson and Pettitt 2018; Lewis-Williams 2002). In this view, there is a complex developmental continuity from the earliest forms of material engagement, such as getting one's hands dirty by leaving finger traces on cave walls, to the appearance of hand stencils and figurative cave art (Froese 2019). In all of these cases a concern for embodied interaction with the cave environment dominated, with the main difference being that eventually this concrete interaction process started to incorporate more conventional forms into the material engagement. Thus, especially when trying to understand the earliest traces of cultural expression of a region, rock art may be more appropriately conceptualized as concrete traces of an interaction process involving graphical acts rather than as abstract graphical signs that were made in order to be read like a text (Malafouris 2007).

As such, the perceived meaning of such traces to prehistoric observers may have had to do with how they were transforming the surface—for example by marking it—while participating in the realization of certain kinds of materially mediated rituals, sometimes even echoing the precise movements that were used. For example, a zigzag line on a cave wall is a material trace left behind by a person's zigzag movement, and the surface can be thought of as a material interface affording such kinds of patterned interactions. While it is possible to interpret this trace in terms of the artist's intention to leave a sign with a particular meaning, say a "water snake" signaling the presence of water to others, we should not ignore the importance of the act itself. Arguably, what also could have mattered to the maker of the sign was the concrete experience of being in that time and place, and personally engaging with the surface, especially if it was a culturally recognized special place. We could even go so far as to say that it mattered less that the graphical patterns also had a representational meaning; what mattered was the brute existential fact of the performance of its making, whereby the mark maker could come into direct contact with the powerful forces that animated the place. The bodily performance of a culturally significant pattern during this concrete material engagement—expressed by the arm and hand movements that embody the pattern in contact with the surface and record it for posterity as a graphical trace—can then be understood as a symbolically mediated way of intensifying this encounter between self and other. An illustration of this hypothetical example is provided in Figure 3.2.2.

A Methodological Challenge

It is methodologically difficult to scientifically arbitrate between the representational and enactive approaches to prehistoric rock art. So far there has been a concern with qualitative

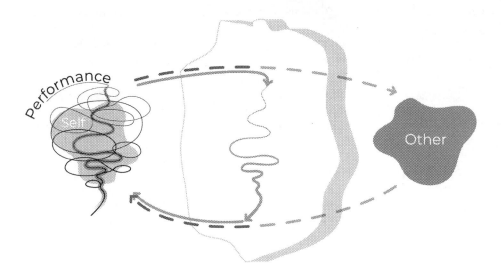

Figure 3.2.2   An enactive approach to prehistoric rock art. The artist intends to interact ritually with the powers that are animating a special place, including by manipulating its surface, and this materially mediated aspect of the performance remains visible as traces on the surface. Observers of these traces can see in them an encounter between Self and "Other," especially if the traces include culturally meaningful patterns that highlight this intention of the engagement. In this way, the traces transform the appearance of the surface, making it stand out from other similar surfaces, and increasing its attraction for future ritual interactions. Diagram by Maria Gohlke.

hypotheses (Froese 2019; Malafouris 2007), as the enactive approach gives rise to a number of general criteria. The earliest forms of rock art tend to involve the following:

- Simple marks and geometric motifs predominate, these likely made without concern for their precise execution (for example, the emphasis was on performing the interaction with the surface rather than on its resulting material trace).
- If figurative motifs are present, they likely are not very realistic.
- The location of the marks suggests an intention to materially engage with the rock's surface (for example, by affording a particular kind of interaction, such as completing naturally suggestive contours or guiding placement of hand stencils).
- The location of the marks suggests a concern for a special place that facilitates interaction with what lives in or lies behind the rock (for example, by literally revealing the rock's interior or by being particularly expressive of its inner character).
- The location of the marks suggests it was chosen with little concern for access or enhanced visibility to external observers.
- When it appears the trace itself was significant, it was likely produced with the aim of enhancing the potency or duration of the interaction—as exemplified by hand stencils that first enhance the resemblance of hand and rock by covering them both with paint and subsequently leave a permanent echo of that direct contact.

Most of these criteria for the earliest forms of rock art have already been discussed in the literature, especially in the context of the shamanic hypothesis (Clottes 2016; Clottes and

Lewis-Williams 1998; Lewis-Williams 2002) and with respect to altered states of consciousness more broadly (Froese 2013, 2015; Froese, Woodward, and Ikegami 2013). Even those rock art researchers who prefer not to speculate about the prevalence of shamanistic cultures in deep prehistory—and who hence do not appeal to the extreme altered states of consciousness assumed by the shamanic hypothesis—are in broad agreement with these qualitative criteria (Hodgson and Pettitt 2018). Nevertheless, the importance of material engagement, and of the entanglement to which it gives rise, has been difficult to measure and quantify.

Here we propose a novel testing method: we argue that the distributions of rock art at a site should reflect whether the artists' intention was focused on the representational *product* of their activity or on the *process* of material engagement itself. The representational approach would expect rock art to be equally spatially distributed across surfaces, like the paintings on the walls of a gallery or text on a page, because the artists were concerned with making the traces more visible or "readable." They would avoid compromising public visibility of an image by reducing clutter and would shun overlapping it with other images (in contrast to what we see in panel A of Figure 3.2.4, for example). However, to the extent that the rock art consists of traces of ritual performances, and that these can serve as signs of previous successful interactions with the sacred via a specific surface of a special place, we can expect that such traces actually get entangled with subsequent performances at the same location. Hence, the enactive approach, and its claim that material engagement with such surfaces was more important than was the artistic outcome per se, leads us to expect a skewed distribution whereby some areas are more crowded with rock art. This preferential attachment produces an accrual of sacred power at particular surfaces. In other words, we expect a self-amplifying effect, akin to the "Matthew effect" (Perc 2014), which is the phenomenon that the rich tend to get richer and the potent even more powerful, an effect that is also studied in sociology in terms of cumulative advantage and "success breeds success." This phenomenon has been intensely studied by network science since the 1990s (Barabási 2002; Watts 2003), and we now know that this kind of skewed distribution, known as a "power law" to refer to its exponential change, tends to consistently emerge in social systems where people select among a broad range of choices according to their preferences. To test this methodological proposal, we analyzed the petroglyph distribution at *El Peñón del Diablo*, Chihuahua, Mexico.

Description of El Peñón del Diablo Site and Petroglyphs

In mid-2014, a series of meetings was held between the authorities of the Municipality of Janos and the staff of the *Instituto Nacional de Antropología e Historia* (INAH) Chihuahua Center with the aim of supporting the management of the municipality's cultural heritage. Among the points that were addressed was a request of support for recording and research at the site known as *El Peñón del Diablo* (The Devil's Crag). Due to the site's proximity to the community, it is a recreation area that is visited and used regularly, so there is neither adequate protection nor control of access, resulting in it being exposed to vandalism. Similarly, by being located within areas of cultivation and livestock breeding, the site is at risk of being lost little by little. In response to these risks, the Municipality of Janos requested the support of archeologists from the School of Anthropology and History of Northern Mexico (EAHNM), Chihuahua, to record the petroglyphs and survey the surrounding site in order to better understand and communicate its importance as well as to contribute to its conservation and promotion as a patrimonial asset of the community (Gallaga and García 2019).

The site *El Peñón del Diablo* is located in the Northwestern portion of the state of Chihuahua, within the municipality of Janos, just 2.6 kilometers southwest of the community of the same name, at an altitude of 1,366 meters above sea level (Figure 3.2.3). The locale, from which the site receives its name, is a natural outcrop of crystalline tuff that stands out in the valley on which a series of images were made, one of which is an anthropomorphic character with horns on the head that stands out and is locally known as *"el diablo"* (Spanish for "the devil") (Figure 3.2.4). The *Peñón* is approximately 18 meters high with a northwest-southeast orientation and a length of 66 meters (Figure 3.2.5). It is located in the geographical region known as the intermountain valleys of Janos and is characterized by grasslands, xerophilous scrub, and oak and coniferous forests (CONABIO 2014; CONANP 2006). The location of the site should not surprise us, since it is located at the center of a fertile valley in which there was a spring—which today is dry, possibly from overexploitation of the aquifer. But in the rainy season the old riverbed fills with water and the valley comes back to life, attracting all the desert wildlife. The site is about 5 kilometers east of the Casas Grandes River and the Cerro Juanaqueña site (a relevant archaic site) (Hard and Roney 1998); the later site of Paquimé is 60 kilometers to the south (Gallaga and García 2019; Gallaga, Moreno Alvarado, and Guzmán Aguirre 2016).

Since the designs of the petroglyphs of *El Peñón del Diablo* are not very deep in the rock—in other words, they did not leave a well-marked groove, but only broke the surface layer of the rock—we know that they were made by a combination of techniques: scraping and crushing/beating. A total of 78 panels were identified, each consisting of one or more rocks, and including a total of 651 petroglyphs. Each one was recorded, drawn, and photographed. As we mentioned, this data was recorded as part of an archaeological survey of the area. Although there is a presence of petroglyphs around all sides of the *Peñón*, most of them are concentrated on the western side—perhaps because that side of it is shadowed in the morning, or because it is well lit at dusk, and thus ideal for ritual activity. In addition, at some placements sunlight shines through cracks in the *Peñón* during sunrise on special days marked by astronomical events, including solstices (Muñoz 2017).

Subsequently, the petroglyphs were categorized through the framework established by Viramontes (2005), resulting in 231 figurative motifs and 420 geometric motifs (Figure 3.2.6). Anthropomorphic (145) and zoomorphic (68) figures predominate the first category; lines (160), circles (99), and triangles (29) were the most common designs in the second category. On top of this, three different rock art styles have been identified: the Desert Abstract (Archaic period 8,500/5,500 BCE to 100/200 CE), the Jornada Mogollon area (Archaic period 8,500/5,500 BCE to CE 100/200), and Medio Period (Paquime ceramic period 1,150–1,450 CE). The Desert Abstract style is associated with the Archaic period and is distinguished by motifs such as zigzag lines, wavy lines, concentric circles, rake shapes, and simple circles with dots and suns with rays—as well as hand and footprints, traces of animals, and anthropomorphic figures (Schaafsma 1980, 1992; VanPool, Rakita, and VanPool 2009: 53). The Jornada Mogollon style is also associated with the Archaic period; it is characterized by its naturalistic character and anthropomorphic representations of "hunting scenes, with animals such as mountain sheep or deer, and humans with headdresses who have shaman like qualities" (Sutherland 2006: 9). The motifs identified for the Medio Period (1,150–1,450 CE) are lizards, snakes, tadpoles, outlines of crosses, circles with rays, and anthropomorphic figures with horns and carrying a staff—as well as human figures with expressive arms and legs (Schaafsma 1980, 1992, 2005; VanPool et al. 2009: 54). The Desert Abstract style was by far the most prevalent at the site, and we therefore do not further distinguish between these petroglyph styles in what follows.

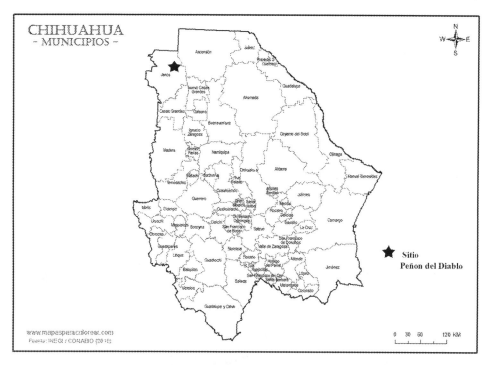

Figure 3.2.3   Location of *Peñón del Diablo* site in the state of Chihuahua, Mexico. The site is located in a municipality bordering the state of New Mexico, USA. Map modified by Emiliano Gallaga, from www.mapasparacolorear.com.

Figure 3.2.4   Some illustrative examples of the petroglyphs at the *El Peñón del Diablo* site: (a) Panel #25, a surface densely clustered with petroglyphs; (b) Panel #18, where the figure locally known as "*El Diablo*" is found. Photographs by Emiliano Gallaga.

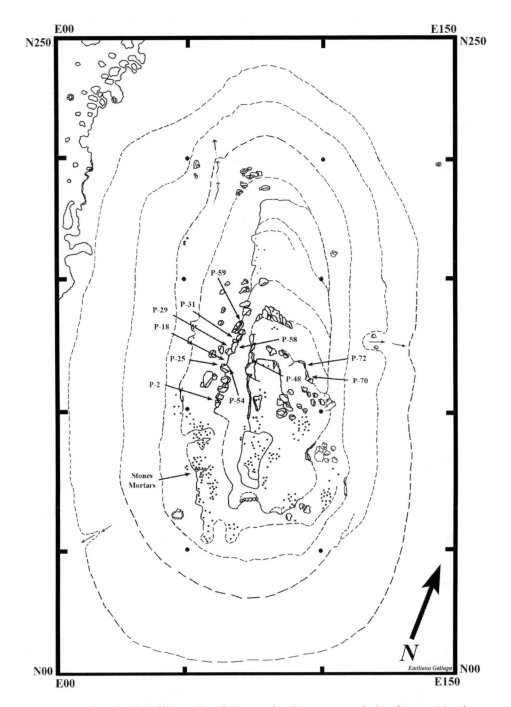

Figure 3.2.5   El Peñón del Diablo map. Details discussed in the text are marked in the map. Map drawn by Emiliano Gallaga.

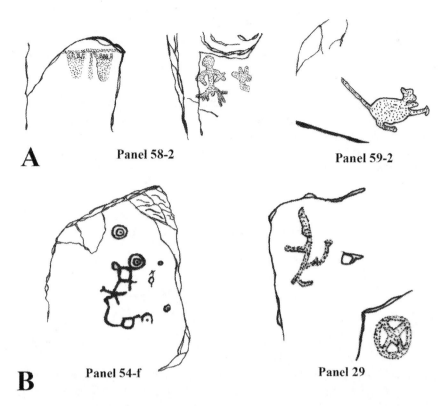

Figure 3.2.6   Some examples of *El Peñón* petroglyphs: (a) Figurative petroglyph examples: panel 58-2 shows motifs from the Desert Abstract style, while panel 59-2 shows a rare example of what seems to be a cat; (b) Non-figurative and geometrical petroglyph examples of the Desert Abstract style from two panels. Drawings by Emiliano Gallaga.

Archaeological Context: Life around El Peñón del Diablo

Investigations at rock art sites often focus on only the rock art, leaving the rest of the site/area unexplored. Yet the rock art may well be part of a broader set of elements and materials that indicate other types of activities carried out by the community that made the petroglyphs, or the community that occupied/used the areas surrounding them. In the present case, it was already known thanks to previous investigations that the site was much more than simply a rock art site. At its base, more than 200 fixed mortars were documented, which have been interpreted as "the center of an extensive mesquite pod processing site during the Archaic Period" (VanPool, Rakita, and VanPool 2015: 145).

Accordingly, the survey also included surface collections in two phases. One total collection is set in a grid of 250 meters by 150 meters; another, less systematic prospection, was made over the surrounding area of the *El Peñón* site using transects set 20 to 30 meters apart. The primary grid yielded 13,137 lithic artifacts (totaling 216 kilograms). The lithic sample consisted of 12,656 flakes, of which 267 were obsidian; and 531 cores, 253 artifacts, and 228 projectile points. Preliminary results indicate that though some materials were prepared at the *Peñón*, the vast majority of the materials were pre-worked at another location, probably at the raw material sources. So far, seven types of projectile point have been identified, most of which have a chronological distribution that places them between the Middle (3,000–1,000

267

BCE) and Late Archaic periods (1,000 BCE to CE 200). In addition, a total of twenty-five ovens (identified as concentrations of fire-cracked rock on the surface), five possible structures, and an eroded human burial were registered, but there was no household in the site (Gallaga and García 2019).

Due to its location and time period, the *El Peñon del Diablo* site would have a strong interaction with the *Cerro Juanaqueña* and related "Cerro de trincheras" (terraced-hill) sites that flourished in the hills around the valley during the Late Archaic period around 3,000 years before the present (Hard and Roney 1998). The massive *Cerro Juanaqueña* site is envisioned as having been a primary base camp mostly used for sleeping and some item production, while other activities were performed in the valley. It is possible that the *El Peñón del Diablo* site was one of the many areas the Juanaqueña people used for ceremonies, social gathering, food consumption, and other social activities. As such, it would show us an important part of the multiple activities carried out by the inhabitants of this community outside the hill, as other researchers have already mentioned (Gallaga and García 2019; VanPool et al. 2009).

The material evidence found around the site supports the claim that *El Peñón del Diablo* was not an isolated site in this part of the valley, but rather part of a larger complex of human presence and activity. In addition to the hundreds of petroglyphs, a large amount of mortars was found around the outcrop. These mortars were slowly carved into the bedrock through repeated grinding; they indicate that large numbers of people repeatedly returned to this site over long stretches of time. Thus, at first glance, one could think that it is only a place of ceremonial or ritual use; however, the investigations carried out both at the *Peñón* and in the surrounding area allow us to come to a different conclusion. Surely there was a ritual use or meaning of the *Peñón*; however, the site was also an area that was occupied, at least temporarily or seasonally. It also shows a great diversity of activities that transformed the natural environment into a cultural landscape recognized by communities that lived in the area for many generations. Accordingly, the activities surrounding the petroglyphs could have been of a communal nature since there is no impediment for them to have been observed by the people temporarily settled at the site (Bech 2017; Muñoz 2017; Murray 2007; Rodríguez 2016). It is plausible that the *Peñón* site served as a special place—that is, a public place at which people from different terraced-hill communities in the wider area would gather for ritual, exchange, and other social activities on solstices (Gallaga and García 2019). This phenomenon of special places serving to integrate broad social networks is consistently found throughout the world and is associated with the rise of stateless social complexity (Stanish 2017).

In sum, we can assume that the activities resulting in this corpus of petroglyphs were diverse. In this region of the Chihuahuan desert, a spring/waterhole would have been a highly attractive, life-giving feature, which presumably also imbued the location with a magical connotation. Accordingly, many of the petroglyphs were most likely associated with ceremonial/ritual activities, some of which were probably astronomical in nature. Others were probably associated with cultural or community affiliation, and/or claiming the place as theirs (Gallaga and García 2019). This last claim is supported by the fact that not all of the cultural groups that frequented the area left their distinctive rock art at the site, such as the Apaches. Unfortunately for us, there is no longer a living community that can claim ties to the archaeological remains of *El Peñon del Diablo*. As an archaic hunter-gatherer group that was experimenting with agriculture, they possibly transformed themselves into a sedentary agricultural community; with the passage of time, they might have become part of the inhabitants of the nearby Paquime site of the Medio period (1,150–1,450 CE).

This archaeological survey allows us to paint a richer picture of life around the *Peñón*. When you are in the highest part of the rock outcrop, your view perfectly dominates the valley around it. With a little imagination, it is not very difficult to glimpse it as it could have looked on a day in the Archaic period. The site would have been blessed with water from the nearby marsh, attracting birds and turtles and, of course, people. Some of those people would be crushing the seedpods of the nearby mesquite trees in the mortars at the base of the *Peñón*; others would be working stones to make projectile points or other stone tools. Looking past the marsh a little further south, one would see smoke over the area where another group of people was sitting around the ovens preparing food—such as agave hearts, and juicy portions of deer meat or rabbit—all of which would be eaten following the next solstice ceremony. Perhaps it was during such ceremonies that the communities' spiritual leaders interacted with the divine forces of nature residing in the site—and thereby leaving traces of new images on the walls of the crag of *El Diablo*.

Methods

We propose that one way to test the enactive approach is to measure the distribution of rock art and examine whether it is skewed in accordance with a power law. Effectively, we argue that if the material engagement with special places is important, then some surfaces will tend to attract more people to connect with them, which in turn makes it even more likely to attract more people, and so forth. If this appeal to preferential attachment is on the right track, then we can adopt measures from network science that are designed to capture the popularity of people or things in terms of the skewed distribution of the numbers of their social connections or followers. To give just one contemporary example, this effect has been observed in the evolution of the structure of the Internet (Huberman 2001), but also in more specialized applications such as in recent social tagging services (Hashimoto, Oka, and Ikegami 2017).

If preferential attachment is at play in a social network, the prediction is that there should be an inverse correlation between the number of connections and the number of nodes with that number of connections: there is a small probability for a node to have a large number of connections, while there is an increasingly higher probability for a node to have an increasingly smaller number of connections. For our purposes, we treated the panels identified by the archaeological survey as the nodes, while the petroglyphs are the connections. For the survey some panels had been divided into subpanels based on different features, but we treated them as a single rock panel for our analysis.

We performed our analysis according to the following procedure: for each possible number of petroglyphs (k) on a panel's surface, which for this site was within the range $k = [1, 25]$, we counted the number of panels whose surface had a particular number of petroglyphs (n_k). This allowed us to calculate the proportion of those particular panels with respect to the total amount of panels (N). We denote this proportion as the probability of a panel surface having a particular number of petroglyphs, $P(k)$, which is given by the following equation:

$$P(k) = n_k / N$$

A secondary aim of our analysis was to take into consideration the specific kind of petroglyph forms associated with the panels. This is not the context in which to do a systematic analysis of all the petroglyph forms, but we can usefully distinguish between figurative motifs and all other, non-figurative (including non-identifiable) motifs. This distinction allows us to test whether there is a bias toward non-figurative forms for the panels containing the largest number of petroglyphs (large k). For if it is indeed the case that more densely worked panels were particularly attractive because of their potential for material engagement, then we might expect more simple graphic elements than elaborated figurative images.

We therefore calculated the average percentage of figurative motifs for each panel petroglyph cluster size k, with the expectation that there will be a decrease of the average percentage of figurative motifs with increasing cluster size.

Results

If the artists had distributed the petroglyphs in a more or less equally spaced manner across these panels, then we would have found the distribution of petroglyphs centered on an average of around 10 petroglyphs per panel. This is not what we found. The distribution of petroglyphs is skewed in the form of a power law, as we had expected, with the highest proportion of surfaces featuring very small numbers of petroglyphs—followed by a quick drop in proportion, and a long tail toward increasingly lower proportions of surfaces with higher numbers of petroglyphs. Some illustrative examples of different cluster sizes are shown in Figure 3.2.7, while the main results of our analysis are summarized in Figure 3.2.8a.

To our knowledge this is the first time that it has been reported that a petroglyph distribution is consistent with an explanation centered around the social phenomenon of preferential

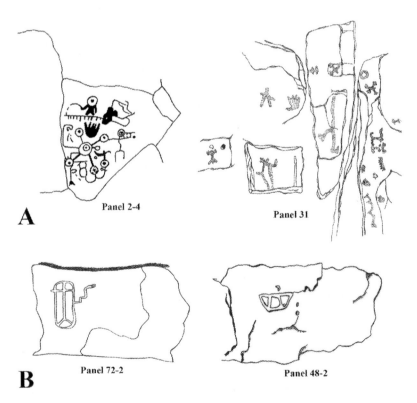

A Panel 2-4

Panel 31

B Panel 72-2

Panel 48-2

Figure 3.2.7   Some examples of the distribution of the panels: (a) Rock panels with several petroglyphs in a cluster; (b) Rock panels with isolated motifs. Drawings by Emiliano Gallaga.

attachment. Admittedly, the fit to the power law curve could be better, but the overall trend is still very suggestive, especially given that the *Peñón* has less than 100 panels, whereas studies of modern social phenomena typically work with cleaner datasets that are larger by several orders of magnitude.

Regarding the distribution of rock art with figurative as opposed to non-figurative motifs, after averaging across all panels of a particular cluster size, we found that the average percentage of figurative motifs is only 38 percent. In other words, most motifs are non-figurative, which is consistent with our general expectation that there was more of a concern with material engagement—and hence comparably less concern with producing elaborate figurative motifs. However, surprisingly, we were unable to confirm our expectation of a decrease in the percentage of figurative motifs with respect to increased petroglyph cluster size: as shown in Figure 3.2.8b, the average percentage of 38 percent is notably independent of cluster size. There is more variation for smaller cluster sizes, but this is expected given that fluctuations around the average will have a comparably larger effect when the total number of motifs is smaller.

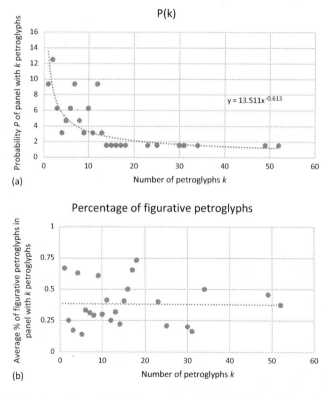

(a)

(b)

Figure 3.2.8a Distributions of petroglyphs. Scatter plot of the probability *P* of a rock panel with a particular number of petroglyphs *k*. Most rock panel surfaces have very few petroglyphs, while very few surfaces contain many petroglyphs.

Figure 3.2.8b Scatter plot of the average percentage of petroglyphs consisting in figurative motifs for a rock panel with a particular number of petroglyphs *k*. Overall, 38% of petroglyphs are figurative; this average is independent of petroglyph cluster size *k*.

What could explain this independence of the ratio of figurative to non-figurative motifs with respect to cluster size? It could indicate that these two kinds of motifs were actually not significantly distinct categories from the perspective of the artists. Thus, perhaps even the figurative motifs should be treated as equally part of the performance. For instance, in the case of figurative paintings in the Paleolithic caves of Europe, Lewis-Williams (2002: 193) has questioned the importance of representational reference: "In all probability the makers did not suppose that they 'stood for' real animals." In addition, the solidity of the rock panels may have also played a role, given that material engagement only resulted in traces if the artists used tools with the aim of penetrating the surface of the rock. Given this material barrier to making rock art, any extra effort of elaborating complex figures rather than simple marks may be negligible. It would be interesting to do a comparative analysis to see if the ratio changes across cluster size if the substrate is softer, like clay cave walls.

Discussion

The distribution of the petroglyph concentrations at the *Peñón* makes a relatively good fit with a power law, but the fit could be improved. Part of the problem is that this is a small site; since the rock art corpus we analyzed is still a comparatively small dataset, deviations of data points from the exact power law distribution are to be expected. Future work could apply this method to rock art datasets that are orders of magnitude larger than ours, which should hopefully provide a better fit. Moreover, in this exploratory analysis we worked with the raw counts of rock panel surfaces and petroglyphs while ignoring other possible factors that could influence the distribution. For instance, thematic relatedness could explain some cases of co-occurrences of petroglyphs on one rock, while smaller rock surfaces and/or larger petroglyphs could tend to decrease co-occurrence. We believe that such factors did not influence our findings in any significant way, but future work could, for instance, divide the rock surface into equally spaced areas in order to eliminate variation in panel size.

We do not know how many people were involved in the creation of this rock art. It would be interesting if we could assign each petroglyph to a particular maker, which would allow us to develop a more detailed account of the entanglement between artists and rocks. However, for present purposes this information about authorship is not essential. Our proposal is that the placement of the petroglyphs was primarily driven by processes akin to preferential attachment in the context of material engagement rather than for representational purposes. This proposal is not dependent on whether the distribution of petroglyphs reflects the preferences of a large group of people that each created only one or few petroglyphs, or of a select number of people that created multiple petroglyphs. Certainly, our proposal would be further strengthened if it could be shown that rocks with high densities of petroglyphs are the product of temporally extended processes, involving multiple people and perhaps even multiple generations. That this expectation is on the right track is indicated by the temporal distribution of the rock art. Most of it was made during the Archaic period (8,500/5,500 BCE to 100/200 CE), but it also attracted artists during the later Medio Period (Paquime ceramic period 1,150–1,450 CE). This is an interesting topic for future research.

Our proposal could also be further strengthened by applying the method to a suitable control case. In particular, when applied to a set of visual signs that we know were mainly made for representational purposes, we should not find evidence of a distribution with a power law. This is intuitively true of modern contexts such as art galleries, which aim to show each artwork in a stand-alone manner and hence have a narrow range of densities of artworks. Nevertheless, this contrasting expectation should also be confirmed with rock art sites, especially if there are more recent ones for which we have good ethnographic information confirming that the artists' primary intent was to create public representations. In this way network science could help to further investigate the relationship between material engagement and material entanglement in prehistoric rock art.

References

Abramiuk, Marc A. 2012. *The Foundations of Cognitive Archaeology.* Cambridge: MIT Press.

Barabási, Albert-László. 2002. *Linked: How Everything is Connected to Everything Else and What It Means for Business, Science, and Everyday Life.* New York: Basic Books.

Bech, Julio A. 2017. *Símbolos de la Lluvia y de la Abundancia en el Arte Rupestre del Desierto de Sonora. Lineamientos Generales para la Interpretación del Arte Rupestre y Estudio de Caso.* Mexico: ENAH-INAH.

Clark, Andy. 2014. *Mindware: An Introduction to the Philosophy of Cognitive Science.* 2nd ed. New York: Oxford University Press.

Clottes, Jean. 2016. *What Is Paleolithic Art? Cave Paintings and the Dawn of Human Creativity.* Translated by Oliver Y. Martin and Robert D. Martin. Chicago, IL: Chicago University Press.

Clottes, Jean and David Lewis-Williams. 1998. *The Shamans of Prehistory: Trance and Magic in the Painted Caves.* New York: Harry N. Abrams.

CONABIO. 2014. *La Biodiversidad en Chihuahua: Estudio de Estado.* Mexico: Comisión Nacional para el Conocimiento y Uso de la Biodiversidad (CONABIO).

CONANP. 2006. *Estudio Previo Justificativo para el Establecimiento del Área Natural Protegida: Reserva de la Biosfera Janos, Chihuahua, Mexico.* Mexico: Comisión Nacional de Áreas Naturales Protegidas (CONANP).

David, Bruno. 2017. *Cave Art.* New York: Thames & Hudson.

Dean, Carolyn. 2010. *A Culture of Stone: Inka Perspectives on Rock.* Durham, NC: Duke University Press.

Di Paolo, Ezequiel A., Thomas Buhrmann and Xiaber E. Barandiaran. 2017. *Sensorimotor Life: An Enactive Proposal.* Oxford: Oxford University Press.

Di Paolo, Ezequiel A., Elena Clare Cuffari and Hanne De Jaegher. 2018. *Linguistic Bodies: The Continuity Between Life and Language.* Cambridge: MIT Press.

Durt, Christoph, Thomas Fuchs, and Christian Tewes, eds. 2017. *Embodiment, Enaction, and Culture: Investigating the Constitution of the Shared World.* Cambridge: MIT Press.

Frith, Chris. 2007. *Making Up The Mind: How the Brain Creates Our Mental World.* Oxford: Blackwell.

Froese, Tom. 2013. "Altered States and the Prehistoric Ritualization of the Modern Human Mind." In *Breaking Convention: Essays on Psychedelic Consciousness,* edited by Cameron Adams, Anna Waldstein, Ben Sessa, David Luke, and David King, 10–21. London: Strange Attractor Press.

Froese, Tom. 2015. "The Ritualised Mind Alteration Hypothesis of the Origins and Evolution of the Symbolic Human Mind. *Rock Art Research* 32 (1): 90–97.

Froese, Tom. 2018. "Ritual Anti-Structure as an Alternate Pathway to Social Complexity? The Case of Ancient Teotihuacan, Central Mexico." *Material Religion* 14 (3): 420–422.

Froese, Tom. 2019. "Making Sense of the Chronology of Paleolithic Cave Painting from the Perspective of Material Engagement Theory." *Phenomenology and the Cognitive Sciences* 18: 91–112.

Froese, Tom, Alexander Woodward, and Takashi Ikegami. 2013. "Turing Instabilities in Biology, Culture, and Consciousness? On the Enactive Origins of Symbolic Material Culture." *Adaptive Behavior* 21 (3): 199–214.

Gallaga, Emiliano, Jesús Emmanuel Moreno Alvarado, and Marisela Guzmán Aguirre. 2016. *Informe Final No Publicado del Proyecto Salvamento del Rancho Santa María, Municipio de Galeana, Chihuahua.* Mexico: Consejo de Arqueología.

Gallaga, Emiliano, and Tobías García. 2019. "El Peñon del Diablo: A Rock Art Site in the Janos Valley, Chihuahua." In *Recent Research in Jornada Mogollon Archaeology: Proceedings from the 20th Jornada Mogollon Conference,* edited by George Mallof, 127–140. El Paso, TX: El Paso Museum of Archaeology.

Garofoli, Duilio. 2017. "Ornamental Feathers Without Mentalism: A Radical Enactive View on Neanderthal Body Adornment. In *Embodiment, Enaction, and Culture: Investigating the Constitution of the Shared World,* edited by Christoph Durt, Thomas Fuchs, and Christian Tewes, 279–305. Cambridge: MIT Press.

Hard, Robert J., and John R. Roney. 1998. "A Massive Terraced Village Complex in Chihuahua, Mexico, 3000 Years Before Present." *Science* 279: 1661–1664.

Hashimoto, Yasuhiro, Mizuki Oka, and Takashi Ikegami. 2017. "Anomalous Popularity Growth in Social Tagging Ecosystems." *arXiv,* 1711.02980v1.

Henshilwood, Christopher S., and Benoît Dubreuil. 2011. "The Still Bay and Howiesons Poort, 77–59 ka: Symbolic Material Culture and the Evolution of the Mind during the African Middle Stone Age." *Current Anthropology* 52 (3): 361–380.

Hodder, Ian. 2012. *Entangled: An Archaeology of the Relationships between Humans and Things.* Chichester: Wiley-Blackwell.

Hodder, Ian. 2018. "Material Entanglement." In *The Encyclopedia of Archaeological Sciences,* edited by Sandra L. López Varela. Chichester: John Wiley & Sons.

Hodder, Ian. 2020. "The Paradox of the Long Term: Human Evolution and Entanglement." *Journal of the Royal Anthropological Institute* 26: 389–411.

Hodgson, Derek, and Paul Pettitt. 2018. "The Origins of Iconic Depictions: A Falsifiable Model Derived from the Visual Science of Palaeolithic Cave Art and World Rock Art." *Cambridge Archaeological Journal* 28 (4): 591–612.

Hohwy, Jakob. 2013. *The Predictive Mind.* Oxford: Oxford University Press.

Huberman, Bernardo A. 2001. *The Laws of the Web: Patterns in the Ecology of Information.* Cambridge: MIT Press.

Hutchins, Edwin. 1995. *Cognition in the Wild.* Cambridge: MIT Press.

Hutchins, Edwin. 2010. "Enaction, Imagination, and Insight." In *Enaction: Toward a New Paradigm for Cognitive Science,* edited by John Stewart, Oliver Gapenne, and Ezequiel A. Di Paolo, 425–450. Cambridge: MIT Press.

Hutto, Daniel D. 2008. *Folk Psychological Narratives: The Sociocultural Basis of Understanding Reasons.* Cambridge: MIT Press.

Iliopoulos, Antonis, and Duilio Garofoli. 2016. "The Material Dimensions of Cognition: Reexamining the Nature and Emergence of the Human Mind." *Quaternary International* 405: 1–7.

Kirchhoff, Michael D., and Julian Kiverstein. 2019. *Extended Consciousness and Predictive Processing: A Third Wave View.* Abingdon: Routledge.

Lewis-Williams, David. 2002. *The Mind in the Cave: Consciousness and the Origins of Art.* London: Thames & Hudson.

Malafouris, Lambros. 2007. "Before and Beyond Representation: Towards an Enactive Conception of the Paleolithic Image." In *Image and Imagination: A Global Prehistory of Figurative Representation,* edited by Colin Renfrew and Iain Morley, 289–302. Cambridge: McDonald Institute for Archaeological Research.

Malafouris, Lambros. 2008. "Beads for a Plastic Mind: The 'Blind Man's Stick' (BMS) Hypothesis and the Active Nature of Material Culture." *Cambridge Archaeological Journal* 18 (3): 401–414.

Malafouris, Lambros. 2013. *How Things Shape the Mind: A Theory of Material Engagement.* Cambridge: MIT Press.

Muñoz, Alan. 2017. "Estudio Arqueoastronomico de los Petrograbados del Sitio El Peñon del Diablo, Janos, Chihuahua." BA thesis, EAHNM.

Murray, William B. 2007. *Arte Rupestre del Noreste.* Mexico: Gobierno del Estado de Nuevo León.

Overmann, Karenleigh A. 2020. "The Material Difference in Human Cognition." *Adaptive Behavior* 29 (2): 123–135.

Perc, Matjaž. 2014. "The Matthew Effect in Empirical Data." *Journal of the Royal Society Interface* 11: 98.

Ramírez-Vizcaya, Susana, and Tom Froese. 2019. "The Enactive Approach to Habits: New Concepts for the Cognitive Science of Bad Habits and Addiction." *Frontiers in Psychology* 10, article 301: 1–12.

Renfrew, Colin. 2004. "Towards a Theory of Material Engagement." In *Rethinking Materiality: The Engagement of Mind with the Material World,* edited by Elizabeth DeMarrais, Chris Gosden, and Colin Renfrew, 23–31. Cambridge: McDonald Institute for Archaeological Research.

Robert, Eric. 2017. "The Role of the Cave in the Expression of Prehistoric Societies." *Quaternary International* 432: 59–65.

Rodríguez, Francisco.2016. *El Arte Rupestre en México: Guía para el Estudio, Conservación e Interpretación.* Mexico: Primer Círculo.

Schaafsma, Polly. 1980. *Indian Rock Art of the Southwest.* Albuquerque, NM: University of New Mexico Press.

Schaafsma, Polly. 1992. *Rock Art in New Mexico.* Santa Fe, NM: Museum of New Mexico Press.

Schaafsma, Polly. 2005. "The Paquimé Rock Art Style, Chihuahua." In *El Arte Rupestre en México: Ensayos 1990–2004,* edited by María Pilar Casado López, 219–240. Mexico: INAH.

Stanish, Charles. 2017. *The Evolution of Human Co-operation: Ritual and Social Complexity in Stateless Societies*. Cambridge: Cambridge University Press.

Stewart, John. 2010. "Foundational Issues in Enaction as a Paradigm for Cognitive Science: From the Origin of Life to Consciousness and Writing." In *Enaction: Toward a New Paradigm for Cognitive Science*, edited by John Stewart, Oliver Gapenne, and Ezequiel. A. Di Paolo, 1–31. Cambridge: MIT Press.

Sutherland, Kay. 2006. *Rock Paintings at Hueco Tanks State Historic Site*. Austin, TX: Texas Parks & Wildlife.

Sutton, John. 2020. "Personal Memory, the Scaffolded Mind, and Cognitive Change in the Neolithic." In *Consciousness, Creativity, and Self at the Dawn of Settled Life*, edited by Ian Hodder, 209–229. Cambridge: Cambridge University Press.

Thompson, Evan. 2007. *Mind in Life: Biology, Phenomenology, and the Sciences of Mind*. Cambridge, MA: Harvard University Press.

VanPool, Todd, Gorden F. M. Rakita, and Christine S. VanPool. 2009. "Cerro del Diablo: Un sitio multi-componente de la Cultura Casas Grandes en la región de Janos." *Espaciotiempo* 3: 50–59.

VanPool, Todd, Gorden F. M. Rakita, and Christine S. VanPool. 2015. "Bedrock Mortars and their Significance at Cerro del Diablo, Chihuahua, México." In *Collected Papers from the 18th Biennial Mogollon Archaeology Conference*, edited by Lonnie Ludma. Las Cruces, NM: University of New Mexico.

Varela, Francisco J., Evan Thompson, and Eleanor Rosch. 2017. *The Embodied Mind: Cognitive Science and Human Experience*. Rev. ed. Cambridge: MIT Press.

Viramontes, Carlos. 2005. *Grafica Rupestre y Paisaje Ritual: La Cosmovisión de los Recolectores-Cazadores de Querétaro*. Mexico: INAH.

Watts, Duncan J. 2003. *Six Degrees: The Science of a Connected Age*. London: William Heinemann.

Wheeler, Michael. 2020. "Cognitive Change and Material Culture: A Distributed Perspective." In *Consciousness, Creativity, and Self at the Dawn of Settled Life*, edited by Ian Holder, 90–106. Cambridge: Cambridge University Press.

3.3

"DISENTANGLING" AS AN EVERYDAY PRACTICE

Material, Visual, Sacred, and Commodity Features of "*Puja* Things"

Vineeta Sinha

Theorizing encounters of religion and the marketplace at the turn of the twenty-first century requires one to transcend modernist frames. It is vital to consider how a context of "post-modernity" or "late/high modernity," marked by recognizably varied and novel socio-cultural formations and consciousness—that have not necessarily supplanted modernity (Lyon 2000: 91)—reconfigure religious expressions and religiosity. Religion's emplacement in a capitalist universe of commodification and commercialization processes, in a highly mediated, digitally connected, and technologically driven context, demands fresh theorizing. Carrette and King remark that the "'market mentality' is now infiltrating all aspects of human cultural expression in (so-called) 'advanced' capitalist societies" (2005: x). Reginald Bibby observes a similar move in Canada, from "religious commitment to religious consumption" (1987), while Grace Davie has called the dominant trend in British religion "believing without belonging" (1994), so that "believers" are also "consumers" who choose the elements of religion that appeal to them and avoid the rest. Presently, the encounter of the spiritual and commercial realms persists globally, especially in novel, reconfigured modes through the emergence of new technological modes and media. But this is far from a "troubled encounter" even as I agree with Strasser that the commodification process can be "conflicting and contradictory" (2003: 7).

In scrutinizing the interpenetration of religious and commercial spheres, it is limiting to approach markets, monetary transactions—indeed—money itself as contaminating and debasing to religious sensibilities. The concern with generating profits and the expansion of a market share does not sit uncomfortably with the potentially and ostensibly "religious"/ "sacred" nature of the commodities being traded, a view that is sometimes expressed in the scholarship (Mitra 2016). The latter is embedded in the sharp distinction that is made between "sacred" and "profane" realms (and extended to apply to commodities) and the assumption of diametrically opposed values associated with these two spheres. Ethnographic data from Hindu, Buddhist, and Catholic contexts challenge this presumption and offer alternative readings: the commodification of religious objects, goods, and commodities as they feed back into the realm of religious practices with charged meanings in effect supports an enchanted field of practices rather than producing mindless consumerism or

DOI: 10.4324/9781351176231-22

disenchanted consciousness. An alternative analytical strategy for theorizing the field of religion, commodification, and consumerism require critical engagement with the scholarship on visual and material culture, which interrogates how and why religious objects are used and how they generate religious meanings, identity, solidarity, and community.

Social scientists have interrogated the complex processes of consumption in cultural realms, highlighting their "symbolic dimensions" (Lyon 2000: 89) with a shift from "use value" to "sign value" of a commodity. Baudrillard popularized this term, arguing that in specific contexts "commodities are given meanings through a logic of signs" (88). Mike Featherstone offers three helpful perspectives on consumer culture that shift the field discursively and complicate the binary of "good" versus "bad" effects of consumption. The first views consumer culture negatively, where consumers are seen to be manipulated and seduced by the marketplace; the second focuses on how people consume—how social relationships and identities are thus forged—and how that consumption delivers satisfaction; the third asks why people consume—with one response being that consumption brings pleasure (cited in Lyon 2000: 78). But, extending this question to religious domains, it has been asked if and how both consumption practices and the merchandising of "religious objects" diminish the sacred itself. Douglas and Isherwood ask "why people want goods" (1979: 4), pointing out that "what happens to material objects once they have left the retail outlets and reached the hands of the final purchasers is part of the consumption processes" (36).

Working across a range of religious traditions, scholars have highlighted the rise of an industry for religious paraphernalia (material objects), religious personnel and expertise, religious practices (rituals, festivals, processions), religious spaces (pilgrimage sites and holy places), and, marginally, to more symbolic religious notions (blessing, charisma, spirituality, efficacy, piety, and devotion)—all of which are treated as "commodities" and mass-produced, and further subjected to branding, packaging, and merchandising techniques. Numerous examples throughout history and across varied religious traditions affirm the existence of intimate links between religious spheres and commercial, worldly concerns. The commodification and commercialization processes have been noted for Roman Catholicism (Geary 1986; Kaufman 2004; McDannell 1995), Islam (D'Alisera 2001; Starrett 1995), Buddhism (Kitiarsa 2007; Yee 1996), Hinduism (Jain 2007, Pinney 2003, Sinha 2010, Smith 1995) and New Age Religiosity (Bowman 1994; Zaidman 2003). The intersections of everyday religious life with processes of commodification and commercialization in Asia have yet to be comprehensively explored. Some notable contributions include P. Kittiarsa's edited volume *Religious Commodifications in Asia: Marketing Gods* (2007) which explores the location of religion in the interstices of capitalism and globalization, drawing on ethnographic work from Malaysia, Vietnam, Thailand, Indonesia, and Singapore. The collection's contributors argue that it is not merely material entities but "blessings," "merit," and "religion" that are subjected to "commodifying tactics." Yeoh's (2006) analysis of material religion at a pilgrimage shrine in Malaysia is a rare work that highlights how religions operate in a world dominated by market forces but without diminishing religious sensibilities. My own *Religion and Commodification: "Merchandizing" Diasporic Hinduism* (2010) uses the lenses of "visuality" and "materiality" to gain insights into the everyday religious lives of Hindus as they strive to sustain theistic, devotional Hinduism in diasporic locations. The work argues that, despite the commodification of ritual objects, for devotees their sacred sensibilities have been far from degraded (Mitra 2016).

Everyday Hindu religiosity relies on a range of accessories and implements—known as *"puja* things" (prayer items)—whose visual and material dimensions are vital in enacting rituals and expressing devotion. These ritual objects are densely entangled bundles of "visuality," "materiality," "divinity," and "commodity"—properties that are brought into sharp focus and acted upon. Their usage requires devotees to "unscramble" and contextually unpack the otherwise jumbled, intermingled attributes of "*puja* things." Sonia Hazard (2013), Dan Hicks (2010), and Soumhya Venkatesan (2009), deriving theoretical insights from ethnographies of religion and crafts, respectively, speak of the "material turn" in research efforts nudging toward rethinking how "materiality" and agency associated with this is theorized. Joyce Flueckiger's latest research project, the exciting "Material Acts: The Agency of Materiality in India," seeks to "articulate an indigenous Indian theory of the agency of materiality through performative and ethnographic analyses of a range of different kinds of material that are not usually included in the study of religion" (Flueckiger n.d.; See also Flueckiger 2020). Here, I follow through the counsel to analytically unpack materiality but, more importantly, to operate outside the binary of the "material"/"non-material" and its logic.

Using ethnographic data from Singaporean and Malaysian Hindu domains, I argue that such "disentangling" is a crucial everyday practice that enables devotees to adopt particular attitudes to the category of "*puja* things" and shapes how these are used/consumed. In the literature on the anthropology of art (Gell 1998, Ingold 2007) and new materialisms (Coole and Frost 2010, Ingold 2007, Pongratz-Leisten and Sonik 2015), calls have been made to problematize the materiality/non-materiality binary, to acknowledge "entanglements" of matter (Keller and Rubenstein 2017, Keurs 2014), and to recognize the agency of materiality—in other words, "agentic realism" (Barad 2003), building on earlier research that had already theorized objects in novel modes (Gosden 2005, Olsen 2010, Spyer 1997). In different ways, the arguments from this rich body of scholarship include the following: an emphasis on holism and seeing connectivities between human and non-human worlds; struggling with the continuous, infinite, entangled nature of lived realities; and, thus, seeing the limits of finite binaries, dichotomies, and mutually exclusive categories and, indeed, calling for novel ways of thinking about ontology and epistemology.

Extrapolating from these ideas but also taking the discussion in a different direction, here I present "disentangling" not as just a concern for the researcher/analyst but, importantly, as an everyday practice that is routine, unproblematic, and indeed necessary for the materialization/accomplishment of everyday religiosity. I further argue that, in such unraveling, practitioners avoid essentialism and reductionism in their approach to "*puja* things." The material, sacred, and visual properties of "*puja* things" are intertwined and knotted in complex modes, even as devotees are fully aware of their identity as commodities. The awareness that objects have biographies and move in and out of commodity states (Appadurai 1986) demands a rethinking of consumption practices in religious domains, as does the recognition that things are marked by fluidity and mobility (Costall 2006, Henare 2007). Through a close scrutiny of the ritual use of fresh flowers and visual representations of Hindu divinity, I demonstrate that it is possible to identify "pre-consumption," "consumption," and "post-consumption" moments in the journey of using "*puja* things." I argue that devotees see these materials as having different properties during a trajectory of usage. At various points, devotees focus on these specific properties in order to express devotion and enact ritual. However, at the end of their ritual usage—when, for instance, flowers are perceived to have served their function (for deity and devotee)—devotees are nonetheless hesitant to treat them in profane terms. Here, flowers that have been offered to divinity accrue blessings that are then passed on to devotees. At the end of this cycle, these flowers do not revert to their "original" profane/secular state. Instead, offered flowers are thought to still embody properties that make it difficult for devotees to discard them as rubbish. Given this logic, it is a limited view to assume that materiality and materials are passive and inert. But it is also problematic to speak simplistically of "agency" of materiality. This ethnographic vignette does, however, allow me to argue that materials used in and through ritual have the capacity to produce particular kinds of embodied, emotive, and sensorial responses and practices—and thus animate and energize everyday religious domains.

Materiality, Commodity, Deity: Intermingled Domains

Religious imagery and symbolism are critical for sustaining theistic and devotional Hinduism in homes and temples. The visualization of deities is essential for individual expression of devotion and functions primarily to concentrate devotees' attention on divinity. The Sanskrit term *murti* connotes "form, likeness, image of a deity" (Fuller 1992) or "the embodied god" (Klostermaier 1989) and is deemed central (although not mandatory) in the act of *puja.* For devotees, icons, paintings, and images of Hindu gods and goddesses genuinely embody divinity. Hindus would agree with Webb Keane that "Religions may not always demand beliefs, but they will always involve material forms" (Keane 2008: 124). What Keane calls the "materiality" of religion (21–23) does not pose a dilemma within the logic of theistic Hinduism. Neither are objectification and materialization of divinity seen to devalue religiosity. As such, representations of the abstract, formless Brahman in a variety of material forms are neither prohibited nor problematic: theoretically, the granting of concrete form to divinity renders it accessible to devotees as a material presence within the human world. However, like Keane, some Hindus argue that, experientially, the materiality of rituals, images, or utterances does not necessarily connote, represent, or signify an abstraction but are meaningful in and of themselves. Visual images of Hindu divinity are woven effortlessly into the fabric of everyday, devotional Hinduism and they (literally) sit comfortably in a variety of physical sites in the human world, including within the domestic domain, and indeed are divine.

The imagination and construction of a deity (including the physical manifestations, size, dimension, color—as well as the materials to be used) are governed by a detailed body of knowledge, principles, and procedures carried in a body of texts known as the *Silpa Sastra,* which are mastered by a category of experts, the *silpi or sthapati,* who translate these conceptualizations into practice. This adherence to a codified grammar applies strictly to the production of Sanskritic deities, whose images are carefully produced according to principles meticulously detailed in these texts. Non-Sanskritic, folk deities, on the other hand, are not bound by any such received codes, and their visualization has routinely seen a free expression of devotees' imagination.

The retail markets in Singapore, Kuala Lumpur, Malacca, and Penang are flooded with an array of visual images of Hindu divinities in the form of painted and sculpted statues (in stone, clay, brass, marble, bronze, and *panchalokam*), paintings, pictures, chromolithographs, and photographs—as well as other symbols associated with them. Iconic and non-iconic representations of Sanskritic deities and folk variants are available to Hindus in the diaspora primarily in the form of mass-produced commodities but also as custom-made, personalized items—and occasionally even self-made ones. As commodities these are imported from India (through both formal and informal mechanisms) or ordered, mainly from different parts of Tamil Nadu in South India. Although devotees remain attached to the idea of India as the core site for securing all things "Hindu," in reality, specific items used in worship are sourced from several other locales. It is thus notable that parts of Malaysia, Indonesia, Thailand, Singapore, and, most recently, China have emerged as important players in these trading, marketing, and distribution networks of items used in Hindu worship, including visual images of deities. In addition to pictorial and iconic depictions, shelves in retail stores are further lined with religious insignia (*yantra, rudraksha* beads). These find their way to domestic prayer altars together with iconic images of deities, and are approached as marked with degrees of sacrality. Hindu symbolism and imagery are now also embossed and imprinted on a variety of everyday "secular" objects—such as wallets, lockets, pendants, key chains, T-shirts, notebooks, bags, pens, cell phone covers, lunch boxes, car decals, and stickers—which are not necessarily rendered "sacred" because of these divine associations. In fact, the items in this category remain functional and are valued perhaps for their decorative and aesthetic value rather than as ceremonial/ritual objects central in worship.

What are then the conceptual parameters of a commodity in the world of religious commerce? How do retailers and consumers approach "*puja* things" that carry a price tag and are sold and bought in a marketplace? What does "consumption" of religious objects signify for practitioners? These are intriguing questions given the complex and nuanced ways in which the category of "puja things" is approached by Hindus. While sitting on a shelf, waiting to be purchased, these commodities may be viewed as objects *of* worship, as objects to be used *in* worship, or simply as objects to be appreciated on "purely aesthetic grounds" (Bowman 1994: 150)—as opposed to what I have denoted "ceremonial, symbolic consumption." In the former the appeal emanates from a sense of aesthetics, artistic and visual appreciation—while in the latter these are procured for their ritual value. Items deemed to be decorative and ornamental are not defined as connoting potential sacrality, and so do not find space at prayer altars. In theorizing everyday consumption of such objects, the idea that individuals are driven to consume these goods for the satisfaction of temporary, superficial, restless, and worldly appetites is clearly irrelevant. The ethnographic material from my research strongly reiterates that materiality, physicality, sacredness, and monetary value are all concurrently packed on to an object—and that these are carefully and contextually separated out by practitioners (producers, sellers, and devotees/consumers).

For a start, it is important to recognize that "*puja* things" are not "trapped" in a commodity state forever. In fact, they have a limited "shelf life" and eventually have the potential to move out from the marketplace into ritual domains, thus activating their potential, other "non-commodity" attributes. I propose that commodities that enter a field of religious activity are accorded and can acquire alternative identities. Extrapolating from this insight, for devotees/consumers "once upon a time" commodities are appreciated and cherished because of their potential, implicit ritual value and are not assessed exclusively in terms of their exchange value. Neither are they rejected or devalued because of their association and contact with the profane world of commerce and entrepreneurship. Thus, the merchandising of "*puja* things" does not lead to mindless, individualistic consumerism; neither is it necessarily a threat to religious and cultural sensibilities. In making these arguments, one needs to be cautious of both the pitfalls of romanticizing consumption practices and the limitations of overstating the case for seeing the meaning and value of participating in consumer culture. Practitioners can transcend the commodity and commercial attribute of objects, and can as easily "forget" this characteristic when their focus shifts to how these facilitate the enactment of religiosity. Indeed, devotees appreciate that "*puja* things" that are deemed indispensable in ritual can be accessed in the marketplace; merchandising of such objects and materials for religious actors has been viewed as enabling rather than debilitating (Sinha 2010). Things used in rituals are undeniably transacted as goods in the marketplace. However, it is problematic to assume that rituals' domains are therefore contaminated by secularity/profaneness due to their prior embeddedness as commodities within a capitalist marketplace. This is not to deny that commodification and consumption processes can sometimes lead to mechanical consumerist behavior. However, in Hindu domains, devotees as consumers often use objects in ways that are unintended by the producers, fashioning them to their own needs; by no means do consumers receive these things passively.

So, what meanings do these items carry: for retailers who display them for sale as commodities, and for devotees who browse as potential buyers? For many retailers a *"puja thing"* is typically approached in terms of its utility, functionality, and exchange value. It carries a price tag, which may or may not be negotiable, and circulates in the marketplace like any other commodity does—to be bought and sold. There is a clear awareness that these are, first and foremost, commodities, and thus they are treated as such. Yet, these players are also aware that, although *"puja* things" exist as commodities and are by-products of cycles of production and distribution in a capitalist marketplace, they are *intended* to be consumed and appropriated as ritual objects. As such, retailers are conscious that they are dealing with a unique category of commodities. Retailers and wholesalers admit that, even though for them these are ultimately just "things" to be transacted, they do potentially embody a non-monetary value. Mr. Raghu Ramaiyya, a Hindu trader whose family runs a business that is a major player in Singapore, acknowledges that "prayer items" must be approached with reverence and that it makes good business to do so. Traders like Mr. Jagan Kumar are quite aware that, even though objects used in religious ritual are produced as commodities, once they enter the sphere of worship they become "animated" and their sacred potential is activated through usage. *"Puja* things" are accorded due respect even as commodities—since their potential as "sacred objects" is acknowledged and constitutes part of the implicit, background knowledge that traders work with.

Other retailers who trade in these items operate with the idea that objects may be used either for worship or for decoration. My discussion with Mr. Ali Karim conveys both the complexity of the issue and the straightforward resolution that he has adopted as a business practice. Here is his response to the question of whether he sees his Muslim identity to be problematic in handling and trading Hindu and Christian religious art:

> Why should there be? After all, I'm only selling art pieces here. Yes, some of the Muslim people have talked to me, have told me that what I'm doing is wrong. But I say, Look, I am not doing anything to them, I'm not praying to them. I'm just selling them.

In this instance, the entrepreneur is attempting to demarcate the boundaries of materiality and spirituality of the deity, while asserting that the commodity is merely a "decorative product." This view is reiterated by another businessman, Mr. Anwar Malik, whose father founded a long-standing business that deals primarily with the framing of pictures, including those of Hindu, Christian, and Buddhist divinity. Despite dealing with religious imagery from a range of different religious traditions, Mr. Anwar explained the predominance of Hindu imagery given the location of the business in an "Indian" area. This is of course a long-standing practice in the Indian context since at least the early twentieth century. One good example of this is the Ravi Varma Press, which mass-produced calendars and posters across different religious traditions. Mr. Anwar noted that, although the shop deals primarily with "Indian prayer things," this was not a problem for him given that Muslims relate to pictures only as "decorative items." He also made the further point that he did not treat the items in his shop in any special way just because they may be considered by customers to be religious objects. For him, objects are just objects, nothing more—and his decision to trade in them is driven by purely pragmatic and instrumental reasons:

> We consider these pictures just as objects. . . There is no such regard for these pictures as anything more. We treat them as any other item we sell.

Ritual practices in the domain of everyday Hindu religiosity reveal the complex intersection of visual and material dimensions of accessories used in the act of worship. Facets of "material," "divinity," and "commodity" are simultaneously implicated and "mixed up" in objects. As we have seen, visual representations of Hindu divinity—both iconic and non-iconic—are available to Hindus in the diaspora in the form of mass-produced commodities as well as personalized, custom-made entities.

Disentangling as an Everyday Practice

This section takes up thematics with regard to the use of "*puja* things" in worship: what renders objects used in Hindu worship "sacred?" And what are the prospects of disentangling the convoluted modes in which facets of "material," "divinity," and "commodity" are "mixed up" in this category of things? Rachel Dwyer (2006: 2) notes the "vivid materiality of popular visual culture," and Christopher Pinney argues that the realm of visual culture "is an experimental zone where new possibilities and new identities are forged" (2003: 8) and as such should be approached as an autonomous field of study. Lawrence Babb observes that:

> mechanical reproduction of pictures of deities (and other sacred entities) has become one of the most ubiquitous manifestations of modern religion in South Asia.
>
> *(Babb 1995: 6)*

Exploring religion's location at the interstices of capitalism, post-modern consciousness, and popular culture offers exciting opportunities for creative research. Notable contributions from the Indian context that theorize the interface of mass-produced religious insignia and Hindu religiosity include Kajri Jain's *Gods in the Bazaar: The Economies of Indian Calendar Art* (2007), Karline McLain's *India's Immortal Comic Books: Gods, Kings, and Other Heroes* (2009), and Sumathi Ramaswamy's *The Goddess and the Nation: Mapping Mother India* (2010). The analytical frameworks available in these works—and in those of H. Daniel Smith (1995) and Stephen Inglis (1995), especially on the history of the "god poster" industry and its phenomenal growth in twentieth-century India—have been pathbreaking. Citing Smith's observation that the emergence of chromolithographic technology was critical for production and dissemination of colored pictures, Babb concurs that this was instrumental in facilitating "the social and spatial mobility of iconic symbols in South Asia" (Babb 1995: 6). My own theoretical leanings resonate with the emphases in Smith's work about attending to how printed pictorial images of divinity are received and consumed by Hindus in practice (Sinha 2010: 136). The treatment of these objects and the attitudes toward them at the various sites of reception is key. Continuing this focus on "doing," Smith (1995: 36) argues that the preponderance of "god posters" and their easy availability, dissemination, and mobility have engendered "new forms of ritual response to images"—which is captured in a term he coins "omnipraxy" (Sinha 2010: 136). Speaking to the theme of the mobility of these religious artifacts, Inglis notes that these printed images have traveled well, not just within India but also beyond—a development that is crucial for sustaining Hinduism in diasporic locales:

> Visualizing the deities through popular depictions links not only virtually all markets, temples, and pilgrimage places in India, but also Hindu residences, workplaces, shops, and places of worship throughout the world.
>
> *(Inglis 1995: 67)*

The generation of mass-produced prints and chromolithographs of deities has revolutionized the domain of Hindu worship in making visual depictions of divinity accessible and afford-able to clusters of Hindus for whom this was previously either impossible or challenging (Pinney 2003). Devotees seem partial to framed prints largely for pragmatic reasons: they are easy to secure and manage—not to mention easily movable should the need arise. Fur-thermore, their ritual maintenance is straightforward, which is crucial in view of reduced time for worship within the home. However, another reason that devotees avoid keeping too many statues at the home altar has to do with the perception of the ritual attention that must be regularly paid to them. Statues are typically found in temples and are consecrated according to Agamic procedures, thus necessitating that religious specialists properly care for them. Statues that are kept at home are not similarly consecrated and thus do not require the same level of ritual notice. Yet, among the Hindus I conversed with, the idea that a three-dimensional statue must be cared for differently and "properly"—as compared to a photograph—is strong. This view is embedded in the further reasoning that a statue is, in the words of many a respondent, "more powerful" than a framed picture. The statue is in fact deemed to be spiritually more energized, but its efficacy can be positive or negative. Countless devotees expressed the view that, should there be any lapses in the care of divinity embodied in a statue (for instance, lack of ritual attention, improper worship, or contact with pollution), the family and household would have to face the wrath and anger of the deity. Some expressly stated that they would be "afraid" of touching the deities directly, an anxiety they explained as being located in the ritual separation of devotees from deities in temples.

The relationship between the image and what it ultimately represents is acknowledged to be a complex one in Indian texts that deal with the construction of images and their consecration before being used in worship. Diana Eck (1981: 38) notes that the *murti,* often inaccurately translated as "likeness," is rather "the deity itself taken form" and that the image is an "embodiment of the divine" serving to focus attention of the devotee (45), a point noted by other scholars—including Heather Elgood (1999: 14–15), who observes that the sculpted image must be both "beautiful" and "unblemished" in order to be fit for the deity. Painted, sculpted, or printed images of gods and goddesses are seen by devotees to carry the divine being's presence and are indeed treated *as if* they were a divinity. My respondents have no illusions about the relationship between an image and its physical representation, nor any confusion about what the latter connotes or its express function. For example, Mr. Suresh Kumar, a Brahmin priest from Singapore, succinctly explained the dialectical relationship between divinity and its imagery—an elucidation that would be easily grasped by lay Hindus as well:

> Yes, the statue or picture is a resemblance of the main god. So it also is a god, but it is only a resemblance. It is like this: If you see my face in the mirror, it is still me, but it's also not exactly me, so it is the same with the statue, it is still god, but also not the same.

From Material to Deity: Indian Rituals of Consecration (2005), a volume edited by Shingo Einoo and Jun Takashima, collects the work of scholars who have analyzed consecration rituals in Hinduism (2005). Citing Jan Gonda's work on the subject, one contributor of the volume, Hiromichi Hikita, identifies two meanings of "*pratistha*": one, to place a definite power in an object, to endow an object with divine faculties, and two, to enable the worshipper to realize the presence of the divine power, god's presence, in the image so that it becomes an effectual means of contact between the divinity and the worshipper (Gonda 1975, cited in Hikita 2005: 143). Hikita's conclusion is especially relevant in the context of teasing out the relationship between "religious objects" and "commodities" and the concomitant meanings they connote for producers and consumers:

> By going through this process of "consecration" the nature of the image changes. They are no longer materials but become endowed with life and supernatural powers.
>
> *(Hikita 2005: 143)*

Certainly for the writers and compilers of Hindu texts that detail consecration ceremonies, there was no ambiguity that there is a difference between the "obvious" *materiality* of an object and the spiritual, divine energy it eventually carries, bestowed upon it through the proper performance of ceremonies—in other words, through human intervention. Lay Hindus too are quite clear that material objects embody divine power and energy only after due ritual attention by religious experts during consecration ceremonies. My respondents noted that statues, for example, are spiritually "empty" unless they are ceremonially galvanized; once thus triggered, the regular performance of ceremonies ensures that the deities remain "enlivened." Even within the home, before statues and pictures are placed at the altar and approached as objects of/for worship, they are either "blessed" (by being taken to a temple) or properly "seated" (through an invitation or invocation ritual by a priest), possessing spiritual energy thereafter. I found Mr. Suresh's interpretation of the difference between material and deity quite illuminating:

> Okay. This stone is, this cement is supposed to be the same cement which made the Saneeswaran, but we don't pray to cement, we pray to the statue of Saneeswaran. This metal is the same metal which made a statue of Murugan, but we don't pray to the metal. Why? Without the invitation for the god to come in, the metal and cement do not have power. It is simple. We must do the ritualistic thing to invite the god to come and sit inside.

Of course these consecration ceremonies are not necessary for the worship of a category of objects that are deemed to be "inherently sacred" such as the *svayambhu* or "self-born images," which may be "discovered *in situ* in the middle of the field or under a tree" (Eck 1981: 55). Eck cites these following examples: the *salagrama* stone, believed to be a natural form of the deity Visnu found in the Gandki River in Nepal; the stones of Mount Govardhan in Vraj; the *svarupa* form of the Hindu god Krishna; and the *bana linga*, a natural form of the deity Siva found in the Narmada River. These objects, which are infused with sacredness indefinitely, are also deemed to be highly efficacious. This important distinction between objects that have intrinsic sacredness and those to which sacredness is attributed through human action is highly relevant to the question about the symbolism of ritual objects and how individuals relate to them on the basis of assigned meanings. Collectively, the noted discussions are insightful in directing attention to how the idea of "sacredness" is *understood and acted upon* by Hindus once a ritual object is deemed to be sacred, whether inherently or through appropriate ritual attention. Just as there are ceremonies enshrining a deity in a visual, material form, Hinduism also provides procedural guidance for their de-consecration. This applies primarily to temple deities but in theory could be applied to domestic deities as well:

> By a reverse ceremony the image can be deconsecrated and if such an image happened to fall into the hands of non-believers it would be less offensive to believers if this was to happen to a consecrated one.
>
> *(Mishra 1999: 219)*

In practice, there are instances of icons being de-consecrated (with the assistance of Brahmin priests) when the temple is being renovated, moved to another site, or demolished altogether—although these instances are rare; they are seen as a last resort, and generate some level of discomfort among Hindus.

Diana Eck's pioneering work *Darsan: Seeing the Divine Image in India* (1981) has highlighted *darsan* as the two-way interaction between devotee and deity in the act of *puja*. Eck translates the idea of "*darsan*" as "seeing," "religious seeing," or "auspicious sight of the divine" (1981: 7), and as being central in Hindu worship, both public and private. The elements of reciprocity and exchange of vision have been further noted, as has the recognition that the act of *darsan* cannot be reduced to "our common-sense understandings of vision as a passive reception of images on the retina" (Mines 2008: 140). Lawrence Babb's (1981) detailed analysis of "glancing" as a mode of visual interaction in Hinduism adds to scholarly works that highlight the contact with the deity and the possibility of communicating with divinity. There is certainly an exchange at work here, and not just a visual one, mediated by devotional gestures and material objects, something that devotees are aware of but that remains condensed. Here, the question of who has "more power" in this interaction is a challenging one. Narratives from my Hindu respondents suggest that, while the image is certainly deemed to be powerful, its spiritual energy remains implicit and "contained" unless it is activated by appropriate and authentic ritual attention from devotees—hence complicating considerably the power relationship between divinity and devotee. The practice of *darsan* in the act of worship rests on the specific meanings that an image carries for devotees. My respondents shared that the spiritual energy of the "home gods" is triggered when devotees "pray" before it; otherwise it remains latent. Devotees request the deity to come and settle in the statue or picture for the duration of the prayer. There is also the view that temple deities are comparatively more powerful—given that they have received the collective attention of many individuals over long periods, and that they have been "properly" consecrated.

Pre-Consumption, Consumption, and Post-Consumption Moments

Ethnographic material from Singaporean and Malaysian Hindu domains have led me to argue that the consumption of "ritual objects" reveals a life cycle of usage/utilization. This directs attention to what I call the "pre-consumption" and "post-consumption" moments of such trajectories. What happens to the "sacredness" of objects at the end of a ritual? Do the objects lose their sacred quality? Can we speak of "degrees" of sacredness of ritual objects? If the efficacy of objects is perceived to be acquired as well as temporary, can it also be "neutralized"? Do institutionalized procedures exist for "deactivating" or "defusing" the sacredness of objects and, if so when does this occur? Do lay Hindus have access to the knowledge of how "used" sacred objects are to be treated? To what extent is this knowledge acted upon, and with what constraints, especially in the Hindu Diaspora? What kind of symbolism, functionality, and value are "*puja* things" seen to embody *before* being used in worship, *during* the *puja* itself, and, in particular, *after* they have served their ritual purpose? The ritual consumption of fresh flowers and visual representations of divinity enable grounded responses to these queries. With respect to the use of *murti(s)*, Heather Elgood observes:

> For the Hindu, the image is an instrument of purpose, significant only in its role as a vessel fit to contain the deity with little consideration as to its intrinsic value. Images are discarded once they have served their spiritual purpose.
>
> *(Elgood 1999: 27)*

Although some "prayer things" (such as metal statues) may be passed down to one's children, by and large they cannot be recycled, exchanged, or re-sold. Scholars have also noted a place in Hinduism of "impermanent images" (Huyler 2003: 549), which are intended for only temporary use for a set period, after which they may be properly disposed of. For Hindus, the sacred can essentially be materialized from literally anything; the material is less important than the attitude with which something is approached. A lump of turmeric, dough, or clay can be fashioned into a representation of a deity. Drawing three horizontal lines (in sandal-wood, ash, or vermillion powder) anywhere (on a person, on a tree, on a wall, on a brick, on fruits, on sweetmeats) marks these with shades of sacrality. Just as readily are these depictions or images of sacrality dismantled and undone—without trauma. Hindus are quite used to the ideas of *making*, *un-making*, and *re-making* sacrality. This logic allows them to avoid the objectification, reductionism, and essentialization of "puja things."

Interestingly, Hindus regularly "change" their collection of visual images over time. But what do Hindus do with "old" icons/statues and pictures of deities? They know it is wrong to simply throw them away. Normatively speaking, depending on the nature of the object, used items are to be disposed of appropriately—ideally returned to nature; they are not to be discarded as rubbish. Framed pictures are typically placed in temples, under trees, in a forested area, or by the seaside. But devotees do not part easily with statues—which tend to remain in the family across generations. Stone or clay statues can be immersed in a body of water, but certainly not metal statues. On rare occasions statues are abandoned. Hindus are aware of the injunctions against picking up "someone else's" statue, as these have already been "prayed to." The underlying rationale is that the rejection of a statue has probably incurred the wrath and anger of the deity, wrath that will be directed to the new owner. As far as I know, Hindus do not perform any ritual before they part with statues and photographs.

The dynamics of living in a highly urban space means that there are few options for easily accessing streams, lakes, rivers, or public spaces for properly discarding "used" "puja things." Another practical complication in Singapore is that dumping is illegal, including into the sea. Yet I heard many stories of how clay statues, flowers, rice, fruit, and the like had been placed in sea waters around Singapore or in canals at the end of a prayer ceremony. Some Hindus I interviewed are against this practice on environmental grounds. For instance, Mrs. Alka Nath, a North India Hindu woman in her forties, says that she has been performing *Deepavali* prayers with the same Lakshmi statue for the last fifteen years and does not believe in "*visarjan*"—the immersion of statues in water. Other devotees expressed anxiety about throwing away prayer objects, worried that doing so was a *paap*—a sinful act. There seems to be a strong preference for leaving statues and pictures within temple premises given that a temple is a "sacred" site where gods "naturally" belong. But my respondents agreed that this was only a partial solution, since that simply transferred the problem to another party. Temple authorities discourage this practice, asking what they are supposed to do with discarded, "orphaned" icons and images. One Brahmin priest I spoke to was extremely candid in expressing his annoyance at the practice of "dumping" statues in temples "quietly, in the middle of the night." He sees this as a nuisance—and admits that he simply throws everything away in a rubbish bin, something that he does not do willingly or with pleasure. This example reveals how, though sacred and profane properties of materials used in ritual are deemed to be entangled, sometimes they have to be carefully separated, often for practical reasons.

Part of my research focused on accessing the meanings of flowers. At what point are they considered sacred? And if/when/how do their secular properties surface? Working backward from the realm of consumption, I asked these simple questions: Where do fresh flowers come from? How do they get to Singapore? Who brings them in and through what channels? Whose daily labor and efforts transform fresh jasmine, marigolds, and roses into floral strings and garlands ready for sale in the shops in Little India? Answers to these questions reveal the key mechanisms and processes through which flowers are secured and the networks through which they are distributed, often involving long distances. It is hardly surprising that flower shops are blooming in Singapore: there is money to be made, there is increased demand in the market, and the profit margin is high—despite the stiff but healthy competition.

Despite having been sold as commodities, flowers and garlands once bought by devotees are by no means tainted from the economic exchange. They are in fact valued even before they are used in the act of *puja*. Sellers are thus aware that the greatest care has to be observed in treating the flowers such that they will be deemed worthy of being offered to gods. In the shops flowers are respected and "pampered," not just as evidence for customers but also because it makes good business sense to do so. Once flowers are used in ritual offerings, they are considered sanctified through divine contact, embodying grace and blessing. But because flowers are organic, they do decay and rot. So what happens to them thereafter? Ideally, according to common-sense Hindu wisdom, they should be disposed of in running water, or in a garden or at the base of trees, to be returned to nature. In urban places like Singapore and Kuala Lumpur, this is seldom possible, and the used flowers and garlands do end up in garbage bins. How is this possible? Clearly, the sacrality or profanity of flowers is not inherent in the objective, essential property of the flowers themselves, but rather carried in the attitudes with which they are approached by devotees. Flowers carry different connotations as they move through the life cycle of a ritual. Before being used in worship they are "potentially sacred," during/after the ritual their sacrality is actualized and enhanced, and at the end of the ritual they are seen to have expended their sacrality and are thus treated accordingly. These slices of ethnography reveal that, as images of divinity and flowers move through "before, during and after" moments of the consumption cycle, they undergo "transformation"—moving from being approached as "material"/"commodity" to "deity"/sacrality and back to "material" again (but perhaps minus the commodity feature) at the end of the consumption cycle.

Concluding Thoughts

I have argued that it is problematic to assume that the world of markets and consumer culture necessarily and inevitably desecrates religious worlds; as such, we must rethink simplistic assumptions about religious actors being consumers. The ethnographic material presented here suggests strongly that, as consumers and customers, religious devotees are not easily manipulated. Instead, the dominant culture of consumption (including in the religious sphere) that defines a post-industrial context is mediated through a range of socially and culturally specific motifs and resonances. This recognition implies that the processes of commoditization and consumption within the religious domain have to be interpreted alternatively—in other words, outside a theoretical logic framed by a moral, righteous critique of consumption and the fear of its pernicious and toxic effects on cultural practices. What is required instead is a fresh perspective on how the very dichotomies of "sacred-profane" and "spiritual-material" are read. For example, it is unhelpful to perfunctorily inscribe destructive and hostile attributes to profane, secular, and material dimensions of social life in terms of their capacity to authoritatively diminish if not eliminate the "sacred." Nor is it feasible to judge the latter as being vulnerable and thus weakening or withering due to the assault of profane, commercial, consumerist pressures that are additionally deemed to be sacrilegious.

Through a focus on the everyday religious lives of Hindus in Singapore and Malaysia, I have articulated human interactions with objects *as they are used in and through* ritual and suggest that, rather than being subjugated, religious practitioners respond to, and appropriate, the logic of the market to achieve their own ends. As such, I specify the everyday use of "*puja* things" and theorize the broader connections between the spiritual and the material in enactments of religiosity. Here I make a call for situating things at the center of human, social, religious experience. For devotees, "*puja* things" encompass a sense of power. But this is not derived from their exchange value in the marketplace; rather, it is derived from the efficacies and other resonances they are seen to embody. Encounters with objects of religion inspire visceral (including emotional) and sensorial responses among practitioners, experiences that typically remain unexplored in analyses of everyday religiosity. Students of religion need to ask how and why religious practitioners use objects, how they engage and interact with them. This discussion needs to be balanced with greater comparative, cross-cultural material from varied religious traditions to complicate and challenge dominant Euro-American discussions (Berger 1990; Taylor 2007) about the intersection of religious domains with commodification and consumption processes. I make a case thus for more concrete, historically and empirically grounded accounts of how religious spheres intersect with commercial spheres. We must contemplate new analytical frames and methodologies for theorizing the sense-making of social actors whose everyday religious lives continue to be enacted evocatively and purposefully in entangled worlds.

References

Appadurai, Arjun, ed. 1986. *The Social Life of Things: Commodities in Cultural Perspective*. Cambridge: Cambridge University Press.

Babb, Lawrence A. 1981. "Glancing: Visual Interaction in Hinduism." *Journal of Anthropological Research* 37: 387–401.

Babb, Lawrence A. 1995. "Introduction." In *Media and the Transformation of Religion in South Asia,* edited by Lawrence Babb and Susan S. Wadley, 1–18. Philadelphia, PA: University of Pennsylvania Press.

Babb, Lawrence A., and Susan S. Wadley, eds. 1995. *Media and the Transformation of Religion in South Asia*. Philadelphia, PA: University of Pennsylvania Press.

Barad, Karen. 2003. "Posthuman Performativity: Towards an Understanding of How Matter Comes to Matter." *Signs: Journal of Women in Culture and Society* 28 (3): 801–833.

Berger, Peter. (1967) 1990. *The Sacred Canopy: Elements of a Sociological Theory of Religion*. New York: Anchor Books.

Bibby, Reginald W. 1987. *Fragmented Gods: The Poverty and the Potential of Religion in Canada*. Toronto: Stoddart.

Bowman, Marion. 1994. "The Commodification of the Celt: New Agearen/Neo-Pagan Consumerism." *Folklore in Use* 2: 143–152.

Carrette, Jeremy, and Richard King. 2005. *Selling Spirituality: The Silent Takeover of Religion*. Oxfordshire: Routledge.

Coole, Diana, and Samantha Frost, eds. 2010. *New Materialisms: Ontology, Agency, and Politics*. Durham, NC: Duke University Press.

Costall, Alan and Ole Dreier, eds. 2006. *Doing Things with Things: The Design and Use of Everyday Objects*. Hampshire: Ashgate.

D'Alisera, JoAnn. 2001. "I Love Islam: Popular Religious Commodities, Sites of Inscription and Transnational Sierra Leonean Identity." *Journal of Material Culture* 6: 91–110.

Davie, Grace. 1994. *Religion in Britain since 1945: Believing Without Belonging*. Oxford: Blackwell Publishers.

Douglas, Mary and Baron Isherwood. 1979. *The World of Goods: Towards an Anthropology of Consumption*. London: Routledge.

Dwyer, Rachel. 2006. *Filming the Gods: Religion and Indian Cinema*. New York: Routledge.

Eck, Diana. 1981. *Darsan: Seeing the Divine Image in India*. New York: Columbia University Press.

Einoo, Shingo and Jun Takashima, eds. 2005. *From Material to Deity: Indian Rituals of Consecration*. New Delhi: Manohar.

Elgood, Heather. 1999. *Hinduism and the Religious Arts*. London: Cassell.

Flueckiger, Joyce B. n.d. https://www.gf.org/fellows/all-fellows/joyce-flueckiger/

Flueckiger, Joyce B. 2020. *Material Acts in Everyday Hindu Worlds*. Albany, NY: SUNY Press.

Fuller, Chris. 1992. *The Camphor Flame: Popular Hinduism and Society in India*. Princeton, NJ: Princeton University Press.

Geary, Patrick. 1986. "Sacred Commodities: The Circulation of Medieval Relics." In *The Social Life of Things: Commodities in Cultural Perspective*, edited by Arjun Appadurai, 169–194. Cambridge: Cambridge University Press.

Gell, Alfred. 1998. *Art and Agency: An Anthropological Theory of Art*. Oxford: Oxford University Press.

Gonda, Jan. 1975. *Vedic Literature: (Saṃhitās and Brāhmaṇas)*. Vol. 1 Fasc. 1 of *A History of Indian Literature*. Wiesbaden: Otto Harrassowitz.

Gosden, Chris. 2005. "What Do Objects Want?" *Journal of Archaeological Method and Theory* 12 (3): 193–211.

Hazard, Sonia. 2013. "The Material Turn in the Study of Religion." *Religion and Society* 4 (1): 58–78.

Henare, Amiria, Martin Holbraad, and Sari Wastell, eds. 2007. *Thinking Through Things: Theorizing Things Ethnographically*. New York and London: Routledge.

Hicks, Dan. 2010. "The Material-Cultural Turn: Event and Effect." In *The Oxford Handbook of Material Culture Studies*, edited by Dan Hicks and Mary C. Beaudry, 25–98. Oxford: Oxford University Press.

Hikita, Hiromichi. 2005. "Consecration of Divine Images in a Temple." In *From Material to Deity: Indian Rituals of Consecration*, edited by Shingo Einoo and Jun Takashima. New Delhi: Manohar.

Huyler, Stephen R. 2003. "Hindu Shrines." In *South Asian Folklore: An Encyclopedia. Afghanistan, Bangladesh, India, Nepal, Pakistan and Sri Lanka*, edited by Margaret A. Mills, Peter J. Claus, and Sarah Diamond, 547–550. New York: Routledge.

Inglis, Stephen. R. 1995. "Suitable for Framing: The Work of a Modern Master." In *Media and the Transformation of Religion in South Asia*, edited by Lawrence A. Babb and Susan S. Wadley, 50–75. Philadelphia, PA: University of Pennsylvania Press.

Ingold, Tim. 2007. "Materials Against Materiality." *Archaeological Dialogues* 14: 1–16.

Jain, Kajri. 2007. *Gods in the Bazaar: The Economies of Indian Calendar Art*. Durham, NC: Duke University Press.

Kaufman, Suzanne K. 2004. *Consuming Visions: Mass Culture and the Lourdes Shrine*. Ithaca, NY: Cornell University Press.

Keane, Webb. 2008. "The Evidence of the Senses and the Materiality of Religion." *Journal of the Royal Anthropological Institute* 14(1): S110–S127.

Keller, Catherine and Mary-Jane Rubenstein, eds. 2017. *Entangled Worlds: Religion, Science, and New Materialisms*. New York: Fordham University Press.

Keurs, Pieter Ter. 2014. "Entanglement: Reflections on People and Objects." In *Social Matters(s): Anthropological Approaches to Materiality*, edited by Tryfon Bampilis and Pieter ter Keurs, 45–60. Zurich: LIT Verlag.

Kitiarsa, Pattana, ed. 2007. *Religious Commodifications in Asia: Marketing Gods*. London: Routledge.

Klostermeir, Klaus. 1989. *A Survey of Hinduism*. Albany, NY: SUNY Press.

Lyon, David. 2000. *Jesus in Disneyland: Religion in Post-Modern Times*. Oxford: Polity Press in association with Blackwell Publishers Ltd.

McDannell, Colleen. 1995. *Material Christianity: Religion and Popular Culture in America*. New Haven, CT: Yale University Press.

McLain, Karline. 2009. *India's Immortal Comic Books: Gods, Kings, and Other Heroes*. Bloomington, IN: Indiana University Press.

Mines, Diane. P. 2008. 'Exchange.' In *Studying Hinduism: Key Concepts* and Methods, edited by Sushil Mittal and Gene Thursby, 139–154. London: Routledge.

Mishra, P. K. 1999. *Studies in Hindu and Buddhist Art*. New Delhi: MS Abhinav Publications.

Mitra, Simontee. 2016. "Merchandizing the Sacred: Commodifying Hindu Religion, Gods/ Goddesses, and Festivals in the United States." *Journal of Media and Religion* 15 (2): 113–121.

Olsen, Bjomar 2010. *In Defense of Things: Archaeology and the Ontology of Objects*, 1–21. Lanham, MD: AltaMira Press.

Pinney, Christopher. 2003. *Photos of the Gods: The Printed Image and Political Struggle in India*. London: Reaktion Books.

Pongratz-Leisten, Beate, and Karen Sonik, eds. 2015. *The Materiality of Divine Agency*. Berlin, Munich, Boston: De Gruyter.

Ramaswamy, Sumathi. 2010. *The Goddess and the Nation: Mapping Mother India*. Durham, NC: Duke University Press.

Sinha, Vineeta. 2010. *Religion and Commodification: Merchandising Diasporic Hinduism*. New York and London: Routledge.

Smith, Daniel. H. 1995. "Impact of 'God Posters' on Hindus and their Devotional Traditions." In *Media and the Transformation of Religion in South Asia*, edited by Lawrence A. Babb and Susan S. Wadley, 26–29. Philadelphia, PA: University of Pennsylvania Press.

Spyer, Patricia., ed. 1997. *Border Fetishisms: Material Objects in Unstable Spaces*. London: Routledge.

Starrett, Gregory. 1995. "The Political Economy of Religious Commodities in Cairo." *American Anthropologist*, New Series, 97 (1): 51–68.

Strasser, Susan, ed. 2003. *Commodifying Everything: Relationships of the Market*. New York and London: Routledge.

Taylor, Charles. 2007. *A Secular Age*. Cambridge, MA: Harvard University Press.

Venkatesan, Soumhya. 2009. "Rethinking Agency: Persons and Things in the Heterotopia of Traditional Indian Craft." *Journal of the Royal Anthropological Institute* 15 (1): 78–95.

Yee, Shirley. 1996. "Material Interests and Morality in the Trade of Thai Talismans." *Southeast Asian Journal of Social Science* 24 (2): 1–21.

Yeoh, Seng-Guan. 2006. "Religious Pluralism, Gender and Kinship in a Pilgrimage Shrine: The Feast of St. Anne in Bukit Mertajam, Malaysia." *Material Religion: The Journal of Objects, Art and Belief* 3 (1): 4–37.

Zaidman, Nurit. 2003. "Commercialization of Religious Objects: A Comparison Between Traditional and New Age Religions." *Social Compass* 50 (3): 345–360.

3.4

BROKEN BUDDHAS

Reflections on (Im)Materiality and Impermanence

S. Romi Mukherjee

What is this?

Zen Koan, Huineng (638–713 CE)

The entanglement is a site of enchantment, but also one replete with danger. Within the rhizomes of the material, one may succumb to the burden of too much ontological identification with things—the entanglement qua entrapment potentially becomes something to be overcome. One is thus brought to ask: To what degree are we beholden to things? What lies beyond the horizon of the material? Can we locate a threshold of overcoming that embraces the immaterial beyond of the object which is not God, nor transcendence, but "no-thing."

Ian Hodder also recognizes the perils of too much entanglement:

> It is in our nature to try and fix our problems now by fiddling and fixing and so becoming more entangled in things and technologies. It is in our very being to devour things. . . . But we have perhaps come close to the end of the sustainability of this human impulse. Perhaps we need to face the possibility that fixing our technologies of co-dependency only increases rather than resolves the problem. The long term perspective of increased entanglement offered by archaeology and human evolution suggests the need to look deep inside ourselves and into what it means to be human. The moral choice is substantial, to change what it is to be human, to become something other than ourselves.
>
> (Hodder 2012: 221)

This chapter asserts that a Buddhist hermeneutics offers one means of imagining "becoming something other than ourselves" through its revealing of a new plane of immateriality that overcomes entanglements. In Buddhism one finds a conceptual apparatus for destabilizing "object agency," the dialectics of devouring, and the human impulse. In refusing to fortify a flawed and ontologically insecure self, a Buddhist approach to (im)materiality evades all reification. Here, nothing, emptiness, and void are not loci of despair, but rather the pre-conditions for ethical life insofar as any authentic engagement with the other can only evolve from the radical openness instantiated by ego dissolution. These concepts are not mystical bromides, but philosophical tensors with implications for the manner in which we imagine something called the self and the world out there—both subject as they are to breakage and breakdown.

DOI: 10.4324/9781351176231-23

A Reddit post began with the following query: "What is the best thing to do with a Broken Buddha Statue?" The owner hesitated to throw the Buddha in the bin, perhaps holding the object to be sacred or, perhaps, unintentionally reposing the problem of materiality and immateriality. Among the responses to the question, one finds:

> Contemplate impermanence.Nothing physical is thrown "away" . . . it goes somewhere.
> I am all thrown away on this blessed day.
> We're all throwed here.
> A great student doesn't attach to either form or emptiness.
>   (Reddit 2018)

Buddhas break—in accidents, acts of iconoclasm, and in the ravages of time. The Buddha is a man, but also the index of the specter of impermanence for all those who are "thrown away," but not thrown out, for all those who have no recourse but to "continue" in the face of malady, death, and constant loss. Yet, he cannot really be broken since, like all things, he has no inherent qualities. The broken Buddha does not die when shattered. He is decomposed in the flux of the composite assemblage of simple bodies that constitute the vitalism of the natural world. Finitude is grasped in his silence. Between the shards of the broken Buddha is the fullness of nothing, the non-essentiality of the material, and the apophatic power of space.

The broken Buddha presences the interval or gap between the ontic and the de-ontic that serve to raze cumbersome philosophical architectures of being. He moves by way of non-dialectical negation and reveals the paucity of the distinction between "it is" and "it is not." Yet, for all of the Buddha's pragmatism and ambivalence toward metaphysics (an outlook unfortunately perverted by some of the inheritors of the tradition), Buddhism is not a materialism. Rather, it is a comprehensive empiricism and naturalism that privileges the sustained examination of the intricate workings of the sensorium.

This is not to say that "things do not exist," but rather that what is being removed or penetrated was never really there. Rather than possessing autonomy and agency, the material comes to appear as mere dross. Something may be misguided in the way we apprehend things, which instantiates the entanglement and emboldens the entrapment. For Lama Thubten Yeshe,

> [O]ur instinctive belief in the self-existence of things is an invalid concept having nothing to do with the way in which things exist. . . . [W]e are so familiar with the apparently concrete nature of things, including ourselves, that it is not easy to switch to a looser, more relaxed vision. . . . [W]ith all this talk of non-existence and the illusory nature of phenomena we might conclude that ourselves, others, the world, and enlightenment are totally non-existent. Such a conclusion is nihilistic and too extreme. It is their concrete and independent manner of existence that is mistaken and must be rejected.
> *(Yeshe 2014: 60–62)*

A "looser vision" reconfigures the heuristic of the entanglement in emptying the object of its illusions, our projections, and our grasping of it. Broken things do not necessarily imply broken selves. The entanglement can be loosened, along with interpersonal and object-oriented knots, through an appeal to Buddhism and its theoretical environs—one that, nonetheless, does not limit itself to social scientific and/or purely philosophical approaches to Buddhism, but rather advocates a practical and polyvalent deployment of Buddhist tropes and dictums.

Engendered in this project is also the apprehension of how Buddhism is not one thing. This also opens the possibility of effecting the Buddhist turn in critical theory or gesturing toward a new critical Buddhist theory. The efficacy of such a project requires that we, on the one hand, battle tirelessly against what Timothy Morton calls Buddhaphobia and the taboo on inner life (which should not be confounded with the interiority of the monotheistic subject); and, on the other hand, following Zizek, refuse the recuperation of Buddhism as supplement to late capitalism (Zizek 2001: 12–14; Morton 2015: 165–185;, see also Dapsance 2018). The Buddhist turn in critical theory must be irreverent and far reaching in its approach, and engage with a polyphony of voices ranging from lamas and practitioners to psychoanalysts and historians. It must resist the tendency to become mired in metaphysical speculation; it must not hesitate to radically reconstruct Buddhism through evoking the "Buddhist theoretical spirit" across a vast array of traditions, epochs, and entanglements.

Getting to the "other side" of the entanglement may take us to "nothing," but nothing may actually be, paradoxically, "groundless ground." And in Buddhism, "place" opposes "ground." In other words, the entanglement is woven from within the contingencies of a house, a job, a marriage, a reputation, a bank account, a good body, and a self. Therefore, it is purely conditional and teetering on various brinks and untenable precipices. Something is always slipping away. On the other side is "groundless ground," which is terrifying in its inability to be secured or to offer ontological security and yet also liberating in its affirmation and acceptance of radical contingency and constant conditionality (Batchelor 2015: 240–241). The entanglement cannot be mastered. It would be foolish to even think to do so. This chapter's argument is deceptively simple—emptiness is not lack and no-thing is not a space of laceration and loss. This space, as we further argue, is not, "lack," "void," or "*nihil*." Rather, it is a psychological, social, and political horizon from where to imagine a radically different future, one where there is serenity in the negative that may be "the ground."

Sand

Tibetan monks of the Tantric tradition labor for weeks in their construction of mandalas. Granule by granule, they lay down an approximation of "absolute reality," a portal to an "unentangled" world. The Mandala, solemn and silent, cuts through all delusion. Upon completion, monks ritually destroy the mandala, deconstructing its labyrinthine contours and wiping away the doorway. The sand is placed in special jars or thrown into rivers. Sometimes the mandala is simply left there to be faded by the elements. The core tenet of Buddhism is evinced here—the transience of all things.

It is in the apprehension of finitude that we become other to ourselves and fully responsible to others. Compassion is predicated on incompletion and groundlessness. For many monks, the throwing of the sands into nature is akin to the pouring forth of compassion and love (concepts unfortunately scoffed at by the Buddhaphobia latent in the social sciences). Herein one finds the mystery of the concrete universal, the concreteness and universality of the other's death, of the broken object. For a moment, we are no longer defined by our primordial roots, or "identities," but by our collective inability to be totality. In the mandala, finitude overflows into plenum and then disappears.

The mandala is a circular index of all phenomena, which reverberate within the infinity of circles within circles within circles. In other words, it is a universal archetype perceived in everything from cellular structures to city planning to cosmic *hermetica*. For scholar of Tibetan Buddhism Robert Thurman, the mandala is a "world-model," "a matter of imaginal world-patterning directly affecting inner structuring of physical and mental senses" (Thurman 1997: 143). As such, we live in mandalas, scurrying through labyrinthine psychic-material entanglements, which are not as entangled as we think. Underneath this is an immanent field which is "another world," right here. As psychologist Rob Preece further suggests,

> [A] mandala, which encompasses our entire worldview . . . this mandala of appearances arises or manifests from the causal mind or clear light mind. When we are unaware that our relative world arises in this way, we believe it to be solid and inherently existent, but when we recognize its momentary, fleeting nature, its lack of inherent existence begins to be understood. This does not imply the relative world does not exist—merely that it is fluid, transitory and illusory.
>
> *(Preece 2006: 236)*

The entanglement may be of the relative world and, perhaps, so too the entire domain of what we call "material culture." The agony of the entrapment stands to be parried by aware-ness of the mandala's existence and the degree to which we are in a state of play between the phenomenal and the "non-existent." For Ajit Mookerjee, the bad forms of dependency engendered by the entanglement may be transmuted into a state of passage when cast against the backdrop of the mandala, as a "cosmic crosspoint . . . in the relative plane, at which the individual encounters the universal *noumena*" (Mookerjee 2003: 15). The mandala reminds us that "reality" can have different iterations or, rather, that "things" are not given.

Hence, the mandala is less a religious symbol than a challenge to ordinary methods of locating ourselves in relationship to things. It foments a way of seeing that is less colored by affective overlays and more in tune with the general economy of nature where cellu-lar mandala, corporal mandala, cognitive mandala, and external mandala strain to enter into correspondence. Of course, it is an esoteric symbol that in Tantric lore evokes the Buddha-Nature, the Buddha families, deities, and the dissolution of samsaric life. One may engage with the mandala as a sacred circle or as just a circle. Yet, ultimately, it is an expres-sion of the non-substantiality of "reality out there," which is, in part, a production of "real-ity, in here." For this reason, the mandala is also a realm of responsibility that asks that we own our productions. At an elementary level, it requires that we become aware of our awareness of things, cognizant in our grasping of things, and attentive to our capacity to be at their mercy. This requires a radical reworking of "view."

Fire

Any cursory appraisal of Buddhist philosophy would begin with the Four Noble Truths (or Tasks) and the last of those truths, the Eightfold Path. The Eightfold Path lies at the heart of Buddhism, for it was the path taken by the Buddha himself. In the *Dhammapada*, he pro-nounces that "This is the path; there is no other that leads to the purification of the mind. Follow this and conquer Mara. This path will lead to the end of suffering. This is the path I made known after the arrows of sorrow fell away" (*The Dhammapada* 2007: 205). While it is generally admitted that the core of the Path lies in its final steps (meditation and mind-fulness), the key to embarking on the path is Right View. Right View refers to a modality of experience that seeks to "see" the true nature of things and engage with material reality without prejudice. Not dissimilar from Stoic dogma as elaborated by Marcus Aurelius, Right View implores one to "remove the judgement" and thus, "remove the thought" (Aurelius 2006: 25; see also Hadot 1998: 36). And in Marcus's *Meditations*, written while walking over the mutilated bodies of his soldiers, and in the Buddha's passage to Right View, arrived after harrowing years of unsuccessful mortification of the flesh, we find two paradigmatic technologies of the self: non-attachment and impermanence.

Non-attachment is the movement through which the ego is collapsed and, with it, the desire to secure the self and the object within the flux of the aleatory. Nothing can be secured in such flux, and attempts to construct a stable relation with the internal and the external are simply deployed to disavow finitude and non-sense. The great obstacle, of course, is found in the fact that this is what we do.

On the contrary, Right View would dictate that the object—be it the other, the breast, the commodity fetish, and/or the religious relic—becomes a placeholder in the desperate attempt to construct "place," which is mistaken for ground. Non-attachment moves in synchrony with the disintegration of and liberation from such securing and "shoring up." Consequentially, the reinforcements of self, status, and security are unsustainable and mediated by phantasy that alienates just as it titillates. Non-attachment is also a buffer against the tragedy of ego-grasping precisely where the satiation of desire leads to the anomic state of permanent insatiability. Non-attachment struggles against Durkheim's *le mal de l'infini*—the hypertrophy of desire beyond measure, the "infinite of the dream,'" "the infinite of desire" promised by capitalist infinity and animated by the egoism of modern societies. Indeed, among the most powerful iterations of anomie is crystallized in the perpetual unhappiness of infinitely desire and the concurrent refusal to accept finitude (Durkheim 1951: 248). The object tantalizes with visions on infinite psychic security and total satisfaction. But death cannot be postponed by the object, be it breast, the other, the commodity fetish, or the religious relic. The object also alienates. Nothing can truly be mastered. *It* was never really "personal."

Non-attachment is bound to the lesson of impermanence. For the Buddha, "All created things are transitory; those who realize this are freed from suffering. . . . [N]either children nor parents can rescue one whom death has seized" (*The Dhammapada* 2007: 205). Buddhism is about "hard-truths" and is defined by a realism that refuses to beat back the reality of impermanence through the fortification of the ego or "coping mechanisms" (the hallmarks of American ego psychology). Yet, it also refuses the journey to the dark heart of trauma that typifies analysis interminable. As psychoanalyst Mark Epstein notes, Right View is where we find the Buddha as a "contemporary behaviourist who taught people to carefully go towards the things they fear the most," but in lieu of occupying the site of the trauma with Freudo-Lacanian grim determination:

> The Buddha found that a simple acknowledgement of the reality of thing could help life become more bearable. Acknowledging impermanence is a paradoxical injunction: it is counter to our most instinctive habits. Ordinarily we look away. We do not want to see death. . . . [W]e pull ourselves away from the traumatic undercurrents of life. . . . [T]he Buddha made Right View the first branch of the Eightfold Path to remind us that a will-ingness to engage with such challenges is the most important thing of all. . . . Things break. People hurt our feelings. Ticks carry Lyme disease. Friends get sick and die.
>
> *(Epstein 2018: 26)*

Yet, when things break something endures beyond them. The last word may not be with death, but rather with the ethical injunctions bound in the community of friends and strangers that is never fully achieved. This being said, there is a need to reconfigure, as Daniel Miller notes, something called society as not a place of fragmented individuals, but as "people who strive to create relationships to both people and things. These relationships include material and social routines which give order, meaning and often moral adjudication to their lives; an order which, as it becomes comfortable and repetitive, may also bring comfort to them" (Miller 2008: 296). People need comforting. But Right View acknowledges that material and social routines are besieged by breakdowns and catastrophes. In the *Addittapariyaya Sutta* (the Fire Sermon), the Buddha exhorted that "everything is always burning," —the mind, the nose, the ears, the tongue, the body, burning with fires of lust, craving, delusion, and finitude. Day-to-day life is a space of burning and constant discomfort. Things break. Right View admits as much. It engages with the traumatic ground of being with a view to eking out moments of sublimity, play, creativity, and care—despite the relentless encroachments of fire.

Silent Note

Buddhism's negation of ontological substance, its apprehension of dependent arising, and the ongoing agonistics concerning these ideas among the Hinayana, Mahayana, Tantra, and Zen, problematized what has come to be known as Buddhist dialectics. These debates aside, Buddhist dialectics outbids its Occidental counterparts in recoding the movement of Being/Negation/Becoming to one of Being/Non-Being/Nothing (which is not lack or the Lacanian Real).[1] As T. R. V. Murti suggests in his appraisal of Madhyamika:

> The Hegelian dialectic is a *conjunctive* or *integrating* synthesis. . . . [T]he Jaina dialectic is a disjunctive synthesis of alternatives. . . . Hegel's thought is *creative*, while for the Jaina it is *representative* of the real. The Jaina's is a logic of realism and pluralism. Hegel's is a logic of idealism and absolutism. . . . The Madhyamika dialectic tries to remove the conflict inherent within Reason by rejecting both the opposites taken singly or in combination. . . . [T]he function of the Madhyamika dialectic, on the logical level, is purely negative analytic.
> *(Murti 2016: 128)*

The Buddhist dialectic's precession is found in its rejection of unities, its refusal of the impasse of identity and difference, and its displacement of dialectics beyond "The Dialectic." It breaks away from the site of epistemological antagonism toward a wholly other space of alterity. Yet this is not trite riffing on the tautologies of the negation of the negation. The movement of being, in its classical philosophical recensions, is halted and ceases to even be possible. And in abandoning being for becoming, there is an encounter with "a reality beyond Reason" (Murti 2016: 135). This reality does not foreclose the possibility of knowledge, but supplants it with another modality of knowing, akin to what some call "intuition." It insists that emptiness is full in the same manner as the impossible is a condition of possibility. Hence, it is misleading to reduce Buddhism to another banal nihilism (Pol-Droit 2010: 68). In this view, nothing can only be annihilation. But nothing was always the non-ontic "plane" upon which all neurotic ontologies, metaphysics, and "Gods" were built. As eminently human constructions, the aforementioned over-code nothing and desperately strain to fill up space (as is our nature).

Hegel, of course, played a type of fort/da game with "empty," begrudgingly accepting nothing at one moment, only to run roughshod over it as *nihil* at another. He refused to traverse being and maintained that, as being erects itself on nothing, nothing opposes the higher realm of Spirit. But Hegel also acknowledges nothing as being substrate and accepts that "everything emerges from nothing, everything returns into nothing" (Hegel 1984: 253). Nonetheless, while Buddhism's nothing remains important for the philosopher, it is nonetheless inferior to "full" recensions of God, wherein total substance is achieved in dialectical redemption. As Timothy Morton suggests, "what Hegel actually produces . . . is a sense of a positive nothingness that exists alongside phenomena. In strictly Buddhist terms, he becomes guilty of the very nihilism he is berating in what he beholds" (Morton 2007). Hence, despite his attraction/repulsion toward nothing, Hegel sides with being and, lazily— or because of the hermeneutic limits embedded in his context—assumes that Buddhism collapses ontology and non-ontology.[2]

Nothing knows nothing of being. It is neither its hidden corollary nor the Absolute. The Buddhist dialectic flees the Hegelian and becomes a dialectic outside of the dialectic that does not posit nothing in relation to being. It negates the dialectic and becomes nothing upon a discordant epistemological plane, contravening conventional understandings of contradiction and beginning beyond the tension of the abstract and the concrete. Philosophy stops. As Morton further observes, Hegel flattens out the "phenomena-thing gap . . . because there is a more basic fear of a weird *presence* in and as nothingness. . . . This is what the Hegelian narrative forecloses . . . a night in which all cows are black still has cows. . . . [I]t not absolutely nothing at all" (Morton 2015: 237–238). Hegelian night is void and not black within black within blacker.

Silence is important in jazz and improvisation, something to be written into the chart. Space is to be used as opposed to filled. In a similar manner, in Indian Classical music the tabla player plays the "khali," the empty. Buddhism too remains agnostic, playing the silence. The Buddhist dialectic refuses to foreclose the gap, and occupies the chasm between negation and affirmation, between motion and rest. In this serene yet bustling interzone, subjectivity is emptied and transformed. For Murti, "the change is epistemic (subjective), not ontological (objective). The real is as it has ever been" (Murti 2016: 273–274). The "Real as it has ever been" illuminates a gap that may not be a gap at all.

Right Condition

Adorno had little tolerance for Buddhism, and was virulent in his assailing of "metaphysics for dunces" and those spiritualisms that spawned contemporary irrationalism (which, for the critical theorist, created the conditions for totalitarianism). Zen and other "restorative philosophies" were "non-conceptual vagary," the "opposite of freedom" (Adorno 1973: 68). Against Nirvana, he opined, "Nothingness is the acme of abstraction, and the abstract is abominable" (Adorno 1973: 380). However, Adorno and Buddhism, in their own ways, shunned both redemptive salves and dialectical happy endings. Nonetheless, for all of their tragic realism, they both also remained steadfast enemies of abjection and "damaged life," past and present. It is not without interest that Adorno also imagined a "place" beyond the dialectic, noting that, "In view of the concrete possibility of utopia, dialectics is the ontology of the false condition. *A right condition* would be freed from dialectics, no more system than contradiction" (Adorno 1973: 11). From Right View to Right Condition, there is the exigence to think of a politico-material frontier disencumbered of the burdens of our epistemological heritage. For Antonio Negri, "Communism refuses the dialectic. . . . [I]t refuses all binary formulae. . . . [D]eny the dialectic: that eternal formula of Judeo-Christian thought, that circumlocution for saying—in the Western world—rationality" (Negri 1991: 189). Communism and Right Condition may simply be names for a disentangled futurology. However, whether driven by radical hope or radical fear, we remain caught in contradiction. How to dismantle reason without lapsing into "irrationalism?" How to envision a redemptive moment, all the while curbing utopianism with the spirit of pessimism? How to engage in "reparations," move out of the depressive position, and praise the "thing" that we destroy? How to confront Adorno's hesitation and be exacting in our treatment of "no-thing," refusing the insipid *ritournelles* that repeat "nothing is something, something is nothing." Above all, how to take nothing out of "abstraction" and with it the Right Condition as well? The entanglement is material. It is also political and epistemological.

One response to these queries may come precisely from the cultivation of "the gap" and a commitment to "staying in the middle" between the affective vortex of the entanglement and the distanced and non-judgmental apprehension of its fundamentally ephemeral nature. And here, as Nagarjuna's "middle way" contends, form and non-form are two sides of the same coin. Stated otherwise, the entanglement as assemblage may be a constellation of causes and conditions, but, for Nagarjuna, insofar as cause and effect are never related, the assemblage has no inherent essence (Nagarajuna 2013: 226). The rhizome cannot be reified because it is in flux—roving, decentered, and without essence. In the end, empty may be simply a way of speaking about non-essence, transience, and impermanence. Following from this, the "Middle Way" refuses both ontology *and* nihilism (Nagarajuna 2013: 161). Yet, the middle path does not really sit in the middle but posits an elsewhere that is neither totally full nor completely empty. Right Condition is a site of struggle and the name of a problem.

One needs to get to zero to begin anew. One needs to drop the story line to fashion a more compelling narrative. Or rather, after all the deconstruction and negative dialectics, there may be a need to put things back together again. And "putting it back together again," does not entail replicating the object or dabbling in antiques. There is a futurology implicit in the middle way (Right Condition), but also, if for Nagarjuna, samsara and nirvana are ultimately the same thing. There is also a strong engagement with the present and affirmation of this world as all we have. But not so quick—our condition cannot be elided so easily. Empty can be full, but it can also just be empty, resonating with the experience of psychic deadness. For Michael Eigen, "Extremes and Middle are not at war. Neither exists without the other. Extremes and Middle are at war. This is part of the way they exist together" (Eigen 2001: 61). The Middle Way instructs us that emptiness is not annihilation. But the threat of annihilation always looms in the descent to groundless ground.

Canyon

Matthew Monahan is a sculptor of ruins whose works, or fabricated "artefacts," are designed to evoke a "futuristic archeology," ancient to the future, wherein the present is blasted out by the vestiges of the deep past—just as that past is constituted in the present, either to be disavowed in presentism's rejection of the hauntological or dissimulated in spectacles of commemoration where ghosts are revived only to be cast out again. Monahan's fragments make ample use of Buddhist iconology, but his Buddhas are severed, decapitated, and broken. The shards cannot be put back together, as they seem to be frozen in a certain prison of "time." Yet, they cause no alarm and, even in the material cacophony of part objects and destroyed things, they invite calm and equanimity. When asked about his Broken Buddhas, Monahan remarks:

> I don't contrive to make Buddhas. . . . But figuration presents certain problems, and these problems led me into all these ancient art forms. . . . My anti-materialism also comes into play. Sculpture is very materialistic. But even as I have a need for a material vessel, I have a desire to liberate it from its ties to materiality. . . . Coming up against the fixity—the boundaries that you need for a recognizable image—creates the urge to have that image disappear into its own background, or to somehow explode it. Once an image becomes an icon or begins to solidify, I start to wonder how to free it or break it down.
>
> *(Monahan 2014)*

To pastiche Winnicott, the Buddha has to survive our destruction. He must be freed from his own materiality in order to be properly used as tensor for our own proper de-reification. In addition, to rethink material culture as a series of vessels reveals that it is less about ontological identification with the totemic structure than a non-ontological-non-identification that breaks down the totem in order to open up another world that is right here (Figure 3.4.1).

Figure 3.4.1 Matthew Monahan. 2014. *The Canyon*. Epoxy resin, floral foam, linen, and stainless steel. Anton Kern Gallery, New York City. 78 1/2 x 25 x 14 inches. © Matthew Monahan. Image courtesy of the Artist and the Anton Kern Gallery, New York.

Immateriality is not sacrificial, but allegorical. In one of the most striking of Monahan's artifacts, the Buddha's head is severed in two, his face set off from his brain and skull. The chasm is indeed the "gap" of Buddhists dialectics, the abyss that is akin to "grace," achieved in the non-form that permeates the vessel. The space between is the interstices of the middle way and, also, just air. From a Zen perspective it may also be, as Paul C. Cooper suggests, indicative of "the rift" or "the precipice," "the gap" that points to, "womb, abyss, death, breast (nourishment, *entanglement,* suffocation, safety), or the unknown" (Cooper 2010: 180, emphasis added). And one must not fill the gap, but "throw oneself down the precipice," caught between "the anxiety engendered by awareness of the gap" and the overwhelmingly infinite possibilities it presents (Cooper 2010: 199). As radically salvational, the gap opens and is experienced "as it is." In Zen parlance: "Just this, Just this!" (Cooper 2010: 119). Perhaps there are gaps in the entanglement, which like the Broken Buddha can alchemically transform sites of alienation into redemptive planes. In jumping into "just this," nothing becomes potentially enabling, since it is no longer a gap to be filled by defense mechanisms. There is only right confronting as overcoming. The gap presages the eternal return. But even if we respond "Yes," we remain liminal.

Addition and Subtraction

The question of being is incarnated and disincarnated in the Buddha's glance. The visage asks the looker to cast off hindrances and strain toward Right View, which may be the first step toward Right Condition, where being cannot be entrapped; the Buddha has no content, but is demanding, like the gap. Hindrances are not simply found in the ego's grasping. They are also the ideological and ontological scaffoldings that erect our default mode of being. The Buddha image asks us to traverse the dialectic, to surpass the substance, to locate new modes of "practice."

Alphonso Lingis stares at a Nepalese Buddha, realizing that "you do not view the Buddha image as an artwork. . . . [T]he Buddha is not intended to represent that particular man named Siddhartha Gautama. . . . [T]he Buddha image is not an icon, but a means of composing one's forces" (Lingis 2000: 20–21). In the composition of forces is found the portal imploring one to act (compassionately), become-singularity (the pre-subjective), and tap into the beyond of the default mode of being. However, these thresholds do not automatically take shape. Lingis further remarks that images of the Buddha "depict an inner life of composure and compassion, which they induce in the viewer" (Lingis 2011: 46). Induction is a means of forcibly stimulating birth. The French equivalent "*déclenchement*" means to cause or "set on the path." The Buddha images induce. This vessel, broken or not, offers an injunction to live another way. And within the injunction is the larger concern of how to reconcile the political with the ethical, whose ultimate starting point should remain the alleviation of suffering. In the induction is also letting go and "throwing away."

Nothing may be a "big problem" bound to "big dialectics," but it may also be a series of habits and a habitus of *ordinary* being. In simpler terms, it may be a means of rethinking our "stuff" and our individual and collective "baggage." In *Immortality,* Milan Kundera contrasts people of addition with people of subtraction:

> There are two methods for cultivating the uniqueness of the self: the method of *addition* and the method of *subtraction*. Agnes subtracts from herself everything that is exterior and borrowed, in order to come closer to her sheer essence (even with the risk that zero lurks at the bottom of subtraction). Laura's method is precisely the opposite; in order

to make herself more visible, perceivable, seizable, sizable, she keeps adding to it more and more attributes (with the risk that the essence of the self might be buried by the additional attributes). . . . The method of addition is quite charming if it involves adding to the self such things as a cat, a dog, roast pork, love of sea or cold showers. But the matter becomes less idyllic if a person decides to add communism, for the homeland, for Mussolini, for Catholicism, for fascism or antifascism.

(Kundera 1990: 100–101)

Buddhism induces a radical subtraction that risks the zero, which is not zero, but a space of passage to a new site of the socio-political—where practice begins on the plane of immanence, which is a type of philosophical shorthand for the Buddha-Nature or nothing. One should never get too attached to an idea, let alone to cats. Subtraction is also a scouring of the political unconscious and a psychology of the political passions. It demands that we examine the degree to which the investment in ideological superstructures may be "craving" or wrong attachment. The political can also be a fetishistic entanglement marshaled to defend against the fear of nothing and the zero. This, of course, does not mean burning the tradition in a world that is on fire, but simply subtracting the political itself—there where communism is a means of inducing the commons and *communitas*, where socialism is the name of an impossibility (the social), where republicanism is a cosmo-politics, animated by a pluralizing people bound by their love of non-domination, nature, and dogs. The displacement of dialectics to "an elsewhere" may present a new distillation of the political. Such a distillation may begin in the radical nothingness that plays the silent note between the shards of the broken Buddha, where everything is subtracted. Here we potentially traverse the spectrum from total destruction to attempted reconstruction, from breakdown to breakthrough, from dead emptiness to a true self that is not flailing in the void but simply persevering, and getting on with the trials of being, in the impossible quest for equanimity in the hardest of times.

Notes

1 In the triptych of the symbolic, the imaginary, and the Real, the latter constitutes the traumatic core of being, the catastrophe that flanks the quotidian of experience/fantasy, and the radical inexorability of desire. It is monstrous excess, incommunicable, and produced outside of the structures of the signified. As such, it is wholly incapable of being properly integrated into consciousness. It controls the always-already fractured subject, but cannot be controlled. It escapes all calculation. Lacan strained to write on the level of the Real, producing a rhetorical style that never ceased to approximate the "gaps" of the pathological topologies that he excavated. For Lacan, the "Real remains in the shadows" (Lacan 2006: 31). As the outside of knowledge, being, and thought, it escapes us, but remains all too present in a sui generis manner as the product of the originary rupture produced by the entrance into language and the piecing together of the part objects of the self. It "does not wait," but is a central void that permeates—the impossible (which is all you can/should ask for). The Real is the misery of being and the melancholia of never being able to be reconciled with the lost object, whose substitutes do little to satiate. The Real is empty, the intractable threat of annihilation and the accident . . . a protracted *il y a*, the broken Other, and *broken thing*. Or as Lacan explains, "in this completely sleeping world, a voice is heard, Father, can't you see that I am on fire" (Lacan 1992: 58). Yet, empty is actually bifurcated between Buddhism's affirmative posture, or rather its pushing through negativity, and the Real's radical negativity which is at once post-linguistic and post-object-relations. In this antinomy, fecund emptiness (Yes) collides against annihilating negativity (No). However, perhaps the antinomy is not as stringent as it appears. Raul Moncayo, for instance, sees semblances between the two "reals,' and, more particularly, locates within the Lacanian nexus a series of Zen resonances. For Moncayo, "the Buddhist notion of no-self does not conflict with the Lacanian paradigm given that this is precisely a point where both traditions coincide to a certain degree. Both could be said to converge on the

Zen formula that true self is no self or the Lacanian-informed formula true-subject is no ego" (Moncayo 2003: 349). Indeed, true self is the product of a host of dyings and deaths and the complete scouring of ego contents and object relations. Indeed, Lacan and Zen both gesture to a site beyond the signifier and the barring and castrating propensities of the symbolic. But the processes of dissolution in the two traditions diverge or, rather, present two unique passages and crossings to get to empty. What cannot be overlooked in the Lacanian Real, inspired as it was by Bataillean heterology and its tragically lacerated visions of immanence, is how it is not an emptiness that overflows with plenum and how the truth of its true self is traumatic and overwhelming. In other words, the real is "the essential object which is no longer an object, where all words stop and all categories exhaust themselves, the object of anxiety par excellence" (Lacan 1954: 164). Buddhism's empty, on the contrary, traverses the object of anxiety, crosses the Real, and displaces the act of depersonalization beyond or after the tragic encounter. In other words, the Buddhist dialectic gets to empty not within The Real, but through surpassing it. And if the threat of annihilation does engulf Buddhist dissolution, it will need to be transmuted and rendered "creative." The Real holds us together, but the lack in the Big Other need not be the occasion for anxiety, nor will it be filled with fetishes and false ego contents. It simply is "the gap."

2 See Hegel 1975: 167; a disconcerting continuum or univocity is all that Hegel perceives in the Buddhist logic. Indeed, as Bernard Faure suggests, Hegel was the original Buddhaphobe for whom India was a culture that simply played semantic games with self and no-self (Faure 2007: 2).

References

Adorno, T. 1973. *Negative Dialectics.* Translated by E. B. Ashton. New York: Seabury Press.

Aurelius, M. 2006. *Meditations.* Edited by M. Hammond. London: Penguin Classics.

Batchelor, S. 2015. *After Buddhism: Rethinking the Dharma for a Secular Age.* New Haven, CT: Yale University Press.

Cooper, P. C. 2010. *The Zen Impulse and the Psychoanalytic Encounter.* New York and London: Routledge.

Dapsance, M. 2018. *Qu'ont-ils fait du bouddhisme?: Une analyze sans concession du bouddhisme à l'occidentale.* Paris: Folio/Gallimard.

The Dhammapada. 2007. Translated by E. Easwaran. Tomales, CA: Nilgiri Press.

Durkheim, E. 1951. *Suicide: A Study in Sociology.* Translated by G. Simpson and J. A. Spaulding. New York and London: Free Press.

Eigen, M. 2001. *Ecstasy.* Middletown, CT: Wesleyan University Press.

Epstein, M. 2018. *Advice Not Given.* New York: Penguin/Hay House.

Faure, B. 2007. *Bouddismes, philosophies et religions.* Paris: Flammarion.

Hegel, G. F. 1975. *Hegel's Logic.* Translated by W. Wallace. Oxford: Oxford University Press.

Hegel, G. F. 1984. *Lectures on the Philosophy of Religion, Volume I: Introduction and the Concept of Religion.* Edited by P. C. Hodgson. Translated by R. F. Brown, P. C. Hodgson, and J. M. Stewart. Berkeley, CA: University of California Press.

Hadot, P. 1998. *The Inner Citadel: The Meditations of Marcus Aurelius.* Translated by M. Chase. Cambridge, MA: Harvard University Press.

Hodder, Ian. 2012. *Entangled: An Archaeology of the Relationships Between Humans and Things.* Chichester: Wiley Blackwell.

Kundera, Milan. 1990. *Immortality.* New York: Harper Perennial.

Lacan, Jacques. 1954. *La Séminaire: le moi dans la théorie de Freud et dans la technique de la psychanalyse, Tome II.* Paris: Seuil.

Lacan, Jacques. 1992. *Le Séminaire: l'identification, Tome XI.* Paris: Seuil.

Lacan Jacques. 2006. *Le Séminaire: la relation d'objet, Tome IV.* Paris: Seuil.

Lingis, A. 2000. *Dangerous Emotions.* Berkeley, CA: University of California Press.

Lingis, A. 2011. *Violence and Splendor.* Evanston, IL: Northwestern University Press.

Miller, D. 2008. *The Comfort of Things.* Cambridge: Polity Press.

Monahan, M. 2014. "Broken Buddhas." *Tricycle.* Fall 2014. https://tricycle.org/magazine/broken-buddhas/.

Moncayo, R. 2003. "The Finger Pointing at the Moon: Zen Practice and the Practice of Lacanian Psychoanalysis." In *Psychoanalysis and Buddhism: An Unfolding Dialogue,* edited by J. D. Saffran, 331–363. Boston, MA: Wisdom Publications.

Mookerjee, A. 2003. *The Tantric Way: Art, Science, Ritual.* London: Thames & Hudson.

Morton, Timothy. 2007 "Hegel on Buddhism." *Romantic Circles: Praxis Series.* February 2007. University of Colorado, Boulder. https://romantic-circles.org/praxis/buddhism/morton/morton.html.

Morton, T. 2015. "Buddhaphobia: Nothing and Fear of Things." In *Nothing: Three Inquiries in Buddhism*, edited by M. Boon, E. Cazdyn, and Timothy Morton, 185–266. Chicago, IL: University of Chicago Press.

Murti, T. R. V. 2016. *The Central Philosophy of Buddhism: A Study of the Mādhyamika System.* Delhi: Motilalal Banarasidass Publishers.

Nagarajuna. 2013. *Nagarajuna's Middle Way: Mulamadhyamakakarika.* Translated and edited by M. Siderits and S. Katsura. Somerville, MA: Wisdom Publications.

Negri, A. 1991. *Marx Beyond Marx: Lessons on the Grundrisse.* Translated by H. Cleaver, M. Ryan, and M. Viano. Edited by J. Fleming. New York: Autonomedia/Pluto Press.

Pol-Droit, R. 2010. *Le Silence du Bouddha: et d'autres questions indiennes.* Paris: Hermann.

Preece, R. 2006. *The Psychology of Buddhist Tantra.* Ithaca, NY: Snow Lion Publications.

Reddit. 2018. "What is the best thing to do with a Broken Buddha Statue?" Reddit. Posted by u/BuddhismJatakamala, December 19, 2017. https://www.reddit.com/r/Buddhism/comments/7ktrj8/what_is_the_best_thing_to_do_with_a_broken_buddha/

Thurman, R. 1997. "Mandala: The Architecture of Enlightenment." In *Mandala: The Architecture of Enlightenment*, edited by D. P. Leidy and Robert A. F. Thurman. New York: Thames & Hudson.

Yeshe, T. 2014. *Introduction to Tantra: The Transformation of Desire.* Edited by J. Landow. Somerville, MA: Wisdom Publications.

Zizek, S. 2001. *On Belief.* London: Routledge.

3.5

BUDDHIST PRACTICE, RECREATION, AND FUN

Entanglements of Popular Culture and Material Religion

Inken Prohl

One dreary November afternoon, I visited the "Return of Buddha" exhibition in the Altes Museum in Berlin.[1] Despite the poor weather, an astonishing number of visitors, primarily women, wandered earnestly through the museum's solemn rooms, examining the figures and sculptures with reverence and respect. The visitors' earnestness stood in sharp contrast to what we were looking at—lots of slim, beautiful men, smiling softly to themselves, seemingly lost in reverie. What a fabulous opportunity to look at attractive, pleasant-looking men with the bonus of a spiritual promise. Visitors' comments and a few conversations provided anecdotal evidence that the Buddhas' beauty and reverie had indeed captured their attention; yet, some of the visitors also articulated a certain unease. Buddhism assumes an anti-materialistic, otherworldly focus. How can this be reconciled with the attractiveness of the figures and sculptures in the exhibition?

A look back into the world of classical Buddhism in ancient India reveals that the visitors' delight is in good company; classical Buddhist texts describe the Buddha as the epitome of masculinity, and his physical beauty is emphasized throughout the Pali canon. The Buddha's body is endowed with the thirty-two signs of a "Great Man." Some of the thirty-two signs are standard elements of Buddha images and statues; particularly noticeable is the protuberance on the crown of a Buddha's head. Therefore, enlightenment has a spiritual dimension and is also "embodied" in the physical form (Powers 2009: 1–23). Men are said to have been moved by his extraordinary beauty, and women are said to have fainted; men admired his physical superiority, and women felt sexually attracted to him. In classical Buddhist literature, the Buddha uses his physical beauty to win followers. If we understand "popular" to mean what is known and loved by the public, the Buddha was an exceptionally popular man, partly due to his reputed beauty and erotic allure, both timeless sources of popularity.

Reactions to his beauty—physical attraction, feeling entranced, and fainting—prompt comparisons with modern celebrity worship. Bruce Springsteen, Britney Spears, Justin Bieber, and other idols use their irresistible allure and charm to attract people and convert them into fans—in other words, followers (cf. Ward 2011, 2017). It is noticeable that the Buddha was able to elicit similar reactions from his followers as modern celebrities do from their fans. This parallel raises several questions: Was the Buddha a premodern version of Justin Bieber? Were Buddhism and its spiritual focus on enlightenment fundamentally misunderstood? Is Buddhism a popular culture phenomenon elevated by the aura of its age? Or

DOI: 10.4324/9781351176231-24

are "Beliebers," as Justin Bieber fans call themselves, part of a new, previously unrecognized religion?

Posing these questions illustrates the difficulties that confront us when, as expounded in approaches to material religion, we consider religions as more than just disembodied texts, dogmas, and teachings. Once our examinations include their materiality and the physicality with which they are expressed, and once we think about what makes them conspicuous, attractive, and beguiling, the borders between what is commonly known as "religion" and what is termed "popular culture" and "popular" become blurred. In this chapter, I seek to play with the categories of "religion" and "popular," shifting Buddhism back and forth between the two. The intention is not simply to examine "Buddhism" and the fields where it intersects with what we perceive as "popular culture," such as Buddhism *and* entertainment, medicine, or consumption. As soon as the material and the body are introduced into our understanding of religion, as shown by the examples above, it becomes much more *entwined* with what is generally termed "popular culture." This is why I take a close look at examples of Buddhist practice itself and the many ways in which neighboring fields in our contemporary world have adopted Buddhist-inspired ideas, practices, and materialities. After briefly clarifying my understanding of the approaches to "material religion" and the term "popular culture," the sections in this chapter focus on the popular worlds of historical Buddhism, the attractions of contemporary Buddhism in Asia, and the global popularity of Buddhist materialities. Then I present reflections on the spheres that open up beyond the dichotomization between religions and popular culture. The conclusion briefly discusses the gender-related asymmetries at play, causing the dichotomization and the dramatic transformation of an assumed transcendental that impacts our life.

Material Religion and Popular Culture—Playing with Theories

My understanding of approaches to material religion is that they seek to understand and describe how religions build affective bonds with their followers. They study how religions make themselves conspicuous, how they inspire commitment in their participants, and how they make their teachings believable. The effects and "meaning" of religious beliefs and actions are composed of the interaction between what participants perceive and what they experience, varying depending on their individual character (Prohl 2006: 43).

In line with most approaches to "material religion," my heuristic view of "religion" is as a set of ideas and practices enabling what participants perceive as "transcendental," "holy," or "beyond the human sphere of influence" that becomes intellectually and physically tangible through religious practice and ritual (cf. Meyer 2008). For example, the supposedly transcendental could be the religious powers of the Buddha Dharma, manifested in the Buddha's beauty, the notion of eternal life, or the fundamental modern belief in the existence of a unique essence in every human being (cf. Harari 2017).

Forms and social formations enable this experiencing of religion. For these, anthropologist Birgit Meyer has coined the term "sensational forms," which means "relatively fixed authorized modes of invoking and organizing access to the transcendental" (Meyer 2008: 707). The material, therefore, pervades all religions, and this chapter retains the term "material religion" only to focus attention on this fact. Materializations of religion are not necessarily all popular; the word "sensational" can be understood as "stimulating" or "startling" an individual. Materializations that manifest as sensational forms can be individual touches or attacks on the senses. However, in order for these individual accessions to a perceived transcendental to be socially efficacious, to initiate institutionalizations, and to be both retained and remembered, they need to be proclaimed to many people and be presented as attractive. In this respect, the religions that we know are popular.

The need to be popular is an appropriate point for taking a closer look at the intrinsically material and attractive forms of Buddhism to discover more about how and where religion interacts with the popular. The following sections focus on the popular worlds of historical Buddhism and the attractions of contemporary Buddhism in Asia, intending to clarify what is "religious" and what is "popular" or whether, in some cases, there is very little difference.

Popular culture refers to goods, products, and everyday practices that have become part of mass culture, particularly since the twentieth century as the world has modernized. These products are manufactured and marketed by a complex network of visual and media industries. Like religious practices, they appeal equally to reason, the senses, and emotions. Critical theorists applied the term "popular culture" pejoratively to this widespread culture (cf. Schofield Clark 2007; Hecken 2012). However, there have always been strong reservations about bringing together religion and popular culture. These are hard to dislodge because religion, both academically and publicly, is seen by many as serious, holy, and otherworldly (Klassen 2014: 2). It is worthwhile bearing these reservations in mind when we consider the field of Buddhism.

In asking the question "What's not popular?," David Morgan directed our attention to the fact that popular culture is so ubiquitous and pervasive that the term is no longer a viable analytical category and should be replaced with the expression "common culture" (Morgan 2007: 21). However, the introduction of the term "popular culture" has led to an abundance of reflections over the last two decades on the relationship between religion and popular culture. Scholars showed that most people spend most of their time as part of this popular, or common, culture. It is precisely through this culture that they organize their lives, build their identities, and manage their place in society (Morgan 2013). People's social and ritualistic endeavors now take place less in temples and churches and more during work and leisure time—the worlds now generally identified as popular culture (Lofton 2017: 9). The divisions between religion and popular culture are thus beginning to topple because popular culture has assumed many of the functions and roles that religions fulfilled in past societies.

Over the twentieth century, Buddhist-inspired semantics, practices, and materialities have made significant inroads into popular cultures worldwide, including films and video games, psychotherapy, medicine, wellness, marketing, and branding. Is this a new form of Buddhism? Or are they secular forms of popular culture with a Buddhist touch? This merging of the material forms of Buddhism with popular culture is also significant when we are considering the relationship between religion and popular culture.

A Walk through the Popular Worlds of Historical Buddhism

It was not just the Buddha's reputed beauty that made him so popular. The accounts of him in the Pali canon and Mahayana sutras also contributed to his appeal. These accounts depict his incredible superhuman abilities, strengths, and miraculous powers (Goméz 2010). His supernatural powers include levitation, the power of divination and telepathy, and the ability to walk on water and through walls, create duplicates of himself, and travel to distant lands and other universes at the speed of thought. In addition, he is said to have defeated and converted non-Buddhist ascetics, sorcerers, and hostile deities with ease. As stated in the sources, the legendary accounts of the Buddha are intended to amaze and entertain.

Stories about the Buddha inspire attention, wonder, and enthusiasm, make religious claims believable, awaken hopes, and encourage the use of Buddhist rituals and identification with Buddhist teachings. The stories and visual depictions have provided universally clear justification for his religious status and that of his followers—Buddhist monks and priests— who are said to be able to mediate between the supernatural world of the Buddha and the Buddha Dharma. Their training, rites, ceremonies, and habitus enable them to grant lay-people access to the Buddha's world. With help from the Buddha's world, the vast majority of Asian Buddhists have promised themselves material blessings in this world and favorable reincarnation for themselves and their relatives in the next.

The legends and visual depictions tell of the places to be visited as part of the essential practice of making pilgrimages in Buddhist countries. These include the Buddha's place of birth, the place of his enlightenment, where he first prayed, and where he died. This explains why these places are still visited today. The legends and depictions establish emotional bonds to these places and evoke the desire to see them. Buddha's presence endows the sites with religious powers and, by visiting them, pilgrims are said to be able to share this power (cf. Trainor 1997). The stories describe the stupa, a building said to contain the Buddha's remains, laying the foundation for the veneration of relics seen throughout Asian Buddhism. According-ing to Buddhism, rituals can transfer the religious power of relics to material objects such as images of the Buddha or slips of paper with quotations from Buddhist literature. These objects have spread throughout the Buddhist world as talismans and amulets, "repositories of power" (Tambiah 1993) that function in the same way as relics. Mass-produced amulets make the healing powers of the Buddha mobile (cf., for example, Dobbins 2001). A range of consecration practices transforms materializations of the Buddha into living entities. For a long time, Buddhist adherents have seen statues, sculptures, and images of the Buddha as sources of religious powers (cf., for example, Sharf and Sharf 2001; Swearer 2004). The pres-ence of icons and the legends surrounding them constitute compelling performances, con-vincing people of the vitality and powers of the Buddha. One popular example is Mikaeri no Amida, a statue in a temple in Kyoto of Buddha Amida looking over his shoulder. According to legend, the Buddha was looking back at a monk who was walking slowly. The posture of his head symbolizes Amida's compassion for all creatures, even those who are slow or who come to faith later on in life (Faure 1996: 244). These premodern forms of multimedia por-trayal made potentially remote deities accessible and familiar to the masses.

Tibetan priests employed Thangkas—Tibetan scroll paintings—to tell the stories of the Buddha's miracles over vast distances, since they are easy to transport. Priests have used these visualizations of the Buddha's life story for "multimedia presentations" about the origin and miraculous powers of their rituals (Bretfeld 2012: 28). The messages in Zen Buddhism are even easier to transport, as they assert teaching beyond words, with the bodies of the priests themselves functioning as the medium of communication. The practice of quiet sitting, often described as meditation, is more accurately understood as an effective method of per-forming the claim that one's own body can be transformed into a replica of the Buddha's body. In assuming this posture, the priests demonstrate their enlightenment. Zen temples resorted to this effective "re-enactment" to create bonds with their followers (cf. Bielefeldt 1988; Okropiridze and Prohl 2018). To attract followers' attention, temples and monasteries host exhibitions of their treasures. In East Asia, this has often happened under the pretense of airing out the objects, like at Daitokuji, a Zen temple in Kyoto where its famous precious statues, scroll paintings, and writings are set up outside the temple halls, attracting many visitors (Levine 2005: 226–286).

Since the thirteenth century, Buddhists in Japan have employed scrolls (*etoki*) to capture the public's attention, to bridge the gulf between the elaborate teachings of Buddhism and the concerns of the wider public, and to convince the public of the superior healing powers of the Buddha. Using "picture-perfect images of the Western Paradise," the paradise depicted in Amida Buddhism beliefs, priests kindled hopes of a favorable afterlife. Disturbing images of hells "made compelling propaganda" for the teachings of Amida Buddhism (Kaminishi 2006: 194). "In essence, etoki and modern audiovisual entertainment are not so different in the way they use visual images to draw the viewer's attention while verbal texts—whether written or spoken—supply propagandizing messages" (Kaminishi 2006: 193).

In addition, priests made use of Buddhist sites for visual depictions of miraculous stories and effective rituals to convey the benefits of this world and the next. On festival days, in particular, they were transformed into places to watch entertainment (cf., for example, Wong 2018). An excellent example of this is Sensōji, a temple of the esoteric Tendai school of Buddhism in Edo, modern-day Tokyo, where from the seventeenth century onward fund-raising temple stewards organized for artists, sumo wrestlers, and street performers to draw people's attention to the temple and encourage them to visit. The temple was famous for *misemono*, shows or exhibitions that were popular at the time. In Japan, there is a long tradition of linking "prayer and play" (Hur 2000). According to Japanese tradition, this is to entertain the gods and attract their attention (Prohl 2006: 313–319). Markets surrounded the temple sold products that the people offered to the gods, such as rice cakes, seaweed, and sake. Also for sale were amulets and talismans, prayer beads, incense, and other objects belonging to Buddhist practice (Hur 2000: 1–29). Buddhists thus used beautiful, entertaining, and popular items to attract people and win them as followers (Hur 2000: 86). To increase profits, Buddhists also employed attractive saleswomen; like other religious places in Japan and elsewhere, prostitution was also part of a temple's attraction (Hur 2000: 88).[2]

One of the typical features of popular culture is seen to be its ability to appeal to, entertain, and win over a large number of people across great distances using mass-produced goods and professionally designed products. Throughout history, Buddhists have made use of powerful stories, performances, and beautiful—occasionally mass-produced—items to capture people's attention and win them as followers. The methods have included offering emotional experiences, entertainment, pleasure, eroticism, and sex—in other words, things that are particularly attractive in modern popular culture and are used to significant effect in contemporary branding (cf. Grant 2000). In this sense, historical Buddhists used popular strategies to generate followers, obtain their loyalty, and create profits, thereby blurring the borders between religion and popular culture. However, it could be argued that Buddhists only used these strategies to communicate their most vital message to all men and women— that Buddhism offers teachings and religious rituals that can benefit people both in this world and the next. Therefore, the popular practices were intended to establish the allegedly transcendental effects of Buddhism and make them accessible. Where is the difference here to popular culture? Do assumed metaphysical ideas, entities, or systems play a part in what is now subsumed under the term "popular culture"? These questions are worth noting as we now look at current relationships between Buddhism and popular culture.

Attractions of Contemporary Buddhism in Asia

Amusement parks, giant statues, manga, films, Hello Kitty talismans, professionally designed websites, Buddha coffee shops, spectacular presentations of rituals and ceremonies, anime, Bollywood performances, sex, robots, professional advertising campaigns, intensive temple retreats, elaborate weddings, funerals, and enormous quantities of delicious food— contemporary Buddhists make use of a vast range of popular practices, technologies, and strategies to attract people's attention, appeal to them, and win them as followers.

The enormous statues of Buddhas and bodhisattvas in many Buddhist countries in Asia are spectacular, clearly visible manifestations of Buddhism in contemporary Asia. Some of the most well-known of these include the Kamakura Daibutsu in Japan (37 feet/11.3 meters high), the Tian Tan Buddha in Hong Kong (112 feet/34 meters high), and the Phuket Big Buddha in Thailand (148 feet/45 meters high). Many of these giant Buddha statues draw a large number of local visitors and tourists, who can participate in specific religious activities such as reciting sutras, taking part in offerings or meditations, or simply walking and chatting with one another, admiring the landscape, shopping, or eating delicious foods (McDaniel 2017: 1–29). At the Big Buddha in Phuket, visitors can buy small shells filled with rice and place them on a conveyor belt, which carries them past a series of miniature versions of the giant Buddha statues. The ritual is said to multiply the ritual blessings granted through the offering. In parks, temples, and stalls people sell all kinds of Buddhist oracles—talismans, amulets, and souvenirs. At the Kamakura Daibutsu, one can buy rice cakes and biscuits shaped like miniature Buddhas. At holy sites in general, people can buy any object from daily life involved in Buddhist practice: health products, incense accessories, Buddhist decorations, clothing, and food considered to be healthy. The Starbucks at Tian Tan Buddha in Hong Kong sells a Starbucks city mug with a picture of the giant Buddha on it.

In these parks with giant Buddha statues, people can entertain themselves by participating in religious activities, relaxing, or simply having a good time with their family and friends. We cannot neatly categorize these practices as either "Buddhist" or "religious," or indeed "popular" or "secular." They rather offer spaces in which the borders between these categories start to dissolve—further evidence of the fact that the categories do not satisfactorily represent the complexity of social realities.

The parks with giant Buddhas are the prototypes for the temples and monasteries in Asia that have successfully built up their reputation of having statues and relics that can bestow powerful blessings for this world or the next. Buddhist institutions use various popular attractions to develop and nurture this reputation, including works of art, local crafts, and culinary delicacies. Huge ceremonies, such as presentations of powerful statues normally not accessible by the public, attract thousands of visitors. In the past, temples have held these events as fundraising campaigns, like the one at the Zen Buddhist Daiyūzan Saijoji in Japan (Williams 2004: 59–85). At these festivals, temples put on a comprehensive program of entertainment, including comedy, magic shows, and musical performances. The joy of sharing in the ritual blends with the magic of the show, the drama, and the music and induces a whole host of positive emotions in the participants (Bodiford 1994: 26). Participants ascribe these emotions to the deities' actions. For example, the 2016 Naropa Festival in Ladakh was announced as a holy Buddhist celebration to remember the Tibetan monk Naropa. There were Buddhist rituals in the morning and, in the evening, performances by renowned Bollywood performers with booming sound and impressive light shows enjoyed by large crowds of monks, nuns, and laity late into the night (cf. Williams-Oerberg 2020).

In the day-to-day lives of prominent Buddhist temples, religious rituals coalesce with leisure activities, offering all different kinds of Buddhist souvenirs, amulets, and talismans (cf. Reader and Tanabe 1998; Kitiarsa 2008; Catanese 2020). These Buddhist materialities are often designed to appeal to contemporary tastes and trends, with the most famous amulets of this kind being those modeled on the cartoon cat Hello Kitty. When asked about the connection between Buddhism and Hello Kitty, a Japanese priest replied, "Buddhism seeks to help people. If people who come here love Hello Kitty and consider her very cute, then it makes sense to choose this form to help them come into contact with the Buddha Dharma."[3] The auras of these objects—their value as receptacles of the divine, as representations of

Buddhist teaching, and as objects of veneration—are still retained even if they are produced and sold en masse. Their auras are not created by goods themselves but by the interaction with them and the qualities attributed to them (Brox 2019: 121–122). As we have seen, appealing figures such as the cute pink cat known as Hello Kitty turn into popular talismans. Temples and shrines offer the Hello Kitty talisman as a carrier of religiously effective powers of protection and the enhancement of luck. The transformation of the figure of Hello Kitty into magic eliminates any differentiation between religion and popular culture.

The team that looks after the Ryōhōji, a Buddhist temple in Tokyo, certainly knows what will appeal to the public, particularly the younger generation. The temple uses visual culture from manga and anime to draw attention to itself and to attract visitors. By using images, well-known anime music, a "Maid Café," and beautiful celebrities from the world of cosplay and videos, the temple has introduced erotic elements into its offerings to the public, presenting Buddhist teaching and practices in seductive packaging that is tantalizingly close to potential users (cf. Thomas 2015). Buddhism, packaged and mixed with sex and eroticism, sells just as well in the present as it did in the past.

On the morning of December 8, in the kitchen at Ganshoin, a Zen Buddhist temple in the Japanese Alps, women roll sticky rice flour to make hundreds of tiny balls—Japanese confectionery known as mini *daifuku*. December 8 is Bodhi Day, on which the Buddha is said to have experienced enlightenment under the bodhi tree. In the afternoon, a celebration takes place in the main hall of the temple, with sutra recitations and prayer rituals in memory of the event. Similar to the Mainz Carnival, at the end of the celebrations the priests pelt the participants with the mini *daifuku*; the participants enthusiastically try to catch as many as possible, since the teachings claim that consuming these sweet treats will make you as wise as the Buddha himself.[4] The enjoyment of the sweets conveys religious efficacy. Here, religion and what people like and enjoy eating are inextricably linked.

In December 2016, a delegation from the Longquan Monastery in Beijing visited Heidelberg and introduced me to Xian'er. They gave me a miniature of Xian'er as a present; he is the little robot monk of the monastery who has achieved worldwide fame since he arrived at the temple at the end of 2015. The robot is designed to resemble a Buddhist monk with a shaven head and an orange robe. The monk robot responds to speech, makes basic movements, recites sutras, and answers simple questions about Buddhism. The monastery hopes that he will make people, particularly the younger generation, interested in and enthusiastic about Buddhism.[5] The Buddhist priests at the Kōdaiji temple in Kyoto have similar hopes. Since 2019, the robot priest Mindar has been giving instructions in Buddhist teaching. He is modeled on the Bodhisattva Kannon, a goddess of compassion, who is highly suitable for robotization as she can manifest in different forms. The priests also intend Mindar, a life-sized humanoid robot, to nudge the public's interest in Buddhism and attract visitors to the temple. In Japan, human Buddhist priests are also putting on commemoration events for Aibo, Sony's robot dog. A software upgrade to AI is planned shortly for both Xian'er and Mindar. Thus, Buddhist institutions are using the captivating powers of these popular figures and technologies to win over more people.

In conclusion, we can state that Buddhists are using a wide variety of elements of popular culture to create bonds with potential participants.[6] These elements, however, are not simply a means of attracting people. Buddhist institutions convey their teaching and practices using the enjoyable, pleasurable, emotionally appealing, and transformative experiences offered by popular culture. This mechanism doesn't cease with death, either. Robots have been conducting funeral rituals for many years in Japan, partly because they are significantly cheaper than human priests. Mourning centers offer Buddhist-inspired mourning ceremonies in which mourners can choose the coffin, food, and theme of the ceremony, including features from the worlds of Star Wars and Walt Disney, making impossible any separation between Buddhism and popular culture.

The Global Spread of Buddhist Materialities

"Mediatized religion" describes the process in which modern media technologies enable individuals, social groups, and institutions to get a hold of religious semantics and materialities; to interpret, mix, and arrange them in new ways; and then redistribute these creative arrangements with the help of media (cf. Stolow 2005; Hoover 2006; Hjarvard 2012). The elements of this pluralistic emergence of supposedly traditional elements of the so-called "world religions," like Buddhism, do not remain confined within certain traditions—people quite happily carry what they consider to be Buddhist over into other fields. In the case of Buddhism, these fields can be medicine, psychology, psychotherapy, self-help, entertainment and lifestyle, and the fields of literature, film, and video games (cf., for example, Borup 2016; Mitchell 2019). In these fields, we find countless examples of the incorporation Buddhist semantics, images, and designs—with the practice of mindfulness being the most popular in contemporary societies.

Elements of what people consider Buddhist are also commonly found in marketing and branding. People in highly industrialized societies are bombarded with thousands of advertisements every day. In 2020, the advertising industry worldwide reached high levels of $650 billion and it is further growing since then.[7] As a result, our contemporary society is thoroughly permeated by an ethos of consumption (Gauthier, Woodhead, and Martikainen 2013: 2), which in turn is driven by marketing and branding, making both industries critical features of our popular, or common, culture. In its search for powerful, compelling images and messages, the advertising industry has discovered religious imagery, with Buddhist messages and imagery becoming particularly popular (cf. Irizarry 2015; Prohl 2020).

A wide range of advertising campaigns uses images of the Buddha, including food, furniture, toys, and cosmetics, with examples found in Buddhist and non-Buddhist countries. Buddha figures grace advertisements for medicine and electronic devices in India, bookshops in Israel, and leisure activities in South Africa. In the American supermarket chain Whole Foods Market, you can find Karma Milk, Lucky Buddha Beer, and Mindful Mayo. Any ambitious German dental or physiotherapy practice now seemingly has to have a statue of Buddha—or at least images of bamboo, stones, and gardens that invoke associations with Buddhism. In many countries, multinational companies like Shiseido or Starbucks advertise their products using the magic of the word Zen. Zen appears particularly frequently in ads for food, gadgets, and cosmetics.[8] The world of fashion has also discovered the power of the Buddha to drive sales. The logo of the fashion brand True Religion features a very happy-looking, laughing Buddha, guitar in one hand, the other giving a thumbs-up.

People in the twentieth and twenty-first centuries have become more and more governed by the idea of the existence of an individual self. The ever-spreading mantra of postmodern societies claims that this individual self must be strong, independent, and always ready to adapt and change. We are encouraged to be responsible for our own lives and continually improve ourselves (cf. Rose 1996; Illouz 2008). The most potent idea of our time is that human beings possess a unique essence (cf. Harari 2017). This idea of the individual self retaining a unique essence has turned into a belief. The practices around this self constitute a formation analogous to religion. Hence, from an analytical standpoint, the sacred does not reside outside ourselves in the realms of God or the gods anymore. Instead, for many people, it rests within themselves. Modern transcendence drifts inside.

Belief in the unique individual essence of humans turns out to be entirely compatible with modern attributes of Buddhism. Ideas about the Buddha finding the truth by himself are decontextualized from the social institutions of his time and chime in with the paradigm of a unique essence in every human being. This paradigm, however, places a heavy burden on people. The assumed unique essence lying at the base of ourselves must be constantly affirmed and improved. The modern field of Buddhism provides all kinds of assistance with this, as it places a strong focus on the practice of self-improvement. Images of a Buddha maintaining a sitting pose of quiet contemplation are ubiquitous in global popular culture. This image implies that it is easy for anyone to come to know themselves and make themselves feel better. This practice, the quiet immersion in oneself, promises an easily accessible way of improving one's life and self.

The icon of the meditating Buddha proves to be particularly suitable for contemporary branding because the figure and materialities of Buddhism evoke an idea of striving for something beyond. It is this very striving that modern forms of marketing and consumption rely on. As Kathryn Lofton puts it, "The product is a material way to access something ineffable" (Lofton 2017: 9). The sitting Buddha has some mystical touch in the eyes of many, communicating the promise of extraordinary experiences and the possibility of transcending everyday life, even transcending this world altogether.

To fuel consumption, marketing and branding strategies employ the allusions Buddhist narrations and materialities evoke. Buddhist images affirm the importance of working on the body, of individual experience, and of the constant drive for optimization. The aesthetics of the field pull on the senses, thereby reassuring consumers that they constantly have to buy commodities to improve and transform themselves. In short, Buddhist narration and imagery can sacralize consumption. Buddhist practices also promise to establish a connection with the unique essence that people are assumed to have. The Buddha is believed to have transcended this world and to have reached nirvana—enlightenment. In this sacralized Buddha, people can see a reflection of their assumed equally sacred essence, thereby continually affirming and reifying the existence of this essence. The Buddha thus becomes one of the superheroes of the "Age of Animation" (Silvio 2019), constantly showing people ideal versions of themselves that they can realize—with the help of consumption.

To summarize, therefore, in the symbiosis of Buddhism and contemporary popular culture we can see a dynamic that can be described as religious. This symbiosis confirms and supports the belief in the existence and essential significance of a unique essence in every person and enables it to be experienced day to day, rendering definitively obsolete any differentiation between religion and popular culture.

Conclusion: Beyond the Dichotomies

"The Buddha that emerges through the medium of the image becomes a grantor of boons, and the Buddha's teaching about nonattachment falls victim to an obsessive preoccupation with sacred objects revered for their protective potency and economic value" (Swearer 2004: 3). Similar to Swearer, a whole host of academic and non-academic commentators bemoan the connection between Buddhism and the material world, the sphere of prosaic entertainment, and the realm of pleasure and entertainment.[9] Scholars trace back the glorification of the anti-materialistic aspect of Buddhism that focuses on this world to the essentializing, orientalizing text-based notions of Buddhism (cf., for example, McMahan 2008). I want to put forward the prevailing androcentrism in Buddhism research as another reason.

Researchers' gender shapes their attitudes toward a chosen area of research and the selection of topics (cf., for example, Schiebinger 2000). In Buddhism research, the endemic striving to discover truths about the meaning of life by studying philosophical works elevated by the aura of age, and then finding them in a dematerialized and disembodied sphere beyond everyday practices and social interactions, reflects the priorities of men's worlds. These worlds focus less on welfare, interpersonal relationships, and the practices of daily life than on interactions with technology, knowledge systems, and the challenges of surviving in the workplace. The choice of research topics very often reflects this gender-specific prioritization. It is a critical factor behind the long-standing ignorance of the daily, material, and popular dimensions of religion (cf. Woodhead 2007). These gender-specific asymmetries affect wide areas of the research on Buddhism. It is open to debate if the Buddhist teachings themselves, with their focus on the self-sufficient hermit, reflect this gender asymmetry. It is, therefore, a highly relevant field for experimentation when it comes to the interplay of material religion and popular culture, as there is a vast gap between its scholarly depiction in academic writing and the social realities of Buddhism.

As we have seen, Buddhism and popular culture are inextricably linked, and it doesn't make sense to keep these spheres separate. Beyond the categorial dichotomization, we can discern that a clear and powerful transformation is taking place. In the past, religions used attractions, pleasures, and sensual and emotional experiences to convince participants of the world of gods and their powers and make this world accessible and familiar. In the modern world, the experience of the popular constitutes, affirms, and preserves the existence of an individual, unique essence in every person.[10]

In his song "Purpose," Justin Bieber sings about trying to be the best version of oneself; this is ultimately all that is within human grasp and those who don't attempt it are betraying themselves. The critical function of popular culture is condensed into the song's lyrics—the sacralization of the self.[11] The differences between Siddhartha Buddha and Justin Bieber, therefore, fall away. What's left is just religion.

Notes

1 The 2001 exhibition in Berlin presented sixth-century Chinese sculptures discovered in Qingzhou (cf. Nickel und Museum Rietberg Zürich 2001).
2 Reflections on this topic and its broadly euphemistic treatment in academic literature present a challenge for future research.
3 Informal interview, Tokyo, 2005. The priest alluded to the Buddhist concept of *upaya*, "expedient means," by which all means of propagating the Dharma can be justified.
4 Fieldwork, Nagano, December 2005.
5 Informal discussions with delegation representatives, Heidelberg, December 2016.
6 Many additional examples can be found in Schedneck 2014; Scott 2009; McLaughlin 2019; Nelson 2013.
7 A. Guttmann, "Global Advertising Revenue 2012–2026," Statista, December 7, 2021, https://www.statista.com/statistics/236943/global-advertising-spending/.
8 You get an idea of the vast array of products if you search for the word "zen" on amazon.com. The search results in the "Beauty and Personal Care" and "Electronics" departments are particularly interesting.
9 An overview of the criticism can be found in Thomas 2015; Scott 2009.
10 The shift from believing in gods to believing in the sacred core in every person can be seen in global modern Buddhism (cf., for example, Scott 2009).
11 The song lyrics and conclusion are taken from Ward 2017: 325.

References

Bielefeldt, Carl. 1988. *Dōgen's Manuals of Zen Meditations*. Berkeley, CA: University of California Press.

Bodiford, William M. 1994. "Sōtō Zen in a Japanese Town: Field Notes on a Once-Every-Thirty-Three-Years Kannon Festival." *Japanese Journal of Religious Studies* 21 (1): 3–36.

Borup, Jørn. 2016. "Branding Buddha: Mediatized and Commodified Buddhism as Cultural Narrative." *Journal of Global Buddhism* 17: 41–55.

Bretfeld, Sven. 2012. "Tibetische Thangkas." In *Von Thangka bis Manga: Bild-Erzählungen aus Asien,* edited by Iris Possegger and Sven Bretfeld, 26–28. Leipzig: E. A. Seemann.

Brox, Trine. 2019. "The Aura of Buddhist Material Objects in the Age of Mass-Production." *Journal of Global Buddhism* 20: 105–125.

Catanese, Alex John. 2020. *Buddha in the Marketplace: The Commodification of Buddhist Objects in Tibet.* Charlottesville, VI: University of Virginia Press.

Dobbins, James C. 2001. "Portraits of Shinran in Medieval Pure Land Buddhism." In *Living Images: Japanese Buddhist Icons in Context,* edited by Robert H. Sharf and Elizabeth Horton Sharf, 19–48. Stanford, CA: Stanford University Press.

Faure, Bernard. 1996. *Visions of Power: Imagining Medieval Japanese Buddhism.* Princeton, NJ: Princeton University Press.

Gauthier, Francois, Linda Woodhead, and Tuomas Martikainen. 2013. "Introduction: Consumerism as the Ethos of Consumer Society." In *Religion in Consumer Society: Brands, Consumers, and Markets,* edited by François Gauthier and Tuomas Martikainen, 1–26. Farnham: Ashgate.

Goméz, Louis O. 2010. "On Buddhist Wonder and Wonder-Working." *Journal of the International Association of Buddhist Studies* 33 (1–2): 513–554.

Grant, John. 2000. *The New Marketing Manifesto: The 12 Rules for Building Successful Brands in the 21st Century.* London and New York: Texere.

Harari, Yuval Noah. 2017. *Homo Deus: A Brief History of Tomorrow.* New York: Vintage.

Hecken, Thomas. 2012. *Theorien der Populärkultur: Dreißig Positionen von Schiller bis zu den Cultural Studies.* 2nd ed. Bielefeld: transcript.

Hjarvard, Stig. 2012. "Three Forms of Mediatized Religion: Changing the Public Face of Religion." In *Mediatization and Religion,* edited by Stig Hjarvard and Mia Lövheim, 21–44. Göteborg: Nordicom.

Hoover, Stewart. 2006. *Religion in the Media Age.* London: Routledge.

Hur, Nam-lin. 2000. *Prayer and Play in Late Tokugawa Japan: Asakusa Sensōji and Edo Society.* Cambridge, MA: Harvard University Press.

Illouz, Eva. 2008. *Saving the Modern Soul: Therapy, Emotions, and the Culture of Self-Help.* Berkeley, CA: University of California Press.

Irizarry, Joshua A. 2015. "Putting a Price on Zen: The Business of Redefining Religion for Global Consumption." *Journal of Global Buddhism* 16: 51–69.

Kaminishi, Ikumi. 2006. *Explaining Pictures: Buddhist Propaganda and Etoki Storytelling in Japan.* Honolulu, HI: University of Hawai'i Press.

Kitiarsa, Pattana. 2008. "Buddha Phanit: Thailand's Prosperity Religion and Its Commodifying Tactics." In *Religious Commodifications in Asia: Marketing Gods,* edited by Pattana Kitiarsa, 120–144. London and New York: Routledge.

Klassen, Chris. 2014. *Religion and Popular Culture: A Cultural Studies Approach.* Ontario: Oxford University Press.

Levine, Gregory. 2005. *Daitokuji: The Visual Cultures of a Zen Monastery.* Seattle, WA: University of Washington Press.

Lofton, Kathryn. 2017. *Consuming Religion.* Chicago, IL: University of Chicago Press.

McDaniel, Justin Thomas. 2017. *Architects of Buddhist Leisure: Socially Disengaged Buddhism in Asia's Museums, Monuments and Amusements Parks.* Honolulu, HI: University of Hawai'i Press.

McLaughlin, Levi. 2019. *Soka Gakkai's Human Revolution: The Rise of a Mimetic Nation in Modern Japan.* Honolulu, HI: University of Hawai'i Press.

McMahan, David L. 2008. *The Making of Buddhist Modernism.* Oxford: Oxford University Press.

Meyer, Birgit. 2008. "Religious Sensations: Why Media, Aesthetics, and Power Matter in the Study of Contemporary Religion." In *Religion: Beyond a Concept,* edited by Hendrik de Vries, 704–723. New York: Fordham University Press.

Mitchell, Scott A. 2019. "Buddhism and Media." *Oxford Research Encyclopedia of Religion.* Oxford: Oxford University Press.

Morgan, David. 2007. "Studying Religion and Popular Culture: Prospects, Presuppositions, Procedures." In *Between Sacred and Profane: Researching Religion and Popular Culture*, edited by Gordon Lynch, 21–33. New York: Taurus.

Morgan, David. 2013. "Religion and Media: A Critical Review of Recent Developments." *Critical Research on Religion* 1 (3): 347–356.

Nelson, John K. 2013. *Experimental Buddhism: Innovation and Activism in Contemporary Japan.* Honolulu, HI: University of Hawai'i Press.

Nickel, Lukas, and Museum Rietberg Zürich, eds. 2001. *Die Rückkehr des Buddha.* Berlin: Frieden-Vertriebsgemeinschaft.

Okropiridze, Dimitry, and Inken Prohl. 2018. "Von der Sinnlichkeit zu Sitzen: Zazen als materialsemiotische Praxis." *Zeitschrift für Religions- und Geistesgeschichte* 70 (3): 254–274.

Powers, John. 2009. *A Bull of a Man: Images of Masculinity, Sex, and the Body in Indian Buddhism.* Cambridge, MA: Harvard University Press.

Prohl, Inken. 2006. *Religiöse Innovationen: Die Shintô-Organisation World Mate in Japan.* Berlin: Reimer.

Prohl, Inken. 2020. "Branding and/as Religion: The Case of Buddhist Related Images, Semantics and Designs." In *Buddhism and Business: Merit, Material Wealth, and Morality in the Global Market Economy*, edited by Trine Brox and Elizabeth Williams-Oerberg, 111–127. Honolulu, HI: University of Hawai'i Press.

Reader, Ian, and George Joji Tanabe. 1998. *Practically Religious: Worldly Benefits and the Common Religion of Japan.* Honolulu, HI: University of Hawai'i Press.

Rose, Nikolas S. 1996. *Inventing Our Selves: Psychology, Power and Personhood.* Cambridge, MA: University of Cambridge Press.

Schedneck, Brooke. 2014. "Meditation for Tourists in Thailand: Commodifying a Universal and National Symbol." *Journal of Contemporary Religion* 29 (3): 439–456.

Schiebinger, Londa. 2000. *Frauen forschen anders: Wie weiblich ist die Wissenschaft?* Munich: C. H. Beck.

Schofield Clark, Lynn. 2007. "Why Study Popular Culture? Or, How to Build a Case for Your Thesis in a Religious Studies or Theology Department." In *Between Sacred and Profane: Researching Religion and Popular Culture*, edited by Gordon Lynch, 5–33. London: I. B. Tauris.

Scott, Rachelle M. (2009) *Nirvana for Sale? Buddhism, Wealth, and the Dhammakâya Temple in Contemporary Thailand.* Albany, NY: State University of New York Press.

Sharf, Robert H., and Elizabeth Horton Sharf, eds. 2001. *Living Images: Japanese Buddhist Icons in Context.* Stanford, CA: Stanford University Press.

Silvio, Teri. 2019. "Introduction: Welcome to the Age of Animation." In *Puppets, Gods, and Brands: Theorizing the Age of Animation from Taiwan*, edited by Teri J. Silvio, 1–17. Honolulu, HI: University of Hawai'i Press.

Stolow, Jeremy. 2005. "Religion and/as Media." *Theory, Culture & Society* 22 (4): 119–145.

Swearer, Donald K. 2004. *Becoming the Buddha: The Ritual of Image Consecration in Thailand.* Princeton, NJ: Princeton University Press.

Tambiah, Stanley Jeyaraja. 1993. *The Buddhist Saints of the Forest and The Cults of Amulets: A Study of Charisma, Hagiography, Sectarianism, and Millennial Buddhism.* Cambridge: Cambridge University Press.

Thomas, Jolyon Baraka. 2015. "The Buddhist Virtues of Raging Lust and Crass Materialism in Contemporary Japan." *Material Religion* 11 (4): 485–506.

Trainor, Kevin. 1997. *Relics, Ritual, and Representation in Buddhism: Rematerializing the Sri Lankan Theravada Tradition.* Cambridge: Cambridge University Press.

Ward, Pete. 2011. *Gods Behaving Badly: Media, Religion, and Celebrity Culture.* Texas, TX: Baylor University Press.

Ward, Pete. 2017. "Celebrity Worship as Parareligion: Bieber and the Beliebers." In *Religion and Popular Culture in America*, 3rd ed., edited by Bruce David Forbes and Jeffrey H. Mahan, 313–327. Oakland, CA: University of California Press.

Williams, Duncan Ryūken. 2004. *The Other Side of Zen: A Social History of Sōtō Zen Buddhism in Tokugawa Japan.* Princeton, NJ: Princeton University Press.

Williams-Oerberg, Elizabeth. 2020. "When Buddhism Meets Bollywood: The Naropa 2016 Festival in Ladakh, India." *Himalaya: The Journal of the Association for Nepal and Himalayan Studies* 39 (2): 104–118.

Wong, Dorothy. 2018. *Buddhist Pilgrim-Monks as Agents of Cultural and Artistic Transmission.* Singapore: NUS Press.

Woodhead, Linda. 2007. "Gender Differences in Religious Practice and Significance." In *The Sage Handbook of the Sociology of Religion,* edited by James A. Beckford and N. J. Demerath III, 566–586. London: SAGE.

3.6

CHRISTMAS GIFTS AT THE TURN OF THE TWENTIETH CENTURY IN SANTIAGO, CHILE

From a Gift Economy to Commodity[1]

Olaya Sanfuentes

During her 1820s visit to Santiago, Chile, Englishwoman Mary Graham admired the fruits and flowers with which she was welcomed:

> I received a magnificent present of fruit and flowers from Doña Rosa O'Higgins. The fruit was watermelons, lucumas, oranges, and sweet limes, no others being as yet in season; and flowers, of all the finest and rarest. They were arranged on trays, covered with embroidered napkins, and borne on the heads of servants in the full dress of the palace livery.
>
> *(Graham 1824: 216)*

The people of 1820s Santiago regularly gifted flowers and fruit as a way of sharing their most prized possessions. For such an agrarian society (Sanfuentes, 2011a), the fruits of nature were not mere objects; they were full of meaning. Fifty years after Graham's visit, Chile, so influenced by its countryside, was still gifting flowers and fruit for Christmas, probably Chile's most important holiday. People enjoyed and preferred flowers, fruits, and handmade items as a way of giving and celebrating. Over time, members of the upper class distanced themselves from this type of gift and showed a preference for foreign merchandise, especially when it suggested their sophistication and connection to modern life.

The presents one chooses to give are greatly influenced by the values one ascribes to them and the principles at the foundation of one's society. Gifts can participate in the gift economy, the commodity economy, or an overlap and coexistence of the two; they are indications of a society's complexity and the gradual transformation a society undergoes over time. This chapter will approach the issue by referencing changes in Christmas gift-giving in Chile from the late nineteenth century to the mid-twentieth century. It will also show how this issue is connected to other themes: the recipients of gifts, the meaning of Christmas, and marketing and consumerism—as well as foreign influence on Chilean culture and charity.

This work is settled in historical evidence as well as the anthropological theories by Marcel Mauss and Arjun Appadurai. I also used ideas developed by Jean Duvignaud (1997),

DOI: 10.4324/9781351176231-25

Lewis Hyde (2007), and Geo Widengren (1976). In his classic book *The Gift*, Mauss (1957) considers the way traditional societies make exchanges and how these choices articulate social relationships. Generally speaking, he maintains that, by gifting or donating an object, the giver creates a tacit obligation for the receiver to reciprocate. This creates relationships of belonging, hospitality, solidarity, protection, and mutual assistance. A gift, therefore, inherently carries the possibility of exchange and relationships. Commerce, on the other hand, has no inherent value except that imposed on it by its users; it is contingent upon them. For Arjun Appadurai in *The Social Life of Things,* objects circulate in time and space through different value systems. Moreover, the author defines the commodity situation of a thing as the situation in which exchangeability (past, present, or future) for some other thing is its socially relevant feature (Appadurai 1986: 29).

Departing from the mentioned authors and historical evidence, I argue that the nineteenth-century Christmas gift in Santiago, Chile, took part in the gift economy and slowly became an actor of the commodity economy, going through intermediate, overlapping stages. Within the first stage, the aim of the gift exchange was primarily happiness, wellness, and social balance. The one who gave something was rewarded with honor, group loyalty, and other forms of gratitude. In the specific case of the Christmas gift, gift exchanges brought collective joy, seen in visual sources of public festivity and through literary sources exhibiting wishes of goodwill. In the second case—the commodity economy—the exchanges are made through fungible goods: they are subject to the market and visualized through advertising of the epoch. Both cases show the importance of the creation of value in the exchange itself. In both cases it is the object that sheds light on the social context.

Mid-nineteenth-century Christmas Gifts

Baby Jesus was the key protagonist in Christmas celebrations during the eighteenth and nineteenth centuries. His loyal followers wanted to present their material gifts to him at the foot of his manger and their spiritual gifts to him through sacrifice and spiritual assets. In this votive context, everything was symbolic: fruit materially symbolized the best of nature, while prayers and praise spiritually symbolized the best of the soul.[2] The literal nature of the gifts offered to the Baby Jesus sheds light on the importance of material forms of adoration. Families gathered each year in the hearths of their homes, convents, and churches to pray the novena—nine days of praying—starting on December 16. Each actor modulated his or her voice to unite with the collective prayer. Then a group of singers, accompanied by harpists and children on improvised instruments, made all kinds of music, sounds, and noise to honor the newborn baby. To this day, Christmas carols convey the enthusiasm displayed by the masses who praised the Baby Jesus. Oil paintings and etchings from the nineteenth and early twentieth centuries also depict the scene richly. Arturo Gordon's *The Praying of the Novena* is a good example of such work (see Figure 3.6.1).

Next came offerings of objects, which were the first summer fruits, beautiful flowers, and miniatures to decorate the nativity scenes. Fruits and vegetables had been harvested from the people's own gardens and orchards or bought at stands along La Alameda, the downtown avenue where religious followers walked, ate refreshments and fried foods, and bought artisanal crafts. The salespeople traveled in carriages over the Mapocho River Bridge to La Alameda from the La Chimba neighborhood (Santiago's current Recoleta neighborhood). On La Alameda, they sold fruits, flowers, and vegetables for weeks on end. Early twentieth-century photographs show salespeople sitting along the Alameda with their baskets of flowers and fruits, waiting for buyers (Sanfuentes 2013, 2014; Serra 2011; Silva 2012).

Figure 3.6.1 Arturo Gordon. Date information unavailable. *The Praying of the Novena*. Oil on paper. ID 2–50, National Museum of Fine Arts, Chile.

It is important to consider the meaning of the gifts given to the Baby Jesus at his birth. As I understand this activity, the gifting of flowers and fruits, objects taken from nature that will eventually rot, clearly implies symbolism at work. The worshippers would not give Baby Jesus something that will perish if it did not have great significance for them. In fact, for a rural society such as that of mid-nineteenth-century Santiago, flowers and fruit represented life. Giving away nature's first crops was a form of sharing sustenance, offering a prized possession. In the context of a community deeply dependent on nature for survival, gifting part of nature indicates a sense of detachment. By giving away products taken from fields, orchards, and gardens worshippers gave thanks for the blessings received throughout the year, showed gratitude for good harvests, and made offerings to Baby Jesus, asking for his help with the year to come. The past, present, and future converged in these natural cycles, when the divine received gifts from followers and, in turn, continued to provide what they needed. In the gift economy, the gift is intended to circulate, not stay in one place, and it should be an agent of transformation (Hyde 2007: 11).

The newborn Baby Jesus came to Earth with a double nature, which in the theological economy explains the meaning behind the people's offerings. God had become human and was embodied in a little boy; this made evident the need to take care of him, feed him, and ameliorate his needs. Visual artists recognized the power in showing Jesus as a human, in his entirety and similar in form to his loyal followers. He was celebrated and recognized while also human and imitable. The artistic styles of realism were consecrated as a form of worship through the arts (Steinberg 1989: 25). Through realism, the three-dimensional object (sculpture) had authority, and awakened tenderness and mercy in those who saw it. Witnesses were affected and transformed by an object that actively influenced them and their surroundings. The object was not seen as a mere piece of sculpted material, but rather as a living, naked boy, who in his nakedness asked for shelter, affection, song, and offers of food. The object was part of people's lives, which is much more powerful than saying the object looked as if it were alive. In this context, the offerings were an opportunity for two spheres, divine and human, to coexist on the same plane for the recipients. Each sphere offered its best, from itself and its surroundings to participate in a coexistence of natures—the divine and human that the mystery of Incarnation made possible in the theological understanding. Emphasis was placed on the possibility for everyone, in the context of their own circumstances, to offer objects from daily life to Jesus. These practices were inserted in the tradition through popular interpretation[3] of the apocryphal gospels or as the fruits of freely offered religious mercy from those who participated in the mystery of the celebration, offering several elements from their natural surroundings.[4]

In a sense, the annual building of nativity scenes is meant to create a participation in the same type of offering as the shepherds and wise men did (Arbeteta 2000: 18). This form of creating symbolic meaning is analogous to that of convent nuns in their rooms with their own votive beacons (Sanfuentes 2011a, 2011b), which are oval capsules housing the Baby Jesus surrounded by small figures. Handmade miniatures of flowers and fruits, among other things, are offered to Jesus. Their miniature nature conveys the meaning of nature—but for the nuns they show humility in the face of divinity's greatness. Like the baskets of fruit in the Nativity paintings from the viceroyalty, they are none other than symbols of the spiritual virtues and gifts being offered. Flowers and fruit symbolize fertility. Followers add their gratitude for this newborn baby, who brought everlasting life into the world, to their song of life. For this reason, agrarian societies choose these elements to offer the Baby Jesus. They have cultural and symbolic value that commune with the value of the object of celebration: Jesus and life itself. The meaning of fruit and flowers in such a society can be deduced from these objects' uses and history. If they come from the earth and are moved into the symbolic space of the nativity scene as intimate gifts, it is because they are considered very good gifts, a gift worthy of life in tandem with the divine. As offerings, flowers and fruit are elevated from daily life to the sacred (see Figure 3.6.2).

Horticulture is evident in the cutting and arrangement in baskets of the fruit. Convents and private gardens were home to orchards throughout Santiago, and they required manual labor. This relationship between work in the natural world and the spiritual life has a long history. Since the Middle Ages, monks and nuns have cultivated the land to provide food and embody their visions of nature. They see working with the Christian god's creation as a pathway to spiritual conversion. This manual labor is similar to that of the artisans making miniature figures for Nativity scenes or that of producing children's toys. The work implies an intention to make something artistic, unique, and original. The desire to transform raw materials carries with it the intention to transform the soul. In this way, craftwork is also part of the gift economy, where a handmade material good is given to please another person.

Something similar occurs with the Nativity scene figures found with the Baby Jesus in nativity scenes. Many of these figures were also acquired on La Alameda at stands that sold well-loved ceramics and porcelain dishes made by the nuns (see Figures 3.6.3a and 3.6.3b).

These little figures were made by female artisans, inheritors of the St. Clare nuns' traditions. In addition to popular stereotypical figures, animals and Chilean artifacts were represented as well. By their miniaturization, these objects acquired a size that allowed them to

Figure 3.6.2 Artist unknown. *Lantern (fanal) of the Christ Child as a doctor with a hen and a basket.* 18th and 19th centuries. Collection of the Universidad de los Andes, Santiago, Chile.

enter the sacred space of the Nativity scene. Therefore, despite the fact that they were small, they were powerful and meaningful. The worshippers took great care of them because they embodied beloved characters. Moreover, each Christmas figure acquirable on La Alameda

(a) (b)

Figures 3.6.3a and 3.6.3b Ca. 1910. Photograph of stands at the Alameda boulevard selling little figures for Nativity Cribs. Domínguez Collection from Patrimonio Fotográfico, Chile.

represented stereotypical characters from Chilean culture. The popular Chilean figures stand alongside the traditional shepherds and other humble people to warm the Baby Jesus and worship him. Every nineteenth century, Chilean Nativity contains a *huaso* (Chilean cowboy), which again confirms the rural nature of Chilean society. The newspaper *El Chileno* offers this description of a Nativity scene in 1897: three Chilean *huasos* on stick horses, with colorful blankets, large *chupallas* (traditional hats), saddle blankets, lassos, and spurs (*El Chileno,* December 14, 1897). On January 7, 1898, the newspaper *El Pueblo* relayed stories of Christmases past and described Doña Liberata's Nativity scene, which, among other figures, contained three horses outside the gate of a ranch and *huasitos* with blankets and spurs.

It was not just the representation of Baby Jesus in the nativity scene who received gifts at Christmas celebrations; women, children, and the poor did as well. Gallant men bought flowers and herbs on La Alameda and gave them to young ladies, reciting a popular poem that appears in numerous descriptions of Christmas: "*Claveles y albahaca para las niñas retacas, Claveles y rosas para las niñas hermosas* (Carnations and basil for the chubby girls; Carnations and roses for the beautiful girls)." To the children they gave sweets, the nuns' figurines, or small handmade toys, which the children played with first and then added to the Nativity scene.

Late Nineteenth-century Developments in Christmas Gift-Giving

One of the new holiday gifts that emerged in Chile at the end of the nineteenth century was the postcard. Christmas and New Year's share a season of festivities, and postcards enabled loved ones to greet one another at the close of one year and the start of the next. Postcards, a relatively recent invention, originated in the mid-nineteenth century in countries such as Austria, England, Germany, and Hungary as a way for people to connect over the holidays (Hoffman 2002: 2). The first Christmas cards did not necessarily contain Christian Christmas-related images but rather flowers, animals, and landscapes. They quickly rose to popularity in Chile: the newspaper *La Época* stated that in 1882 the Chilean Post Office delivered

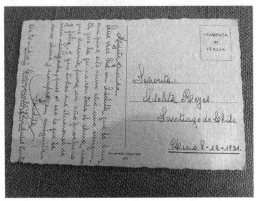

Figures 3.6.4 and 3.6.5 Christmas postcards from a private collection. Ca. 1930–1940. Santiago, Chile.

60,000 cards (*La Época*, December 18, 1882). The newspaper *El Correo* reported that, in 1887, 95,852 postcards were delivered. Some of these cards were imported from the United States or Europe; others were printed elegantly in Chile on fine cardboard (see Figures 3.6.4 and 3.6.5).

The appearance of the postcard is an early indicator of the changes to come in Christmas gift-giving, especially since postcards as gifts involved reading and writing. In anthropological terms, because society had become increasingly language based, the postcard was perceived as having added value. Meanwhile, nature-based gifts (fresh flowers and fruit, for example) continued to represent and symbolize social values. To some degree, the use of writing weakened individuals' relationships to nature while strengthening those they had with social constructs. According to sociologist Pedro Morandé, this shift from a nature-centered culture to a literacy-centered culture inevitably affects humans' relationships with nature as they begin to be mediated by the social constructs of language: nature becomes an externalization of culture (Morandé 2010: 58). While sending a Christmas card implied care and remembrance of the recipient by the sender, one mass-printed Christmas card was the same as another. For this reason, what made each card unique and meaningful was the specific loving message accompanying it as well as the fact that money had been spent on it, both on its purchase and its delivery.

Despite attempts by the government to expand education in 1860 (Serrano and Jaksic 2000), the reality of the majority of the population living in rural areas made these reforms difficult to enact (Ponce de León 2010). Literacy remained, therefore, restricted to the highest classes of urban society. Given that fact, it is astonishing to consider *La Época*'s report that 60,000 postcards were delivered in 1882.

The postcard led to the development of a profitable market reflecting the changing tides. While some people made their own cards, others bought them at stores that sold both local and imported cards, the majority of which came from the United States and Germany and depicted the winter scenes of the Northern Hemisphere. This was one of the first examples of the strong influence the United States was to have on Chilean cultural imagery.

The size of the Christmas-card market during the late nineteenth and early twentieth centuries, the methods of producing the cards, and the simplicity of card messages suggest that it was a gift with a mass audience, a gift fit for a consumerist society. It seems that during holidays season people no longer wanted to write long letters directed at specific loved ones; the Christmas card allowed them to offer simple, standardized greetings during the holidays. Production, consumption, and marketing methods steadily increased.

Christmas Trees in Chile at the Turn of the Twentieth Century

Around the 1880s, Christmas trees began to be mentioned in print. Earlier on, in the mid-1800s, Chinese lanterns and candies were hung from the branches of Chilean fruit trees themselves, but soon Christmas pines arrived. As early as December 1887 the store *Las novedades Parisienses* announced the arrival of different gadgets to decorate the Christmas tree (*El Estandarte Católico*, December 24, 1887) In terms of marketing, the Christmas tree was the visual image consumers most associated with the Christmas season. Santa Claus joined the tree to compete against the Nativity scene, as detailed below. Advertisements from 1902 feature children interacting joyfully with the tree as a way to encourage adults to purchase gifts to set under it. Other products also used the Christmas tree image in their marketing, such as the food company Meyer (*Revista Zig-Zag*, December 1920). In all likelihood, relating a product to the tree made the product more attractive. In many photographs of private Christmas celebrations from the time, families pose with huge trees filled with sparkling ornaments.[5] Presents are arranged under or next to the tree.

Christmas trees had to be decorated with fake snow because December in Santiago falls in the summer season. However, imitations of the Northern Hemisphere, such as trees and winter items, went to extremes. The result was ostentation. Previously, families and communities had competed to have the most spectacular and complete Nativity scene; as of [[time marker]] they did so with Christmas trees and the amount of presents under the tree. Families and friends took pictures of themselves in formal wear next to Christmas trees for the social pages in newspapers and magazines. Chilean historian Jorge Rojas considers that, during the 1920s, immigrants from the Northern Hemisphere were most likely to include trees in their celebrations (Rojas 2005: 378)—a custom that in time was widely adopted by the Chilean elite. Photographs from that time show Christmas trees along Chilean public avenues and in private homes.

According to the magazine *Zig-Zag*, the Christmas tree was introduced gradually to all Chilean homes, even the poorest homes (*Revista Zig-Zag*, December 1930). In 1918, the writer Antonio Acevedo Hernández wrote a Christmas comedy in which the narrator laments that children no longer remember that the presents under the Christmas tree were originally brought by Jesus (Acevedo Hernández 1918: 368). In other words, by that time Santa Claus had replaced Jesus for this task.

The situation was cause for concern. In fact, the *Asociación de Juventud Católica Femenina* (Young Women Catholics) organized a campaign to encourage Christian families to continue

Figure 3.6.6   Chilean elite family around a Christmas tree. 1908. General Collection of the Patrimonio Fotográfico, Chile.

to use the Nativity scene with Jesus, not Santa Claus, as the protagonist of the celebration and to not partake in the use of Christmas trees. In order to carry out this idea, the Association sold inexpensive Nativity scenes made of cardboard and plaster. The point was to involve children by having them make their own cardboard mangers. In *Revista Católica* (Catholic Magazine), the Association asked Catholic families to collaborate and make the campaign a success in order for the Nordic Santa Claus—which they considered an entirely sensationalized, unintellectual, and pagan custom—be substituted by the new "Birth of Jesus," which very clearly conveyed God's sacrifice of the second member of the Holy Trinity. Given that "God does not like lies," the Association wanted to protect the delicate minds of children from non-Christians and teach them the truth: knowledge that Christmas is the day on which God, King of Heaven and Earth, descended to save us and for this reason he was born in a manger in Bethlehem, poor and humble (*Revista Católica*, December 1940, 635).[6] The following year, the magazine included advertisements for home delivery of plaster Nativity scenes at an affordable price (48 cents for a twelve-piece set).

These complaints and concerns demonstrate that Nativity scenes and the Baby Jesus had lost their former protagonist status in favor of objects like the Christmas tree. The fact that Christmas trees appeared in photographs, articles, and descriptions of all kinds from the 1920s into the 1940s, reveals their gradual adoption by Santiago society. The elite and entertainment arts copied foreign trends and introduced them to the country, dictating fashion and taste (*Ecran*, December 1947).

The Era of Advertising and Consumerism

Toward the end of the nineteenth century, gift choices slowly began to change, with handmade, unique gifts making way for commercial and industrial gifts. By the 1920s, the advertising discourse had begun to take hold, inviting people to consume. Advertised toys included stuffed animals, wire and cloth clowns, balancing [rocking] horses, carriages, dolls, and play kitchens. During World War I, toy soldiers, rifles, machine guns and pistols joined the other toys. The press also began to take note of the novelties and special gifts that appeared each year in store windows. In 1892, for example, the newspaper *El Porvenir* sang the praises of magic flashlight games and curious mechanical figurines (*Diario El Porvenir,* January 1892). *El Chileno* mentions how the variety of toys and artwork available made for an excellent memento of friendship or family ties (*El Chileno,* December 15, 1892).[7]

In *The Social Life of Things,* Arjun Appadurai discusses how, in the experienced tension suffered by a society that moved between a mercantilizing economy and its traditional morality, advertisers created a discourse to connect such gifts to expressing love, not contributing to the economy. A 1915 advertisement recommended the purchase of a Victrola for peace at home: "Morality and appreciation for art will enter the home through this object, so bring home a VICTOR VICTROLA, connecting Family Love and the Divinity of Art" (*Revista Zig-Zag,* 1915).[8] It was as if by labeling new merchandise "Christmas gifts" or adding a discourse of concern for the family, the objects would be sacred (Belk 1989). Similarly, the city's department stores introduced the concept of Christmas gifts, and invested energy and creativity in the decoration of their windows—thus elevating mere merchandise into something special and symbolic. Some gifts were wrapped in special paper, another strategy to add value through the perception of a personal touch.

Some advertisements invited people to buy items that only the elite could afford: expensive crystal, silver pieces, fine jewelry, and elaborate suits. A fantastical discourse convinced customers to stroll the aisles of department stores and fairs to purchase luxury items; many of the main department store windows were converted into fairy castles, Arabian gardens, and charming caves *(La Época,* December 24, 1887). Essentially, when customers bought certain types of gifts—expensive and imported—they were also buying a lifestyle and social status that further separated societal groups. The higher classes looked at Europe and the United States as cultural models, and these cultures were therefore very influential when it came to Christmas gift-giving. That advertising in newspapers and magazines included expensive and imported items revealed their ability to represent status and define classes. This imitation completed a dual function: it made the upper class equal in their imitation of the European aristocracy while differentiating and distancing them from the country's other social classes (Henríquez 2013: 153). Products with foreign names—especially French, German, and English—were part of this dynamic as a way of guaranteeing their quality. The products that were most gifted at Christmas during the first years of the twentieth century were Krauss toys, Hardy silver pieces, Belgian lamps, silver items imported by Wescott, toys and other gifts from the Casa Francesa, photography equipment ordered from the Hans Frey catalogue, items from Morrison and Company Meyer food products, toys by Muzard, Weil gramophones, Kodak cameras, PathéBaby Christmas and New Year's presents; Parker feathers, Lionel electric trains, and Gillette razors, they all appear in the advertising of the epoch. Buying gifts for adults and children became a requirement of Christmas celebrations.

Throughout the twentieth century, children's status grew as they gained autonomy and their own identity became separate from adults. This materialized in a sort of "cult of childhood" and an even more compulsive purchasing of toys (Rojas 2005: 351). Department stores began to segment their customers, offering certain gifts to wealthier clients and less expensive ones to others. Privileged classes preferred anything that came from abroad. Even the verbal and visual discourse for selling toys was borrowed from the Northern Hemisphere. By [[time marker]], advertising was full of Christmas trees, Santa Clauses, and European or North American Christmas scenes. Chilean commerce took advantage of Europe's engagement in WWII by selling war-related toys and using military language to attract buyers. One advertisement referred to the world as an "army" of toys "marching" toward homes and the expectant eyes of children (*Revista Zig-Zag*, December 1941).

Advertising also focused on the objective that pooling every resource toward the purchase of toys and gifts was the mark of a good parent (Cavieres 2001: 32), and that parents were doing a good job in their role when they satisfied the needs—and whims—of their children.

Toys were assumed to guarantee play and happiness, but they were also a vehicle to instilling values regarding femininity, masculinity, childhood, and adulthood. Toys prepared children for their adult lives, putting within their reach small pleasures that later become duties (Rojas 2005: 352). Toys were not just a way of enjoying play, but also a way for children to imagine their future. A pewter soldier introduced the possibility of military life and strategies, a ship the possibility of a future of sea-related endeavors. It was thought that toys could truly influence children's futures, offering a way to know the world. It is difficult to imagine another interpretation for the section "Games and Professions" in *Zig-Zag* magazine. The December 1941 issue included a photograph of a girl playing with a doll in its stroller with the following caption: "Latent maternal tendencies are clear from the way this girl treats her doll" (*Revista Zig-Zag*, 1941).[9] Another photograph from *Zig-Zag* showed a girl watering flowers. The caption reads: "Carefully watering her plants, this little girl imagines her future as a housewife."[10] Games and toys were related to social representations of gender. At home, the roles and functions of family members were determined by social pressures. For this reason, toys represented systems of affection and protection, a kind of tacit commitment between an adult and a child (Perrot 1994).

The Charity Gift[11]

The gifts described in the previous section benefited only small groups of society. Poorer Santiago children accessed imported, expensive gifts only as recipients of charity. Upper-class parents recommended that their children save one of their toys to give to the less privileged—thus using toys to cultivate "love for thy neighbor" in their children. These mothers insisted their children's greatest happiness at Christmas come from sharing their toys (*Revista Zig-Zag*, December 1905). This logic can be used to understand the image on the first page of the newspaper *Diario Ilustrado*'s 1922 Christmas edition depicting a wealthy child giving a gift to a poor child (*Diario Ilustrado*, December 25, 1922). Other evidence of the elite's interest in teaching their children charity is the fact that mothers took their sons and daughters to a variety of institutions to hand out gifts to poor children as can be seen in all the local newspaper Christmas season social pages of the times.

Literature spanning several decades demonstrates great concern for poor children at Christmas time and the encouragement of charity among the wealthy. Social classes were extremely polarized; the luxuries enjoyed by some contrasted starkly with the terrible poverty experienced by others (Romero 1997: 10). Migration in high numbers from the country to the city significantly increased urban population, which only worsened the poor living conditions of these new inhabitants. The government's concern for this social issue focused on workers who held employment but could barely maintain a family. Under these conditions, gift-giving among the poor was impossible. The charity of the elite, the Church, and the State offered a variety of solutions to this social problem, awareness of which was at its height during the 1930s after the stock market crash of 1929.

In 1907, writer Antonio Orrego Barros wrote a poem expressing his compassion. In it, children ask Baby Jesus to bring them some simple gifts, and their mother suffers knowing that at daybreak they will find only the truth of their poverty. However, two girls appear bearing gifts to alleviate this poverty—because they have received more than they need. Another important example of concern with charity as a value inculcated during the child-drearing of the elite can be found in the magazine *El Peneca*. As of 1921 it was published by Elvira Santa Cruz, who emphasized the importance of moral education in upper-class children and that they ought to show concern for those of low income (Rojas 2004: 199). A reporter from the magazine *Zig-Zag*, after describing the sadness and resignation felt by the poor upon seeing shop window toy displays, recommended a solution to the miserable situation: that wealthy children reserve a few of the many toys they receive to give to the poor.

These intentions are reflected in moralistic Christmas stories told by Chileans and in special seasonal writings. In 1937, for example, the magazine *Ecran* included a letter written by a father suggesting to his son that, along with enjoying his new toys over Christmas, he consider the poor children who have no toys and, worse yet, have neither clothes nor food (*Revista Ecran*, December 14, 1937). Another eloquent example of the elite's attitude toward the poor being embodied in the Christmas gift can be found in 1918 theater comedy *Navidad* by Acevedo Hernández. Among other family conversations in this work is one shared by siblings regarding their "happy family." Magda, one of the girls, says it is important to love and take care of poor children; one of the other girls says that she is going to give to the poor half of what she receives at Christmas. One of the brothers then asks how she can even consider giving her things to those "barbarians," to which the mother responds with an apologia stating that one must love others because all humans are the same and not everyone is so fortunate as to have parents and a comfortable home. Then, the children say they will give to the poor: one of the girls will give away a doll and one of the boys a shotgun to a boy named Luis (Acevedo Hernández 1918: 367).

Magazines from the beginning of the 20th century intentionally made poor children visible in order to encourage charity (Rojas 2010: 209). In a religious society, as Chile was at that time, charity was a theological virtue the people felt was important to inculcate and develop in their children's private education. Those who practiced charity felt their consciences lightened, assured they were behaving in highly moral ways. In the second volume of *Revista Historia*, Chilean historian Macarena Ponce de León claims that upper- and middle-class women provided assistance by way of religious associations. Each had her own reasons for doing so, with altruism, charity, reformism, and/or feminism standing out. However, there is one more motive I would like to add to this list: concern with social status. The press regularly profiled those leading social initiatives of this nature. Acts of charity enjoyed a high profile thanks in particular to social magazines. The January 1911 issue of *El Peneca*, for example, publicly congratulated all of the generous women who showed concern for the poorest of children. These types of activities gave women their own space at a time when men dominated all other social activities (Ponce de León 2010: 70–71). Additionally, as the elite relied heavily on the press, models of behavior were established and promoted through public recognition. News about generous donors and their social initiatives was ingested by children and adults alike.

In terms of institutions, the State, the Church, and other organizations also took it upon themselves to make sure poor children received Christmas gifts. *La Sociedad Protectora de la*

Infancia (Childhood Protection Agency) handed out gifts each year, and some upper-class women organized collections for Christmas. The Women's Club organized a party for poor children in Recoleta in 1920, which the press reported as well attended, glitzy, and highly morally significant (*Revista Zig-Zag*, December 1920). *Zig-Zag* featured some photographs of a large, lively event in Plaza Bulnes, where tables of toys and sweets provided by the city of Santiago were laid out. The magazine calculated five thousand children had benefited from the wonderful Christmas this initiative offered them. In 1923, Chile's President and his Minister of the Interior visited the Orphan House at Christmas, where a group of children was photographed with their Christmas gifts and sweets (*Revista Zig-Zag*, January 1923). In 1939, an initiative was started by First Lady Juanita Aguirre de Aguirre Cerda, who understood the great magnitude of the tragedy experienced by parents who had no money to buy their children a simple painted doll or a clown figure filled with sawdust (*Revista Zig-Zag*, December 1939).[12] For this reason, she asked for donations from the entire country to ensure a festive, hopeful December 25th for every family in Chile.

Momentum slowly gathered behind what was to become known as *La Pascua de los niños pobres* (The Poor Children's Christmas). Coordination began in 1910, and by 1917 a commission was functioning that collected money in addition to toys, books, sweets, and necessary goods to be distributed in poorer neighborhoods, orphanages, and hospitals. By 1920 the coordinators had established seventeen sites throughout Santiago for the distribution of toys (Rojas 2005: 379). In 1939, the First Lady organized commissions to hand out gifts to thousands of children. A photograph of this activity appearing in a social life magazine shows children moving quickly toward the tables holding the gifts (see Figures 3.6.6 and 3.6.7). In 1949, Cardinal José María Caro publicly praised the work of the First Lady in the organization and sponsorship of the distribution of Christmas gifts to lower-income children (Figure 3.6.8). He said that it not only paid homage to the Baby from Bethlehem, but was a gift to Chile, their beloved country (Caro 1949).[13]

While charity was traditionally reserved for the Church, the State in Chile also began to participate in its own form: "benefit" became the term used for a secular State-led initiative (Ponce de León 2011: 26), whereas "philanthropy" was the term for donations from individuals not associated with a particular religion. During the 1930s, the State's public assistance for children became more active. This did not eliminate Catholic charity, but the Church did find itself relegated to more private and specific acts (Rojas 2005: 204). Furthermore, Christmas gifts for children became so fundamental and indispensable that many institutions were involved in providing them. Chilean newspapers and magazines from the first half of the twentieth century were full of news items about every type of institution providing Christmas for children. The magazine *Zig-Zag* organized Christmas events for the children of its employees—as did municipalities for their residents, the military for its families, the RCA Corporation for its personnel, and the chauffer's union for orphans in port cities. Each institution had its own version: the tobacco workers, the French ladies, the gas company, *Caritas*—the women of the Red Cross, the Brazilian embassy, the *Compañía de Cervecerías Unidas Providencia* (Company of United Breweries Providencia), the Salvation Army, the police, Chileans Abroad, etc. Even the *Estadio Nacional* (National Stadium) sponsored a sports festival to benefit The Poor Children's Christmas.

This transfer of gifts through works of charity speaks volumes about the power dynamics among groups of people. The wealthier gave what they had in excess as a way to narrow economic and social gaps. At exceedingly luxurious parties, money and gifts were collected to transfer to the poor (*Revista Zig-Zag*, January 1906).[14] Even raffles and high-stakes lotteries were held to collect money for those most in need. Disparity in material wealth was

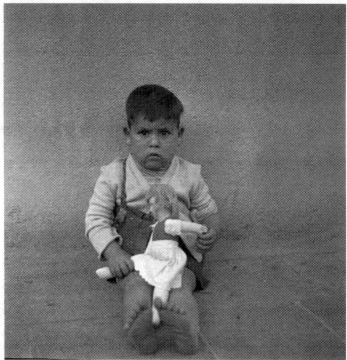

Figures 3.6.7 and 3.6.8 Photographs of Christmas gift distribution for poor children. 1950. National History Museum, Chile.

immense, but through Christmas gifts for the poor the wealthy hoped to create a bridge. This was one form of social connection between groups that had once shared public space but, with the passage of time and urban segregation, were living ever more distantly; it was a strategy for the most marginalized social groups of the time to feel a sense of belonging in a festive atmosphere.[15] It was also a way of transmitting cultural values from the higher classes to the less privileged (Ponce de León 2011: 17). Despite Macarena Ponce de León's argument that charity created connections by which poverty found an opportunity to integrate itself into society (27), I believe that the asymmetry between those who gave gifts and those who received them instead highlighted, within an attractive package, the social gap between the powerful and the poor. As Luis Alberto Romero writes, the intention of charity from the elite toward the poor—including Christmas gifts—had a moralizing result (Romero 1997: 10). Christmas gift-giving *en masse* was a way of temporarily alleviating poverty and its difficulties—but not really an intent to eradicate it at its root. A quote from *Zig-Zag* magazine on the issue is quite representative:

> That they share their happiness with those less fortunate; that among them, from birth, this feeling of social love, of noble and simple fraternity, of complete fruitfulness, incapable of making social differences disappear, given that such a feat was impossible, remedied in great part the sadness associated with them.
>
> *(Revista Zig-Zag, January 1906)*

Final Reflections

The new characteristics of Santiago Christmases did not mean the loss of popular Christmas traditions on La Alameda. For a long time, in fact, popular celebrations and those of the elite coexisted, but, starting in the first decades of the 20th century, the latter increasingly chose private venues for their celebrations. The *Club de la Unión*, the *Club Santiago*, the *Club Italiano, Club Hípico*, the *Club de Golf*, among others, hosted dances where the wealthy could keep to themselves. These venues were located on the city's east side, quite a distance from where the popular celebrations were held.

We know from sources of the time that popular Christmases on La Alameda had not ended. The picturesque sales carts still stood, as did "improvised businesses," where toys for a *peso* were sold, along with other merchandise (*Revista Zig-Zag*, January 1941). Likewise, photographs show that many age old customs were still in practice: couples dancing *cueca* on La Alameda, sales of Talagante ceramics, and groups drinking *ponche*, an alcoholic drink, popular to this day (*Revista Zig-Zag,* December 1928).

The coexistence of these two styles of celebration for a holiday that was previously celebrated more uniformly produced varied reactions. Some, those who tended to think the past was better, remembered it nostalgically. Others—concerned that, with the new Northern Hemisphere fashions, Chilean traditions could be lost—implored their compatriots to maintain the tradition of homemade gifts. In this context, it is clear why magazines printed many recipes for Christmas cookies and instructions for kids to make Christmas gifts, including how to make a low-cost cloth pig (*Ecran*, December 7 and 14, 1937, December 20, 1938).

Many 1940s intellectuals and writers complained that children no longer respected the tradition of receiving their toys on Christmas Day, and that the dizzying pace of the time made them nervous and caused them to ask for their gifts ahead of time. Richard Latcham, feeling that German and English influence had impinged on Chilean customs, lamented the loss of traditions that had not been replaced by anything of value. He also regretted that innocent toys had become complicated, elegant works of art imported at high costs (Latcham 1944). He also expressed that Christmas had changed for the worse and that the *nouveau riche* gave ostentatious gifts to their friends around overly produced dinner tables where they drink expensive whiskey, champagne, and wine.

From today's perspective, we might say that this was an era of gradual changes where gifts and offerings for the Baby Jesus and handmade gifts for giving others were giving way to industrial, serial gifts—Chilean and imported. The former bore witness to a society linked to values of the land and the dynamic cycles of nature. And not just any nature, but Chilean nature that honored the Baby Jesus; a nature whose elements functioned as gifts from the Santiago society of that time. In addition to fruit, flowers, and crafts, what people wanted to offer to Jesus and give among themselves were spiritual gifts, material security, health, and friendship. Expensive, mass-produced, imported gifts demonstrated that the society had urbanized, and during this process had sprung up stores, specialty shops, advertising, and consumerism. In tandem with these gifts, new complementary values emerged, such as status, group identification, and hoarding. People and gifts began to take their value from how much was spent on them—the more expensive the better. In order to be seen as men and women of the world, foreign customs and objects had to be acquired. Because money made tangible the modernization experienced by the county, it was not within everyone's reach. Therefore, different strategies were developed to blur the differences during important times such as Christmas.

The research for this chapter was funded by Fondecyt Project 1200553.

Notes

1   This chapter does not aim to look deeply at the complexities of the theoretical discussion about the concepts of traditional and modern. What is of greatest interest here is to look at a process (changes in gift-giving) that sheds light on certain characteristics associated with that which is considered traditional and that which is considered modern—opposing binomials that define the differences between societies that coexist in time and the evolution of a specific community over time. In general, the traditional is related to the public and collective, while the modern is related to the private and the individual. The traditional is embodied by the earth and agriculture or livestock, while the public is in industry and manufacturing. Traditional societies communicate orally and through images, while modern societies do so through writing. Traditional societies appear to be more religious and prioritized celebrations, while modern societies are more secular and prioritize work.

2   The symbolic function of gifts for Baby Jesus refers to the historic interpretation each time period makes of the gifts and offerings that were supposedly brought to Jesus at the time of his birth. According to the apocryphal gospels, each of the Wise Men's gifts had a different meaning. The shepherds brought animals and baskets of flowers and fruit. The apocryphal gospels are not considered divinely inspired and are therefore not part of the Church's official canon. In 1546 at the Council of Trent, a definitive distinction was made between the canonic and apocryphal books. However, the latter very much influenced the popular mentality and artistic representations of the most important events in the life of Christ. In terms of Christmas, the canonic gospels are very short and offer little iconographic material. The apocryphal gospels, however, provide many elements because they developed through oral tradition, which is rich in imagery. Their influence falls on fertile soil among the popular classes to create a detailed Nativity scene.

3   This is a general description of popular worship. "Popular" refers to worship that comes spontaneously from the heart and from the spiritual experience of a culture. This is not an official, established worship, nor one led by ecclesiastical hierarchy. It is spontaneous, not regulated or directed. It is not meant to show symbolically one type of Church or another, but is rather a form of religion that springs forth from feelings, not from dogma. Official worship's value lies in its use of grandiose elements to show the majesty of divinity and the institution that manages it. Popular religiosity, however, fully emphasizes the possibilities of a Godborn poor among the hay and equal to others, and its value, therefore, lies in its intimacy of expression.

4 Iconographic inspiration for representations of Baby Jesus in the manger appears to have three main sources, ranging from the most canonic to popular imagination and interpretation: firstly, the narration of the birth of Christ by Luke in his gospel; secondly, the apocryphal gospels; and thirdly, the popular imagination where local idiosyncrasies are introduced into the narration of the moment at which universal Christianity began. This can also be understood as oral tradition from the apocryphal gospels, which is adapted by loyal followers in accordance with their location and circumstances.

5 Photograph Catalog, *Centro Nacional del Patrimonio Fotográfico,* visited March 3, 2016, http://catalogo.patrimoniofotografico.cl/fichas/show/6152.

6 Translated by Suzanne Roberts from the original Spanish: "Se sustituya en los hogares la leyenda nórdica de Santa Claus, costumbre pagana que solo halaga a los sentidos y que nada dice a la inteligencia por el antiguo y nuevo "Nacimiento del Niño Dios," que nos hable muy claro del sacrificio del Redentor, de la segunda persona de la Santísima Trinidad que vino a la tierra para redimirnos del pecado. Y muy en particular, que las débiles inteligencias de los niños desviadas por personas poco católicas hacia las ideas del viejo pascuero. Las mentiras nunca son agradables a Dios se enderecen hacia la verdad y sepan que el día de pascua es el día en que el mismo Dios, Rey del cielo bajó a la tierra para salvarnos y por eso nació en el establo de Belén, pobre y humilde."

7 Translated by Suzanne Roberts from the original Spanish: "Que constituyen un excelente aguinaldo como recuerdo de amistad o de familia."

8 Translated by Suzanne Roberts from the original Spanish: "Lleve usted a su hogar una VICTOR VICTROLA y habrá conseguido un sólido vínculo entre el Amor de su familia y la Divinidad del Arte."

9 Translated by Suzanne Roberts from the original Spanish: "Latente espíritu maternal se hace visible en la manera como esta niña trata a su muñeca."

10 Translated by Suzanne Roberts from the original Spanish: "Mientras riega las plantas minuciosamente, esta niña piensa en su futuro como dueña de casa."

11 "Charity" refers to donations individuals and groups made to people in need that were imbued with a Christian religious connotation.

12 Translated by Suzanne Roberts from the original Spanish: "Ha comprendido en toda su magnitud cuan grande es la tragedia de aquellos padres que por falta de dinero no pueden ofrecer a sus hijos una humilde muñeca pintarrajeada o un payaso burlón de aserrín."

13 Translated by Suzanne Roberts from the original Spanish: "No sólo un homenaje al Niño de Belén, sino como un obsequio a la patria querida."

14 Translated by Suzanne Roberts from the original Spanish: "Every year, Santiago charity reveals more layers of its splendid and tireless fruitfulness. Our society knows how to duly recognize and award these efforts. This year we have had the evening parities in Cousiño Park. They have been truly splendid. A crowd exceeding all calculations and predictions has gathered over several nights to stroll in the park's new garden, next to the lagoon and its capricious shores, in the glow from the electric lightbulbs and thousands of colorful lanterns. After the party and the last chords of the military band, hundreds of carriages have flooded the nearby streets amid happy, motley confusion, lending new picturesque colors to the vast park in the midst of the deep calm of night painted by that crowd of loud and happy people who have saved, with warm, joyous treatment, their societal counterparts, whose misfortune is usually ignored, from much bitterness and sadness."

15 In fact, at the end of the nineteenth century, the elite distanced themselves from the rest of the classes in the public spaces to live in the southern part of the city, meet in clubs, and copy the European lifestyle in elegant cafés and private homes where talks were held. Their physical and cultural differences with poorer classes became more obvious.

References

Acevedo Hernández, Antonio. 1918. "Navidad." *Revista de Artes y Letras*, August.

Appadurai, Arjun, ed. 1986. *The Social Life of Things: Commodities in Cultural Perspective.* Cambridge: Cambridge University Press.

Arbeteta, Letizia. 2000. *Oro, Incienso y Mirra. Los Belenes en España.* Madrid: Fundación Germán Sánchez Ruipérez.

Belk, Russell W. 1989. "Materialism and the Modern US Christmas." In *Interpretive Consumer Research*, edited by Elizabeth Hirschman. Provo, UT: Association for Consumer Research.

Caro, José María. 1949. "La Pascua de Navidad y los Niños." *Revista Católica*, December. Santiago, Chile.

Cavieres, Eduardo. 2001. "Ser infante en el pasado. Triunfo de la vida o persistencia de estructuras sociales. La mortalidad infantil en Valparaíso, 1880–1950." *Revista de Historia Social y de las Mentalidades* 5: 31–58.

Diario Ilustrado. 1902, 1906, 1922. Santiago, Chile.

Duvignaud, Jean. 1997. *El sacrificio inútil*. Mexico: Fondo de Cultura Económica.

Ecran. 1932, 1935, 1937, 1938, 1941, 1947. Santiago, Chile.

El Chileno. Santiago, Chile, 1897.

El Peneca. Santiago, Chile, 1911.

El Porvenir. Santiago, Chile, 1892, 1904.

Graham, Mary. 1824. *Journal of a Residence in Chile During the Year 1822. And a Voyage from Chile to Brazil in 1823*. London: Printed by A. & R. Spottiswoode.

Henríquez, María Regina. 2013. "Oferta comercial, publicidad e imágenes en torno a la élite. Valparaíso 19001940." *Universum* 28 (1): 149–172.

Hoffman, Robert C. 2002. *Postcards from Santa Claus: Sights and Sentiments from the Last Century*. Garden City, NY: Square One Publishers.

Hyde, Lewis. 2007. *The Gift: How the Creative Spirit Transforms the World*. Edinburgh: Canongate Books.

Latcham, Ricardo. 1944. "La Pascua de antaño." *Revista Zigzag*, December. Santiago, Chile.

La Época. Santiago, Chile. 1882, 1885, 1887.

Mauss, Marcel. 1957. *The Gift: Forms and Functions of Exchange in Archaic Society*. New York: W. W. Norton.

Morandé, Pedro. 2010. *Ritual y Palabra, Aproximación a la religiosidad popular latinoamericana*. Santiago: Instituto de Estudios de la Sociedad.

Perrot, Jean. 1994. "Play Prepare Father's Christmas Future." *Children's Literature Association Quarterly* 19 (3): 128–133.

Ponce de León, Macarena. 2010. "La llegada de la escuela y la llegada a la escuela. La extensión de la educación primaria en Chile 1840–1907." *Revista Historia* vol. II, n. 42.

Ponce de León, Macarena. 2011. *Gobernar la pobreza. Prácticas de Caridad y beneficencia en la ciudad de Santiago, 1830–1890*. Santiago: Editorial Universitaria.

Revista Católica. Santiago, Chile, 1940, 1949.

Revista Zig-Zag. Santiago, Chile, 1905, 1906, 1908, 1909, 1916, 1920, 1923, 1928, 1930, 1939, 1941, 1944.

Rojas Flores, Jorge. 2004. *Moral y Prácticas Cívicas en los niños chilenos, 1880–1950*. Santiago: Ariadna.

Rojas Flores, Jorge. 2005. "Juegos y alegrías infantiles." En *Historia de la vida privada en Chile*, coordinated by Rafael Sagredo and Cristián Gazmuri. Santiago: Taurus.

Rojas Flores, Jorge. 2010. *Historia de la Infancia en el Chile Republicano, 1810–2010*. Santiago: JUNJI. https://www.aacademica.org/jorge.rojas.flores/9.

Romero, Luis Alberto. 1997. ¿Qué hacer con los pobres? Elites y sectores populares en Santiago de Chile, 1840–1895. Buenos Aires: Sudamericana.

Sanfuentes, Olaya. 2011a. "Agricultura y cultura en el convento de monjas. Una especial devoción al Niño Jesús en el siglo XIX." *Estudios Avanzados* 15: 161–180.

Sanfuentes, Olaya. 2011b. "Artes y prácticas votivas. La devoción al Niño Jesús entre monjas de convento en Chile durante el siglo XIX." In *Devozioni, Pratiche e Immaginario religioso. Espressioni del Cattolicesimo Tra 1400 e 1850. Storici italiana e cileni a confront*, edited by René Millar and Roberto Rusconi, 109–127. Rome: Viella.

Sanfuentes, Olaya. 2013. "Tensiones navideñas. Cambios y permanencias en la celebración de la navidad en Santiago durante el siglo XIX." *Revista Atenea* 507: 149–163.

Sanfuentes, Olaya. 2014. "Pesebres en acción. Representación y performance en el análisis de los nacimientos decimonónicos en Santiago de Chile." In *De nombres y obras. El arte monástico gallego a través de sus autores. Opus Monasticorum VII*, coordinated by Carme López Calderón and edited by Ana Goy Diz and Juan Manuel Monterroso, 353–368. Santiago de Compostela: Andavira.

Serra, Daniela. 2011. "Hoy es Nochebuena y la ciudad está de fiesta. La celebración de la Navidad en Santiago. 1850–1880." *Revista de Historia Iberoamericana* 4 (2): 112–130.

Serrano, Sol, and Iván Jaksic. 2000. "El poder de las palabras: la Iglesia y el estado liberal ante la difusión de la escritura en el Chile del siglo XIX." *Revista Historia* 33: 435–460.

Silva, Elisa. 2012. "La Noche buena en La Alameda. Descripción de una tradición en tiempos de modernización. Santiago de Chile, segunda mitad del siglo XIX." *Revista Historia* 45 (1): 199–246.

Steinberg, Leo. 1989. *La sexualidad de Cristo en el arte del Renacimiento y en el olvido moderno.* Madrid: Hermann Blume.

Widengren, Geo. 1976. *Fenomenología de la Religión.* Madrid: Cristiandad.

3.7

THE JEWEL OF MEN

Weaponry as Material Religion among Muslim Communities

Younes Saramifar

Since the ninth century CE, the Muslim worlds of West and Central Asia produced numerous treatises *(risālah)* on ethics, etiquette, religious practices, civil law, and governance. These treatises covered all aspects of social life and were authored by Muslim literati and learned jurists across the early Caliphates and the later Ottoman and Mughal Empires. Ebn al-Nadī, a learned Muslim in tenth-century Baghdad, in his famous compendium *Al-fehrest*, which claims to catalogue the knowledge possessed by Muslim scholars, traces citations of weapon-handling treatises to manuscripts written as late as the Sassanid Empire (Malyeri 1973). Iranian historians such as Afshārī and Moravijī (2017: 21) suggest these weapon-handling treatises turned orally transmitted knowledge and practices of local champions into written generational wisdom. However, governing authorities rarely ordered the treatises about making weaponry—manuals on bow-carving and general weapon-handling. Curious-minded elites or rebellious literati such as Ibn Baqāl (d. 1162 CE), who encouraged peasant mobilization against feudal or ruling Caliphs, penned most of the treatises on weaponry and weapon craft. They spoke less about warring and military strategies than on the elaboration of weapons, weapon-craftsmanship, rituals of applying weapons, and how to choose from a variety of deadly options—such as long swords, curved swords, double-edged knives, lances, and the short, long, or composite bow with different arrow-types. Most of these treatises promote the use of the bow and arrow among Muslims. The authors supposed archery is the best and most elegant form of war-making according to the traditions prescribed for Muslims by the prophet Muhammad (Afshārī and Moravijī 2017).

These treatises, which I mention in the next section, are my opening exemplars to go beyond the historical importance of weaponry and war-making among Muslims. I open them to show how crafting weapons and their combat applications are intertwined with religion and the senses. These treatises elucidate how, up to today, calling upon divine forces while crafting weapons, drawing swords or bows, or placing arrows embodies the enduring entanglement of worship and warship, which is encouraged by rituals that materially express warriorhood. By focusing on weaponry as socioculturally situated objects that enact religion, I elucidate how the entanglement of subject and object reproduce and repackage religiosity and militancy. This chapter expands my argument from historical instances to the present time, in which rifles such as the AK-47 and the Dragunov sniper rifle are familiar icons of transnational Islamist militias. I begin by exploring the entanglement of Islamic

DOI: 10.4324/9781351176231-26

traditions with ergonomics and affordances of weaponry and by highlighting the notions of masculinity that shape the social life of weaponry in the present. Weaponry, I argue, explain the emergence of warrior subjectivities from subject–object relationships cultivated in the name of God.

Weaponry's Islamic Historicity

Writing and circulating treatises on weapon-handling were popular among Arabic-speaking Muslim literati and learned jurists. Historians of the Arabic peninsula acknowledge Abū Ya'qūb 'Isḥāq ibn 'Isḥāq's treatise on weaponry (d. 1037 CE) as being one of the earliest works on weapon-handling (Salmān 1989). Abū Ya'qūb, a transmitter of hadith and a jurist, authored the *Virtues of Archery* (*Faḍā'il al-Ramī*); other Arab literati, such as the lesser-known poet and historian Ibn Baqāl (d. 1162 CE), continued this genre from the tenth century CE onward (Sāmīrani 1997). Farsi-speaking Muslim literati like Muḥammad ibn Manṣūr, the author of the *Treatise on the Etiquette of War and Warriorhood* (*Risālah fī Ādāb-i Ḥarb va Al-Shajā'a*), showed interest in this genre from the mid-fourteenth century onward. Ibn Manṣūr's writings on weapon-handling were inspired by the Arthaśāstra, a third-century BCE Sanskrit treatise covering, among other topics, military strategy. The rise of interest in weaponry treatises coincided with the growth of Sufi and dervish orders. They became explicitly inclined toward small-scale partisan-armed resistance against the Mongol rulers, who ruled Persia—current Iran, Afghanistan, and some other Central Asian regions like Tajikistan and Azerbaijan—in the early fourteenth century (Matin 2007). Dervish mobilized in different groups; the most prominent groups—such as the *Sarbidārān*, literally translated as "heads for the gallows"—encouraged the public to see Islam as a lifestyle and ideological ground. Rather than limiting Islam to prayers and chanting in solitude, they believed Islam should be practiced in the form of a mobilizing ideology to confront Mongol tyrants (see Pistor-Hatam 2014).

Sarbidārān were the most prominent of the dervish who mobilized across Persia as armed rebels against the ruling Mongol Empire (Zabih 1986). Gradually, the treatises popularly known as *Chapters in Chivalry* (*Futuwat-Nāmah*) and *Treatise on Archery* (*Risālah Kamāndārī*) were written and distributed across the Persianate cultural territories such as the current Afghanistan, Iran, and Tajikistan. They elaborated on warrior ethics, weapon-handling, and chivalry and became the widespread mode of educating subversive groups who claimed to be the champions of the weak against the feudal and landowning rulers. These often handwritten manuscripts produced for armed rebels a common language and articulation of weaponry. Archers and dervish rebels such as Najm ad-Dīn Kubra, who fought against Mongols (Hanif 2002), gained access to new social imaginaries of war-making and theaters of conflict.

The authors of these treatises were literati par excellence. They did not write instruction manuals in the narrow sense of the word. Rather, they infused the prose with mystic-religious poetry meant for the readers' edification. The treatises convey the literati's vast knowledge of the Qur'an, Islamic jurisprudence, and sociocultural practices, which entangled with weaponry craft skills and ideals of warriorhood. The Islamic canon and poetic cosmology of Islamic mysticism were the language of weaponry and weapon-handling. For instance, Sayyid Mīr 'Alavī, dedicates the fourth chapter of his *Instruction in Archery* (*Hidāyat al-Ramī*) to poetry and the poetic articulations of placing an arrow in a bow, and the optimum force for drawing a bow. His poetry is combined with explanatory prose that refers to Hadith and Quranic lines that encourage resisting and mobilizing against enemies. Military objects approved and promoted by religious sensibilities can, therefore, suggest how religion facilitated the armed mobilizations of rebels, subversive groups, and non-state actors. For example, various types of bows and arrows were the most advised weapons approved by Islamic sentiments and traditions because of the numerous sayings by Muhammad demonstrating the Prophet's affinity for archery (cf. McEwen 1974; for more about Turco-Iranian archers see Latham 1970). Additionally, bows and arrows were the weapons of choice for unorganized rebels and low-intensity warfare (Allsen 2002).

Tracing historical modes of articulating the meaning of archery highlights how militancy and Islam intertwined through weapons. Sayyid Mīr 'Alavī, the author of *Instruction in Archery* (*Hidāyat al-Ramī*), dedicates a good portion of his treatise to the obligations and intentions in archery according to Islamic jurisprudence and sayings of the Prophet. He compiles views of Muhammad on archery and interprets Qur'anic verses accordingly—for instance, suggesting that "archery is a form of worship which an archer should not practice without first purifying himself through Islamic ablution" (Afshārī and Moravijī 2017: 121). The instructions are not limited to rituals and chanting Qur'anic names while handling weapons. They especially pay attention to mental preparation and shaping the mindset of the weapon users, who may achieve a blessed alliance with the weapon under *divine interventions* (*fazl-i ilāhī*). Sayid Mīr 'Alavī stresses that "each act of shooting is shaped by *nīyat* (intention) and then, the skills of a weapon user. Therefore, his practice would be only a *la'b* (play) or *bāzī* (a game) without any divine value if he does not intend to shoot wholly in the way of God" (cited in Afshārī and Moravijī 2017: 122). The intention: recalling and reciting the divine turn, then shooting—applying the weapon to a sacred act. By handling weapons the believer becomes the agent of God. The work of God, in other words, is a modality of handling lethal equipment.

The treatises do not focus on weapon users and fighting equipment alone. They also highlight how weapons are the crafts forged collectively, which will eventually lead the community of Muslims to paradise (Khorasani 2006). Sharaf al-Dīn 'Alī Yazdī (d. 1454 CE), the author of the *Etiquette of War* (*Ādāb-i Jang*), repeats the Prophet's saying that "three people, at least, enter into the paradise by one arrow that is thrown in the name of God; the one who crafts it, the one who buys it, and the one who shoots it" (Afshārī and Moravijī 2017: 53). An arrow, or simply the object of war, traverses across a society infused with religious sensibilities, and it becomes more than an arrow—a thing or a matter without content. An arrow or a sword emanates "semiotic materiality" (Law 2009) overarched by religion and religiosity—from the moment of production, to circulation, and finally when it arrives into an archer's quiver or a swordsman's scabbard. Though arrows and swords have fallen out of military use, the remanence of this semiotic materiality constructed in the past remains tangible to this day. The Shah Jahan Mosque in the United Kingdom organized archery lessons to attract younger generations of the Muslim community by reminding them that archery is a *Sunnah* (tradition) recommended and beloved by the Prophet of Islam.[1]

Weapons have moved, crawled, and traveled in the everyday practices of Muslims. They became part and parcel of religious sensibilities, which permit them to vibrate beyond their aesthetics, design, and craftsmanship. However, I do not suggest that a weapon can be entirely reduced to the meanings that it represents according to the sociocultural settings. The craftsmanship and effective, pragmatic design facilitated the production and intensification of meanings. For instance, short composite bows became the craft of Muslim communities whose warriors rode Arab or Persian breeds of horses. These horses were shorter than European varieties, and short composite bows allowed the archers to maintain their balance well while riding (Khorasani and Bede 2018; Loades 2019). Through these affordances which bodies, animals, and the waring tool entangled with each other, the short composite bow became the blessed craft, and the longbow became the weapon of the non-Muslim other (Paterson 1966). The design, the mechanism, and the matter in itself contribute to the meanings' and semiotics' stickiness in holding on to the associated objects. The entanglements, therefore, are enabled by the ergonomics of the matter of weaponry rather than only ideological and religious grounds alone.

Objective Agency

The warriors of the past and the Muslim militants and self-proclaimed resistance fighters of the present emerge in the oscillation between the subject (weapon user) and the object (weapon). This emergence is not solely based on the Islamic canon or the supposed inherent violence associated with Islam and Muslims (Sidahmed and Ehteshami 1996). Warrior subjectivities do emerge, however, in the enactments that make a thing or a person to become *Islamic* (cf. Ahmed 2016). The emergence of a Muslim warrior subjectivity is the process of the embodiment of material religion in which objects such as weapons acquire agentive capacity. The acts of analyzing weapons' agentive capacities and tracing the emergence trajectories of warrior subjectivities make it possible to understand violence in the name of Islam.

The entanglement of violence and Islam became apparent to me during interactions I had with Hezbollah combatants in Lebanon, Mujahedin in Afghanistan, and PMF fighters in Iraq. Members of all three militants utter particular Qur'anic verses before shooting at their selected target. Sniper marksmen and combatants who were assigned the RPG (rocket-propelled grenade) recited the seventeenth verse of the eighth chapter of the Qur'an while locking their sight on the target. They would utter: "It was not you who threw, but it was Allah who threw" and then pull the trigger. The weapon lends its agentive capacities to users and facilitates the emergence of the warrior. In other words, the object and the subject complement each other; they entangle and become a performative social unit by way of religion and religiosity. The conflation of a subject and an object by way of religion renders the divine tangible during combat. Accordingly, a weapon becomes a material expression of religion in the midst of blood and mayhem.

A weapon, as the material expression of Islam for a Muslim combatant, becomes the objective agent (the object that acts as an agent) that joins him and allows God to operate through a combatant. A weapon is a vital link—*the* actor who connects a combatant to God by providing the possibility of resigning his active agency. A weapon encourages a combatant to vacate his own agentive capacity and initiate the divine to work through him. This process explicitly demonstrates how entanglement occurs via material expressions of religion in Islam. To tease out the entanglement and portray subject-object conflation, I will break down the steps into a more detailed articulation. (1) A combatant picks up the weapon and selects the target. This is the primary military performance, embodied through repetitive practice. (2) At the very moment, the weight of the RPG is felt on the combatant's shoulder, or the pressure of the sniper rifle is felt on the collar bone, the warrior begins reciting the appropriate verse. (3) While he recites one eye is shut, the target is fixed, and the breath and body posture are stabilized. (4) The trigger is half-pressed. (5) With the uttering of the verse, the RPG shooter exhales or slowing down the breath for the marksman—then, trigger is fully engaged. (6) The weapon is disengaged from the body.

These steps occur effortlessly, and are continually repeated with no break in their rhythm[2]. Recalling God, uttering the Qur'anic verses, and evoking the divine are the processes bonded to the material entity known as the weapon. Combatants allow God to operate through them via a weapon. In other words, weaponry mediate God and empowers combatants only by way of compliance and acknowledging the divine. I noticed Iraqi Shia combatants themselves performed such compliance when they answered my question as to why they run toward the enemy's post before calculating risk: "We left ourselves in the embrace of Allah and trusted our weapons; we just run to the enemy." These men were deployed to the eastern coast of Syria, an unfamiliar territory for which they received no training. Stuck in the crossfire, they held on to their guns in frustration, uttering, "nothing may occur without the force of God," then screaming while running toward the enemy. Fortunately for them, their tactic worked, causing fear and unexpected chaos along the enemy's lines. Combatants submit to the lethal object and expand their subjectivity by calling on God to dissolve (*hulūl*) in an entanglement that cannot be fulfilled without a weapon.

The six steps noted above are the performative contours of a militant subjectivity that falls apart without the weapon that is shrouded with religiosity. A weapon and a combatant who handles the weapon according to the necessary method and strategy are not isolated, interacting entities or merely cooperating components. The weapon is desired ideologically and religiously far before the union. Hence, the entanglement of subject and object becomes socially tangible and performatively vibrant in the materiality of combat as God steps in to validate the act of shooting. The materiality of combat and God's presence in wars would not occur without the agentive capacities of a weapon. I stress that it is the agentive capacity of an object such as a weapon that allows the enactment of the divine and the emergence of militant subjectivities, yet it demands submission from its human user to entangle. In sum, the agency of a combatant is not only based on his individuated participation in combat. His agency is located in an assemblage of objects such as weapons and intangible forces such as the divine operation that appears in the union of a combatant and his weapon.

A Muslim combatant is constituted neither solely by his ideological and religious motivations nor entirely by his warcraft equipment. It is the materiality of the objects of warcraft, the semiosis based on Islam, and the sociality produced around the objects of a war waged in the name of Allah that lead to the emergence of a Muslim combatant. This emergence is not wholly ideological or cosmological; it is also shaped by an object and its material mode of existence (read: design).

Entanglement and Symbolic Potency

Weaponry carries material expressions of religion among Muslim communities beyond wars, conflicts, and resistance. These material expressions leak into everyday forms of piety, mediate meanings, and shape political consciousness. For instance, Islamic jurisprudence (*fiqh*), regardless of sects and schools of interpretation, strongly recommends that clergymen who lead Friday prayers hold a weapon while offering their sermons before the prayers (Calder 1986). This contemporary practice is based on extending Muhammad's habit of delivering sermons while leaning on a sword, a walking cane, or a bow. The practice goes as far back as to Ibn Ḥayyūn, also known as Nuʿmān Maghribī (910–974 CE), the high jurist of the Fatimid dynasty, who suggested that Muhammad's habit was a tradition that should inspire Muslim clergymen. He emphasized the combination of words (sermon) and sword (the performative object) during the rituals so as to convey to enemies that the sword shall come if the words are not accepted (Poonawala 2001). The weapon, or the lethal object, became part of the clergymen's ensemble and supplied meanings to his spoken metaphors and indirect hints. For instance, in most Friday sermons the term "other" does not always imply the enemy to whom believers should react with aggression. However, it does refer to the antagonistic other if it is uttered by a clergyman holding a weapon. This inference is based on how a weapon, as material expression, lends itself to the ritual and exudes performative intensity into sermons.

Jurists welcomed Nuʿmān Maghribī's intervention, continuing his legacy across Islamic territories. His interpretation was especially disseminated and propagated by the branches of Islam such as Ismaili and Twelver Shias, which emphasized armed resistance. A prominent example is the careful attention paid to the weapon carried by Ali Khamenei, Iran's highest religious authority. After prayers, those in attendance, via social media or in political forums, discuss the type and the manufacturing country of the weapon Ali Khamenei had held and circulate extensive guesswork about why he chose that specific weapon. These conversations and attempts at decoding are not idle and vain chatter; they indicate how specific social imaginaries of the community of believers are tied to weapons as political objects and lethal crafts.

From the time that he has assumed the role of Iran's highest religious authority in 1989, Ali Khamenei has often held the Heckler and Koch G3 during his Friday sermons—whereas other clergymen across Iran carry the AK-47 or the decommissioned bolt-actioned rifle colloquially called Brno because it was manufactured in Brno, Czechoslovakia (the manufacturer refers to the rifle as the Karabiner 98 kurz). The AK-47, which is considered the weapon of resistance, was used widely during the Iran-Iraq war (1980–1988). It is also the official weapon issued to the personnel of the Iranian Revolutionary Guard under the command of Ali Khamenei. However, he avoids holding the AK-47, preferring the G3 which is the official weapon issued to Iran's national defense forces, Ali Khamenei, as the leader of the nation, holds the weapon carried by the national defense forces while addressing the *nation*—thus attending to the national dimension of his leadership instead of projecting a wholly religious persona. The weapon speaks to the crowd; its implication: he who carries it presents himself to the nation.

In 2013, the Dragunov sniper rifle was famously associated with Iranian forces deployed abroad to fight against ISIS (Islamic State of Iraq and Syria). Consequently, this weapon was recognized by some Iranians as the weapon used against ISIS. In turn, Ali Khamenei began holding a Dragunov sniper rifle during the Friday prayer sermons. The weapon gained more notoriety as Iranian marksmen's pictures circulated across social media. When some of them were killed in action, the dedicated revolutionaries' perception of the Dragunov changed—it was no longer a lethal rifle, but the attribute of martyrs in the war against ISIS.

The weapon gained symbolic potency among the community of dedicated believers of the Islamic Republic and Iranian revolutionaries committed to armed resistance. The symbolic potency of weaponry is taken very seriously by some clergymen, who, rather than holding a single weapon, instead pray fully armed during the sermon. Gholam Reza Hasani, the late representative of Ali Khamenei in one of the northern provinces of Iran, always carried a weapon and held an additional handgun during prayers. He would famously hold the handgun in his palms during a specific part of his prayers as if offering it to God. Gholam Reza Hasani does this against the advice of Nuʿmān Maghribī, who warns that the allure of symbolically potent and lethal weaponry can enchant to the extent that carrying a weapon supersedes the words of the prayers and sermons, which are supposed to come before any display of power (Daneshgar 2014).

The symbolic potency is not only the representation of meanings and conveying of political messages. The symbolic potency (read: material semiosis) refers to capacities that an object exhibits, which is entangled in social interactions and contributes to militant subjectivities. I understand these capacities through the use of an object and its treatment in the everyday lives of Muslim communities. The capacities of a weapon appear due to its place as a "transitional object" (Bollas 1987) in the everyday lives of some Muslim believers and Islamic revolutionaries. The transitional object (weapon) is the enviro-somatic transformer for those who subscribe to armed resistance and martyrdom in Islam.

Social Demarcations and Becomings

Taking weaponry as transitional objects accounts for the entanglements in material religion, modes of subjectivities, and everyday life. Additionally, my approach offers an account of the entanglement to ask why certain objects that operate as the material expression of a religion stick to users. Thus, I have argued, religion as a system of belief is not only founding principles (*Uṣūl-i Dīn*, cf. Amir-Moazami et al. 2011; Coleman 2013); or even following founding principles words by words but believers appropriate, reshape, and translate those principles into their own socialities. The everydayness of religious practices and ways of being religious sets the stage in becoming men, especially for young men who present one's own gender *along* with weaponry in some Islamic societies (cf. Schielke and Debevec 2012).

Tracing gender expressions by researching how weaponry are handled in Muslim communities, highlights the fact that religion does not produce social demarcations in isolation from sociocultural settings, which, in turn, shape religion. For instance, most young men and teenagers in the town of Najrāb, Afghanistan—less than 100 km from Kabul—ride motorcycles to school sporting well-maintained AK-47s. These students are neither militants nor members of subversive groups against the Afghan state, and nor do they belong to the Taliban or any other Islamist organization. Weapons, especially the AK-47, are part of the everyday attire of those in the process of becoming men in the eyes of the community. Motorcycles and weapons signal coming of age for young men who acquire sufficient masculine credibility and male sociability to possess a mode of transportation and also be trusted with a lethal object.

A weapon, as a transitional object, marks that a boy is becoming a wise "man," someone who recognizes the value and worth of life itself—someone trusted to respect life at large even as he is equipped to take a life. The AK-47 becomes the mark of transitioning and transforming from boyhood to manhood because, eventually, the respected men—the middle-aged and elderly men in Najrāb—do not need to carry weapons since they are already the measure of masculinity in their community. The weapon and its physical presence serve these young Afghan men for a specific transitional period from adolescence into early adulthood. The perpetuation of conflicts in Afghanistan, however, does not allow weaponry to vanish completely from adults' lives and social imaginaries.

Women become those who offer life by virtue of giving birth. Men in their "masculine" wisdom determine the worth and value of life by virtue of their privilege to tote weapons that terminate life. These ideas and social demarcations are condensed into the subject-object relationships such as the one between a man and his weapon.

Weaponry as the mark of gender expression is not a recent phenomenon; it has been noted in various territories where communities of Muslims dwell back to the time of the Prophet of Islam (seventh century CE). Indeed, his saying "the weapon is the jewel of men" is well known—and well cited by Muslim men to justify their enthusiasm for weaponry and their open carry of weapons. His approval of this cultural tradition loaded with gender demarcation eased its entry into the *Sunnah,* which was already patriarchal in its design. For instance, Heinze (2014) and Khalaf (1990) describe the *Janbiya,* the small dagger fashionably carried by some Arab men, as a mark of masculinity in Yemen. The dagger, worn on their right side or on the front, becomes a gender expression that inspires "gun culture" among Muslim men in Yemen (Heinze 2014). Muhammad's *Sunnah* affirms gender expression based on cultural practices and the historical trajectory of local identities. The entanglement of an object in the lives of Muslim men via Islam, and the facilitation of encounters with the divine, is more than an affair of men and God, and can be disentangled by analyzing how social actors and their gender expressions emerge from the weaponry-subjectivity nexus.

The possession and carrying of weapons in Yemen—the second most heavily armed nation in the world—is not necessarily based on the idea of self-defense or armed resistance in the name of God. Weapons are "part of the national character and more linked to heritage, traditions, and norms than to violence" (Miller 2003: 3). The historical background, cultural settings, social contracts, and religious framework strengthen the role of weaponry as the agent of gender expression. However, the more interesting question is how social demarcations such as gender expression explain why weaponry become sticky objects in Muslim men's lives. Why do lethal objects—weapons such as the AK-47, the Dragunov, or the G3—become the material expression of religion for Muslim men? These questions by no means deny prejudice, bias, and media framing of Muslim men in Western media (Melki 2014). These questions can be understood better by tracing how socialization *in* violence encourages Muslim men to craft relationships with lethal objects.

To elaborate on the connections between weaponry, masculinity, and socialization *in* violence within an Islamic framework I return to Iran and its religious authority. Shia jurists refer to the chapter on Jihad from volume 32 of Saḥīḥ Muslim, especially "the weapon is the jewel of men," to approve the open carry of weaponry for Muslim men. There are numerous fatwas (Islamic ordinances) that consider carrying a weapon openly in public permissible by Islam. However, these fatwas are overridden by whoever assumes the role of the *Valī-i Faqīh*—the Guardian Jurist—or any leader recognized locally as the highest religious authority and politically accepted jurist for Shia Muslims. Basically, a certain learned man can seize the religiously given rights of some Muslim men. He can administer all relationships that his followers would establish with lethal objects by virtue of God, his office, law, and social acceptance. *Valī-i Faqīh* is the man enabled by law, society, and God to precede all men and their desires (Kadīvar 1998). It seems he is the most "masculine" man who can either permit raising arms or prohibit their usage. The *Valī-i Faqīh* and his relationship with weaponry turn him into the highest model of masculinity inspired by Islam. He is able to administer, permit, and prohibit the socialization *in* violence via his authority over the lethal objects. Additionally, Muslim militias accept the authority of *Valī-i Faqīh* because their belief in him legitimizes the act of killing and the use of weaponry.

The combatants whom I encountered during my fieldworks in various parts of West and Central Asia displayed contradictory relationships with weaponry. Our conversations always began with flamboyant excitement or macho comments about their weapons—tones that often changed the longer we talked (Saramifar 2015, 2018a, 2018b). Many sniper marksmen had long-winded stories about their deep affection for rifles, describing how each weapon reminds them of the legacy of martyrs, martyrdom, and finding the path to salvation (*ras-tigārī*). And yet, for some, their "dear old friend" smelled like death. With bitter expressions marksmen mentioned the unpleasantness of their rifles heating up—unpleasant because, as one man shared: "The smell of hot steel alerts me to the corpses which we leave behind."

In such moments in these conversations, the weapon, the very material expression of religion that so often connoted desire, could also provoke disgust—which invariably led to a short, uncomfortable silence. Whenever one marksman hinted at the functional reality of the weapon, reflecting on the fact that weapons kill, another marksman would break the silence by cracking a joke. The joke would bring back sexual innuendos and gender demarcations. For instance, one Lebanese marksman from the Hezbollah Resistance Movement described the relationship with his rifle as resembling his relationship with his wife. The laughter stopped him from continuing, but someone else clarified sarcastically that both relationships are based on a hole (Note that there is a hole in the telescopic sight mounted over the rifle.) The sniper rifle, along with its accessories, slips into the joke and gendered everyday imaginaries of these marksmen. The sequential process of this slippage explains the stickiness of weaponry as the material expression of religion.

When the weapon provokes moments of disgust despite its allure it becomes an abject object—but just briefly, since it is then immediately pulled back from abjection by way of humor, sexually loaded satire, and vulgarity (Entirely unlike Julia Kristeva's conception of the abject [1941], which remains as such in a fixated mental state). The profanity restores the object and its capability of facilitating encounters with the divine among Muslim men. Put differently, gender demarcations and religiosity are not infused into the weapon just so as to render possible the bearing of the abject lethal tool in the midst of conflict, pain, loss, and mayhem. Additionally, the infusion permits Muslim men to sustain and keep intact meanings and materiality already at work. The weapon becomes an integral part of the process of masculinity and becoming a Muslim man, which forces the men to craft strategies and tactics for coping with the lethal object. The modes of accepting and handling weaponry as masculine acts are not set by fixed cultural or religious scripts but are formed by other dynamics and interactions too.

All these historical conditions, cultural settings, and heteronormative worldviews contribute to these gender demarcations. However, for the social scientific understanding of religion, it is not enough to keep returning to these broad factors and repeating the same old tune. Instead, the queries should break open complexities by asking what other conditions reproduce and consolidate the demarcations in each era.

The Weapon in Itself?

Allen Feldman writes in his analysis of IRA militants, "The masked paramilitary holding a weapon is a tool holding a tool" (1991: 53). His attempt to identify the exact conceptual location where the weapon performs and the paramilitary appears reduces human and nonhuman to juxtaposed, decorated entities in opposition to each other. In this chapter, I showed that nonhuman agents such as weapons hold allure and agentive capacities in the formations of male Muslim warrior subjectivities. I stress weaponry are material expressions that some Muslim men interact with and the symbolic potency of their interactions is shaped by sociocultural dynamics *as well as* founding principles that shaped Islam since Muhammad. Weapons enact religion. They neither wholly constitute religion nor entirely fall in the domain of religiosity and individual piety. Therefore, it can be illuminating to analyze how weaponry become sticky material expressions for Muslim men in historical and contemporary settings. I substantiated my framework at three different levels; first, the subject-object relationship and the production of warrior subjectivities; second, the symbolic potency of weaponry and their political use; and, finally, the abject nature and gendered meaning of weaponry. These three levels account for the entanglement of things/objects and people. I disentangled the entanglement of lethal objects in the everyday lives of some Muslims and showed that lethal objects do not serve mere academic fascination for social complexities. Instead, they demonstrate how socialization *in* violence falls beyond Islamic (or any other religion's) principles. In sum, the study of religion's understanding of religious and political violence can be furthered by a focus on weapons as nonhuman agents.

Notes

1 Islamic archery revived in Surrey mosque. *BBC Asian Network*. March 6, 2012.
2 They do not utter the same Qur'anic verses if they switch to a weapon that requires far less concentration while shooting toward the enemy.

References

Afshārī, Mihrān, and Farzād Moravijī. 2017. *Risālah-i Tīrandāzī: Usṭūrah va Tārīkh*. Tehran: Nashr-i Chashmah.

Ahmed, Shahab. 2016. *What Is Islam? The Importance of Being Islamic*. Princeton, NJ: Princeton University Press.

Allsen, Thomas. 2002. "The Circulation of Military Technology in the Mongolian Empire." In *Warfare in Inner Asian History (500–1800)*, edited by Nicola Di Cosmo, 265–293. Leiden: Brill.

Amir-Moazami, Schirin, Christine M. Jacobsen, and Maliha Malik, eds. 2011. "Islam and Gender in Europe: Subjectivities, Politics and Piety." *Feminist Review* 98 (1): 1–8.

Calder, Norman. 1986. "Friday Prayer and the Juristic Theory of Government: Sarakhsī, Shīrāzī, Māwardī." *Bulletin of the School of Oriental and African Studies* 49 (1): 35–47.

Christopher, Bollas. 1987. *The Shadow of the Object Psychoanalysis of the Unthought Known*. London: Free Association Books.

Coleman, Simon. 2013. "Afterward: De-exceptionalising Islam." In *Articulating Islam: Anthropological Approaches to Muslim Worlds*, edited by Magnus Marsden and Konstantinos Retsikas, 247–258. Dordrecht, Netherlands: Springer Science and Business Media.

Daneshgar, Majid. 2014. "Review: The Early History of Ismaili Jurisprudence: Law Under the Fatimids." Edited and translated by Agostino Cilardo. *Journal of Shi'a Islamic Studies* 7 (1): 110–112.

Feldman, Allen. 1991. *Formations of Violence: The Narrative of the Body and Political Terror in Northern Ireland*. New York: Columbia University Press.

Hanif, Door. 2002. *Biographical Encyclopaedia of Sufis: Central Asia and Middle East*. New Delhi: Sarpus & Sons.

Heinze, Marie-Christine. 2014. "On 'Gun Culture' and 'Civil Statehood' in Yemen." *Journal of Arabian Studies* 4 (1): 70–95.

Kadivar, Muḥsin. 1998. *Ḥukūmat-i vilāyī*. Tehran [publisher unknown].

Khalaf, Sulayman N. 1990. "Settlement of Violence in Bedouin Society." *Ethnology* 29 (3): 225–242.

Kristeva, Julia. 1941. *Powers of Horror: An Essay on Abjection*. New York: Columbia University Press.

Latham, Derek. 1970. "The Archers of the Middle East: The Turco-Iranian Background." *Iran: Journal of the British Institute of Persian Studies* 8 (1): 97–103.

Law, John. 2009. "Actor Network Theory and Material Semiotics." In *The New Blackwell Companion to Social Theory*, edited by Brian S. Turner, 141–158. Oxford: Wiley-Blackwell.

Loades, Mike. 2019. *War Bows: Longbow, Crossbow, Composite Bow and Japanese Yumi*. Oxford: Osprey Publishing.

Malyeri, Muhammad. 1973. *Farhanq Irani pish as Islam va Athār e ān dar Tamadūn Islami*. Tehran: Nashr-Tūs.

Matin, Kamran. 2007. "Uneven and Combined Development in World History: The International Relations of State-Formation in Premodern Iran." *European Journal of International Relations* 13 (3): 419–447.

McEwen, Edward. 1974. "Persian Archery Texts: Chapter Eleven of Fakhr-I Mudabbir's 'Adab Al-Harb.'" *Islamic Quaterly* 18 (3): 76–87.

Melki, Jad. 2014. "The Interplay of Politics, Economics and Culture in New Framing of Middle East Wars. *Media, War & Conflict* 7 (2): 165–186.

Miller, Derek B. 2003. *Demand, Stockpiles, and Social Controls: Small Arms in Yemen*. Geneva: Small Arms Survey.

Moshtagh Khorasani, Manouchehr. 2006. *Arms and Armor from Iran: The Bronze Age to the End of the Qajar Period*. Tubingen: Legat.

Moshtagh Khorasani, Manouchehr, and Bede Dwyer. 2018. "El Manuscrito Persa Sobre Tiro Con Arco Izá (Revelación) Por Tāher Māwarā al-Nahri." *Gladius* 38: 125–158.

Paterson, W. F. 1966. "The Archers of Islam." *Journal of the Economic and Social History of the Orient* 9 (1/2): 69–87.

Pistor-Hatam, Anja. 2014. "Historische Erzählungen von mongolischer Eroberung und Herrschaft in Iran." In *Geschichtsschreibung und Sinngeschichte in Iran,* edited by Ali Gheissari, Yann Richard and Christoph Werner, 102–208. Amsterdam: Brill.

Poonawala, Ismail K. 2001. "A-Qadi Al Numan and Islamili Jurisprudence in Daftari Mediaeval Isma'ili History and Thought." In *Mediaeval Ismaíli History and Thought,* edited by Farhad Daftary, 117–143. Cambridge: Cambridge University Press.

Salmān, Mashhūr Hasan Mahmūd. 1989. *Faā'l ūl-Ramy fy Sabylī Ta'ālā.* Alzarqad: Maktabah Al-Nār.

Sāmīrani, Ībrāhym. 1997. *Al-mūqtarīh fy Al-mūstalīh fy Saydī Taiyr.* Dubai: Mārkāz Jūm' Al-mājīd le-saqāfah va Torās.

Saramifar, Younes. 2015. *Living with the AK-47: Militancy and Militants in Hezbollah's Resistance Movement.* Newcastle upon Tyne: Cambridge Scholars Publishing.

Saramifar, Younes. 2018a. "Enchanted by the AK-47: Contingency of Body and the Weapon Among Hezbollah Militants." *Journal of Material Culture* 23 (1): 83–99.

Saramifar, Younes. 2018b. "Tales of Pleasures of Violence and Combat Resilience Among Iraqi Shi'i Combatants Fighting ISIS." *Ethnography* 20 (1): 550–577.

Schielke, Samuli, and Liza Debevec, eds. 2012. *Ordinary Lives and Grand Schemes: An Anthropology of Everyday Religion.* New York: Berghahn Books.

Sidahmed, Abdel Salam, and Anoushiravan Ehteshami, eds. 1996. *Islamic Fundamentalism.* Boulder, CO: Westview Press.

Zabih, Sepehr. 1986. *The Left in Contemporary Iran: Ideology, Organisation, and the Soviet Connection.* London and Sydney: Croom Helm; Stanford, CA: Hoover Institution Press.

3.8

HUMAN-ANIMAL ENTANGLEMENTS AND THE ANTHROPOLOGY OF SACRIFICE

Practicing Qurbani in Mumbai

Shaheed Tayob

It was a bustling Friday evening in Mumbai, ten days before the annual Muslim festival of sacrifice, locally known as Bakri Id (lit: goat festival). Walking with two friends through the majority Muslim neighborhood of Dongri, we chanced upon an increasingly common scene wherein a particularly large black-and-white goat was the center of attention of a group of men feeding it and talking about it. One of them, who was feeding corncobs to the goat, noticed us. We asked him whether it was his goat. He motioned towards the owner, Aziz, a quiet man in his mid-forties who, together with "uncle," ran the ittar (perfume) store in front of which we stood. The goat's name was Kuvran, but his nickname was Kurkure, after the popular spicy snack.

Aziz stood aside quietly as the group of men entertained themselves with Kurkure. He said that easily two hours of "time-pass" was spent like this each evening. One of the men alternated between pinching Kurkure's hide so that he would charge and tapping his head to entice him to rise up onto his hind legs into striking position. The sight of a goat standing tall on its hind legs excites onlookers, drawing gasps of delight. It is a pose associated with goat-fighting, a common practice that is mostly avoided during the days preceding sacrifice. A goat in striking position offers a view of its full size and stature, allowing for comparison to fully grown men. The other form of play is the act of pushing back with one or two hands against the charge of the goat. Whenever Kurkure chased too aggressively or became agitated, Aziz was on hand to pacify him either by touch or by summoning him away from the group with the click of his tongue. Aziz himself never engaged in these practices of play.

As we watched the scenes unfold, a delivery of tea arrived in a plastic bag. The tea was poured into a metal cup. Aziz motioned to Kurkure to step forward. He then offered him some tea. Kurkure drew a sip and pulled away. Aziz realized that the tea was too hot for him to drink. He began to blow on the tea to cool it down, a practice common when offering hot food to children. "Woh thanda ho gaya" ("it is cold now"), he said as he presented the cup to Kurkure again. Kukure took another sip. In between sips, Aziz continued to blow on the tea to cool it down. Kurkure drank for a while, then, apparently satisfied, turned to leave. Aziz grabbed a cloth and wiped his mouth before allowing him to go. Goats are, after all, not cup-trained.

DOI: 10.4324/9781351176231-27

Aziz told us that Kurkure was 22 months old. He had been born in the alley behind the ittar shop. His mother had been bought four years ago and his father sometime after. Kurkure had four siblings. One had died at a few months of age, one had been stolen, and another two had been sold along with their mother to someone in the area. While recounting the story, Aziz showed us a picture on his phone of two tiny, two-month-old twin goats.

Kurkure was due to be sacrificed in ten days time for the annual Muslim festival of sacrifice (Qurbani ki Id/Bakri Id). The play, care, and intimacy between Aziz and Kurkure is a practice through which a particular understanding of sacrifice is produced. Performing sacrifice (Urdu: *qurbani*) with feeling (*ehsaas*) is a virtue. The feeling of loss is the ultimate test of submitting one's desires and attachments to the will of God. This is a subjective experience of sacrifice. However, the celebration of sacrifice is also a social event. Not all individuals have the time, space, or inclination to raise goats from a young age. Also important are market practices of purchasing goats that include an arduous search and tough negotiation. In the neighborhood goats are paraded and compared. A shared aesthetic appreciation for goats, along with recognition of the value of human-animal practices of care, mean that discussions about price and admiration of the beauty of particular breeds is common, as are comments on the character traits of individual goats.

The practice of sacrifice in Mumbai resonates with sacrifice theory as it has developed in anthropology, religious studies, and philosophy. Animal sacrifice is a re-enactment and commemoration of the great sacrifice of the Prophet Ibrahim. It represents Ibrahim's original sacrifice, a founding violence that establishes and maintains the order of the Abrahamic faith (Derrida 1992: 55). As a duty demanded of those who are financially able (*istitaa'at*), ritual sacrifice is understood as an exchange demanded by God for which the practitioner will receive reward in the hereafter. Substitution and identification are central, since Aziz's sacrifice entails the sacrifice and slaughter of Kurkure's life—and the fascination with the strength and size of goats clearly reflects a masculine idea of power. Through the sacrificial exchange, meat is rendered "sacred" and distributed to the poor, circulated amongst friends and family, and prepared as communal meals. The practice also clearly reflects and produces gendered roles about access to public space. However, the forms of play and intimacy between Aziz and Kurkure that precede the act of sacrifice are not reducible to symbolic and universal theories of sacrifice and its nature and function as informed by Christian theological debates. Absent from the dominant discussions is a consideration of animal sacrifice beyond the act of slaughter, the allocation of resources, and the choice of sacrificial animal. Prevailing theories of sacrifice sideline the importance of human-animal entanglements, intimacy, and care as central to sacrificial practice (Govindrajan 2015). Sacrifice as a material practice of religion turns attention to the human-animal relations and notions of value that inform sacrificial activity. Human-animal selfhood and subjectivity within an Islamic sacrifice practice provide an opportunity to theorize intimacy, violence, and love as constitutive of sacrifice.

This chapter begins by identifying a lack of attention to human-animal entanglements and embodied material practices of sacrifice beyond an implicit Christian theological frame. Qurbani as sacrifice emphasizes intimacy and value, forcing an embodied and material consideration of sacrifice, intimacy, and love. The Islamic discursive tradition of sacrifice, intimacy, love, and care unsettles Christian-centric models towards an appreciation of human-animal intimacy and embodied sacrifice. The confluence of intimacy, love, and violence between Aziz and Kurkure unnerves the certainty of moral conviction urging us to dwell in the complexity and messiness of an entangled life.

Sacrifice in Philosophy and Anthropology

For almost three years Aziz cared for and lived with Kurkure. His daily life turned around Kurkure's needs, health, and behavior. Kukure responds to Aziz's touch and voice. The intimacy between the two urges us to consider animal sacrifice as a discursive and material embodiment of both religion and human-animal relations in everyday life. The specificity of an Islamic discursive tradition of sacrifice in Mumbai and the unique intimacy between Aziz and Kukure unsettles the largely abstract, symbolic, and Christian-centric analysis of sacrifice and human-animal relations.

For Dennis Keenan, the notion of a pure, uninterested sacrifice as the sacrifice of Jesus forms the locus around which evolutionary theories of sacrifice have developed (Keenan 2005). The potential and impossibility of sacrifice in Christian theology entails anxiety over sacrifice as the pure, uninterested devotion and willingness to give to God against covert self-interest marred by original sin. The biblical articulation of secrecy and sacrifice requires giving such that you "do not let your left hand know what your right hand is doing" (Matthew 6:3), so "your Father, who sees what is done in secret, will reward you" (Matthew 6:6). The terrestrial sacrifice in secret, an aneconomic sacrifice, is in the end an economic exchange with God (Keenan 2005). Sacrifice by humans pales in comparison to the only true sacrifice: that of Jesus, the infinite gift, the gift that cannot be returned (Derrida 2008: 56–57). In Derrida's reading of Kierkegaard, Abraham's sacrifice of Isaac is the moment at which he sacrifices his ethical relationship with his son in lieu of his secret responsibility to God. Sacrificing ethics, Abraham institutes the formation of the Christian subject, the individual responsible before a God who sees in secret. Except God, who sees in secret, interrupts the sacrifice with the gift of a sheep, suspending the sacrifice and "reestablish[ing] an economy that was interrupted by the dividing of heaven from earth" (2008: 98). This phenomenological and theological reading of sacrifice is a symbolic analysis of Christian theology devoid of flesh-and-blood entanglements.

The anxiety of Christian sacrifice became transformed by nineteenth- and early-twentieth-century theory into an evolutionary model that progresses from primitive religions that engage in material sacrifice in anticipation of reward toward the symbolic sacrifice of the Eucharist—all ultimately insufficient before the epitome of sacrifice, the sacrifice of Jesus (Milbank 1996). For E. B. Tylor, sacrifice developed from a gift to appease the Gods into an offering with no expectation of return—before finally reaching its immaterial incarnation as renunciation (Tylor 1871). For William Robertson Smith, sacrifice is a means through which a community achieves communal unity through the sacrifice of a totem animal, usually one that is revered, then slaughtered in a time of emergency in the aim of achieving communion with each other and God (Robertson Smith 1995). James Frazer reverses the evolutionary model, finding Christianity a perversion of an earlier truth of sacrifice: the sacrifice of the God-King in exchange for the political state's future (George Frazer 2009).

In *Sacrifice: Its Nature and Function* (1899), Henri Hubert and Marcel Mauss emphasize exchange as a means through which the boundary and communication between the sacred and profane are established and sacralization effected. Arguing for sacrifice as "a religious act which, through the consecration of a victim, modifies the condition of the moral person who accomplishes it or that of certain objects with which he is concerned" (Mauss and Hubert 1964: 13) means recognizing that practices of exchange in religious rituals affect the things and beings in the world. This important insight, however, gives way to the Christian sacrifice of Jesus as the evolutionary end-point, the end of sacrifice. Durkheim also linked sacrifice and exchange as a communion and offering that ensures the periodic rejuvenation of society and the Gods (Durkheim 1995: 344–354). For Robert Yelle, sacrifice in these early theoretical accounts is indebted to post-Reformation Protestant-Catholic polemics that sought to discredit the notion of the Eucharist as sacrifice in favor of the Eucharist as "communion" (Yelle 2019). Without denying these insights' potential relevance, it is clear that questions of intimacy and embodiment feature very little in abstract symbolic analyses.

Early theories on evolution, transcendence, violence, and value continue to resonate in much recent scholarship. To René Girard (2005), sacrifice is understood as a way of stemming the human societal tendency toward violence and vengeance through the sacrifice of a scapegoat. And for Maurice Bloch (1992), sacrifice is a means to achieve an element of transcendental vitality in preparation for further violence against neighbors. Even ethnographic studies of sacrifice in specific contexts—such as E. E. Evans-Pritchard on the Nuer (Evans-Pritchard 1953), Gregory Lienhardt on the Dinka (Lienhardt 1961), and M. E. Combs-Schilling on Morocco (Combs-Schilling 1990)—apply symbolic sacrifice theory such that non-human animals, blood, and violence are all related to questions of primordial symbolic power rather than to flesh and blood entanglements. Raymond Firth's survey of sacrifice and everyday economic organization is ultimately encapsulated within a Christian evolutionary frame that understands cost-saving and substitution as the driving force toward the mystification of sacrifice (Firth 1963).

Recent work in anthropology and religious studies demonstrates the pitfalls of trying to apply universal theory and symbolic analysis for understanding everyday life. For example, Karen McClymond argues against definitions of sacrifice in favor of a dynamic interchange between key "elements" or "general types: selection, association, identification, killing, heating, apportionment, and consumption" (McClymond 2008: 29). But her argument is abstract and textual, and tells us very little about affective and embodied practice in specific historical and political contexts. For Michael Lambek, sacrifice as a "gift that cannot be returned, or cancelled, or withdrawn" (Lambek 2007: 29) instantiates a new moral order against which all future acts will be judged. Drawing attention to the ethics of sacrifice, he rejects the economization of sacrifice in arguing for economic value and ethical value as two realms of consideration that are incommensurable to each other (Lambek 2008: 145). Differentiating ethical value and economic value, his argument remains a symbolic analysis of origin and myth. And Maya Mayblin and Magnus Course recognize that sacrifice theory suffers from a symbolic and Christian bias in focusing on "the sort of violent blood ritual that Christianity denigrates" (Mayblin and Course 2013: 312). In appreciating sacrifice as discourse and practice beyond the notion of exotic primitive violence, they simply avoid the question of animal sacrifice altogether.

Radhika Govindrajan's analysis of kinship and human-animal relations in a Himalayan Hindu sacrifice community draws attention to embodied intimacy, care, love, and sacrifice (Govindrajan 2018). Raising an animal from a young age and dedicating it for sacrifice forges affective bonds that remain long after the sacrificial act has taken place. Taking us beyond a normative Christian theological frame that posits the end of animal sacrifice in pursuit of less-material forms allows for an appreciation of the "practices of care and love—that made the sacrificial moment such a compelling occasion for self-reflection" (Govindrajan 2018: 53). For Govindrajan, situating sacrifice within the Himalayan Hindu eschatological context of life, death, and rebirth together with everyday practices of human-animal care and intimacy is crucial for appreciating the ethics of sacrifice in practice.

Returning to Aziz in Dongri: for Aziz the violence of sacrifice pierces the intimacy and love nurtured between himself and Kurkure. Yet, contrary to liberal sensibility that deems violence an affront to the sanctity of the self, for Aziz and others the *ehsaas* (feeling) of pain and loss is the very condition of sacrifice. The etymology of the word *qurbani* (sacrifice)—as explained to me—provides insight into the entanglement of religious discourse, language, and everyday practice. Taariq, a freelance translator who has worked in Mumbai for the past twenty years, is proficient in Arabic, English, Farsi, Hindi, and Urdu. He explained the Arabic root of *qurban* is *q-r-b*—pronounced "qaraba"—from which the words *qurb* (close), *qarib* (he who is close), and *qurbat* (closeness) are derived. The suffix *-aan* indicates "double," so *qurban* means "double close." He offered an example to emphasize the relation between "double close" and the importance of objects of worldly intimacy, love and value. Though aimed at attaining closeness to God, acts of prayer do not constitute instances of sacrifice. Doing Qurbani is thus the act of "spending on things that are valuable and valued in one's own view in the aim (*maqsad*) of seeking proximity and nearness to Allah." "Double close-ness" refers to the "closeness" to the offering that is given up and sacrificed in order to seek "closeness" to God. Taariq then added a series of verbs and adjectives contained in his English use of valuable and valued, namely: *pyaari* (beloved), *qadar karna* (to value), *pasand karna* (to like), and *chahna* (to desire). His emphasis on verbs highlights the importance of embodied practice in cultivating the intimacy and love necessary for sacrifice.

Taariq's etymology resonates with common explanations of Qurbani in Mumbai that are usually accompanied by reference to the Quranic verse in which God orders the Prophet Ibrahim to make an offering of his most beloved thing (*sab se pyaari cheez*): his son. The link between practices of care, exemplary prophetic action, and animal intimacy is further emphasized by the assertion that all of the prophets—including Ibrahim, Moosa, Isa, and Muhammad—had been pastoralists. Pastoral care here is not metaphor; it references the ethical practices of care for animals through which "you can learn everything about life by looking after goats, watching them, caring for them, feeding them." In this view, animals are creations of God, each with an individual consciousness, set of habits, and unique personality. Becoming attuned to these individual habits is an ethical practice through which *sabr* (patience) and *tawajoh* (concentration/attention) are embodied and cultivated.

Qurbani as sacrifice is not reducible to a symbolic economy of violence and meaning. Sacrifice understood through human-animal intimacy offers reflections on what it means to live a life entangled with non-human others. An Islamic discourse of love, care, and submission to the will of God embodied in relations of human-animal intimacy during sacrifice destabilizes the normative aversion to sacrifice rooted in modernist philosophy and Christian theology—while questioning some of the latent assumptions of post-humanist theory.

Human-Animal Entanglements

Increasing attention to human-animal entanglements has been at the forefront of post-humanist efforts to move beyond modernist conceptions of the human as autonomous individual subject. The animalization of the human (Tamimi Arab 2019) is the solution to the modern Enlightenment conception of the human implicated in processes of dehumanization and animalization wrought by colonialism and capitalism (Fanon 2004: 7). For post-humanist theorists, the figure of the animal as conceived by Cartesian philosophy and capitalist practice—as being devoid of reason and thus reduced to mere use-value—is in need of rehabilitation. Donna Haraway thus urges a consideration of the microbial interactions between human and non-human bodies through which to rethink the very category and materiality of the human as autonomous bounded subject (Haraway 2008). The ways in which human and non-human beings are always entangled in a "material-semiotics" of becoming (Haraway 2008: 4; Kocelman 2011) has much to offer a material, embodied approach to animal sacrifice (Govindrajan 2018b).

As Radhika Govindrajan has noted, the practice of sacrifice features unfavorably in post-humanist research. Haraway positions sacrifice beyond her ethical-philosophical deliberations as a "guilt-free form of killing, [which] cannot capture the contingent and complex nature of inequality between two beings who 'have face'" (Haraway 2008: 76, quoted in Govindrajan 2015). Drawing on a Levinasian reading of "face," "responsibility," and "guilt," the notion of sacrifice as being "guilt-free" is thus an abomination to any kind of human-animal ethics. Importantly, guilt, horror, disgust, emotional distress, and the search for emotional comfort are often central to the way in which scholars of human-animal relations position their work and lives, as intertwined processes of ethical becoming (Calarco 2019: 192; Wolfe 2019: 12, 29–30). The emphasis on suffering and emotion implicates this literature in the emergence of what Didier Fassin calls "humanitarian reason": where violence, suffering, and inequality induce feelings of compassion as the motivation for moral action (Fassin 2012: 5). As Amira Mittermaier has argued, the position of guilt and compassion in "humanitarian reason" exposes a Christian ethics of self, responsibility, and pity that need not be the only impetus for ethical acts (Mittermaier 2019). It is not surprising then that Haraway's ethical-philosophical articulations take place after sacrifice "when God is not addressed and sacrifice is not practiced" (Haraway 2008: 75), a teleological assertion that places her well within modern Western conceptions of sacrifice (Keenan 2005). To follow Haraway's and others' philosophical ethics we have to sacrifice "sacrifice" toward a post-humanist becoming. How are we to understand the intimacy and love between Aziz and Kurkure where God is addressed and sacrifice is practiced? What does the sacrifice of Kurkure offer in thinking beyond the implicit Christian theological and Eurocentric assumptions that linger in post-humanist philosophy?

For Derrida, "the industrial, mechanical, chemical, hormonal, and genetic violence to which man has been submitting animal life for the past two centuries" (Derrida 2002: 395) has reached levels that "previous generations would have judged monstrous" (Derrida 2002: 394). His analysis of the figure of the animal in modern philosophical thought thus centers on the novelty of capitalist production. As Talal Asad has argued, we should be cautious of the erroneous assumption that modern philosophical and material developments have been totalizing the world over (Asad 1986a). Pacing over the specificity of post-Enlightenment philosophical and economic development risks reducing the complex arrangement of human, non-human, and capitalist relations in modernity to a simple question of hierarchy between human and non-human animals. Yet for Derrida and Haraway, this slippage is central to their ethical-philosophical deliberations. Pointing to the specificity of post-Cartesian, industrial animal treatment, Haraway maintains the root cause in "the logic of sacrifice that undergirds all versions of religious or secular humanism" (Haraway 2008: 78), and that instantiates the notion that animals can be killed but not murdered. The call to recognize "animal death as murder" is a moral and emotional appeal to justice for non-human animals that in effect criminalizes sacrifice by universalizing a particular religious and historical understanding of the act. The oscillation between European specificity and universal theory supports the claim that hierarchy between human and animals is ubiquitous in all religious and cultural traditions and is equally problematic regardless of place and time. It allows for grand assertions and a sense of embodied moral action against the supposed "solace of Sacrifice" (Haraway 2008: 76)—all without the need to investigate or consider actual practices of animal sacrifice and human-animal relations that do not conform to ideological and material post-Enlightenment developments. This is a Eurocentric approach that once again seeks to be at the forefront of a universal human ethics (Wolfe 2019: 4) without paying sufficient attention to the complex histories of race and colonialism as entangled in questions regarding the animal and the human (Wolfe 2019: 5). It forecloses the possibility for considerations of human-animal relations and sacrifice that are not simply about "making beings killable" (Haraway 2008: 81). It offers little space for a nuanced consideration of other religious traditions, nor for an appreciation of the intimacy and violence between Aziz and Kurkure, a violence that, I argue, destabilizes the solace of moral conviction.

Critical voices from scholars working on various regions and religions of the world have been pushing back against the automatic assumption that hierarchy or ontological difference between humans and non-human animals equals domination and use-value. Paul Nadasdy and Radhika Govindrajan have shown how Himalayan Hindu agrarian and North American hunter communities hold complex views of animals as being both individual agents in the world and beings who are cared for, hunted, and killed for food (Nadasdy 2007; Govindrajan 2015). Here, the co-implication of care, love, intimacy, and violence in human-animal relations does not equate to indifference to animal death, nor to the reduction of animal life to use-value. The discursive tradition of Islam regarding animals offers a similar resource for thinking about ethics in the context of human-animal relations, care, and violence. It illuminates how care for animals is an ethical practice, and how sacrifice through love unsettles the certainty of self and world. This is an opportunity to take seriously the theocentric worldview of Muslims as a factor in moral and ethical reckoning against ever-present Orientalist associations of Islam with un-freedom, violence, and irrationality (Said 1978). It calls for sustained attention to the discursive and material entanglements of human-animal intimacy and sacrifice embodied in ritual practice and everyday life.

Decolonial Perspectives

The intimacy, affection, and inevitable violence of sacrifice evident in the relationship between Aziz and Kukure testifies to the entanglements of bodies, language, and affects. As Ian Hodder argues, "humans are always already involved in the 'external' world of biological, physical and chemical processes" (Hodder 2016: 3). And since "words and ideas are both things . . . and their meanings are always entangled in other words, ideas, and meanings, as well as usually in different forms of material practice" (2016: 4), we can approach the study of material religion as the entanglements afforded by specific formulations of language and materiality. In doing so, we must remain cautious of reintroducing Enlightenment conceptions of religion as offering "practical solutions to deal with matters of social and emotional import that are difficult to make sense of" (2016: 94). This move ultimately reduces the lives and lifeworld's of the people we study to mere data for analysis to be incorporated into universal theories that, as we have seen, are very often indebted to Euro-Christian normativity. As critical scholars of material religion have noted, the modernist philosophical orientation that emphasizes ideas over things entered the study of religion as a deep Protestant bias that distinguished higher moral religions from primitive material religion (Meyer 2011). As with sacrifice, this scholarly genealogy of religion—its essence, nature, and function—was entangled in Catholic-Protestant polemics and the imperial encounter (Chidester 1996, 2013; Strenski 2003; Yelle 2019).

For Talal Asad, the imperial and Christian-centric assumptions in the study of religion require caution (Asad 1993). He argues instead for religion as a discursive tradition, one replete with a complex history of debate, difference, and contestation and with implications for the way moral personhood (Asad 1986b)—and, by extension, human-animal subjectivity— are conceptualized and formed. This move seeks to sidestep the pitfalls of essentialist definitions of religion, drawing attention to the embeddedness in the world of religion as idea, embodiment, and practice (Mahmood 2011). Religious actors are "beings inevitably enmeshed in a relational world" (Strathern 2018: 8) where their "mode of doing things" (Meyer 2009: 10) is informed, authorized, and implicated in discursive and material formations. However, where some scholars take the discursive tradition of religion as a vantage point through which to provincialize the claimed universality of secular European norms (Hirschkind 2006; Mahmood 2011), I argue instead for appreciating how notions of body, personhood, human–animal relations, and God may offer alternative ways of theorizing sacrifice, violence, and human–animal relations. We must remain open to the possibility for alternative notions of sacrifice and human–animal entanglements to offer other ways of being in the world not reducible to nineteenth-century secular modernist or twenty-first-century post-structuralist philosophical reflection. I am indebted to a strand of decolonial anthropology that urges us to think beyond the usual treatment of other lifeworlds as being mere "cultural constructions" (Nadasdy 2007: 26) or as data for analysis; requiring instead an openness to the ethical and philosophical lives of the people we study as a resource for developing non-Eurocentric theory (Nadasdy 2007; Govindrajan 2018: 6; Tallbear 2011; Tayob 2018).

This chapter therefore argues for more attention to the complex ways in which people of different religious persuasions engage and interact with non-human animals as fellow beings—and to do so not only to provincialize Western or European experience but to theorize an epistemologically inclusive, heterogeneous, and complex world of care, love, intimacy, and violence.

A Discursive Tradition of Human-Animal Hierarchies and Care

The intimacy and care between Aziz and Kurkure belies arguments about the solace of sacrifice or indifference to animal life. Performing sacrifice with feeling (*ehsaas*) includes practices of care and attention (*tawajoh*) through which a sacrificial animal becomes a companion species (Haraway 2008). The way Kurkure responds to the touch and voice of Aziz speaks to the years of intimacy through which their lives became entangled with each other. Aziz had assisted with the birth of Kurkure, had cared for him and reprimanded him, and now faces the inevitability of his death. Situating this practice of Qurbani requires an engagement with the ethical-philosophical deliberations of scholars of Islam on the value of animal life—as well as a consideration of both the ethical import of ritual prescription and the guidelines of sacrifice and ritual slaughter (Tayob 2019: 15–16).

Richard McGregor offers a close reading of the tenth-century philosophical epistle entitled "The Case of the Animals versus Man before the King of the Jinn." The text is attributed to an anonymous collective of authors known as the Brethren of Purity (*Ikhwan al-Safa*), and is one among a collection that covers the mathematical sciences, the sciences of natural bodies, the psychological and rational sciences, and theology (McGregor 2015: 225). In the narrative animals take humans to court for their systematic abuse and ill-treatment. The humans defend themselves by making claims to "categorical superiority for their race, which they assume would give them rights over all animals." The king rejects their claim through "a model of providential creation that sees every creature, even the weakest and most vulnerable, as perfect in its own way and as endowed with precisely what it needs to flourish in its environment" (2015: 228). The humans eventually win the case by arguing that among them are saints, whose spiritual rank places them alongside the angels. Thus, ontological difference is articulated through the human potential for virtue rather than an innate disposition or hierarchy of value. For McGregor, the narrative is anthropocentric in orientation, replete with notions of state and society as the "height of human achievement."

Yet, contrary to Enlightenment thinking, "it does not follow that animals are to suffer forever as slaves of the humans, and certainly there is no license here for cruelty or abuse" (2015: 229). Jeremy Bentham's supposedly profound insight about the capacity for animal suffering (Derrida 2002: 396) has for many Islamic thinkers never been in doubt.

Similarly, Sarra Tlili, who has conducted the most extensive investigation of pre-modern Islamic exegetical reflections on the status and nature of animals, argues that the Quran clearly presents animals as "spiritual, moral and psychologically complex beings" (Tlili 2012: 42). For Tlili, the secondary literature oscillates between recognizing the unique capacity and potential of animals and the hierarchy between human and non-human animals (2012: 49–50). Although the Quran does indeed authorize the "practical useability" of non-human animals through the concepts of *tashkir* (subjugation), *tadhlil* (servitude), and *maskh* (becoming animal as divine punishment, 2012: 69–72), humans are not "given free rein to do anything they may want with these species" (2012: 91). For Tlili, this complexity is the basis from which to undo the Platonic Great Chain of Being that, she argues, distorts the Quranic vision (2012: 54–56).

In seeking an egalitarian reading of the Quran, Tlili conflates hierarchy, use-ability, and ontological difference between humans and animals. She too fails to appreciate the specificity of Enlightenment humanism as being entangled with nation-state formation, capitalist development, and colonial expansion that posit hierarchies of being as relations of domination and use-value. Crucial to this discussion are Aime Cesaire's insights into modernity and colonialism as a process of "thingification" (Cesaire 2001: 42) that transforms human and animal life as objects subject to capitalist production. The human propensity to make use of the material environment (Hodder 2016) is not the same as the reduction of other humans, animals, and the natural world to use-value. Issues aside, Tlili's theocentric reading of the Quran foregrounds the limits of human dominion in Islam and offers a basis from which to provincialize the post-Cartesian treatment of animal life. While Tlili gestures toward the Islamic modernist comfort in expounding human dominion over the earth (Tlili 2012: 120), it is clear that these articulations have not been totalizing for the way Muslims relate to the non-human animal world in everyday life in South Asia (Taneja 2015).

In Mumbai, care and intimacy during sacrifice are inseparable from the recognition of animals as "lively material-semiotic beings" (Govindrajan 2015: 507). The point of bringing sacrificial animals into the home in the days, weeks, and years before slaughter is aimed at cultivating worldly love (*muhabbat*) and attachment. A specific emphasis on "treating them as children" aims at commemorating and embodying the affection between the Prophet Ibrahim and his son Ishmael. As with the etymology of *qurbani*, animal care and sacrifice are considered affectively distinct from the donation of money or other offerings. Money as a unit of exchange entails alienation from the deep entanglements of debt and obligation (Graeber 2011), possible only through practices of human-animal intimacy and care. For my discussants in the city, an Islamic discourse of hierarchy distinguishes animals and plants from humans through their supposed lack of a fully functioning rational capacity (Foltz 2006: 15–17). However, as Tlili shows, notions of hierarchy are ultimately subject to a theocentric worldview where all creation is bound under the authority of the creator (God). The primacy of the creator and the ultimate deference to divine authority and divine judgment mean that hierarchy is accompanied by an ethics of care, not domination.

One morning after a game of football, I was at a local restaurant having breakfast with Adeem, a friend in his mid-twenties who is familiar with Aziz and Kurkure. Adeem often expressed fascination at my interest in Qurbani in Mumbai, and held great respect for the care, patience, and emotional labor of Aziz. Reflecting on the relationship between Aziz and Kurkure, he noted both the care and attention—as well as Aziz's occasional tendency to reprimand Kurkure for pursuing particular kinds of bad behavior. He proceeded with a comparison between goats and children who are *be zaban* (without language), *bad dimagh* (of bad mind), and *na samaj* (without understanding): "they are simply animals, they don't have the ability to choose and decide what is right and wrong." For Adeem, this series of lacks translates into the responsibility—as with children—to guide and care for them through repetition, instruction, and reprimand. Being *bad dimagh* (of bad mind), both children and goats tend to pursue undesirable behavior. This includes goats' inclination toward feasting on rubbish in the street and dueling with each other to demonstrate status. Adeem's comparison of goats to children reflects the Quranic differentiation between humans and animals, as well as between different kinds of humans and different kinds of animals (Tlili 2012). Through care, attention, and reprimand, individual animals' biographies become entangled with those of their human companions, rendering sacrifice a moment for reflection on the inevitability of care, violence, love, and death in everyday life.

The recommended guidelines for ritual slaughter further reinforce this analysis. Before slaughter, the animal should be offered a sip of water. The area must be clean and the knife sharp. The animal must not see the knife before slaughter nor witness the slaughter of other animals. Contained herein is recognition of the sensory awareness of animals—their capacity for fear, anxiety, and even solidarity with their fellows. The hierarchical, ordained violence of sacrifice includes an ethics of care and consideration toward animals. The animal is then placed on the ground facing Mecca, the tasmiya "*bismillah Allahu akbar*" (in the name of God, God is great) is recited, and the slaughter proceeds. The significance of the tasmiya is that usually before performing an action the words "*bismillah ir Rahman ir rahim*" (in the name of God the most beneficent and most merciful) are uttered. With slaughter, the action about to be performed is one of power, strength, and violence. Invoking the greatness of God defers ultimate responsibility for slaughter on to a God who is indeed great, but who, in ordering slaughter, is not engaging in mercy. As we will see, the semiotics of the prayer is particularly significant in cases where the intimacy between humans and their companion sacrificial animals makes slaughter a hard act to follow.

Kurkure and Aziz: Human-Animal Biographies in Sacrifice

Two days before the day of sacrifice I was on my way to visit Aziz and Kurkure. Given the surge of activity and goats on the streets that evening I nearly walked directly past the store—only for Aziz to call me back. "Where is Kurkure?" I asked, expecting to see him. Aziz replied somberly, "after one more day there is no more Kurkure." He pointed to his right, where Kurkure was being tended by some of the regulars. Suddenly Kurkure started bleating. Aziz immediately turned to look and said that he was feeling warm. As we chatted a friend arrived with some tea. This time Aziz allowed it to cool before walking over to Kurkure, who stood up expectantly. Aziz offered him some tea and crackers, keeping a few for himself.

The next night I was back at Aziz's store. Many in the area were busy preparing their knives for the following morning. The atmosphere was palpably less buoyant and festive than it had been in the previous weeks. Aziz was alone in the shop sitting with his arm around Kurkure in a warm embrace. As I started speaking to Aziz, Kurkure began misbehaving, attempting to chew the cardboard on the shop counter. Aziz reprimanded him and took him over to a ledge a few meters away. Many who passed commiserated that it was Kurkure's last day. Aziz was clearly not happy at having to hear this repeatedly, and shook his head each time. He seemed pensive.

On the day of Id, slaughter usually begins after the morning prayers. When I arrived at the family home where the slaughter is performed, Aziz informed us of a problem in the day's proceedings. The *qasai* (butcher)—whom he had contracted the day before for the price of 2,000 rupees—had arrived in the morning, taken one look at Kurkure, and decided Kurkure was too large for him. The delay of finding another *qasai* would eventually cost two hours, during which Aziz was impatient. Mostly quiet, he periodically returned to Kurkure's side to feed him by hand and stroke him affectionately.

Eventually, the *qasai* employed by a neighbor announced that he was ready to proceed with the slaughter of Kurkure. There was a discussion about who would hold Kurkure during slaughter. One brother immediately left the building in distress. Another two agreed to help. Aziz was clear that he would not be involved in the restraint nor the slaughter. "Uncle" would wield the knife. Aziz, visibly tense, posed with Kurkure one last time as his brothers and I took pictures. He removed Kurkure's decorative collar and passed him on to the two brothers to lead him toward the slaughter area. Aziz urged me forward but refused to watch. He paced nervously behind me.

Kurkure was dropped to the ground and held firmly in place by the brothers. One grabbed his hind legs and placed pressure on his body. The other grabbed his front legs and did the same. The *qasai* grabbed Kurkure's head, pulled it back, and twisted it to the side to reveal the neck and make the skin taut, enabling the knife to penetrate with ease. Kurkure bleated and writhed. Aziz was tense. He shouted, "*Ek dam zabiha karo!*" (slaughter quickly, in one go), looking over my shoulder to see what was taking so long. The brothers and the *qasai* increased their grip and "uncle" laid the knife on Kurkure—but he did not apply enough pressure, or the knife was not sharp enough, so an incision was not made. Kurkure struggled and bleated again. "*Ek dum maro!*" (strike now, quickly), Aziz cried out as he paced behind me. "Uncle" firmed his grip and recited the takbir (*Allahu Akbar*), loudly, and this time the incision was clean and deep. The blood gushed forth. With the knife the *qasai* made sure that all veins and arteries had been severed to ensure the quick flow of blood from the body. The brothers continued to hold fast as Kurkure went through his final convulsions. With the slaughter complete, Kurkure was no more. Aziz immediately turned to leave the building.

Later in the evening, I met Aziz for a meal of home-cooked mutton that had been gifted by a friend. Aziz donated all of the meat of Kurkure as he could not bear to ingest it. His abstinence demonstrates the personal attachment and feeling that had developed between him and his sacrificial animal. But, I noticed, the emotional discomfort cultivated through sacrifice did not translate into a desire to forgo all meat consumption. It instantiated a relationship to a particular animal life clearly irreducible to mere use-value. For Aziz and others, the practice of care, attachment, and sacrifice offered a visceral and intimate experience of the ephemerality of life and worldly attachment.

The following year, Aziz did not raise a goat for sacrifice, and said that he may never do it again. "Uncle" had purchased from the market a goat that was being cared for at the store. One evening, a few days before Bakri Id, Aziz was tending to the new goat. He had just returned from a nearby market to buy some chicken for the family and some off-cuts of skin and fat to feed his adopted stray cat. I began to talk to him about his experience of the previous year. "It was three years I had him," he shared. "Anything you have for three years with you, then when it goes you feel it. We live, but they have to go, so it makes us think." He then went on to re-affirm what I had heard many times before. "Actually, this is nothing," he said, pointing to the goat grazing beside the shop, "cradling a goat from a young age for sacrifice, that is the real meaning of sacrifice" (*bakra pal kar qurbani kar ke, woh asli qurbani ka meaning hai*).

Against the Solace of Moral Conviction

Sacrifice as a trope of abnegation is ubiquitous in religious discourse, nationalist ideology, and everyday life. The sheer diversity of evocations around sacrifice, in addition to countless material and discursive nuances, tend toward the recognition that there is no universal theory or vantage point available to capture its nature and function. Nevertheless, as many scholars have argued, simply avoiding the question of sacrifice leaves us much poorer in appreciating the complexity of religious and secular life (Mayblin and Course 2013). In this chapter I have argued for an analysis of sacrifice theory as entangled with colonial hierarchies of value. I juxtapose these discursive and material entanglements with an ethnography of sacrifice in Mumbai made legible through the discursive tradition of Islam as offering a resource for critical reflection on what it means to live with non-human animal life.

Universal theories of sacrifice are entangled in hierarchies of value. To be "after sacrifice" is to be modern. "Lower" material religions practice animal sacrifice, whereas "higher" forms of moral religion engage in symbolic sacrifice. The irony is that the analysis of sacrifice engages in a symbolic analysis through which to posit the superiority of symbolic sacrifice. This chapter has thus drawn attention to an embodied material approach to sacrifice that remains aware of the hierarchies of value within Eurocentric theory, and that offers a different avenue for appreciating the entanglements of intimacy, care, love, and violence in the practice of sacrifice. A critical engagement with contemporary human-animal studies, a field that has been crucial to appreciating the material-embodied practice of sacrifice, itself reveals the tendency to slip into a post-sacrificial teleology of ethical progress and becoming. In so engaging, I am following scholars working on human-animal relations from a decolonial perspective in their willingness to theorize with ethnographic interlocutors who live, love, and learn with animals in intimate and therefore sometimes violent ways (Nadasdy 2007; Govindrajan 2018).

The practice of care and sacrifice by Muslims in Mumbai is evidence of how a discursive tradition of sacrifice in Islam is embodied. The intimacy and sacrifice between Aziz and Kurkure point to the complexity of human-animal entanglements, which are not reducible to the polar extremes of imperative vegetarianism and the normativity of non-violence or the reduction of human and animal life to mere use-value. Dwelling in this in-between offers neither the solace of moral conviction nor the indifference of teleology. It urges instead a nuanced and humble way of theorizing our relation to each other and to the world. It gestures to the recognition that perhaps our ability as middle-class urban subjects to think about the materiality of non-human animal life is circumscribed by our very limited engagement with non-human animal life in modern urban contexts. And it forces us to consider how living with non-human animal life, in all its complexity and liveliness, may in fact be a solution to the indifference to death and destruction as a feature of our contemporary world. After all, as Haraway and others have argued, it is much easier to stand firm in abstract moral conviction than to dwell in the messiness and complexity of an entangled life.

References

Asad, T. 1986a. "The Concept of Cultural Translation in British Social Anthropology." In *Writing Culture: The Poetics and Politics of Ethnography,* edited by J. Clifford and G. E. Marcus, 141–164. Berkeley, CA: University of California Press.

Asad, T. 1986b. *The Idea of an Anthropology of Islam.* Washington, DC: Center for Contemporary Arab Studies, Georgetown University.

Asad, T. 1993. *Genealogies of Religion: Discipline and Reasons of Power in Christianity and Islam.* Baltimore, MD and London: Johns Hopkins University Press.

Bloch, M. 1992. *Prey into Hunter: The Politics of Religious Experience.* Cambridge: Cambridge University Press.

Calarco, M. 2019. "Living Philosophically." In *Messy Eating: Conversations on Animals and Food,* edited by S. King, R. S. Carey, I. Macquarrie, V. N. Millious, and E. M. Power, 188–203. New York: Fordham University Press.

Cesaire, A. 2001. "Discourse on Colonialism." In *Discourse on Colonialism,* translated by J. Pinkham, 31–78. New York: Monthly Review Press.

Chidester, D. 1996. *Savage Systems: Colonialism and Comparative Religion in Southern Africa.* Cape Town: University of Cape Town Press.

Chidester, D. 2013. *Empire of Religion: Imperialism and Comparative Religion.* Chicago, IL: University of Chicago Press.

Combs-Schilling, M. E. 1990. *Sacred Performances: Islam, Sexuality and Sacrifice.* New York: Columbia University Press.

Derrida, J. 1992. "Force of Law: The 'Mystical Foundation of Authority.'" In *Deconstruction and the Possibility of Justice,* edited by D. Cornell, C. Rosenfeld, and D. Gray Carlson, 3–67. New York and London: Routledge.

Derrida, J. 2002. "The Animal That Therefore I Am (More to Follow)." *Critical Enquiry* 28 (2): 369–418.

Derrida, J. 2008. *The Gift of Death and Literature in Secret.* Translated by D. Wills. 2nd ed. Chicago, IL: University of Chicago Press.

Durkheim, E. 1995. *Elementary Forms of Religious Life.* Translated by K. E. Fields. New York: Free Press.

Evans-Pritchard, E. E. 1953. "The Sacrificial Role of Cattle among the Nuer." *Journal of the International African Institute* 23 (3): 181–198.

Fanon, F. 2004. *The Wretched of the Earth.* Translated by R. Philcox. New York: Grove Press.

Fassin, D. 2012. *Humanitarian Reason: A Moral History of the Present.* Berkeley and Los Angeles, CA: University of California Press.

Firth, R. 1963. "Offering and Sacrifice: Problems of Organization." *Journal of the Royal Anthropological Institute of Great Britain and Ireland* 93 (1): 12–24.

Foltz, R. C. 2006. *Animals in Islamic Tradition and Muslim Cultures.* Oxford: Oneworld Publications.

George Frazer, J. 2009. *The Golden Bough: A Study of Magic and Religion.* Auckland: Floating Press.

Girard, R. 2005. *Violence and the Sacred.* Translated by P. Gregory. London and New York: Continuum Books.

Govindrajan, R. 2015. "'The Goat that Died for Family': Animal Sacrifice and Interspecies Kinship in India's Central Himalayas." *American Ethnologist* 42 (3): 504–519.

Govindrajan, R. 2018. *Animal Intimacies: Interspecies Relatedness in India's Central Himalayas.* Chicago, IL and London: University of Chicago Press.

Graeber, D. 2011. *Debt: The First 5,000 Years.* New York: Melville House Publishing.

Haraway, D. J. 2008. *When Species Meet.* Minneapolis, MN and London: University of Minnesota Press.

Hirschkind, C. 2006. *The Ethical Soundscape: Cassette Sermons and Islamic Counterpublics.* New York: Columbia University Press.

Hodder, I. 2016. *Studies in Human-Thing Entanglement.* Online book. http://www.ian-hodder.com/books/studies-human-thing-entanglement.

Keenan, D. K. 2005. *The Question of Sacrifice.* Bloomington and Indianapolis: Indiana University Press.

Kocelman, P. 2011. "A Mayan Ontology of Poultry: Selfhood, Affect, Animals, and Ethnography." *Language in Society* 40: 427–454.

Lambek, M. 2007. "Sacrifice and the Problems of Beginning: Meditations from Sakalava Mythopraxis." *Journal of the Royal Anthropological Institute* 13: 19–38.

Lambek, M. 2008. "Value and Virtue." *Anthropological Theory* 8 (2): 133–157.

Lienhardt, G. 1961. *Divinity and Experience: The Religion of the Dinka.* London: Oxford University Press.

Mahmood, S. 2011. *Politics of Piety: The Islamic Revival and the Feminist Subject.* Princeton, NJ, and Oxford: Princeton University Press.

Mauss, M., and H. Hubert. 1964. *Sacrifice: Its Nature and Function.* Translated by W. D. Halls. Chicago, IL: University of Chicago Press.

Mayblin, M., and M. Course. 2013. "The Other Side of Sacrifice: Introduction." *Ethnos* 79 (3): 307–319.

McClymond, K. 2008. *Beyond Sacred Violence: A Comparative Study of Sacrifice*. Baltimore, MD: Johns Hopkins University Press.

McGregor, R. 2015. "Religions and the Religion of Animals: Ethics, Self, and Language in Tenth-Century Iraq." *Comparative Studies of South Asia, Africa and the Middle East* 35 (2): 222–231.

Meyer, B. 2009. "From Imagined Communities to Aesthetic Formations: Religious Mediations, Sensational Forms, and Styles of Binding." In *Aesthetic Formations: Media, Religion, and the Senses,* edited by B. Meyer, 1–28. New York: Palgrave Macmillan.

Meyer, B. 2011. "Mediating Absence—Effecting Spiritual Presence: Pictures and the Christian Imagination." *Social Research* 78 (4): 1029–1056.

Milbank, J. 1996. "Stories of Sacrifice." *Modern Theology* 12 (1): 27–56.

Mittermaier, A. 2019. *Giving to God: Islamic Charity in Revolutionary Times*. Berkeley, CA: University of California Press.

Nadasdy, P. 2007. "The Gift in the Animal: The Ontology of Hunting and Human-Animal Sociality." *American Ethnologist* 34 (1): 25–43.

Robertson Smith, W. 1995. "Lectures on the Religion of the Semites." *Journal for the Study of the Old Testament* 183: 33–58.

Said, E. W. 1978. *Orientalism*. New York: Pantheon Books.

Strathern, M. 2018. "Relations." In *The Cambridge Encyclopedia of Anthropology* (online), edited by F. Stein, S. Lazar, M. D. Candea, J. Robbins, A. Sanchez, and R. Stasch. Cambridge: University of Cambridge.

Strenski, I. 2003. *Theology and the First Theory of Sacrifice*. Leiden: Brill.

Tallbear, K. 2011. "Why Interspecies Thinking Needs Indigenous Standpoints." *Fieldsights*. Society for Cultural Anthropology. November 18. https://culanth.org/fieldsights/why-interspecies-thinking-needs-indigenous-standpoints.

Tamimi Arab, P. 2019. "Spinoza, Arch-Father of the Material Religion Approach and New Materialisms." *Material Religion: The Journal of Objects, Art and Belief* 15 (5): 624–626.

Taneja, A. V. 2015. "Saintly Animals: The Shifting Moral and Ecological Landscapes of North India." *Comparative Studies of South Asia, Africa and the Middle East* 35 (2): 204–221.

Tayob, A. 2018. "Decolonizing the Study of Religions: Muslim Intellectuals and the Enlightenment Project of Religious Studies." *Journal for the Study of Religion* 31 (2): 7–23.

Tayob, S. 2019. "Disgust as Embodied Critique: Being Middle Class and Muslim in Mumbai." *South Asia: Journal of South Asian Studies* 42 (6): 1192–1209.

Tlili, S. 2012. *Animals in the Qur'an*. Cambridge and New York: Cambridge University Press.

Tylor, E. B. 1871. *Primitive Culture: Researches into the Development of Mythology, Philosophy, Religion, Art, and Custom*. London: Bradbury, Evans, Printers, Whitefriars.

Wolfe, C. 2019. "Turning Toward and Away." In *Messy Eating: Conversations on Animals and Food,* edited by S. King, R. S. Carey, I. Macquarrie, V. N. Millious, and E. M. Power, 19–35. New York: Fordham University Press.

Yelle, R. 2019. "From Sovereignty to Solidarity: Some Transformations in the Politics of Sacrifice from the Reformation to Robertson Smith." *History of Religions* 58 (3): 319–346.

3.9

BORRANDO LA FRONTERA

Ana Teresa Fernández's
Transborder Communion[1]

Barbara Sostaita

It was fall and the air was crisp—October or November 2011, as the artist Ana Teresa Fernández recounts. A cool sea breeze stung her skin as she placed a ladder against the eighteen-foot-tall metal beams dividing Playas de Tijuana and San Diego and painted the border wall a sky blue, disappearing the barrier against the horizon. Wearing a black tango dress and matching stilettos, the artist conjured—if only for a moment—a landscape where borders are irrelevant to movement. Fernández recalls how quickly Border Patrol agents arrived on the scene; green-striped pickup trucks sped down the beach as officers shouted orders through a loudspeaker, demanding that she stop painting at once (Fernández 2021). They considered detaining the artist, but—according to Fernández—they eventually relented, at least partly because of her choice of clothing. As I argue in this chapter, femme practices and performances invite alternative worlds in the present. Fernández used Behr's "Seashore Dreams" paint color for the six-hour-long performance (Tedford 2017). Her own dream was to facilitate transborder touch (Figures 3.9.1 and 3.9.2).

Since the first performance, Fernández and her collaborators have led similar projects in Nogales, Sonora (2015), Mexicali, Baja California (2016), Agua Prieta, Sonora (2016), and Ciudad Juárez, Chihuahua (2016). Later iterations of the project have taken place in collaboration with deported migrants and binational artists. The insistence on finding each other across borders—residents from both sides of the line painting, erasing, and defacing together—is a reaction to state practices of containment, confinement, and capture. In this chapter, I invite scholars of material religion to take touch and performance seriously as modes of engaging with the sacred. While many scholars have recently turned their attention to devotional objects such as altars and prayer cards on the migrant trail, I suggest that performance—its ephemerality and "hapticality" (Moten and Harney 2013)—facilitates generative and prefigurative ways to think about material religion in the borderlands. By erasing the border, Fernández makes tangible its absence, activating sacred forces that deface the profane world—or the everyday, routinized violences of border enforcement. In creating a hole, she actually makes the wall more visible.

Peter Andreas refers to the southern border as a "ceremonial practice"—a series of performances and rituals that are less about deterring unauthorized drugs and migrants than about reaffirming a state's territorial authority (Andreas 2000: 11). Detention centers, militarized checkpoints, and surveillance infrastructure produce an image of an impermeable

DOI: 10.4324/9781351176231-28

Figures 3.9.1 and 3.9.2   Ana Teresa Fernández. 2011. *Borrando la Frontera (Erasing the Border).* Courtesy of the artist and Catharine Clark Gallery, San Francisco.

border and reassure citizens of state sovereignty. Barriers and technologies redirect migrants to desert terrain with less accessible sources of water (De León 2015), militarizing Indigenous lands and continuing a project of settler colonialism—eliminating and disappearing migrants, many Indigenous, who are increasingly dispossessed by extractive capitalism and neoliberal development. But migrants, *coyotes* (human smugglers), and other travelers contest and transgress borders every day. And *Borrando la Frontera* enlists the wall itself as a participant in the performance, showing how it can be challenged, undone, and "redressed," to use the artist's language. In erasing the border, she shows its impermanence. Through a performance based in collectivity and touch, she interrupts the project of militarization— *even if only briefly*. Here, I study her performance alongside a weekly border Eucharist, showing how Fernández's interventions are also communion scenes: a collective becoming that disrupts national borders and a prefigurative performance in which the future interrupts the present.

Fernández staged the 2011 performance near Friendship Park, a binational recreation area where a commission met to delineate the international boundary following the Treaty of Guadalupe Hidalgo, which dispossessed Mexico of over half of its territory and fractured Indigenous lands. *Borrando la Frontera* was a response to the Obama Administration's limits on transborder touch at the park, a site where families separated by the border have historically gathered and embraced—even if under the surveillance of customs and border enforcement agents. In an interview with *Artsy*, Fernández—who herself is a Mexican migrant—explains:

> I did it as a protest when they applied the third layer of mesh and didn't allow people to touch anymore. [Friendship Park] was the area where people used to be able to congregate and share meals and touch each other. In 2011 that was no longer allowed, the mesh was implemented, and now you can only touch your fingertips.
>
> *(Fernández, cited in Artsy Editors 2017)*

Fernández longed for transborder touch, and her performance intended to create "the illusion of a huge hole in the fence, a visual pause, so that people who came to the beach could have moments of rest from the beast separating Mexico from the United States" (Fernández, cited in Dubrock n.d.). Calling *Borrando la Frontera* a "visual pause" suggests the performance is temporary, though the first iteration was recorded and archived on YouTube (Favier 2014). Even still, the footage hints at its own ephemerality: the time-lapsed video's accelerated speed emphasizes the performance's impermanence. The hours-long performance is collapsed into a few minutes. Time rushes past the viewer and the artist's body soars upwards—almost as if she is dancing in the air. Permanence, on the other hand, is the language of enforcement. Borders are measured by their staying power or their longevity. Politicians frame campaigns and run administrations on the promise of "sealing" and "securing" the southern border, implying that the walls they build will be impermeable and indestructible. Fernández suggests that borders are themselves performances; they are continuously reinforced, remade, and undone. In this case, the performance takes place through a spray gun and a pair of stilettos.

According to John Fanestil, a minister who weekly administers the Eucharist at Friendship Park, no barriers of any kind existed in the area for over a century after the Treaty of Guadalupe Hidalgo. As late as the 1960s, the site was marked "by nothing more than a few cement posts and a low-hanging metal chain" (Fanestil 2013: 163). In 1994, as part of Prevention Through Deterrence, which increased the number of agents and barriers at urban ports of entry, steel metal panels replaced the chain-link fence (De León 2015). Fanestil explains the panels were recycled from the landing mats of retired US aircraft carriers—quite literally militarizing the border (Fanestil 2013: 164). In 2009, the US closed Friendship Park and installed a second fence with barbed wire, surveillance cameras, and motion sensors. Before the construction of the second fence, families met to exchange food and souvenirs across the wall, pressing their faces against or forcing their arms through metal slats to touch loved ones. As Border Patrol vehicles idled in the background, families would bellow greetings to each other, savoring their long-anticipated conversations. They could get physically close enough to touch cheeks and feel the warmth of each other's bodies, close enough to observe the fine lines and sun spots that had formed on their loved one's faces. Friendship Park simultaneously accelerated and paused the passing of time.

Since the park's reopening in 2012, Border Patrol has enforced "very rigidly" that nothing shall be passed across the border, warning Fanestil that distributing bread and wine constitutes a "customs violation" (Fanestil 2021). Before the COVID-19 pandemic shut down visits entirely, Border Patrol limited gatherings to weekends from 10:00 a.m. to 2:00 p.m. Only ten adults were granted entry to the US side of the park at any one time, and their admission was contingent on proof of legal residence. Friendship Park—a sacred space that interrupts profane time—is heavily policed, enclosed, surrounded by taboos and prohibitions. Given increased restrictions at Friendship Park, Fanestil and his Mexican collaborator,

Guillermo Navarrete, improvised other ways to touch across the border. Now, they place a table or altar on the Mexican side and another on the opposite side of the wall, each with their own bread and cup. Consecrating the Eucharist at the same time only a few footsteps away from each other, the priests imagine they are "converting the border from a wall into a table." This, too, is a form of transubstantiation. Through collective ritual, they transform cold steel bars into a space of touch and intimacy. They pursue proximity.

Borrando la Frontera pulses with a desire to touch—a queer longing in the sense proposed by José Esteban Muñoz: as "not here yet" and as a "horizon of being" only momentarily accessible through intimacy and performance (Muñoz 2009: 23). Like Fanestil's subversive sacrament, Fernández's performance leaves fleeting traces of an otherwise world without borders. Like the Eucharist, her performance is a transmutation: instead of changing the bread and wine into the body and blood of Jesus, she transforms the wall into a "visual pause." When the artist learned that welded railway track had been used to build a section of the wall, she was determined to

> reshift the [rails'] purpose by painting them sky blue; it's almost like I am pulling down the sky and putting a costume on the train tracks, so they can be performers and become something else again. They were built to allow people to move. Maybe now they can allow visually for people to keep moving.
>
> *(Fernández 2021)*

The artist repurposed the metal rails so that they, too, can be performers. Fernández yearned to engage with the train tracks as active participants in her intervention, as collaborators and co-conspirators. She saw the tracks as agents, who not only make possible movement but also move themselves. They can "become something else again." "Redressing" the railway track used to build the wall, she intended to "pull down the sky," an eschatological vision also expressed in the Eucharist. Indeed, as William Cavanaugh writes, "in the Eucharist the heavens are opened, and the church of all times and places is gathered around the altar" (Cavanaugh 1998: 225). By way of performance, Fernández pulled down the sky or opened the heavens, emboldening her audience to envision and make possible a time to come or a time that has escaped. She invites her collaborators to reach across the wall and commune with those on the other side.

The Decolonial Femme and "How We Usually View Things"

Footage of the 2011 performance opens with Fernández's back turned to the camera. She wears a form-fitting black dress that falls slightly above her knee. The artist holds a paintbrush, and she bends and rises to paint the steel wall ritualistically, reverently even. Fernández is physically able to paint several bollards at a time, and she is seen climbing a ladder to reach the tallest parts of the eighteen-foot wall. The camera focuses on the artist as enforcement agents approach and question her; when they leave, the camera fixates on her stilettos and prompts the viewer to pay close attention to her body. Fernández's stilettos emphasize her precarity. The ladder is shaky, and the artist is vulnerable—an experience highlighted by the ways that women's labor has been made invisible and, even, that women were historically not allowed on scaffolding. While painting, Fernández wears a black dress, hinting at her femme sensualities and her experiences *en luto*, or mourning. It is clear that the artist has suffered a loss. For most of the performance, Fernández conceals her face, and the audience is not granted access to her expressions or reactions. She simultaneously emphasizes the use of her body and renders the body invisible—transforming herself into a black dot that travels up and down the canvas.

Fernández explains that by "amplifying" the use of her own body, her performances "challenge the history and perspective of how we usually view things. . . . I dress in Tango attire, altering a space or myself within a space, performing actions that use my body as a measuring device" (Fernández 2015). The black dress and stilettos are key to the project of seeing differently. Fernández wants to challenge our ways of moving through the world, activating femme senses and sensualities that disrupt the movements of everyday life.

Religious studies scholars, especially those researching Latin American and Latinx communities, have written on performance and sacred space. Alysia Gálvez's edited volume *Performing Religion in the Americas* and Elaine Peña's *Performing Piety* and *Viva George* take seriously what the latter terms "devotional labor" (Gálvez 2007; Peña 2011, 2020). Peña attends to the ways devotees' bodies—their movements, gestures, wounds, aches, words—transmit memory and produce knowledge. This chapter extends these methodologies and focuses primarily on how Fernández centers femme's potential to disrupt borders and facilitate communion. As Jill Holslin observes, Fernández's project "situates the sensual/laboring female body in the specific context of the U.S.-Mexico border, a site where personal, national, and gender histories intersect" (Holslin 2011). This contextualization is important—women, queer, trans, and femme migrants at the border are uniquely vulnerable to the dangers of border-crossing journeys, gender-based violence, and workplace abuses. Their racialized, gendered, and sexualized bodies are constructed as a biological threat to the nation-state—migrant women reproduce migrant babies, and their transnational and cross-border lives pose challenges to citizenship (Segura and Zavella 2007). Emphasizing the "sensual/laboring female body," and widely known as the artist who erased the border in a little black dress, Fernández performs what Macarena Gómez-Barris terms a "decolonial queer femme methodology" (Gómez-Barris 2017: 9).

Gómez-Barris's *The Extractive Zone* is an experiment in seeking out submerged perspectives that exist despite and beyond practices of extraction in Latin America. The book's case studies show how rivers refuse capture and Indigenous communities mobilize against oil drilling. In the book's opening pages, Gómez-Barris proposes a decolonial femme methodology, which "attends to lived embodiment as world-shaping activities" (Gómez-Barris 2017: 9). *The Extractive Zone* is attentive to movement and performance, detailing the ways both human and more-than-human actors create other worlds in the present—worlds that defy and exceed militarization and occupation. This methodology "subverts and exceeds the colonial sight of the normative. The multiple perspectives of the female eye perceive in opposition to the extractive gaze, the singular, patriarchal, and hierarchical organizing vision of gendered capitalist economies" (124). Gómez-Barris's methodology requires embracing multiple perspectives and multiple worlds—or, in other words, seeing beyond a heteronormative and masculinist vision. In the borderlands, steel slats penetrate the land; government contractors dynamite nature refuges, and crews extract sacred groundwater to mix concrete that holds the border wall in place. This masculinist viewpoint insists on a singular vision; it seeks to not only restrict mobility, but to control or supervise movement—to tame an unruly and wayward process. On the other hand, decolonial femme methodologies affirm these mobile ways of moving through the world, embracing the ephemeral, the fragile, the not here yet. Like Fernández's artistic practice, decolonial femme methodologies challenge "how we usually view things" (9).

In centering the touching, dancing, and laboring female body, Fernández "valorizes nonnormative embodied femininity as sources of knowing and perceiving" (Gómez-Barris 2017: 9). She explains:

> My body has become the vehicle in which I investigate spaces, push/pull against it, or tango with it. I try to insert value with these movements in landscapes of labor that go under-recognized or *unseen*. And by sensuality, I mean, provoking and awakening your senses.
>
> *(Fernández, cited in Murga 2015)*

Fernández wants to awaken the audience's senses, and she plots ways to "tango with" land and territory. Notably, as Julie Taylor describes this style of dance, the Argentine tango is shaped by ongoing histories of violence and loss, rupture and terror. As an apprentice, Taylor learned that tango demands an "emotional response" to music, an "exchange of energy," or what she calls a *puta entrega* that embraces the danger in the dancer handing herself "over to [her] own body" (Taylor 1998: 87, 111, 113). This dance is fully sacred, simultaneously negative and positive—"profoundly pleasing and profoundly disturbing, something that both rendered me visible and disappeared at the same time, something that I was afraid to touch for fear that I would no longer exist" (Taylor 1998: 76). Touch, and the intimacy it demands, threatens to undo the performer, to unmake them. By describing her work as a form of tango, Fernández suggests that she, too, hopes to evoke an emotional response or to provoke a *puta entrega*. She invites the viewer to give themselves over to possibility, potentiality. The pause in the fence compels the spectator to squint, to look twice, to second guess what they assumed to be natural and inflexible (i.e., the singular masculinist vision). A passerby might even see the hole in the wall and wonder if it is actually there; to confirm their suspicions they would have no choice but to approach the wall and feel the cold, steel bars. Her intervention is almost like a magic trick, a disappearing act that makes the border wall hypervisible.

Borrando la Frontera taps into senses and impulses disciplined out of us by borders and walls. While border militarization projects constrain transborder touch, Fernández's project nurtures this proximity. The artist facilitates an ephemeral intimacy—recruiting volunteers from both sides of the border to labor together and collectively imagine alternatives to militarization. Greeting each other the morning of the performance, perhaps by shaking hands or exchanging a kiss on the cheek, brushing the border wall with paint and brushing (up) against each other, bumping against and smelling other bodies while laboring together, sharing food, sharing space, and sharing *testimonio*—the act of coming together to erase a wall makes tangible that which is no longer. Fernández and her volunteers refuse to accept the permanence of colonial boundaries, the endurance of borders.

Queer Pause or a Return to "Lost Intimacy"

Borrando la Frontera is a practice of care, offering brief moments of refuge to border residents and crossers scarred by the violences of enforcement. According to Fernández, the "militarization of the border is forcing these train tracks to become something they weren't born into," and her intervention is to "allow them to transcend that and become something else, to offer a respite for *like a second*" (Fernández 2021). The artist hoped to facilitate imagination, prompting passersby to ask, "What if the wall disappeared?"

The "what if" is a sacred impulse that disrupts the profane or, in other words, the everyday world of law, order, security, and sovereignty. If the sacred is what is set apart from the mundane and routine, then I define the sacred as those performances and moments that flee the present and its insistence on stability and sameness. Here, I draw inspiration from Georges Bataille, who in *Theory of Religion* observes that the sacred is unruly and ungovernable—an attempt to grasp at "lost intimacy" (Bataille 1992: 53). *Borrando la Frontera* was inspired by the artist's longing for this lost intimacy stolen by layers of mesh and steel bars. Not to romanticize or glorify this intimacy, the sacred is both positive and negative, tender and destructive, or to return to Taylor, "profoundly pleasing and profoundly disturbing" (Taylor 1998: 76). Fernández's performance brings the audience closer to this dangerous practice of intimacy, erasing or interrupting the lines that keep us separate—the prohibitions and exclusions that divide families and tribal nations like the Tohono O'odham. But this communion scene is only temporary. It offers a reprieve from borderization for, *like, a second.* In the end, human beings can access the sacred world only for brief moments and in fleeting glimpses. As Roger Caillois insists in *Man and the Sacred*, "This state cannot be maintained for very long" (Caillois 1939: 38). Caillois writes of the dangers of accessing the sacred and of the need to purify oneself before and after entering the ungovernable world. The sacred is unsustainable and human beings must be cautious when approaching the world of "lost intimacy." Communion, too, is ephemeral. At the end of the day, participants return to their homes and communities. The barriers remain in place, and many cannot cross to the other side.

Touch facilitates the visual pause. It longs for a time to come or perhaps even, a time that once existed and that will exist again. Before the layers of mesh were added at Friendship Park, loved ones clung to each other, gripped each other's faces, stroked each other's hair, refused the everyday or routine forms of distance or division imposed by borders. In the art world, touch also transgresses the profane; in galleries and exhibitions, touch is typically prohibited, the subject of a taboo. While visiting St. Xavier Mission in the Sonora-Arizona borderlands, I noticed various signs asking visitors to respect sacred space by abstaining from touch. Even before the COVID-19 pandemic, these signs encouraged devotees to be "prudent" and reminded guests that hands transmit germs and disease. Touch is infectious, transmissible, and, therefore, sacred—to draw from Émile Durkheim's definition of the sacred as "extraordinarily contagious" (Durkheim 1995: 327). A sacred force, touch easily slips out of the control of religious leaders and immigration authorities—transgressing borders and barriers. (Figures 3.9.3 and 3.9.4).

Cat Lachowskyj insists that conversations around touch and defilement haunt the art world: "As soon as objects enter a museum, the priority is to freeze them in time, which is prioritized over access (despite access being the claim of many collections)" (Lachowskyj 2020). According to this framework, touch disrupts the integrity of art; it interrupts the process of preservation. Lachowskyj continues:

> If a museum acquires nitrate negatives or color negatives and prints, they are often obligated to immediately put them into cold storage for preservation and safety. Cold storage is notoriously inaccessible because there are various sealed freezer bags. There is definitely a great divide, especially with vernacular and ritual objects which are essentially meant to be touched and to circulate.

The everyday world of museums and galleries is designed to protect art from sacred touch, which threatens the object's authenticity and purity. Yet, there are many art forms—including performance—that disrupt this division between proximity and preservation. Fernández's performance plays with one of these genres; *Borrando la Frontera* can be read as an optical illusion, or *trompe l'oeil*. French for "to deceive the eye," *trompe l'oeil* is an art technique popularized in the Renaissance era that plays with perspective and misleads viewers into

Figures 3.9.3 and 3.9.4 Holy Reminders at St. Xavier Mission. 2020. Photographs by Barbara Sostaita.

seeing three-dimensional objects in a painting or creates imagined architectural elements in a room. Like Fernández, *trompe l'oeil* asks, "What if?" It is an exercise in changing "how we usually view things." This technique invites audiences to blur boundaries between what is depicted on a canvas or a mural and what exists in the material world. It facilitates the imagination, and refuses the normal, the mundane, the ordinary in favor of otherwise worlds. *Trompe l'oeil* begs to be touched, prompting viewers to engage with their senses, to enter into intimacy with the work itself.

Fernández's transborder touch is a pause or queer trace, not a permanent installation. In fact, only a decade after Fernández's intervention, the paint that erased the border wall at Playas de Tijuana has seemingly disappeared. Or, more accurately, it has transformed into something else (again). The sky blue has been weathered by the sun and covered with other projects, including an interactive mural bearing the portraits of childhood arrivals to the United States. The *trompe l'oeil* is no more. Touch escapes; it fades. José Esteban Muñoz insists that queer performance, too, refuses preservation and permanence. It is a disruption of normative and normal time, fleeing the confines of the here and now.

The late Cuban theorist insists that queerness is future-oriented. It rejects the present, which is all too often unlivable and uninhabitable for queer folks and people of color. In *Cruising Utopia*, Muñoz suggests that queer time disrupts straight time, living within but imagining beyond the present. According to Muñoz, straight time is the dominant order, the heteromasculinist vision described by Gómez-Barris in *The Extractive Zone*. Muñoz insists it is settled and settler time. It operates within the profane world of borders, walls, and boundaries. It is legible, fixed, and preoccupied with the present (Muñoz 2009: 35). *Borrando la Frontera* interrupts straight time. Uninterested in permanence, the performance only leaves a queer trace, one that will fade and disappear with time. Behr's Seashore Dreams paint will continue to chip and scenes of transborder touch will become only a distant memory. Crowds will gather at Friendship Park and then return to their homes on opposite sides of the fence. The performance's ephemerality points to an alternative marking of time and a restless yearning for intimacy, *if only for a second.*

Fernández interrupts the present or profane world, which is invested in maintaining and reinforcing borders. Through transgressive touch, the artist and participants in her performances refuse the routine world of enforcement. Queer time, as a reminder, refuses the singular vision of the present. It is a "critique of the present by casting a picture of what can and perhaps will be" (Muñoz 2009: 35). This is what *Borrando la Frontera* accomplishes—it transgresses the present and insists on another world in the now. This is also eucharistic time, in which the past and future interrupt the present, in which the sky is pulled down, in which the heavens are opened.

Up the sandy hill where Fernández first performed *Borrando la Frontera*, John Fanestil and Guillermo Navarrete lead devotees in a weekly border Eucharist. Even before taking the actual elements, participants engage in the acts of confession and the passing of the peace. Fanestil explains the importance of touch in the ritualized liturgy that precedes communion:

> Everybody [present] places their hands on the wall for a time of confession. We'll often encourage people to find somebody on the other side of the wall if they can. First, we confess our sins as individuals, as communities, as churches, and as nations and then we invite people to offer their own confessions in silence. But people are commonly very moved by that experience because they're touching somebody's fingertips on the other side of the wall and praying together in a very intimate way. We then invite them to raise their hands and look at the sky as a reminder that God's grace is greater than the structures humans create for ourselves.
>
> *(Fanestil 2021)*

Fanestil says that the impulse to offer the Eucharist came from the awareness that the space has been one of communion for decades. According to him, the border Eucharist is an attempt to "mark" and "protect" space, to set it apart or consecrate it as sacred—through labor, touch, and ritual. For him, eucharistic time ruptures the profane or the everyday and its insistence on militarization and separation. He notes that, since its inauguration, Friendship Park has been a refuge from enforcement—a meeting place to pause or disregard, if not outright refuse, border enforcement. During confession, Fanestil invites participants to lock eyes with someone on the other side, to lay their hands on the steel bars and poke their fingertips through the barriers.

In *Theory of Religion,* Bataille imagines the religious impulse as the desire for immanence or being "in the world like water in water." Bataille details how the profane world of order, utility, law, and productivity alienates humans from each other and from land (Bataille 1992). Bataille insists that religion can be understood as a practice and performance of transgression, of accessing—if only momentarily—a world of sacred energies, forces, and powers. Religion is the desire to lose yourself in the other, to touch and feel beyond individuation, to defy the limits imposed by the profane world. *Borrando la Frontera* embraces this impulse, bringing bodies into communion across borders and defying state-sponsored taboos. The performance facilitates a queer temporality and a defiant sociality, a touch that exceeds taboos.

Conclusion

In this chapter, I have theorized *Borrando la Frontera* as scenes of communion. During our conversation, the artist compared her act of erasing the border with the Eucharist's promise to erase sin and suffering. The sacrament is, according to Cavanaugh's *Torture and Eucharist,* an interruption of profane time, a refusal to engage with history as a linear series of events. "In the Eucharist, past and future simultaneously converge, and the whole Christ, the eschatological church of all times and places, is present" (Cavanaugh 1998: 234). Cavanaugh suggests that the rite of communion—as a commemoration of the incarnation, death, and resurrection of Christ—lifts participants from this world and offers a glimpse of the heavenly Kingdom (14). It is another world in the present, a time to come in the here and now.

Asked about the lessons she gained from erasing the border, Fernández answered, "What I learned is that many people do not allow themselves to dream of other options, of other ways of seeing what is possible. I also realized that many people are afraid of how strong imagination can be" (Fernández, cited in Dubrock n.d.). Believing there are other ways of experiencing and moving through the world, the artist puts into practice Macarena Gómez-Barris's notion of decolonial femme methodologies that exist beyond extractive zones—in this case, the "layers of mesh" and steel fences that divide families and communities (Gómez-Barris 2017: 12). Borders are not permanent, and they are not inevitable. Fernández's project argues that a different world is possible, and, in fact, it is already being lived every day.

Despite recent interventions, the study of Latinx material religion continues to focus disproportionately on altars, images, and devotional objects. While these are also tactile, I suggest that taking performance seriously facilitates other ways of thinking about the sacred. Performance invites participants to touch and commune, to interrupt the routine by imagining the future in the here and now. *Borrando la Frontera* in particular illuminates how ritual and repetition, touch and transgression deface the profane world and conjure other possibilities. By staging the performance at Friendship Park, the artist makes clear that she is interested in pauses and interruptions, in gaps and holes that facilitate lost intimacies or unruly attachments. With her tango dress and pair of stilletos, Fernández offers a temporary glimpse at a world of intimacy and immanence, where borders and barriers do not limit possibilities for intimacy and proximity.

In arguing for decolonial femme methodologies, Macarena Gómez-Barris notes that "the dream of 'another world' is not merely a future-oriented utopia but it is already in motion, teeming with the alternatives we desire" (Gómez-Barris 2017: 134). In seeing through, beyond, and underneath the "mesh" of border walls—the infrared cameras, heat sensors, surveillance drones, and steel fences—Ana Teresa Fernández likewise puts into motion a world where borders are irrelevant to movement. After erasing the border in 2011, as she collected empty cans of paint and tore the stilettos off her swollen feet, Fernández noticed a woman and her young daughter coming out of their home and eagerly approaching the fence. The woman addressed the artist wide-eyed and awe-struck.

> You know, I've lived here for a very long time, and I've seen protests and demonstrations against the wall. But before today, I never actually stopped to see the wall itself. By you erasing it, I see what a nuisance it is. I never really stopped to think about it, about what this place would be like without a fence.
>
> *(Fernández 2021)*

Postscript: As of the publication of this book, activists are engaged in a campaign to save Friendship Park. Earlier this year, the Biden administration began construction on two thirty-foot walls through the historic site. Activists insist that this surveillance infrastructure will severely limit the ways people from both sides are able to gather and commune.

Note

1 Thanks to Mary Stephens of *Performance in the Borderlands* for connecting me with Ana Teresa, and to the artist herself for this intervention, which has sparked my imagination and invited so many others to dream otherwise. Thanks to China Medel, for the feedback on this chapter when it was first a seminar paper and to Todd Ramón Ochoa for introducing me to many of the theorists I have cited here and for teaching me how to ask questions, how to celebrate the "what if?". And, lastly, I will forever be grateful for Alex Morelli, my partner and editor, whose eye for detail makes me a more cautious and thoughtful writer.

References

Andreas, Peter. 2000. *Border Games: Policing the US-Mexico Divide*. Ithaca, NY: Cornell University Press.

Artsy Editors. 2017. "For Artists, the U.S.-Mexico Border is Fertile Territory." *Artsy*, March 6, 2017. https://www.artsy.net/article/artsy-editorial-mexican-artists-threat-trumps-wall-fuel-inspiration.

Bataille, Georges. 1992. *Theory of Religion*. Princeton, NJ: Princeton University Press.

Caillois, Roger. 1939. *Man and the Sacred*. New York: Free Press of Glencoe.

Cavanaugh, William. 1998. *Torture and Eucharist*. Malden, MA: Blackwell Publishing.

De León, Jason. 2015. *The Land of Open Graves: Living and Dying on the Migrant Trail*. Berkeley and Los Angeles: University of California Press.

Dubrock, Francesca. n.d. "Erasing the Border Is Possible." *Sol de Medianoche*. Accessed December 17, 2021. http://www.soldemedianochenews.org/erasing-the-border.html.

Durkheim, Émile. 1995. *The Elementary Forms of Religious Life*. New York: Free Press.

Fanestil John. 2013. "A Divided Friendship: Friendship Park: The Past, Present, and Future of the U.S.-Mexico Border." In *Religion and Politics in Americas Borderlands*, edited by S. Azaransky, 161–175. Lanham, MD: Lexington Books.

Fanestil, John. 2021. Zoom interview with Barbara Sostaita, March 30, 2021.

Favier, Sylvie. 2014. "Borrando la Frontera/Erasing the Border." April 19, 2014. YouTube video, 3:38. https://www.youtube.com/watch?v=NLRAP4GmZ4Q&ab_channel=sylviefavier.

Fernández, Ana Teresa. 2015. Commentary on *White Sins, 2014*. Humboldt University. Spring 2015. http://www2.humboldt.edu/third/exhibitions/2015/atf/whitesins.html.

Fernández, Ana Teresa. 2021. Zoom interview with Barbara Sostaita, August 31, 2021.

Gálvez, Alyshia, ed. 2007. *Performing Religion in the Americas: Media, Politics, and Devotional Practices of the 21st Century*. Chicago, IL: University of Chicago Press.

Gómez-Barris, Macarena. 2017. *The Extractive Zone*. Durham, NC: Duke University Press.

Holslin, Jill. 2011. "Borrando la Frontera." https://anateresafernandez.com/borrando-la-barda-tijuana-mexico/.

Lachowskyj, Cat. 2020. Facebook Messenger interview with Barbara Sostaita, October 6, 2020.

Moten, Fred, and Stefano Harney. 2013. *The Undercommons: Fugitive Planning & Black Study*. Brooklyn, NY: Minor Compositions.

Muñoz, José Esteban 2009. *Cruising Utopia: The Then and There of Queer Futurity*. New York: New York University Press.

Murga, Tamara. 2015. "Ana Teresa Fernández on Erasing the U.S.-Mexico Border." *The Athenian Print*, November 4, 2015. https://theathenianprint.wordpress.com/2015/11/04/ana-teresa-fernandez-on-erasing-the-u-s-mexico-border/.

Peña, Elaine. 2011. *Performing Piety: Making Space Sacred with the Virgin of Guadalupe*. Berkeley and Los Angeles, CA: University of California Press.

Peña, Elaine. 2020. *Viva George: Celebrating Washington's Birthday on the US-Mexico Border*. Austin, TX: University of Texas Press.

Segura, Denise, and Patricia Zavella, eds. 2007. *Women and Migration in the U.S.-Mexico Borderlands: A Reader*. Durham, NC: Duke University Press.

Taylor, Julie. 1998. *Paper Tangos*. Durham, NC: Duke University Press.

Tedford, Matthew Harrison. 2017. "Ana Teresa Fernández Erases the U.S.-Mexico Border." *Sculpture Nature*, January 20, 2017. http://www.sculpturenature.com/en/ana-teresa-fernandez-erases-the-u-s-mexico-border/.

PART IV

Hyperobjects, or How Ginormous Things Affect Religions

4.1

THE ERIE CANAL AND THE BIRTH OF AMERICAN RELIGION

Infrastructure as Hyperobject

S. Brent Rodríguez-Plate

If you drive into Palmyra, New York, today you will see a site not unlike what the Mormon founder Joseph Smith saw two hundred years ago: a cluster of four tall steeples rising from four Protestant churches. Presbyterians, Methodists, Baptists, and Episcopalians confront each other at adjacent corners of the town's crossroads. Though they aren't the same steeples as in Smith's day, the inter-denominational face-off was already in force, leading Smith to reflect: "There was in the place where we lived an unusual excitement on the subject of religion. . . . Priest contended against priest, and convert against convert so that all their good feelings one for another were entirely lost in a strife of words and a contest about opinions" (Smith 1839: 2). In a newly settled land rife with old and new religious movements in direct competition for people's souls, Smith turned the discord to his advantage. As is well known through contemporary caricature and acclaim alike, he forged one of the most powerful religious traditions operating in the world today.

What is not so well known is that the origins of Mormonism, like the origins of many U.S. religious practices and beliefs, are deeply bound up with the birth of the Erie Canal.[1] Palmyra is situated on the canal, fifteen miles south of Lake Ontario and twenty miles east of Rochester. Smith's family moved from New England to the Palmyra area in 1817 when Joseph was twelve years old, the same year Erie Canal construction began between the towns of Rome and Utica a hundred miles east. Two years later he began having visions of heavenly beings as he walked in the pristine forests surrounding the small Yankee settlement. In 1823, the Erie Canal was opened between Palmyra and Rochester, establishing the outpost as a regional commercial center: prosperity grew along with the population. In another two years the Canal would stretch the entire 363 miles from Albany to Buffalo, creating economic boomtowns along the way and generating strong spiritual excitation and experimentation as settlers moved further from the ecclesiastical authorities of the East (see Figure 4.1.1).

In *A History of the American People*, Paul Johnson suggested the Erie Canal is "the outstanding example of a human artifact creating wealth rapidly in the whole of history" (1997: 248). We might amend this analysis to suggest the Erie Canal is the outstanding example of a human artifact creating new religious movements rapidly in the whole of history. Simply put, without the canal—a geological, geographical, artistic, technological, and religious hyperobject—deeply engrained beliefs about free will, sex, science, manifest destiny, equal

DOI: 10.4324/9781351176231-30

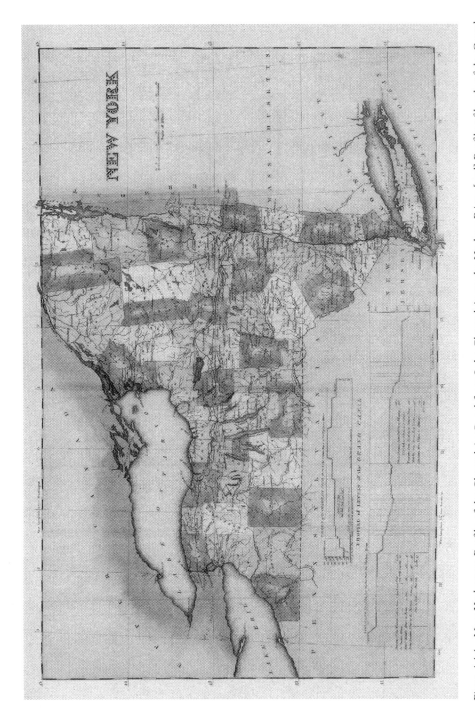

Figure 4.1.1   New York state: Profile of the Champlain Canal from Lake Champlain to the Hudson River [and] Profile of levels of the Grand [i.e. Erie] Canal. Published by New York State, Albany, 1825.

rights, the environment, the afterlife, and the imminent end of the world would not retain such a hold on the U.S. religious imagination.

Within two decades of its opening, this "psychic highway" (Klees 2001; Keene 2016), cultivated extraordinary experimental groups including the Mormons; the Seventh-day Adventists; Spiritualism; a revived Apocalypticism in general; utopian communal societies such as the Oneida Community, the Amana Colony, and the Shakers; as well as the emotion-laden revivals of the Second Great Awakening. The canal also engendered the religiously infused social movements of abolition, women's suffrage, and temperance. In most cases, the origins can be traced elsewhere, to lands further east, but it was the fecund space of upstate New York in which new movements coalesced and surged into mainstream American life. Little wonder the preacher Charles Finney eventually named this area the "Burned-over District" (see Cross 1950). Even so, this moniker belies a deeper truth: out of the ashes rose a uniquely U.S. faith that continues to exist through the present day.

In the following, I offer some brief sketches regarding the immense impact of the Erie Canal on religious life in the United States. The infrastructural work is, in one strong sense, a "hyperobject," to borrow Timothy Morton's term. That is, the canal is "massively distributed in space and time relative to humans" (Morton 2013: 1), "almost impossible to hold in mind" (58), an "interconnected" mesh (82–83), that is ultimately "nonhuman" (199). Morton's analysis is firmly set within twenty-first century accounts about climate change and the Anthropocene, but there is a kinship to the impact of the Erie Canal on early nineteenth-century perspectives because of its daunting and history-shifting materiality. I am not concerned to systematically align the Erie Canal with Morton's hyperobjects, but I do hold some of these ideas in mind as I investigate the older infrastructural technology.

This chapter offers an argument for the place of the materiality of geography and technology as a hub of innovation for religious life and practice, exemplified in the Erie Canal. The overview is brief, but the intent here is to show the vast range of influence of one hyperobject such as a canalway. What I offer is a bird's eye view, flying over one strip of land over a few short decades of history in upstate New York, in an attempt to show how religious tradition is deeply enmeshed with its geographical and technological environment, and the far-reaching effects and affects that may have.

Out of the Wild: A New Eden

At the beginning of grand mythologies about the creation of the world, water is the source of all things, as well as a potent force of chaos and destruction. The European colonizing of the American continent is often discussed in similar terms. Beginning in the seventeenth century, clusters of Europeans began crossing the great body of water that is the Atlantic, as they sought freedom from restrictions on religious and economic practices, with the promise of a newer, freer life ahead. "New" England becomes a new creation. Likewise, the mythology of the Erie Canal begins out of chaos, carved into what was nominated the "wilderness."

Disgusted by what she saw in the rapidly industrializing United States, the English novelist Frances Trollope wrote a deeply unfavorable work called *Domestic Manners of the Americans* ([1832] 1984). She found nuevo-Americans rude, crude, and lacking in social skills, not least of whom included the workers of the Erie Canal passenger boats. Yet, when she ceased demeaning Americans on the canal boats, she looked to the scenery around and noticed the "magnificent cliffs," the "lovely scene," the "fantastic" form of the river running over rocks. At almost the same time, Alexis de Tocqueville was making his famed jaunts through the American countryside, traveling the path of the Erie Canal, but when he ventured just a few miles from the canalway he found "one of those deep forests of the New World whose somber savage majesty strikes at the imagination and fills the soul with a sort of religious terror" (quoted in Bernstein 2005: 203). There is a paradox of the wild, both beautiful and terrifying, seen in the literature and the arts of the time.

The Erie Canal cut through this imagined and sometimes real wilderness, connecting not just the east coast of the continent with points west, but simultaneously connecting "nature" and "civilization," the domestic and the wild. Passengers would sit on canalboats and view the expanses of wilderness that unfolded for hours in between the cities of the canalway. European artists and writers coming to the States were in awe of the untouched, primal nature that they saw: the cliffs of the Hudson River Valley, and the rugged Catskills and Adirondacks. The canalways forged routes into remote areas where Hudson River School painters Asher Durand and Thomas Cole would seek the wild in the midst of rapid industrialization. In short, as many writers have noted, upstate New York became a place not only where one could see the wilderness, but where the wilderness was indeed *invented*. Yet, the canalboats were also a transportation source for the Underground Railroad, suffragettes, and many other people invested in social reform.

In actuality, the canal ran through the Native American settlements of the Haudenosaunee in what were the western reaches of the young country, and use of the term "wilderness" became charged with white colonialist land grabbing. For those colonizers, the United States was emerging as a cosmic continent, but the chaos of the "wild" waters and forests had to be domesticated for the conveying of commerce and concepts. To do so, many Haudenosaunee people were displaced. Governor DeWitt Clinton, central to the institution of the canal itself, predicted that "before the passing away of the present generation, not a single Iroquois [Haudenosaunee] will be seen in this state" ("Dispossession and Disruption").

Begun in 1817 and completed in 1825, the Erie Canal stretched from Buffalo, on the edge of the Great Lakes, to Albany, on the banks of the Hudson River, with eighty-three locks in between. It was one of the greatest civil technological feats in world history, made all the more amazing since there was little expertise in manners of engineering for such a grand project. From Albany it was a quick 150 miles by steamboat to New York Harbor, and this aquatic connection is what turned New York into a world-renowned city. Timber, grain, and goods came from Western New York to expand the lively seaport (NYC's population increased nearly 700% from 1820 to 1860), as markets for New York City's goods opened up in western regions of the continent as well as Europe (for overviews, see Sheriff 1996; Bernstein 2005; Koeppel 2009).

The Erie Canal follows the only significant gap in the Appalachian Mountain chain extending from Maine to Georgia, a geographical fact attributed by George Washington and his contemporaries to the goodness of "Providence." This navigable break, this narrow strip of land in a vast country, was God's gift to the fledgling nation, inspiring citizens to move west, push the frontier, and glean benefits from the natural riches of the continental interior. Intellectual ideas about Manifest Destiny flowed from the geographical realities of this place. Even so, this divine gift needed improvements, as nature did not offer an immediately accessible ride: too many portages and navigation of rapids challenged human and commercial transport. With the Erie Canal and its ingenious set of locks, came the ability to travel from New York all the way to Cleveland (eventually) with unheard-of ease. When canal construction commenced under the work of New York Governor Clinton with state funding (after President Jefferson vetoed federal funding), the waterway exceeded its basic geographical and transportation use to become an empire builder (McGreevy 2009). Indeed,

Washington himself is often attributed as being the first to nominate New York the "Empire State." The political-economic empire was inextricable from a spiritual empire.

Of note is the sense of freedom that was encouraged as Europeans moved ever farther from their homelands across the Atlantic and into the frontier. This prompted what became thought of as heroic action on the part of preachers, politicians, canal diggers, and Bible readers. From out of this freedom, new styles of economic, as well as spiritual, marketplaces were developed in which an individual could roam free and exercise choice in manners of faith and life.

The Spiritual Marketplace

Competing commercial goods took their place alongside competing moral goods in upstate New York in the nineteenth century. The Erie Canal created an unprecedented environment for economic growth, as raw materials and foodstuffs from western regions traveled across the canal to New York City and beyond, and technological tools from the Eastern seaboard cities traveled west. "Choice" (for those who had access to it) became the buzzword of the free market economy, just as it was the mantra of free market religions. As the young United States began to build on its still-recent independence, reaffirmed in the War of 1812, and as New Englanders migrated across the canalway—some stopping to set up homes and shops, and others continuing further west—economic systems were dramatically changed.

As much as new canal cities like Utica, Syracuse, Rochester, and Buffalo were economic centers, they were also religious boomtowns, primed for innovation and new spiritual experiences (see Johnson 1978). The "market" was not a passive place where people were consumers, but an active place perpetually being remade. Ideas and newspapers, new tools and new ways of worshipping, were passed from person to person, and town to town, generating a host of opportunities in sacred and profane life alike.

Building on a free economic market, mixed with the wide-open spaces of the western frontier, the Christian doctrines of Free Will began to challenge the older Calvinistic determinism. Nowhere was this fleshed out more than in the preachings of Charles Finney, whose revivals in canal towns such as Utica, Rome, Syracuse, and Rochester forever shaped U.S. Christian beliefs and practices (Cross 1950: 151–169; Perciaccante 2003). A do-it-yourself theology emerged from out of the do-it-yourself economy, which itself rested on a natural landscape forever altered by human hands. God loved humans just the same, but humans now were seen to have an urgent ability to change their ways, and the ways of others, and create their own paths toward salvation, just as people were believed to forge their own economic destiny. As Cross suggests, "if Finney had happened upon Utica in 1822, perhaps, or upon Rochester about 1825, neither town would have been so well prepared to listen" (Cross 1950: 75). When freedom from the past meets a marketplace mentality, and that is matched with abilities to reshape the natural environment through work and engineering, anything might be possible. Moral improvement, even to the point of potential "perfection," emerged within the range of human capabilities.

While freedom seems to be a "natural" right, there is a flip side of too much freedom, as people began to seek out new and alternative authority structures to replace the old ones. Self-styled prophets arose up and down the corridor, taking the old theologies and practices, and with a little tweaking remaking them in their own image and quickly gaining followers. Through it all, one of the clearest new authorities became the individual self.

Awaiting the End of the World

A land "given by God" comes with a serious set of responsibilities. Many European settlers, steeped in Christian traditions, saw the growing American continent not only as a New Eden, a place to start over, but also as a New Jerusalem, a place that marks the coming Kingdom of God. Which also meant that the end of the world was soon to come and there was work to be done to prepare. At the same time, freed from the shackles of church authorities that dominated European life for centuries, this land along the canal provided ample imaginative possibilities for working out one's salvation and ushering in the coming Millennium, the reign of God's kingdom on earth. Apocalyptic fever ensued, making way for a series of charismatic leaders who believed themselves to be voices crying in the wilderness, like Jeremiah and St. John before them. Joseph Smith was one, and this is the reason Mormons are the "Latter-day" Saints.

Others, like John Humphrey Noyes, responded by creating a utopian Christian community on the principle of "biblical communism," meaning that *all* things were shared equally among members, including children and spouses. The Noyes-led Oneida Community was established in 1848 in the central region of the canalway, with a special building that hosted up to 300 members. A communal child care facility and carefully delineated system of sexual partnering made this an unusual arrangement, and Noyes himself coined the term "free love" more than a century before the Hippies of the 1960s. The Oneida Community's metalworking skills sustained them, and even after their community life faded their well-known silverware has continued to grace tables around the world (Wonderley 2017).

The "New Eden" was also a New Jerusalem. The creation mythology of the new world turned into a glorious retelling of the coming end of the world. Many colonists and those of the early Republic toiled under the impression that their work here on earth was coming to a close. With new technologies and theologies demonstrating the ways one could work out one's own salvation, Americans realized they could bring about the Millennium, and usher in the second coming of Jesus Christ (Barkun 1986).

Noyes and Smith were careful to not be too specific about the coming end of the world. Others not so much. Around the same time, down the canal, a wheat-farmer-turned-Baptist minister named William Miller predicted the Second Coming of Jesus to occur on March 21, 1843, based on his extensive study of the numerology of the Bible. When the end did not come, he revised his calculations for October 22, 1844. The failed prediction led to what would become known as the "Great Disappointment." Many of Miller's numerous followers lost faith, at least in his cause, and turned to the Shakers and other rapidly growing Christian sects for connection. Others, like Ellen G. White, took up where Miller left off, and the Adventist tradition was born through an Albany-based meeting in 1845 (Rowe 1985). The Adventist sects that followed from this meeting were based on, among other things, healthy bodies (many groups promoted vegetarianism) and an understanding of Jesus's imminent return (i.e., the "advent"). Some of their followers went on to Battle Creek, Michigan to found the famed Sanatorium there.

The idea of the impending end of the world was shared among most of the religious communities of upstate New York in the nineteenth century. How the apocalypse would happen became a point of contention and difference. While many made predictions about when the end would come, others set to work on being sure people got their lives in order and were prepared morally and physically. Joseph Smith and the Mormons, William Miller and the Adventists, John Noyes and the Oneida Community, and the many working for social justice, saw the coming end, and organized themselves appropriately. With Finney's ideas of free will and human improvement in the background, and the revolutionary technology of the canal linking the world together in the foreground, the perfectible state of earthly life, and hence the new Millennium, was in range.

With freedom comes responsibility, so prophets and preachers, teachers and activists endeavored to create a more equitable world in the here and now, inspiring each other in socio-religious work. The canalway of the nineteenth century was where former slaves and outspoken abolitionists Frederick Douglass and Sojourner Truth mingled with women's rights activists Elizabeth Cady Stanton and Susan B. Anthony in Rochester and Seneca Falls, as they all sought to articulate social applications for the religious roots of freedom and equality. Over in Syracuse, Stanton's and Anthony's colleague Matilda Joslyn Gage gleaned feminist values from the Haudenosaunee, becoming a member of the wolf clan of the Mohawk Nation (Wagner 1996). Stanton, in turn, was the cousin of Utica native and Christian reformer Gerrit Smith, who funded John Brown's raid on Harpers Ferry, promoted the Underground Railroad along the Erie Canal, and worked alongside Frederick Douglass in publishing anti-slavery newspapers in Syracuse and Rochester (see Sernett 2002). These social meshes proliferated in central and western New York in the fifty years after the completion of the canal, and would have been impossible without the waterways.

There are the stories of well-known workers like Douglass and Stanton, and their connections in the canalway, but there were also lesser-known figures like Jermain Loguen, Austin Steward, Matilda Joslyn Gage, and Amy Post (see Rodríguez-Plate 2017a, 2017b). The former two escaped slavery early in life and found a better, freer life in the canal cities, where they helped publish anti-slavery papers, and worked on the Underground Railroad as the canalboats often provided passage for fugitive slaves. The latter two worked closely with the women's rights movement, as well as anti-slavery movements. The two social struggles were deeply intertwined as Christian values interlocked with social reform.

Amassing the Media via Infrastructure

Besides religious movements, many new media developed along with the Erie Canal at this time, and the media and religious movements had a synergistic impact. New media at the time includes Samuel Morse's telegraph in the 1830s. Morse's early work on the telegraph took place in New Jersey, but he married the Utica-born Sarah Elizabeth Griswold and spent a good deal of time in central New York. Morse helped launch the first telegraph company in the world in 1845, The Buffalo, Albany and New York Telegraph Company, which ran across the same lines that the canal ran, linking New York City to Buffalo and ultimately with the West (Reid 1879: 300). The telegraph, in turn, radically influenced the newspaper industry, which was now able to get the latest news across great distances. Four decades later, George Eastman's Kodak Company and the birth of mass photography was founded in Rochester. Ultimately, the canal, and then the railroad, as many literary historians have argued, helped create a national literature. Nineteenth-century literary figures Harriet Beecher Stowe, James Fenimore Cooper, Nathaniel Willis, Nathaniel Hawthorne, and Herman Melville traveled the canal for periods of time, enchanted by what they saw, writing about their experiences and bringing readers into the collective worlds (see Hecht 2003). And it was in the canalway that L. Frank Baum grew up, son-in-law to the great feminist writer Matilda Joslyn Gage, eventually writing the great American mythology, *The Wonderful Wizard of Oz* at the start of the twentieth century.

French diplomat and writer Alexis de Tocqueville traveled the United States, spending time on the packet boats of the Erie Canal, and noted that there was "scarcely a hamlet which has not its own newspaper" (Tocqueville [1835] 2019: 116). The canal not only helped create mass industry and mass commercial capitalism; it was also instrumental in the generation of mass media. Newspapers, tracts, pamphlets, and magazines proliferated as new markets were available via the canal linking east and west. Canalboats made costs of shipping cheap, and supplied connections across New York State, and beyond as the nation moved ever further into the west.

New media's impact on religious life was clear. In 1830, the editor of the *Baptist Register* spoke of the burgeoning religious movements in relation to the infrastructure needed to circulate the ideas: "we need constant excitement. . . . And in what way can this be done so effectively, as by the circulation of a religious paper?" (Quoted in Cross 1950: 108). The American Bible Society was founded in 1816, and as historian John Fea notes, in ways that harken back to the mythological beginnings of the canal and the "new world" itself,

> The ABS owed much of its distribution success to a burgeoning American infrastruc-
> ture. Fitting with a nation committed to building itself through travel across rivers,
> lakes, and canals, the ABS and its auxiliaries often used water metaphors to describe the
> distribution process. . . . Both literally and figuratively, the ABS was using water to link
> remote and scattered settlements into a Bible nation. Fitting with a nation committed to
> building itself through travel across rivers, lakes, and canals, the ABS and its auxiliaries
> often used water metaphors to describe the distribution process.
>
> *(Fea 2016: 31–32)*

Many religious leaders realized that print media could become vital to the spread of fervor and social reform, and the canalway created notable new publishing venues that codified much of the early Republic and its attendant religiosities. The most important preacher of the nineteenth century, Charles Finney, sparked revivals in canal cities as part of the Second Great Awakening, while the many religious newspapers that began at this time dispersed Finney's and other's charged messages by way of the canalboats. William Miller's end-of-times predictions would have remained nothing but the rants of local preacher were it not for the publishing work of Joshua V. Himes and others: millions of "Millerite" tracts and papers are estimated to have been distributed across the country in the 1840s and his rhetoric was amplified by newspapers such as *Signs of the Times* and others (O'Leary 1994: 93–110). The year of the opening of the Erie Canal, 1825, was also the year of the opening of the evangelistic American Tract Society in New York City; within a decade, millions of printed ATS products were being shipped around the world, with large numbers of them targeted for seamen and boat crews. And just a year before Finney's massive revival in Rochester, a few miles down the canal, Joseph Smith had five thousand copies of the Book of Mormon printed in Palmyra, a number that far exceeded literate souls in the town, but that would launch a global religious movement. The nearly one-ton iron press that printed the Book of Mormon arrived in Palmyra from New York City on the Erie Canal—its mass nearly impos-sible to transport overland. All of these activities led to a rapid rise in literacy rates in the young nation which in turn created demand for more printed material, which various reli-gious organizations gleefully helped supply, aided by efficient transportation across the canal.

With literacy and publishing on the rise, and an influx of new immigrants, the Erie Canal generated a symbiotic relation between the arts, education, and religious sensibilities. The European writers Alexis de Tocqueville and Harriet Martineau traveled the same canalboats that American writers Hawthorne and Melville did, coming to different conclusions about the young Republic and its religiosity. Hudson River School painters Asher Durand and

Thomas Cole found inspiration not just along the Hudson, but also through the "wilderness" that the Erie Canal made more accessible just as it ironically helped lead to its demise. The cities that overtook the wilderness along the waterway became sites where Fredrick Law Olmstead would unveil some of his utopian visions of urban parkspace, and other architects created novel living environments for communal societies like the Shakers, Oneida Community, and Amana Colony, as they sought to remake traditional family structures; they knew that you can't just talk about community, you have to build differently.

In educational circles, with the engineering success of the Erie Canal in mind, Amos Eaton founded one of the first universities of science and technology in the English-speaking world, the Rensselaer School outside Albany. From there Eaton established a traveling summer science school along the canal (Rezneck 1959). Further up the waterway, Elizabeth Cady was taking classes at Troy Seminary, the first school to teach mathematics and science to women. Well before the Civil War and Emancipation Proclamation, African Americans were learning at the Presbyterian-founded Oneida Institute (Sernett 1985). Denominationally minded "continuing education" turned ecumenical in the far-western reaches of the canalway at Chautauqua, sparking a movement of Chautauquas that stretched across the country by the early twentieth century. At the far-east end of the canal, a penniless Irish immigrant named William James settled in Albany early in the century, made a fortune on canal-based real estate, and passed it on to his descendants who included the Harvard philosopher and psychologist William James, and the writers Alice and Henry James. The younger William James was one of the most prominent philosophers of religion in American history, and became intrigued by Spiritualism, a movement that grew from the supernatural accounts of the Fox sisters communing with the dead in their house near Rochester in 1848: from there Spiritualism became a global phenomenon that is very present in the contemporary day (Braude 1989).

When railroad lines were established in the middle of the nineteenth century, the canal's influence began to decline. However, some of these new lines followed the routes of the canal and fed off what were deeply established urban areas by then: canal towns became rail towns, and what were once new spiritual experiments became part of the establishment, primed and ready for export. The religious practices, behaviors, and beliefs that emerged in the second quarter of the nineteenth century in the canalway continued their influence into the westering country. As the railroad and telegraph extended far into the American continent, they brought many of the innovative religious practices from the Erie Canal corridor into the new settlements. The canal—like the railroad, coach, and airplane after it—was also communicative. Media materials do not just "arrive" at various places in ethereal distribution systems, they are transported from one place to the next through infrastructure.

Conclusion: The Erie Canal in Modern Oblivion

Like other infrastructural hyperobjects—the Silk Road in Asia, the Incense Trail in Arabia, and the Panama Canal in the Americas—the Erie Canal established physical links across geographic regions, while actively reforming the social environments that spread out beyond the immediate transportation paths. New York's network of canals and cities, rivers and farmlands made the world smaller and more easily accessible than ever before. Newspapers and immigrants, novelists and painters, grain and lumber, suffragists and fleeing slaves, revivalists and new technologies all traveled and lived on the canalway together, creating new connections and establishing unique currents of American religious life. This generated, in the words of Joseph Smith, "an unusual excitement on the subject of religion" (Smith 1839: 2).

To this day U.S. citizens are still obsessed with the apocalypse, "family values," and dis-ease about sexual matters permeate politics, while conflicts between science and religion occur in educational settings, American exceptionalism continues, religion is thought to be a personal individualistic matter, and the connections between social activism and religious belief are constantly shifting. All of this can be traced to influences from the Erie Canal and its tributaries, both real and metaphorical. The canalway had a profound impact on the religious life of upstate New York in the second quarter of the nineteenth century, but because of its key location and function as the link between "east" and "west," the repercussions of canal-formed spiritual experiments rippled across the continent with westward expansion.

Today's Erie Canal is a study in ruins. There are still boat tours of sections of the canal (or, of the third version of the canal, redug in the early twentieth century when waterways had already passed their prime usefulness), New York State tourist offices have attempted to fit the canal into their hospitality industry, and every few years someone kayaks the length of the canal, taking advantages of the locks and smooth waters, and then writing about the experience with a mix of wistfulness and triumph. Overall, nostalgia remains.

The old canalway became the path for the railroads in the 1860s (Walker 2019), which began the canal's decline in importance, and then the interstate highways, which made overland travel the choice of transportation through the twentieth century. Technology is layered on technology and the canalway is today a geographic palimpsest, a surface on which is written older histories: the stories have been erased but are still legible between the lines.

The religious groups took various routes out of town, via rail, water, wagon, and foot. Many, like the Mormons and Spiritualists, spread to remote corners of the globe. Others slowly faded into the landscape. But regardless of whether the religions moved, survived, or disappeared, particular beliefs and behaviors continued to flow from this ribbon of land and have remained part of the peculiar mixture of practices across the pluralistic United States.

Note

1 Materiality and geography are still largely understudied in religious histories. I have found no overview of U.S. religious history, or even studies focusing on the "burned-over district" that mention much at all about the Erie Canal. Histories continue to be written from an intellectualist standpoint and treat geography and technology as if they are incidental. Whitney Cross's work (Cross 1950) is still the best work in this regard, as Cross notes the presence of the canal at many points (esp. pp. 55–77), though the direct impact of the canal is often underplayed, almost as if it was miraculous that so many new religious movements started within a few hundred miles of each other in only a couple decades.

References

Barkun, Michael. 1986. *Crucible of the Millennium: The Burned-Over District of New York in the 1840s.* Syracuse, NY: Syracuse University Press.

Bernstein, Peter L. 2005. *Wedding of the Waters: The Erie Canal and the Making of a Great Nation.* New York: W.W. Norton.

Braude, Ann. 1989. *Radical Spirits: Spiritualism and Women's Rights in Nineteenth Century America.* Boston, MA: Beacon University Press.

Cross, Whitney R. 1950. *The Burned-Over District.* Ithaca, NY: Cornell University Press.

"Dispossession and Disruption," Erie Canalway National Heritage Corridor website: https://eriecanalway.org/learn/history-culture/native-americans.

Fea, John. 2016. *The Bible Cause: A History of the American Bible Society.* New York: Oxford University Press.

Hecht, Roger W. 2003. *The Erie Canal Reader, 1790–1950.* Syracuse, NY: Syracuse University Press.

Johnson, Paul. 1997. *A History of the American People.* New York: HarperCollins.

Johnson, Paul E. 1978. *A Shopkeeper's Millennium: Society and Revivals in Rochester, New York, 1815–1837.* New York: Hill & Wang.

Keene, Michael T. 2016. *The Psychic Highway: How the Erie Canal Changed America.* Fredericksburg, VA: Willow Manor Publishing.

Klees, Emerson. 2001. *The Crucible of Ferment: New York's "Psychic Highway."* Rochester, NY: Cameo Press.

Koeppel, Gerard T. 2009. *Bond of Union: Building the Erie Canal and the American Empire.* Cambridge, MA: Da Capo Press.

McGreevy, Patrick. 2009. *Stairway to Empire: Lockport, the Erie Canal, and the Shaping of America.* Albany, NY: State University of New York Press.

Morton, Timothy. 2013. *Hyperobjects: Philosophy and Ecology after the End of the World.* Minneapolis, MN: University of Minnesota Press.

O'Leary, Stephen D. 1994. *Arguing the Apocalypse: A Theory of Millennial Rhetoric.* New York: Oxford University Press.

Perciaccante, Marianne. 2003. *Calling Down Fire: Charles Grandison Finney and Revivalism in Jefferson County, New York, 1800–1840.* Albany: State University of New York Press.

Reid, James. 1879. *The Telegraph in American: Its Founders, Promoters, and Noted Men.* New York: Derby Brothers.

Rezneck, Samuel. 1959. "A Traveling School of Science on the Erie Canal." *New York History,* 40.3: 255–269.

Rodríguez-Plate, S. Brent. 2017a. "Did the Erie Canal Help Put an End to Slavery?" *America.* September 18, 2017. https://www.americamagazine.org/arts-culture/2017/08/16/did-erie-canal-help-put-end-slavery.

Rodríguez-Plate, S. Brent. 2017b. "What a Forgotten 19th Century Suffragist Can Teach us About Women's Rights vs. the Religious Right." *Religion Dispatches.* March 8, 2017. https://religiondispatches.org/what-a-forgotten-19th-century-suffragist-can-teach-us-about-womens-rights-vs-the-religious-right/.

Rowe, David L. 1985. *Thunder and Trumpets: Millerites and Dissenting Religion in Upstate New York, 1800–1850.* Chico, CA: Scholars Press, 1985.

Sernett, Milton C. 1985. "Oneida Institute's Role in the Fight Against American Racism and Slavery." *New York History* 66(2): 101–122.

Sernett, Milton C. 2002. *North Star Country: Upstate New York and the Crusade for African American Freedom.* Syracuse, NY: Syracuse University Press.

Sheriff, Carol. 1996. *The Artificial River: The Erie Canal and the Paradox of Progress, 1817–1862.* New York: Hill and Wang.

Smith, Joseph. 1839. "History, Circa June 1839–Circa 1841 [Draft 2]," *The Joseph Smith Papers,* https://www.josephsmithpapers.org/paper-summary/history-circa-june-1839-circa-1841-draft-2/2.

Tocqueville, Alexis de. 2019 (1835). *Democracy in America. Volume 1.* Democracy in America. New York: SNOVA.

Trollope, Frances. 1984 (1832). *Domestic Manners of the Americans.* Richard Mullen, ed. New York: Oxford University Press.

Wagner Sally Roesch. 1996. *The Untold Story of the Iroquois Influence on Early Feminists: Essays.* Aberdeen, SD: Sky Carrier Press.

Walker, David. 2019. *Railroading Religion.* Chapel Hill, NC: University of North Carolina Press.

Wonderley, Anthony. 2017. *Oneida Utopia: A Community Searching for Human Happiness and Prosperity.* Ithaca, NY: Cornell University Press.

4.2

THE KUMBH MELA AS HYPEROBJECT

Sound, Scale, Nation, Environment

Amanda Lucia

The Kumbh Mela is the largest religious gathering on earth. In 2019, the Ardh Kumbh Mela (the half-*melā*) drew 150 million people to *sangam*, the confluence of three rivers—the Ganga, the Yamuna, and the mythological Saraswati—at Prayagraj (Allahabad) in northern India.[1] There is a rich mythological history to the benefits of bathing in the *sangam*. Hindu scriptures, such as the Purāṇas, list hundreds of examples, as in the following passage:

> If one bathes and sips water where the Ganga, Yamuna, and Sarasvati meet, he enjoys liberation, and of this there is no doubt.
>
> *(Padma Purāṇa Uttara Khanda 23.14, cited in Eck and Bhatt 2015: 36)*

Many Hindus believe that the Kumbh Mela has been occurring at the *sangam* at Prayag since time immemorial. There is evidence that a gathering of ascetics (renunciates) from different religious orders and sects have gathered for a Magh Mela at Prayag annually since ancient times. In more recent histories, both Mughal and British rulers have provided descriptive accounts of annual gatherings at Prayag in the winter months of Magh (January/February, beginning when the sun enters Capricorn).

However, the first Kumbh Mela in the modern sense of the term, meaning a special gathering that occurs once every twelve years at Prayagraj, likely occurred in 1870, according to Kama Maclean's historical research (Eck and Bhatt 2015: 37; Maclean 2008). Today, the gathering that occurs every twelve years at Prayagraj is called the "Maha Kumbh Mela" (the big/great Kumbh Mela). At the half-point, every six years, there is a similar gathering at Prayagraj called the "Ardh Kumbh Mela" (the half Kumbh Mela). There are also quadrennial events in Naisik, Ujjain, and Haridwar that are also called "Kumbhs" that host large gatherings of ascetics from the various *akhāras* (sects of renunciates).

Recently, Yogi Adityanath, the Minister of Parliament of Uttar Pradesh (UP)—the Indian state in which Prayagraj is located—renamed the *melās* held at Prayagraj, designating the twelve-year *melā* as the "Maha Kumbh Mela" and the six-year *melā* as simply the "Kumbh Mela." Traditionally, the total duration of Kumbh assembly is forty-four consecutive days in the month of Magh, beginning with Paush Purnima and continuing through Mahashivaratri (Tripathi 2007: 211). The *nāgā sādhus* (naked ascetics) of the *akhāras* arrive before Paush Purnima and leave after Vasant Panchami (mid-February), while *kalpavāsis* (resident pilgrims) stay

DOI: 10.4324/9781351176231-31

for all forty-four days and leave only after Mahashivaratri. Most other pilgrims attend for much shorter stays.

In the past twenty years, the Kumbh Mela at Prayagraj has exponentially increased in size and scale. It has become a global media spectacle, with teams of international photographers and photo journalists literally chasing after bands of *nāgā sādhus* to capture their image as they rush into the holy waters of *sangam* on the most auspicious bathing days. The domestic tourism boards of India are just as fervent in their attempts to capture the Kumbh Mela and exploit its allure. In the months leading up to the event, images of the *nāgā sādhus* appear on corporate- and government-sponsored billboards and on the sides of trains, advertising products and inviting pilgrims to attend.

The images capture the profoundly local experience of individual ascetics removing their sins through an auspicious bath. But as these images are reproduced in time and space around the globe, they become microcosmic examples of the diffusion and defiance of locality and thus vivify the experience of the Kumbh Mela itself (see Figure 4.2.1).[2] As an "ephemeral megacity" (Mehrotra and Vera 2015), the Kumbh Mela is both located and dislocated, built and destroyed, stationary and expansive. It exists in the individual through the personal experiences of sacrality and purification of the hundreds of millions of pilgrims who wander its streets. It exists in the national imagination through global and domestic tourism campaigns. It exists as a promise of environmental progress and as evidence of environmental catastrophe (Lucia 2023). It exists as a hyperobject not only because it defies the boundaries of the senses: it extends to the horizon farther than the eye can see and restores "spectral

Figure 4.2.1   Amrit Giri Tyagi Baba, Mahanirvani Akhara, Kumbh Mela 2013. Photo taken just before the most auspicious bathing day (*śahi snān*). Photo courtesy of author.

intimacy" (Morton 2013: 193) to the object through the cacophony of auditory overwhelm. But it also exists as a hyperobject because it defies its own existence. It is produced and dismantled, only to be reproduced and dismantled once again, both in its physical form as a temporary megacity and in its ephemeral form as memory, imagination, and ideology.

Sound

In 2019, in the midst of the Ardh Kumbh Mela, while walking down an alleyway in Sector 13, I passed a man unrolling a large spool of wire from a utility box to a camp several hundred feet away. As he prepared to pass it to his fellow worker positioned at the top of a high ladder, I asked him what it was for. Amidst the cacophony of blaring *bhajans* (devotional songs), *homas* (Vedic sacrifices), recitations of Hindu scriptures, and informational and safety announcements, he shouted to me over the din, exclaiming proudly, "It is for the speakers! We will be playing recitations of the *Bhagavad Gītā* 24/7!" The overwhelming soundscape of the Kumbh Mela assaults one's auditory faculties through multi-layered, overlapping, and competing devotional sounds detonating from nearly every encampment. But for this *melā* celebrant, the extant cacophony of devotional sounds could be augmented further still by an added layer of sacred Hindu scripture recitations. This collective auditory onslaught bathes *melā* participants in the sacred sounds of Hindu religiosity and engulfs them in an intensely deafening religious world.

Pilgrims walking along the roads of the Kumbh hear a camp before they see it. The cacophony of sacred sound invites pilgrims traversing the *melā* on foot into particular camps. It invites them to sing *bhajans*, take in the recitations of religious discourses and scriptures, and observe plays and productions, such as Ram or Krishna *līlās*. Many stop for a reprieve from the hot sun of the street to cool themselves in the shade of a camp.

The projected orations that can be heard from the street function as an advertising tool asserting both the social capital and the spiritual messages of particular gurus and religious organizations. Once the auditory allure has drawn pilgrims inside a camp, they are exposed to the advertising, pamphlets, and publications of that particular camp, many of which strive to impress through the scale and grandeur of their productions. Microphones are connected to loudspeakers, which are then attached to the tops of tall poles to broadcast the happenings of a particular camp. The loudspeakers trace back to microphones placed alongside raised stages hosting plays, dances, and *bhajan* performances, in the center of collective *kīrtans*, at the seat of priests conducting *homas*, and at the side of gurus giving religious discourses during *satsaṅgs* (religious gatherings). They are also placed in the hands of MCs who serve as hawkers to the unseen crowd, notifying passersby of upcoming events and free meal distribution (*prasād*), of the efficacy of particular medicinal remedies, or of the importance of a particular guru or spiritual practice.

When I first arrived at the Maha Kumbh Mela in 2013, a man in a neighboring camp was singing into a microphone connected to a loudspeaker turned to full volume to broadcast the *bhajan*, "*Shree Ram Jai Ram, Jai Jai Ram, Sita Ram, Sita Ram.*" His intoning voice bathed the entirety of the neighborhood in its sacred sound. That night, I fell asleep to his repeating incantation only to wake the next morning hearing it still. As I stepped out of my large canvas tent, I saw the entire camp was blanketed by a deep winter fog blinding me to my surroundings. The only measure of orientation was the ever-present lilting *bhajan*: "*Shree Ram Jai Ram, Jai Jai Ram, Sita Ram, Sita Ram.*"

Day and night, I bathed in "*Shree Ram Jai Ram, Jai Jai Ram, Sita Ram, Sita Ram*"—for several weeks. Amazed at this dedication, I inquired of Dr. D. P. Dubey, a life-long participant and scholarly expert on the Kumbh Mela, why our neighboring camp maintained this broadcast. He gave a devotional answer, explaining that the resonance of the sacred music protects the Kumbh and its participants. It purifies pilgrims' thoughts and directs their minds and attentions to god (*bhagvān*). He noted as well that if there were not sacred music being broadcast at all times, there might be more of a tendency toward crime or mischief (*badmāś*). In his reasoning, pilgrims would not want to commit crimes in the auditory presence of god.[3]

The constant auditory stimulation of sacred sound resonates day and night throughout the *melā* grounds, carried on the wind, penetrating the fog, seeping into dreams. It is the soundtrack of the *melā* itself, the walking pace of pilgrims, the echoes of anticipation, and the reminder of sacred presence. The lilting and yearning voices of the *kīrtan* musicians supply the underlying ethic of the festival and provide an active method of disciplining errant behavior, just as powerful—or perhaps even more powerful—than the regulatory signage and law enforcement intended to keep the peace.

The sonic onslaught beckons divine presence, inviting the metaphysical sacred to enter into and conjoin with the ordinary. This invocation of the divine wafts through the air and the ether complementing the sacrality of the land and the joining of the three sacred rivers (*triveni*) at their confluence (*sangam*). In their book *Hyperobjects: Philosophy and Ecology after the End of the World*, Timothy Morton writes of Hindu sacred music as offering a "profound range of materiality," in part because it "evokes a hugely expanded sense of what in musical language is called timbre: the material that generates a sound." They expand their argument by referring of the multidimensional resonances of Hindu mantras more generally. They write:

> The singing of Sanskrit syllables, such as "OM" (a sound that Hinduism and Buddhism associate with the material universe as such), evokes the materiality of the singing body and of the breath that circulates within and outside that body while it remains alive. These syllables are made to vibrate with as subtle as profound a range of harmonics as possible, evoking the vastness of the universe. Devotional singing, then, is a form of hyperobject, one that meets the intimacy with the other and with the distant future that hyperobjects such as plutonium force on us.[4]

Following this, pilgrims might imagine the cacophony of devotional music that permeates the Kumbh Mela crafting an intersectionality of hyperobjects. The *melā* grounds and *sangam* expand vertically into the imagined sacred landscapes of the gods. The *bhajans* and *mantras* invoke the vastness of the universe while pulsating in the rhythmic and synchronous breaths of more than one hundred million people. The metaphysical world of divine actors intersects the ordinary lived realities of pilgrims on the streets of Prayagraj, drawn to earth through staged exhibit and invocation. The devotional soundscape of the Kumbh Mela, designed with ancient components that aim to resonate with the frequencies of the universe, draws participants close and invites them to enter into the devotional space of the *melā*. The experience destabilizes convention and situates anew, recalibrating the senses to the aural pulsations of the sacred.

Scale

In addition to the simultaneously broadcasting cacophony of *bhajans*, *kīrtans*, *satsangs*, and *līlās*, the soundscape of the Kumbh Mela is accompanied by the uproarious sounds of rickshaw, motorcycle, Jeep, and water tank engines, horns, bleating goats, squealing children, hollering adults, police whistles and carnival whistles, and conversations. Just nearly drowned in the din, the repeating refrain broadcast from the multiple Emergency Lost and Found offices courses over the crowd: "Ravi Thakur [or Priya Mukherjee] has gotten lost. Please meet your party at the Emergency Lost and Found Office in Sector 4." Historically, the Kumbh has gained a notorious reputation as a place where one can be irrevocably lost. In 2013, I met a young boy who had been adopted by the *sādhus* of an *akhāṛā* (renunciant sect) because he had gotten separated from his parents and subsequently lost at the Maha Kumbh Mela in 2001 (see Figure 4.2.2). Today, with conservative crowd estimates ranging from 120 to 150 million people attending over the course of the two-month-long *melā*, the loudspeaker announces lost persons twenty-four hours a day. The announcer's voice shrills and accelerating to a fever-pitch on peak bathing days, when more than 30 million converge at the epicenter of the *saṅgam* in an attempt to bathe there at the most auspicious astrological time.[5]

On peak bathing days, it is common to see long strings of villagers clutching the clothing of the person in front of them as their group navigates the pressing crowds. The advent of cellular phones has somewhat mitigated the very real threat of becoming lost in the mass of humanity assembled at the *melā*. But with only 64 percent of Indians owning cellular phones and a widening gender, education, and age gap,[6] it is no wonder that elderly, uneducated, rural village women at the Kumbh Mela still clutch tightly to the woman's sari walking in front of them. Many village groups travel long distances to the *melā*, by bus and by foot, aided by a leader who manages transportation and lodging. Some speak regional dialects, or travel from regions where Hindi is not the local language. If they are not from urban centers

Figure 4.2.2 A young renunciate novice and his mentor. The mentor recounted that the boy had become lost at a previous Kumbh and had since been adopted by the Juna Akhara, Kumbh Mela 2013. Photo courtesy of author.

of India, they may have never seen such a mass of humanity as they will encounter at *sangam* on the most auspicious bathing days. Even for those who have seen the likes of Mumbai, Sao Paolo, or Cairo, the population density on the small strip of land at *sangam* is extraordinary (see Figure 4.2.3). It is a sea of heads as far as the eye can see, jostling, dressing, undressing, carrying bundles, holding close to loved ones so as not to become separated. People stand on railings, pole stanchions, and temporary structures to attempt to escape the morass. At times the crowd is so thick that the slow forward motion toward *sangam* turns to simply standing, pressed against other human bodies on all sides. The threat of stampede looms darkly on the horizon.

On the most auspicious bathing day (Mauni Amawasya) in 2019, I awoke at the most auspicious hour (around 3:00 am) to frantic announcements from the emergency services center. There was an edge of fear in the announcer's voice as she attempted to maintain order, and the loudspeakers crackled with the sound of an immense, tumultuous, uncontrollable crowd in the background. The shrillness of her voice also reverberated across history, surfacing into memory the Kumbh Tragedy of 1954, when a crowd rush on the same most auspicious bathing day ended in mass death. Official reports by UP government officials reported 316 deaths, while other accounts raised the figure to over 10,000 (Maclean 2008: 192; Tripathi 2007: 210). Kama Maclean, a historian of the Kumbh Mela, writes that the 1954 Kumbh Tragedy continues to loom large over the event, creating a specter of the danger and violence that could erupt in such a mass assemblage of humanity. Then too, amidst other logistical errors, "some pilgrims who had already bathed sat down to watch the processions instead of leaving the area, occupying valuable space and adding to congestion" (Maclean 2008: 193,

Figure 4.2.3 Crowds at *sangam* during an auspicious bathing day. Photo courtesy of author.

201). In 2019, a shrill voice broadcast from hundreds of loudspeakers urged pilgrims to take their holy bath quickly and to immediately leave the vicinity of *sangam*.

That year, sprawling across a gargantuan space of forty-five kilometers, the Ardh Kumbh Mela was geographically immense, and the massive influx of crowds incited a similar threat of danger undergirding the peak bathing days (PTI 2018). Even though it was only an Ardh Kumbh Mela, the crowds superseded any previous Kumbh Mela in history. The increased geographical footprint of the *melā* also resulted in farther distances for pilgrims to walk to get to *sangam,* and demanded an increase in road infrastructure to accommodate subsequent vehicle traffic. Some *kalpavāsis* were offered government-supplied tent-housing more than twelve kilometers from *sangam*. Rickshaws were in high demand and commanded exorbitant prices; lines formed at intersections, where eager passengers bid with each other to secure rides. Motorcycles and mopeds sped through the streets, while VIPs traveled through the *melā* in a long caravans of TATA jeeps. *Kalpavāsis* and other pilgrims walked dozens of kilometers through the *melā,* often barefoot, carrying their supplies in bundles on their heads and children on their hips.

The ephemeral megacity of the Kumbh is laid out in a rectangular grid, extending from *sangam* along the banks of the river Ganga. Most of the nineteen different Sectors spread from those banks, while several others are located on the far banks of the river Yamuna (see Figure 4.2.4). On the streets, pilgrims both produce and are enmeshed in the text of the city. As Michel de Certeau writes of walkers in the city, "The networks of these moving, intersecting writings compose a manifold story that has neither author nor spectator, shaped out of fragments of trajectories and alterations of spaces: in relation to representations, it remains daily and indefinitely other" (de Certeau 1984: 93).

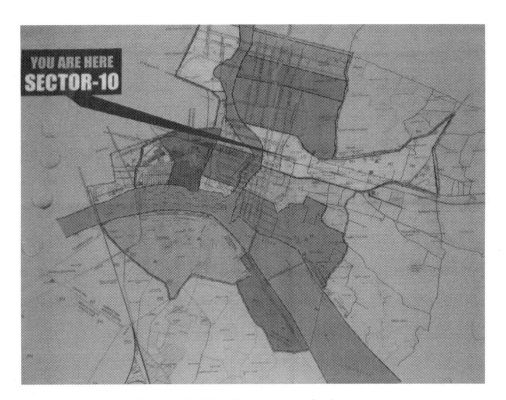

Figure 4.2.4 Map of the Kumbh Mela 2013. Photo courtesy of author.

In constructing the Kumbh Mela, the Indian government establishes the city grid, including its networked mesh of wide boulevards, drainage ditches, trash receptacles, toilets, camps, tents, electrical poles, water tanks, emergency stations, and cellular towers. But the pilgrims of the Kumbh Mela produce the city, creatively building on its ephemerality. As an impermanent city, the Kumbh Mela is inherently temporary, and thus more malleable to creative interventions. It is also a performative space for pilgrims and religious organizations. Large-scale processions to the holy rivers erupt from the landscape with incessant regularity. Rituals, hawkers, and circus performers overflow into the streets. Large groups of pilgrims squat for rest and to organize their next venture. Temples and *Maths* (religious sects) establish feeding kitchens on the streets in front of their camps, wherein they seat hungry pilgrims in long rows and dollop out dal, rice, and *sabzī* (vegetable) as a form of *prasād* (religious offering). Toward *sangam*, petty merchants establish their wares along the roadsides selling ritual supplies, empty water bottles, *mālās* (prayer beads), and carnivalesque trinkets for children. More inland, the street merchants supply that which is needed for tent living: fruits, vegetables, spices, rice, kitchen instruments, clay stoves, clothing, blankets, and luggage. On each and every lane, amulet makers, fortune tellers, Ayurvedic medicinal suppliers, and *kalpavāsi* family camps that have found no other place to reside all spill into the streets, altering the formal grid of the city. In de Certeau's framing, these overflows of people produce "anti-texts" from "within the structured space of the text" (de Certeau 1984: 107).

Because the primary intention of the *melā* is the holy bath at *sangam*, there is a constant stream of pilgrims in motion to and from that holy confluence, and their constant influx in turn creates the "anti-text" of a city in motion, teeming with life. As a part of their ascetic practice, *kalpavāsis* bathe in the sacred waters in the early morning for each day of their residence at the *melā* (Tripathi 2007: 211–212). This reverence for the sacred waters creates additional patterns of motion in the city as hundreds of thousands of pilgrims walk daily to and from the river banks, carrying bundles of dry, then wet, clothing and bathing supplies. The riverbanks are bustling spaces, with families in various stages of undress. Women change from their dripping saris with modest precision, while men and boys emerge from the river wet and in their underclothes. The waters are usually cold, and there is much revelry among family and friends as they wash away their sins in communal celebration. The riverbanks, even more than the city streets, are places in motion. During the most auspicious bathing times, the motion accelerates, the anti-text threatening to eclipse the strategically-planned textual grid of the city. Shrill like the announcer's voice, its vibrant energy becomes frenetic. In contrast, on the routine daily bathing ritual, it is constant, pulsating, but often playful and fun.

Walking through the city affords pilgrims a sequential exposure to the extraordinary diversity of sectarian traditions of Hindu religions, more than could be found in any other place in India. In walking one city block, one might first encounter the thunderous recitations of sixty yellow-robed Vaishnava renunciates reciting the *Bhagavatām,* their words echoing across the wind for the next hundred meters. One hundred meters away in the neighboring camp, one might find the UP Boy Scouts Association organizing for their *sevā* mission. Walking along the same block after another twenty-five meters, uniformed officials congregate over *chai* at the fire station, after which is the neighboring tea and snacks shop. Neighboring the chai stall, stands a massive camp of 100 Dandi *samnyāsīs*, orange-robed renunciates from one of the oldest Hindu sects, which measures more than 100 meters long, and just as deep. The block closes with a camp that boasts an alluring exhibition of three-story-tall automaton Hindu deities, and then a towering pyramid structure, funded by a powerful guru, within which a 1,000-firepit Vedic *homa* (fire ritual) is being recited. All the while in the street, traffic, hawkers, merchants, pilgrims, and processionals intersect in a synchronous dance of nearly missed collisions. Without interval, the next block begins—and the cacophony and extravaganza continues.

During the course of the *melā*, adventurous pilgrims (and professional photographers) climb to the mid-point of the suspended highway bridge to gaze over the *melā* grounds spreading across the dried riverbed in a colorful panoply of yellow and blue tents as far as the eye can see. From that elevated vantage, the participants step back from their role as walking creators of the ephemeral city and to take on the role of voyeur. As de Certeau explains, the elevation puts the observer at a distance and "transforms the bewitching world by which one was 'possessed' into a text that lies before one's eyes. It allows one to read it, to be a solar Eye, looking down like a god" (de Certeau 1984: 92). But, it is impossible to capture the city; even from this vantage point, one must turn to in circles to view the expanse. Only from an airplane can one see its entirety.

But even then, the Kumbh Mela extends far beyond the structures temporarily posted in the geography of the dried river bed. As Morton describes, we can only ever see fractions of hyperobjects at a time. This is in part because they are so diffuse (as in a tsunami or radiation sickness), but also because what we experience is fluid, metaphorical, and symbolic. Hyperobjects are expressions of "higher dimensions of structure, which is where the hyperobjects live" (Morton 2013: 70). In the case of the Kumbh Mela, the event also extends into the annals of Mughal and British colonial history; and even further in the cultural understandings of Hindu folklore (Dubey 2013: 20). It extends into the religious imagination of hundreds of thousands of pilgrims who walk for miles on foot to bathe in the sacred waters. It extends as a media spectacle, celebrated globally on billboards and in travel advertisements. Most significantly, it extends into the national imagination, at the intersection of religion and politics in India.

Nation

As the largest gathering of Hindus in India, the Kumbh Mela has always been intimately related to the government. In 1567, the Mughal king Akbar witnessed a famous battle between Shaiva and Vaishnava ascetics at Thaneshwar, a Hindu holy site on the banks of the Saraswati River. The sectarian groups of militant yogis fought to the death for the honor of bathing first during the auspicious eclipse—and thus receiving the larger share of alms from devotees (Diamond 2013: 172–175; Mallinson 2013: 76–77). Such altercations between religious sects at the Kumbh Mela are "a well-known fact of Indian religious history" (Dubey 2013: 20). Famously, in 1760, Shaiva and Vaishnava warrior ascetics battled for supremacy on at the Kumbh Mela in Haridvāra (Haridwar), in which purportedly 18,000 persons perished (Maclean 2008: 61). During the British colonial period, militant bands of *sādhus* (ascetics) gathered at the Kumbh were often accused of anti-colonial activity, while princely pilgrimages to the Kumbh Mela, such as Ranjit Singh's in 1809, were intentional "belligerent marches through British territory" (Maclean 2008: 60–62). The British colonial government deployed multiple strategies in its attempts to contain the possibility of violence, disease, and nationalistic subversion that the Kumbh Mela signified. In 1820, when 400 pilgrims died at the Haridwar Kumbh Mela, the British undertook extensive repairs to the main bathing steps (*ghāt*) descending to the river in order to elicit governmental support from pilgrims. In 1888, the British *rāj* rejected Christian missionary demands to disavow support for the *melā*, and instead asserted paternalistic control of the event.

The Kumbh Mela of 1954 marked the first Kumbh Mela in Prayagraj (Allahabad) that had no state-imposed restrictions or barriers attached to attendance. As the first Kumbh

Mela to occur after Indian independence in 1947,[7] the "*melā* was the message" as the newly formed independent Indian government "attempted to turn it into a positive statement of a vibrant and Independent India" (Maclean 2008: 191). While the Kumbh Mela has enjoyed a long history of celebration among Hindu ascetics and pilgrims, the exponentially increased crowds of the past twenty years have made it even more influential in the national narrative. Calculating the number of pilgrims on only the most auspicious bathing day (Mauni Amavasya), the Indian government estimated that, between 1989 and 2001, the number of bathing pilgrims doubled from 15 to 30 million (Maclean 2008: 186). In general, official figures claimed that the Kumbh Mela doubled in size from 2001 to 2013, expanding from 60 to 120 million pilgrims. At the Ardh Kumbh Mela in 2019, reports totaled the figure at 150 million.

But the Indian government's estimations of the number of pilgrims present at the *melā* are inseparable from the larger governmental project of celebrating a vibrant Hindu India through the successful orchestration of the Kumbh Mela. In 2019, Prime Minister Narendra Modi rightly assessed that the Kumbh Mela (which fell just before the elections in April/May) would be an excellent opportunity to demonstrate both the Indian government's commitment to building India's infrastructure and the success of his *Swachh Bharat* (Clean India) Campaign. The Indian government initiated the theme "*Swachh Kumbh, Surakshit Kumbh*" (Clean Kumbh, Secure Kumbh) and was determined to make the Kumbh a phenomenal success. To ensure this, the Indian government poured resources into the *melā*, and the UP government provided the Kumbh Mela with Rs 4,300 crore ($597.8 million USD) to build and maintain facilities.[8]

The ways in which the national elections, environmental concerns, and the Kumbh Mela are interrelated provide an example of what Morton discusses as the interobjectivity of hyperobjects. They write, "Hyperobjects provide great examples of interobjectivity—namely, the way in which nothing is ever experienced directly, but only as mediated through other entities in some shared sensual space" (Morton 2013: 86). Along these lines, the nation and the environment might both be considered hyperobjects that are encountered in the tactile space of the Kumbh Mela, a hyperobject in itself. Teams of government-employed workers wearing Swacch Bharat vests and sweeping street trash at the Kumbh Mela signified the government's commitment to an environmentally conscious India, employment opportunities, the disavowal of street-cleaning as caste-determined labor, and the celebration of India as a Hindu nation. Signifying far beyond the local event, the Kumbh generates religio-national pride and confirms to millions of Hindu voters that the government of India, led by the Bharatiya Janata Party (BJP), supports their best interests for India's present and future Hindu generations.

Historically, aside from the cleansing bath, the primary function of the Kumbh Mela was to provide an opportunity for the thirteen *akhāṛas* to gather in order to initiate new members and host administrative meetings, wherein they elect officers, discuss policies, and manage financial exchanges (*dakṣiṇā*) (Eck and Bhatt 2015: 43; Hamaya 2018). In recent years, it has also become a central node in the administrative orchestration of India's most powerful Hindu groups, a place for representatives from powerful Hindu temples, ashrams, and religious organizations to congregate for meetings on pressing religious and political issues. The Vishwa Hindu Parishad (VHP) has a camp there, as does the Rashtriya Swayamsevak Sangh (RSS), as do each of the Śankarāchāryas, the Hindu ascetic leaders who serve as heads of the four major Maths of Advaita Vedanta first established by Adi Shankaracharya. Most of the celebrity gurus in India have camps there—including contemporary influencers like Baba Ramdev and Sri Sri Ravi Shankar, as well as deceased yet still revered gurus like Neem Karoli Baba and Sathya Sai Baba. With everyone assembled in one location, the *melā* also supplies an opportunity for politicians to align themselves with these powerful religious figures (see Figure 4.2.5).

Figure 4.2.5 Sriprakash Jaiswal, former member of Parliament (1999–2014) and Minister of Coal (2011–2014) (Left) with Swaroopananda Saraswati, Sankaracharya of Dwarka (1982–2022) (Right). Photo courtesy of author.

Thus, we can understand the Kumbh Mela as a mesh, in Morton's sense of the term, a system of networked relationships that form the substantive and sensual connectivities for a wide variety of things: the nation, the environment, Hindu religiosity, and so on. Morton explains meshes as being "potent metaphors for the interconnectedness of things"—but, importantly, ones that allow for losses and absences, permeations and gaps. They argue that the links and gaps of the mesh "enable causality to happen" (Morton 2013: 83). But what forms of causality might emerge from the interconnectivities of the Kumbh Mela?

Conclusion

On the one hand, the Kumbh Mela is a generative signifier of Modi government's activation of his high-profile environmental campaign for Swachh Bharat. However, the environmental success of the 2019 Kumbh Mela was just a thin veneer, enabled by the release of massive amounts of water from the Tehri Dam and the temporary closure of tanneries upriver. Furthermore, fifty percent of the sewage from the 122,500 newly constructed eco-friendly toilets was allowed to enter the river Ganga without treatment (Kaur 2019). A tribunal also reported that the groundwater had been polluted because thirty-six temporary ponds at the bank of the river had not been lined, and thus dirty sewage water percolated underground (Kaur 2019). Quite literally, the massive hyperobject that was the Kumbh

Mela was uncontainable, seeping into the earth and rivers. Its impact extends into an unseen future, diffused into multiple forms of eco-catastrophe.

On the other hand, the Indian government's subsidization and support for the Kumbh Mela also signifies a new era in Indian politics that is dangerous for India's religious minorities—an era in which being Indian is increasingly equated with identifying as Hindu. In 1954, when the newly established Indian government overtly supported the Kumbh Mela, a detractor argued that "as a secular government they should have not done anything in the nature of a propaganda to attract people [to attend the Kumbh Mela]" and that such a campaign exploited the religious sentiments of "illiterate, superstitious unsophisticated people."[9] Today, as the Indian government slides away from its pluralistic ideals and toward overt support for a new form of Hindu theocracy, the secular government routinely subsidizes Hindu religious activities. As I have written elsewhere (Lucia 2023), the Kumbh Mela has become a platform for state-sponsored Hindu nationalism, in particular, political organizing to establish a Ram temple upon the location of the demolished Babri Masjid in Ayodhya.[10]

In this sense, too, the Hindu nationalist sentiment that generatively accelerates through the Kumbh Mela is uncontainable in its causality.[11] Walking down one of the wide boulevards at the Kumbh in 2019, I encountered a Muslim man, identifiable by his white skull cap (Arabic: *takīyah*/Urdu: *topī*) and *kurta-pajama*, and *mojarī* (traditional leather-crafted shoes). I asked him if he felt safe at the Kumbh. He replied, "Of course. This is *our* Mother India. This *melā* is for all the people of India." Later, dining back at my camp in Sector 13, I was warned by a senior Hindu man that "all Muslims are terrorists and if you turn your back on them, they will slit your throat." As he said this, he sliced his finger across his throat in a gruesome gesture. While I felt immediate horror, I saw that my Hindu dinner companions all nodded in agreement. What are the unforeseeable causalities of such an uncontainable and interobjective sentiment? And, which of these two narratives signifies the Kumbh Mela? Likely it is both. As a hyperobject that expands in multiple and fractal directions, extending in its causality beyond the range of sight and sound, both sentiments prevail, overflowing in signification with its expansive effects. As Morton argues, "Locality is always a false immediacy" (Morton 2013: 48). The Kumbh Mela is, after all, an ephemeral city. At its close on Mahashivaratri, its millions of temporary inhabitants disperse across India and, to a lesser extent, across the globe. What they carry with them could be the religious passion conjured by the absorption of sacred mantras, or a newfound commitment to environmental conservation, or a vision of a religiously pluralistic "Mother India," or the militant fervor of Hindu chauvinism. Viewed as a hyperobject, the Kumbh Mela becomes a catalyst for infinite possibility, as pilgrims encounter themselves, each other, the divine, the land, and the imagined spaces of the nation in this largest gathering of humanity in recorded history.

Notes

1 This chapter is based in my ethnographic field work at the Kumbh Melas in Prayagraj. I attended the Maha Kumbh Mela in 2013 (with 120 million attendees) and the Kumbh Mela in 2019. I am grateful to the Society of Pilgrimage Studies (SPS) camp for their support and for housing me in their camp in 2013 at the Kumbh Mela for five weeks, and at the Ardh Mela in 2019 for three weeks. Independent of the SPS, I also attended the Magh Mela in 1997.

2 In 2013, I befriended a *nāgā sādhu* from the Mahanirvani Akhara (see Figure 4.2.1). By 2019, the image of his holy bath in 2013 had been captured and disseminated on billboards in Prayagraj and Paris, and was used by a tourism organization advertising the Kumbh Mela as one of the "Hidden Treasures of India," https://htoindia.com/blog/allahabad-kumbh-melā-2019/, accessed September 9, 2020.

3 Dr. Dubey. Conversation with author. February 18, 2013. Kumbh Mela, Prayagraj, India. See also D. P. Dubey 2013.

4 See Morton 2013: 169. Morton correctly observes that there is purported cosmic significance of *mantras* and Sanskrit syllables, such as *Oṃ* in the Indian Hindu context, and that popular belief holds that these syllables resonate powerfully in concert with the energetic vibrations of the universe. See also Gerety 2015, Beck 1993, and Padoux 1990. Hindu devotional music can be regarded as a kind of hyperobject in that it is intended to circulate in body, mind, and breath and to connect those features of the human with cosmic frequencies of the universe. However, some of Morton's assertions regarding "Hindu music" are incorrect. They write, "The augmented fourth chord is considered sacred in Hindu music precisely because it allows the ear to access a vast range of harmonics, a range that evokes a hugely expanded sense of what in musical language is called timbre: the material that generates a sound, such as the wood and strings and open body of a sitar" (Morton 2013: 168–169). Without delving too deeply, suffice to say that the notion of "Hindu music" is somewhat of an untenable category in their reference. Rather, it is Indian classical music (not specifically Hindu) upon which the music theory they are referring to is based. Further, the notion of "chord" is not an applicable concept in Indian musical forms, nor is the augmented fourth considered to be sacred. I am grateful to Max Katz, a scholar of Indian classical music, for discussing this passage with me and deepening my knowledge of Indian classical music theory (Max Katz, personal email communication, August 13, 2019).

5 Maclean 2008: 186. In their research on the 2013 Maha Kumbh Mela, Jukka-Pekka Onnela and Tarun Khanna analyzed the meta-data of the festival based on cellular phone use. On the peak bathing day, February 10, 2013, there were 800,000 unique SIMs (SIM cards) in use at Prayag (Onnela and Khanna 2015: 214).

6 Women, the uneducated, and the elderly (fifty-plus) are the least likely to own a cell phone in India, according to a recent twenty-seven-country survey conducted by the Pew Research Institute (Krishnan 2019).

7 Indian media reports at the time largely proclaimed the 1954 *melā* as the first Kumbh Mela of independent India, despite the fact that there was a Kumbh Mela observed in Haridwar in 1950. Many Indians consider the Kumbh Mela to be the *melā* that occurs every twelve years in Prayagraj. This common understanding persists despite the fact that there are quadrennial Kumbh Melas that occur in Naisik, Ujjain, and Haridwar, as well as annual gatherings in Prayagraj and the Ardh Kumbh Mela held in Prayagraj every six years (Maclean 2008: 193).

8 For a more precise discussion of budget projections as of July 26, 2018, see Sharma 2018. For more on the pre-election politicization and negative environmental impacts of the 2019 Kumbh Mela, see Lucia, 2023.

9 Letter from Vir Nandanjindal, *Pioneer*, February 10, 1954, quoted in Maclean 2008: 204.

10 In his travelogue account of the Kumbh Mela in 1971, Tully recounts how the VHP (Vishwa Hindu Parishad) used the Kumbh Mela as a forum through which to accelerate Hindu fervor and to call for the destruction of the Babri Masjid (Tully 1991). Hindu militants ultimately destroyed the mosque in 1992.

11 While Hindu chauvinism has accelerated under the current BJP-led Indian government, the Kumbh Mela has a long history of Hindu exclusivism. In 2013, the Dalai Lama planned to attend the Kumbh Mela, but cancelled his visit in response to Hindu threats. As early as 1906, there were calls to ban Muslims and Christians from the *melā* grounds (Maclean 2008: 127).

References

Beck, Guy. 1993. *Sonic Theology: Hinduism and Sacred Sound*. Columbia, SC: University of South Carolina Press.

de Certeau, Michel. 1984. *The Practice of Everyday Life*. Berkeley, CA: University of California Press.

Diamond, Debra, ed. 2013. *Yoga: The Art of Transformation*. Washington, DC: Arthur M. Sackler Gallery, Smithsonian Institution.

Dubey, D. P., ed. 2013. *Kumbh Mela: Pilgrimage to the Greatest Cosmic Fair*. Allahabad, India: Society of Pilgrimage Studies.

Eck, Diana, and Kalpesh Bhatt. 2015. "Understanding the Kumbh Mela." In *Kumbh Mela: Mapping the Ephemeral Megacity,* edited by Rahul Mehrotra and Felipe Vera, 30–56. New Delphi: Niyogi Books; Cambridge, MA: Harvard University South Asia Institute.

Gerety, Finnian. 2015. "The Whole World is OM: Song, Soteriology, and the Emergence of the Sacred Syllable." PhD diss., Harvard University.

Hamaya, Mariko. 2018. "The Circle of Gift Giving: A Case Study of Female 'Lay Ascetics' and Holy Feasts in Haridwar, North India." *Contemporary South Asia* 26 (1): 34–50.

Kaur, Banjot. 2019. "Kumbh Brought Allahabad to Verge of an Epidemic, Says NGT." *Down to Earth,* April 25. https://www.downtoearth.org.in/news/waste/kumbh-brought-allahabad-to-verge-of-an-epidemic-says-ngt-64139.

Krishnan, Varun B. 2019. "24% of Indians have a Smart Phone, Says Pew Study." *The Hindu.* February 8. https://www.thehindu.com/news/national/24-pc-of-indians-have-a-smartphone/article26212864.ece.

Lucia, Amanda. 2023. "Economies of Wonder: The Production of Spectacle at the Kumbh Mela." In *Wonder in South Asia: An Anthology,* edited by Tulasi Srinivas. Albany, NY: SUNY Press.

Maclean, Kama. 2008. *Pilgrimage and Power: The Kumbh Mela in Allahabad 1765–1954.* New York: Oxford University Press.

Mallinson, James. 2013. "Yogis in Mughal India." In *Yoga: The Art of Transformation,* edited by Debra Diamond, 69–84. Washington, DC: Arthur M. Sackler Gallery, Smithsonian Institution.

Mehrota, Rahul, and Felipe Vera (eds.). 2015. *Kumbh Mela: Mapping the Ephemeral Mega City.* Berlin: Hatje Cantz.

Morton, Timothy. 2013. *Hyperobjects: Philosophy and Ecology after the End of the World.* Minneapolis, MN: University of Minnesota Press.

Onnela, Jukka-Pekka, and Tarun Khanna. 2015. "Investigating Population Dynamics of the Kumbh Mela through the Lens of Cell Phone Data." In *Kumbh Mela: Mapping the Ephemeral Megacity,* edited by Rahul Mehrotra and Felipe Vera, 202–225. New Delphi: Niyogi Books; Cambridge, MA: Harvard University South Asia Institute.

Padoux, André. 1990. *Vāc: The Concept of the Word in Selected Hindu Tantras.* New Delhi: Sri Satguru Publications.

PTI. 2018. "Kumbh Mela 2019 to Be Spread Over Larger Area." *Indian Express.* December 4. https://indianexpress.com/article/india/allahabad-prayagraj-kumbh-mela-spread-over-larger-area-5507305/.

Sharma, Aman. 2018. "Kumbh 2019 Budget Estimate: Over Rs. 4,200 Crore." *Economic Times.* July 26. https://economictimes.indiatimes.com/news/politics-and-nation/kumbh-2019-budget-estimate-over-rs-4200-crore/articleshow/65142214.cms.

Tripathi, B. D. 2007. *Sadhus of India: The Sociological View.* New Delhi: Pilgrims Publishing.

Tully, Mark. 1991. *The Kumbh Mela.* Varanasi: Indica Books.

4.3

SONIC RELIGION

The Analysis of Atmospheric Half-Things

Patrick Eisenlohr

Reviews of the study of sound in religion tend to start with the observation of the marginality of this field, especially in contrast to the burgeoning field of visual culture in the study of religion (Hackett 2011: 448, 2012: 11–12; Laack 2015: 221). Often this is attributed to a legacy of deeply engrained European ocularcentrism, which turns sound and the sonic into a mysterious other that is difficult to grasp. Since the turn of the millennium, the "deafness" in the study of religion (Weiner 2009: 897) seems less pronounced than it used to be, with the topic of sound and religion receiving a new wave of attention. Nevertheless, the study of sound raises deeper questions for scholarly engagement with material religion at large. It points to a weakness in its very approach to materiality, a bias to imagine materiality along the lines of objects, things, and images—while sidelining eventful energetic forces such as the sonic.

Even though founding figures in the academic study of religion, such as Rudolf Otto (Otto [1917] 2014), considered sound and music fundamentally important, the study of religion long suffered from a dearth of compelling accounts of what exactly sound and the sonic contribute to religious practice and experience. Its approach to the materiality of the religious is also a direct result of this difficulty to understand sonic materiality and its effects. The recent shift in academic interest away from belief and textual content toward the sensual and material dimensions of religion has only highlighted this limitation, although it has provided a much more hospitable environment for the study of sound in its own right. Much of this new surge in interest in material religion has focused on the roles of objects, images, and things in religious life. Sound and sonic events are indisputably material. However, as they are not objects or things, their impermanence and fleeting nature call for a different analytic in order to make sense of how they contribute to religious world-making. This also necessitates a method that goes beyond the study of discourse about religious sounds, which is still the dominant approach. Of course, it is very important to take into consideration the variety of cultural discourses on sonic religion. For example, some of the Indic traditions grouped together under the label Hinduism since the nineteenth century are especially notable for their highly elaborate sonic metaphysics and cosmologies, according to which the sonic as a vibratory and anterior force pervades all and is responsible for the emergence of all entities (Beck 1993; Wilke 2017; Wilke and Moebus 2011). These traditions exemplify the necessity to take the sonic seriously as a mode of knowledge and meaning-making of its own,

DOI: 10.4324/9781351176231-32

including but also going beyond its verbal renderings. After all, the whole point of the sonic is that it is not reducible to language—even if scholarly conventions in the end force us to account for its effects through language, and to translate them into learned discourse. Moreover, as the sonic exceeds language, it is the locus of non-verbal knowledge that encompasses but also goes beyond hearing as technologically mediated (Sterne 2015) and beyond listening as learned bodily techniques of attention (Rice 2015). The upshot of this is that the sonic as a material modality of the religious includes as well as exceeds auditory culture, and appears to be difficult to grasp. In going beyond both language and directed techniques of the body— such as listening—the sonic cannot be fully understood though these more commonly studied avenues of cultural analysis, including the study of religion. This points to the necessity of an alternative approach to the sonic in religion.

The materiality of religion matters because of human embodiment. In European intellectual traditions, phenomenology is among those traditions that have contributed most to the analysis of embodiment and its consequences for knowledge about the world. In fact, a minor tradition within phenomenology, one that centers on the analysis of atmospheres and the way they mingle with sentient bodies, offers a promising perspective on the sonic that can also be useful for an improved understanding of sonic religion. In this chapter, I discuss research on sonic religion along these lines, making a case for the analysis of half-things and atmospheres as being central to an understanding of religion.

Religious Sounds, Belonging, and Emotions

The making and marking of spaces as belonging to a particular group, as well as the articulation of identities and political stances, are among the most explored aspects of sound in religious settings, especially in urban contexts. Religious sounds can suffuse urban environments and establish the presence of a particular group with which this kind of sound is conventionally associated. The recognized presence of a group through sonic performance and claims of political belonging and citizenship can be tightly interwoven (Eisenberg 2013). A sonic "sacralizing [of] the city" (David 2012) through technologically enhanced "amplified piety" (Gerety 2017: 6) also factors in the literature on the azan—the Islamic call to prayer. The azan is among the most notorious flashpoints of contention in religiously plural urban environments (Lee 1999; Tamimi Arab 2017; Weiner 2014). It provides an impressive testimony to the spatiality of sound and the making of "acoustic territories" (Labelle 2010) that in turn become the focus of contestation over issues of belonging and citizenship (Oosterbaan 2009; Sykes 2015). Originally, the use of the notion of religious soundscapes in urban and religious settings pointed to processes of ethical self-fashioning through mediated sermons, with an emphasis on their poetic and sonic aspects (Hirschkind 2006). However, soundscape has also become a fruitful analytic for spatialized and territorialized forms of religious and urban belonging, including claims of citizenship (de Witte 2016). For reasons I will explain below, the notion of soundscape is of limited use when it comes to grasping the atmospheric and other emotive dimensions of sonic religion. It is, however, highly evocative in drawing attention to the spatial and territorial aspects of sonic religion, as well as to possible conflicts surrounding them. Nevertheless, music and other sonic practices need not always be tied to territorial contest or the affirmation of distinct identifications with their associated claims for recognition. As Jim Sykes has shown in his investigation of the "musical gift" in Sri Lanka, musical performances can also foreground and perpetuate histories of exchange and conviviality across ethno-religious lines, weakening the latter in the process (Sykes 2018). Ultimately, the power of sonic religion to produce or dilute religious and political forms of belonging rests on the performative power of sound. Its eventful unfolding has a transformative character, helping to bring about links among people, spaces and territories, and forms of identification and belonging. The fact that these aspects of sonic religion have drawn wide attention raises the question of where the specific sonic contribution to the building of such connections lies. Surely, the sonic work behind the making or unmaking of such links is more than the provision of a symbolic marker—a conventional and thereby arbitrary sign for the presence and claims of a particular religious group. This is because there is a strong emotive dimension in sonic performance, a bodily feeling of a certain presence—such as, for example, the presence of religious others—that invests such presence with a particular self-evident character. This intertwining between the sonic and the emotive in sonic religion calls for closer investigation.

The emotive power of the sonic is among the prime reasons why sound matters in religious contexts (Amy de la Bretèque 2016; Becker 2010; Brennan 2018: 150–154; Jarjour 2018). This insight was already at the base of Abu Hamid al-Ghazali's reasoning about the permissibility of music from an Islamic perspective. His reasoning took as a starting point the notion, inherited from ancient Greek traditions, that the character of the music was sufficient to account for the emotional effects of music on listeners. Al-Ghazali combined that with a highly context-sensitive consequentialist view that music is permitted if it leads listeners closer to God and proscribed if it leads them astray (Shehabi 1995: 119–131). In Christian contexts, a culturally constructed contrast between visuality as being supposedly distancing, intellectualizing, and objectifying and aurality as being immersive and directed to the inner soul has long been a dominant paradigm. As Jonathan Sterne has shown, this Graeco-Christian "audiovisual litany" (Sterne 2003: 15–17) has had an enormous impact on modern North Atlantic scholarship on sound and orality. The notion that emotions and types of music, or modal components within them, are intrinsically intertwined is enormously widespread. It can already be found, for example, in al-Farabi's *Great Book of Music* (Shaw 2019: 44). Also, Indian raga music has long been built on the presupposition that the performative actualization of a raga and listeners' emotional states are linked (Jairazbhoy 1971; Kaufmann 1965). A similar link underlies compositional techniques in European Baroque music, explicitly formulated as *Affektenlehre*, in which artful sonic events bring about certain feelings and passions (Großmann 2014: 192–194). More recently, however, the theme of emotions in sonic religion has been approached from the perspective of sensible religious media and their materiality. The role of vocal sound as a medium of the divine is crucial here, such as in "a mystical continuity between the voices of God, celestial beings and human beings" characteristic of Orthodox Christianity (Engelhardt 2017: 60). Also, Muslims have long regarded Qur'anic recitation as the site where God reveals himself in this world (Gade 2006; Graham and Kermani 2006). More specifically, Sufi traditions of Islam have made rituals of remembering God (*dhikr*) that often involve recitation of prayers or short phrases—as well as the performance of particular genres of music—a central technique for establishing a closer-felt connection with the divine (Kapchan 2007; Qureshi 1986; Waugh 2005). The sonic dimensions of sensual religion have also featured in discussions of prayer (Blanton 2015; Engelhardt 2017) and glossolalia (Bialecki 2017; Harkness 2017; Remme 2019) where the blurring of the boundary between language and non-language is of crucial significance. In a related manner, the materiality of religious architecture can contribute to this suspension of the boundary between verbal and non-verbal vocal sound, generating the effect of a deeply felt proximity of the divine. As Bissera Pentcheva has shown, the large reverberation times of vocal sound in the Hagia Sophia cathedral building were unsuited for making speech intelligible, but turned the sound of melismatic choral singing in the liturgy into a "liquid" action that was felt to be inspiriting, bringing about a pneumatic descent of the divine into the matter of the cathedral (Pentcheva 2017: 9).

This range of studies has made a compelling case for the centrality of the sonic in generating powerful sensations and emotions in religious settings. There appears to be wide agreement that religious sounds' emotive effects rest on their materiality. Accordingly, there is a need for a compelling analytic that could account for the coupling of sonic materiality and religious sensations and emotions. How do the material particularities of the sonic as a mode of knowledge produce the efficacy of sonic performances in religious contexts? If the materiality of religion matters, sonic materiality also needs to be taken seriously in its specificity. As I will try to show, an analytic of atmospheres as developed in more recent strands of phenomenology can provide an enhanced understanding of material religion, especially its sonic dimensions, by drawing attention to the entrainment of sonic movement with motion as sensed by the felt-body.

Sonic Atmospheres in Religion

The phenomenologist Hermann Schmitz defines atmospheres as spatially poured out emotions that envelop and intermingle with felt-bodies (Schmitz 1969: 98–106; Schmitz et al. 2011: 247, 255). According to him, atmospheres are the "occupying of a nondimensional space or area within the range of experienced presence" (Schmitz 2014: 30, author's translation). From this perspective, emotions are not subjective, interior phenomena, but quite literally forces in the world. They are atmospheres that are "out there" and that seize people and their bodies. The phenomenological distinction between the physical body (*Körper*) and the felt-body (*Leib*) is crucial in this respect, as the latter can also include that which is felt to pertain to the body even though it is outside the boundaries of the physical body. Having a felt-body is the condition for the somatic intermingling that atmospheric sensibility revolves around. For Schmitz, atmospheres are also "half-things" (*Halbdinge*), fleeting phenomena that come and go, such as the weather, wind, feelings of warmth and cold, pain, voices, or musical figures. They can also be distinguished from things not only because they can be interrupted, but also by the fact that their presence and their effects are directly linked, such as a pain's paining, or warm weather's warming. In contrast to things and objects, whose effects require an intervening causal link between presence and effect—such as in the case of a rock causing an injury where the fall of the rock is the intervening causal link—the presence of half-things and their effects are one and the same.

> First, [half-things] differ from complete things (*Volldingen*), things in the ordinary sense, in their duration and extent. The duration of things is maximally steady in time; they also move steadily in space. Half-things can interrupt their duration and can shift their location in space in an unsteady fashion. Second, they are different from things in the causality particular to them. Things can be distinguished as causes from their effects. In the case of half-things cause and effect become one in immediate causality—while one could not ask, following Hume, for a link between cause and effect. In a related fashion, feelings or emotions (*Gefühle*) can be awakened—for example, by individual or collective experiences. Attitudes, and fates, can disappear and awake again at another time at the same or another place, like a voice that falls intermittently silent. Feelings and emotions can at first only be perceived and can then also take hold of and shift on to the perceiver. Yet even in this case the atmosphere does not cause such seizing of the perceiver through an intervening act of seizure, like the stone causing the smashing or shifting

of the object hit through its impact, or the medicine through the injection. Rather, the feeling or emotion (*Gefühl*) turns itself into felt-bodily-affectedness (*leiblich-affektives Betroffensein*) without additional action as mediating link.

(Schmitz 2014: 75, author's translation)

Building on recent work on sound, music, and atmospheres (Abels 2013, 2017, 2022; see also Eisenlohr 2018; Riedel 2015), I stress that sound and sonic events, like the voices mentioned by Schmitz, are prime examples of atmospheric half-things in this phenomenological sense. They come and go, can restlessly shift their location; they envelop and intermingle with felt-bodies, and they are energetic flows that act on felt-bodies. Even as they are fleeting, they are profoundly material. Their effects on sentient bodies and their presence are one and the same, not requiring a third causal material link. Like warmth and the weather, they intermingle with bodies and can be perceived simultaneously through more than one modality of the senses. They can be sensed in a holistic way, by the entire body, such as through vibratory motion. This is why it makes sense to speak of sonic atmospheres instead of acoustic atmospheres, because the acoustic is limited to the range of wave phenomena that humans can ordinarily perceive with their hearing apparatus. In contrast to the notion of soundscape—which in analogy to the idea of a landscape surveyed by an observer is still indebted to a subject-object divide (compare Ingold 2007)—sonic atmospheres as half-things intermingle with and act on felt-bodies without respecting their boundaries. Sound and sonic events' effects are as diffuse as they are powerful, and they are not easy to pin down through discursive means. Their holistic effect on the felt-bodies of those exposed to them can be understood through the suggestions of movement they exert (Schmitz 2014: 85). Sound and sonic events as atmospheres work through the nudges of motion that they contain and that their presence suggests to felt-bodies.[1]

The basic idea behind this is a resonant coupling of the sonic and felt bodies that is not unlike affect.[2] These couplings and interminglings make it possible for the sonic as energetic flows to seize felt bodies, to exert suggestions of movement on them—often in a collective setting—and to provoke emotions and other feelings in the process. These couplings are consequential because the sonic is a force of transduction. Transduction is not only at work in such couplings in the ordinary sense of the conversion of one modality of energy into another, such as repeated differences in air pressure converted into neuronal impulses by the hearing apparatus. The sonic is also transducive in Gilbert Simondon's sense as a force that generates new potentials and phenomena across physical, biological, and human domains through processes of "individuation" out of an inchoate material milieu (Simondon [1964] 1992). Transduction as material and energetic interaction results in the creation of the new; in the religious settings discussed here, these include both sensations and the psychic phenomena linked to them. The forces of transduction and the new entities and phenomena created by them stand in a relation of analogy, as in the sonic movements and the felt-bodily affectedness caused by them.[3]

Sonic atmospheric seizing of felt bodies has a quality that is both diffuse and powerful, and it frequently escapes verbal rendering. The coupling of the sonic and felt-bodies discussed here raises several questions. Can we understand the effects of the sonic as automatic? Would this not contradict a broad array of findings from anthropology and ethnomusicology that have stressed the cultural and historical contexts of sound and sonic perception? In other words, the analysis of sonic religion as atmospheric half-things brings to light a split between the notion of sound and the sonic as having power in itself—as argued in parts of sound studies—and the idea that human actors and their cultural discourses and practices invest sound and the sonic with power. The latter is typically argued by anthropologists, ethnomusicologists, and historians, as well as scholars in the field of sound studies. The question is whether it is possible to reconcile the facticity of the sonic as atmosphere and its somatic effects with the existence of auditory cultures and the relational ways of knowing that Steven Feld has called acoustemologies (Feld [1996] 2015), including those that are part of religious formations.

The theme of auditory cultures brings into play the meaningfulness of the sonic. Contrary to ideas about the sonic as a material flux that is prior to any kind of signification (Cox 2018),[4] a notion of the sonic that aligns with Massumi's "autonomy of affect" from meaning and other forms of qualification through the social dimensions of human life (Massumi 2002: 35), sonic atmospheres are highly meaningful. Their power does not lie in a putatively non-representational presence; it lies precisely in their meaningfulness (Abels 2022). The sonic movements they contain do not comprise discursive meanings, but are nevertheless iconic and indexical in Peircean terms.[5] In contrast to symbols, which are signs that depend on socio-cultural convention for their functioning; the meaningfulness of indices and icons is part of their materiality—as in causality and contiguity in the case of indices, or inherent qualitative likeness as in the case of icons. Atmospheres' "internally diffuse meaningfulness" (Schmitz 2014: 53) is largely composed of these materially ingrained forms of signification, and is also of a more vague and dispersed kind than the meaning-making found in the discourse of many auditory cultures—such as, for example, in sonic theologies. Sonic movement, especially when felt simultaneously with others in a social setting, provides emotive undergirding for the more qualified kind of meaningfulness elaborated in the discourses of religious traditions.[6] In such a way, sonic motion can deliver somatic evidence for the claims of religious traditions and the performative transformations enacted in religious practices. To sum up, sonic religion comprises a continuum of meaningfulness—from the diffuse meaningfulness of atmospheric sonic motion at one end, through the more clearly defined auditory cultures found in religious traditions, and on to the most qualified forms of meaningfulness found in the discourse of religious traditions at the other end.[7] To return to the question of whether sonic half-things are powerful in themselves—or whether human actors invest the sonic with power—the answer is that both positions are correct and not mutually exclusive. Sonic atmospheres and auditory culture can be found and interact on the same cline of meaningfulness in religious contexts. The former is more diffuse in its holistic seizing of the felt-body, while the latter more defined around notions of sonic theology as components of religious traditions. The interplay among discursive religious traditions, culturally attuned audition, and atmospheric sonic suggestions of movement accounts for the power of sonic religion.

In my own research on the recitation of na't—Urdu poems that eulogize the Prophet Muhammad among Mauritian Muslims, poems that are also very popular in South Asia—I have investigated such interplay among sonic suggestions of movement, sonic theologies, and their discursive elaborations in the context of a South Asian Islamic reformist tradition (Eisenlohr 2018). The poetry expresses deep love and longing for the Prophet, profusely praises his wonderful attributes, and articulates the wish to be close to him. In these poems the city of Madina, frequently regarded as the Prophet Muhammad's favorite city, often features as a metaphor for the presence of the Prophet. In this tradition, the poetic rendering of the wish to travel to Madina is an expression for the desire to personally encounter the Prophet. This in turn resonates with the doctrine of *hazir-o nazir* (present and observant) espoused by the Sufi-inclined Ahl-Sunnat va Jama'at reformist movement, whose followers belong to the most avid practitioners of the recitation of na't. According to this doctrine, the Prophet was no ordinary human being, and long after his death continues to be present as pure light—a concept along the lines of the Sufi idea of the *nur-e muhammadi*. The artful and emotionally invested recitation of na't can address the Prophet and literally bring about his presence among those poetically and affectionately invoking and praising him. In the poetic recitation's text, "Madina" is a stock theme for this kind of personal encounter with the Prophet. The sonic aspects of the recitation are not only important because they point to the great significance of artful vocal recitation as the site where God reveals himself in this world in Islamic traditions—a sonic theology that is based on the paradigm of Qur'anic recitation. My interlocutors in Mauritius used metaphors of transport and motion to describe the sensations that the vocal sounds of the poetic recitation provoked for them: the feeling of being carried away to a better place. As it happens, detailed spectrographic analysis of the vocal recitation also shows that the performance of this genre of devotional poetry revolves around movements of rising pitch, volume, and the shifting of acoustic energy to higher frequency bins, leading to the building of sonic intensities followed by relaxation. These sonic movements can be sensed by felt-bodies as suggestions of motion that align with the doctrinal and textual emphasis of spiritual travel to Madina to be in the presence of the Prophet. In semiotic terms, these sonic movements are diagrams of such travel, a type of icon "which represent[s] the relation . . . of the parts of one thing by analogous relations in their own parts" (Peirce 1932: 157). In other words, sonic movements turn into meaningful atmospheres that envelop and intermingle with those exposed to them, bringing about powerful sensations and emotionally charged experiences of transcending the self and traveling to a desired place. In the recitation of na't poetry, sonic atmospheres act as somatic and emotional evidence for the spiritual journeys and encounters that religious doctrine and poetic discourse both describe and praise.

To be thorough, an investigation of the aural aspects of material religion cannot be confined to the study of discourses of auditory culture; instead, it must offer close consideration to the sonic materiality of religious practices. For this, one needs to analyze the morphology of sonic half-things in religious contexts, as well as the suggestions of motion they contain. This is of key importance for understanding both the emotive dimensions of religion and the prominent position of sound and the sonic in them. As mentioned, theorizing about an intimate relationship between religion and music on the basis of a joint directedness to the "numinous" goes back to the beginnings of religion as a scholarly field of study (Otto [1917] 2014; see also Lehrich 2014). However, it is important to note that there is nothing specifically "religious" about the sonic as atmospheric half-things—even though Hermann Schmitz at some points in his work appears to suggest otherwise. Schmitz has actually drawn a link between atmospheres as spatially poured out emotions and the Homeric notions of divine rage and erotic love that the gods of ancient Greece literally sent down to mortals, who were powerless to resist them. He also views Biblical accounts of divine rage or love as illustrations of such an atmospheric understanding of emotions (Schmitz 2014: 45–47). Nevertheless, I maintain that atmospheres' diffuse meaningfulness refuses to be fully captured by religious traditions. As I noted regarding recitation of na't devotional poetry among Mauritian Muslims, the holistic but unspecific meaningfulness of atmospheric suggestions of motion that the intermingling of the sonic with felt-bodies involves blends with more qualified forms of signification. The latter are found in more standardized forms of religion, such as in my example of a particular South Asian reformist tradition of Islam. There, the feeling of being moved somewhere else in moments of sonic intensification along several dimensions aligns with spiritual travel to Madina in the context of a particular Islamic tradition. The latter stipulates the possibility of such travel and of a personal encounter with the

Prophet Muhammad. Sonic movements in atmospheric half-things are also distant from the invention of religion as a universal category and its attendant opening of an academic field of study. Atmospheric half-things as sonic motion are especially unrelated to the frequently attested Christian and more particularly Protestant bias that has shaped thinking about religion in the academy of the North Atlantic world, manifest in a modern concept of religion centered on belief (Asad 1993; Masuzawa 2005). If anything, the more recent interest in the materiality of the sonic dimensions of religion is part of the broad academic turn away from such a belief-centered understanding of religion. In other words, there are no necessary links between sonic motion and religious traditions; such motion has nothing "religious" about it. Nevertheless, sonic motion frequently mingles and converges with the discourses and auditory cultures of religious traditions. The sonic as atmospheric half-things is prima facie a multidirectional and open force. In contexts we tend to regard as religious, sonic atmospheres can then in a second step undergo further qualification through the interplay with religious discourse and learned, directed techniques of the body that form part of religious traditions.

Conclusion

The sonic cannot be grasped by approaches suited to objects, things, and images. Its special kind of materiality calls for a different mode of investigation, one that does justice to sonic events as half-things. Unlike objects and things, half-things can intermingle with felt-bodies, resulting in a holistic mode of perception where the atmospheric half-thing poured into space and the feeling of having a body become one and the same. Sonic atmospheres as half-things also vividly exemplify suggestions of motion as a primary mode of atmospheric action. As with the recitation of devotional poetry among Mauritian Muslims, sonic atmospheres are also emotions poured out in space that can take hold of people through somatic intermingling. In such a way, an analytic of atmospheres provides an answer to the old question where the often-remarked emotional effects of sound and music come from (Böhme 2000: 16), including in contexts defined as religious. Understanding the sonic dimensions of religion as atmospheric half-things that exert suggestions of motion on felt-bodies therefore helps to account for what exactly sound and the sonic contribute to the making of religious worlds. It also helps to widen the analysis beyond discourse on religious sound and the investigation of auditory cultures. At the same time, I have stressed that atmospheric half-things' enacting of suggestion of movement is no manifestation of an ontological force prior to signification. On the contrary, the suggestions of movement that atmospheric half-things exert on felt-bodies are highly meaningful. The indexicality and iconicity that make up the diffuse meaningfulness of atmospheric half-things are part of their material morphology. In sonic religious practice, their more dispersed kind of meaningfulness interacts and blends with more qualified kinds of signification such as those found in the auditory cultures, acoustemologies, and discourses circulating in religious settings. In such a way, they do not only imbue such settings with a certain feel, but can also provide somatic evidence for the states and transformations that religious performances bring about.

Notes

1 See also Heidemann (2017) for an analysis of a South Indian pilgrimage that foregrounds the links between atmosphere and proprioception.
2 See Eisenlohr (2018: 124–128) for a critique of the identification of the sonic with affect.

3   Simondon explains the generation of the new in a material milieu through analogous structuration in the following way: "This term [transduction] denotes a process—be it physical, biological, mental, or social—in which an activity gradually sets itself in motion, propagating within a given area, through a structuration of the different zones of the area over which it operates. Each region of the structure that is constituted in this way then serves to constitute the next one to such an extent that at the very time this structuration is effected there is a progressive modification taking place in tandem with it." (Simondon [1964] 1992: 313).

4   Christopher Cox draws on Nietzsche and Deleuze in formulating his metaphysics of a sonic flux. An understanding of the sonic as an immemorial, "primary flux" (Cox 2018: 31) that precedes everything and is responsible for the individuation of all entities was anticipated much earlier as the notion of Nada-Brahman by Indian theorists, most notably by the musicologist Sharngadeva (1175–1247) (Wilke 2017: 325–329).

5   It hardly needs to be reiterated that discourse is shot through with indexicality and iconicity as well.

6   This perspective is not incompatible with recent research on musical emotion at the interface of neuroscience interested in supraindividual, cross-subject processes and music studies: "The changes in the neurophysiology of the listener are not attributable simply to the brain/body of a self-contained individual. They occur through the group processes of recurrent interactions between co-defined individuals in a rhythmic domain of music" (Becker 2010: 149). The approach I am arguing for here extends such insights from the domain of listening to the more holistic realm of the sonic.

7   This is not an argument against the pivotal role of language and discourse in religious contexts. The performance of religious language can actually comprise a whole continuum of meaningfulness at once, from the diffuse meaningfulness of sonic atmospheric suggestions of motion—the meaning-making that the poetic function of religious language affords—to the foregrounding of highly qualified referential meanings in language. For such an interplay, see my example of the performance of devotional poetry among Mauritian Muslims later in this chapter.

References

Abels, Birgit. 2013. "Hörgemeinschaften. Eine musikwissenschaftliche Annäherung an die Atmosphärenforschung." *Musikforschung* 66 (3): 220–231.

Abels, Birgit. 2017. "Musical Atmospheres and Sea-Nomadic Movement Among the Sama Dilaut: Sounding Out a Mobile World." In "Atmospheres and Mobilities." Special issue, *Mobile Culture Studies: The Journal* 3 (3): 21–36.

Abels, Birgit. 2022. *Music Worlding in Palau: Chanting, Atmospheres, and Meaningfulness.* Amsterdam: Amsterdam University Press.

Amy de la Bretèque, Estelle. 2016. "Vocalisation des émotions dans les funérailles yézidies d'Arménie." In *Mythes, rites et émotions, les funérailles sur la route de la soie*, edited by Anna Caiozzo, 265–279. Paris: Honoré-Champion.

Asad, Talal. 1993. *Genealogies of Religion: Discipline and Reasons of Power in Christianity and Islam.* Baltimore, MD: Johns Hopkins University Press.

Beck, Guy L. 1993. *Sonic Theology: Hinduism and Sacred Sound.* Columbia, SC: University of South Carolina Press.

Becker, Judith. 2010. "Exploring the Habitus of Listening: Anthropological Perspectives." In *Handbook of Music and Emotion: Theory, Research, Applications*, edited by Patrik N. Juslin and John A. Sloboda, 127–157. Oxford: Oxford University Press.

Bialecki, Jon. 2017. *A Diagram for Fire: Miracles and Variation in an American Charismatic Movement.* Oakland, CA: University of California Press.

Blanton, Anderson. 2015. *Hittin' the Prayer Bones: Materiality of Spirit in the Pentecostal South.* Chapel Hill, NC: University of North Carolina Press.

Böhme, Gernot. 2000. "Acoustic Atmospheres: A Contribution to the Study of Ecological Aesthetics." *Soundscape: The Journal of Acoustic Ecology* 1 (1): 14–18.

Brennan, Vicki L. 2018. *Singing Yoruba Christianity: Music, Media, and Morality.* Bloomington, IN: Indiana University Press.

Cox, Christoph. 2018. *Sonic Flux: Sound, Art, and Metaphysics.* Chicago, IL: University of Chicago Press.

David, Ann R. 2012. "Sacralising the City: Sound, Space and Performance in Hindu Ritual Practices in London." *Culture and Religion* 13 (4): 449–467.

de Witte, Marleen. 2016. "Encountering Religion through Accra's Urban Soundscape." In *Encountering the City: Urban Encounters from Accra to New York*, edited by Jonathan Darling and Helen Wilson, 133–150. London: Routledge.

Eisenberg, Andrew. 2013. "Islam, Sound and Space: Acoustemology and Citizenship on the Kenyan Coast." In *Music, Sound, and Space: Transformations of Public and Private Experience*, edited by Georgia Born, 186–202. Cambridge: Cambridge University Press.

Eisenlohr, Patrick. 2018. *Sounding Islam: Voice, Media, and Sonic Atmospheres in an Indian Ocean World*. Oakland, CA: University of California Press.

Engelhardt, Jeffers. 2017. "Listening and the Sacramental Life: Degrees of Mediation in Greek Orthodox Christianity." In *Praying with the Senses: Contemporary Orthodox Christian Spirituality in Practice*, edited by Sonja Luehrmann, 58–79. Bloomington, IN: Indiana University Press.

Feld, Steven. 1996. "Waterfalls of Song: An Acoustemology of Place Resounding in Bosavi, Papua New Guinea." In *Senses of Place*, edited by Steven Feld and Keith Basso, 91–135. Santa Fe, NM: School of American Research Press.

Feld, Steven. 2015. "Acoustemology." In *Keywords in Sound*, edited by David Novak and Matt Sakakeeny, 12–21. Durham, NC: Duke University Press.

Gade, Anna M. 2006. "Recitation." In *The Blackwell Companion to the Qur'an*, edited by Andrew Rippin, 481–493. Malden, MA: Blackwell.

Gerety, Finnian M. M. 2017. "The Amplified Sacrifice: Sound, Technology, and Participation in Modern Vedic Ritual." In "Crafting New Horizons: South Asian Folklore in Transition." Special issue, *South Asian History and Culture* 8 (4): 560–578.

Graham, William A., and Navid Kermani. 2006. "Recitation and Aesthetic Reception." In *The Cambridge Companion to the Qur'ān*, edited by Jane Dammen McAuliffe, 115–42. Cambridge: Cambridge University Press.

Großmann, Rolf. 2014. "Sensory Engineering: Affects and Mechanics of Musical Time." In *Timing of Affect: Epistemologies, Aesthetics, Politics*, edited by Marie-Luise Angerer, Bernd Bösel, and Michaela Ott, 191–205. Zürich and Berlin: Diaphanes.

Hackett, Rosalind I. J. 2011. "Auditory Materials." In *Handbook of Research Methods in Religious Studies*, edited by Michael Stausberg and Steven Engler, 447–458. New York: Routledge.

Hackett, Rosalind I. J. 2012. "Sound, Music, and the Study of Religion." *Temenos* 48 (1): 11–27.

Harkness, Nicholas. 2017. "Glossolalia and Cacophony in South Korea: Cultural Semiosis at the Limits of Language." *American Ethnologist* 44: 476–489.

Heidemann, Frank. 2017. "Social Aesthetics, Atmosphere and Proprioception." In *Aesthetics of Religion. A Connective Concept*, edited by Alexandra K. Grieser and Jay Johnston, 457–464. Berlin: De Gruyter.

Hirschkind, Charles. 2006. *The Ethical Soundscape: Cassette Sermons and Islamic Counterpublics*. New York: Columbia University Press.

Ingold, Tim. 2007. "Against Soundscape." In *Autumn Leaves: Sound and the Environment in Artistic Practice*, edited by A. Carlyle, 11–13. Paris: Double Entendre.

Jairazbhoy, Nazir Ali. 1971. *The Rags of North Indian Music: Their Structure and Evolution*. London: Faber and Faber.

Jarjour, Tala. 2018. *Sense and Sadness: Syriac Chant in Aleppo*. Oxford: Oxford University Press.

Kapchan, Deborah. 2007. *Traveling Spirit Masters: Moroccan Gnawa Trane and Music in the Global Marketplace*. Middletown, CT: Wesleyan University Press.

Kaufmann, Walter. 1965. "Rasa, Raga-Mala, and Performance Times in North Indian Ragas." *Ethnomusicology* 9 (3): 272–291.

Laack, Isabel. 2015. "Sound, Music and Religion. A Preliminary Cartography of a Transdisciplinary Research Field." *Method and Theory in the Study of Religion* 27: 220–246.

Labelle, Brandon. 2010. *Acoustic Territories: Sound Culture and Everyday Life*. New York: Continuum.

Lee, Tong Song. 1999. "Technology and the Production of Islamic Space: The Call to Prayer in Singapore." *Ethnomusicology* 43 (1): 86–100.

Lehrich, Christopher I. 2014. "The Unanswered Question: Music and Theory of Religion." *Method and Theory in the Study of Religion* 26: 22–43.

Massumi, Brian. 2002. *Parables for the Virtual: Movement, Affect, Sensation*. Durham, NC: Duke University Press.

Masuzawa, Tomoko. 2005. *The Invention of World Religions: Or, How European Universalism Was Preserved in the Language of Pluralism.* Chicago, IL: University of Chicago Press.

Oosterbaan, Martijn. 2009. "Sonic Supremacy: Sound, Space and Charisma in a Favela in Rio de Janeiro." *Critique of Anthropology* 29 (1): 81–104.

Otto, Rudolf. (1917) 2014. *Das Heilige. Über das Irrationale in der Idee des Göttlichen und sein Verhältnis zum Rationalen.* Munich: Beck.

Peirce, Charles Sanders. 1932. *Collected Papers of Charles Sanders Peirce. Volume II: Elements of Logic.* Cambridge, MA: Harvard University Press.

Pentcheva, Bissera V. 2017. *Hagia Sophia: Sound, Space, and Spirit in Byzantium.* University Park, PA: Pennsylvania State University Press.

Qureshi, Regula Burckhardt. 1986. *Sufi Music of India and Pakistan: Sound, Context and Meaning in Qawwali.* Cambridge: Cambridge University Press.

Remme, Jon Henrik Ziegler. 2019. "The Problem with Presence: The Ambiguity of Mediating Forms in Ifugao Pentecostal Rituals." *Ethnos* (9 December).

Rice, Tom. 2015. "Listening." In *Keywords in Sound*, edited by David Novak and Matt Sakakeeny, 99–111. Durham, NC: Duke University Press.

Riedel, Friedlind. 2015. "Music as Atmosphere. Lines of Becoming in Congregational Worship." *Lebenswelt* 6: 80–111.

Schmitz, Hermann. 1969. *System der Philosophie*, 3/2. Der Gefühlsraum. Bonn: Bouvier.

Schmitz, Hermann. 2014. *Atmosphären.* Freiburg, Germany: Alber.

Schmitz, Hermann, Rudolf Owen Müllan, and Jan Slaby. 2011. "Emotions Outside the Box—The New Phenomenology of Feeling and Corporeality." *Phenomenology and the Cognitive Sciences* 10: 241–259.

Shaw, Wendy M.K. 2019. "Seeing with the ear, recognizing with the heart: rethinking the ontology of the mimetic arts in Islam." In *Figurations and sensations of the unseen in Judaism, Christianity and Islam: contested desires*, edited by Birgit Meyer and Terje Stordalen, 37–56. London: Bloomsbury.

Shehabi, Fadlou. 1995. *Philosophies of Music in Medieval Islam.* Leiden: Brill.

Simondon, Gilbert. (1964) 1992. "The Genesis of the Individual." In *Incorporations*, edited by Jonathan Crary and Sanford Kwinter, 297–319. New York: Zone.

Sterne, Jonathan. 2003. *The Audible Past: Cultural Origins of Sound Reproduction.* Durham, NC: Duke University Press.

Sterne, Jonathan. 2015. "Hearing." In *Keywords in Sound*, edited by David Novak and Matt Sakakeeny, 65–77. Durham, NC: Duke University Press.

Sykes, Jim. 2015. "Sound Studies, Religion and Urban Space: Tamil Music and the Ethical Life in Singapore." *Ethnomusicology Forum* 24 (3): 380–413.

Sykes, Jim. 2018. *The Musical Gift: Sonic Generosity in Post-War Sri-Lanka.* Oxford: Oxford University Press.

Tamimi Arab, Pooyan. 2017. *Amplifying Islam in the European Soundscape: Religious Pluralism and Secularism in the Netherlands.* London: Bloomsbury.

Waugh, Earl H. 2005. *Memory, Music, and Religion: Morocco's Mystical Chanters.* Columbia, SC: University of South Carolina Press.

Weiner, Isaac A. 2009. "Sound and American Religions." *Religion Compass* 3 (5): 897–908.

Weiner, Isaac A. 2014. "Calling Everyone to Pray: Pluralism, Secularism, and the Adhān in Hamtramck, Michigan." *Anthropological Quarterly* 87 (4): 1049–1077.

Wilke, Annette. 2017. "Moving Religion by Sound: On the Effectiveness of the Nada-Brahman in India and Modern Europe." In *Aesthetics of Religion. A Connective Concept*, edited by Alexandra K. Grieser and Jay Johnston, 323–346. Berlin: De Gruyter.

Wilke, Annette, and Oliver Moebus. 2011. *Sound and Communication: An Aesthetic History of Sanskrit Hinduism.* Berlin: De Gruyter.

4.4

MORTANDAD AS HYPEROBJECT

Colonial Death Worlds and Epidemic Cataclysm in Las Américas

Jennifer Scheper Hughes

Ritual relations with material sacra ground many iterations of Mexican and Mexican American religion, historically and through the present. In the Mexican Catholic analogical imagination, the sacred is immanent and discoverable in the world (Tracy 1981). This quality is especially perceptible in intimate and tender relations between human beings and materially manifest sacred entities: the vital matter of Catholic practice. In previous work, I have explored such material-human relations. In a small community in the mountains of the Mexican state of Morelos, a beloved ancestral image of the crucified Christ has oriented religious faith and practice over five centuries. Today devotees care for him with familiar and tender regard, understanding the sculpted saint as a living and agentic guardian of their pueblo. Elsewhere in Mexico, ritual practice is sometimes oriented instead around images of the infant Jesus and other child saints. The feelings evoked in these practices are similarly warm and affectionate, as these diminutive images are cradled in the crook of an arm, or lovingly placed in a crib to sleep at night (Hughes 2010, 2012a, 2012b). I have argued that these are traceable to ritual trajectories rooted in pre-invasion, Mesoamerican object-oriented ontologies (Hughes 2016).

However, the study of material religion should not only consider relational intimacy with small and sacred things. Not all objects of material religion are diminutive, physically accessible, familiar, and proximate, nor tenderly regarded, including in the Mexican context. Some are large and unwieldy, massive in scale, so much so that their shape and impacts, including violent ones, have been only partially discernable to scholars of religion. We might term these "hyperobjects," following ecological theorist Timothy Morton. Morton coined the term to analyze global warming: to explain how we are both caught up within, and at the same time oblivious to, the real threat that looms all around us (Morton 2013). Perhaps it is not surprising that scholars of religion have largely failed to capture such objects within our analyses and interpretations. After all, hyperobjects are by definition elusive: "massively distributed in time and space," they are at once acutely experienced but never fully knowable, "uncanny," Morton says (2013: 48). But scholars of religion have inherited a particular distortion of scale that likely exacerbates the problem of perception. In many of the world's religious traditions, the balance of religious relations skews between the finite (the human, the tangible, the here and now) and the infinite (God "himself," the ultimate, the unknowable, the immaterial), with a vast chasm void in between. Within the formal theological

DOI: 10.4324/9781351176231-33

structures of the major monotheistic traditions, God is the only "hyperobject," dwarfing and eclipsing all other massive forms. But thinking of the hyperobject, it is no longer God who defines the infinite and unknowable, but rather the man-made material realm itself.

In the post-invasion history of religion in *Las Américas*, there are many things that might be analyzed as hyperobjects, the global imperial church, for one: with the imposing physicality of its networked buildings and tentacle reach of its myriad institutions. Even the colony itself, the kingdom of New Spain, might be considered as such: a vast territorial and institutional mass that was at once mystical and fleshy (Hughes 2020). To my mind, one hyperobject looms largest and most terribly: the sixteenth-century demographic cataclysm; what Spanish witnesses termed the *mortandad*, or death event. In the *mortandad* disease pathogens ravaged Indigenous bodies and lives, not once but many times over: more than six periods of epidemic crisis scarred the century. The Mexican *mortandad* is the subject of my recent book, *The Church of the Dead: The Epidemic of 1576 and the Birth of Christianity in the Americas* (2021) in which I focus on the religious impact of a particular disease outbreak called "*cocoliztli*" in 1576–1581. The *mortandad* ruined and then remade human institutions in its likeness: among these is what I have termed the *ecclesia ex mortuis*, the church of the dead: a settler church that built its sovereignty on a condition of death. I conclude that the Indigenous mortality crisis of the sixteenth century was the founding condition of the church in the Americas.

Here, I return to reconsider the *cocoliztli* epidemic, but this time framed as hyperobject.[1] My purpose is not to test the potency of the idea of hyperobject against the *mortandad*. Instead, I work to coax the concept into a critical analytic useful for the study of religion in contexts of extremity, one that perhaps helps us reckon with the American death event more deeply. With respect to the *mortandad*, Morton's philosophy of the hyperobject clarifies the problem of scale and perceptibility, provides language to explore the appearance of its attendant affects in the historical record, and illuminates the complex nature of temporality, including the ambiguity of catastrophic beginnings and end times. Historical sources for this study, both Spanish and Indigenous, come from the epoch of epidemics; they are documentary materials that emerge from what I term the "archive of cataclysm." Adapting Morton's category of hyperobjects, I refer to those things of immense size that bear down upon us in history, through time and space, both constraining and refracting religious experience. The Mexican *mortandad* is, in fact, the original hyperobject.

The First Hyperobject: *Mortandad* and the End of the World

When Europeans arrived in the Americas in 1492, the Indigenous population stood at 100 million people. In Mexico alone, one of the most populous regions on Earth, there were no fewer than twenty-two million persons. Mexico's political and spiritual capital, Tenochtitlan, one of six major urban centers of the world, had a population of about 400,000. The Valley of Mexico was so densely occupied that in many regions, homes were contiguous, one abutting the next without interruption. (In comparison, Sevilla was a relative backwater in 1492, with a population of no more than 35,000.) By the end of the sixteenth century, the population of Mexico had plunged to less than two million (Figure 4.4.1).

By far, the most well documented of the early colonial period, the second *cocoliztli* pandemic beginning in 1576—*Cocoliztli* II, as we might call it—has often been identified as the most destructive, striking what seemed to be a final blow, and it is here that my attentions rest. For centuries, the deadly illness was thought to be typhus or a form of the smallpox that had struck in 1520. In the first decade of the twenty-first century, as Ebola threatened the African continent, epidemiologists concluded that the historic *cocoliztli* epidemic, with

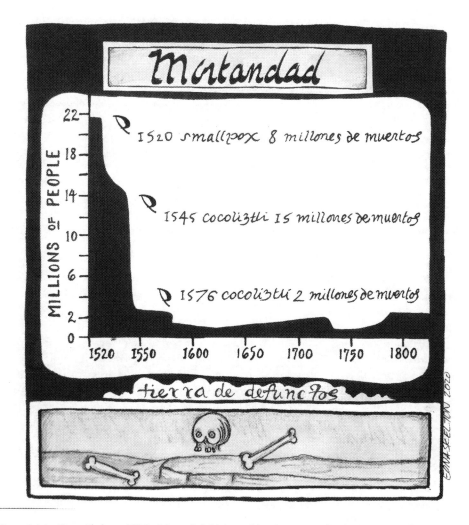

Figure 4.4.1 Eona Skelton. 2020. *Mortandad*. Major epidemic catastrophes in Mexico in the sixteenth century. Drawing from the author's private collection.

its familiar bloody symptoms, must have been hemorrhagic fever. Others have suggested that there was not a single disease agent but rather that the Great Death stemmed from a constellation of causes. Most recently, new technological instruments have made it possible for paleoarcheologists to trace agent pathogen DNA. Scientists have identified the presence of a strain of bacterial *Salmonella enterica* (a paratyphoid fever, *S. Paratyphi C*) in individuals who were buried in a plague cemetery in Oaxaca during the first *cocoliztli* outbreak in 1545 (Vågene 2018). Perhaps *Salmonella enterica* was indeed also the culprit in 1576. To be absolutely clear, the *mortandad* was never reducible to a virus or bacteria, but always connected to even larger webs of significance: first among these, the imperial apparatus and its lethal interaction with disease pathogens.

During the 1576 *cocoliztli* outbreak and its aftermath, Spanish witnesses grieved that in some sense the world as they knew it had come to an end, the world that they hoped and labored for was no more. Facing the threat of Indigenous annihilation, they confronted the raw precarity of the Spanish colonial project in the New World. For the imperial church, the *mortandad* contradicted its utopian expectation that the discovery of the Americas signaled a new age. Millennial hope dissolved into apocalyptic despair (Phelan 1970).

Hyperobjects are often inherently and intimately related to end times. For Morton, the end time in question is the impending apocalypse wrought by global warming: "For what comes into view for humans at this moment is precisely the end of the world brought about by the encroachment of hyperobjects." "The end of the world has already occurred," they continue: the origins of global warming are in April 1784, when the steam engine was patented, chugged to life, and began churning its carbon into the atmosphere. But "since for something to happen it often needs to happen twice," Morton also identifies the end of the world in the testing of the first atomic bomb in 1945 (Morton 2013: 7). These twin events demarcate the geological period of the Anthropocene, our current geological age. The emergence of the hyperobject thus signals the human-wrought environmental apocalypse that entraps human beings in the "jaws of death."

Scholars of religion, all too familiar with apocalyptic religious phenomena across traditions, will surely find Morton's elaboration of end times as these relate to hyperobjects suggestive, as I have. But with respect to the earthly impacts of human beings, it is not the carbon/nuclear fallout cataclysm that is the original hyperobject catastrophe, but rather the sixteenth-century *mortandad*. Two centuries prior to the invention of the steam engine, and almost half a millennial before the first atomic test, the demographic cataclysm suffered by Indigenous peoples across this hemisphere made itself manifest in the geological record. The so-called Orbis Spike refers to a measurable drop in carbon dioxide levels recorded in the Antarctic glacial ice core in the precise period of sudden population decline: 1570–1620. Some climate change scientists have read the mortality crisis suffered by Native peoples in the spike (Lewis and Maslin 2015; Koch et al. 2019). The icy geological landscape records a solemn imprint of human loss. It is a stratographic section, a boundary marker, between geological epochs. This cataclysm led to a near cessation of Indigenous agriculture followed by a period of rapid reforestation: "A genocide-generated drop in carbon dioxide."[2] After the colonial cataclysm, the earth appeared to gasp as the Indigenous population tumbled—a sharp intake as if in response to trauma. It is precisely this moment of catastrophe that signals the current geological epoch, in which human activity is the dominant influence on climate and the environment. Tragedy is written on geological landscapes, captured in ice and earth.

Five centuries ago, the world ended in the *mortandad* hyperobject. In fact, both Indigenous survivors and Spanish observers remember the *cocoliztli* cataclysm as punctuating history, as rending time. With *mortandad* Spanish observers pronounced a mortality crisis of apocalyptic scale. Many historical sources from the late sixteenth and early seventeenth centuries position the *cocoliztli* outbreak as the end of history. *Cocoliztli* is the final historical event referenced in the *General History of the Things of New Spain*, the twelve-volume encyclopedic study that the Franciscan Bernardino de Sahagún coauthored with Nahua elders and experts. The culmination of decades of labor, the *Historia general* was a compendium of Nahua history, culture, and society written not in scholarly Latin but rather in the New World vernacular—that is, in Nahuatl with Spanish translation. Capturing and preserving centuries of accrued Indigenous knowledge, the volumes have been lauded as the first work of American anthropology, and as such are integral to the history of Mexico. The achievement recorded the very world disintegrating around its creators. It was a labor of decades that came to its conclusion as the cocoliztli *mortandad* raged.

In the *Historia general*, the cocoliztli outbreak appears as a temporal disruption, as an interruption to the narrative of the work overall that also identifies cocoliztli as the final, concluding event of the *Historia*. This happens twice, the first occurrence is at the hand of the Indigenous authors, and the second by Sahagún himself (which I discuss below). The first of these is in the appendix of Book III, in a Nahuatl section of the *Historia general* explaining traditional customs pertaining to the dead. *Cocoliztli* carried away so many people that Nahua elders described a particular path to Mictlán, the place of the dead, especially for those who died of the disease: "*auh in umpa ui, Mictlan / iehoantin, in ixquichen tlalmiqui / in zan coculitzli ic miqui / in tlatoque, in maceoalti*" —by that way they go to Mictlán, those who died on the earth, those who from *cocoliztli* died, whether they were lords or commoners.[3] In subsequent centuries, the word *cocoliztli* came to refer to epidemics more generally. But here, at this historical juncture, it named a specific ailment, the affliction that Mexico was facing at the time of the text's writing. Cocoliztli stands as the final chronological event in the twelve-volume opus, as the end of the *Historia*, and perhaps even of history: an event that sets people on their journey to the afterlife, into post-history, we could say.

The *Anales de Tecamachalco* chronicles two hundred years of community history, from 1398 to 1590. Here again cocoliztli appears as the end of a Nahua history. Written in Nahuatl as a collective account, the *Anales* records seventy years of Spanish invasion and corresponding *mortandad* and population loss, concluding with years of the *cocoliztli* pandemic and its aftermath (Corteguera 2012). For the years 1577–1580, the *Anales* remembers the people of Tecamachalco's embodied experience of *cocoliztli* as a collective and shared affliction. In a third example, the Nahua annalist Chimalpahin Quauhtlehuanitzin—who was born in 1579, amid *cocoliztli*'s second surge—identified the *cocoliztli* epidemic of 1576 not precisely as the end of history but, rather, as the beginning of a new era. He opens his history of Mexico with this epidemic, *the* notable event for 1577 (Chimalpahin [1615] 2006: 27).[4]

Spanish witnesses similarly responded to the temporal uncertainty wrought by the *mortandad*. The Dominican chronicler Augustín Dávila Padilla concluded his missionary history with the cataclysm of *cocoliztli* (Dávila Padilla 1625), as does another Dominican friar, Diego Durán, whose account of Aztec history was based upon written and oral Indigenous sources. Finally, Sahagún himself, the editor and translator of the *Historia general* referred to above, further affirms *cocoliztli* as the end of history from a Spanish missionary perspective. In a largely unstudied section of the penultimate volume of *Historia general* (the eighth chapter of Book 11), he poured out his emotional and theological reflections on the devastation of the *cocoliztli* epidemic. Overcome, Sahagún departed from faithful translation of the Nahuatl to consider instead the consequences of the current epidemic for the future of the church. Engaging with the theme of the text before him even as he diverged from it, Sahagún mourned that *cocoliztli* had brought Christianity to the "end of its road" in the New World:

> There was once a great diversity of peoples in this land, but these are pretty much finished. And those that remain are on the *road* to their end as well.. It seems to me that the Catholic faith is not long for these lands because the people head to their end with great haste not only for the bad treatment they receive because of the diseases that god has sent upon them.[5]

Then Sahagun adds a startling footnote, as an asterisk, in which he prays: "Pray to our lord to remedy this great plague because if it lasts much longer all will be lost!"

The Invisible *Mortandad*: The Problem of Perception

The *mortandad* hides in plain sight. But then, this is one of the identifying qualities of all hyperobjects: even as human persons suffer their immediacy, hyperobjects are simultaneously large and nonlocal, and we cannot fully perceive the web in which we are caught. "Hyperobjects occupy a high-dimensional phase space that results in their being invisible to humans for stretches of time," Morton writes (2013: 70). Witness testimonies of those who survived Hiroshima may be helpful here. Morton describes how each testimony is at once local and distant, or remote. The bomb in memory is both "distant and close at the same time."

The absence and inaccessibility of the *mortandad* hyperobject loom in the work of historians who have not grappled with the reality of the *mortandad* beyond the traditional demographic and epidemiological studies that have dominated academic inquiries of sixteenth-century epidemics. Most scholars have set aside the death event as they pursue other lines of historical inquiry. It has been until now completely feasible to write specific cultural, social, or economic histories of Mexico with scant reference to the fact that the *mortandad* was the defining context for every historical action. The field has lacked a critical apparatus capable of confronting the ways in which the Indigenous mortality crisis, the fact of mass death, defined and shaped all dimensions of colonial life.

The problem of perceptibility of the colonial death world also pertains to the archive. Imperial archives frequently obscure more than they reveal. That is, the archive itself obscures the outbreak even as it mourns it. For example, the minutes of the *cabildo* (governing council) of Mexico City during the years of *cocoliztli* have startlingly little to say about the world that was crumbling around local administrators, who tried as they could, plodding along, to continue business as usual.

The slippery illusiveness of the *mortandad*, an echo of its nonlocality, is further evident in historical descriptions of *cocoliztli*. To Spanish witnesses, the erratic epidemic defied known patterns of disease contagion and seemed to have a mind of its own, to be animate. In 1577, the viceroy Martín Enríquez wrote that it "affects one town just a league away from another where it rages for a long while and later returns to it so that it appears as if it is a living thing and that it goes in search of towns so that none remain."[6] The next year, the bishop of Michoacán similarly worried:

> Almost half of the Indians of this province have been taken. When the pestilence enters a town, for ten months or a year it jumps from *barrio* to *barrio* and house to house. And it was without order even though divine disposition would have had it well ordered. Because it struck one neighborhood and then jumped to another far away, sparing the one closer by. And in the same home it took some and spared others, only to return four or six months later to claim the healthy. This was observed by all.[7]

That is to say, as hyperobject the *mortandad* transgressed and defined typical spatial logics. It also manifested a temporal slipperiness.

Spanish missionaries deployed the word *mortandad* to indict each ravaging epidemic that threatened the Indigenous communities they sought to convert and evangelize. Each *mortandad*, each "Great Death," was both a singular event and part of an extended epoch of loss and devastation that defined and transgressed centuries. In colonial sources, *mortandad* was used variously to refer to particular locally bounded outbreaks of disease, to pandemics affecting all of Mexico, and to the entire colonial demographic cataclysm wrought by disease, violence, and extractive labor. Each wave of disease represented its own traumatic punctuation of history, each historically unique and specific. At the same time, the accumulated effect was so profoundly disorienting that at times multiple episodes blurred together to become one horror, appearing as one accrued cataclysm in historical memory. The bishop of Michoacán observed of *cocoliztli*, "The *Indios* are coming to their end with great haste because everywhere they are falling ill and dying [. . .] a slow and sly pestilence *never ceases*."[8] Morton explains, "Hyperobjects envelop us, yet they are so massively distributed in time that they seem to taper off, like a long street stretched into the distance. Time bends them and flattens them" (2013: 55). This might help explain both the haphazard appearance of the *mortandad* in the archive, as well as the historians' inability to grasp the colonial *mortandad* in all its terrible dimensions.

Affects as Traces of the Hyperobject

In the Spanish record and in the archive, the *mortandad* makes itself known most immediately through the affects, the feelings that it evokes for observers. Hyperobjects, as elusive as they may be, also are acutely experienced through the perceptible and sensorial world. They leave trails and traces: "The octopus of the hyperobject emits a cloud of ink as it withdraws from access. Yet this cloud of ink is a cloud of effects and affects" (Morton 2013: 39). Searching the imperial archive for word about the *mortandad* is an exercise in exegesis. Mundane letters of colonial administration are the documentary maintenance of bureaucracy. The affective regime of the colonial archive surfaces emotion only to contain it; emotions are made visible even as their full expression is constrained and limited. The archive's power, then, resides in its capacity to police and patrol the boundaries of emotion and reduce human suffering to so many marks captured on a page. One of the most potent modes of reading against the grain, of subverting the effacing power of the archive, might be to enter the colonial archive armed with affective approaches to reading and narrating history. Rather than accepting that the archive is empty of affect, what if we allowed emotion, our own and that of historical others—others whose feelings haunt us even from the distant past—to penetrate our sources and ourselves? This hermeneutic is especially pressing when we realize that sometimes affects are the "cloud of ink" that echoes the hyperobject's very absence.

Rereading the colonial archive through the lens of cataclysm, emotion is evidence of the collateral violence of colonial rule. Morton explains that the hyperobject is knowable (or I could say, historically accessible) via the feelings that it evokes; for example, by the affects that emerge around "climate change" (which Morton calls a failed term) or "global warming." It is precisely through affects and senses that the *mortandad* leaves its trace in the historical record.

Filled with pathos and sentiment, the written testimonies of Spanish missionaries document their encounters with the *mortandad*. Their emotions rebounded and resounded off this hyperobject. Grief and dismay, despair and dread: these religious feelings flood the documentary record. Mexico City had become a valley of tears, "un valle de lágrimas." Missionaries recoiled at the empty desolation of the landscape of the *mortandad*, a *horror vacui*: dread at the vacant canvas of Mexico. These are telluric affects, emotions born of place: cloaked and communicated in the earthy, tectonic language of space and scape. The Franciscan friar Pedro de Oroz, an eyewitness to *cocoliztli*, remembered:

> This land that was once to be the foundation of Christianity, the patrimony for which Christ put himself on the cross, is now in the hands of the enemy that seeks to destroy all of the children [the *Indios*] of this mother, the Church. The church watches, wakefully,

417

to find some remedy, some cure to these great many miseries and calamities. One thing related to this, please forgive how I say it with pain and feeling, the *Indio* vassals of your majesty suffer great miseries of *mortandad* and hunger.[9]

In other colonial contexts, emotions such as those that surface here have been identified as colonialist lament for colonial destruction. Unexpected emotions leveraged as regimes of affect contributed to the complicated, multifaceted work of colonial rule.

Recalling the epidemic, the Jesuit Juan Sánchez Baquero found recourse in the language of Jeremiah's biblical lamentation. He offered another powerful pairing of lament and land to articulate the destruction of the *mortandad*:

> And after that it never completely ceased, it never stopped taking lives here and there, now in these towns, now in those. In this way it could be said that which Jeremiah lamented so deeply for a single city applied to an entire land, how lonely the city stands [*quo modo sedet sola civitas plena populo*]. Because according to the great number of people and the populated areas that were contiguous, Mexico [once] seemed as if it were truly a single city rather than many, and today it is alone and finished.
>
> (Sánchez Baquero [1571–1580] 1945: 89)

Preserving the power of the Latin phrase, Sánchez Baquero echoes Jeremiah's despondent cry, "How doth the city sit solitary, that was full of people! How is she become as a widow! She that was great among the nations, and princess among the provinces" (Lamentations 1:1). Fragmented by the *mortandad*, Mexico suffered a terrible and final blow. Desolated by *cocoliztli*, the land was widowed, lonely, abandoned. For both colonial observers, lament is related to their perception of end times. The epidemic leaves its traces in the affective response of these missionaries: "There is an essence, and it's right here, in the object resplendent with its sensual qualities yet withdrawn" (Morton 2013: 158).

We can understand, then, that the imperial project is an affective labor. The emotions elicited in the *mortandad* make clear the "affective dimensions of the regimes of social maintenance" (Madra). Catholicism transformed into a colonial institution driven by new theologies and affects directed toward the absence of the bodies of the Indigenous people who died in the *mortandad*. Most pronounced among these were feelings of grief and despair over the deterioration and disappearance of those bodies amid a ruined landscape. It is important to remember that these emotions, these epic-in-scale affects, refer to a conglomeration of individual, specific encounters with persons and communities. Even more urgently, the lives of those who died from *cocoliztli* were never encompassed within nor defined by the emotional worlds of Spanish observers, no matter how heartfelt, wrenching those Spanish reports were. The *mortandad* reoriented and restructured Christian sentiment, generating particular affective attachments both to the people known as *Indios* and to their territories. This affective labor coupled and conjoined colonial people—subjects—to the religious and political infrastructures that sustained the colony, another hyperobject itself.

American Necropolis: Hyperobject Conclusions

Las Américas are built on a vast necropolis, over the mortal remains of those who died in the colonial *mortandad*. As hyperobject, the mortandad, these long-ago deaths, continues to shape our current socio-political settlements, even as they push against the limits of collective memory and remembrance. There appears to be little to aid us in our recollection—no national rituals or rites inspired by material memory, no commemorations of memory sites. With respect to man-made mass death in the sixteenth through eighteenth centuries, archeologists have been slow to identify and excavate sites of cataclysm, violence, and collapse in Latin America, with few exceptions. If we are haunted by the material presence of the dead, we are also haunted by their absence. In reflecting on the *mortandad* as hyperobject, the dead are brought to the surface, "to the notice of the living" (Laqueur 2015: 32), so that aggrieved ancestors from the long past might speak to us more clearly across the centuries.

Notes

1 Here, I revisit data presented in my book, *The Church of the Dead: The Epidemic of 1576 and the Birth of Christianity in the Americas*. Some sections of interpretation from the book reappear here as well. However, the application of the analytic of hyperobjects is original to this essay.
2 https://www.ucl.ac.uk/news/2019/feb/great-dying-americas-disturbed-earths-climate
3 This translation of the Nahuatl is from, López Austin, "Los caminos de los muertos," 142. López Austin is analyzing material from the appendix of book 3 of Sahagún's treatise. The original Nahuatl can be found there. Note that in the original, Sahagun translates cocoliztli with the non-specific "enfermedad" and translates "*mictlán*" as "*infierno*." The original document folio is available here: https://www.loc.gov/resource/gdcwdl.wdl_10614/?sp=48&st=image
4 *Cocoliztli* appears alongside the publication of *Interior Castle*, a guide to prayer written by the Spanish mystic St. Teresa of Ávila, and the brief arrival and immediate departure of a group of discalced friars on their way to China.
5 For my study of Sahagún's opus, I use the digitized version of the original manuscript volumes provided by the Biblioteca Medicea Laurenziana Library, Florence, Italy, and made available via the World Digital Library: www.wdl.org. "General History of the Things of New Spain by Fray Bernardino de Sahagún," book 11, folios 237r–239v.
6 Letter from viceroy Martínez, AGI, México, 20, n.1, Item 11, 19 de octubre de 1577.
7 Letter from bishop Juan de Medina Rincón, AGI, México 374, Cartas y expedientes de Michoacán 1561–1700, 23 de febrero de 1578.
8 Emphasis mine. Letter from Fray Juan de Medina Rincón, AGI, México 374, Cartas y expedientes de Michoacán 1561–1700, 8 de marzo de 1581. "Ban se acabando con prisa porque en todas partes enferman muchos y mueren mas q los ordinarios/nunca çesa una lenta y disimulada pestilencia."
9 Letter from Fray Pedro de Oroz to the King, AGI, México 283, Cartas y expedientes de personas eclesiásticas 1575–77, noviembre de 1576.

References

Chimalpahin Cuauhtlehuanitzin, Domingo Francisco de San Antón Muñón. [1615] 2006. *Annals of His Time: Don Domingo de San Antón Muñón Chimalpahin Quauhtlehuanitzin*. Edited by James Lockhart, Susan Schroeder, and Doris Namala. Stanford, CA: Stanford University Press.

Corteguera, Luis R. 2012. *Death by Effigy: A Case from the Mexican Inquisition*. Philadelphia, PA: University of Pennsylvania Press.

Dávila Padilla, Agustín. 1625. *Historia de la fvndación y discurso de la provincia, de Santiago de México, de la Orden de Predicadores por las vidas de sus varones insignes y casos notables de Nueva España*. Brussels: Luan de Meerbeque.

Hughes, Jennifer Scheper. 2010. *Biography of a Mexican Crucifix: Lived Religion and Local Faith from the Conquest to the Present*. Oxford: Oxford University Press.

Hughes, Jennifer Scheper. 2012a. "The Nino Jesús Doctor: Novelty and Innovation in Mexican Religion." *Nova Religio: The Journal of Alternative and Emergent Religions* 16 (2): 4–28.

Hughes, Jennifer Scheper. 2012b. "Mysterium materiae: Vital Matter and the Object as Evidence in the Study of Religion." *Bulletin for the Study of Religion* 41 (4): 16–24.

Hughes, Jennifer Scheper. 2016. "Cradling the Sacred: Image, Ritual, and Affect in Mexican and Mesoamerican Material Religion." *History of Religions* 56 (1): 55–107.

Hughes, Jennifer Scheper. 2020. "The Colony as the Mystical Body of Christ: Theopolitical Embodiment in Mexico." *Social Analysis* 64 (4): 21–41.

Hughes, Jennifer Scheper. 2021. *The Church of the Dead: The Epidemic of 1576 and the Birth of Christianity in the Americas*. New York: New York University Press.

Koch, Alexander, Chris Brierley, Mark M. Maslin, Simon L. Lewis. 2019. "Earth System Impacts of the European Arrival and Great Dying in the Americas After 1492." *Quaternary Science Reviews* 207: 13–36.

Laqueur, Thomas Walter. 2015. *The Work of the Dead: A Cultural History of Mortal Remains*. Princeton, NJ: Princeton University Press.

Lewis, Simon L., and Mark A. Maslin. 2015. "Defining the Anthropocene." *Nature* 519: 171–180.

Madra, Yahya M. "Affective Economies of Capitalism: Shifting the Focus of the Psychoanalytical. Debate." *Surplus Thought* (blog). http://www.surplusthought.net/ymadra/affective.pdf, accessed November 18, 2022.

Morton, Timothy. 2013. *Hyperobjects: Philosophy and Ecology after the End of the World*. Minneapolis, MN: University of Minnesota Press.

Phelan, John L. 1970. *The Millennial Kingdom of the Franciscans in the New World*. Berkeley, CA: University of California Press.

Sánchez Baquero, Juan. [1571–1580] 1945. *Fundación de la Compañia de Jesús en Nueva España*. Mexico City: Editorial Patria.

Tracy, David. 1981. "The analogical imagination." *Religious Studies* 19 (4): 552–553.

Vågene, Åshild J., Alexander Herbig, Michael G. Campana, Nelly M. Robles García, Christina Warinner, Susanna Sabin, Maria A. Spyrou et al. 2018. "Salmonella Enterica Genomes from Victims of a Major Sixteenth-Century Epidemic in Mexico." *Nature Ecology & Evolution* 2 (3): 520–528.

4.5

VIRUS AS HYPEROBJECT

Early Atlantic World Jews and Yellow Fever Epidemics

Laura Arnold Leibman

When the dreaded yellow fever epidemic of 1822 finally passed, religious leaders around New York paused to both write down their gratitude for deliverance and dole out the blame for lives lost. Death has long been the domain of religion, and demise by yellow fever was no exception. When facing death, humans grapple with the meaning of life, revealing "what we value most" (Garces-Foley 2006: ix). Yet scholarly discussions of epidemics in early America have generally downplayed the role of religion, except when discussing inoculation controversies (Minardi 2004; Finger 2012). In this chapter, I use a variety of print, archival, and material sources from New York's 1822 yellow fever epidemic to show how this oversight is a mistake. Religion tinged people's view of the disease, and the disease reshaped local Jewish practice.

My analysis draws on Timothy Morton's discussion of hyperobjects: entities such as global warming, nuclear materials, natural disasters, and even plastic bags that tend to be nonlocal, viscous, and bond breaking (Morton 2017). Massively distributed through time and space, yellow fever wore down interfaith alliances, ruptured local Jewish practice, and transformed the Jewish liturgical calendar's season of hope into a season of despair. The hyperobject model illuminates why viruses fragmented New York's Jewish community. Traditionally, scholars have argued that periods of cultural stress culminate in productive religious awakenings (McLoughlin 2013). Temporally, hyperobjects refuse to conform to our expectations about the "natural" lifetime we expect from physical things, thereby muddying the boundary between the mortal (material) and immortal (immaterial) realms. Hyperobjects produce cultural stress: their vast size causes a "quake in being" (Mentz 2015: 31). Yet, rather than being clearly productive, hyperobjects "reveal human hypocrisy, lameness, and weakness" (Mentz 2015: 31). While these qualities can awaken religious sentiments, they also force people to question whether the future will bring destruction or transformation. A hyperobject model of religious change reveals how pandemics differ from other kinds of social stress.

Using hyperobject theory to analyze yellow fever underscores why large-scale environmental issues impact American religions differently. Not enough has been said about how yellow fever, typhoid, and cholera fed the Second Great Awakening (Jortner 2007; Whooley 2013; Heinrichs 2017). Considering how the 1822 pandemic affected Jews illuminates why religious responses to disease vary. As Kathryn Long notes, "each of the various revival traditions in North America maintained an internal rhythm shaped by its own characteristic

DOI: 10.4324/9781351176231-34

religious rituals" (Long 1998: 50). The "internal rhythm" of the Jewish ritual calendar heightened Jewish despair. Yet, Jewish responses were not formulated in isolation: Protestant antisemitism exacerbated Jewish anguish.

I explain the challenge of yellow fever to early American Judaism in four sections. In the first, I set the stage by examining how Jews became entangled with the 1822 epidemic. In the second, I examine how Protestant New Yorkers used antisemitism to master yellow fever. In the third, I look at how antisemitism and the virus fractured New York's Jewish community. In the concluding section, I address how Morton's theory elucidates religion's ensnarement with disease.

Setting the Stage

They thought they had the virus contained. Yellow fever struck terror everywhere it landed, and between June 25 and July 1, 1822, it landed in lower Manhattan. Four boats freighting sugar arrived from Havana with an infected crew. The city was prepared. Though the ships had sneaked past Staten Island's quarantine zone, when they arrived at the city's docks they were immediately sequestered. Only sailors with proven immunity left the boats to unload the sweet cargo. City officials also cautiously quarantined the sugar in warehouses along Rector Street wharf. The sugar boxes, they explained, were made of rough pine, which presented "an exterior surface of porous or bibulous natures . . . for which the contagious poison of yellow fever is known to have so strong an affinity" (Townsend 1823: 23–25).

Their precautions proved useless. By July 10, the fever had escaped: unlike pine boxes, local mosquitos easily flew among the ships, businesses, and homes along the wharves. The fever began its work where Rector and Washington Streets intersected the piers (Townsend 1823). For a couple of weeks, denial reigned. Then despair spread across the town. The symptoms left little doubt: first, the victims' skin took on a yellow cast. Then, blood seeped from their faces. Finally, seizures set in (Figure 4.5.1). Death grasped over half of infected New Yorkers. Many of those who did not die wished they had (Townsend 1823; Geggus 1979; Leibman 2021).

For New York's Jews, the disease held specific challenges. You would think few Jews would have been caught unprepared: newspapers such as the *New-York Gazette, New-York Daily Advertiser,* and the *Evening Post* all covered the pandemic's Atlantic journey. But two New York Jews would later receive specific ire for withholding "intelligence" about the disease. Previous evacuations had caused economic woes, and few wanted to risk unnecessary disruption (Townsend 1823: 77). Yet when the attending doctor told the mayor, the

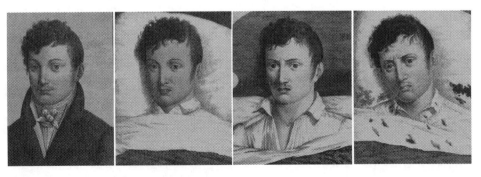

Figure 4.5.1 Four illustrations show the Progress of Yellow Fever. *Observations sur la fièvre jaune, faites à Cadix.* Paris: Etienne Pariset and André Mazet, 1820. National Library of Medicine.

board of health, and "Messrs. Phillips and Noah, the editors of the National Advocate," that these were "unequivocal cases of yellow fever," all the men expressed doubt. Consequently, the city lost crucial days in containing the epidemic (Townsend 1823: 27, 32). Phillips and Noah—the only men blamed by name in the report—were Jews.

When Peter Townsend wrote up his *Account of the Yellow Fever*, he did not state outright that Phillips and Noah were Jewish, because he did not have to. Naphtali Phillips was the *parnas* (president) of the city's sole synagogue. His religion was common knowledge. When Phillips became the vice president of New York's Democratic-Republican Society in 1795, his opponents slandered him for being from the "tribe of Shylock" (Rock 2015: 109; Eisenstadt 2005: 92). Likewise, Mordecai Manuel Noah was "easily the most prominent and influential Jew in the United States" and the first public figure "to demand continuous recognition as both a devoted American and a devoted Jew" (Sarna 1980: 159; Weingrad 2007: 75). Throughout the 1820s, antisemites repeatedly attacked Noah (Figure 4.5.2). Noah and Phillips were so visibly Jewish that critics mocked the *National Advocate* as a "kasher [kosher] newspaper" (Marcus 1975: 50).

Less prominent Jews also became entangled with the disease's spread. Jews lived, worked, and prayed in the area hardest hit. On August 5, death knocked on Naphtali Phillip's door.

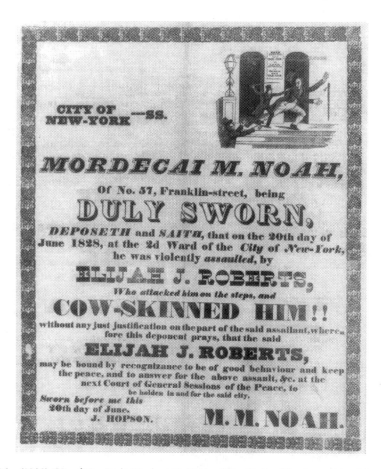

Figure 4.5.2 (1828) *City of New York. Mordecai M. Noah, of No. 57, Franklin-Street, being duly sworn.* New York City, 1828. [Woodcut]. Courtesy the Library of Congress, LC-USZ62–40912.

His wife, Rachel Hannah Seixas Phillips, was one of 1822's first fever victims ("Mortuary Notice," 1822).

Likewise, the virus crisscrossed the Hebrew calendar in troubling ways. The four infected ships were quarantined during the Three Weeks, a traditional period of mourning. This tribulation culminates with Tisha B'Av—the day when the Temple fell and Jews were exiled—after which traditionally begins a period of consolation. Yet in 1822, like other years when the virus fell upon New York, Tisha B'Av passed without any release. The following month (Elul) typically overflowed with rituals of return, but instead terror reigned. Tishrei, the month when God restored his covenant, found Jews still exiled (Townsend 1823).

Jews who lived through the 1792, 1793, 1795, 1796, 1799, 1803, and 1819 epidemics found the reworked calendar painfully familiar. Yellow fever *always* hit New York in the summer, and never left until the first frost, typically at least a month after the High Holidays ended. Thus, the virus consistently turned the Jewish ritual program on its head. Yellow fever had mutated the community's sense of end-times: apocalyptic upheaval returned at irregular intervals but never culminated in redemption. Protestant attempts to cast Jews out of local community-building deepened this trauma. I begin, then, by looking at how white, Protestant writers deflected concerns about the disease on to Jews.

Jews and the Yellow Fever through Non-Jewish Eyes

Though Yellow fever's global migrations also threatened white Protestant New Yorkers, those New Yorkers resolved much of the shock by spotlighting Jewish culpability. Yellow fever undercut the status of the United States as a redeemer nation by suggesting the nation had spiritual work left to do. The question remained: Whose work was it (Tuveson 1968)? Ultimately white Protestant New Yorkers turned their fevered gaze to Jews, offering them up as scapegoat. Jews became entangled with the virus until Jews themselves seemed to be hyperobjects. Jews as much as fevers became a pox on the city.

Ironically, "Old Testamentism" bolstered the white Protestant position. As Eran Shalev has noted, the story of Exodus "functioned as a towering narrative and trope, fundamental in shaping the form and content of early American biblicalism" (Shalev 2013: 6, 10). Old Testamentism depicted the United States as a place of salvation—though others had objected to this story. For example, African Americans, when invoking Exodus, depicted America as Egypt, not Israel (Glaude 2000). Yellow fever also threated the myth of the United States as a "promised land," since the disease's repeated visitations "served as final proof to the defenders of the faith that divine wrath had at last taken notice of the great apostasy in America" (Khalaf 2012: 24). Yet who were these apostates, and what had they done? While, in 1799, Jews and Protestants had united in interfaith thanksgiving ("Sermons by Gershom Mendes Seixas," 1799), by 1822, white Protestants scapegoated Jews.

Morton's attention to the nonlocal illuminates why yellow fever threatened white Protestants' redemption narrative and why Protestants blamed Jews. Like other hyperobjects, yellow fever reflected humans' rise as a global, geophysical force. The same doomed ships used in the triangle trade carried fever-laden mosquitoes to the Americas. Global trade networks kept the virus in circulation. Outbreaks in Spain and Gibraltar were soon transferred to Spanish Havana, and then on to New York. Equally crucial, yellow fever ravaged time: it materialized, left, then randomly reappeared.

Yellow fever's nonlocal attributes highlight why it disrupted religion's spatiotemporal cosmology. Apocalypticism relies on global thinking, but redemption insists that local events are meaningful. Hyperobjects, however, "evaporate" the local (Morton 2017: 54). Yellow fever reminded New Yorkers that "there is no such thing, at a deep level, *as* the local" (Morton 2017: 47, emphasis added). Disintegrating relations between the local and the cosmos undercut local efficacy. In some years the disease appeared in the city, regardless of safeguards; other years it stayed away. Time no longer seemed to linearly progress toward a telos. The calendar's predictable cycles dissolved: when the virus reappeared, time folded back upon itself, rupturing a providential sense of the cosmos.

New Yorkers questioned whom to blame for the cosmic wrenching. White abuse of Blacks could easily explain God's wrath. After all, though in 1822 New York State condemned slavery, it still practiced it. Moreover, white writers understood yellow fever's tie to the slave trade. Some also noticed Blacks' greater immunity to the virus (Bancroft 1811; Johnson 1824). Long after abolition, the idea that yellow fever was a "righteous punishment" for slavery *did* occur to both British and American writers (Senior 2018: 196). Yet, I have found no instances of this idea in white Protestant New Yorkers' discussion of yellow fever from the 1820s. Instead, by 1822, white Protestants indicted Jews.

Jews—Protestants argued—were partially to blame for the chaos of 1822. Like many divisive stereotypes, there was a sliver of truth to this. To a certain extent, early critics *were* correct that the Jewish press had delayed suggesting evacuation. On August 2, Phillips and Noah still touted the Board of Health's line that "nothing . . . can justify any alarm, or create any apprehension that the disease . . . will spread" ("Public Health" 1822). By August 10, however, the *National Advocate* changed its tune, reporting that "the inhabitants should remove forthwith and all intercourse cease" with the infected district ("Public Health" 1822). The alarm now rung, twenty thousand New Yorkers evacuated the city in four short days (Duffy 1974).

Maps of lower Manhattan had long featured Jewish locales, but New Yorkers mapped the "city in exile" as Christian space. The northern exodus's size forced the city to issue an emergency map of the exiled banks, Custom House, Post Office, Merchants Exchange, Dutch Church, Episcopal Church Yard, and coffee houses in Greenwich Village (Stout 1822). Although, starting in 1730, New York maps typically featured the Mill Street Synagogue, and even included drawings of the building (Cohen and Augustyn 2014), no synagogue lay on the Greenwich map.

In part, the missing synagogue reflected how the evacuation fractured the Jewish community. Some Jews relocated southeast, renting an apartment for a "temporary Shule" across from the Chatham Street cemetery. Other wealthier congregants prayed in a minyan at Isaac Moses's Mount Listen estate, just north of Greenwich Village ("Items Relating" 1920; De Sola Pool 1953). Equally important to understanding Jews' absence in the Greenwich map, however, is how Christian New Yorkers imagined Jews as being "stuck" to the fever. As Morton notes, hyperobjects are sticky (Morton 2017). But for Jews, their involvement was largely metaphorical. Through metaphor, individual Jews lost their local meaning, becoming Jews writ large. Protestant print media helped to adhere Jews to the virus.

As early as 1814, the Wandering Jew and yellow fever appeared side-by-side in Atlantic World newspapers (Morton 2017). By the 1850s, the association was so normal that the *New York Medical Gazette and Journal of Health* warned that "contagionists" in the medical profession had "indoctrinated multitudes of our population into the belief that Yellow Fever . . . 'travels' north by land and sea, like the Wandering Jew" ("Yellow Fever" 1856: 366). Medieval Christians invented the Wandering Jew, citing John 21: 22–23 (Edelmann 1965). Reportedly cursed by Christ during the Crucifixion for having scorned him, the Wandering Jew was doomed to circumambulate the globe until the second coming (Andrews 1957). Longevity was as crucial to the Jew's punishment as diasporic movement was (Edelmann

1965). An early hyperobject, Wandering Jews violated norms of space and time. Their sinful rejection of Christ made them a pollutant, cast out from Christian society everywhere they landed.

Moral pollution was often associated with disease; thus, from the medieval era onward, Jews were seen as carriers of epidemics—whether the plague, tuberculosis, cholera, or, in this case, yellow fever. As Susan Sontag notes:

> Any important disease whose causality is murky, and for which treatment is ineffectual tends to be awash in significance. First, the subjects of deepest dread (corruption, decay, pollution, anomie, weakness) are identified with the disease. The disease itself becomes a metaphor.
>
> *(Sontag 1978: 58)*

This metaphor is then placed on other items, such as Jews. Like many metaphors that rely on emotions, Jews' connection to yellow fever proved remarkably sticky (Percy et al. 2011). Between 1764 and 1820, the Wandering Jew haunted gothic literature and took on vampiric associations. So did yellow fever—that "yellow-fanged monster" (Senior 2018: 122–123). Like the vampire, the Wandering Jew was both mortal and immortal, demonically spreading death though never dying (Davison 2004). While some writers in the long eighteenth century claimed to have met the Wandering Jew, the itinerant Israelite was generally understood not as "an individual person, but rather as the entire Jewish people, who had been dispersed and were wandering all over the world . . . to remain alive until the End of Days" (Baron 1952: 374; Andrews 1957). The virus's victim's yellowed skin merged in the Christian imagination with the vampire's undead skin, and the diseased, "black-yellow skin" of the Jew (Pellegrini 1997: 21; Gilman 2003: 141).

Townsend wrote his 1822 yellow fever report in this context. In it, Townsend ponders whether Jewish "habits and mode of life" predisposed Jews to yellow fever (Townsend 1823: 231). In the end, he decided Jews' religious practices condemned them and, consequently, their neighbors. As proof, Townsend turned to Sir James Fellowes's study from Gibraltar. Fellowes noted that Gibraltar's Jews "were not generally attacked by the prevailing disorder, until after the eighteenth of September, the day of atonement, on which the Hebrew nation meet together in the synagogues." For Fellowes the holiday, like the "Feast of Tabernacles" (Succot), created problems because

> it is customary at this time for the friends and acquaintance[s] to meet at each other's houses and to enter the synagogue. . . . This assemblage of the Jews, and the communication which followed evidently facilitated the propagation of the malady, and afterwards occasioned such a mortality, that between seven and eight hundred fell victim to its fury.
>
> *(Townsend 1823: 231–232)*

Jewish ritual incited cosmic punishment.

Early Protestant ministers in New York spun the same "data" differently. Jews were once again singled out when ministers looked for causes of the pandemic, but now moral failings rather than ritual alone were behind the spread. Paschal Strong of the Reformed Dutch Church in New York, for example, spoke about how "the nation of Jews" were "living witnesses," and how God would heap "vengeance" upon those who were disobedient (Strong 1823: 4). Strong felt his job was not to speak of "smooth things" but rather "to declare unto . . .

Israel his sin" (Strong 1823: 5). The new emphasis on "hard truths" suggests some of the problems that Christian ministers faced as the epidemics continued to rock the upper Atlantic coast. Methodist Francis Asbury, for example, who kept a preaching journal during the early yellow fever epidemics, also found himself having to change tactics when yellow fever kept reappearing. During the 1793 epidemic, Asbury had been hopeful (Ashbury 1821: I.176); yet the next year, Ashbury's trust wavered, as he became anxious that ships coming from the West Indies would once again spread the disease north (Ashbury 1821: I.203). By September 1796, most of Ashbury's audience stayed away out of fear (Ashbury 1821: I.1:265, III.174). Seen through the lens of the hyperobject, the nonlocal aspect of the epidemic had worn down Protestants' hope, breaking the bonds of early interfaith alliances.

In terms of preaching genres, yellow fever shifted Protestant rhetoric out of the sphere of jeremiads (which encouraged congregants to look inward and repent) and into the language of execution sermons (in which sins are heaped on the dead, who are then cast out). By the 1820s, white Protestants blamed yellow fever on weak bodies, which they conflated with loose morals. As Townsend explains, "the indulgence of the venereal appetite . . . and the state of pregnancy in women, strongly predispose the system to be acted upon by the contagion of yellow fever" (Townsend 1823: 238). Weak bodies contaminated the body politic, dragging everyone into the mire. Like many contemporaries, Townsend believed miasma and effluvia were "powerful conductors and contagion of yellow fever" (Townsend 1823: 231). Like miasma, effluvia was an invisible, disgusting stench. Yet while miasma came from contaminated water and decaying animals and plants (Townsend 1823), effluvia came from human bodies—more particularly the wrong kind of bodies ("Effluvium"). The inability to get far enough away from those bodies exacerbated the problem. As Townsend notes, "the contagious matter must be accumulated to a certain amount, and circumscribed to a confined and crowded neighborhood, the atmosphere of which is more or less charged with human effluvia" (Townsend 1823: 231). In the short term, retreat was necessary; but in the longer term, Protestant New Yorkers would seek to limit contact with the dead and "undesirables" in the city center.

Protestant New Yorkers blamed Jews for the city's excessive effluvia. Historians had long noted that Jews in antiquity did not embalm. Thus, dead Jews were more likely to produce effluvia (Pascalis Ouviere et al. 1823: 18–19). Scottish theologian Adam Clarke singled out modern Jews for their healthy attempts to protect themselves and others from this effluvia by burying their dead at a distance (Holy Bible 1817), but changes in New York's demographics brought the Jewish dead closer. As the 1822 epidemic drew to a close, Jewish funerary rites came under attack. By 1825–1826, the city closed cemeteries in lower Manhattan from fear of effluvia. Effluvia haunted Jews even after their dying breaths. The impact of this metaphoric thinking would weigh heavily on New York's Jewish community as they struggled with the epidemic.

In sum, white Protestants dealt with the cosmic threat of yellow fever by scapegoating a small portion of the city's population. This strategy was not new. As Thelma Lewis Foote notes, white New Yorkers had similarly blamed Black New Yorkers for the "desecration of the pure body politic" during Independence Day festivities. Black New Yorkers were also blamed by the city for excessive effluvia. In 1807, for example, the all-white Common Council closed African Zion Methodist Episcopalian Church's vaults. Blacks were required to bury their dead in the Potter's Field, among "strangers" and yellow fever victims (Folpe 2002: 56–57; Hartog 2018: 71–72). This mandate suggests the council correlated Black bodies, outsiderness, yellow fever, and effluvia. Yet whereas Black New Yorkers responded to discrimination by drawing together (Foote 2004), the city's Jews splintered into divisive subgroups.

Jewish Response to Yellow Fever

The 1820s divided Jewish New Yorkers like no previous decade had. Jews had responded to prior yellow fever epidemics in New York by refastening ties, but by 1822, disagreement regarding the virus reigned: one camp fled in terror, while the other turned to mysticism. By 1824, the mystics irrevocably left to form the city's second synagogue, B'nai Jeshurun. I am hardly the first scholar to notice the fractures that wretched Jewish New York apart in the 1820s (Gurock 2014; Rock 2015). Yet, while previous historians have blamed an Ashkenazi influx and "Jeffersonian republicanism" for rupturing the "homogenous synagogue community" (Gurock 2014: 41; Rock 2015: 126–129), I argue that yellow fever and the accompanying antisemitism contributed to the cleaving. Minute books, sermons, personal letters, and rituals provide evidence for my discussion of yellow fever's divisive impact on Jewish communal life.

Previous visitations of the yellow fever had hit New York Jews hard, but the 1822 epidemic fractured the community. The main places Jews worked, lived, and prayed were all at the center of the fever map. By September 1, everything below Fulton street closed (Townsend 1823). As the community fled, it splintered. Many of the old guard of Portuguese Jews escaped North, while more fervent members of the congregation moved East, praying in rented rooms near the old cemetery. The eastern group was largely Ashkenazi, but not entirely so (Wetherill 1916; Goldstein 1930; Stern 1978; Swierenga 1994). Over half of eastern minyan were recent immigrants, and at least two were known for their passionate defense of Judaism ("Israel Vindicated" 1823; Kohn 1965; Lerman 1998). When the first frost killed the mosquitoes in November, many of those who moved eastward did not return to Lower Manhattan near the synagogue. Since congregants walked to services, the eighteen sectarians argued that they needed a "new place of worship in a more convenient situation for those residing uptown" (De Sola Pool and de Sola Pool 1955: 437). By "uptown," they meant the area around the Chatham Street Cemetery, where eventually they would build congregation B'nai Jeshurun (Goldstein 1930). The two rival yellow fever minyans remapped Jewish New York.

Death preoccupied the sectarians. In 1826, before B'nai Jeshurun had even built a synagogue, the congregation bought a separate burial ground on Thirty-second Street and Seventh Avenue, near where the Mount Listen minyan had prayed (Goldstein 1930). In 1828, when Anshe Chesed splintered off of B'nai Jeshurun, they also stayed on the east side, nesting two blocks east of the Oliver Street minyan (Gurock 2003; Rock 2015). Once again, burying the dead was paramount. Rather than let their dead rest with the dead of B'nai Jeshurun, Anshe Chesed petitioned Shearith Israel to use their new burial ground in Greenwich Village (De Sola Pool 1953).

Yellow fever pierced the vision of the cosmos espoused in Jewish theology. As a nonlocal phenomenon, yellow fever reminded early Americans that humans were not the measure of time and space—but, in a way, that fact defied larger meaning rather than reinforced it. Eighteenth-century Atlantic world theologians like Moses Ḥayyim Luzzatto argued that providence and human agency drove the cosmos, connecting spiritual and physical realms. While humans could never fully grasp God's plan—as it was beyond humans' notion of time and space—God micromanaged the world's functions through an elaborate hierarchy of angels (*malachim*) and Transcendent Forces (*Kochot*). Hyperobjects like yellow fever, however, undermined providence by revealing everything as being hopelessly embedded in chaotic, random "flowing movement" (Morton 2017: 43). Yellow fever ruptured bonds between God and Jews—leading some into despondency and others into obsessive mysticism.

Yellow fever's temporal spread increased Jewish despair. Between 1792 and 1803, Shearith Israel's hazan Gershom Mendes Seixas united the community in thanksgiving; by 1822, however, the message had soured. Early on, Seixas had argued that "the many existing commotions throughout the world" signaled the "glorious restoration of Israel" was near (Kessner 1969: 467). Jews might be dispersed "outcasts," but soon they would be ingathered (Kessner 1969: 466). Likewise, Seixas emphasized that the fever revealed God's providence as well as his mercy in allowing the survivors to escape death (Kessner 1969). He also promoted community-building actions. In 1798, for example, Seixas established Kalfe Sedaka Mattan Besether to "distribute charity and 'undisclosed gifts' to Jewish epidemic victims and survivors" (Amanik 2019: 56). Likewise, in 1802 in response to yellow fever, Seixas helped restart the congregation's burial society, now called Hebra Hased Va-Emet (Kindness and Truth Society). They built a *metaher* (*tahara*) house at Chatham Square in which to properly prepare the dead (De Sola Pool and de Sola Pool 1955). Both societies used rituals to tie the dead to the living and the world-to-come. Yet, even then, cracks began to show in Seixas's upbeat message. His response to grief was dispiriting. Diseases like yellow fever, Seixas argued, resulted from sin. Moreover, he urged people not to expect God to intervene (Kessner 1969). His congregants must have felt God had abandoned them.

By 1815, Seixas was more dour. Once hopeful about the promise about Jewish delivery by the Messiah, he now confessed himself uncertain, and "disagreed with those who thought that the world was close to the last days" (Kessner 1969: 467). By July 1816, his consolations had ceased altogether, as he had died at the beginning of the year's fever season. The congregation was similarly weary. Gershom's sister Grace Seixas Nathan (1752–1831) depicts the virus's heart-wrenching impact on Jewish family life in 1805. Although evacuations saved lives, they increased Grace's anguish. Lower Manhattan, once a place of comfort, now bred sorrow. "Farewell," she proclaims, "I go—where Sickness & Death Have spread their dire influence around" (Nathan family 1805: 8–9). Loss followed Nathan's family as they fled. Watching over "her agonized child," a mother can only suppress a "heart-rending sigh"; her feelings are "so acute [they] made her wild / In madness" (Nathan family 1805: 8–9). Nathan's fears become a prayer: "Oh God!" she pleas, "may my prayer ascend / And be heard in thy Mighty Domain, / My city, oh deign to defend / Let millions not lose thee in vain" (Nathan family 1805: 9). Ambiguity mars the tidiness of the rhyme. Is the lost "thee" the city, the dead child, or both?

This poisoning of hope divided the community regarding Jewish burial practices. Because the Jewish afterlife (*olam haba*, "the world-to-come") is inherently spatiotemporal, Jewish death rites are particularly susceptible to hyperobjects. Jews had to work closely with the dying, despite "medical" concerns about effluvia, in order to transition the dead into the afterlife (de Sola Pool 1953: 125–126). When a Jew died, she was buried quickly, but not before the *hebra kadisha* had washed and prepared the *meit* (מת) for its voyage. While *meit* is sometimes translated as "corpse," this translation undercuts the *meit's* status. A corpse is the "vilest 'object' of abjection," but the *meit* "remains holy or perhaps becomes more holy than ever" (Amanik 2019: 3). The work of the burial societies—in this case Hebra Hased Va-Emet—is to connect God, the *meit*, and survivors through *tahara* (ritual purification). Transformation of the *meit* took place in the *metaher* house. There, as the members of the *hebra* washed the *meit*, they would speak to the soul who hovered nearby. During the ceremony, the leader of the burial society led the living in seven circuits (*acafoth*) around the *meit* (Emmanuel 1957). These circuits embedded the dead into the memory of the community, strengthened the *meit's* eternal bonds to God, and reinforced death as a transformation (Leibman and Goldblatt 2012). Yellow fever made these ceremonies more urgent, not less so.

Yet disputes over death rites during epidemics split the community. In 1812, Gershom Mendes Seixas, Israel Baer Kursheedt (the *mohel*), Moses L. Moses, Aaron Levy, and *National Advocate*–owner Naphtali Phillips revised Hebra Hased Va-Emet's constitution (de Sola Pool and de Sola Pool 1955). With added fines for members of the *hebra* who refused duties, the new constitution reinforced that the *hebra* needed to attend the dying and dead, perform the Tahara, and attend funerals (Congregation Shearith Israel 1812). Grace Nathan's poetry suggests fears of contagion contributed to the need of fines. Although she was well educated in religious subjects, including mystical ideas about the "Cabala" and afterlife (Nathan 1816: 2), when it came to yellow fever, Nathan deferred to science, noting the "Disease was inhaled with the breath" (Nathan 1805: 8). This "scientific" belief was problematic, as *hebras* worked closely with the dead, inhaling the effluvia-contaminated air as they sat with sick and prepared the *meit*.

Yet, while some fearfully shirked their duties, others doubled down, adding more rituals to the mix. In 1822, Kursheedt and seventeen others broke ranks and formed the Hebrew Benevolent Society Hebrah Gemilut Hesed to "aid the needy, visit the sick, help new immigrants and assist in burials" (Jackson et al. 2010). The eighteen men of the new *hebra* became charter members of B'nai Jeshurun three years later (Goldstein 1930). Usefully, they recorded what motivated the change: a more elaborate, mystical approach to death.

While the rift between B'nai Jeshurun and Shearith Israel is typically understood as one between "German and Polish" and Portuguese rites (de Sola Pool and de Sola Pool 1955), B'nai Jeshurun's minute books suggest yellow fever created a deeper theological rift that cut across these ethno-religious groups. The sectarians—those who chose to wait out the epidemic near the cemetery where they could bury the dead—had turned to mystical texts for guidance on surviving pandemics. They noted that they were particularly interested in "administering such comforts as dying persons and afflicted survivors may require in having the various duties prescribed in Sephar Hachayim properly performed" (de Sola Pool and de Sola Pool 1955: 275–277).

This work was almost certainly Prague Rabbi Ḥayyim ben Betzalel Loew's 1593 *Sefer ha-Ḥayyim*, which combined two hallmarks of Prague Judaism: attention to death rites and practical kabbalah (Katz 2000; Sherwin 1975). During the long eighteenth century, burial societies typically modeled themselves on the Eastern Sephardic-inspired *hebra kadisha* Rabbi Eliezer Aschkenazi had founded in 1564 in Prague. Aschkenazi's guidelines were then codified in the *Pinkas ha-takanot* (1692), which became the model for regulations like the 1812 New York constitution (Jacobs 2008). *Sefer ha-Ḥayyim* enhanced Aschkenazi's work by adding mystical traditions. Rabbi Ḥayyim ben Betzalel Loew and his brother the Maharal rejected Rabbi Ashkenazi's assertion that God could be understood through human reason, and instead resorted to practical kabbalah (magic) to interact with the divine (Levin 2008). It was practical kabbalah that had caused the rift in 1822 New York, not the "rational" statutes outlined in the pinkas that Rabbi Aschkenazi had inspired.

Sefer ha-Ḥayyim shows how Jews can use practical kabbalah to compensate for quotidian despair. As Gideon Aran notes, "a bad death—such as a death by terror—requires 'theodization'" (Huss et al. 2010: 400). *Sefer ha-Ḥayyim* used mysticism to address deaths during epidemics. Rabbi Loew composed the book during the bubonic plague of 1578, when he lost three members of his household while antisemitism ravaged the city (Sherwin 1975). *Sefer ha-Ḥayyim* emphasizes the effects of supernatural forces and explains how to protect those dying from demonic creatures. "Because the ill are especially susceptible," Rabbi Lowe warns, a sick person should be careful not to allow his limbs to extend outside the bed where evil spirits are lurking. Should one of his limbs be outside the bed at the moment of death, the demons would grab it, and the sick person would not go to the grave a whole man with all his limbs.

(Sherwin 1975: 47)

Amulets, Rav Ḥayyim suggests, could also keep demons at bay (Sherwin 1975).

Taken as a whole, the "duties prescribed in Sephar Hachayim properly performed" require a more mystical attention to the dying than the 1812 constitution had (Congregation Shearith Israel 1812: 12). *Sefer ha-Ḥayyim* provided solace to survivors. According to Rabbi Lowe, clues to God's providence were everywhere. By paying attention to omens and astrological data, people could glimpse how "God controls the fate of the heavenly spheres, [and] the heavenly sphere[s] have power to influence human lives and make some times more propitious than others" (Sherwin 1975: 48). The sectarians' mystical worldview belittled fears about effluvia and miasma: mysticism's hyperpowers defeated the hyperobject.

Given that all the Jews who died in the 1822 epidemic were interred in the Chatham Square cemetery, they were likely buried by the new, more mystical *hebra* that resided nearby. Shearith Israel had two northern cemeteries established in 1802 and 1805 for people who died of "Pestilential disorders" (de Sola Pool 1953: 122–124), but the 1822 dead were buried in Chatham because the newer cemeteries were in Greenwich Village, where Protestants had set up the city in exile. While a few Jews died before the August 1822 evacuation, most died after. Equally damning for those who promoted Jewish redemption was the fact that a cluster passed away around the time of the high holidays (Minutes of the Trustees 1810). Grace Nathan's husband was one of the unlucky; a month after evacuation, Simon Nathan died of yellow fever (de Sola Pool 1953). For effluvia believers, the cluster of deaths around the high holidays undoubtedly reinforced their suspicions.

When Protestants returned to Lower Manhattan, they brought back fears of contagious smells. While Chatham Square had once been surrounded by orchards, by 1822 the area was residential. The burial ground's "leakiness" had become a constant source of worry (de Sola Pool 1953). In 1805, the congregation installed spikes and a trespassing sign to warn small boys and dogs off the property, and in 1816, the city complained that the fence was "very much out of repair" (de Sola Pool 1953: 33). Neighbors, too, encroached upon the space, drying clothes in the burial ground. Miasma trespassed the fence as neighbors deposited "disagreeable filth" among the grave markers (de Sola Pool 1953: 45–49). Fence work and nearby construction caused coffins to give way, scattering the remains of the dead (de Sola Pool 1953).

By March 1823, the city had had enough. Hoping to avoid another yellow fever season, the mayor and aldermen drew a line across the city. As of June 1, no graves or vaults would be opened anywhere south of Canal Street. Any violators would be penalized $250 (Amanik 2019). Chatham Square fell well within the forbidden zone. By 1827, the ban was extended, closing Shearith Israel's Greenwich Village cemeteries (de Sola Pool 1953). The ban ruptured families, who had long fought to be buried alongside each other. Those who could, paid the fines. Others petitioned to move dead kin so eventually they might "rest side by side" (de Sola Pool 1953: 85, 127). Such measures were often temporary. When she died in 1831, Grace Seixas Nathan's son paid the fine to bury Grace next to Simon. Twenty-five years later, roadwork forced Grace's remains to be moved the congregation's newest cemetery in Queens (de Sola Pool 1953).

The epidemic's chaos and Chatham Square's uncertainty meant the 1822 fever victims went largely uncommemorated. Earlier Jewish yellow fever victims received elaborate and optimistic tombstones (de Sola Pool 1953; Leibman 2020), but Simon Nathan received a "bare bones" epitaph that has since disappeared. Naphtali Phillips's wife's grave has no marker, nor does that of 1822 victim Esther Gomez. The paltry memorialization reflects the congregation's disarray in 1822–23 ("Minutes of the Trustees" 1810). The inability to process death during pandemics is not unique. As Kathryn Lofton has so eloquently written, epidemics overturn normal rites surrounding loss, signaling "when we can't handle speaking aloud the society that made this loss on this scale" (Lofton 2020). By 1822, repeated loss wore the Jewish community down, fragmenting the "homogenous synagogue community" into two distinct groups characterized by scientific dread on one side, and radical mysticism on the other.

Conclusion

Applying Morton's theory to New York's 1822 yellow fever epidemic underscores the intertwining of diseases and material religion. Religion was a lens through which city dwellers viewed both the virus and each other. Nineteenth-century white Protestants entwined yellow fever and Jews. By displacing their fears on to Jews, white Protestants could shrug off the virus's tendency to "reveal human hypocrisy, lameness, and weakness" (Mentz 2015: 31). White Protestants deemed Jews weak, and thrust them to the body politic's margins, alongside other disenfranchised New Yorkers.

This displacement meant that Jewish New Yorkers suffered from antisemitism alongside yellow fever and theological turmoil. Yellow fever's unrelenting visits eventually splintered the Jewish community of New York. One side ingested fears about contamination from the dead; the other side used mysticism to argue for increased interactions with the dying. In the years that followed, this split permanently fractured the city's small Jewish community, becoming the basis of a new synagogue that followed a new religious rite. The 1822 dispute forever remapped Jewish New York.

Pandemics, like other hyperobjects, can threaten providential views of the universe. How religious groups respond to that threat, however, varies based on a variety of factors, including rituals, theology, and relations to power. During the yellow fever epidemic of 1822, we see three different responses to hyperobjects' religious threat: (1) a shifting of the chaos on to the bodies of "others" (such as Jews and Blacks), (2) a retreat into medical theories and despair, and (3) mysticism that endowed rituals with hyperpowers. A similar pattern emerged in the COVID-19 epidemic of 2020–21. As COVID-19 spread in the summer of 2020, so did antisemitic and racist tropes associated with the virus. The tendency for those in power to shift hyperobjects' chaos on to the bodies of "others" emphasizes how the police brutality of the summer of 2020 was part of a pattern of response to epidemics, and magnifies why rejecting attempts to displace chaos on to racial and ethnic others is crucial to group survival.

The divide between medicine and mysticism continues to beleaguer Jewish responses to pandemics. Although science's understanding of contagion has changed since 1822, in 2020 *hebra kadishas* tackled the same question: Should one place one's trust in God or science? In 2020, *hebra kadishas* debated whether personal protective equipment (NASCK) was necessary, as well as who would provide it. Was it halachically acceptable to modify the *tahara* procedure to protect *hebra* members ("Coronavirus and Jewish Death Practices" n.d.)? Radical mysticism likewise flourished in the recent pandemic. *Sefer ha-Ḥayyim* made a small comeback (Katz 2000), and new voices emerged. Kabbalist Joel Bakst of the "City of Luz," for example, spread his message about the COVID-19's "Messiah Code" via social media (Figure 4.5.3). Bakst has a small but growing group of followers, and plans to publish his

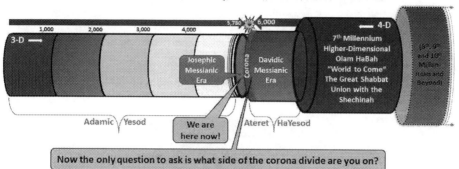

The Messiah Code of the Corona Virus
(According to the Gaon of Vilna and *Leshem Shevo VeAchlamah*)

Adamic Yesod Timeline of the Josephic and Davidic Messianic Eras

Figure 4.5.3 Joel Bakst (2020). 7 April. The Messiah Code of the Corona Virus. https://www.face-book.com/107446807549469/photos/a.112880327006117/125825892378227/

message regarding "The Cosmic Virus" in book form. Bakst's messages and "good news" may appear fanciful to the uninitiated, but time will tell. Perhaps several hundred years from now, Bakst's book will lead a new revival against the latest plague.

References

Amanik, A. M. 2019. *Dust to Dust: a History of Jewish Death and Burial in New York*. New York: New York University Press.

Andrews, S. G. 1957. "The Wandering Jew and the Travels and Adventures of James Massey." *Modern Language Notes* 72 (1): 39–41.

Bancroft, E. N. 1811. *An Essay on the Disease Called Yellow Fever, with Observations Concerning Febrile Contagion, Typhus Fever, Dysentery, and the Plague, Partly Delivered as the Gulstonian Lectures, before the College of Physicians, in the Years 1806 and 1807*. London: T. Cadell and W. Davies.

Baron, S. W. 1952. *A Social and Religious History of the Jews*. 2d ed. New York: Columbia University Press.

Cohen, P. E., and R. T. Augustyn. 2014. *Manhattan in Maps: 1527–2014*. New York: Dover.

Congregation Shearith Israel 1812. "Second Constitution of the Hebra Hased Va Amet, 1812." Box: 2, Folder: 2. American Jewish Historical Society. Center for Jewish History. https://archives.cjh.org/repositories/3/archival_objects/580689.

Davison, C. M. 2004. *Anti-Semitism and British Gothic Literature*. New York: Palgrave Macmillan.

De Sola Pool, D. 1953. *Portraits Etched in Stone. Early Jewish Settlers, 1682–1831*. New York: Columbia University Press.

De Sola Pool, D., and T. de Sola Pool. 1955. *An Old Faith in the New World; Portrait of Shearith Israel, 1654–1954*. New York: Columbia University Press.

Duffy, J. 1974. "Nineteenth Century Public Health in New York and New Orleans: A Comparison." *Louisiana History: The Journal of the Louisiana Historical Association* 15 (4): 325–337.

Edelmann, R. 1965. "Ahasuerus, the Wandering Jew: Origin and Background." *Proceedings of the World Congress of Jewish Studies* 4: 111–114.

Eisenstadt, P. R., 2005. *The Encyclopedia of New York State*. Syracuse, NY: Syracuse University Press.

Emmanuel, I. S. 1957. *Precious Stones of the Jews of Curaçao: Curaçaon Jewry: 1656–19*. New York: Bloch.

Finger, S. 2012. *The Contagious City: The Politics of Public Health in Early Philadelphia*. Ithaca, NY, and London: Cornell University Press.

Folpe, E. K. 2002. *It Happened on Washington Square*. Baltimore, MD: Johns Hopkins University Press.

Foote, T. W. 2004. *Black and White Manhattan: The History of Racial Formation in Colonial New York City*. New York: Oxford University Press.

Geggus, D. P. 1979. *Yellow Fever in the 1790s: The British Army in Occupied Saint Domingue*. London: Medical History.

Glaude, E. S. 2000. *Exodus!: Religion, Race, and Nation in Early Nineteenth-Century Black America*. Chicago, IL: University of Chicago Press.

Goldstein, I. 1930. *A Century of Judaism in New York: B'nai Jeshurun, 1825–1925: New York's Oldest Ashkenazic Congregation*. New York: Congregation B'nai Jeshurun. See also *Journal of American History* 18 (1) (June): 138.

Garces-Foley, K. 2006. "Introduction." In *Death and Religion in a Changing World*, edited by Kathleen Garces-Foley, ix–xiv. Armonk, NY: MESharpe.

Gilman, S. L. 2003. *Jewish Frontiers: Essays on Bodies, Histories and Identities*. New York: Palgrave Macmillan.

Gurock, J. S. 2003. "The Orthodox Synagogue." In *The American Synagogue: A Sanctuary Transformed*, edited by J. Wertheimer, 37–84. Cambridge: Cambridge University Press.

Gurock, J. S. 2014. *American Jewish History, Vol. 1: The Colonial and Early National Periods, 1654–1840*. London and New York: Routledge.

Hartog, H. 2018. *Public Property and Private Power: The Corporation of the City of New York in American Law, 1730–1870*. Ithaca, NY: Cornell University Press.

Heinrichs, E. A. 2017. *Plague, Print, and the Reformation: The German Reform of Healing, 1473–1573*. London: Routledge.

Huss, B., M. Pasi, and K. von Stuckrad. 2010. *Kabbalah and Modernity: Interpretations, Transformations, Adaptations*. Leiden: Brill.

Israel Vindicated; Being a Refutation of the Calumnies Propagated Respecting the Jewish Nation; in Which the Objects and Views of the American Society for Ameliorating the Condition of the Jews, Are Investigated. By an Israelite. 1823. New York: Abraham Collins.

"Items Relating to the Moses and Levy Families, New York." 1920. *Publications of the American Jewish Historical Society* 27: 331–345.

Jackson, K. T., L. Keller, and N. Flood. 2010. The Encyclopedia of New York City: Second Edition. New Haven, CT: Yale University Press.

Jacobs, J. 2008. *Houses of Life: Jewish Cemeteries of Europe*. London: Frances Lincoln.

Johnson, J. 1824. *The Influence of Tropical Climates on European Constitutions: Being a Treatise on the Principal Diseases Incidental to Europeans in the East and West Indies, Mediterranean, and Coast of Africa*. Philadelphia, PA: Kite.

Jortner, A. 2007. "Cholera, Christ, and Jackson: The Epidemic of 1832 and the Origins of Christian Politics in Antebellum America." *Journal of the Early Republic* 27 (2): 233–264.

Katz, D. 2000. "R' Chaim, Brother of the Maharal (1520–1568): Profound Literary Critic of Halakhic Literature." *Jewish History with Rabbi Dr. Dovid Katz*. Podcast, MP3 audio, 57:51. May 26. https://podbay.fm/p/jewish-history-with-rabbi-dr-dovid-katz/e/1590507552.

Kessner, T. 1969. "Gershom Mendes Seixas: His Religious 'Calling,' Outlook and Competence." *American Jewish Historical Quarterly* 58 (4): 445–471.

Khalaf, S. 2012. *Protestant Missionaries in the Levant Ungodly Puritans, 1820-1860*. New York: Routledge.

Kohn, S. J. 1965. "Mordecai Manuel Noah's Ararat Project and the Missionaries." *American Jewish Historical Quarterly* 55 (2): 162–196.

Leibman, L. A. 2020. "Jewish Healers and Yellow Fever in the Eighteenth-Century Americas." *Jewish Social Studies* 25 (4): 77–90.

Leibman, L. A. 2021. *Once We Were Slaves*. New York: Oxford University Press.

Leibman, L. A., and S. Goldblatt. 2012. "Grave Matters: Childhood, Identity, and Converso Funerary Art in Colonial America." *Sephardic Horizons* 2 (3).

Lerman, L. P. 1998. "Solomon H. Jackson's 'The Jew': A Contemporary American Jewish Response." *Studies in Bibliography and Booklore* 20: 43–53.

Levin, L. 2008. *Seeing with Both Eyes: Ephraim Luntshitz and the Polish-Jewish Renaissance*. Leiden and Boston: Brill.

Lofton, K. 2020. "The Profound Horror of the Mass Grave." *Yale Review* 108 (2) (Summer). https://yalereview.yale.edu/profound-horror-mass-grave.

Long, K. 1998. *The Revival of 1857-58 Interpreting an American Religious Awakening*. New York: Oxford University Press.

Marcus, J. R. 1975. *Memoirs of American Jews, 1775-1865*. New York: Ktav Pub. House.

Mentz, S. 2015. *Shipwreck Modernity: Ecologies of Globalization, 1550-1719*. Minneapolis, MN: University of Minnesota Press.

McLoughlin, W. G. 2013. *Revivals, Awakenings, and Reform*. Chicago, IL: University of Chicago Press.

Minardi, M. 2004. "The Boston Inoculation Controversy of 1721–1722: An Incident in the History of Race." *William and Mary Quarterly* 61 (1): 47–76.

Morton, T. 2017. *Hyperobjects: Philosophy and Ecology after the End of the World*. Minneapolis, MN: University of Minnesota Press.

Nathan, G.S. 1805. "Poetry Manuscript—Grace Seixas Nathan." Nathan Family Papers. Box: 1, Folder: 10. American Jewish Historical Society. Center for Jewish History. http://digital.cjh.org/webclient/DeliveryManager?pid=3804178.

Nathan, G.S. 1816. "Letter, New York, August 16, 1816." Correspondence—Sara Sexias Kursheedt and Grace Sexias Nathan, 1814-1821. Nathan Family Papers. Box: 1, Folder: 2. American Jewish Historical Society. Center for Jewish History. https://archives.cjh.org/repositories/3/archival_objects/968143.

Pascalis Ouviere, F., F. Vicq-d'Azyr, and S. Piattoli. 1823. *An Exposition of the Dangers of Interment in Cities: Illustrated by an Account of the Funeral Rites and Customs of the Hebrews, Greeks, Romans, and Primitive Christians*. New York: W. B. Gilley.

Pellegrini, A. 1997. *Performance Anxieties: Staging Psychoanalysis, Staging Race*. London: Routledge.

Percy, E. J., J. L. Hoffmann, and S. J. Sherman. 2011. "Sticky Metaphors and the Persistence of the Traditional Voluntary Manslaughter Doctrine." *University of Michigan Journal of Law Reform* 44 (2): 383–428.

"Public Health." 1822. *National Advocate*. August 2.

Rock, H. B. 2015. *Haven of Liberty: New York Jews in the New World, 1654–1865*. New York: New York University Press.

Sarna, J.D. 1980. *Jacksonian Jew: The Two Worlds of Mordecai Noah*. New York: Holmes & Meier.

Senior, E. 2018. *The Caribbean and the Medical Imagination, 1764-1834: Slavery, Disease and Colonial Modernity*. Cambridge: Cambridge University Press.

Shalev, E. 2013. *American Zion: The Old Testament as a Political Text from the Revolution to the Civil War*. New Haven, CT: Yale University Press.

Sherwin, B. L. 1975. "In the Shadows of Greatness: Rabbi Hayyim Ben Betsalel of Friedberg." *Jewish Social Studies* 37 (1): 35–60.

Sontag, S. 1978. *Illness as Metaphor*. New York: Farrar, Straus and Giroux.

Stern, M. H. 1978. *First American Jewish Families: 600 Genealogies, 1654–1977*. Cincinnati, OH: American Jewish Archives.

Stout, J. D. 1822. *Plan of Greenwich from Actual Survey 1822*. New York: New York Historical Society.

Strong, P. N. 1823. *The Pestilence, a Punishment for Public Sins: A Sermon Preached in the Middle Dutch Church, Nov. 17, 1822, After the Cessation of the Yellow Fever, Which Prevailed in New-York in 1822*. 2nd ed. Open Collections Program at Harvard University. Contagion. New York: HSage. http://galenet.galegroup.com/servlet/Sabin?af=RN&ae=CY112695375&srchtp=a&ste=14.

Swierenga, R. P. 1994. *The Forerunners: Dutch Jewry in the North American Diaspora*. Detroit, MI: Wayne State University Press.

Townsend, P. S. 1823. *An Account of the Yellow Fever, as It Prevailed in the City of New-York . . . 1822*. New York: Printed by Samuel Marks. US National Library of Medicine Digital Collections. http://resource.nlm.nih.gov/35020010R.

Tuveson, E. L. 1968. *Redeemer Nation: The Idea of America's Millennial Role*. Chicago, IL: University of Chicago Press.

Weingrad, M. 2007. "Messiah, American Style: Mordecai Manuel Noah and the American Refuge." *AJS Review* 31 (1): 75–108.

Wetherill, S. P. 1916. *Philadelphia History, Vol. 2: Samuel Wetherill and the Early Paint Industry of Philadelphia*. Philadelphia, PA: City History Society of Philadelphia.

Whooley, O. 2013. *Knowledge in the Time of Cholera: The Struggle over American Medicine in the Nineteenth Century*. Chicago, IL: University of Chicago Press.

"Yellow Fever." 1856. *New York Medical Gazette and Journal of Health* 7 (6): 365–367.

4.6

ON HUMAN EXTINCTION

Evander Price

In an essay published posthumously in *The Varieties of Scientific Experience*, Carl Sagan meditated on the concept of human extinction. He wrote:

> Now, extinction seems to me serious. Hard to think of something more serious, more worthy of our attention, more crying out to be prevented. Extinction is forever. Extinction undoes the human enterprise. Extinction makes pointless the activities of all of our ancestors back those hundreds of thousands or millions of years. Because surely if they struggled for anything, it was for the continuance of our species.[1]

He went on to muse that extinction is not only possible, but probable, part of the "ordinary course of events." What would human extinction mean and how are we not-yet-extinct denizens of the present to understand such an unthinkable concept?

Extinction is the apocalypse of a species. Extinction is the absence of something, a void. It is difficult to perceive what is not there, to reckon with these absences, these gaps in the fabric of ecosystems, to account for the genetic libraries of Alexandria that are lost when an unbroken thread of thousands of millions of years of continuous evolutionary experimentation is suddenly—snipped. Extinction is everywhere on a scale too large to easily see or comprehend. It therefore falls into the category Tim Morton calls a "hyperobject," an enormous *thing*, both spatially and temporally, ungraspable by the human senses, yet physically real and "responsible for . . . *the end of the world*" (Morton 2013: 2). Robert Nixon's related concept of "slow violence" is another useful way to frame extinction, which he defines as

> a violence that occurs gradually and out of sight, a violence of delayed destruction that is dispersed across time and space, an attritional violence that is typically not viewed as violence at all. . . . [A] violence that is neither spectacular nor instantaneous, but rather incremental and accretive, its calamitous repercussions playing out across a range of temporal scales.
>
> *(Nixon 2011: 2)*

Both hyperobjects and slow violence highlight the invisibility of the many collective small actions (and some very large ones) that build toward an enormous vector of catastrophe.

 DOI: 10.4324/9781351176231-35

Global warming, nuclear radiation, migration, heatwaves, droughts, industrial agriculture, evolution, the Chicxulub impactor, and the Pleistocene ice age are all hyperobjects bound to extinction.[2] They are big, slow, terrifying; difficult to perceive, measure, or apprehend; and, so far as they are outside of the range of the empirical senses, they are a matter of faith, real as they are. A fossil, for example, is not extinction in the same way that a soldier is not a World War II—it is just one edge of the greater hyperobject, one node of a larger network of fossils that were once organisms that evolved over a tremendous amount of time in a particular environment that were, by chance, encased in some oxygen-deprived environment ideal for the mineralization of organic material over another tremendous period of time. In contemplating such fossils, one faces the terrifying and humbling realization that individual death can be and has been exploded into the catastrophe of species-wide extinction. One writer, penning an obituary to the Heath hen—a bird native to Martha's Vineyard—captured this difference between death and extinction:

> [S]omething more than death has happened, or, rather, a different kind of death. There is no survivor, there is no future, there is no life to be created in this form again. We are looking upon the uttermost finality which can be written, glimpsing the darkness which will not know another ray of light. We are in touch with the reality of extinction.
>
> *(Hough 1933)*

This chapter surveys the relationship between deep time, extinction, and some of the fictions and theologies that have developed in response to an ever more present end-to-things—in the words of Frank Kermode: what fictions are invented now that "the End is immanent" and "no longer imminent" (Kermode 1967: 25)? The first section of this chapter considers how the omnipresence of fossil seashells, those ubiquitous *memento mori* blanketing the planet, has challenged anthropocentric assumptions as far back as ancient Greece, and served as the material evidence undergirding theories of creation and apocalypse. The second section touches on Ken Ham's denial of evolution in favor of the Young Earth creationism. The third section considers what it means to accept as valid the geological fact of mass extinction, and the ramifications of the extinction of that most precious material of religion—human beings. The final section considers the possibility of *de*-extinction and technophilic faith in the power of human ingenuity to achieve godlike powers to undo and—quite literally— resurrect extinct species. In each of these sections, we see that the hyperobject of extinction pushes belief systems into a tortured and often paradoxical reconciliation with the abyss of time and death.

The Humble Seashell

In "'Ancient Episteme' and the Nature of Fossils," J. M. Jordan traces the history of a common assumption propagated across twentieth-century geology textbooks that mistakenly claims that, until the seventeenth-century Enlightenment, fossils were considered *lusus naturae*, "games of nature"—jokes, jests, random quirks serendipitously generated from rocks. This theory is a gentle dodge because, if fossils are mere games, then one need not confront the frightening deductions that follow. In fact, a number of ancient philosophers had already deduced the organic origins of fossils (Jordan 2016).[3] Jordan cites Xenophanes, among others, who asserted that the "earth, as it is being carried down continuously and gradually, in time gives way to the sea." This erosive action explains "the fact that sea shells are found in the midst of earth and in mountains, and in the quarries of Syracuse impressions of fish and seaweed have been found . . . [I]n Paros . . . and in Malta fossils of all sea creatures." For Xenophanes, fossils were evidence that what is now land must have once been under water, that some sort of cycle of creation and destruction must have occurred for seashells to be found on mountain tops, and this transition must have taken a very long time indeed (Jordan 2016: 93).[4]

Historian and folklorist Adrienne Mayor argues that fossils likely served as the inspiration for mythology. Those fossilized seashells, dinosaur bones, and remains of Pleistocene megafauna that periodically surfaced across the Mediterranean were evidence of a lost world of titans, cyclopes, centaurs, and worldwide diluvian catastrophes. Griffins and centaurs were not mere fanciful poetic metaphors; Greek mythology is nonfiction (Mayor 2011). Though some historians overlooked and underestimated the interest the ancient world took in fossils, many ancient philosophers (Mayor points to Empedocles, Theophrastus, and Apollonius, among others) developed sophisticated theories to explain their presence, deducing the existence of a fluid, changeable world that long preceded the introduction of humans, a world in which mountains ebbed and flowed; and diverse, now-extinct creatures roamed far and wide; and that some of them (centaurs) perhaps still lived in far off yet undiscovered lands (Mayor 2011: 226–227).

Nor was the antediluvian origin of the seashell lost on philosophers of the Middle Ages. To Avicenna, writing at the turn of the first millennium, the ubiquity of the humble seashell was evidence of "ages of which we have no record" (Jordan 2016: 95).[5] What one natural philosopher, John Ray, saw in petrified seashells he examined in the seventeenth century were creatures unlike any he had seen alive, yet not so random as to be a mere *lusus naturae*:

> Among these petrified shells are many sorts, which are not at this day that we know of any where to be found; nay some proceed so far as to affirm, that there is not the like of any one of these supposed petrified shells to be found among our present shell-fishes. If it be said, that these species be lost out of the world: that is the supposition which philosophers hitherto have been unwilling to admit, esteeming the destruction of any one species to be a dismembering the universe rendering it imperfect, whereas they think the divine providence is especially concerned to preserve and secure all the works of the creation.
>
> *(Ray 1738: 107)*

John Ray looked into the void of the fossil seashell and saw the possibility of "dismembering the universe." For Ray, the extinction of a species would reflect the fallibility of an imperfect Creator. In imagining such an expanse of time and extinction, he wrote to a colleague, "There follows such a train of consequences, as seem to shock the Scripture-History of ye novity of the World" (Ray 1695). Petrified shells petrified Ray, shaking his Young Earth assumptions with the implication that the fate of the seashell is not a singular one.

In *The Sixth Extinction* (2014), Elizabeth Kolbert dives deep into the void. "The fossil record," she observes, "is incredibly incomplete. One rough estimate holds that we've only ever found a tantalizing 0.01 percent of all species that have ever existed" (Kolbert 2014: 247). Mass extinction is not just a fact—it has happened more than once (Brannen 2017). So far as can be ascertained from the geologic record, the world has ended at least five times before—John Ray's god took multiple mulligans—and if all this were not enough, the current rate of extinction is "on the order of 10,000 times greater than the naturally occurring background state" (Kolbert 2014: 186). In the hyperobject of extinction, Morton captures the dilemma of Dr. Frankenstein magnified to species-wide scales: "What has happened so far has been the gradual realization by humans that they are not running the show, at the very moment of their most powerful technical mastery on a planetary scale" (Morton 2013: 164). The challenge, then, is how to stop the next asteroid from hitting Earth, when human beings are both the source and destination of the asteroid. It is the existential paradox of asking: how do we become not us?

Extinction Anxiety

For many, this existential threat is best met with denial, which can manifest in willful ignorance (why think about what cannot be changed?), or confabulation (choosing a happier narrative). A Gallup poll from 2017 found that 38 percent of Americans believe in Young Earth creationism: the idea that the planet is six thousand years old; this amount is down from 42 percent of Americans in 2014 (Gallup 2014, 2017). This is the position of Ken Ham, founder of the Creation Museum in Kentucky, where dinosaurs are exhibited living happily alongside early Adamic tribes.

Ham makes the distinction between "experimental" science—that is, science that "uses the method of *repeatable, observable* experiments to determine how [something] *operates* or functions *in the present*," versus "historical science," which "includes historical geology, paleontology, archaeology, and cosmology"—all of which attempt to reconstruct "*past, unobservable, unrepeatable* event(s)" (Ham 2017: 30).[6] Since, in Ham's view, the past is fundamentally inaccessible, one can and should choose a preferable narrative from a reliable eye-witness source, and Ham has chosen *Genesis*. The museum finds evidence for dinosaurs-alongside-humans in the myth of St. George and the Dragon, the Epic of Gilgamesh, and others—thus forwarding an argument a bit like Adrienne Mayor's concerning the relationship of fossils to Greek mythology, though without evidence. The Creation Museum spent millions to build a 510-foot replica of the biblical ark, the "Ark Encounter," a monument born from profound extinction anxiety and denial (see https://arkencounter.com/about/).[7] At the museum, there is no need to fear the ubiquitous humble seashell. It is neither evidence of extinction nor proof of the enormous incomprehensible age of the Earth; it merely demonstrates the veracity of Noah's flood and assures the indispensable centrality of human beings (Ham 2017: 31–41). For Young Earthers, the fierce adherence to a particular reading of biblical scripture provides a reassuring belief system that promises human beings a central role of a temporally tiny cosmos, one that is approximately six thousand years old—an easily comprehensible age, a number that a person can count up to in an hour or so, should one extend the effort.

The popular cosmologist Carl Sagan felt such views reflect a sort of cultural childishness. In *Pale Blue Dot* (1994), he wondered, "What do we really want from philosophy and religion? Palliatives? Therapy? Comfort? . . . Reassuring fables?" The answer for Ken Ham and many others is a resounding *yes* (Sagan 1994: 46). For Sagan, choosing to "believe" in a religion or philosophy versus choosing to "explore" the universe through scientific inquiry is a choice between the blue pill and the red pill, and many would prefer humankind had collectively taken the blue pill.[8] Conversely, "modern science" is the red pill, taking us into a "voyage into the unknown, with a lesson in humility waiting at every stop" (Sagan 1994: 19). In Chapter 3, "The Great Demotions" (one might call it "The History of Anthropocentric Apologism"), Sagan outlines this series of humbling de-centerings, each followed by a corresponding human re-centering in an ever-growing universe. Summarized:

• [Ptolemaic universe] The Earth is the center of the universe. Therefore, human beings are special.

- [Copernican universe] Even if the Earth is not the center, the sun is, so human beings are very close to the center of the universe. Therefore, human beings are special.
- [Galilean universe] The sun is not the center of the universe, but the Milky Way is. Therefore, human beings are special.
- [Hubble universe] Sure there may be hundreds of billions of Galaxies, but ours is the center of them all. Therefore, human beings are special.
- [Einsteinian universe] Well if there is no center to the universe, no other stars have planets. Therefore, human beings are special.
- [Wolszczanian universe] Even if other stars have planets, none of them has life. Therefore, human beings are special.
- [Darwinian Universe] We might be related to animals, but we are still special and separate from them somehow.[9]

Sagan points to the fossil shell as the most humbling step of all, an idea that moved him so much that he repeats the line twice:

> [I]t is clear from the fossil record that almost every species that has ever existed is extinct; extinction is the rule, survival is the exception. And no species is guaranteed its tenure on this planet.
>
> *(Sagan 2006: 196, 66)*

Given that at each of these cosmos-expanding, human-humbling demotions "the gods were disappointingly hard to find" (Sagan 1994: xv), and seashells hard *not* to find, Sagan proposes replacing religion with scientific humanism—essentially Spinozan awe and pursuit of knowledge of the universe so far as it is possible to apprehend. It is time, Sagan explains, to quit clinging to the reassuring fantasy of a universe that, seen from the individual perspective, intuitively seems to be all about the human—and embrace the awesome hugeness of a cosmos in which, if there is a god at all, such a god "must be even greater than we dreamed" (Sagan 1994: 50). In Sagan's encomium to scientific exploration, we hear echoes of Marlowe's *Faustus*, Milton's Satan, and Erskine's "The Moral Obligation to Be Intelligent." Sagan exhibits a type of stubbornness that refuses to look away from something terrifying—in this case the harrowingly large number that is the age of the planet relative to the smallness of human beings. When it comes to such incomprehensible swathes of time, it is not enough to simply call the void "forever." Forever is without beginning or end. Morton notes the difference:

> The timescale is a Medusa that turns us to stone. These gigantic timescales are truly humiliating in the sense that they force us to realize how close to Earth we are. Infinity is far easier to cope with. . . . I can think infinity. But I can't count up to one hundred thousand. . . . There is a real sense in which it is far easier to conceive of "forever" than a very large finitude. Forever makes you feel important.
>
> *(Morton 2013: 60)*

Sixty-five million years (or more) of seashell extinction is precisely the finite sort of timescale that is not forever. It is instead terrifyingly big. It is a hyperobject that one cannot fully grasp, one that fundamentally destabilizes any notions of the centrality of human beings to the whole endeavor. As the temporal horizon of the past ever expands deeper and deeper, from the 6,000 years deduced from the Bible by James Ussher, to the geologic millions of years re-discovered in the nineteenth century, to the cosmic billions estimated by modern astronomers, a tension arises with the reciprocal compression of the future—which seems, in comparison, terrifyingly imminent. Given that so much past has passed, it becomes impossible to conceive of human beings as being in the "middle" of time—and much easier to conceive that extinction is a rule from which human beings are not an exception.[10] The ostrich's strategy only augments the hyperobject; the void grows whether or not one chooses to peer into it.

Accepting Extinction

The other side of extinction denial is radical extinction acceptance. Such acceptance means to admit, as Roy Scranton does in *Learning to Die in the Anthropocene* (2015), that our civilization (if not species) is already dead. Scranton writes:

> As we struggle, awash in social vibrations of fear and aggression, to face the catastrophic self-destruction of global civilization, the only way to keep alive our long tradition of humanistic inquiry is to learn to die.

> *(Scranton 2015: 108)*

Scranton gestures toward an ethics derived from the *Hagakure: The Book of the Samurai*. It is an ethics predicated on accepting death so that one can live fully, and not—as many do—in a perpetual arrested state of fear, paralyzed by the promise of the future (and present) onslaught of never-ending environmental trolley problems.[11] For Scranton, only when human beings come to accept the inevitability of human extinction can the species possibly find a way (Scranton doesn't specify how) to avert the self-fashioned asteroid, to avoid the fate of the fossil seashell, possibly by means of some massive restructuring of the very assumptions that comprise the foundations of anthropocentrism—a hyperobject that has origins, Morton argues, situated as early as 12,000 years ago during the Agricultural Revolution in the Fertile Crescent. In other words, what sort of all-encompassing changes would be necessary for a species that now sees the ramifications of the Agricultural Revolution as a big mistake (Morton 2016: 43, 52–59)?

Scranton's acceptance of extinction can be taken further. Rather than accept extinction, why not embrace it? Kolbert closes her book with a quote she attributes to Paul Ehrlich, author of the neo-Malthusian book *The Population Bomb* (1968): "in pushing other species to extinction, humanity is busy sawing off the limb on which it perches" (Kolbert 268). If, as Peter Brannen argues, "humanity's gain has been biodiversity's loss since birth" (Brannen 224); and if, as Michel Serres argues, the relationship between human beings and the planet is fundamentally parasitical (Serres 1980), then might it be ethical to remove, inhibit, or prevent the proliferation of the primary material of religion: human beings? The Voluntary Human Extinction Movement (VHEMT) argues precisely that.

Embracing Extinction

VHEMT is an online community founded in 1991 by Les Knight that advocates for the extinction of the human species.[12] Nor are they alone in this project. Far more radical online groups include the "Church of Euthanasia," UNAPACK (a 1996 presidential write-in campaign for Ted Kaczynski), and the H.P. Lovecraft-inspired "Cthulhu for America" ("Awaken Cthulhu for Big Apocalyptic Change")—all of which advocate for the same goal as VHEMT, but without the condition "voluntary." Any means necessary will do: nuclear war, sterilization, violence, whatever (see Korda 1992; and https://cthulhuforamerica.com/).[13] Compared to the rhetoric of the Church of Euthanasia, the VHEMT sounds sober. To achieve the goal of a planet without humans, their followers simply pledge to not have children. In ideal circumstances, a world where everyone committed to not reproducing would lead to the end of the human species in a generation or so, which would be of great boon to all other species, and thus the planet as a whole. Given that there are already so many children that are being uncared for, and so many people living in poverty, is there an ethical argument that justifies bringing more children into the world before attending to the ones who are already here? Are human beings good? Good for whom? Good for the planet? Good for each other?

The motto of VHEMT displayed proudly on their webpage is "May we live long and die out," a prayer of sorts that inverts the Vulcan salute, "Live Long and Prosper."[14] Bumper stickers are available for purchase. But though they may joke, the acolytes at VHEMT are deadly serious. They argue:

> Phasing out the human species by voluntarily ceasing to breed will allow Earth's biosphere to return to good health. Crowded conditions and resource shortages will improve as we become less dense.
>
> *(Knight 1991a)*

In addition to outlining an extensive array of arguments and rebuttals to a wide range of challenges from natalists, the website also serves as a repository of anti-breeding propaganda, bumper stickers, and awards (Knight 1991b). VHEMT strategically redefines the parameters of the discussion by controlling the diction: a person without children is not child*less*; rather, that person is child*free*. People who have children are not called "parents"; rather, parents are demoted to "breeders," a particularly loaded word. Consider the difference between "breeder/ing" and "procreator/ion/ing." In the same way "pro-life" casts opponents, by implication, as "anti-life" or "pro-death," so too does "procreation" imply an antithetic "anti-creation" or "pro-destruction." By demoting procreation and other such "breeder rhetoric" (MacCormack 2020: 173) to breeding, sex with the intent to reproduce is divorced from idea of love, passion, creation, or any metaphysical notions that might uniquely separate the human version of sex from the animal version of sex. A breeder is a breeder, whether the breeder is a human being or a dog, or horse, or rabbit—such copulation is just another animal behavior (Knight 1991c).

VHEMT features the work of Nina Paley, an award-winning animator and childfree advocate. One animation, "Fertco" (Paley 2002a), juxtaposes a chic blonde white woman walking confidently into a fertility clinic, while images of emaciated babies flash behind her and frenetic electronic music punctuates her every step. Lyrics blare, "Buy! Consume! Be happy! Buy *more*!" A zygote divides as the baby factory thumps and pulses, churning out babies with industrial, exponential celerity. Another short film, "The Stork" (Paley 2001), retells the Hans Christian Andersen folktale that is normally a useful story for too-curious toddlers. In Paley's rendition, bright-eyed smiling storks fly over a forest, dropping their bundles of joy, which explode like bombs decimating the trees and transforming them into a sprawling suburbia. The saccharine tune of Edvard Grieg's "Morning Mood" plays in the background; Paley could have used Malvina Reynolds's "Little Boxes" to similar effect. Bambis flee the onslaught of baby bombs, multiplying Chevrolet Suburbans (a pun on suburbia), and smiling babies copy-pasted *ad*—disturbing and uncanny—*nauseum*. At last, the whole Earth explodes into one giant, smiling baby head. A third film, "The Wit and Wisdom of Cancer" (Paley 2002b)—set deep in the brain of a dying patient named "Gaia"—depicts conversations of ethics-arguing cancer cells meant to represent the relationship between human beings and the planet. One doubting cancer cell forwards the VHEMT position, complaining, "It's crowded! There's too many of us!" A breeder cancer rebuts his doubting interlocutor with a barrage of natalist arguments:

> You can't have too many of us. . . . Unrestrained growth is the philosophy of the cancer cell!
> You value other cells over cancer cells?
> Other cells wouldn't have any value without cancer cells to appreciate them!
> Cancer cells are the pinnacle of evolution! We can think. We're more successful be-cause we are smarter.
> If smart cancer cells like us don't reproduce, then we will only have dumb cancer cells!

Paley's point of course is that arguments about human exceptionalism, natalism, and dominance over nature follow the same logic of the bloviating natalist cancer cell. It is the thoughtless, confidant, unreflective, self-centered, self-assured, unexamined faith in cultural norms as being good—even as the whole system heedlessly careens toward a Malthusian limit (Paley 2009). Paley argues that humans are a cancer to the planet, a parasite that realizes too late it is killing the very thing that sustains it (Serres 1980, 2007).[15]

Pro-extinction arguments are difficult to grapple with because they attack natalist assumptions that are deeply engrained in culture (as in, babies are good), and contradict foundational assumptions of many religious belief systems (such as go forth and multiply). They are easy to dismiss because at first glance they appear nihilist and impossible to imple-ment. Nonetheless, the ethics of the pro-extinction worldview is worthy of serious consider-ation. After all, if it is ethical to reduce one's carbon footprint, then surely the greatest ethical choice an individual could make would be the choice not to create more carbon-consuming things.[16] Philosopher Patricia MacCormack addresses many of these concerns in *The Ahuman Manifesto: Activism for the End of the Anthropocene* (2020), in which she sums up her essential argument in a quasi-poem (MacCormack 2020: 10):

A call to
forsake human privilege;
practice abolitionist veganism;
cease reproduction of humans;
develop experimental modes of expression beyond
anthropocentric signifying systems of representation and
recognition and
care for this world at this time until we are gone.

For MacCormack, "ceasing reproduction of humans . . . need not be considered 'unthink-able' but can be welcomed as affirmative of earth life" (144). The choice to not have chil-dren should not be read as a misanthropic act of self-erasure but rather a life-affirming act embodying how Michel Serres defines *grace*:

> Whoever is nothing, whoever has nothing, passes and steps aside. From a bit of force, from any force, from anything, from any decision, from any determination. . . . Grace is nothing, it is nothing but stepping aside. Not to touch the ground with one's force, not to leave any trace of one's weight, to leave no mark, to leave nothing, to yield, to step aside. . . . [T]o dance is only to make room, to think is only to step aside and make room, give up one's place.

(*MacCormack 2018: 156; Serres [1985] 2008: 45*)

In this definition of grace, one hears echoes of the Beatitudes, those blessings delivered by another famously childfree philosopher; one hears echoes of Carl Sagan's Great Demotions, for "stepping aside" is surely an act of de-centering. If each demotion de-centers the human species one rung further down from its presumed place at the top of things in the ladder of creation, then the final de-centering is the grace of making way for all other things. In essence, grace is the conscious act of not doing something, of not firing one's gun, of holding the jaws of the lion shut—in precisely the way that Samson does not.[17] Violence, then, is the anthropocentric principle that demands more me-me-mes. Having children is an act of violence. The Voluntary Human Extinction Movement is life-affirming in the broadest sense of what is considered alive (in other words: biodiversity; non-human life; life that is already here and now). It is a version of Roy Scranton's acceptance and embrace of death that might be the very thing that can shake the foundations of the hyperobject. In Knight's words, "We have been fruitful and multiplied, now it is time to mature and nurture" (Knight 1991b).

Extinction Denial

What if extinction could be undone? For Stewart Brand and the many scientists affiliated with the Revive & Restore project, de-extinction is a viable way to re-tie those genetic lines now lost. This belief in engineering technology is a type of technophilia that promises to undo the casualties of the Anthropocene, with all the confidence of Jesus raising Lazarus from the dead. Such technophilia is first and foremost a manifestation of extinction denial that embraces an illusion of a human-centered world in which, in Brand's words, "We are as gods, and *have* to get good at it" (Brand 2009: 20).[18]

In 2013, Brand hosted a TEDx conference on the topic of de-extinction, inviting speakers such as George Church (the Mammoth guy), Ben Novak (the Passenger Pigeon guy), Beth Shapiro (ancient DNA), and many other scientists who are the main proponents of de-extinction (Biello 2016: 106–107; Shapiro 2015).[19] The greatest success to date of these so-called "Lazarus species" or "chimeras" is Przewalski's horse, which "never went completely extinct" (Revive & Restore 2020). Before that was the Pyrenean ibex, or *bucardo*, the last of which (named "Celia") died in 2000. The DNA of the extinct ibex was extracted from Celia, and injected into the ovum of a domestic goat, which then acted as a surrogate for the ibex (Fernandez-Arias 2013).

Greek myths are rife with science-fictional stories about the perils of genetic engineering. The Minotaur, for example, was a half-man/half-bull whose teratogenesis was a result of his mother, Pasiphaë, using an elaborate contraption that would allow her to copulate with a bull. Proponents of de-extinction see no irony in the fact that the original Chimera—the one their chimeras are named after—was a monster, a fire-breathing thing with a lion's head, a goat's body, and a serpent's tail. The hero Bellerophon had a time of troubles killing the Chimera. In the end, however, he managed to suffocate the Chimera to death. The first de-extinction suffered the same fate. Celia's genetic stuff was reborn from the domestic goat. The resurrected ibex was born with collapsed lungs. After ten minutes of suffering, it too died of suffocation. Aside from "Kurt," the Przewalski's horse born in August 2020, other de-extinction prospects are not showing much better promise.[20]

Even if de-extinction were possible, would it be good? These "Lazarus species" give way to a different reading of the details of the story of Jesus resurrecting Lazarus. The story is quite dark when considered from the perspective of Lazarus. Jesus first let Lazarus die—he did not think to spare Lazarus the pain of dying.[21] And then he waited four days while Lazarus's body festered. Only when Jesus is challenged by his followers ("But some of them said, 'Could not he who opened the eyes of the blind man have kept this man from dying?'"), does the idea of a miracle occur to him—not for the sake of Lazarus, but "for the benefit of the people standing here, that they may believe that you [God] sent me" (John 11:44). Lazarus has no agency here; the whole point of the resurrection is to glorify the resurrector. One might infer that Lazarus's fate was the same as the Iberian Ibex. Lazarus, resurrected into his old, failing body, four days festered, would have to suffer and die all over again. Jesus killed Lazarus twice, simply to prove his own power. Victor Frankenstein might have a word to say. One wonders whether de-extinction is for the good of the species or for the good of the scientist.

Brand admits that "preventing extinction is a bargain compared to reversing extinction. . . . [I]f the Passenger pigeons are brought back, what is to stop us from eating them to death again?"[22] But doing the hard work necessary to preventing the death of a species does not fulfill de-extinction narcissism. De-extinction means doubling-down on the Mesopotamian principles (geo-engineer more, re-create nature so it conforms further to human needs) that, Morton argues, entangled us in the hyperobject in the first place. Brand might agree with the idea that Matthew Yglesias entertains in his panegyric to cornucopianism, *One Billion Americans*: Have children. Have a billion of them. Out-do China. More human minds mean more thought-power directed toward solutions to the problem of too many people (Yglesias 2020). Fear not the void of extinction, Brand tells us:

> The headlines are not just inaccurate. As they accumulate, they frame our whole relationship with nature as one of unremitting tragedy. The core of tragedy is that it cannot be fixed, and that is a formula for hopelessness and inaction. Lazy romanticism about impending doom becomes the default view.
>
> *(Brand 2015)*

For Brand, the genre of extinction is somehow not tragedy. Surely, it is not comedy, either. Faced with the prospect of extinction, Brand takes precisely the opposite position of Serres's "grace" or of Scranton's stoic acceptance of death as a "formula for hopelessness and inaction."

The idea that human beings will save themselves from their own self-created apocalypse with some future, not-yet-invented-but-just-in-time technology is a sort of technophilic, cornucopian faith that re-centers the human in the Anthropocene. Lauren Berlant calls such faith a "cruel optimism," inherent "when something you desire is actually an obstacle to your flourishing" (Berlant 2011: 1). In other words, cruel optimism is an attachment to an unattainable, or unsustainable, idea of the good life. Berlant outlines many flavors of cruel optimism, but the faith in the *deus ex machina*, the faith implied by de-extinction or massive geo-engineering, seems to be precisely the faith that powers the engine of the hyperobject in the first place (Berlant 2011: 23–24). Historian Naomi Oreskes defines what could be called a subset of cruel optimism, "human adaptive optimism":

> The belief that there are no limits to human adaptability—that we can either adapt to any circumstances, or change them to suit ourselves. Belief in geoengineering as a climate "solution" was a subset of HAO.
>
> *(Oreskes 2014: 58)[23]*

The End of Extinction

Extinction means confronting the end of things—to have what Frank Kermode calls "a sense of an ending." From this perspective in the middle of things, Kermode explains:

> [People] make considerable imaginative investments in coherent patterns which, by provision of an end, make possible a satisfying consonance with the origins and with the middle. . . .
>
> The matter is entirely in our own hands of course; but our interest in it reflects our deep need for intelligible Ends. We project ourselves—a small, humble elect, perhaps—past the End, so as to see the structure whole, a thing we cannot do from our spot of time in the middle.
>
> *(Kermode 1967: 17, 7–8)*

"Considerable investments" indeed, though "satisfying consonance" may be elusive. I offer no judgments on any of these responses elicited by extinction, but I do mean to point to contradictions underlying each, which are related to the paradox of being both the cause and the destination of the thing itself—of becoming not us, or of "see[ing] the structure whole" from some Archimedean standpoint. Invariably, what one chooses to believe must be continually revised as the complexity of the hyperobject of human apocalypse is further known—layer by layer, shell by shell, degree by degree. Denying the existence of something so bleak seems in a way the most reasonable response, whether that denial takes the shape of an ark or faith in some *deux ex machina* technology and the human capacity for infinite ingenuity—an optimism that philosopher Peter Sloterdijk describes as a characteristic of the human condition: the conundrum of being perpetually "presented with tasks that are too difficult for [human beings], without the option of avoiding them because of their difficulty" (Sloterdijk 2009). One might ask what benefit the proverbial frog-in-the-pot gains from understanding the properties of the pot and the water that is slowly beginning to boil around it. Yet, there exists a sort of Pascal's wager with extinction denial that precludes the Young Earth response. Or perhaps what is necessary is some sort of new religion, such as Marcia Bjornerud's temporal awareness—*timefulness*—born from her experience as a geologist (Bjornerud 2018); or Carl Sagan's mysticism reified in his Golden Record and his famous "Pale Blue Dot" speech (Sagan 1994: 6–7); or even May Lin's extinction-awareness work, *What is Missing?* (Lin 2009). Tim Morton argues that "hyperobjects are a great candidate for what [Martin] Heidegger calls 'the last god,'" before dismissing such an "eschatological solution . . . or revolution in consciousness" as belated (Morton 2013: 21). Roy Scranton's radical acceptance of extinction suffers from the critique leveled by Stewart Brand and others of causing paralyzing fatalism and inaction, though Scranton would reply that the acceptance of the fatalism is precisely what liberates one from it. None of these views seem readily translatable from theory to practice; nor does some degree of population-control via voluntary human extinction, as Knight imagines, nor the ahuman ethics that MacCormack proposes. And yet the effort to avert the anticipated extinction vector resulting from global warming surely necessitates something as big as a collective change of consciousness, a new religion, a new technology, voluntary human extinction—something—before massive migration, food and water shortages, superstorms, fires, pandemics, and wars (Lustgarten 2020; Wallace-Wells 2019) compel the involuntary sorts of extinction.

Notes

1 Sagan (2006: 204).
2 These two concepts have a remarkable overlap. Nixon cites many examples of slow violence in common with hyperobjects, including: "Climate change, thawing cryosphere, toxic drift, bio-magnification, deforestation, the radioactive aftermath of wars, acidifying oceans, and a host of other slowly unfolding environmental catastrophes."
3 Jordan ultimately attributes this error to a twentieth-century tendency to "exaggerate the intellec-tual achievements of modernity . . . against the abyss of religious superstition and ignorance that supposedly dominated preceding eras" (Jordan 2016: 91).
4 For a thorough exploration of this topic, see Rudwick, 1985, 2014.
5 Jordan further quotes Avicenna: "Mountains have been formed . . . probably from agglutinative clay which slowly dried and petrified during ages of which we have no record. It seems likely that this habitable world was in former days uninhabitable and, indeed, submerged beneath the ocean . . . it is for this reason that in many stones, when they are broken, are found parts of aquatic ani-mals, such as shells, etc."
6 For Ham, the past is a matter of faith, and the only things that can be "scientifically known" in the sense that he proposes are things and events that can be directly witnessed.
7 One social psychology study found that people are more likely to believe in intelligent design when confronted with *momento mori* (Tracy, Hart, and Martens 2011). In Bjornerud's words, "[R] esistance to the concept of evolution is rooted more in existential dread than religious doctrine" (Bjornerud 2018: 174). One might say that fossil seashells scare people into believing in god.
8 I allude here to a scene in *The Matrix* (Wachowski and Wachowski 1999) in which the Genesis story of the Tree of Knowledge of Good and Evil (Genesis 2–3) is re-imagined in a postapocalyptic dystopian setting. In this scene, Morpheus gives the protagonist the choice between the learning the difficult knowledge of the truth (the "red pill") or maintaining the easy ignorance of a lie (the "blue pill").
9 The descriptions of "Ptolemaic, Copernican, Galilean, etc.," universes are added by the author for the sake of rough categorization.
10 One experiences a similar feeling of the uncanny gap between "infinity" and "really big" when looking at the population clock: https://www.census.gov/popclock/.
11 Scranton does not mince his words: "We're fucked. The only questions are how soon and how badly" (Scranton 2015: 16). David Biello too acknowledges the "resigned fatalism of working scientists, many of whom will tell you after a few beers, 'We're fucked'" (Biello 2016: 269).
12 Though often credited as such, Les Knight has repeatedly denied being the founder of VHEMT because he feels anti-natalism has a history that far precedes him. He thinks of himself more as a promoter of the cause.
13 Perhaps the most jarring example is that Chris Korda, the musician-provocateur at the center of these groups, regularly performs a techno song celebrating the fall of the World Trade Centers.
14 Scroll to the bottom of the webpage and you will find another motto: "Thank You For Not Breeding."
15 Agent Smith makes a similar argument in *The Matrix*, comparing human beings to a virus (Wachowski and Wachowski 1999: https://www.youtube.com/watch?v=IM1-DQ2Wo_w).
16 One infographic on VHEMT's website estimates that having one fewer child per family saves 58.6 tons of CO_2 emissions per year, far outstripping all other individual carbon-reduction methods (Wynes and Nicholas 2017).
17 I allude here to the "Strength" Tarot card.
18 Brand overtly denies the existence of a sixth mass extinction (Brand 2015).
19 Incidentally, Revive & Restore is interested in de-extincting the Heath hen memorialized in Hough's lament (Hough 1933).
20 "Mammoth DNA is more like confetti that's been run over by a herd of mammoths in the rain" (quoted in Biello 2016: 117).
21 I gleaned this reading of the Lazarus story from Bud Foote (Foote 1991: 6–7); Stefan Skrimshire offers a resonant reading in "Rewriting Mortality" (Skrimshire 2016: 120).
22 Quoted in Biello 2016: 127.
23 Oreskes's definition recalls Voltaire's/Pangloss's definition of "optimism" in *Candide*: "'What is that, optimism?' 'Why it is the madness of maintaining that all is well, even when you are feeling bad.'"

References

Answers in Genesis. 2021. "About the Ark." Ark Encounter website. https://arkencounter.com/about/.

Berlant, Lauren. G. 2011. *Cruel Optimism*. Durham, NC: Duke University Press.

Biello, David. 2016. *The Unnatural World: The Race to Remake Civilization in Earth's Newest Age*. New York: Scribner.

Bjornerud, Marcia. 2018. *Timefulness: How Thinking like a Geologist Can Help Save the World*. Princeton, NJ: Princeton University Press.

Brand, Stewart. 2009. *Whole Earth Discipline: An Ecopragmatist Manifesto*. New York: Viking.

Brand, Stewart. 2015. "Rethinking Extinction." Revive & Restore. https://reviverestore.org/rethinking-extinction/.

Brannen, Peter. 2017. *The Ends of the World: Volcanic Apocalypses, Lethal Oceans, and Our Quest to Understand Earth's Past Mass Extinctions*. New York: Ecco.

"Cthulhu for President 2024." (2015) 2021. Cthulhu for America website. https://cthulhuforamerica.com/.

Fernandez-Arias, Alberto. 2013. "The First De-extinction: Alberto Fernandez-Arias at TEDxDeExtinction." TEDxDeExtinction. Filmed in Washington, DC, March 15, 2013; posted April 1, 2013. Video, 12:08. https://www.youtube.com/watch?v=5eMqEQw9Fbs.

Foote, Bud. 1991. *The Connecticut Yankee in the Twentieth Century: Travel to the Past in Science Fiction*. New York: Greenwood Press.

Gunther, Robert T., ed. 1928. *Further Correspondence of John Ray*. London: Ray Society.

Ham, Ken. (2007) 2021. "What Really Happened to the Dinosaurs?" Answers in Genesis website. https://answersingenesis.org/dinosaurs/when-did-dinosaurs-live/what-really-happened-to-the-dinosaurs/.

Ham, Ken. 2017. *Four Views on Creation, Evolution, and Intelligent Design*. Grand Rapids, MI: Zondervan.

Hough, Henry Beetle. 1933. *Vineyard Gazette* 87, no. 51 (April 21). Quoted in "Never Say Never; Heath Hen May Get Its Boom Back," by Sara Brown, April 3, 2014. Martha's Vineyard Magazine. https://vineyardgazette.com/news/2014/04/03/never-say-never-heath-hen-may-get-its-boom-back.

Jordan, Jason M. 2016. "'Ancient Episteme' and the Nature of Fossils: A Correction of a Modern Scholarly Error," *History and Philosophy of the Life Sciences* 38 (1): 90–116.

Kermode, Frank. 1967. *The Sense of an Ending: Studies in the Theory of Fiction*. London and New York: Oxford University Press.

Knight, Les. 1991a. The Voluntary Human Extinction Movement (VHEMT) website. http://www.vhemt.org/.

Knight, Les. 1991b. "Biology and Breeding." The Voluntary Human Extinction Movement (VHEMT) website. http://www.vhemt.org/biobreed.htm.

Knight, Les. 1991c. "Politics." The Voluntary Human Extinction Movement (VHEMT) website. http://www.vhemt.org/politics.htm.

Kolbert, Elizabeth. 2014. *The Sixth Extinction: An Unnatural History*. New York: Henry Holt.

Korda, Chris. 1992. Church of Euthanasia website. https://www.churchofeuthanasia.org/.

Lin, Maya. 2009. What Is Missing? website. http://whatismissing.net.

Lustgarten, Abrahm. 2020. "How Climate Migration Will Reshape America." *New York Times*, September 15, 2020. https://www.nytimes.com/interactive/2020/09/15/magazine/climate-crisis-migration-america.html.

MacCormack, Patricia. 2018. "The Grace of Extinction." In *Michel Serres and the Crises of the Contemporary*, edited by Rick Dolphijn, 147–168. London: Bloomsbury Publishing.

MacCormack, Patricia. 2020. *The Ahuman Manifesto: Activism for the End of the Anthropocene*. London and New York: Bloomsbury Academic.

Mayor, Adrienne. 2011. *The First Fossil Hunters: Paleontology in Greek and Roman Times*. Princeton, NJ: Princeton University Press.

Morton, Tim. 2013. *Hyperobjects: Philosophy and Ecology After the End of the World*. Posthumanities, 27. Minneapolis, MN: University of Minnesota Press.

Morton, Tim. 2016. *Dark Ecology: For a Logic of Future Coexistence*. New York: Columbia University Press.

Newport, Frank. 2014. "In U.S., 42% Believe Creationist View of Human Origins." Gallup.com. June 2. https://news.gallup.com/poll/170822/believe-creationist-view-human-origins.aspx.

Nixon, Robert. 2011. *Slow Violence and the Environmentalism of the Poor.* Cambridge, MA: Harvard University Press.

Oreskes, Naomi. 2014. *The Collapse of Western Civilization: A View from the Future.* New York: Columbia University Press.

Paley, Nina. 2001. "The Stork." Video, 3:05. https://archive.org/details/NinaVision/The_Stork. mpeg.

Paley, Nina. 2002a. "Fertco." Video, 2:53. https://archive.org/details/NinaVision/Fertco.mpeg.

Paley, Nina. 2002b. "The Wit and Wisdom of Cancer." Video, 4:29. https://archive.org/details/ NinaVision/The_Wit_and_Wisdom_of_Cancer.mpeg.

Paley, Nina. 2009. NinaVision. http://archive.org/details/NinaVision.

Ray, John. 1695. John Ray to Edward Llwyd, October 8, 1695. Bodleian Library, University of Oxford. https://tinyurl.com/y8tfmxwd.

Ray, John. 1738. *Travels Through the Low-Countries, Germany, Italy and France, with Curious Observations Natural, Topographical, Moral, Physiological, &c.* Vol. 1. 2nd ed. London: J. Hughs.

Revive & Restore. 2020. "The Przewalski's Horse (Takhi) Project." https://reviverestore.org/ projects/przewalskis-horse/.

Rudwick, Martin J. S. 1985. *The Meaning of Fossils: Episodes in the History of Palaeontology.* Chicago, IL: University of Chicago Press.

Rudwick, Martin J. S. 2014. *Earth's Deep History: How It Was Discovered and Why It Matters.* Chicago, IL: University of Chicago Press.

Sagan, Carl. 1994. *Pale Blue Dot: A Vision of the Human Future in Space.* New York: Random House.

Sagan, Carl. 2006. *The Varieties of Scientific Experience: A Personal View of the Search for God.* New York: Penguin.

Scranton, Roy. 2015. *Learning to Die in the Anthropocene: Reflections on the End of a Civilization.* San Francisco, CA: City Lights Books.

Serres, Michel. 1980, 2007. *The Parasite.* Posthumanities 1. Minneapolis, MN: University of Minnesota Press.

Serres, Michel. 1985, 2008. *The Five Senses: A Philosophy of Mingled Bodies,* translated by Margaret Sankey and Peter Cowley. London and New York: Continuum.

Shapiro, Beth A. 2015. *How to Clone a Mammoth: The Science of De-extinction.* Princeton, NJ: Princeton University Press.

Skrimshire, Stefan. 2016. "Rewriting Mortality: A Theological Critique of Geoengineering and De-Extinction." In *Theological and Ethical Perspectives on Climate Engineering: Calming the Storm,* edited by Forest Clingerman and Kevin J. O'Brien, 103–126. Lanham, MD: Lexington Books.

Sloterdijk, Peter. 2009. "Rules for the Human Zoo: A Response to the Letter on Humanism." Translated by Mary Varney Rorty. *Environment and Planning D: Society and Space* 27 (1): 12–28.

Swift, Art. 2017. "In U.S., Belief in Creationist View of Humans at New Low." Gallup.com. May 22. https://news.gallup.com/poll/210956/belief-creationist-view-humans-new-low.aspx.

Tracy, Jessica L., Joshua Hart, and Jason P. Martens. 2011. "Death and Science: The Existential Underpinnings of Belief in Intelligent Design and Discomfort with Evolution." *PLoS ONE* 6 (3): e17349.

Wachowski, Lana, and Lilly Wachowski. 1999. *The Matrix.* Burbank, CA: Warner Bros. Village Roadshow Pictures, Groucho Film Partnership.

Wallace-Wells, David. 2019. *The Uninhabitable Earth: Life After Warming.* New York: Tim Duggan Books.

Wynes, Seth, and Kimberly A. Nicholas. 2017. "The Climate Mitigation Gap: Education and Government Recommendations Miss the Most Effective Individual Actions." *Environmental Research Letters* 12 (7): 074024.

Yglesias, M. 2020. *One Billion Americans: The Case for Thinking Bigger.* New York: Penguin Random House.

INDEX

Note: **Bold** page numbers refer to tables; *Italic* page numbers refer to figures and page numbers followed by "n" denote endnotes.

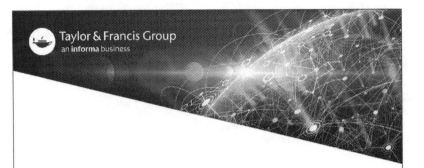

Printed in the United States
by Baker & Taylor Publisher Services